Contemporary Industrial/Organizational Psychology

Third Edition

Contemporary Industrial/Organizational Psychology

Third Edition

L. N. Jewell

Brooks/Cole Publishing Company

I⊕P®An International Thomson Publishing Company

Pacific Grove • Albany • Belmont • Bonn • Boston • Cincinnati • Detroit • Johannesburg • London • Madrid
Melbourne • Mexico City • New York • Paris • Singapore • Tokyo • Toronto • Washington

Sponsoring Editor: *Marianne Taflinger*
Marketing Team: *Christine Davis, Michael Campbell, Deanne Brown*
Marketing Representative: *Diana Morgan*
Editorial Assistant: *Scott Brearton*
Production Editor: *Marjorie Z. Sanders*
Manuscript Editor: *Lorraine Anderson*
Permissions Editor: *May Clark*
Design Editor: *Roy R. Neuhaus*

Interior Design: *Detta Penna*
Cover Design: *Susan Horovitz*
Interior Illustration: *Lori Heckelman, Lisa Torri*
Cover Photo: *Toyohiro Yamada/FPG International*
Art Editor: *Lisa Torri*
Photo Editor: *Kathleen Olson*
Typesetting: *Carlisle Communications, Ltd.*
Printing and Binding: *The Courier Co., Inc./Westford*

For more information, contact:

BROOKS/COLE PUBLISHING COMPANY
511 Forest Lodge Road
Pacific Grove, CA 93950
USA

International Thomson Publishing Europe
Berkshire House 168-173
High Holborn
London WC1V 7AA
England

Thomas Nelson Australia
102 Dodds Street
South Melbourne, 3205
Victoria, Australia

Nelson Canada
1120 Birchmount Road
Scarborough, Ontario
Canada M1K 5G4

International Thomson Editores
Seneca 53
Col. Polanco
11560 México, D. F., México

International Thomson Publishing GmbH
Königswinterer Strasse 418
53227 Bonn
Germany

International Thomson Publishing Asia
221 Henderson Road
#05-10 Henderson Building
Singapore 0315

International Thomson Publishing Japan
Hirakawacho Kyowa Building, 3F
2-2-1 Hirakawacho
Chiyoda-ku, Tokyo 102
Japan

Printed in the United States of America

10   9   8   7   6   5   4   3

Library of Congress Cataloging-in-Publication Data

Jewell, Linda N.
    Contemporary industrial/organizational psychology / Linda N.
Jewell.—3rd ed.
      p. cm.
    Includes bibliographical references and index.
    ISBN 0-534-34971-4
    1. Psychology, Industrial.   I. Title.
HF5548.8.J48   1998   97-17615
158.7—dc21   CIP

Contents in Brief

Contents

Organizations Cited in the Text

Professional Societies and United States Government Organizations Cited in the Text

Preface

The dawn of the 20th century coincided approximately with the beginnings of that field of study we now know as industrial/organizational (I/O) psychology. The dawn of the 21st century finds I/O an established and respected discipline of international scope. The years between have been years of evolution and expansion in response to the many advances in all areas of psychological research and theory, to the practical challenges presented by organizations of all kinds, and to the skills, interests, and experiences of an increasingly diverse professional community.

The objective of the third edition of *Contemporary Industrial/Organizational Psychology,* like that of previous editions, is to assist the individual professor in guiding his or her students through an overview of what is now some 100 years of theory, research, and application in I/O psychology. Priority is given to helping the reader appreciate the topics, the issues, and the methods of I/O psychology in a way that reveals the big picture as well as the details, the *why* as well as the *what.*

Application

For the various subject areas, the text introduces the reader to the objectives of application, the decisions to be made and the alternatives available for achieving those objectives, and the issues involved in choosing among the alternatives. Many examples from a wide variety of contemporary organizations help to illustrate the discussion. The section that begins each chapter—*Psychology at Work*—adds the flavor, if not the specifics, of applying I/O psychology knowledge in contemporary organizations. For example, the development of a structured job interview specifically for the Big Brothers-Big Sisters of Chicago organization by a human resources consulting firm is described in Chapter 4.

Theory

The important relevant psychological theories are summarized or discussed in context as alternative explanations and foundations for studying certain phenomena. They are not treated as subject matter in and of themselves, and there is no advocacy for any particular point of view. Rather, every effort has been made to put these theories into a perspective that accurately reflects current mainstream consensus regarding their research support and practical utility.

Research

Running through the discussion of theory and practice in I/O psychology is a "research stream" emphasizing the building of knowledge through the cumulative results of many thousands of individual research investigations through the years. The empirical literature, both new and classic, is used to make and illustrate points, with many of the figures, tables, and other exhibits reproduced directly from this literature.

The concept of scientific research, which may be unfamiliar to some students, is brought to life by means of the regular chapter feature *Spotlight on Research,* which presents a relevant study in a modified real-life journal format. In Chapter 14, the Spotlight shines on an investigation of how the success of an organization change effort is affected by varying degrees of employee participation in its planning and implementation. Additional research-oriented features may speak to the professor as well as the student.

- A brief history of the changes in thinking and research directions in important topic areas: In Chapter 6, for example, the evolution of the job satisfaction research is traced from early attempts to prove that "a happy worker is a good worker" to current ideas regarding the role of personality in this attitude and related behaviors.

- The identification of research opportunities in the form of "holes" in the knowledge base in important I/O areas: Employee socialization is a research area of growing interest and importance, for instance, yet there is virtually no research into employee orientation, the first step in socialization for most employees (Chapter 5).

- Suggested new arenas for I/O psychology research: The number of telecommuters is large and growing, but this option does not work for everyone, even when they do the same work. What makes the difference in success or failure? What "kind" of individual is a good telecommuting bet? What "kind" of manager does it take to be effective without being able to supervise employees directly (Chapter 8)?

- The identification of "settled" questions that deserve a new look: The long-accepted explanation for a well-documented modest negative correlation between job satisfaction and absenteeism is that absenteeism is a way of coping with low job satisfaction. There is some interesting evidence, however, that the process may actually work the other way, with absenteeism being a cause of lower job satisfaction rather than a consequence of it (Chapter 7).

- Citations of recent reviews of the research literature for many important topics, including: absenteeism, turnover, workplace violence, stress, team job design, the measurement of workload, organizational commitment, personality testing, training evaluation, meta-analysis techniques, and goal setting.

Looking Ahead

The advancement of knowledge requires the courage to question, and *At Issue*—a forum for the new, the speculative, or the controversial (appearing at the end of each chapter)—challenges professors and students alike to do so. Some *At Issue* topics are so new that their implications for the study of human behavior in organizations are only now beginning to be explored. For instance, the problem of employee privacy in the electronic communication age is considered in "Is Anybody Listening?" (Chapter 12). In other cases, *At Issue* presents the views of those who are questioning mainstream or traditional approaches to topics of established importance. Examples include "Leadership and the Loch Ness Monster" (Chapter 14) and "Equal Employment Opportunity and Affirmative Action—Catch 22?" (Chapter 4).

Features

Psychology at Work, Spotlight on Research, and *At Issue* are signature features of this text that remain user favorites. Also back are the popular margin references that offer students an instant "refresher course" in central I/O terms and concepts by referring to the page(s) of the original definition and discussion earlier in the book. A related easy access feature is the end-of-chapter references. Multiple-purpose Questions for Review and Discussion may be used for take-home assignments, general class discussion, small group projects, essay exams, or self-study. Each chapter's set of questions is constructed to be of varying difficulty and complexity to meet a range of needs. New to this edition is a list of key terms and concepts at the end of each chapter.

Content

The third edition offers the comprehensive and objective coverage of traditional and contemporary I/O subject matter on which adopters have come to rely. A revised arrangement of chapters begins with an introduction and coverage of basic conceptual and measurement concepts. It then progresses from "I" to "O," beginning with the individual employee and his or her job, moving on to the broader context of the organizational environment, and finally stepping back still further to consider organization change and development.

No topics have been eliminated from the third edition, but all have been updated and many have been expanded to reflect the more central role they occupy in today's world of work and I/O psychology research. Among these topics are work teams and team job design, family/work issues, organizational culture, personality and personality testing, recruiting and staffing strategies, computer-assisted training, and organizational commitment. The subjects of employee health, safety, and well-being in general, and work-related stress in particular, have been expanded to a complete chapter.

Topics that are new to the third edition include meta-analysis and multiple correlation, workforce diversity, workplace flexibility, computerized testing, self-efficacy, electronic performance monitoring, workplace violence, sexual harassment, mentoring, procedural justice, and electronic communication. The third edition also reflects such important current trends in the field as increased emphasis on measurement and measurement issues; a transition from simple questions of "if" to questions of "why"; the integration of material from cognitive psychology into many subject areas including training, job design, and performance appraisal; and the importance of the "two-way-street" concept in understanding such phenomena as socialization, training, and organizational leadership.

Instructor Support

CNN Applied Psychology Video

Brooks/Cole will offer an accompanying 25-minute CNN video that specifically focuses on workplace issues and how psychologists study them. For example, one segment features the study of construction workers on site by psychologists at the University of Massachusetts–Lowell to analyze specifically what they do, the physical stresses involved, and what can be done to rearrange the site for maximum efficiency and minimum stress to the workers. A short narrative will set up each segment and conclude each segment so students know what to look for and what they've seen.

Instructor's Manual/Test Bank

The Instructor's Manual/Test Bank is being prepared by Scott Johnson, a veteran author of high-quality supplements. It contains chapter overviews, chapter outlines, lecture activities, homework activities, and transparency masters. There are 10 essay/discussion questions, 30 multiple-choice questions, and 10 true/false questions for each chapter. There will be a computerized test bank for both Windows and Macintosh.

Acknowledgments

A textbook is a group effort, and I have been fortunate in working with the best on this edition. It would be difficult to say enough good things about senior editor Marianne Taflinger or production supervisor Marjorie Sanders and her team. Closer to home, I offer heartfelt thanks to William Goodyear for his patient technical support, to Marc Siegall for his insightful editorial assistance, and to my research associate, Karen King O'Connor, for a job well done. Last, but most definitely not least, I wish to express my appreciation to all of those who gave of their time, experience, and talents to contribute many helpful ideas, suggestions, and comments at various stages of manuscript preparation.

John F. Binning	Illinois State University
Timothy DeChenne	University of California at Riverside
Donald L. Fischer	Southwest Missouri State
Ernest B. Gurman	University of Southern Mississippi
Richard K. Kimball	Worcester State College
Jean P. Kirnan	The College of New Jersey
Michael McCall	Cornell University
Lawrence R. Murphy	Xavier University
Charles S. Peyser	University of the South
Gerald L. Quatman	Xavier University

L. N. Jewell

Introduction and Basic Concepts

CHAPTER 1
An Overview of Industrial/Organizational Psychology

CHAPTER 2
The Scientific Study of Human Behavior

CHAPTER 3
Reliability, Validity, and Testing in Organizations

Part I of *Contemporary Industrial/Organizational Psychology* provides an overview and a foundation for the material that follows in Parts II through IV. Chapter 1 is a brief introduction to the field of industrial/organizational (I/O) psychology, its subject matter, development, training requirements, and career opportunities. Chapters 2 and 3 introduce major concepts, terminology, and principles basic to understanding the theory, research, and practice of I/O psychology.

An Overview of Industrial/Organizational Psychology

A Quick Walk Through Hawthorne

In the relay assembly test room, as Roethlisberger wrote in *Management and Morale,* ". . . the idea was very simple. A group of five girls were placed in a room where their condition of work (assembly of a telephone relay) could be carefully controlled, where their output could be measured, and where they could be closely observed. It was decided to produce at specified intervals different changes in working conditions and to see what effect these innovations had on output. Also, records were kept, such as the temperature and humidity of the room, the number of hours each girl slept at night, and kind and amount of food she ate for breakfast, lunch, and dinner." Over a two-and-a-half year period, tons of material were collected and analyzed.

What did the data show? The key point was that with each variable—shorter rest periods, longer but fewer rest periods, the five-day week, introduction of group incentive pay, reversion to original working conditions—production increased period after period in an almost unbroken line. This confirmed the puzzling—to the researchers—result of an earlier illumination experiment in which either raising *or* lowering the light levels had consistently positive impact on productivity, except for one phase in which employees were compelled to work in semidarkness. . . .

One reason for the continuing rise in productivity lay in the changing social environment. An ordinary group of workers, performing routine, low-status jobs with little or no recognition, had been transformed into important people. "Their physical health and well-being became matters of great concern. Their opinions, hopes, and fears were eagerly sought," observed Roethlisberger.

Nor was this all. They were questioned by investigators—frequently in the superintendent's office—sympathetically and at length about their reactions to working conditions. They traded an oppressive production-centered supervisor for a trained observer sympathetic to their needs. They could chat as they wished, and they set their own productivity quotas.

A change in morale occurred with the development of feelings of group responsibility. All labor turnover stopped and casual absences fell to a fraction of the rate in the department outside the test room. The "layabout" girl, for example, who had been absent 85 times in the 32 months before the experiment, went for 16 months thereafter without an absence.

Excerpt reprinted by permission of the publisher, from "Hawthorne Revisited: The Legend and the Legacy." *Organizational Dynamics,* Winter 1975, *3,* 66–80. Copyright © 1975 American Management Association, New York. All rights reserved.

THE EXCERPT in Psychology at Work describes one phase of some of the most famous and controversial experiments that have been conducted in the field of industrial/organizational psychology. The Hawthorne studies, conducted over a period of several years at the Western Electric plant in Hawthorne, Illinois, by Fritz Roethlisberger, Elton Mayo, William Dickson, and others (Roethlisberger, 1941; Roethlisberger & Dickson, 1939), have been the subject of an extraordinary number of articles, lectures, seminars, and books in the more than 70 years since they began. At the center of this activity is the question of what brought about the dramatic production, attendance, and morale improvements observed in the relay assembly room at Western Electric.

One early explanation for the effects observed at Hawthorne was that they were a natural consequence of singling out individuals for special attention. This phenomenon became known as the **Hawthorne effect,** which can be defined as changes in behavior that are brought about through special attention to the behavior. An alternative explanation was that improvements were due to the increased participation in work-related decisions that the experiments gave employees.

Both of the early explanations for the results of the Hawthorne studies focused on the social environment of the workplace, an influence on work performance that had not received widespread attention in I/O psychology prior to that time. If the importance of social factors was not an entirely new idea, it was an idea whose time had come. Neither the study of the behavior of people at work nor the practice of management has been the same since.

Hawthorne has stimulated an almost unbroken line of controversy, debate, reanalysis, and research that continues to this day (e.g., Chant, 1993; Stafford & Stafford, 1993). This extensive examination has raised many questions about the conduct of the experiments, the data presented, and the conclusions reached. Currently, the consensus of opinion seems to be that the productivity improvements at the Western Electric plant can be explained fairly simply in terms of the important changes that were made in working conditions. Feedback about performance and positive reinforcement for good performance appear to have been of particular importance (Parsons, 1992).

Despite the fact that almost every aspect of the Hawthorne experiments has been questioned and many inaccuracies have been identified, the significance of these studies for I/O psychology is not in question. The interventions at Hawthorne were undertaken with the intent of making production at Western Electric more efficient. Unlike many such efforts in other companies, however, they were planned by academic behavioral scientists, who made pioneering efforts to exercise statistical and experimental controls in an applied undertaking.

The Hawthorne studies focused attention on the social environment at work (paving the way for the *organizational* part of industrial/organizational psychology), changed the practice of management in enduring ways, and stimulated an enormous amount of valuable research relevant to the behavior of people at work. As well as any event in the history of the field, the Hawthorne experiments and subsequent debates illustrate the dynamic, evolving character of research and theory in I/O psychology. For all of this, they were only one milestone in the development of the field.

The Development of Industrial/Organizational Psychology

Psychology is the study of human behavior. As a formal scientific discipline, it began in European laboratories in the 1800s. There, early psychologists used experimental methods borrowed from the physical sciences to search for the laws they believed governed behavior. As they gained experience and confidence, they began to broaden and diversify this new science and to develop their own methodologies. Gradually, they began to extend the study of behavior to natural as well as laboratory settings.

Today, a large number of special interest applications, each with its own characteristic approach to the study of behavior, makes up the discipline of psychology. The major coordinating professional society, the American Psychological Association (APA), has more than 50 divisions for these special interests. Division 14 is the Society for Industrial and Organizational Psychology, Inc. (SIOP). The Society is also affiliated with the American Psychological Society (APS) and is incorporated separately as a nonprofit organization. It defines its goals as follows:

> . . . to promote human welfare through the various applications of psychology to all types of organizations providing goods and services, such as manufacturing concerns, commercial enterprises, labor unions or trade associations, and public agencies. The purposes of the Society are scientific, professional, and educational and not for financial gain. (Society for Industrial and Organizational Psychology, Inc., 1986)

The "Specialty Guidelines for the Delivery of Services by Industrial/Organizational Psychologists" (APA, 1981) defines the services offered by psychologists in Division 14 as follows:

> **Industrial/organizational psychological services** involve the development and application of psychological theory and methodology to problems of organizations and problems of individuals and groups in organizational settings. (p. 666)

The definition clearly portrays the traditional status of mainstream industrial/organizational psychology. These psychologists have a dual allegiance to research and practice. As part of a recognized scientific discipline, they develop psychological theory and methodology. As practitioners, they apply what is developed to solving problems or creating innovations in organizational settings.

A good summary source of information about the history of the field of psychology in general is the special February 1992 issue of the American Psychological Association's journal, the *American Psychologist*. Interesting personal views about this history, as well as about the present and the future of the field, are found in articles by Boneau (1992) and Wiggins (1994). A brief review of these issues as they relate specifically to industrial/organizational psychology is presented here.

The Early Years of Industrial Psychology

Relative to other sciences and to other areas in the field of psychology, I/O psychology has a short history. Like the formal study of organizations, it dates back only to the turn of this century (Wren, 1987). In the early days, it was simply called industrial psychology and its scope was considerably narrower than the definition in the "Specialty Guidelines"(APA, 1981).

Mainstream industrial psychology in the first third of this century might be summed up by the title of one of the earliest textbooks in the field: *Psychology and Industrial Efficiency* by Hugo Münsterberg (1913). Münsterberg, a charter member and onetime president of the American Psychological Association, was trained in Germany and came to the United States to oversee a psychological laboratory at Harvard. His professional interests were broad, but it is for his leadership in the application of psychology to business and industry that he is best remembered today. Among his other contributions to the field, Münsterberg was a pioneer in the study of safety in the workplace and of aptitude and work sample testing for employee selection. He also was one of the first to introduce validation as a formal standard for checking the accuracy of such work (Landy, 1992).

As the title of Hugo Münsterberg's 1913 book implies, the early industrial psychologists were very concerned with efficiency in the workplace. They believed that better employee selection methods, training methods, job design, and work layout strategies were the keys to achieving this efficiency. Walter Dill Scott, a psychologist trained in Germany in the classical tradition, was a pioneer in these efforts. Scott conducted psychological research in the field of advertising, in the selection and placement of salespeople, and in the testing and classification of Army officer candidates (Scott, 1911a, b).

Their emphasis on efficiency meant that the work of the early industrial psychologists tended to overlap with and be influenced by the work of industrial engineers. The principles of time analysis and motion study, developed and refined by Frederick Taylor, Frank and Lillian Gilbreth, and others, were particularly relevant, and the engineering approach to job design and problems in the workplace is still very much a part of I/O psychology.

The practical concerns of the early industrial psychologists were accelerated by America's entry into World War I in 1918. Robert Yerkes, then president of the American Psychological Association, actively encouraged psychologists to respond to the military's pressing need to classify and assign large numbers of new personnel to appropriate war work. The intelligence, psychomotor, and personality test data they collected as they worked to develop and validate sound large-scale selection and placement methods gave psychologists interested in the measurement of human characteristics years' worth of test development material.

The Years Between the Wars: 1920–1940

There were only about 100 industrial psychologists by the end of the 1930s, but the field nevertheless experienced important developments in the decades between the two world wars. On the academic scene, what is generally believed to be the first doctoral degree in industrial psychology was granted by the Carnegie Institute of Technology in 1921 to one Bruce V. Moore (Katzell & Austin, 1992). On the career front, industry was becoming an important employment choice. The Hawthorne studies were conducted at Western Electric during this time, and Macy's department stores, Proctor & Gamble, and Aetna Insurance, among other firms, were hiring full-time staff psychologists. Companies that did not want or need in-house service could employ psychologists through consulting firms, such as the Psychological Corporation, which was founded in 1921. (Today the Psychological Corporation is primarily a test development and distribution firm; it is owned by Harcourt, Brace, Jovanovich.)

In a broader view, several things were happening in the United States of the 1920s and 1930s that changed the world of work and ultimately expanded the scope of I/O

The personnel requirements of the armed forces have played a significant role in the development of I/O psychology.

psychology. This period saw the rapid development of unionism in this country. It also brought the Great Depression and the publication of the Hawthorne studies, but the impact of these events on I/O psychology was not felt immediately.

In the beginning, labor union activities were of more interest to factory owners and managers than to psychologists, and most people seemed to think that the high levels of unemployment created by the Depression were solely the government's problem. Even the Hawthorne experiments, as far-reaching as their results turned out to be, did not receive widespread attention from psychologists when the first report appeared in 1939. The United States entered World War II in 1941 and pressing practical concerns assumed top priority.

Industrial Psychology and World War II

Like the First World War, the second put an enormous strain on military personnel functions. Large numbers of new recruits had to be assigned to work that they would be able to perform satisfactorily. Many had to be trained in a very short time to use highly sophisticated equipment. At home, women went to work to fill the vacancies left by their husbands, fathers, brothers, and friends; civilian organizations cried for help in training these inexperienced members of the work force. At the same time, advances in technology were creating a critical demand for human factors psychologists to coordinate human and machine capabilities.

World War II challenged the resources of industrial psychology as never before. Both military and civilian selection, placement, and training problems were more complex and more immediate, and their scale could be staggering; more than 12 million soldiers and Marines took the Army General Classification Test developed by psychologist M. W. Richardson (1940). Hundreds of psychologists were employed by the military to address these and other issues, including team development strategies, performance appraisal procedures, and attitude change methods to increase morale.

Not all industrial psychologists in the first half of the 20th century were involved with the problems created by U.S. military involvement in global conflict. Still, it cannot be denied that these problems were a significant stimulus to the growth of the field and to the advancement of its knowledge (Harrell, 1992). Nor did the end of World War II bring about an end to the military's contribution to the field. A significant portion of the research reviewed in this book has been carried out in military settings. A recent example is the comprehensive Project A, the U.S. Army's development of a sophisticated experimental test battery for making selection and classification decisions for entry-level enlisted personnel. A detailed description of Project A is found in the Summer 1990 issue of the *Journal of Personnel Psychology*.

I/O Psychology Today

The three main roots of I/O psychology had been developing somewhat separately prior to World War II, but since that time they have come together to create a discipline with a broad base. To industrial efficiency and its related selection/placement issues have been added human factors engineering and the psychological concerns brought into prominence by the Hawthorne experiments. These concerns include worker motivation, job satisfaction, leadership, and group influence on individual employee behavior.

Today, there are few areas that touch on human behavior or concern organizations that have not captured the interest of I/O psychologists. In addition to traditional issues, they study employee substance abuse, the behavior of consumers, career paths, stress, the special problems of minority employees and minority-owned organizations, the impact of work demands on home and family (and vice versa), and a host of other questions and problems.

Many of today's I/O psychologists do their research in association with an academic institution, a choice that has become increasingly common since the end of World War II. Working in an academic setting provides stimulation from the theoretical interests of colleagues pursuing other lines of research as well as from the practical problems of organizations. This stimulation has both assisted and strengthened the dual theoretical-applied nature of I/O psychology.

Most I/O psychologists today believe that theory, research, and practice cannot be separated in this field. Theories are useless unless they are tested, and the test of a work behavior theory must be carried out in a work setting. Practice, on the other hand, is a valuable source of information and insight but it is not science if it stops there. Science carries with it a responsibility for communicating knowledge to others.

Industrial/Organizational Psychology as an Academic Discipline

Industrial/organizational psychology shares the goal of achieving greater understanding of human behavior with all of the other special interest areas in psychology. What sets I/O psychology apart is its focus on the behavior of people in organizational settings. This focus, in turn, gives it something in common with the study of management, particularly with those areas called organizational behavior and personnel management.

I/O Psychology and Organizational Behavior

Organizational behavior (OB) is the application of psychology, sociology, anthropology, and related fields to the study of organizations and the people in them. It has certain roots in common with industrial/organizational psychology, but the two disciplines differ in emphasis and in academic context.

Organizational behavior is a special interest area within the academic discipline of management. Its scholars and practitioners place relatively more emphasis on organizational variables (such as organization structure) than do I/O psychologists, whose *primary* emphasis remains on individual variables. This distinction is by no means hard and fast. In practice it is almost impossible to study people without regard to setting or vice versa. The American Psychological Association formally recognized this interrelatedness in 1973. At that time, the old designation *industrial psychology* was replaced with the term now in standard use—*industrial/organizational psychology*.

I/O Psychology and Personnel Management

Personnel are the employees of an organization, and these employees are the focus of I/O psychology. They are also the focus of management, and it is usual to find one or more courses in personnel (or human resource) management in an academic management curriculum. These courses cover such topics as compensation, government regulations affecting human resource policies, and union-management (industrial) relations.

Personnel management courses also cover topics central to the subject matter of I/O psychology, including selection, training, health and safety, and performance appraisal. Accordingly, these courses sometimes are called personnel psychology, and they may be taught in the psychology department in addition to (or instead of) being offered in the management department curriculum.

From this brief review it is clear that drawing firm lines to set the subject matter of I/O psychology apart from related areas would be difficult. Industrial/organizational psychology remains a separate and identifiable academic discipline, but I/O psychologists are not confined by rigid boundaries, either in research or in applied activities.

Industrial/Organizational Psychology as a Career

In this section, the training, work settings, and activities of I/O psychologists are summarized. There is also an overview of employment in this field. The employment statistics available are based on American Psychological Association surveys of its membership, which means that people who are performing the same kind of work but are not members of the APA are not represented in the data. Nevertheless, these statistics probably are representative of overall employment opportunities in the field.

Employment in I/O Psychology

On a percentage basis, I/O psychologists are one of the smallest groups in the field of psychology. According to most estimates, they represent 10% or fewer of all psychologists. This figure remains fairly consistent from year to year, as does the demand for I/O psychology programs in colleges and universities. Employment figures for college graduates

I/O psychologists today are interested in every aspect of the interaction between individuals and organizations, from recruiting through employee performance, satisfaction, and well-being.

with an undergraduate degree in I/O psychology are not available, but those holding advanced degrees have few problems finding employment.

The American Psychological Association maintains a research office that conducts periodic surveys of the APA membership on various issues, including employment. Of the Division 14 members who responded to the most recent published survey, fewer than 1% with master's degrees or Ph.D.'s reported being unemployed and seeking employment (Stapp & Fulcher, 1983). These results are consistent with earlier reports (e.g., Gottfredson & Swatko, 1979) as well as with more recent unpublished data compiled by APA (1995a). Employment opportunities in this field have been and remain good, and they may be looking even brighter. The U.S. Department of Labor identifies psychology as one of the occupational groups expected to grow much faster than the average for all occupations through the year 2005.

More information about psychology in general or I/O psychology in particular is available from many sources. Woods and Wilkinson (1987) offer a useful discussion of psychology as an undergraduate major. Up-to-date information on careers in this field is provided by the American Psychological Association in a booklet/video package entitled *Psychology: Scientific Problem Solvers, Careers for the 21st Century* (APA, 1995b). APA also publishes a guide to graduate programs in I/O and other areas of psychology. Some departments of psychology make these materials available to students, and many college/university libraries carry all or some of them. American Psychological Association publications can be purchased directly from the association (see Appendix A).

Training for I/O Psychology

The statistics quoted for employment in I/O psychology are based on surveys of members of APA Division 14. Certain criteria must be met to obtain membership in APA, and most of these standards relate to training. An individual with a master's degree may hold associate membership status, but full membership currently requires a Ph.D. This degree does not have to be in psychology provided that an individual has demonstrated interest and competence in this discipline through his or her doctoral research.

Most of the I/O psychologist members of APA are in agreement that they are psychologists first and psychologists with an interest in organizations second, and this position has strong implications for their views on training. Exhibit 1–1 describes the APA-recommended components of a doctoral study program in I/O psychology. Note that both broad training and specific experience are included; bachelor's and master's programs are modified as appropriate.

Activities and Work Settings of I/O Psychologists

The dual nature of I/O psychology is reflected in career opportunities as well as in training specifications. Industrial/organizational psychologists may be found doing purely theoretical work in research organizations or exclusively applied work as self-employed consultants to organizations. Many do work that is a mixture of both the theoretical and the applied.

In the mid-1980s, roughly one third of I/O psychologists with advanced degrees were employed in academic settings (Howard et al., 1986). According to data collected by the American Psychological Association, this percentage had changed little a decade later

Exhibit 1–1
APA Standards
for Doctoral
Training in I/O
Psychology

A fully qualified *I/O psychologist* has a doctoral degree earned in a program primarily psychological in nature. This degree may be from a department of psychology or from a school of business, management, or administrative science in a regionally accredited university. Consistent with the commitment of I/O psychology to the scientist-professional model, I/O psychologists are thoroughly prepared in basic scientific methods as well as in psychological science; therefore programs that do not include training in basic scientific methods and research are not considered appropriate educational and training models for I/O psychologists. The I/O psychology doctoral program provides training in (a) scientific and professional ethics, (b) general psychological science, (c) research design and methodology, (d) quantitative and qualitative methodology, and (e) psychological measurement, as well as (f) a supervised practicum or laboratory experience in an area of I/O psychology, (g) a field experience in the application and delivery of I/O services, (h) practice in the conduct of applied research, (i) training in other areas of psychology, in business, and in the social and behavioral sciences, as appropriate, and (j) preparation of a doctoral research dissertation.

From "Specialty Guidelines for the Delivery of Services by Industrial/Organizational Psychologists," by the American Psychological Association, *American Psychologist,* 1981, *36*, 665–666.

(APA, 1995a). Typical activities of I/O psychologists on a college or university campus include teaching various courses, conducting research, supervising student research, publishing research reports or other articles in professional journals, attending conferences, presenting papers, and being on panels or symposia at professional meetings. Many I/O psychologists in academic settings also do independent consulting with private industry, hospitals, military services, and local, state, or federal government agencies.

Most industrial/organizational psychologists whose primary employment is not in an academic setting are to be found working for business or government organizations (or working with them in a self-employed capacity). They are not alone there. Psychologists from other specialties, such as clinical or experimental psychology, also choose to work in organizational settings and many of these workplace psychologists are concerned with the same problems as their I/O colleagues.

The activities of I/O psychologists in applied settings vary according to the size and type of organization, but they may include any or all of those listed in Exhibit 1–2. These psychologists also publish the results of their research in professional journals, and many participate in professional meetings alongside their academic colleagues.

Employment opportunities for job seekers whose training in I/O psychology stops at the undergraduate level seldom include academic positions, but there are many possibilities in applied settings, particularly in private industry. Human resource departments are the obvious choice. Employees with I/O training often perform such activities as selection testing, job analysis, and equal employment opportunity documentation research.

Organizations also employ people who have training in I/O psychology in general management positions. Some companies believe this training is an advantage for managers and excellent preparation for work in customer relations. Students with undergraduate training in I/O psychology also find employment in large companies where they work under the supervision of one or more full-time advanced-degree psychologists; in

I/O Psychologists Work with Organizations in the Areas of

Exhibit 1–2
Activities of I/O Psychologists in Applied Settings

- Selection and Placement
  - Developing assessment tools for selection, placement, classification, and promotion of employees
  - Validating test instruments
  - Analyzing job content
  - Developing and implementing selection programs
  - Optimizing placement of personnel
  - Identifying management potential
- Training and Development
  - Identifying training and development needs
  - Formulating and implementing technical training and management development programs
  - Evaluating the effectiveness of training and development programs relative to productivity and satisfaction
  - Career planning
- Organization Development
  - Analyzing organizational structure
  - Maximizing the satisfaction and effectiveness of individuals and work groups
  - Facilitating organizational change
- Performance Measurement
  - Developing criteria
  - Measuring utility
  - Evaluating organizational effectiveness
- Quality of Work Life
  - Enhancing the productive outputs of individuals
  - Identifying factors associated with job satisfaction
  - Redesigning jobs to make them more meaningful
- Consumer Psychology
  - Assessing consumer preferences
  - Identifying consumer reactions to new products
  - Developing market segmentation strategies
- Engineering Psychology
  - Designing work environments
  - Optimizing person-machine effectiveness
  - Developing systems technologies

From *The Science and Practice of Industrial and Organizational Psychology* by the Society for Industrial and Organizational Psychology, Inc. College Park, MD: Society for Industrial and Organizational Psychology, Inc., 1986. Reprinted by permission.

marketing research; in advertising; and in a variety of government and public sector agencies, such as hospitals.

The Regulation of I/O Psychologists

Psychologists have a tradition of and a preference for self-regulation, but as concern for consumer product protection has spread to consumer services as well, they have been drawn with other professionals into the issues and debates raised by the matter of external regulation. Industrial/organizational psychological services are not as controversial as those supplied by other applied psychologists (such as those who work in public mental health), but I/O psychologists must still have a license or a certificate to offer certain applied services to the public at large.

> Licensing is a legal process which regulates the use of a title and defines the activities that constitute the practice of a particular profession. . . . Certification . . . involves . . . a regulation designed only to limit the use of a title, such as "psychologist;" it does not define the scope of the practice. (Howard & Lowman, 1982, p. 1)

At present, the licensing or certification of psychologists is done on a state-by-state basis (see Appendix D). Few states offer the less stringent certification option. Most require licensing, and every state has a mandatory examination for acquiring this license. The process is similar to that of state bar exams for attorneys or certified public accountant exams for accountants. Certain basic educational or training requirements (or both) must be met before the exam may be taken. Once granted, the license must be renewed periodically; in some states, this is every year.

The subject matter and the scope of the questions industrial/organizational psychologists face in acquiring or renewing a license are illustrated in Exhibit 1–3. This exhibit lists the workshop material covered by one of several organizations that offer license exam review programs to psychologists.

Industrial/Organizational Psychology in the Future

For more than a century, industrial/organizational psychology has existed as a distinct and identifiable discipline within the field of psychology. I/O psychologists have devoted themselves to the study of human behavior in organizational settings, both for the knowledge they acquire about behavior (science) and for the usefulness of that knowledge to organizations (practice). A great deal has changed during those 100 years. The world of work has steadily become more complex, more fast-paced, and considerably less predictable than it once was. This trend will continue into the 21st century, but with a new wrinkle. Organizations of the future are not just going to be increasingly more sophisticated, faster, and more turbulent; many are going to be *different* in some very fundamental ways from all of the organizations that have come before them.

In the pages to come, many aspects of the changes sweeping through the world of work are encountered. For a variety of reasons, companies are making themselves smaller ("downsizing") and putting increasing pressure on employees to do more with less. How does this affect the motivation and job satisfaction of the 21st century worker? How can selection and training methods be modified to be effective in organizations where tasks and responsibilities are not fixed but fluid, depending on the needs of the moment?

Exam Strategies: Structure and content of the EPPP; study schedule. Practice exams with discussion. Strategies for reducing test anxiety.

Correlation Analysis and Research Design: Pearson r, types of correlation coefficients; simple and multiple correlation and regression; multivariate correlational techniques; experimental and quasi-experimental designs; case studies; developmental research, single subject research; sampling procedures; internal and external validity.

Statistics: Descriptive and inferential statistics; central limit theorem; hypothesis and significance testing; parametric and nonparametric tests; univariate vs. multivariate analyses; post-hoc analyses.

Test Construction and Interpretation: Scales for psychological measurement; standard scores and the standard deviation curve; speed and power tests; item analysis; reliability; standard error of measurement; factors that affect reliability; content, construct, and criterion-related validity; factor analysis; norm-referenced versus criterion-referenced interpretation.

Industrial/Organizational Psychology: Job analysis; performance appraisal; job selection and validity of methods; decision theory; EEOC regulations; adverse impact; leadership style and philosophy; motivation and satisfaction; communication networks; training; ergonomics.

Learning Theory and Behavior Therapy: Classical and operant conditioning; positive and negative reinforcement; punishment; extinction; schedules of reinforcement; counterconditioning; systematic desensitization; flooding; implosion; aversive therapies; token economies; shaping; modeling; stimulus control; cognitive therapy; behavioral medicine; biofeedback.

Clinical and Abnormal Psychology: DSM-IV Diagnoses including: major affective, schizophrenic, anxiety, and personality disorders; theories of personality; schools of psychotherapy; group psychotherapy; systems theories and family therapy; cross-cultural psychology; psychological factors affecting physical conditions; crisis intervention; effects of psychotherapy; treatments for: sexual dysfunctions, eating disorders, suicide, hypertension; psychopharmacology; psychological assessment; community psychology.

Ethics and Professional Practice: APA's Ethical Standards; General and Specialty Guidelines; the ethics complaint process; licensure and certification; professional relations.

Developmental and School Psychology: The "nature vs. nurture" debate; cognitive, personality, social, and language development; adult development; school psychology; intellectual assessment and the IQ controversy; effects of divorce; recent research in child psychology.

Social Psychology: Field theory; attribution theory; attitude research; cognitive dissonance; prosocial behavior; crowding; social facilitation theory; role theory; obedience to authority; group dynamics; interpersonal attraction; prejudice; psychology of gender.

Printed through the courtesy of Academic Review, Inc., Educational Services, 30 East 60th Street, New York, NY 10022.

Exhibit 1–3
The Curriculum of a Licensing Review Program

Another change in the world of work that is already well under way is a new role for management. The rigid organizational hierarchies of the past are disappearing at an accelerating rate. What does this mean for traditional notions of leadership in organizations? How is this leadership affected by technology, which is not only eliminating many jobs but also making it possible in some cases to eliminate organizations themselves in the usual sense? Instead of a factory or an office full of people, there may be a "virtual office" whose functions are "outsourced." What do absenteeism and turnover mean in such a context?

The list could go on, but the point has been made. What do such radical changes mean for I/O psychology in the next century? One member of the profession answers the question this way:

> As psychology in general, and industrial and organizational psychology in particular, stands poised on the brink of the 21st century, I believe that our greatest challenge will be to change the way we as a field think about organizations and their people. (Cascio, 1995, p. 931)

Changing the way they think about the world of work will require I/O psychologists to break with many of their traditional practices, to examine old questions from fresh perspectives, and to find creative ways to conduct meaningful research in settings that bear little or no resemblance to those they are accustomed to examining. These requirements do not mean that the past must be abandoned. To the contrary, the body of knowledge that is I/O psychology today is the most powerful tool available for meeting the challenges of tomorrow, and it is that work that is described in this book.

At Issue

One, Two, or Many Psychologies?

The American Psychological Association was founded in 1892 with 31 members. Slightly more than a century later it has almost 85,000 members, nearly 60,000 affiliates, and 51 special interest groups ranging from General Psychology (Division 1) to the Society for the Psychological Study of Men and Masculinity (Division 51). The increasing size and specialization within psychology, as reflected in the growth and diversity of APA membership, is generating increasing debate about the appropriate way to conceptualize the field. Is psychology one discipline with numerous areas of application, as the traditional view holds (Matarazzo, 1987)? Or is it really a group of many related but distinct disciplines that Koch (1993) calls "the psychological studies"?

The significance of a debate about the true nature of psychology is perhaps most easily recognized when it comes to training. The basic issue can be stated very simply. If psychology is one discipline, training must be broader than if it is not. In particular, psychology students must be exposed to a core of basic subject matter before moving on to areas of specific interest.

As the 21st century approaches, the tradition of one psychology is clearly more mainstream than Koch's advocacy of many psychological sciences. There is a third alternative, however. Perhaps psychology is neither one discipline nor many, but two. However it might have *begun*, maintain some psychologists, what psychology has *become* is two basic and largely nonoverlapping fields with different values, methodologies, and agenda. On the one hand is research-oriented scientific psychology and on the other is pragmatically oriented applied psychology. This view is not new, but it seems to be finding expression in the literature much more frequently of late. Some who write about it are approving, some are disapproving, and a minority (e.g., Schönpflug, 1993) maintain that it has always been so.

What would it mean if a majority of psychologists accepted the view that the science and practice of psychology are not just two different orientations within one field but two different fields? The implications are far-reaching and, to many, very disturbing. One of the more profound effects would, again, lie in training and in the associated licensing requirements. There is already considerable pressure in the mental health field for people with master's degrees to be recognized as fully qualified psychologists. It is not much of a stretch to envision the doctoral degree ultimately becoming the science degree while the master's degree becomes an applied degree.

Industrial/organizational psychology would be profoundly affected by any significant "remaking of psychology" (Bevan & Kessel, 1994) in the direction of a recognized and accepted science/practice split. Some individual members would disagree, but the profession in general has always endorsed an interdependent relationship between science and practice. As Morris Viteles, who began publishing in the field in the early 1920s, expresses it: "If it isn't scientific, it's not good practice, and if it isn't practical, it's not good science" (quoted in Katzell & Austin, 1992, p. 826).

The fact that people who call themselves psychologists work in many different places doing many different things is a perfectly natural consequence of the maturing of a science, according to Bower (1993). It is also perfectly natural that people who do very different kinds of work in very different places should have very different views on some issues. In particular, there will probably always be some divergence between the perspectives of psychologists who do work that is primarily or exclusively applied and those who do not. Nevertheless, "the scientific account of behavior is very different from ordinary ways of thinking" (Kimble, 1994, p. 510). The question seems to be: Is allegiance to this way of thinking strong enough to hold the field together?

Summary

Industrial/organizational psychology is a relatively small specialty within the discipline of psychology, with a history going back some 100 years. Advanced degree industrial/organizational psychologists work in a variety of academic and applied settings. Training is rigorous, stressing both the theoretical and applied aspects of the discipline, and every state now requires that those who offer applied I/O services to the public be licensed or certified, or work under the supervision of a licensed psychologist.

Questions for Review and Discussion

1. The two world wars have had a significant impact on the field of industrial/organizational psychology, but World War II ended more than 50 years ago. Suggest at least two major events or developments in America since that time that you think have important implications for the study of people in organizations. Explain briefly.

2. In your own words, describe the major differences between an I/O psychologist's perspective on organizations and that of a management scholar. Do you believe these fields should be combined to create an industrial/organizational/management field (as industrial psychology became industrial/organizational psychology)? Why or why not?

3. Assume that you have an undergraduate degree with a major in industrial/organizational psychology. Using what you know about career opportunities in this field, what would you do next and why?

4. Distinguish between licensing and certification for I/O psychologists and briefly discuss your personal opinion of external regulation for professionals in psychology.

Key Terms

American Psychological Association

certification

Hawthorne studies

industrial/organizational psychological services

licensing

psychology

Society for Industrial and Organizational Psychology, Inc.

References

American Psychological Association (1981). Specialty guidelines for the delivery of services by industrial/organizational psychologists. *American Psychologist, 36,* 664–669.

American Psychological Association (1995a). Unpublished survey data.

American Psychological Association (1995b). *Psychology: Scientific problem solvers, careers for the 21st century.* Washington, DC: APA Education Directorate and Office of Public Communications.

Bevan, W., & Kessel, F. (1994). Plain truths and home cooking: Thoughts on the making and remaking of psychology. *American Psychologist, 49,* 505–509.

Boneau, C. A. (1992). Observations on psychology's past and future. *American Psychologist, 47,* 1586–1596.

Bower, G. H. (1993). The fragmentation of psychology? *American Psychologist, 48,* 905–907.

Cascio, W. F. (1995). Whither industrial and organizational psychology in a changing world of work? *American Psychologist, 50,* 928–939.

Chant, G. (1993). The Hawthorne effect. *Journal of the Market Research Society, 35,* 279.

Gottfredson, G. D., & Swatko, M. K. (1979). Employment, unemployment, and the job search in psychology. *American Psychologist, 34,* 1047–1060.

Harrell, T. W. (1992). Some history of the Army General Classification Test. *Journal of Applied Psychology, 77,* 875–878.

Hawthorne revisited: The legend and the legacy. (1975). *Organizational Dynamics, 3,* 66–80.

Howard, A., & Lowman, R. L. (1982). *Licensing and industrial/organizational psychology: Background and issues.* Prepared for the Executive Committee of the Division of Industrial/Organizational Psychology. Washington, DC: American Psychological Association.

Howard, A., Pion, G. M., Gottfredson, G. D., Flattau, P. E., Oskamp, S., Pfafflin, S. M., Bray, D. W., & Burstein, A. G. (1986). The changing face of American psychology: A report from the committee on employment and human resources. *American Psychologist, 41,* 1311–1327.

Katzell, R. A., & Austin, J. T. (1992). From then to now: The development of industrial-organizational psychology in the United States. *Journal of Applied Psychology, 77,* 803–835.

Kimble, G. A. (1994). A frame of reference for psychology. *American Psychologist, 49,* 510–519.

Koch, S. (1993). "Psychology" or "the psychological studies"? *American Psychologist, 48,* 902–905.

Landy, F. J. (1992). Hugo Münsterberg: Victim or visionary? *Journal of Applied Psychology, 77,* 787–802.

Matarazzo, J. D. (1987). There is only one psychology, no specialties, but many applications. *American Psychologist, 42,* 893–903.

Münsterberg, H. (1913). *Psychology and industrial efficiency.* Boston: Houghton Mifflin.

Parsons, H. M. (1992). Hawthorne: An early OBM experiment. *Journal of Organizational Behavior Management, 12,* 27–43.

Richardson, M. W. (1940). *Plans for the construction and validation of the Army Classification Test: A report to the Test Committee, National Research Council.* Washington, DC: National Research Council.

Roethlisberger, F. J. (1941). *Management and morale.* Cambridge, MA: Harvard University Press.

Roethlisberger, F. J., & Dickson, W. J. (1939). *Management and the worker.* Cambridge, MA: Harvard University Press.

Schönpflug, W. (1993). Applied psychology: Newcomer with a long tradition. *Applied Psychology: An International Review, 42,* 5–30.

Scott, W. D. (1911a). *Increasing human efficiency.* New York: Macmillan.

Scott, W. D. (1911b). *Influencing men in business.* New York: Ronald Press.

Society for Industrial and Organizational Psychology, Inc. (1986) *The science and practice of industrial and organizational psychology.* College Park, MD: Author.

Stafford, T. F., & Stafford, M. R. (1993). Reaction effects in participant observation: A response. *Journal of the Market Research Society, 35,* 280–281.

Stapp, J., & Fulcher, R. (1983). The employment of APA members: 1982. *American Psychologist, 38,* 1298–1320.

Wiggins, J. G., Jr. (1994). Would you want your child to be a psychologist? *American Psychologist, 49,* 485–492.

Woods, P. J. (Ed.), with Wilkinson, C. S. (1987). *Is psychology the major for you? Planning for your undergraduate years.* Washington, DC: American Psychological Association.

Wren, D. (1987). *The evolution of management thought* (3rd ed.). New York: Wiley.

2

The Scientific Study of Human Behavior

PSYCHOLOGY
AT WORK

College Students Weigh the Costs and Benefits of Deceptive Research

Excerpted from
C. B. Fisher and D.
Fryberg,
"Participant
Partners: College
Students Weigh the
Costs and Benefits
of Deceptive
Research."
*American
Psychologist,* 1994,
49, 417–427.
Copyright © 1994
by the American
Psychological
Association.
Reprinted by per-
mission.

Since . . . [the early 1960s], the use of deception in psychological research has gained popularity and drawn ethical debate. . . . The APA guidelines . . . while recognizing that deceptive research practices require ethical concerns, leave to the judgment of the individual psychologist about how best to contribute to scientific knowledge and protect human welfare. . . .

In practice, the ethical advice that researchers receive is obtained informally from colleagues and formally through institutional review board (IRB) approval or disapproval of research proposals. Equally important but relatively untapped resources for ethical advice are members of the population who will serve as research participants. . . .

[Our study was] designed to gather information on how prospective participants evaluate . . . elements of deceptive research. . . .

Following informed consent procedures, an equal number of men and women were randomly assigned to read and answer questions about one of . . . three studies. . . .

. . . three articles were selected from the *Journal of Personality and Social Psychology* typifying different forms of deceptive research procedures. . . .

The descriptions of each study followed identical format sections designed to complement the students' introductory background in research design and to provide them with sufficient information to answer the questions that followed. The sections covered the purpose of the study, participants, experimental procedures, measurement of participant reactions, and results. . . .

The majority of students thought the societal benefits of the study they reviewed were greater than the costs to participants. . . . On this basis, most also thought that the study they evaluated should be conducted.

. . . However, they also believed that participants would be discomforted by the study and that forewarned individuals would be less likely to participate.

THE PURPOSE of this chapter is to introduce the basic principles of the scientific study of human behavior. Because the subjects of this study are people, psychologists have special ethical concerns not shared by researchers in other sciences. These concerns are especially critical if a research project involves deceiving subjects in some way until the research is complete.

As discussed by the authors of the article from which the excerpt in Psychology at Work is taken, the basic ethical decision in any research project involving deception requires weighing the welfare and rights of the subjects against the scientific value of the research. Fisher and Fryberg's (1994) study is one of the few that approaches this question *about* research *through* research, rather than philosophically.

The data Fisher and Fryberg got from their student subjects lends support to the safeguards used by psychologists in research involving deception (most subjects believed the three studies were worth carrying out). At the same time, they highlight an issue that disturbs many investigators who use human subjects. Put simply, the majority of subjects believed many people would have refused to participate in these research projects involving deception if they had understood them well enough in advance.

Different forms of deception are used in psychological research, but the basic purpose of all forms is to avoid introducing unwanted error into data collection. Consider the difference between the way students in a class might approach a test they believe is going to affect their final course grade and the way they might approach it knowing in advance that the test is for research purposes only. If the investigator giving the test is trying to answer a question about real-life test-taking behavior, it is unlikely that he or she will obtain appropriate data in the second case.

The task of designing and conducting a study that allows for collecting appropriate data and making valid inferences about the question of interest is the focus of this chapter. The basic tool used by most scientists, including I/O psychologists, is a set of principles for research called the scientific method.

The Scientific Method

Researchers in I/O psychology rely on the principles of the scientific method whether they are trying to answer questions about why bosses listen more to certain subordinates, what training methods work best for a particular set of tasks, how to raise the level of employee motivation, or any of hundreds of other topics. The **scientific method** is the investigation of phenomena by an orderly process of observation, inference, and verification. It has four very important characteristics that set it apart from other approaches to solving problems or acquiring knowledge.

1. It requires a precise vocabulary.
2. It has rules for collecting and organizing data.
3. It is based on a system of logic for making decisions (called inferences) about the meaning of observations.
4. It requires verification of these inferences.

The basic research process that comprises the scientific method is shown in Figure 2–1, which depicts the relationships among the four characteristics of the scientific method and the three critical elements of the research process—observation, inference, and verification. This process is a cyclical one; theoretically, the verification stage has no limits. There is always more to learn in any field, and I/O psychologists are still

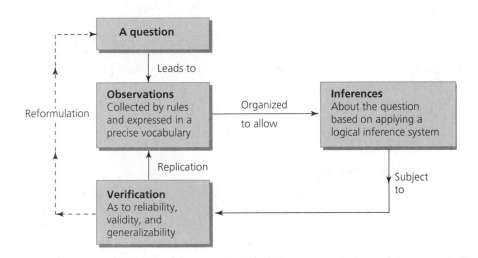

Figure 2–1
The Scientific
Method

trying to discover and integrate some rather basic relationships in a world that stubbornly refuses to stand still and wait until they catch up.

The dynamic environment in which I/O psychologists work makes it all the more critical that they apply rigorous standards to their research efforts to understand or bring about changes in organizations and the behavior of people in them. That research is the foundation of this book, and understanding it will be easier if there is some familiarity with the vocabulary and more common methods of research in I/O psychology. The discussion is organized around the three cornerstones of the scientific method—observation, inference, and verification.

Observation: *Research Design*

All knowledge starts with the immediate conscious experience of an individual—that is, with observation. The scientific approach to knowledge requires investigators to use a precise vocabulary to describe their observations. Where a supervisor might say that a particular employee is good with his or her hands, an I/O psychologist would describe the same employee in terms of "a high level of manual dexterity."

A recognized scientific vocabulary serves an important function in research: it enables scientists to describe their observations clearly and precisely. This precision makes it possible for others with similar interests and appropriate training to understand exactly what was observed. It also allows them to make meaningful comparisons with their own observations.

In addition to requiring that scientists use a common scientific vocabulary, the scientific approach to knowledge requires them to make observations in a systematic fashion according to certain rules. These rules concern the nature and number of observations needed, the way these observations are measured, and the conditions under which the observations are made. They serve to control sources of error that could make it difficult or impossible to infer answers to the questions under investigation (or that could allow for a variety of equally likely inferences about what is observed). Thus, the rules serve both as a standard against which to evaluate research results and as a source of assistance for scientists planning research.

Laying out a plan for making observations consistent with the rules of the scientific method is called **research design**. Four important questions must be answered at this planning stage: What is to be observed? Who is to be observed? Where are the observations to be made? How are the observations to be made? Together, these questions summarize a plan for data collection—that is, for making a defined set of observations according to a particular plan.

What Is to Be Observed?

All scientific research starts with a question. Sometimes this question is as broad as "I wonder what would happen if . . .." Often, however, it is a specific question that has been raised by a theory, a problem, or just plain curiosity. "I wonder if more break periods would reduce symptoms of stress among employees?" is an example of the kind of specific question that might interest an I/O psychologist.

Exhibit 2–1
A Research
Hypothesis

"Employees in autonomous work groups show lower levels of absenteeism and turnover than their counterparts in traditionally designed jobs."

From J. L. Cordery, W. S. Mueller, and L. M. Smith. "Attitudinal and Behavioral Effects of Autonomous Group Working: A Longitudinal Field Study." *Academy of Management Journal*, 1991, *34*, 464–476.

Hypotheses

To answer a question such as that about work breaks and symptoms of stress, an investigator following the rules of the scientific method would begin by restating the question in the form of an hypothesis. An **hypothesis** is a statement of a predicted answer to a research question. Such a statement about the question of work breaks and stress might read: "Employees given frequent work breaks will show significantly fewer symptoms of stress at the end of six months than those given fewer work breaks." An actual research hypothesis taken from a published research report is shown in Exhibit 2–1.

Cordery, Mueller, and Smith (1991) were investigating the question of the relationship between (a) type of work group (traditional vs. autonomous), (b) absenteeism, and (c) turnover for employees of two minerals processing plants in Australia. Their hypothesis about this relationship was that both absenteeism and turnover would be lower among workers in autonomous groups. This way of organizing work allows employees a high degree of self-regulation in matters usually given over to management, such as allocating work tasks, determining priorities, and hiring new members into the group.

Hypotheses come from theories, experience, published research on similar or related questions, or sometimes just from "educated guesswork." It is usual to explain the source of an hypothesis when publishing the results of a research investigation. Cordery and his colleagues were attempting to confirm the results of earlier studies, and so the hypothesis shown in Exhibit 2–1 had its source in published reports of research into the same question.

Determining if the prediction made by an hypothesis is confirmed by observation is called hypothesis testing. Conclusions about this testing are based on the statistical analysis discussed in a later section. The next step in research design is to state the variables to be observed and how they are to be measured.

Variables

One of the advantages of stating a research question as a formal hypothesis is that it highlights the variables to be observed in the research. A **variable** is some aspect of the world that can take on at least two different measured values. The variables specified by the hypothesis in Exhibit 2–1 are (a) type of work group, (b) level of absenteeism, and (c) level of turnover. Among the other variables studied frequently in I/O psychology research are motivation, job satisfaction, and job performance.

The theoretical opposite of a variable is called a constant, but when the subject is human behavior there are few, if any, real constants. Most variables may be *held constant* for research purposes, however. For example, sex may be held constant in an investigation by observing only male or only female subjects. In this case, sex, which is a variable in the world, is a constant in the scientific study.

An hypothesis provides a clear statement of the variables to be observed in a research investigation, but remember that this observation must conform to certain rules. One of these rules is that what is observed must be defined unambiguously so that others can understand and repeat the observations if they desire. In the scientific method, such a definition is called an operational definition.

Operational Definitions

An **operational definition** defines a variable to be observed in terms of the process by which it is measured. The following are among the operational definitions that are used frequently in I/O psychology research:

- *Intelligence:* a score on a particular intelligence test
- *Work performance:* a supervisor's evaluation on a standard evaluation form
- *Turnover rate:* the percentage of newly hired employees who leave the company voluntarily within six months

Each of the variables in the list can be and often is defined in a different way. This is true of many research variables. In their study of absenteeism, for example, Haccoun and Jeanrie (1995) defined absenteeism in terms of a flat count of days absent from work. Two alternatives to this operational definition often found in the research literature are (1) the ratio of time absent to time worked and (2) a count of absence incidents in a given time period (three successive days missed would be only one incident).

All of the operational definitions of absenteeism— ratio, flat count, incident count— are equally valid. The definition that is used in a particular study is the one that best serves the researcher's purpose at that time. It is for this reason that understanding and evaluating reports of research would be very difficult and replicating (duplicating) a study would be impossible if specific operational definitions of variables were not provided.

To summarize to this point, research design starts with a question. The investigator states this question in terms of a research hypothesis that specifies the variables to be observed. He or she then goes on to determine the operational definitions for these variables. The focus of research in I/O psychology is the behavior of human beings; therefore, the next step is to decide who they will be.

Who Is to Be Observed?

There are some exceptions, as when an entire organization is the "subject," but most research in I/O psychology uses individual human subjects (also called participants). Given that the purpose of this research is to gain knowledge about the behavior of people in organizations, it would seem that the best subjects would be organizational employees. Unfortunately, it is not always possible to gain access to such subjects. Finding organizations willing to allow the possible disruption of their normal activities can be a problem. In addition, many variables cannot be controlled in real-life settings. For some purposes, then, subjects other than organizational employees are more appropriate.

Even when it is possible and desirable to use employees as research subjects, other questions must be answered. How many employees in what jobs in what organizations? What characteristics must these subjects (the sample) have to be representative of those to whom research findings are intended to apply (the population)?

Exhibit 2–2
Describing the
Subjects of
Research
Observation

"This study was conducted in a private organization that owns and operates 77 super-markets in four northeastern states. . . . The final sample included 104 managerial trainees, 104 supervisors, and 297 coworkers. . . . For the trainee sample, the mean age was 32 years and 57% were women. They had been with the company an average of 8 years and had been in their current position an average of 3 years. . . . The peer and su-pervisor samples had similar demographic characteristics."

From J. B. Tracey, S. I. Tannenbaum, and M. J. Kavanagh, "Applying Trained Skills on the Job: The Importance of the Work Environment." *Journal of Applied Psychology,* 1995, *80,* 239–252.

In research design, the term **population** refers to all of the people (organizations, de-partments, or other units) that have the characteristics relevant to the research question of interest. This means that for research purposes, a population is defined by the investi-gator. In a 1981 study by Dalton and Perry, for example, the population was defined to be employees of all organizations that had unionized personnel.

Very few researchers in any field have the resources to study an entire population. In most cases, they must select a defined portion of the population called a **sample.** Each in-dividual (or other unit) in a sample is called a **subject,** and one of the most important considerations in the choice of subjects is that they be *representative* of the population de-fined by the investigator. If the population is defined as all employees of Company X, the sample should include employees of both sexes who represent the full range of jobs, lev-els of experience, ages, salaries, and ranks.

If the subjects in a sample are not representative of the population of interest, it is not possible for the researcher to extend conclusions from the research to this population with much confidence. The very common use of students as subjects in psychology re-search illustrates the problem. If the population a researcher is interested in is organiza-tional personnel, inferences from research with undergraduate psychology students as subjects are severely restricted (Landy, Shankster, & Kohler, 1994).

To help the reader of a research report evaluate the extent to which reported results may be generalized to the relevant population, it is usual for the sample to be described in detail. One such description is shown in Exhibit 2–2. Tracey, Tannenbaum, and Kavanagh (1995) tell the reader the kind of organization their subjects were employed in and how many people of what age, sex, tenure with the company, and level of job expe-rience participated in their study.

Where Are Observations to Be Made?

There are two basic strategies for making observations in I/O psychology research. First, researchers may go to the subjects and make observations in their usual surroundings. In such a case, the research is being carried out in a field setting. Second, subjects may come to the researchers and be observed in surroundings that the researchers have created. This research is being carried out in a laboratory setting.

Sometimes the decision as to whether to conduct field or laboratory research is made for the researcher by the nature of the question being investigated. If the behavior of em-ployees involved in a wildcat strike is the focus of the investigation, the researcher will go to the site of the strike (a field setting) to make observations. Other times a researcher has a choice of setting; the assembly of watches could be observed either in a watch factory or in a laboratory.

There are trade-offs in deciding whether to observe watch assembly in the field or in a laboratory. The factory setting offers the advantage of reality, but in the typical organizational setting it can be difficult to obtain appropriate samples and to get permission for control groups. Another problem is that field settings limit a researcher's ability to control variables that are not being investigated. Some of these variables will have little or no effect on the research; others may affect both the observations and the conclusions significantly.

A **confounding variable** is an extraneous variable (a variable not of interest to the researcher) that can affect conclusions from research through its effect on a variable that *is* being investigated. Suppose that an I/O psychologist wants to find out if different kinds of magnifying instruments have predictable effects on the accurate assembly of watches. If he or she takes this question to the floor of a watch factory (a field setting), there most likely will be varying conditions of lighting, noise, social interaction, and supervision for different subjects.

The varying conditions for subjects in the watch factory setting are confounding variables. They affect the vision and the concentration of the subjects, which, in turn, affect the accuracy of watch assembly. Therefore, it would be difficult to determine to what extent observed differences in assembly accuracy actually were due to differences in the magnifying instruments.

If the researcher in question makes the other decision, he or she might study watch assembly in the psychology behavior laboratory at a university, where potentially confounding variables can be controlled. In this setting, it is possible to get a clearer picture of the actual performance differences associated with various types of magnifying instruments. On the other hand, "working conditions" now are very different from real ones, and there is room for doubt as to whether the conclusions reached in the laboratory would hold up in the factory.

The example of watch assembly illustrates the basic point that the advantages and disadvantages of laboratory and field settings for research contrast sharply and an either/or choice can be very difficult. Many researchers believe it is better not to make such a choice, but to use a combination of settings in order to take advantage of the strengths of each (e.g., Ackerman & Kanfer, 1993; Katzell & Austin, 1992; Robbins & DeNisi, 1994; Tepper, 1994).

To use a combined strategy in the present example, controlled observations could be made in the laboratory and then compared with subsequent observations under real conditions at the watch factory. At this point, the researcher might draw conclusions with more confidence as to which magnifying instrument is most effective for increased watch assembly accuracy.

How Are Observations to Be Made?

The classic method by which scientists make their observations is by performing experiments in a laboratory (or, more recently, in a field setting). Experimentation is not the only way to make such observations, however. A scientist may go into a particular setting and simply record the observations of interest; that is, he or she may do field observation.

Alternatively, observations may be collected by questionnaires or from the records of others. These methods are known as survey research and historical studies, respectively. Along with experimentation and field observation, they make up the primary methods by which I/O psychologists collect data.

Experimentation

In an **experiment**, observations of subject behavior are made under different states of the environment that are created by the experimenter's manipulation of specified variables. The manipulated variable in an experiment is called an **independent variable**. The particular states created by the manipulations in an experiment are called **treatments** or **experimental conditions** (both terms appear in this book as both appear in the I/O psychology literature). The subject behavior of interest in an experiment is called the **dependent variable**. In the watch assembly example, the magnifying instrument is the independent variable, the different types of magnifying instruments are the various experimental conditions, and the accuracy of subject watch assembly is the dependent variable.

The great advantage of experimentation over other ways to investigate questions about human behavior is that it allows a researcher to make inferences about cause and effect. If predicted (hypothesized) changes in a dependent variable follow specified manipulations of an independent variable, there is evidence that the manipulated variable is a causal factor in the observed behavior. To illustrate the concept of experimentation, a summary of a laboratory experiment in I/O psychology appears in Spotlight on Research.

SPOTLIGHT ON RESEARCH

Improving Group Performance by Training in Individual Problem Solving

Summarized from P. C. Bottger and P. W. Yetton, "Improving Group Performance by Training in Individual Problem Solving." *Journal of Applied Psychology*, 1987, 72, 651–657.

Research hypothesis "The problem-solving performance of groups whose members are trained with an individual-based task intervention is superior to groups with untrained members" (p. 652).

Type of study Laboratory experiment.

Subjects Three hundred seventy-six male and female managers and business students.

Independent variable
■ Training or no training in problem solving by experimenter.

Dependent variable
■ Accuracy of the group solution to the Moon Survival Exercise as measured by deviance from standard solution.

General procedure Ten minutes of individual problem-solving training were given to 127 subjects, who then were formed into 53 groups of 4 to 6 members each. The remaining 249 subjects were formed into 53 groups of like size without members having received instruction in problem solving. All groups were instructed to generate a *group* solution to the Moon Survival Exercise. In this problem, subjects imagine themselves as having crash-landed on the moon 200 miles from home base. The task is to rank the 15 pieces of equipment they have with them in order of importance to survival. Rankings were compared to expert ranking to calculate an accuracy score.

Results Hypothesis supported.

Conclusion "The individual-ability intervention improves group resources and performance. . ." (p. 654).

The Spotlight feature also outlines the decisions that the researchers made about the other research design questions that have been discussed.

Bottger and Yetton (1987) were interested in group problem solving, an area of research that is increasingly important as more organizations use groups or teams to accomplish tasks and projects (rather than individuals overseen by supervisors). In the study summarized in Spotlight on Research, the investigators examined the effect that training individual group members in problem-solving skills might have on subsequent group problem-solving performance. A laboratory setting was chosen. The task was a group decision-making exercise of a type that long has been used in this kind of research. This task has the advantage of being a controlled one with a standard solution, although it bears little resemblance to most real work tasks.

One strategy for making use of some of the advantages of a laboratory experiment such as that of Bottger and Yetton (more control) *and* the advantages of a field experiment (more reality) that works for some research questions is called a **simulation experiment**. In this case, the experimenter reproduces certain important aspects of the real world while exercising control over the more critical potential confounding variables.

In some simulation experiments, subjects are aware of the experimental nature of the situation; in others, they are not. A classic example of the second case is a simulation experiment by Ilgen, Nebeken, and Pritchard (1981). These researchers were studying the effects on task performance (the dependent variable) of manipulating (a) task difficulty and (b) method of pay (the independent variables). Subjects in this simulation experiment were obtained through a newspaper advertisement, and they worked at what they believed was an actual temporary job. In other words, a fairly common employment situation was *simulated* by the investigators. The difference was that they "hired" only those subjects with certain characteristics in order to control potentially confounding variables such as age, sex, and scores on the selection tests they used. In a field setting, these researchers would have been limited to choosing subjects from among people already employed.

Laboratory, field, and simulation experiments are alternative settings/strategies for carrying out experimentation. For a study to be a genuine experiment, two conditions must be met. First, the researcher must be able to manipulate one or more independent variables. Second, the subjects must be assigned randomly to the various treatments. In practice, it often is not possible to meet both of these criteria. An investigator may be able to manipulate the independent variable but not to carry out random assignment of subjects to the various experimental conditions, for example. In this instance, a quasi-experiment might be conducted. A **quasi-experiment** is similar to the real thing, but it does not meet the standards for pure experimentation (Cook & Campbell, 1979).

The question of how the pay system affects productivity in manufacturing plants offers an illustration of a quasi-experiment. Suppose that an I/O psychologist is able to convince the management of one plant to change the pay system from an hourly wage to a piece rate (the employee is paid for each unit produced); this is one experimental condition. A second plant that is similar in size, product, and current productivity level is located, and the general manager agrees to cooperate in the study. The hourly wage system that exists in this plant is left alone; this is the second experimental condition.

In the study outlined, the researcher is manipulating the pay system. If this is to be a true experiment, however, it is also necessary for the total sample of subjects to be assigned randomly to each treatment (piece rate or hourly). This condition cannot be fulfilled; current employees in the two plants are the subjects, and their assignment to experimental treatment is based upon their current plant of employment. For this reason, the experiment is a quasi-experiment, not a true one.

The major drawback to a quasi-experiment appears after the investigator conducts the study and analyzes the data. In the current example, he or she gives the new wage system in the first plant a chance to take hold, then measures the productivity in the two plants. As hypothesized, it is higher under the piece rate. Did the piece-rate pay system cause the greater productivity? There is no way to be sure with this research design.

The two plants in the investigator's study may be similar, but no two plants are exactly alike in terms of employee characteristics, supervision style, and other variables. Therefore, the researcher must be very cautious about making inferences that the new wage system caused the higher productivity observed in the first plant, because it was not possible to assign subjects at random to the two experimental conditions. A quasi-experimental design yields more information about possible causes and effects than many of the alternative procedures, but its failure to conform to the standards for a pure experiment limits the extent to which such inferences may be made.

The quasi-experiment is an option when an experimenter has some control over independent variables. There are times, however, when an independent variable specified by a research question cannot be manipulated at all. This problem may arise for practical reasons. An I/O psychologist interested in the effect of (a) total work force size on (b) employee turnover rate cannot manipulate the size of a work force in a company, for instance. Other variables are not subject to experimentation for ethical rather than practical reasons. It would be possible to manipulate job stress by giving people impossible work goals or by implying, falsely, that their jobs were in jeopardy, but such strategies are entirely outside the bounds of ethical research practice in I/O psychology. In such cases, one of the field observation research methods may be a useful alternative.

Field Observation

Examples of other variables of interest to I/O psychologists that cannot, or should not, be manipulated are employee morale, organization structure, volume of business, and employee friendship patterns. These are variables, nonetheless; they exist in different quantities or states in the world. One way to study such variables is to seek out subjects who already are different with respect to them and to conduct what is called a field study.

In a **field study**, the researcher relies on existing circumstances to provide clues to the relationships between important variables. For example, an I/O psychologist might be interested in how the degree of decision-making autonomy given to employees affects their job satisfaction. The hypothesis is that individuals with more decision-making autonomy are more satisfied with their jobs. The investigator cannot manipulate company policy or employee job satisfaction, but he or she can make systematic observations of job satisfaction in several companies with measurably different policies about decision-making autonomy. Statistical procedures can then be used to make an inference about the hypothesized relationship between these two variables.

In addition to serving as a way to get around the problem of variables that cannot be manipulated, field studies are useful to psychologists as a way to investigate the effects of events over which they have no control (such as strikes, massive layoffs, company mergers, and so on). An I/O psychologist might take the opportunity to study workers' attitudes toward their jobs in two plants belonging to the same company, one of which has full employment and one of which is experiencing large numbers of employee cutbacks, for instance.

Not all psychologists can or want to conduct field studies, although they are interested in what is happening in field settings. An alternative field method is simply to observe and record what happens with respect to some aspect of the situation that is of interest. The researcher interested in attitudes might do in-depth interviews with the remaining employees in the plant experiencing the layoffs, for example. Such observations frequently appear in the form of the familiar observational, or case, study.

The distinguishing characteristic of a case study as a research strategy is that it focuses on intense examination of a current event in its natural environment without interfering with the event (Yin, 1981). Such studies are time-consuming to carry out and difficult to write in such a way that the reader really shares in the experience. If they are done well, however, they can be especially rich sources of experimental research hypotheses (e.g., Hackman, 1989). There are also methods under development for subjecting case studies themselves to statistical analysis (e.g., Larsson, 1993).

One important use of case studies is providing verification (or lack thereof) of observations made in other settings. In addition, such observations are useful in helping organizations avoid the pitfalls into which others may have stumbled. This last possibility is illustrated by the excerpt from a well-known case study in Exhibit 2–3. The author of that study, T. A. Wise (1966), describes the IBM Corporation's experiences in marketing and manufacturing what was at the time an entirely new line of computers.

IBM's System/360 consisted of six new models of a sophisticated technology that had not been tested previously in the marketplace. As Wise's report makes clear, selling this equipment was one of the least of the company's problems. The corporation also encountered internal resistance to change, production problems, and management problems. A clear and detailed description of such problems can be very useful to I/O psychologists as well as to companies about to market new products.

Historical Studies and Survey Research

Observational studies, field studies, and experiments are methods of making observations in which a researcher interacts with subjects in some fashion. In historical studies and survey research, by contrast, subjects may never be seen by the investigator. In an **historical study**, research observations are made from records kept by others. An I/O psychologist might use such records to investigate the nature of the relationship between sex and absenteeism in a company, for example. He or she would not need to see any employees, only to obtain the appropriate information from the company's files.

In **survey research**, observations are made by means of questionnaires. Subjects may be chosen on the basis of membership in some group (as in the American Psychological Association studies of employment reported in another chapter) or on the basis of some particular characteristic (such as having been employed by a particular company for at least five years). The data in survey research are self-report data; in most cases, the questionnaires are filled out by the subjects without their ever seeing the researcher. (Occasionally the data are obtained in an interview, but this method is properly called field survey research.)

Both historical studies and survey research offer investigators the advantage of being able to collect large numbers of observations in less time and with less disruption to the normal activities of subjects or organizations than other methods. There are drawbacks, however. In historical research, the investigator is dependent upon the accuracy and completeness with which records have been kept, and this can be a frustrating experience.

When Tom Watson, Jr. made what he called "the most important product announcement in company history," he created quite a stir. International Business Machines is not a corporation given to making earth-shaking pronouncements casually, and the declaration that it was launching an entirely new computer line, the System/360, was headline news. . . .

By 1963, with the important decisions on the 360 being implemented, excitement about the new product began to spread through the corporation. . . . But this rising pitch of interest by no means meant that the struggle inside the company was settled. . . . The System 360 Concepts plunged IBM into an organizational upheaval. . . . The General Products Division (for example) really bristled with hostility. Its output, after all, accounted for two-thirds of the company's revenues for data processing. It had a popular and profitable product in the field, the 1401, which the 360 threatened to replace. . . .

Production of the 360 line was . . . held up by a maddening series of shortages. There were, for example, critical shortages of epoxy glass, copper laminate, and contact tabs. . . . IBM representatives suddenly began appearing at tab plants late in the evening or early in the morning with suitcases. They would pack all the tabs they could and then fly to Endicott to keep the production line moving.

Around mid-1965, however, the company gradually became aware that production problems were not its only, or even its greatest, obstacle to getting the 360 program on schedule. While there had been no disposition to underrate the technical difficulties in preparing the programming, no one, it appears, foresaw the appalling management problems that would be associated with them. . . .

Exhibit 2–3
Excerpt from a Case Study

Excerpted from T. A. Wise, "The Rocky Road to the Marketplace." *Fortune,* 1966, *74,* 138–212. Copyright © 1966 Time Inc. All rights reserved. Reprinted by permission.

One person has forgotten to record attendance or production figures for a critical time period. A long-departed administrative assistant had handwriting like hen scratchings. The files for three years in the middle of the time period being studied were erased by a new computer data entry assistant.

Similar problems arise in survey research. Some questions are left unanswered, some have two answers, and the truthfulness of still others is open to question for one reason or another. One respondent's handwriting may be illegible while another respondent may have spilled coffee on the form, blotting out several replies. Many questionnaires simply vanish, never to be returned to the hopeful investigator.

The problems described have led some I/O psychologists to dismiss survey research entirely (e.g., Campbell, 1982). Others are trying to identify areas in which the weaknesses of self-report data are particularly likely to create serious inference problems (e.g., Crampton & Wagner, 1994) and to discover methods for minimizing the impact (e.g., Arnold, Feldman, & Purbhoo, 1985). Still other investigators are working on ways to reduce the problems with survey research in general. In a series of five studies, Brennan (1992) found that offering a 50-cent monetary incentive was an effective and cost-efficient way to increase both the number of questionnaires returned and the speed with which they were returned.

The truthfulness of self-report data presents a greater problem for researchers than does return of questionnaires. In any study there could be many reasons for some subjects to answer questions in ways that serve a purpose of their own rather than that intended by the investigator. One of the more common is a desire to appear in a favorable light. A subject who is very dissatisfied with his or her job might prefer to report a high degree of job satisfaction because of a perception that people who admit to being dissatisfied are "being negative." Being negative, in turn, is considered undesirable behavior in many segments of the American culture.

The tendency to underreport personal characteristics and feelings that are perceived to be socially undesirable (such as a negative attitude) and overreport characteristics perceived to be socially desirable (such as liking one's job) is known as the social desirability bias (Crowne & Marlowe, 1964). A number of investigators have explored the effects of such bias on relationships described in I/O research. The consensus seems to be that if self-report data are central to a study, a measure of social desirability bias should also be included (Ganster, Hennessey, & Luthans, 1983). Over time, accumulated data from these studies would alert researchers to settings and variables that are especially vulnerable to this form of bias. Ways to control for it or to separate its effects from other relationships might then be devised.

Even when people are trying very hard to be accurate in filling out a questionnaire, they may have difficulty understanding some of the questions or remembering the information needed to answer them. There also can be influences on their responses that arise out of the conditions under which questionnaires are administered. An interesting example is a study in which the investigators found they could influence job satisfaction questionnaire responses in a positive direction simply by distributing cookies at questionnaire administration sessions (Brief, Butcher, & Roberson, 1995).

Results from studies such as that cited add weight to Johns's (1994) proposal that psychologists study self-report data as a source of unique information about human behavior rather than using it as a data collection tool. The idea is an interesting one that seems worth following up on its own merit rather than as an alternative strategy. Despite

Naturally occurring events, such as strikes, offer I/O psychologists op portunities to conduct useful field and observational studies.

the problems described, both historical studies and survey research remain popular for their many advantages; it seems unlikely that they will ever be abandoned as research methods.

Inference: Statistical Analysis

Research design can be a long, complex process. Scientists put in all of this planning time so that they can make inferences about their research questions with some confidence after observations have been made. **Inference** is the process by which scientists derive conclusions from observations. In I/O psychology, the means for making an inference usually is statistical analysis that allows one or more hypotheses to be tested. Analytical procedures vary, but the concept central to all is that of significance.

Statistical Significance

When it is very unlikely that the results obtained from a defined research procedure are due to chance, the results are said to have **statistical significance**. A simple coin toss illustrates this concept. Suppose that a coin is tossed into the air 30 times; it comes down heads 17 times and tails 13 times. Is this a *significant* departure from the expected result of 15 heads and 15 tails or was it obtained by chance? One way to answer the question is to repeat 30 tosses of the same coin over and over and note how many times a ratio of 17:13 is observed. Statistical analysis makes this tedious process unnecessary. An estimate of the number of times that a 17:13 result would be obtained by chance can be made after the first 30 tosses. This estimate is called a probability statement.

In the I/O psychology research literature, a probability statement is designated by the combination of symbols and numbers p (for probability) $<$ (less than) $.05$ (5%), which is read "the probability is less than 5%." In the example of the coin toss, this statement would signify that the researcher could expect an observed ratio of 17 heads to 13 tails to be obtained by chance fewer than 5 times out of 100 sets of 30 tosses. This would be considered a statistically significant result, because .05 and .01 ($p < .01$) are the two long-accepted standards for significance in I/O psychology. This fact is important to understanding the literature, but it should not be taken to mean that other observations are worthless. So-called nonsignificant research results (observations that would be obtained by chance *more* than 1 or 5 times out of 100) can be very useful as signposts to trends and guidelines for future research.

It also should be noted that the traditional standards and procedures are not accepted by all psychologists (e.g., Cohen, 1994; Sauley & Bedeian, 1989). Measurement itself is the primary area of interest to many researchers, who examine the assumptions and accuracy of existing methods and standards as well as work to develop new techniques and tools. At some time in the future, it is possible that research in this area may lead to a generally accepted change in the traditional standards for statistical significance. (Division 5 of the American Psychological Association is the division for psychologists with a special interest in evaluation, measurement, and statistics.)

In research reports, a probability statement such as $p < .05$ is attached to some **statistic**, a number that is the result of a defined set of mathematical computational procedures.

The probability statement is arrived at by comparing this statistic with special tables published for this purpose. Among the statistics encountered frequently in I/O psychology research are r, F, t, $x2$ (read "chi square") and R (read "multiple r"). In each case, the statistic (one number) obtained from analysis of a set of observations can be compared with numbers in a published table. It is then possible to form a probability statement about the likelihood that this number was obtained by chance—that is, to make an inference about the significance of the observations.

It is not necessary to know how to calculate the statistics mentioned in order to understand the research in this book, as long as the concept of significance is clear. It will be useful, however, to discuss an assumption that is basic to all of these procedures. This assumption is that the variables observed are distributed so as to approximate a normal curve. In addition, three other concepts that are met often in reading reports of I/O research are important—one is correlation and correlational relationships, a second is determinant/predictor variables and analysis of variance, and the third is a group of statistical techniques called meta-analysis.

The Normal Curve

Most of the statistical analysis procedures in common research use are based on the assumption that the variables observed have a normal distribution in the population at large. If a variable is normally distributed, a graph of a large number of observations of that variable will have a particular bell shape called a **normal curve**. If the height (a variable) of a large number of men or women chosen at random on a busy street corner one morning is measured, for example, a relatively small percentage of the sample will be very short or very tall. The remainder will bunch up together in the middle. Graphically, this set of observations will produce the normal curve shown in Figure 2–2.

All normal curves can be described in terms of two numbers. One of these numbers is the average obtained measurement on the scale being used—that is, the **mean** (μ) of the distribution. As shown in Figure 2–2, it lies at the center of the curve. The other number that describes a normal curve is a measure of the variability, or spread, of the curve around

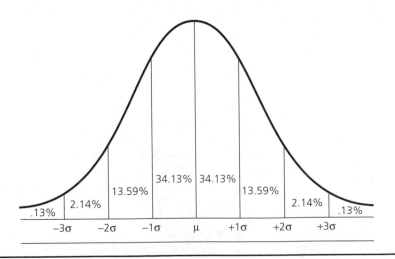

Figure 2–2
The Normal
Curve

the mean. By a process of mathematical transformation, the variability of all such curves can be expressed in a standard unit called a **standard deviation** (σ).

If the mean and the standard deviation of a normal curve are known, anyone can reproduce the curve accurately, because exact percentages of the observations in any normal curve fall within each standard deviation, plus or minus, from the mean. These percentages are seen in Figure 2–2; for example, 68.26% of all of the observations in a normal curve lie within one standard deviation of the mean (34.13% on each side).

The normal curve has a number of uses beyond that of serving as a foundation for formal statistical analysis. One of the more important of these uses is helping people understand the meaning of their scores on tests. If the mean for a standardized test of mathematical ability is 50 and the standard deviation is 10, for example, someone who scores 70 on the test has done better than approximately 95% of the people who might take the test. A score of 70 is two standard deviations above the mean (50 + 10 + 10 = 70).

Most statistical procedures are based on the normal curve assumption, but some important variables in research do not conform to this distribution. Sex has a bimodal distribution; that is, there are two measured values—male and female. Other variables have what is called a skewed distribution, one in which observations tend to bunch up at a point on the scale other than the middle. In the United States, body weight has a skewed distribution; for any particular height and sex (that is, *controlling* for height and sex), there are more people at the higher ends of the distribution than at the lower ends.

Special statistical procedures are necessary for bimodal, skewed, and other non-normal variable distributions, but with a few exceptions (such as sex), these variables are encountered rarely in I/O psychology. A particular observed *sample* distribution may be non-normal, however, due to design decisions or sampling error.

Correlation and Correlates

Correlation refers to a relationship between variables such that they change in a predictable manner with respect to one another. A familiar occurrence of such a relationship in the I/O literature is that between age and expressed job satisfaction. Over the years, many studies have found a tendency for these variables to be positively correlated; that is, increases in one go with increases in the other. As age increases so, in general, does expressed satisfaction with work. Job satisfaction and absenteeism, on the other hand, are often found to be negatively correlated; that is, as one goes up, the other goes down. As expressed job satisfaction increases, absenteeism generally decreases.

There are a variety of procedures for determining whether two variables, such as age and job satisfaction, are correlated at all and whether this correlation is positive or negative, but all share the same basic technique. A measurement is taken for each subject on each variable and a defined computational procedure is applied to the resulting measurements. This procedure yields a **correlation coefficient**, the r mentioned earlier.

In some research, one of the two measurements taken for each subject in a correlation analysis is actually a group of measurements. An I/O psychologist might be interested in the relationship between scores on five employment screening tests and performance in a job training program, for example. To investigate this relationship, he or she could use a multiple correlation procedure. One of the measurements for each subject is the measure of training performance. The other measurement is a composite test score (one number) that is derived mathematically from the five different screening tests. When the correlation coefficient for these two variables is calculated, the result is written as R (read "multiple r") to make it clear that more than the usual two variables are involved.

All correlation coefficients, regardless of the method by which they have been calculated, range between -1.00 and $+1.00$. (In the remainder of this text, the convention of omitting the plus sign for positive coefficients is followed.) The number indicates the strength of the relationship; the closer it is to 1.00, plus *or* minus, the stronger the relationship.

A correlation coefficient is calculated mathematically, but it is often depicted graphically by what is called a scattergram. The variables are plotted on a two-axis graph, and a dot representing each subject's position is placed appropriately. A scattergram showing the relative position of 18 subjects with respect to their scores on a grammar test and a vocabulary test appears in Figure 2–3. One subject (Subject 5) made a score of 60 on both tests. Most of the other subjects had different scores on the two tests, but there clearly is a strong tendency for high scores on one test to go with high scores on the other.

The calculated correlation coefficient for the data in Figure 2–3 is $r = .94$. The fact that this is a positive correlation can be seen in the pattern of the dots, which slants from the lower left corner of the graph to the upper right corner. If the correlation were negative, the slant would be from upper left to lower right.

Correlational Relationships

The relationship between the variables in Figure 2–3 is a linear relationship; that is, the line that best fits all of the points is a straight line. Not all correlational relationships are linear, however. Some research suggests that the relationship between completed level of education and reported job satisfaction is curvilinear, for example. This means that higher job satisfaction is associated with higher *and* lower levels of education. Lower job satisfaction is associated with middle levels of education. This pattern is shown graphically in Figure 2–4.

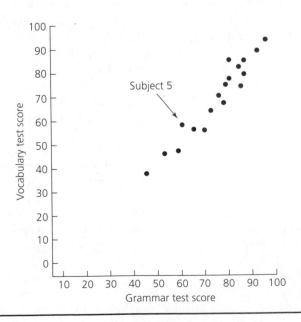

Figure 2–3

A Scattergram
Showing Scores
on a Grammar
Test and a
Vocabulary Test

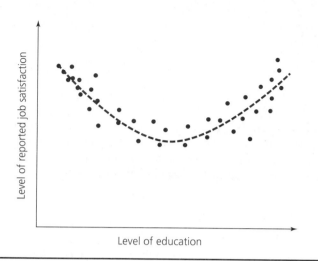

Figure 2–4
A Graphic Depiction of a Curvilinear Correlational Relationship

If a researcher were to apply standard correlation computation procedures to variables that actually are curvilinearly related, it might very well appear that there is no relationship at all between the variables. In this case, he or she would make the incorrect inference that there is no relationship between job satisfaction and level of education. To guard against this possibility, it has become standard procedure for researchers to perform a test for curvilinearity before inferring that there is no association between variables.

In addition to the possibility that the true relationship is actually curvilinear, the presence of a strong moderator variable can also obscure the relationship between two variables and lead to an incorrect inference if undetected. A **moderator variable** is a variable that has a predictable influence on the nature of the relationship between two other variables. For instance, Hackman and Oldham (1976) hypothesize that the nature of the relationship between (a) job enrichment (making a job more meaningful) and (b) improved job performance and/or satisfaction is *moderated* by (c) individual needs for personal growth and achievement. Where such needs are low, there will be little or no association between variables *a* and *b;* where they are high, there may be a strong positive correlation.

In situations where important moderators are operating, the strength of the relationship between an independent variable and a dependent variable depends on the level of a moderator variable. If the Hackman and Oldham hypothesis is correct, an investigator who failed to account for different levels of individual needs for personal growth would most likely find little or no correlation between his or her measures of job enrichment and job performance/satisfaction. Like curvilinearity, moderator variables represent a step forward from simple correlational relationships in addressing the complexities of human behavior.

A Note on Cause and Effect

Correlation is a basic concept that is encountered often in I/O psychology research, but it is a measure of association only. No matter how obvious it may seem that one of two strongly correlated variables is causing the other, such an inference simply cannot be made on the basis of the usual procedure for calculating correlation. If a high positive correlation exists between two variables, x and y, the true cause-effect situation may be any of the following:

- x causes y.
- y causes x.
- Both x and y are caused by a third variable, z.

As an example of this important point, consider the positive correlation noted by some social scientists between the rate of alcoholism in a particular geographic area (x) and the rate of unemployment in the same area (y). On the basis of this simple correlation alone, the cause-effect relationship between these two variables may be any of the following:

- The alcoholism causes the unemployment.
- The unemployment causes the alcoholism.
- Both the alcoholism and the unemployment are caused by a third variable.

The various causal possibilities that underlie an obtained correlation between two variables means that it is not accurate (on the basis of this procedure alone) to refer to "causes" and "effects." The correct term for x and y in this case is *correlates*. **Correlates** are variables found to be associated with one another in a predictable fashion. It is a term encountered many times in this text and other I/O psychology reading, because much psychological research is correlational in nature. A review of the issues and problems and a checklist for evaluating the validity of this type of research in organizations can be found in a well-known 1985 article by Mitchell.

As well as frequent mention of correlates, the I/O psychology literature also contains many references to the "antecedents" of some behavior or attitude. Antecedents are variables (or groups of variables called antecedent conditions) that are believed to lie at the causal end of a cause-effect relationship, rather than at the effect end. The positive correlation that is often found between absenteeism and turnover serves as an example.

A significant correlation between absenteeism and turnover means only that these two variables are correlates, not that one causes the other. Absenteeism always comes before turnover, however, so obviously turnover cannot cause absenteeism. In this case, it is acceptable to call absenteeism an antecedent of turnover. It is not acceptable, however, to call absenteeism a *cause* of turnover. Again, standard correlational analysis does not provide this information.

Determinants, Predictor Variables, and Analysis of Variance

Inferring cause and effect where two variables are concerned is a matter of figuring out which of the two has the effect on the other. An examination of the causal factors behind a positive height-weight correlation, for example, would lead to the conclusion that the height must "cause" the weight. Weighing more cannot make people taller, but being taller gives them more skeleton to cover and so they will tend to weigh more, other things being equal.

A fact of research life is that other things are seldom equal. Many important factors other than height determine what a particular individual weighs. Among these are heredity, metabolism, activity level, percentage of body fat versus percentage of muscle, and amount of food consumed. These factors, together with many of lesser importance that are not listed, explain the **variance** (differences) in observed body weights. A complete list of these factors would be a list of the **determinants** of human body weight, and this complete list would explain 100% of the variance in body weights.

A complete list of the determinants of any particular attribute (such as weight) or behavior is very unlikely. There are simply too many unknowns. Nevertheless, there are many instances in I/O psychology research in which a researcher is interested in identifying at least some of the more important determinants of observed differences among people on some variable. To do so, he or she draws on experience, theory, and previous relevant research to form an hypothesis about the variables that might be relevant. These variables are called predictor variables.

A **predictor variable** is a variable that explains a significant portion of the variance observed in measuring another variable. One way to illustrate this concept is in terms of the extent to which two variables overlap or share a common space (called common variance). In the diagram in Figure 2–5, job experience and job performance are shown to have a modest common variance, as indicated by the area common to the two circles. In this case, job experience would be a predictor variable for job performance.

In research, the predictor variable resembles an independent variable in that it is a variable of interest (not irrelevant or confounding) and it is not a dependent variable. However, predictor variables are not manipulated (as in experiments), nor are they sought at particular levels (as in field studies); instead, they are measured as they exist for the particular subjects in a sample.

As an illustration of the use of predictor variables, consider a dependent variable called job involvement, defined here as the extent to which a person is personally, or psychologically, invested in his or her current job position. The research question is: What variables account for the observed differences (variance) among people on measured job involvement? An examination of the previous research on job involvement suggests that level of education, level of work performance, amount of work experience, and a personality variable called locus-of-control (Rotter, 1966) may be relevant.

When observations on the variables listed are collected and analyzed, all except work performance are related significantly to job involvement. Together, level of education, amount of work experience, and locus-of-control are found to account for 23% of the variance in job involvement for subjects in the study. This is a respectable percentage in this type of research, but some important determinants were missing from the hypothesis, because a large percentage of the variance (100% − 23% = 77%) in job involvement was *not* explained.

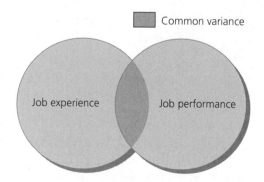

Common variance

Job experience   Job performance

Figure 2–5
The Concept of
Common
Variance

Part of the unexplained or missing variance in the example is accounted for by unidentified determinants left out of the hypothesis, but part is due to error. Some of this error is measurement error, while some stems from the particular subjects chosen for the study. Both measurement and subject error are present in all I/O psychology research. Much can be done to reduce this error by giving careful attention to research design, but it cannot be eliminated. It becomes important, therefore, to estimate how much error actually may be present.

A very common procedure for estimating how much of the variance in a particular set of observations is due to error is called **analysis of variance** (ANOVA). There are a number of variations on ANOVA, but all are based on the concept of comparing the amount of variance (in the dependent variable of interest) explained by experimentally manipulated variables to the amount explained by error. This concept is illustrated by the graph in Figure 2–6.

The large circle in Figure 2–6 represents the total observed variance (100%) in measurements of the dependent variable—the average number of errors made by pilot subjects in reading an instrument panel. The three sectors of the circle represent proportions of variance explained by each of the following:

- the independent variable, which is the variable of interest (different instrument panel configurations)

- error stemming from the particular characteristics of the subjects in the sample (such as differences in visual acuity)

- error stemming from other sources, such as measurement problems (error in recording a subject's response, for example)

Even without knowing the actual figures, one can see that more of the variance in pilot instrument reading performance is explained by differences in the instrument panels

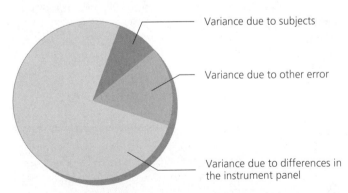

Subjects: Helicopter pilots
Type of experiment: Simulation
Dependent variable: Average number of reading errors
Independent variable: Arrangement of instrument panel

Variance due to subjects

Variance due to other error

Variance due to differences in the instrument panel

Total observed variance in average number of reading errors

Figure 2–6
A Graphic
Illustration of
Simple Analysis
of Variance

Data from R. E. Kirk, *Experimental Design: Procedures for the Behavioral Sciences,* Brooks/Cole Publishing Company, 1968.

than by error. This is a desirable outcome in research, but there is still error in the graph, and in some experiments this error will be statistically significant.

Meta-Analysis

As the body of accumulated research in any area grows, the question of what the findings considered together, rather than separately, mean becomes increasingly important. I/O psychologists and others have been studying job satisfaction for many years, for example. What have they learned about the overall significance and impact of this variable on the behavior of people in organizations? One way to answer this question is to look at the individual research reports and then to make judgments regarding consensus or trends. This procedure has a long tradition in psychology in the form of special articles in journals called review articles.

Review articles are cited many times in this book, usually introduced by a phrase such as "In their review of the literature . . . ." In the larger sense, this book is itself a form of review article; for each of the various topic areas, it reviews the questions, the research to date, the answers that research has provided, and the direction future research might take to help fill in gaps or find answers to new questions.

An alternative or supplement to the traditional literature review is a group of statistical procedures called meta-analysis. **Meta-analysis** is the use of quantitative methods to summarize findings across independent research studies. For example, Ones, Viswesvaran, and Schmidt (1993) were interested in the relationship between scores on a type of employment screening test called an integrity (honesty) test and certain aspects of work behavior. A literature search yielded more than 600 correlation coefficients relevant to this relationship. Meta-analysis allowed Ones and his co-investigators to combine the results from these many different studies statistically and then to estimate that the correlation coefficient between integrity test scores and later supervisory ratings of job performance in their data pool was .41.

Since their introduction in the 1970s (see Glass, 1976; Schmidt & Hunter, 1977), meta-analysis techniques have come to occupy a prominent position in the research methodology of industrial/organizational psychology. It must be kept in mind, however, that the results of investigations using this technique are only as good as the individual studies that go into them (Russell et al., 1994). Accordingly, authors who publish such reports should describe the rationale and criteria for the selection of the studies they include in the analysis and provide a list of these studies so that readers can place them in the appropriate context (Rosenthal, 1995).

Verification: Reliability, Validity, and Generalizability

So far, this chapter has reviewed the basic process of scientific inference—drawing conclusions about a research question from a particular set of observations. In I/O psychology, this inference is usually based on statistical analysis, and it rests on the concept of significance. Achieving significant results is not enough for the scientific method, however. It also is necessary to verify results. **Verification** means confirming or substantiating results. Verifying the results of a particular research investigation requires answering three questions.

1. Is the inference reliable? That is, if the investigation were repeated exactly as carried out, would the observations allow for the same inference?

2. Is the inference valid? That is, did the investigator measure the variables he or she intended to measure, control for the more important confounding variables, and use appropriate techniques for inference? If so, there should be no obvious plausible alternative explanation for the findings.

3. Is the inference generalizable? That is, can results be extended to people (a population) other than the particular ones (the subjects) used in the investigation (the sample)?

A study of absenteeism by Kim and Campagna (1981) serves to illustrate how these three questions are applied to the inferences made from a research study. These investigators conducted a field experiment in which they manipulated a particular aspect of working conditions (the independent variable) and observed employee absenteeism rates (the dependent variable). They looked at employee absenteeism under flexitime (where people have some choice in their working hours) and under the standard work hour arrangement (where everyone works the same set hours). On the basis of their analysis of the observations, they arrived at the inference that "flexitime significantly reduces employees' unpaid absences in general" (p. 739).

If the inference made by Kim and Campagna is *reliable,* the same or different investigators would reach the same conclusion if the experiment were repeated under the same conditions. If the inference is *valid,* an examination of their methods, observations, and data analysis would allow obvious alternative explanations for the lower absenteeism rate under flexitime to be ruled out. Possible competing explanations for the results of this

Behavior at work is the result of a complex interaction of individual and situational factors. To ensure that they capture this complexity, I/O psychologists are very careful to verify their research findings.

study include statistical problems, biased measures of absenteeism, and uncontrolled relevant differences between subjects observed under flexitime and subjects observed under normal working hours. Finally, if these researchers' inference about flexitime and absenteeism is *generalizable,* the same inference would be drawn from an investigation using different subjects in different organizations.

Some of the aspects of verifying the inferences made from research observations can be evaluated by a close scrutiny of the research design, the execution of the study, and the data analysis. The real test of **generalizability**, however, rests on further research of a similar nature with different subjects—that is, upon replication. Such replication, with and without design changes, is an important way for scientists to increase their confidence in any research finding.

The standards for evaluating inferences made about observations should reinforce the importance of following common rules for using known and understood analytical procedures in research. Without them, there would be no foundation for agreement as to reliability, validity, and generalizability. Each researcher could bring his or her own individual methods and biases to the process, and there would be no basis for combining these individual efforts to build a solid body of knowledge.

Ethics in the Conduct of Research

The term *manipulation* has appeared several times in this chapter. Many people have a negative reaction to this word and, by association, a negative attitude toward the scientific investigation of human behavior. The stereotype of the cold, calculating researcher going about manipulating situations and people against their wills in a relentless pursuit of science may be with us still in some quarters, but it is entirely alien to the spirit and conduct of contemporary psychological research.

Professional I/O psychologists, together with their colleagues pursuing other interests in the field of psychology, are committed to the ethical conduct of research. Debates over the exact meaning of this conduct are frequent, but this is as it should be. New ethical issues arise and old ones persist; debate is the means by which the issues may be clarified and consensus as to the relevant and appropriate ethical standards may be reached. Some psychologists, as the excerpt in Psychology at Work that opens this chapter illustrates, are beginning to collect empirical data to aid in this process.

The American Psychological Association maintains a standing Ethics Committee to assist in the clarification of issues, investigate alleged violations of ethics, and formulate ethical principles that satisfy the consensus of its membership. In published form, these constitute the "Ethical Principles of Psychologists and Code of Conduct" (APA, 1992). This document is revised at intervals, as is *Ethical Principles in the Conduct of Research with Human Participants* (APA, 1982), the APA standard guide to the conduct of psychological research involving human subjects.

At Issue

Inspirer or Perspirer—Who Gets the Glory When the Study Ends?

A characteristic of all science is the sense of community among the mainstream of its practitioners. The majority of scientists in any field see themselves as a group dedicated to the accumulation of knowledge in their discipline. Professional meetings serve as one mechanism for maintaining and strengthening this bond and aiding scientists in sharing the results of recent work with one another. Professional journals extend this communication to all interested parties as well as to those who attend the meetings.

Because they are accessible to everyone, professional journals are the lifeblood of any science. They allow busy practitioners to keep current, provide newcomers to the discipline with a "feel" for what is going on, and form the backbone of research progress. With few exceptions, reports in professional journals begin with a review of previous research and thinking relevant to the topic under discussion. In this review, the author (or authors) of the report explains how current work builds on or connects to that done previously.

Because professional journals are so important to science, many universities some years ago began to encourage their faculty members to publish in them, expecting that this activity would benefit students as well as the university and the various sciences themselves. Encouragement most often took the form of reduced classroom loads and/or more rapid advancement through the academic ranks for faculty who devoted some part of their time to research and publishing.

The policy of rewarding people for publishing in professional journals has been successful by many criteria, but this success has not been without costs to individuals whose talents do not lie in research or writing. "Publish or perish" has gone from being an in-group catch phrase to hard reality in al-most every corner of the academic world. Nor is just publishing necessarily enough to avoid perishing. In many settings, more credit is given for publishing in some journals than in others. If the research report is a joint one, there is often more credit attached to being listed as the first ("senior") author (Floyd, Schroeder, & Finn, 1994).

There are no known data to support the position, but it seems likely that most scientists believe the benefits of publish-or-perish to their fields outweigh the problems it creates for some individuals. But the issue has implications that go beyond the careers of individuals. This aspect can be illustrated by the case in which the idea for research comes from someone other than the researcher who carries it out. As Webb (1983) asks in the article from which the title of this feature was borrowed: "Who gets the credit, the inspirer or the perspirer?" (p. 5).

In studies of team research discussed by Webb, as few as 6% of questionnaire respondents believed that coauthorship should be given to the person who had the original idea (the "inspirer") if he or she did not take part in the research itself. Even when it was stated that the idea included specific design and methodology, only slightly more than half of the respondents would give the inspirer coauthorship.

Most authors of journal articles now give acknowledgment, if not coauthorship, to those who helped in some way with the research being reported. The number who do not, even though such credit is due, is unknown, but not the issue. The issue is that by making credit matter so much, we are putting ourselves at risk of wholesale idea guarding or even of idea stealing (Hunt & Blair, 1987), to the ultimate detriment of the entire discipline.

Title taken from the article of the same name by W. B. Webb, *APA Monitor,* 1983, *14,* 5.

Summary

Psychologists carry out their search for knowledge about human behavior within the context of the scientific method, which is characterized by commonly understood and accepted terminology and research methods. In I/O psychology, inferences from this research usually are based on statistical tests of significance. Within the framework of the scientific method, verification of these inferences—evaluation of the reliability, validity, and generalizability of a researcher's conclusions—is mandatory. Some philosophers argue that nothing can really be proved, but scientists seek to obtain as much proof as possible.

Questions for Review and Discussion

1. Compare and contrast the acquisition of knowledge about human behavior through the scientific method with learning about such behavior through everyday experience.

2. Describe a research question for which you would choose a laboratory setting over a field setting and another for which you would do the reverse. Explain your answer.

3. Demonstrate by example that you understand the difference between the following: independent variable, dependent variable, confounding variable, predictor variable, moderator variable.

4. After months of planning and more months of work, you have finished collecting data for an important research project. Statistical analysis of these data yield nonsignificant results. What will you do now and why?

5. In the example of the correlation obtained between rate of alcoholism (x) and rate of unemployment (y) in a particular geographical area, it was noted that either might cause the other *or* both might be caused by a third variable (z). Offer two suggestions as to what z might be and explain your answer.

Key Terms

confounding variable

correlation/correlate

experiment

field observation

hypothesis

independent/dependent variable

inference

moderator variable

operational definition

predictor variable

research design

scientific method

statistical significance

variable/constant

verification

References

Ackerman, P. L., & Kanfer, R. (1993). Integrating laboratory and field study for improving selection: Development of a battery for predicting air traffic controller success. *Journal of Applied Psychology, 78,* 413–432.

American Psychological Association. (1982). *Ethical principles in the conduct of research with human participants.* Washington, DC: APA Committee for the Protection of Human Participants in Research.

American Psychological Association. (1992). Ethical principles of psychologists and code of conduct. *American Psychologist, 47,* 1597–1611.

Arnold, H. J., Feldman, D. C., & Purbhoo, M. (1985). The role of social-desirability response bias in turnover research. *Academy of Management Journal, 28,* 955–966.

Bottger, P. C., & Yetton, P. W. (1987). Improving group performance by training in individual problem solving. *Journal of Applied Psychology, 72,* 651–657.

Brennan, M. (1992). The effect of a monetary incentive on mail survey response rates: New data. *Journal of the Market Research Society, 34,* 173–177.

Brief, A. P., Butcher, A. H., & Roberson, L. (1995). Cookies, disposition, and job attitudes: The effects of positive mood-inducing events and negative affectivity on job satisfaction in a field experiment. *Organizational Behavior and Human Decision Processes, 62,* 55–62.

Campbell, J. P. (1982). Editorial: Some remarks from the outgoing editor. *Journal of Applied Psychology, 67,* 691–700.

Cohen, J. (1994). The earth is round ($p < .05$). *American Psychologist, 49,* 997–1003.

Cook, T. D., & Campbell, D. T. (1979). *Quasi-experimentation: Design and analysis issues for field settings.* Boston: Houghton Mifflin.

Cordery, J. L., Mueller, W. S., & Smith, L. M. (1991). Attitudinal and behavioral effects of autonomous group working: A longitudinal field study. *Academy of Management Journal, 34,* 464–476.

Crampton, S. M., & Wagner, J. A. III. (1994). Percept-percept inflation in microorganizational research: An investigation of prevalence and effect. *Journal of Applied Psychology, 79,* 67–76.

Crowne, D. P., & Marlowe, D. (1964). *The approval motive.* New York: Wiley.

Dalton, D. R., & Perry, J. L. (1981). Absenteeism and the collective bargaining agreement: An empirical test. *Academy of Management Journal, 24,* 425–431.

Fisher, C. B., & Fryberg, D. (1994). Participant partners: College students weigh the costs and benefits of deceptive research. *American Psychologist, 49,* 417–427.

Floyd, S. W., Schroeder, D. M., & Finn, D. M. (1994). "Only if I'm first author": Conflict over credit in management scholarship. *Academy of Management Journal, 37,* 734–747.

Ganster, D. C., Hennessey, H. W., & Luthans, F. (1983). Social desirability response effects: Three alternative models. *Academy of Management Journal, 26,* 321–331.

Glass, G. V. (1976). Primary, secondary and meta-analysis of research. *Educational Researcher, 5,* 3–8.

Haccoun, R. R., & Jeanrie, C. (1995). Self-reports of work absence as a function of personal attitudes toward absence, and perceptions of the organization. *Applied Psychology: An International Review, 44,* 155–170.

Hackman, J. R. (1989). *Groups that work (and those that don't).* San Francisco: Jossey-Bass.

Hackman, J. R., & Oldham, G. R. (1976). Motivation through the design of work: Test of a theory. *Organizational Behavior and Human Performance, 16,* 250–279.

Hunt, J. G., & Blair, J. D. (1987). Content, process, and the Matthew effect among management academics. *Journal of Management, 13,* 191–210.

Ilgen, D. R., Nebeken, D. M., & Pritchard, R. D. (1981). Expectancy theory measures: An empirical comparison in an experimental simulation. *Organizational Behavior and Human Performance, 28,* 189–223.

Johns, G. (1994). How often were you absent? A review of the use of self-reported absence data. *Journal of Applied Psychology, 79,* 574–591.

Katzell, R. A., & Austin, J. T. (1992). From then to now: The development of industrial-organizational psychology in the United States. *Journal of Applied Psychology, 77,* 803–835.

Kim, J. S., & Campagna, A. F. (1981). Effects of flexitime on employee attendance and performance: A field experiment. *Academy of Management Journal, 24,* 729–741.

Kirk, R. E. (1968). *Experimental design: Procedures for the behavioral sciences.* Belmont, CA: Brooks/Cole.

Landy, F. J., Shankster, L. J., & Kohler, S. S. (1994). Personnel selection and placement. *Annual Review of Psychology, 45,* 261–296.

Larsson, R. (1993). Case survey methodology: Quantitative analysis of patterns across case studies. *Academy of Management Journal, 36,* 1515–1546.

Mitchell, T. R. (1985). An evaluation of the validity of correlational research conducted in organizations. *Academy of Management Review, 10,* 192–205.

Ones, D. S., Viswesvaran, C., & Schmidt, F. L. (1993). Comprehensive meta-analysis of integrity test validities: Findings and implications for personnel selection and theories of job performance. *Journal of Applied Psychology, 78,* 679–703.

Robbins, T. L., & DeNisi, A. S. (1994). A closer look at interpersonal affect as a distinct influence on cognitive processing in performance evaluations. *Journal of Applied Psychology, 79,* 341–353.

Rosenthal, R. (1995). Writing articles for *Psychological Bulletin. Psychological Bulletin, 118,* 183–192.

Rotter, J. B. (1966). Generalized expectancies for internal versus external control of reinforcement. *Psychological Monographs, 80* (Whole No. 609).

Russell, C. J., Settoon, R. P., McGrath, R. N., Blanton, A. E., Kidwell, R. E., Lohrke, F. T., Scifres, E. L., & Danforth, G. W. (1994). Investigator characteristics as moderators of personnel selection research: A meta-analysis. *Journal of Applied Psychology, 79,* 163–170.

Sauley, K. S., & Bedeian, A. G. (1989). .05: A case of the tail wagging the distribution. *Journal of Management, 15,* 335–344.

Schmidt, F. L., & Hunter, J. E. (1977). Development of a general solution to the problem of validity generalization. *Journal of Applied Psychology, 62,* 529–540.

Tepper, B. J. (1994). Investigation of general and program-specific attitudes toward corporate drug-testing policies. *Journal of Applied Psychology, 79,* 392–401.

Tracey, J. B., Tannenbaum, S. I., & Kavanagh, M. J. (1995). Applying trained skills on the job: The importance of the work environment. *Journal of Applied Psychology, 80,* 239–252.

Webb, W. B. (1983). Inspirer or perspirer—who gets the glory when the study ends? *APA Monitor, 14,* 5.

Wise, T. A. (1966). The rocky road to the marketplace. *Fortune, 74,* 138–212.

Yin, R. (1981). The case study crisis: Some answers. *Administrative Science Quarterly, 26,* 58–65.

Reliability, Validity, and Testing in Organizations

PSYCHOLOGY AT WORK

The Money Test

Excerpted from F. L. Schmidt and J. E. Hunter, "Employment Testing: Old Theories and New Research Findings," *American Psychologist,* 1981, *36,* 1128–1137. Copyright 1981 by the American Psychological Association. Title, "The Money Test," from the article of the same name by F. L. Schmidt and J. E. Hunter, *Across the Board,* 1982, *19,* 35. Title used through the courtesy of the Conference Board, New York.

Tests have been used in making employment decisions in the United States for over 50 years. . . . the most commonly used employment tests have been measures of cognitive skills; that is, aptitude or ability tests. . . . In the middle and late 1960s certain theories about aptitude and ability tests formed the basis for most discussion of employee selection issues and, in part, the basis for practice in personnel psychology. . . .

One such theory—The Theory of Low Utility—holds that employee selection methods have little impact on the performance and productivity of the resultant work force. . . . The basic equation for determining [if this were true] had been available for years, but it had not been employed because there were no feasible methods for estimating one critical equation parameter: the standard deviation of employee performance in dollars (SDy). SDy indexes the magnitude of individual differences in employee yearly output of goods and services. The greater SDy is, the greater the payoff in improved productivity from selecting high-performing employees.

During the 1970s, a method was devised for estimating SDy based on careful estimates by supervisors of employee output. Applications of this method showed that SDy was larger than expected. For example, for entry-level budget analysts and computer programmers, SDy was $11,327 and $10, 413, respectively. This means that a computer programmer at the 85th percentile in performance is worth $20,800 more per year to the employing organization than a computer programmer at the 15th percentile. Use of valid selection tests substantially increases the average performance level of the resultant work force and therefore substantially improves productivity. For example, use of the Programmer Aptitude Test in place of an invalid selection method to hire 618 entry-level computer programmers leads to an estimated productivity improvement of $54.7 million . . . over a 10-year period if the top 30 percent of applicants are hired.

IN FORMER times, federal government pressures on companies to undertake expensive test validation programs led many organizations to abandon employment testing; management was just not convinced of its worth relative to its cost. Industrial/organizational psychologists know better. When they are well planned and executed, testing programs for employment screening and selection provide organizations with employees who are better suited to learn, perform, and stay with their jobs. Employment testing also benefits employees by making it more likely that they can achieve job success and the rewards that go with it. It is difficult to put a dollar value on such benefits, however, so the development of a possible way to estimate the cost effectiveness of good employment testing was a welcome event.

In the years since the appearance of the article from which Psychology at Work is excerpted, I/O psychologists have been busy investigating the potential of the Schmidt-Hunter utility analysis procedure. Efforts to refine the original procedure are also under way (e.g., Judiesch, Schmidt, & Mount, 1992; Roth, 1994), as is the search for alternative ways to demonstrate the economic impact of testing on human resource management (e.g., Raju, Burke, & Normand, 1990; Russell, Colella, & Bobko, 1993).

Employment testing is one application of measurement techniques in organizations. Other organizational activities based on measurement are performance appraisal, job evaluation, and the assessment of job training effectiveness. If these activities are to be carried out effectively, the measurements on which they are based must be both reliable and valid. These topics—reliability, validity, and tests and testing in organizations—are the subject matter of this chapter.

Tests and Testing in Organizations

The systematic assessment of individual differences by means of tests as we know them today generally is agreed to have begun in the late 19th century, and the development of I/O psychology has been closely allied with the development of testing. In this context, a **test** is a defined procedure for making an estimate of an individual's relative or absolute position on some physical, psychological, or behavioral scale of measurement. Physical characteristics of interest to I/O psychologists include eyesight, hearing, strength, and manual dexterity. Attitudes, needs, and personality traits are among the more common psychological characteristics of interest. Behaviors often assessed include communication ability, work attendance, and job-related skills.

There are any number of ways for I/O psychologists to go about estimating, or testing, the amount or state of individual characteristics and behaviors. A person's typing skill might be estimated in absolute terms on the basis of the number of words typed in a given time period. Alternatively, it might be estimated in relative terms by comparing the amount of material typed in a given time to a standard for the same time set by a group of typists. Some ways of measuring are better than others for particular testing purposes, but all contain measurement error.

Measurement is the assignment of values to observations according to some defined system. (The values are often, but not always, numerical.) There are countless such systems, or measuring instruments, in everyday use. Familiar examples include rulers, thermometers, the gadgets that tell people the air pressure in their automobile tires or how much oil is left in their engines, and those ubiquitous multiple-choice exams taken by millions of students every year.

In I/O psychology, measurement is the foundation of all research and a great many applied activities, so that its accuracy is a matter of primary concern. This accuracy is a relative matter, however. Theoretically, it is possible to obtain a true measurement of the individual attributes and behaviors of interest, but a basic assumption underlying any measurement activity in psychology is that all such measurement contains error. It may be useful to take a look at measurement error more closely in a context that is familiar—the classroom exam.

When a professor administers an examination to a class of students, he or she is attempting to measure student knowledge and comprehension of a particular body of material. As is true of all measurement, this measurement will contain error. Some of this error originates in the exam, some with the person taking the exam, and some in the conditions under which the exam is given. Any of these sources may produce errors that are constant in the sense that they affect everyone taking a test in the same way (or the same individual all the time).

Sources of error in the exam situation may also produce errors that are unpredictable in the sense that they have differential effects—whether the error will occur and whose exam scores it will affect are not known in advance. Some obvious examples of possible constant and unpredictable errors that might affect the scores of students taking a classroom exam are shown in Table 3–1.

Classroom examinations and psychological research are relatively complex measurement situations, but even "objective" measuring instruments have the potential for error. The measurement of length by a standard yardstick or tape measure would seem to be very simple, straightforward, and accurate, for instance. But a wooden yardstick can be warped, a metal one can bend or contract or expand with the temperature, and

Table 3–1		Examples of Constant and Unpredictable Errors in Classroom Testing
Source of Error	**Constant**	**Unpredictable**
Test	Typographical error	Uneven reproduction; some copies of tests clearer than others
Person	Fear of tests	Temporary loss of memory; mind "goes blank"
Situation	Crowded room	Intermittent noise from lawn mowing equipment outside room

a cloth tape measure can stretch. Is it possible to get a true measurement with such an instrument?

In considering the accuracy of the measurement obtained with a measuring instrument, it is also important to consider how it is used. Is the measuring instrument lying flat? Is the sight line straight? Must the thickness of the measuring instrument be considered in the result? Of course, anyone who has done any carpentry work will be getting impatient about now. "Measure twice, cut once" is the rule. This commonsense advice leads directly to the first of the standards by which the adequacy of any measuring instrument or method is evaluated—reliability.

Reliability

Variance
See pages 40–42

The most widely accepted definition of reliability rests on the relationship between the variance of a set of observed measurements and the variance that exists in the true measurements (Nunnally, 1978). Unfortunately, a true measurement is a theoretical concept; in practice, it can never be known, and this makes the technical definition of reliability a rather difficult one for most people to grasp.

Saal and Knight (1988) offer one useful paraphrase of the technical definition of reliability: "reliable measures are relatively free of errors or mistakes that are random or without any discernable pattern" (p. 139). How is it possible to know if a measurement is relatively free of these errors? Follow the carpenter's advice and measure twice, cut once. If the two measurements are the same, cut with confidence. If a pocket calculator in good working order produces the same sum when a column of figures is added three times, this number probably is the correct answer.

As the examples suggest, in practical terms, **reliability** is understood as consistency or stability of measurement. If a particular measuring instrument is reliable, the result will be consistent from one measurement to the next and/or when different people take the measurement. By contrast, unreliable measuring instruments produce different results depending upon circumstances.

Reliability is a general requirement for any kind of measurement in any setting. In organizations, much of this measurement takes the form of tests, such as employment screening tests, ability tests to determine training needs, and competency tests to determine suitability for promotion. As a result, I/O psychologist practitioners often become involved in questions of test reliability.

Correlation
See pages 37–39

There are several ways to estimate the extent to which a test yields reliable measurements. The three methods that are used most commonly in I/O research are all correlational procedures, yet they often yield different results because the sources of error included in each calculation differ. Therefore, measurements of reliability, like test scores themselves, must be regarded as estimates of the true state of affairs. In practice, an investigator's choice of one method of estimating test reliability over another depends to some extent on which source of error is least unacceptable for the particular purpose at hand. It also depends to some extent on practical considerations stemming from the procedural requirements that are met as each method is reviewed.

The Test-Retest Reliability Estimate

One of the most commonly used operational definitions of test reliability is the test-retest procedure. The variables correlated with this procedure are two measurements from two administrations of the same test to the same people at two different times. Like all correlation coefficients, the resulting coefficient is designated r, but it is called a co-efficient of stability. The closer this coefficient is to 1.00, the greater the confidence in the reliability of the scores produced by a test.

Operational definition
See page 26

Variables
See pages 25–26

The test-retest procedure is quick and easy from the viewpoint of a researcher. It may be less popular with subjects who must take the test twice. As Smith and George (1994) emphasize, motivation to do well on a test is an important aspect of test taking. It is possible that some additional error is introduced into the second score of a test-retest procedure by subject impatience or boredom. Many researchers also report that attrition is a problem—some number of subjects simply disappear between the first and second test administrations.

Other things may happen in the time between test administrations in a test-retest reliability study as well. If the time is too short, the coefficient of stability can be affected by memory or a practice effect, as well as by reduced subject interest. If the time period between test administrations is too long, subjects may change in some way relevant to the test (they may receive training, gain experience, study the material, and so on).

If practice or changes affected all of the subjects in a reliability study in exactly the same way, these effects would present no major problem. This is extremely unlikely, however. Some subjects will have good memories, others poor ones. Some subjects will have their curiosity aroused by the test and study what they missed (even if they do not know that the test will be given again); others will not bother to do so.

The effect of uneven subject responses to the time interval between test and retest is to add error to the reliability estimate of the test. For this reason, this method is most useful for estimating the reliability of tests of skills that are not likely to benefit from the brief practice of the first test administration and that have little to do with memory. Examples of such tests include tests of hearing acuity, problem-solving skills, and finger manipulation dexterity.

The Internal Consistency Reliability Estimate

Some of the problems of subject motivation, memory, and practice raised by the test-retest method of estimating reliability can be avoided by using the internal consistency method. This procedure focuses on consistency among items rather than on consistency in scores over time. In one common approach, a number of subjects take a test once. Afterward, the test is divided for scoring purposes into two parts; each subject now has two scores, and it is these two scores that are correlated with one another.

Research subject
See page 27

The most usual division of a test is to use the odd-numbered items as one subtest and the even-numbered items as the other. When the two "scores" are correlated, the resulting coefficient, *r*, is called a coefficient of internal consistency, or sometimes a split-half coefficient. (This procedure actually yields an estimate of reliability for a test of half length, and results should be corrected statistically to estimate the reliability of the full test.)

The internal consistency procedure circumvents the problems of giving the same test twice, but it has drawbacks of its own. Unless a test is very long, the split-half coefficient is likely to be on the conservative (low) side. This procedure also requires that the two "tests" be of equal difficulty. Unequal halves are less likely if the test is split odd/even than if it is split first-half/last-half (as once was common practice), but this is not a guarantee of equality.

The internal consistency reliability estimate rests on the assumption that whatever method was used to make the split, the two halves of the test are of equivalent difficulty. This assumption is difficult to verify and the careful test evaluator will make use of one of the statistical formulas that yields what might be called a generic estimate of a test's internal consistency—a reliability coefficient that is not dependent upon the *particular* split of the test used in the calculations. The most well known of these formulas are the K-R formulas 20 and 21 (Richardson & Kuder, 1939) and Cronbach's Alpha coefficient (Cronbach, 1951). A detailed discussion of the strengths and weaknesses of such procedures is offered by Cortina (1993).

The Equivalent Forms Reliability Estimate

An alternative to the internal consistency procedure is to begin with two different tests. If the tests cover the same material and are equivalent in form and difficulty, reliability can be estimated by the equivalent forms procedure. Each subject takes each form of the test and the resulting score correlation, *r*, is called a coefficient of equivalence. This name provides a clue as to the greatest drawback of this method—constructing equivalent test forms. The question of reliability is a question of consistency with the same measuring instrument. If the different forms of a test are not equivalent, then the same instrument is not being used and the estimate of reliability will be lowered accordingly.

Equivalent test forms can be difficult and time-consuming to construct. In addition, the alternate forms must be tested for equivalence on a different sample of subjects before they can be used to estimate test reliability. Once the test has been shown to have adequate reliability, however, having equivalent forms on hand can be useful. If testing is done in a group, for example, one potential source of measurement error is reduced if subjects sitting next to one another have different forms of the test.

The discussion of equivalent test forms thus far has been based on the traditional situation in which two or more forms of a paper-and-pencil test are constructed. An interesting variation on this situation is arising with the increasing use of computerized versions of tests that were developed for paper-and-pencil administration. Is the same thing being measured when a test is given by means of a computer as when the (supposedly) identical test is given by conventional methods? The answer, as the laboratory experiment summarized in Spotlight on Research demonstrates, may be no.

**Laboratory
experiment**
See pages 27–28

**Independent/
dependent
variable**
See page 29

Van de Vijver and Harsveld (1994) used the General Aptitude Test Battery (GATB), a test of general intelligence developed by the U.S. Department of Labor that has been given to many thousands of subjects, to investigate a simple question: Does the form of administration (independent variable) affect performance (dependent variable) on the GATB? The

SPOTLIGHT ON RESEARCH

The Incomplete Equivalence of the Paper-and-Pencil and Computerized Versions of the General Aptitude Test Battery

Summarized from F.J.R. Van de Vijver and M. Harsveld, "The Incomplete Equivalence of the Paper-and-Pencil and Computerized Versions of the General Aptitude Test Battery." *Journal of Applied Psychology,* 1994, *79,* 852–859.

Research question   Are the paper-and-pencil and computerized versions of the General Aptitude Test Battery equivalent?

Type of study   Laboratory experiment.

Subjects   250 male and 76 female applicants to the Royal Military Academy in the Netherlands ranging in age from 16 to 31 years.

Independent variable   Computer versus paper-and-pencil administration of the test.

Dependent variables   Number of items completed and proportion of items completed that had correct answers.

General procedure   One-half of the subjects were administered the computerized version of the General Aptitude Test Battery (GATB); the other half took the test in original paper-and-pencil form. The two groups of subjects were matched for age, sex, and scores on a test of general intelligence.

Results   The computer administration subjects worked faster and completed more items. Standard administration subjects answered fewer items but got a higher proportion of those they did answer correct; the effect was strongest on simple tests.

Conclusion   "`. . . equivalence of paper-and-pencil and computerized versions of a test should be demonstrated rather than assumed. . . ."(p. 858).

answer for their subjects, even when past experience with computers was controlled for, was yes. The authors' conclusion that test form equivalence must be *demonstrated* rather than assumed serves as a fitting close to the discussion of the equivalent forms estimate of reliability.

To recapitulate, there are three common ways to estimate the reliability of a test. Each has certain advantages and disadvantages. Administratively, the internal consistency method is the simplest because subjects take one test once. For shorter tests, however, the test-retest method or the equivalent forms method may be preferable. Finally, it should be noted that the selection of one method over another may depend to some degree on the purpose of the investigator.

Interpreting a Reliability Coefficient

The three methods described for estimating the extent to which a test is a reliable measuring instrument all yield a single number, a correlation coefficient. This number, designated *r,* varies between 0 and 1.00, but what does it mean? For example, does $r = .60$ indicate acceptable test reliability or not?

Most psychologists would agree that a test reliability coefficient in the high .80s is acceptable, with figures in the .90s being more desirable. There is less consensus as to the minimally acceptable figure because tests are used for so many different purposes. For example, Dreher and Mai-Dalton (1983) concluded that an internal consistency estimate of .60 on a test called the Manifest Needs Questionnaire is "minimally useful."

An *r* of .60 is low by ideal standards, nor does it conform to the .70 that traditionally has been a lower limit for the Cronbach's Alpha estimate of internal consistency (Nunnally, 1978). But the Manifest Needs Questionnaire is used most often for research purposes, and standards of reliability tend to be more flexible in that context. When test results are to be used for making decisions about people's lives, as for employment or college entrance, the traditional higher standards apply. To a certain degree, then, standards for evaluating an estimate of reliability, like choice of a method, depend on the investigator's purpose.

The considerations involved in evaluating the evidence for a test's reliability are discussed in detail in textbooks devoted to the subject of testing. Without comprehensive knowledge, the safest rule of thumb is probably "the higher the better," because the reliability of a test has a direct bearing on the test's standard error of measurement. This statistic, in turn, has important implications for the practical use of a test.

The Standard Error of Measurement

Estimates of test reliability are estimates of the error made in assessing an individual's true position on the scale of measurement. Theoretically, if that same person were given the test a large number of times, the obtained test scores would be spread out around the true score. Some of these test scores would be closer to this true score than others, because some test administrations would include less error than others. If all of these obtained scores were subjected to certain statistical transformations, the results of these many test administrations could be shown in the form of a normal curve. The **standard error of measurement** is the standard deviation of that curve, as shown in Figure 3–1.

Normal curve
See pages 36–37

The standard error of measurement relates to the distribution of scores that would be obtained if one person were given a test many times (although it is not obtained this way). The larger the standard error of measurement, the more spread out the score distribution is around the true score (the mean of the distribution). In Figure 3–1, the standard error of measurement of Test A is approximately one-half that of Test B. What this means is that a test score from Test A is *more likely* to be near a person's true score than a score from Test B.

A test's standard error of measurement is not just a theoretical concept; it can affect any person who is subject to decisions made on the basis of test scores. If a particular college entrance examination has a standard error of measurement of 30, there is a fairly good chance that an obtained score of 530 on the test represents a true score as low as 500 or as high as 560. In this case, a college or university that requires a score of 550 for admission could reject an applicant with a score of 525 solely on the basis of test measurement error.

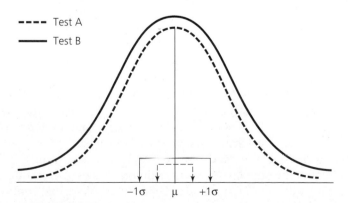

Figure 3–1
The Standard
Error of
Measurement
for Two Tests

There are ways to increase the reliability of a test and thus to decrease the standard error of measurement. The most common is to increase the length of the test in order to achieve a more stable sample of the characteristic being measured (such as scholastic potential).

Validity

According to its dictionary definition, validity is founded on truth or fact, while reliability is founded on consistency. There is a great deal more discussion of validity than of reliability in the I/O psychology literature, but this emphasis in no way diminishes the importance of reliability. It is critical for a very simple reason: an unreliable measurement cannot have any validity. A reliable measuring instrument is not necessarily valid, but unless it is reliable, the issue of validity is irrelevant. An example should help to make the distinction clear.

Suppose that a professor wants to measure the intelligence of the students in a class. He or she decides to do so by measuring the size of each individual's head with a tape measure, reasoning that larger heads contain bigger brains and bigger brains are bound to be more intelligent brains (an argument and a procedure that actually were employed in the past). If the procedure described were followed, would the professor obtain reliable measurements? The answer is yes; if the tape measure were a good one, the professor could measure each head three times and obtain about the same measurement each time. Would these measurements of intelligence be valid? Of course not. There is no evidence that more intelligent people have bigger heads than less intelligent people. The measurement would be consistent but not founded on truth or fact.

At this point, the preliminary definition of validity must be abandoned. It has served its purpose but it is inadequate to the task of discussing measurement validity in I/O psychology, because it implies that something either is or is not valid or true. In fact, validity is very much a matter of context. This statement will be discussed in relation to test validity but, again, remember that validity is a standard to be applied to all measurement situations.

In relation to testing, **validity** is defined as "the appropriateness, meaningfulness, and usefulness of the specific inferences made from test scores" (American Educational Research Association et al., 1985, p. 9). There are different reasons for giving tests, even the same kind of test, so the specific inferences whose validity is of concern differ. When a test is given for employment screening purposes, the relevant inference concerns some aspect of an individual's future behavior. An inference about an employee's current level of job performance is the focus if the test is in the form of a performance evaluation instrument. In both cases, the validity of the test is the extent to which the evidence supports the inferences that are made from the test results.

Inference
See pages 35–43

It is traditional to partition the evidence for the validity of inferences that can be made from a test into three categories based on the kind of inference to which the evidence is most relevant. If there is evidence that the test captures the meaning of the characteristic being measured, there is construct-related evidence of validity. If it can be demonstrated that the items on a test are representative of all of those that are defined as relevant to the test, there is content-related evidence of validity. Finally, if there is a systematic relationship between test scores and some external criterion (such as future job performance), there is criterion-related evidence of validity.

The categories described are convenient, but they should not be taken to mean that there are different types of validity. Rather, each aspect refers to a kind of evidence that might be accumulated to draw conclusions about the overall validity of the measuring device. Ideally, psychologists might like as much of this evidence as possible. Research is time consuming and expensive, however, and test validation is more often a matter of collecting the evidence that is most necessary in light of the intended inferences to be made from the test.

A Word About Terminology

The phrases "construct-related evidence of validity," "content-related evidence of validity," and "criterion-related evidence of validity" are accurate but cumbersome. These phrases continue to appear occasionally, but most of the time the more convenient terms "construct validity," "content validity," and "criterion validity" are used, in accordance with convention. In similar fashion, the term "test validation" appears many times in this and later chapters, but this phrase is merely shorthand for the process of acquiring evidence relevant to inferences that might be made from test scores.

Construct-Related Evidence of Validity

A fundamental question to ask about any test used for any purpose is: Does it measure what it is intended to measure? If the answer is yes, the test has **construct-related evidence of validity**. This concept can be difficult to grasp in the abstract, but Kraiger's (1989) example and related discussion should help to make it clearer.

Determining the nature of the relationship between playing the piano and success on certain kinds of job tasks requires collecting construct-related evidence of validity.

During World War II, I/O psychologists discovered that one of the best predictors of fighter pilot success was whether the individual had had piano lessons as a child. This information could be used with justification as a "test" for screening fighter pilot candidates, because the fact of having had piano lessons as a child was correlated positively with shooting down enemy planes as a pilot. The relationship, however, is purely empirical; it arises out of data that were collected and has no theoretical foundation.

The fact that piano lessons usually develop eye-hand coordination seems to be a reasonable explanatory link between the lessons and success as a fighter pilot, but this is an hypothesis. Specifically, it is an hypothesis that the question "Did you have piano lessons as a child?" is really an indicator, or test, of a psychological construct. To provide evidence of construct validity for this "test" would require more than simply a correlation between it and a behavior criterion (such as success as a fighter pilot), however.

Hypothesis
See page 25

There are many studies that might be carried out to examine the question of whether a test is indeed an indicator of a particular construct. One common approach is to correlate scores on the test with scores on a different, well-accepted measure of the same construct. For example, a large number of people could be given one of the several validated eye-hand coordination tests available and also asked the question about piano lessons. A strong positive association would suggest evidence of construct validity. As an alternative to this procedure, scores on the test for two groups of subjects who logically would be expected to differ on the construct might be compared. It seems likely that there would be significant differences in eye-hand coordination between successful data entry clerks and clothing salespersons, for example. Do responses to the piano lessons question differ significantly between people in these occupations as well?

**Statistical
significance**
See pages 35–36

To accumulate meaningful evidence of construct validity, a researcher would have to do a number of studies to build up confidence that scores on a test (in this case, the piano lessons question) permit inferences regarding the intended construct (hypothesized to be eye-hand coordination). This is one likely reason that construct validation research has long been less common than criterion validation studies.

Despite the infrequency of relevant studies in the past, construct-related evidence of validity is considered by most I/O psychologists to be fundamental to the question of validity (Carrier, Dalessio, & Brown, 1990), ". . . the beacon to steer toward" (Landy, Shankster, & Kohler, 1994, p. 284). Today, increasing numbers of I/O psychologists seem to be undertaking such research. King and King (1990) present a detailed analysis of the construct validity of a variable called role ambiguity (uncertainty about what is expected in a given organizational position), to take one example. Other investigators have taken on the broader task of assessing construct validity in organizational research in general (Bagozzi & Phillips, 1991; Barrett, 1992). As interest in this area of research grows, there may be a new emphasis on construct-related evidence of validity in the theory and practice of I/O psychology in the future.

Content-Related Evidence of Validity

Construct-related evidence of validity is relevant to making inferences about what a test measures (the construct underlying it). **Content-related evidence of validity** is relevant to making inferences about the specific items on a test (its content). The content validity of a test is usually defined in one of two ways. One is the relevance of what is on the test to what is being measured. For example, a multiplication problem is relevant to a test of arithmetic computational ability but asking someone to spell *multiplication* is not.

The other standard for content-related evidence of validity is ". . . the degree to which the sample of items, tasks, or questions on a test are representative of some defined universe or domain of content" (American Educational Research Association et al., 1985, p. 10). In other words, this standard is concerned with the representativeness of what *is* on the test relative to everything that *might* be appropriate to be on it—the **domain** of the test.

Again, the college exam is a convenient vehicle for illustrating a concept, in this case the concept of a test that is representative of its "defined domain of content." Suppose that a professor gave a test that was to cover Chapter 2 of the textbook. Suppose further that all of the questions on the test came from one section in the middle of the chapter. The cry "Unfair!" would ring down the halls, and it would be justified. The questions on such a test would not constitute a representative sample of the questions that could be asked to evaluate knowledge of the assigned chapter. As a measure of that knowledge, therefore, such a test would have low content validity.

Content-related evidence of test validity, as defined by relevance and representativeness, is illustrated in Figure 3–2. The square is the appropriate domain of the test—the material in Chapter 2, to continue with that example. Dots inside the square represent relevant test items. The areas labeled A, B, and C encompass items that might constitute three possible tests on this material. These tests may be described as follows:

- Test A contains items that are not *relevant* to the domain; perhaps the professor included some questions from Chapter 3.

- Test B contains items that are relevant, but not *representative*; they all come from one section of the domain. This might be the test on which all of the items are from one section of the chapter.

- Test C has the greatest content validity. All of its questions lie inside the square, and it includes questions from all sections of the domain. The professor may have divided the content of the assigned chapter into sections corresponding to the major headings and written two questions from each section, for example.

Although Figure 3–2 is based on an example from an academic setting, the principle is the same whatever kind of measurement is involved. A performance appraisal in-

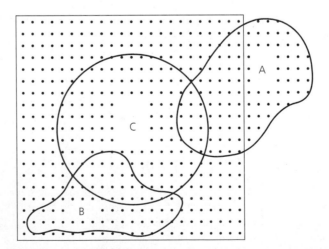

Figure 3–2
The Concept of
Content
Validity

strument that asked questions only about the quantity of an employee's work output would have low content validity—its "items" would be relevant, but they would not be representative of all aspects of the employee's job. Unless quantity were the only concern and aspects of job performance such as quality, timeliness, and the ability to work with others were not relevant for this job, the appraisal instrument would be *deficient.*

Establishing content-related evidence of validity requires making judgments about the correspondence between test content and test domain. In Figure 3–2, the domain is the material in a specified chapter of a textbook, but domain is not always so well defined. In a study for the Oklahoma Department of Corrections, Hughes and her colleagues (1989) undertook to develop a physical performance test for selecting and evaluating corrections officers. The four-step process they used began with establishing the domain of the test.

1. Define the job content domain.

2. Demonstrate a correspondence between the content of the job and the proposed content of the test.

3. Support the soundness of the process used to construct the test with appropriate data.

4. Provide and support a rationale for scoring the test items (that is, the physical qualification standards that are established).

Physical performance has a great many dimensions and so it was necessary to determine which of these are relevant to the work of a corrections officer (the domain) before a test of physical performance could be developed for that job. By way of interest, the six appropriate and basic performance requirements identified by these investigators were as follows: whole body rapid response, body drag and rescue, lifting and carrying weight, response time, grip strength, prolonged physical activity, and push-away force.

Criterion-Related Evidence of Validity

When there is **criterion-related evidence of validity** for a test, there is evidence that scores on the test (the predictor variable) are related in a systematic and significant fashion to a criterion. A **criterion** is an external measurement of some attribute or behavior against which to make an evaluation. Frequently used criteria in I/O psychology include turnover, absenteeism, job performance, training progress, and rate of job advancement.

Predictor variable
See pages 41–42

As an example of a situation in which criterion-related evidence of validity is important, consider a large organization that proposes to use a test of arithmetic computational ability to help select payroll department trainees. The company wants to use this test to predict individual performance in a training program to avoid wasting training money on unsuitable job candidates. If the predictions (inferences) made from this test are valid, people who score better on the test also should (1) learn the training material more quickly and (2) make fewer errors. These are the criterion variables.

Figure 3–3 is a scattergram made by graphing the arithmetic computation test scores of 16 payroll trainees against the performance evaluations they received after two weeks of training. It is clear that higher test scores tend to go with higher evaluations, a graphic picture of criterion-related evidence of validity for making predictions (inferences) on the basis of the test.

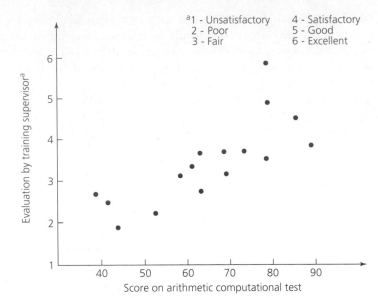

Figure 3–3
A Graphic
Illustration of
Criterion-
Related Validity

The Predictive Design

Criterion-related evidence of validity means that scores from a test may be used to make inferences in the form of predictions. The basic procedure for acquiring this evidence, therefore, is called a predictive design. Test scores taken now are correlated with measures made later on some criterion for the same subjects. This is the design that was used in Figure 3–3; arithmetic test scores obtained *before* hiring were correlated with supervisor evaluations obtained *after* hiring and two weeks of job training.

The predictive design has traditionally been considered the preferred design for obtaining criterion-related evidence of validity, but it has drawbacks in applied settings. A major one has to do with the subjects available. To be carried out correctly, the predictive design requires that the subjects in the validation sample have a full range of scores on the test in question. Accordingly, it is necessary to hire some job applicants with low scores on the test. This can be a difficult requirement to sell to those who do the hiring. If the test is going to be used for employment screening, a natural assumption is that people with low scores are not going to do well on the job—so why hire them?

Another possible problem associated with a predictive design for obtaining criterion-related evidence of validity is the time span between the collection of test data (predictor) and the collection of criterion data. The farther into the future predictions about behavior (such as job performance) are extended, the less accurate they are likely to be (Henry & Hulin, 1987; Hulin, Henry, & Noon, 1990). Supervisor evaluations, which probably are the most common criterion measures in such studies, may be particularly vulnerable because they are so time and job specific. One way around such problems is to use a concurrent design for establishing criterion-related evidence of validity.

The Concurrent Design

The concurrent design for establishing criterion-related evidence of validity uses the people already employed in an organization as subjects; therefore, it is not necessary to hire new employees with low test scores. The test in question is given to current employees, and the scores are correlated with the appropriate criterion measures for the same employees. This procedure has at least two major advantages. First, it does not affect the hiring of new employees until after the validation study is complete. Second, it eliminates the time lag between collecting the test scores and collecting the criterion measurements. This gets around the problem mentioned of trying to make long-term predictions in a dynamic situation. It also gets the test into use more quickly if the results of the study are positive.

The concurrent design solves some criterion validity research problems, but it too has drawbacks. One has to do with motivation. To use current employees in a validation study, it is necessary to reassure them that test results will not affect their jobs. It cannot be assumed that these subjects, with nothing riding on the results, will approach the test in the same way a job applicant would. But the population for which the test is intended is job applicants, not current employees.

Another problem created by the concurrent design for acquiring criterion-related evidence of validity is related to the very issue this procedure is used to get around—having to hire people with very low test scores. This is not done with the concurrent model, and in consequence the validation sample may very well not include any subjects at the low end of the test score distribution.

Research sample
See page 27

When an I/O psychologist sets out to get evidence that a test can be used for prediction, he or she has some reason to believe that there is a relationship between what is measured by the test and the behavior to be predicted. If this is true in the case of an employee screening test, most of those employees who would have scored at the lowest levels (had they been given the test) should no longer be on the job. Accordingly, the range of scores for the employees who remain to be eligible for a concurrent validation study is restricted.

Restriction of Range

The graph in Figure 3–4 illustrates the inference problem that can be created by **restriction of range** of test scores in a study designed to find criterion-related evidence of validity. The full graph shows the relationship between scores on a selection test (predictor) and six-month performance evaluation measures (criterion) for a full range of test scores. The correlation coefficient between these two measures is approximately $r = .40$.

The boxed portion of Figure 3–4 highlights the scattergram for those subjects in the sample who scored 60 or above on the test (a restricted range). The almost circular pattern of the dots in this restricted range is the classic depiction of no correlational relationship between two variables. This particular test would be rejected as an employment screening device if it happened that most of the people who took the test scored above 60 (the situation that might arise in a concurrent design study).

There are statistical procedures for dealing with restriction of range under certain conditions (e.g., Dobson, 1988; Raju, Burke, & Maurer, 1995), but a full range of actual scores remains preferable. A compromise for obtaining criterion-related evidence of validity in an applied setting is to use a mixed strategy. A limited concurrent design study can be used to get an idea of the test's potential. If findings are encouraging, the test can

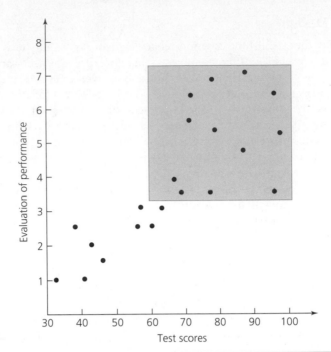

Figure 3–4
The Problem
of Range
Restriction in
Correlation

**Correlation
coefficient**
See pages 37–38

then be used on incoming employees who are hired on the basis of other screening methods. Over time a sufficient number of cases will be accumulated to carry out the standard predictive design study.

Interpreting a Validity Coefficient

Like estimates of reliability, estimates of test validity appear in the form of correlation coefficients. To a considerably greater degree than is involved in interpreting a reliability coefficient, however, interpreting a validity correlation coefficient involves both theoretical and practical concerns. For purposes of illustration, the discussion will be confined here to the interpretation of criterion-related evidence of validity, the situation encountered most frequently by the majority of I/O psychologists .

The discussion of test reliability noted that most psychologists will accept an estimate of reliability that lies in or above the upper .80 range, provided it is based on competent research. Things are not so straightforward with respect to criterion-related evidence of validity. In some 90 years of employment testing, these coefficients seldom have exceeded $r = .50$, a number that looks rather small compared with reliability coefficients that lie in the .80- or .90-plus range. Remember, however, that a reliability estimate is essentially a correlation between two measures of the same thing. By contrast, a criterion-related validity coefficient is an estimate of the correlation between two different things—a test score and some other measure of behavior.

All behavior has multiple and complex causes and it is unlikely that any test measures more than a very small number of the factors relevant to the behavior it is being used to predict. Measures of job satisfaction have often been used to predict absenteeism from work, for example, but anyone who has worked knows that the decision to be absent on a particular day may have nothing to do with job satisfaction or the lack of it. In terms from Chapter 2, job satisfaction may be one determinant of absenteeism, but it explains a limited part of the variance in this criterion variable.

Determinant
See page 41

The amount of variance in a criterion that a given test score can explain is expressed as a percentage called the coefficient of determination. Mathematically, this number is calculated as the square of the correlation coefficient between test and criterion. For a test that correlated $r = .50$ with a measure of job performance (criterion), the coefficient of determination would be .25 (25%). In other words, about 75% $(1.00 - .25)$ of the variance in job performance is *not* accounted for; there are many factors other than that measured by the test that determine how people perform on the job.

The size of any coefficient of determination is limited, and to date this limit appears to be about 25%. Therefore, it may seem that there is little reason to commit significant resources to constructing, validating, and using tests for predictive purposes in organizations. The prediction that has been under discussion, however, is statistical prediction, which is determined by the amount of variance in the criterion (such as job performance) accounted for by the predictor variable (test score).

In practice, I/O psychologists often find a test with a criterion-related validity coefficient of .30 (9% of the variance) to be useful for adding to the effectiveness of decision making in many situations. The concept of usefulness, or utility, is relevant to any kind of measurement for any kind of personnel decision, but it can be seen most clearly in the context of an organization's success rate for hiring.

The term **success rate for hiring** refers to the proportion or percentage of employees hired who are considered to be successful on the job. Two types of selection errors, or mistakes, can lower this percentage. Hiring people who do not work out is a false positive error. The opposite situation—deciding not to hire people who would have worked out—creates a false negative error. The relationship between these errors and good hiring decisions is shown in Figure 3–5.

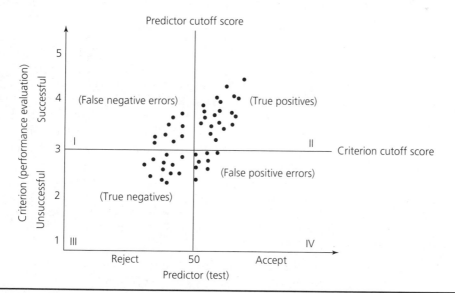

Figure 3–5
Errors in the Selection Process

Figure contributed by John F. Binning, Ph.D., Department of Psychology, Illinois State University, Normal, IL. Reprinted by permission.

The base of Figure 3–5 is a graph showing the relationship between scores on an employment screening test (the predictor) and a general evaluation of job performance (the criterion). For purposes of illustration, it is assumed that all new employees hired into this company for a given period of time were given the test. The scores were not used for selection, however, but were filed away to be used later when performance evaluations were available for these employees. (This, of course, is the same procedure as the predictive design for acquiring criterion-related evidence of validity.)

There are two more assumptions about the situation behind the graph in Figure 3–5. The first is that *if* the test had been used to help select employees, applicants who scored below 50 would not have been hired. Fifty (50) is the predictor cutoff score. The second assumption is that employees who receive a performance evaluation above the midpoint (3) on the scale are considered by the organization to be successful and the rest to be unsuccessful employees. Three (3) is the criterion cutoff score.

On the basis of the information provided about Figure 3–5, the meaning of false positives, false negatives, and good hiring decisions is clearer. Each dot in the scattergram represents one employee's position with respect to test score and performance evaluation. The employees in quadrant IV were above the predictor cutoff score and should have been good employees, but they were given low performance evaluations; hence, the label "false positives."

The opposite situation holds true for the employees in quadrant I of Figure 3–5. They would not have been hired had their test scores been considered at the time, but they are above the criterion cutoff score; hence, the label "false negatives." Finally, the employees in quadrants II and III performed according to prediction and represent good decisions (true positives or negatives).

When making selection decisions, people in organizations focus on the case represented in quadrant II of Figure 3–5—successful employees who can be identified in advance. The extent to which an employment screening test can increase the number of cases in quadrant II relative to quadrant IV depends on three factors:

1. The success rate for hiring without the test (sometimes called the base rate)

2. The criterion-related validity coefficient of the test

3. The proportion of applicants who must be hired for every job (the selection ratio)

The number of applicants from among which to choose one individual to fill one job position is called the **selection ratio**. If this ratio is 1:1 (only one applicant for a position), there is no decision to be made and no reason to use a test. If, on the other hand, there are more job applicants than there are positions, there is a decision to be made. The question of the utility of a particular test is the question of whether the test will help whoever makes this decision to do a better job.

There are published tables that make it possible to answer the question of a test's utility at a glance if the current success rate for hiring, criterion-related validity coefficient of the selection test, and selection ratio are known. A portion of the original Taylor-Russell tables (Taylor & Russell, 1939) is reproduced in Figure 3–6. The situation depicted in that figure is as follows:

1. The success rate for hiring *without* a new test that is being considered for use is 50% (half of the employees hired have been successful).

2. A validity study has estimated the criterion-related validity of the new test to be $r = .41$ (accounts for about 17% of the variance in performance on the job in question).

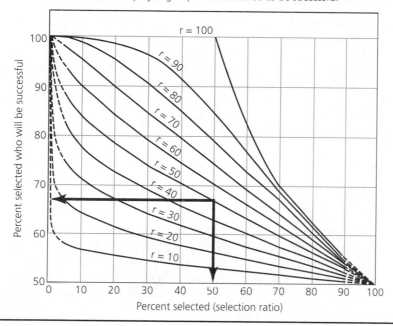

Predictive value of r for various selection ratios when 50 percent of the employee group are considered to be successful

Figure 3–6
An Excerpt from the Taylor-Russell Tables

From H. C. Taylor and J. T. Russell, "The Relationship of Validity Coefficients to the Practical Effectiveness of Tests in Selection: Discussion and Tables." *Journal of Applied Psychology,* 1939, 23, 565–578.

3. The selection ratio is 50% (there are, on average, two applicants for every job opening).

As indicated by the heavy dark line in Figure 3–6, a company that only has to hire half of the people who apply for jobs (a 50% selection ratio) can push its success rate from 50% to more than 65% by using a screening test with a criterion-related validity coefficient of $r = .41$. The impressive monetary savings that might go along with such an improvement are discussed by Schmidt and Hunter (1981) in the Psychology at Work feature that opened this chapter.

The Taylor-Russell tables have assisted I/O psychologists and others in evaluating the utility of tests for more than 50 years. It is for this historical value that one of the original graphs is reproduced here; tabular forms of the tables are usually employed today. Those developed by Ghiselli and Brown (1955) show the percentage increase in job efficiency at different validity coefficients directly. Tables by Naylor and Shine (1965) are especially useful when it is not possible to make the clear-cut distinction between success and failure on the job that is required to use the Taylor-Russell tables.

Test Validity: Putting It All Together

To recapitulate, the evidence relative to the validity of the inferences that can be made from a test traditionally is separated into three categories. These are not different types of validity; with respect to any given test, the different approaches to collecting evidence of validity should lead to consistent conclusions. The ideal in test construction is the use of multiple procedures employed sequentially at different stages of test development.

> Validity is thus built into the test from the outset, rather than being apparently limited to the last stages of test development. . . . The validation process begins with the formulation of trait or construct definitions, derived from psychological theory, prior research, or systematic observation and analyses of real-life behavior domains. . . . Test items are then prepared to fit the construct definitions. Empirical item analyses follow, with the selection of the most valid items from the initial item pools. . . . The final stage includes validation . . . against external, real-life criteria. (Anastasi, 1989, p. 475)

Issues in Test Validation Research

The process of validating a test can be a long one and it ends with one number—a correlation coefficient. Important decisions may be made on the basis of this number, and I/O psychologists must remain alert to problems that might introduce error into validation research. Two such problems are discussed here—sampling error and differential validity. It is also important to find ways to make validation research more efficient. One possible answer is validity generalization.

Sampling Error

The theme that all measurement incorporates error has been a recurring one throughout this chapter. One consistent source of error is the subjects who are observed. There are many ways in which the particular subjects of an experiment (including test takers in a reliability or validity study) may differ in some important aspect from other subjects who might have been observed. If these differences are critical, **sampling error** is introduced. This bias reduces the extent to which a sample is representative of the relevant population.

Generalizability
See page 45

The effect of sampling error is to reduce the extent to which inferences from a set of observations can be generalized beyond the sample on which they were made. For example, suppose that for some reason an I/O psychologist can administer an experimental employment screening test only to job applicants who come into a company's human resources office between three and five in the afternoon. In such a case, any estimate of the test's criterion-related validity would most likely be based on a biased sample.

The exact nature of the bias is unknown, but the sample described would almost certainly include a disproportionate number of both late starters and applicants who got going early in the day and have already applied (and perhaps been tested) at other companies. The applicants who got an early start are likely to be tired and perhaps discouraged as well. Those who did not get out of bed until noon may not really be all that interested in working. Either way, the researcher collects a sample of test scores that differs from the one that would be obtained by testing job applicants over a full day. The extent to which a future criterion-related validity coefficient obtained on the basis of these subjects can be generalized to the "applicants to this company" population is questionable.

The example depicts an obvious sampling error that is easy to avoid, but the realities of conducting research mean that some kind of sampling error usually is a foregone conclusion. This is one reason the scientific method stresses verification. In validity research, this verification requires checking the first estimates of validity on another sample—that is, replicating the study. Unless there is some reason to suspect that an entire sample is biased (as in the example), this replication frequently is carried out with some portion of the total available subjects. This "sample of a sample" is called a hold-out sample; it consists of a random sample of the original sample of subjects. The remaining subjects in the research sample are tested first and results are replicated with the hold-out sample.

Scientific method
See pages 23–24

The hold-out sample method saves time. If time is not critical, or if there is some problem with the original sample, a replication study can be carried out by doing the same study again at a different time with a different sample of subjects. However it is accomplished, one replication is considered the absolute minimum required if a test is to be used in an applied setting. If the test is used for any length of time, reevaluation at intervals is necessary. Jobs change, standards change, and the characteristics of individuals applying to a particular organization change.

Verification
See pages 43–45

Differential Validity

The purpose of conducting research to establish criterion-related evidence of validity is to establish a relationship between a predictor variable and one or more criterion variables. An interesting chapter in the history of employment testing was written when it was suspected that another member of the variable family—the moderator variable—might be affecting studies of this relationship.

Moderator variables, variables that have a predictable influence on the nature of the relationship between two other variables, captured widespread attention when employment testing first came under fire for its suspected role in perpetuating racial bias in organizations. The question arose when it was pointed out that racial minorities were being left out of jobs in disproportionate numbers even when tests with demonstrated criterion-related validity were being used for screening. It looked as if race might be modifying the basic test score–job criterion relationship established by the validity studies.

Moderator variable
See page 39

A simple illustration of race as a moderator variable in selection testing is shown in Figure 3–7. Graph A of that exhibit depicts the results of an hypothetical criterion-related validity investigation that includes both whites and nonwhites in the sample. The trend of these data, a more or less straight line from lower left to upper right, suggests a modest but acceptable positive correlation. Actual calculations probably would show sufficient criterion-related evidence of validity for selection utility.

Graph B in the figure is a scattergram that separates the white subjects from all subjects, and Graph C does the same for the nonwhite subjects. Note that the positive correlation shown in A holds and looks stronger in B, but disappears in C. This is a picture of the concept of **differential validity**: the degree of criterion-related validity is significantly different for subgroups of subjects. It is acceptable for whites, but close to zero for nonwhites; race *moderates* the test score–job performance relationship.

The graphs in Figure 3–7 are typical of what many I/O psychologists found in their data when they began examining them for differential validity. The implications for equal employment opportunity led to an intense but short-lived revolution in I/O psychology testing research. Moderator variable research (often called subgroup analysis) became part of every testing program. Sex, education, social class, and various personality traits as well as race were subject to scrutiny as possible moderator variables.

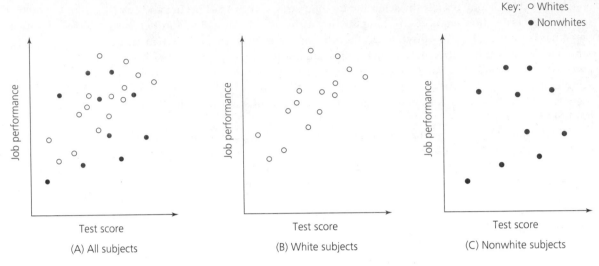

Figure 3–7
The Concept of Differential Validity

As often happens in applied psychology, the initial excitement over moderator variables was followed by a more sober examination of the results of this research. These new analyses suggested that the appearance of differential validity more often than not is due to chance or to statistical problems. The consensus in mainstream I/O psychology today is that differential validity is not a major cause for concern in employment testing.

There will probably always be situations in which a test does not predict as well for one broad grouping of subjects as it does for another. Most of the time, however, plain old criterion-related evidence of validity remains the issue, as it always has been. The matter of white/nonwhite differences in test scores and the way these scores are used continues to concern many people, however. More on this subject is found in At Issue.

Validity Generalization

In the broadest sense, validity generalization refers to the ability to extend inferences from an empirical validation study beyond the original sample and setting. Most applied use of tests requires such generalization; testing conditions are seldom identical to those under which the original validity data were gathered. As it is more often used in the I/O psychology literature today, however, the term has a narrower meaning. **Validity generalization** (VG) refers specifically to extending or transporting criterion-related evidence of validity for a test from the job for which it was established to other jobs without conducting separate validation studies.

The Equal Employment Opportunity Commission takes the position that it is lawful to generalize criterion-related evidence of validity beyond the particular job for which it is established, *provided* it can be demonstrated that the various jobs require "essentially the same work behaviors" (Equal Employment Opportunity Commission, 1978, Section 7B). This demonstration begins with job analysis—the process of breaking a job down into its component behaviors to reveal what job holders actually do.

Often, job analysis reveals that jobs with quite different titles, such as bank teller and customer service clerk, actually require about the same work behaviors from the people who perform them. A test that has been validated for selecting employees for one of the jobs can legally be used to screen employees for the other—but will it do this effectively? Can success as a billing clerk in the parts department of a large, busy automobile repair shop be predicted effectively with the same test used to predict job success as a billing clerk in a quiet upscale department store? The job behaviors are similar, but the work situations are very different.

The idea that the context in which a job is performed (the situation) is so important that it affects the ability to predict job success is known as the situational specificity hypothesis. From this perspective, the billing clerk in the auto parts department and the billing clerk in the department store have two similar, but different, jobs. In practical terms, this means that a separate validity study should be conducted for every job for which a test might be used as a predictor, even if job analysis suggests that the jobs themselves are made up of very similar tasks.

The situational specificity hypothesis was accepted by most I/O psychologists for many years, and there seemed to be ample evidence to support it. When the same tests were used to predict performance on the same or similar jobs in different companies (or even different parts of the same company), the obtained validity coefficients varied widely. The conclusion that work setting was acting as a moderator variable in the predictor-criterion relationship seemed inescapable. For example, Brown (1981) estimated that over a third of the variance in predicting the performance of life insurance agents was due to differences in their work situations.

Beginning in the 1970s, some investigators started taking a hard look at the situational specificity hypothesis. Aided by new techniques of meta-analysis, they examined the possibility that what *appeared* to be significant differences in validity coefficients

Meta-analysis
See page 43

Generalizing employment test validity from one job situation to another requires demonstrating that the two jobs call for "essentially the same work behaviors."

across situations might actually be variation created by the methods and procedures used to collect and analyze the data; that is, the variation might be a "statistical artifact" rather than a true phenomenon. In one of the earlier investigations, Pearlman, Schmidt, and Hunter (1980) reexamined the data from some 700 studies of predictive validity for clerical jobs and concluded that the true validity coefficients tended to be consistent across studies and situations.

The tests examined in the early studies of validity generalization were tests of cognitive (mental) abilities. Less than a decade after the first published research report, the conclusion that the validity of such tests in employment situations is generalizable had achieved widespread acceptance (e.g., Anastasi, 1988; Society for Industrial and Organizational Psychology, 1987). This is an important element of the body of knowledge being accumulated about selection testing and good news for organizations that use or could use cognitive ability tests for selection.

The success of validity generalization research to date has stimulated a great deal of additional research, discussion, and controversy concerning the many associated measurement, theoretical, and practical issues. These are not of concern here except by way of reminder that scientific investigation is an ongoing process. The ability to transport criterion-related evidence of the validity of a cognitive ability test across situations suggests that validity coefficients in general may be hardier than has been assumed. There are still many questions, however, and it would be premature to dismiss situational specificity altogether (James, DeMaree, Mulaik, & Ladd, 1992; Lance, Stennett, & Mayfield, 1992).

An Overview of Employment Screening Tests

The discussion to this point has taken employment testing in organizations as its frame of reference without discussing specific screening tests. The reason for this order is not unlike the old problem of whether the chicken or the egg came first. Reliability, validity, restriction of range, validity generalization, and the other topics covered thus far in this chapter are general measurement issues. They could as easily be discussed in an educational context, for example, as in an organizational one. Most people find they do need *some* context, however, as these concepts can be very difficult to understand in the abstract.

This book is about behavior in organizations, and therefore an organizational context for measurement issues is appropriate. Within that context, employment testing provides a useful framework for demonstration. At the same time, some understanding of measurement basics is a necessary foundation for any discussion of specific employment screening tests. These basics have been reviewed, and the major categories of tests used to help select employees for organizations can now be examined. Nontest selection methods are reviewed in Chapter 4.

Ability Tests

An **ability test** is designed to assess the potential of an individual for learning something or performing some activity. The Scholastic Aptitude Test and the College Entrance Examination Board tests were developed to assess ability to master academic material at the college level. In organizations, ability tests are used to assess abilities necessary to perform or to be trained to perform particular jobs. Among those used more frequently are tests of mechanical, psychomotor, and mental abilities.

The ability to acquire and use skills that are mechanical in nature is required by many jobs, even in the so-called information age. Psychologists who have studied this ability have found that it has two distinct aspects. One aspect is a general potential for understanding mechanical concepts; the other is the more specific ability to grasp spatial relationships. A sample item from a general mechanical aptitude test is shown in Exhibit 3–1. This test might be used to screen applicants for semiskilled jobs involving simple tools or machinery. Except for the directions, which may be read or explained by the examiner, the test is nonverbal; that is, an individual's score is not dependent on

---

Use of Tools and Materials
Time 10 Minutes

Exhibit 3–1

A Test of General Mechanical Ability

The five pictures in this sample group include: D. a needle, N. a plumb bob, M. a thimble, V. a pair of scissors, and A. a spool of thread. The needle, thimble, scissors, and the thread are the most common articles in a sewing kit. The plumb bob is used mostly in construction work and would be out of place in a collection used for sewing. Therefore, letter "N" is written in the block on the right.

SAMPLE:

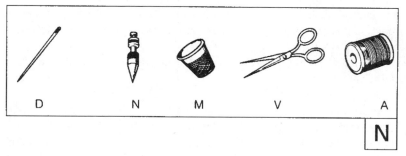

| D | N | M | V | A |

N

DIRECTIONS: This is a test of ability to identify the proper use of some common tools and materials. Below, there are twenty groups of pictures. In each group of five pictures across the page, there is one item which does not properly belong to the group. Each picture is marked with a letter. Write in the small block on the right in each group the letter of the picture which does not belong in the group.

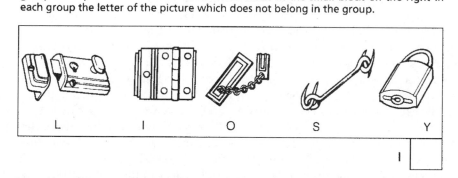

| L | I | O | S | Y |

I

From the Acorn National Aptitude Tests, Test 4, Mechanical Aptitude Test: Non-Verbal. Published by Psychometric Affiliates, 1620 E. Main Street, Murfreesboro, TN 37130. Reprinted by permission.

language skills. This feature makes this test useful for job applicants with poor basic education skills or whose first language is not English.

Tests of mechanical ability are but one of the many kinds of specialized ability tests used in organizations. For example, tests of perceptual abilities (such as eyesight and hearing) and psychomotor abilities (such as general manual dexterity, reaction speed, and eye-hand coordination) are used in screening applicants for pilot training (e.g., Kantor & Carretta, 1988). Tests of general physical capabilities are also useful in many employment testing situations (e.g., Blakley, Quiñones, Crawford, & Jago, 1994). Arvey and his colleagues (1992) found eight physical ability tests that were related significantly to two basic aspects of police officer performance, for example.

Despite their unquestioned utility in many situations, the use of physical ability screening tests is likely to discriminate unfairly against women, given the well-documented differences in general male-female physical abilities (Astrand & Rodahl, 1986). One way around this problem that works for some tests is illustrated in a study by Peters, Servos, and Day (1990). These investigators found that all sex differences on a test of finger dexterity disappeared when statistical controls for index finger and thumb size were added to the scoring process.

Another approach to the problem of systematic sex bias in tests of physical ability is to give more attention to the lowest level of the ability actually required by the job (rather than looking for candidates with the highest possible level of ability). Alternatively, the role of work aids might be factored in. Most women cannot shift as much weight as most men, for example, but with assistance from a hand truck or other device, this fact might be unimportant to on-the-job performance. It seems likely that this approach will receive significantly more attention in physical testing since the passage of the Americans with Disabilities Act of 1990.

The oldest type of ability test used in organizations is the test of mental ability (often called an intelligence test). Verbal ability, logical reasoning, abstract reasoning, mental adaptability, problem-solving ability, and numerical reasoning are among the aspects of mental ability that may be assessed in this way. A sample item from a nonverbal test of logical reasoning ability is shown in Exhibit 3–2. This test might be used to help screen trainees for a job in which they would need to use judgment to sort or arrange items or materials.

Specific aspects of mental ability have been shown to predict both training success and work performance in a wide variety of occupations. Distefano, Pryer, and Crotty (1988) conclude that vocabulary and verbal ability test scores show promise for improving the selection of hospital psychiatric aides without increasing adverse impact on minorities. In another study, scores on the Science Problems and Reading Skills subtests of the Medical College Admission Test predicted a measure of physician competence (scores on written certifying examinations), but scores on the Quantitative Skills subtest did not (Glaser, Hojat, Veloski, & Blacklow, 1992).

These and other findings reinforce the concept of mental ability as a composite, or mosaic, of abilities. One reviewer identified more than 70 different abilities measured by tests that were available at the time of the search (Carroll, 1993). The authors of a recent article on the subject speak for those psychologists who believe that it is important to distinguish among the various components of mental ability in this way: "A growing body of research . . . suggests that differential success in academic and nonacademic environments reflects, in part, differences in the intellectual competencies required for success in these arenas" (Sternberg, Wagner, Williams, & Horvath, 1995, p. 912).

Few I/O psychologists argue with the basic premise that there are many facets of intelligence, but the majority probably accept Spearman's (1904) two-factor theory of mental ability. One factor (*s*) is the sum of specific abilities (such as those identified by Carroll) while the other is a general cognitive ability (*g*). The relative importance of *s* and *g* in predicting job performance has been and remains a matter of controversy (e.g., Olea & Ree, 1994; Ree, Earles, & Teachout, 1994; Sternberg & Wagner, 1993). The extension of mental ability test validity across a variety of job situations has stimulated still more interest in this debate.

Most of the validity generalization research has involved tests of general cognitive ability, a measure of *g*. The success of such measures in predicting success on many kinds of jobs lends some support to the position that *g* is relatively more important in selection than *s*, but it does not prove it conclusively. Given that some level of cognitive ability is necessary to perform most jobs, it is not surprising that cognitive tests usually work as predictors.

The usefulness of general cognitive ability measures also should not be taken to mean that other kinds of tests have no role in screening job applicants and selecting employees. To quote the authors of one review: "The challenge [to I/O psychologists] lies

---

Practice Items

For each item, find the picture that goes best with the picture in the first box. Draw a dark line from the upper right corner to the lower left corner in the proper box to show the right answer.

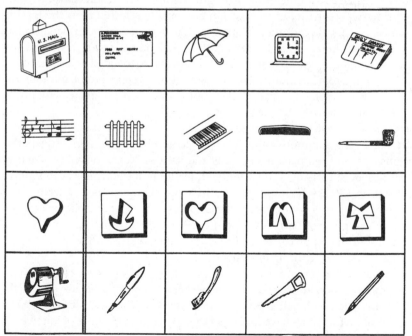

Exhibit 3–2
A Test of
Logical
Reasoning
Ability

From the Non-Verbal Reasoning Test developed by R. J. Corsini, 1957. Published by London House Press, 1550 Northwest Highway, Park Ridge, IL 60068. Reprinted by permission.

in accounting for more performance variance through the combination of cognitive tests with other job-related predictors" (Smith & George, 1994, p. 85).

In short, a test of cognitive ability may be a good base for prediction, but other screening measures can add to this base and produce what is called incremental validity—an increase in the ability to predict successful job-related behaviors over that provided by the base measure. One kind of test that is showing promise in this regard is the personality test.

Personality Measures

A **personality test** is a test intended to compare an individual with the "average" individual (the "norm") on one or more personality traits such as conscientiousness or extraversion. Such tests once were very popular with organizations for screening applicants for salespeople and jobs at upper levels of management for the traits believed to be important to successful job performance. In particular, personality tests were often used to try to identify applicants who were highly motivated to work hard and achieve success.

The premise that personality is important to performance in many jobs makes sense to most people, but the scattershot approach to personality testing (different organizations using different tests for different purposes with different scoring standards) prevented the accumulation of sufficient evidence for the criterion-related validity of these tests (Guion & Gottier, 1965). In consequence, applied personality testing all but disappeared from mainstream I/O psychology until the development of meta-analysis techniques.

Meta-analysis makes it possible for investigators to examine the findings from the personality research as a whole in a meaningful fashion. The results of this research suggest five primary personality factors, which are usually referred to as the Big Five. The basic premise of this classification system is that personalities can be summarized in terms of five basic dimensions (Digman, 1990). The names given to these dimensions differ somewhat among researchers, but the terms and associated characteristics shown in Exhibit 3–3 are representative. This classification system is not without its critics (e.g., Block, 1995; Schmit & Ryan, 1993), but it has been accepted by many I/O psychologists (Mount, Barrick, & Strauss, 1994).

The great advantage of an accepted classification system for personality traits is that it gives researchers a common frame of reference within which to investigate the possible relationships between personality traits and various work behaviors. Their research to date has proved surprisingly consistent; while different traits have been found to have modest criterion validity for some criteria in some occupations, the trait of conscientiousness (see Exhibit 3–3) appears to be a consistently valid predictor across criteria and occupational groups (Barrick & Mount, 1991). The runner-up, so to speak, is extraversion, a trait that appears to be most important in jobs with a large social component, such as sales and working in teams.

With the identification of at least two personality traits that have criterion-related validity in many work situations, researchers have begun exploring the use of tests that measure these traits, such as the NEO Five-Factor Inventory (Costa & McCrae, 1992). In the process, several investigators have found personality tests to be more predictive of job behavior in combination with cognitive ability tests than alone (e.g., Baehr & Orban, 1989).

Using cognitive ability tests as well as personality tests in screening individuals for jobs may also help to offset negative reactions from job applicants who do not see the relevance of personality tests to future job performance (Rosse, Miller, & Stecher, 1994).

Phrasing personality test items so that they refer specifically to work also seems to help make the connection for job applicants (Schmit, Ryan, Stierwalt, & Powell, 1995). "I have always gotten along well with others" might be changed to "I have always gotten along well with my co-workers." In a work situation, the second item has more "face validity," meaning that it *appears* to the test taker to be more appropriate for its purpose.

Tests that generate scores on the Big Five personality traits are by no means the only personality tests available for use in personnel selection. For example, Caliper Human Strategies Inc. has developed an instrument specifically for employment testing use. The Caliper Profile has more than 150 questions and is intended to provide an overall picture of a job applicant's fit with job and organizational requirements.

The measurement issues surrounding personality testing in general are not settled. Nevertheless, as Hogan, Hogan, and Roberts (1996) note in their review of the most frequently asked questions about personality measurement in employment situations: "(a) well-constructed measures of normal personality are valid predictors of performance in virtually all occupations, [and] (b) they do not result in adverse impact for job applicants from minority groups" (p. 469).

The restoration of personality testing to mainstream I/O psychology research and practice is good news to the many organizational hiring personnel who have long believed that personality is a vital part of adaptation to, and success in, many occupations. Among these occupations are those of salesperson, customer service representative, air traffic controller, police officer, and psychiatric hospital aide. The behavior trait of honesty is also vital in these and other job contexts, and instruments for assessing this quality, called integrity tests, are seeing increasingly widespread use.

Integrity Tests

An **integrity test** (sometimes called an honesty test) is an employment screening device intended to identify people likely to be dishonest or to engage in other behaviors that create problems on the job (disruptiveness, for example). Such tests, and many are available, are now used routinely for screening job applicants for a wide variety of jobs in which employees have security duties or access to merchandise or cash. The practice

---

Agreeableness
    Cooperative, good-natured, trusting
Conscientiousness
    Achievement-oriented, dependable, organized, persistent, responsible
Emotional Stability
    Calm, secure
Extraversion
    Active, ambitious, assertive, sociable, talkative
Openness to Experience
    Artistically sensitive, imaginative, intellectual

Note: Different researchers use different labels for the five factors. Those listed here, together with the associated descriptive terms, are representative. Listing is alphabetical and does not suggest relative importance.

Exhibit 3–3
The "Big Five"
Personality
Dimensions

raises a number of issues. Most important, it is appropriate to ask whether integrity tests have sufficient criterion-related validity to offset concerns about invasion of privacy and restriction of job opportunities.

It is probably accurate to say that most I/O psychologists were doubtful about integrity tests in the beginning. One result of this skepticism is that these instruments have been subjected to close examination. To date, this examination has yielded generally favorable results (e.g., Goldberg, Grenier, Guion, Sechrest, & Wing, 1991; Ones, Viswesvaran, & Schmidt, 1993). In one study, for example, scores on an integrity test successfully predicted detected (actual) theft for 111 convenience store employees (Bernardin & Cooke, 1993).

Estimates of the economic costs of employee theft to American businesses range from $15 billion to $125 billion a year. Even at the lowest estimated figure, it is obvious that the ability to screen out individuals likely to be dishonest can be important to the very survival of some companies. Nevertheless, there are issues surrounding this employment screening device that need to be addressed. A primary one concerns who administers the tests and evaluates the results.

Given the implications of failing an "honesty test," it seems glaringly obvious that integrity test scoring should be done only by people who are qualified to evaluate test results. Yet nearly 60% of the integrity test publishers responding to a comprehensive APA survey had no controls of any kind on the purchase of these tests at the time of the study (Camara & Schneider, 1994). The related potential for misuse led Massachusetts to ban these tests, and other states are expected to follow suit. At the other end of the controversy scale is the work sample test, a screening method that is accepted by almost everyone.

Work Sample Tests

A **work sample test** is a measuring instrument consisting of a sample of some behavior that is important to performing a particular job successfully. To be considered a test, this sample must be taken under standardized conditions and scored on a standardized, defined scale of measurement. As with more typical paper-and-pencil screening tests, the measurement must be reliable and valid. Work sample tests for typing and shorthand have been around for a very long time, but the concept has expanded considerably in recent years.

- American Telephone and Telegraph Company developed work sample screening tests of number transcription, coding, area code usage, and filing.

- Some regional transportation (bus) districts find direction tests useful in selecting information operators. These test the ability of job applicants to use maps to give directions between one city location and another.

- A northern California data processing firm requires potential managers to spend two days developing a business plan detailing how they would solve described organizational problems.

- A computer consulting and training firm requires applicants to give a speech on any subject (except computers) to demonstrate their training skills.

Unlike most tests that are used for screening, a work sample test is a direct measure of some important behavior that is needed on a job. A young cooking school graduate showed his understanding of the attractiveness of this approach to organizations. He walked away with the job of cook in a New Jersey prison by bringing (unasked) two full-course dinners to his employment interview.

In the past, work sample tests were used primarily to screen applicants with experience in, or training for, the job in question. Under pressure from the Equal Employment Opportunity Commission to validate screening tests, however, organizations showed interest in their more general use. An early study by Cascio and Phillips (1979) illustrates this screening test in an interesting setting.

Cascio and Phillips investigated work sample testing for amusement park concession stand attendants. After their subjects had been shown how to use the cash register, they were asked to count change, fill out a revenue report, make public announcements, and deal with several irate customers. The authors report that this screening method was less expensive, better liked by job applicants, and as effective as the paper-and-pencil tests used earlier to help select successful employees.

An investigation of work sample tests in a different kind of setting was carried out by Schmitt and Ostroff (1986), who developed tests for specific job behaviors needed by emergency telephone operators. These work sample tests included written tests in which applicants were required to answer specific questions about material presented in tape recordings, and role-playing exercises in which applicants responded to simulated emergency calls. The researchers concluded that these tests possessed high content validity, demonstrated good reliability, and were helpful in presenting job applicants with a realistic preview of actual job duties.

As illustrated by the examples, the most frequently used methodology for work sample testing is hands-on testing. This can be a problem in some job situations. Tasks may take too long to complete to be feasible for work sample testing or expensive parts or equipment may be wasted or damaged. In some cases there can also be a risk to the job applicant if he or she does not have related training and/or experience.

A possible way around these problems has been developed by Hedge and Teachout (1992). In walk-through performance testing (WTPT), job applicants describe in detail how they would do a job task. This interview is checked against a detailed step-by-step checklist of behaviors, standards, and conditions for successful task accomplishment. In their study of almost 1,500 Air Force personnel, Hedge and Teachout conclude that WTPT is useful and may have wide applicability, including serving as an alternative to more traditional job interviews.

Concluding Remarks

The formal study of tests and testing includes a variety of important topics, such as test development, not covered in this chapter. There are many useful books and articles on this subject, including Haney's (1981) well-regarded discussion of testing from the standpoint of social concerns and Guion's (1980) classic article on the concept of validity as it applies to making inferences from tests. A thorough examination of test validity in the context of personnel decisions in organizations can be found in Binning and Barrett (1989).

The categories of tests reviewed here include the primary kinds of tests used to help make employment selection decisions such as hiring, promoting, and providing advanced training to selected individuals. Some organizations with special requirements use specialized tests. Most also use information other than tests in their decision-making process; other screening methods are reviewed in Chapter 4.

At Issue

Test Fairness

There are numerous definitions of *test fairness* in the I/O psychology literature and some complex statistical models as well (e.g., Anastasi, 1989; Millsap & Everson, 1993; Sackett & Wilk, 1994). The essence of the issue, however, may be stated simply. The theory of test unfairness holds that "even if validity coefficients are equal for minority and majority groups, a test is likely to be unfair if the average test score is lower for minorities" (Schmidt & Hunter, 1981, p. 1131).

Schmidt and Hunter go on to note that the theory of test unfairness is based on the assumption that the causal factors lying behind lower test scores for minorities are not related to job performance. While some researchers have found that job performance differences are smaller than score differences on these tests (e.g, Ford, Kraiger, & Schechtman, 1986), the evidence as a whole contradicts the premise that test scores and job performance are not related.

There are many factors that influence job performance. In general, however, ability and skill differences revealed by tests are associated with differences in job performance just as they are associated with differences in school performance (Neisser et al., 1990); they are real, not created by "unfair" tests. This means that tests that reveal such differences are doing what they were designed to do— assessing differences among individuals. Efforts to construct and use tests in order to make these differences disappear in the name of "fairness" destroy both the purpose and the utility of the tests.

Many of those who struggle with the problems that plague the use of tests in organizations believe that ideas about test fairness or unfairness have led to some important issues becoming thoroughly confused. Many people in our country have not had (or have not taken advantage of) the educational and cultural experiences that are generally associated with better test performance. This is a fact that no amount of sophisticated test validation research or legal haggling will change, and efforts to do so only waste valuable resources.

Tests, as tests, are neither fair nor unfair. They are simply more or less good at measuring what they are intended to measure; that is, they are more or less reliable and valid. As a result, some are more vulnerable to being *used* unfairly than are others. Efforts to improve tests and the way they are used should not, and will not, be abandoned. But guaranteeing equality of opportunity does not guarantee equality of results; attacking employment tests on which some groups predictably score lower than others is attacking a serious social problem from the wrong end.

Summary

Measurement is the assignment of values to observations according to some defined system, such as a test. The basic standards for evaluating the adequacy of a test as a measuring instrument are reliability (consistency of measurement) and validity (confidence in test-related inferences).

The assessment of reliability and validity can be a long, expensive process subject to a variety of situational difficulties and constraints. Newer analytic techniques suggest that the validity of certain kinds of tests can be transported from the job for which it was established to other jobs, making the standard employment tests reviewed considerably more attractive to organizations with slender resources.

Questions for Review and Discussion

1. Describe three measuring instruments not mentioned in this chapter and give one example of a possible source of measurement error associated with each.

2. If you were asked to measure the height of each of your classmates and give an estimate of the reliability of your measurements, explain how you would go about it.

3. You and some colleagues have developed a new test. Results of early reliability research have not been encouraging, so you decide to quit wasting time and move on to validity testing. Discuss.

4. In a few sentences, demonstrate that you understand the essential differences between construct-, criterion-, and content-related evidence of validity.

5. What does the term *validity generalization* mean and why is it considered to be an important breakthrough in I/O psychology?

Key Terms

construct validity	reliability
content validity	screening test
criterion	selection
criterion validity	test
domain	validity
measurement/measurement error	validity generalization

References

American Educational Research Association, American Psychological Association, & National Council on Measurement in Education. (1985). *Standards for educational and psychological testing.* Washington, DC: American Psychological Association.

Anastasi, A. (1988). *Psychological testing* (6th ed.). New York: Macmillan.

Anastasi, A. (1989). Ability testing in the 1980's and beyond: Some major trends. *Public Personnel Management, 18,* 471–485.

Arvey, R. D., Landon, T. E., Nutting, S. M., & Maxwell, S. E. (1992). Development of physical ability tests for police officers: A construct validation approach. *Journal of Applied Psychology, 77,* 996–1009.

Astrand, P., & Rodahl, K. (1986). *Textbook of work physiology.* New York: McGraw-Hill.

Baehr, M. E., & Orban, J. A. (1989). The role of intellectual abilities and personality characteristics in determining success in higher-level positions. *Journal of Vocational Behavior, 35,* 270–287.

Bagozzi, R. P., & Phillips, L. W. (1991). Assessing construct validity in organizational research. *Administrative Science Quarterly, 36,* 421–458.

Barrett, G. V. (1992). Clarifying construct validity: Definitions, processes, and models. *Human Performance, 5,* 13–58.

Barrick, M. R., & Mount, M. K. (1991). The Big Five personality dimensions and job performance. *Personnel Psychology, 44,* 1–26.

Bernardin, H. J., & Cooke, D. K. (1993). Validity of an honesty test in predicting theft among convenience store employees. *Academy of Management Journal, 36,* 1097–1108.

Binning, J. F., & Barrett, G. V. (1989). Validity of personnel decisions: A conceptual analysis of the inferential and evidential bases. *Journal of Applied Psychology, 74,* 478–494.

Blakley, B. R., Quiñones, M. A., Crawford, M. S., & Jago, I. A. (1994). The validity of isometric strength tests. *Personnel Psychology, 47,* 247–274.

Block, J. (1995). A contrarian view of the five-factor approach to personality description. *Psychological Bulletin, 117,* 187–215.

Brown, S. H. (1981). Validity generalization and situational moderation in the life insurance industry. *Journal of Applied Psychology, 66,* 664–670.

Camara, W. J., & Schneider, D. L. (1994). Integrity tests: Facts and unresolved issues. *American Psychologist, 49,* 112–119.

Carrier, M. R., Dalessio, A. T., & Brown, S. H. (1990). Correspondence between estimates of content and criterion-related validity values. *Personnel Psychology, 43,* 85–100.

Carroll, J. B. (1993). *Human cognitive abilities: A survey of factor-analytic studies.* Cambridge, England: University of Cambridge Press.

Cascio, W. F., & Phillips, N. F. (1979). Performance testing: A rose among thorns? *Personnel Psychology, 32,* 751–766.

Cortina, J. M. (1993). What is coefficient alpha? An examination of theory and applications. *Journal of Applied Psychology, 78,* 98–104.

Costa, P. T., Jr., & McCrae, R. R. (1992). *NEO/PI/FFI professional manual.* Odessa, FL: Psychological Assessment Resources.

Cronbach, L. J. (1951). Coefficient alpha and the internal structure of tests. *Psychometrika, 12,* 1–16.

Digman, J. M. (1990). Personality structure: Emergence of the five-factor model. *Annual Review of Psychology, 41,* 417–440.

Distefano, M. K., Pryer, M. W., & Crotty, G. B. (1988). Comparative validities of two cognitive ability tests in predicting work performance and training success of psychiatric aides. *Educational and Psychological Measurement, 48,* 773–777.

Dobson, P. (1988). The correction of correlation coefficients for restriction of range when restriction results from the truncation of a normally distributed variable. *British Journal of Mathematical and Statistical Psychology, 41,* 227–234.

Dreher, G. F., & Mai-Dalton, R. R. (1983). A note on the internal consistency of the Manifest Needs Questionnaire. *Journal of Applied Psychology, 68,* 194–196.

Equal Employment Opportunity Commission (1978). Adoption by four agencies of the "Uniform Guidelines on Employee Selection Procedures." *Federal Register, 43,* 38290–38315.

Ford, J. K., Kraiger, K., & Schechtman, S. L. (1986). Study of race effects in objective indices and subjective evaluations of performance: A meta-analysis of performance criteria. *Psychological Bulletin, 99,* 330–337.

Ghiselli, E. E., & Brown, C. W. (1955). *Personnel and industrial psychology* (2nd ed.). New York: McGraw-Hill.

Glaser, K., Hojat, M., Veloski, J. J., & Blacklow, R. S. (1992). Science, verbal, or quantitative skills: Which is the most important predictor of physician competence? *Educational and Psychological Measurement, 52,* 395–406.

Goldberg, L. R., Grenier, J. R., Guion, R. M., Sechrest, L. B., & Wing, H. (1991). *Questionnaires used in the prediction of trustworthiness in pre-employment selection decisions: An APA task force report.* Washington, DC: American Psychological Association.

Guion, R. M. (1980). On trinitarian doctrines of validity. *Professional Psychology, 11,* 385–398.

Guion, R. M., & Gottier, R. F. (1965). Validity of personality measures in personnel selection. *Personnel Psychology, 18,* 135–164.

Haney, W. (1981). Validity, vaudeville, and values: A short history of social concerns over standardized testing. *American Psychologist, 36,* 1021–1034.

Hedge, J. W., & Teachout, M. S. (1992). An interview approach to work sample criterion measurement. *Journal of Applied Psychology, 77,* 453–461.

Henry, R. A., & Hulin, C. L. (1987). Stability of skilled performance across time: Some generalizations and limitations on utilities. *Journal of Applied Psychology, 72,* 457–462.

Hogan, R., Hogan, J., & Roberts, B. W. (1996). Personality measurement and employment decisions: Questions and answers. *American Psychologist, 51,* 469–477.

Hughes, M. A., Ratliff, R. A., Purswell, J. L., & Hadwiger, J. (1989). A content validation methodology for job-related physical performance tests. *Public Personnel Management, 18,* 487–504.

Hulin, C. L., Henry, R. A., & Noon, S. L. (1990). Adding a dimension: Time as a factor in the generalizability of predictive relationships. *Psychological Bulletin, 107,* 328–340.

James, L. R., DeMaree, R. G., Mulaik, S. A., & Ladd, R. T. (1992). Validity generalization in the context of situational models. *Journal of Applied Psychology, 77,* 3–14.

Judiesch, M. K., Schmidt, F. L., & Mount, M. K. (1992). Estimates of the dollar value of employee output in utility analysis: An empirical test of two theories. *Journal of Applied Psychology, 77,* 234–250.

Kantor, J. E., & Carretta, T. R. (1988). Aircrew selection systems. *Aviation, Space, and Environmental Medicine, 59,* 32–38.

King, L. A., & King, D. W. (1990). Role conflict and role ambiguity: A critical assessment of construct validity. *Psychological Bulletin, 107,* 48–64.

Kraiger, K. (1989). Personal communication.

Lance, C. E., Stennett, R. B., & Mayfield, D. L. (1992). A reexamination of selected meta-analysis results: Has the generalizability of research findings been overstated? Presented at the Seventh Annual Meeting of the Society for Industrial and Organizational Psychology, Montreal.

Landy, F. J., Shankster, L. J., & Kohler, S. S. (1994). Personnel selection and placement. *Annual Review of Psychology, 45,* 261–296.

Millsap, R. E., & Everson, H. T. (1993). Methodology review: Statistical approaches for assessing measurement bias. *Applied Psychological Measurement, 17,* 297–334.

Mount, M. K., Barrick, M. R., & Strauss, J. P. (1994). Validity of observer ratings of the Big Five personality factors. *Journal of Applied Psychology, 79,* 272–280.

Naylor, J. C., & Shine, L. C. (1965). A table for determining the increase in mean criterion score obtained by using a selection device. *Journal of Industrial Psychology, 3,* 33–42.

Neisser, U., Boodoo, G., Bouchard, T. J. Jr., Boykin, A. W., Brody, N., Ceci, S. J., Halpern, D. F., Loehlin, J. C., Perloff, R., Sternberg, R. J., & Urbina, S. (1990). Intelligence: Knowns and unknowns. *American Psychologist, 51,* 77–101.

Nunnally, J. C. (1978). *Psychometric theory* (2nd ed.). New York: McGraw-Hill.

Olea, M. M., & Ree, M. J. (1994). Predicting pilot and navigator criteria: Not much more than g. *Journal of Applied Psychology, 79,* 845–851.

Ones, D. S., Viswesvaran, C., & Schmidt, F. L. (1993). Comprehensive meta-analysis of integrity test validities: Findings and implications for personnel selection and theories of job performance. *Journal of Applied Psychology Monograph, 78,* 679–703.

Pearlman, K., Schmidt, F. L., & Hunter, J. E. (1980). Validity generalization results for tests used to predict job proficiency and training success in clerical occupations. *Journal of Applied Psychology, 65,* 373–406.

Peters, M., Servos, P., & Day, R. (1990). Marked sex differences on a fine motor skill task disappear when finger size is used as a covariate. *Journal of Applied Psychology, 75,* 87–90.

Raju, N. S., Burke, M. J., & Maurer, T. J. (1995). A note on direct range restriction corrections in utility analysis. *Personnel Psychology, 48,* 143–149.

Raju, N. S., Burke, M. J., & Normand, J. (1990). A new approach for utility analysis. *Journal of Applied Psychology, 75,* 3–12.

Ree, M. J., Earles, J. A., & Teachout, M. S. (1994). Predicting job performance: Not much more than g. *Journal of Applied Psychology, 79,* 518–524.

Richardson, M. W., & Kuder, G. F. (1939). The calculation of test reliability coefficients based on the method of rational equivalence. *Journal of Educational Psychology, 30,* 681–687.

Rosse, J. G., Miller, J. L., & Stecher, M. D. (1994). A field study of applicants' reactions to personality and cognitive ability testing. *Journal of Applied Psychology, 79,* 987–992.

Roth, P. L. (1994). Group approaches to the Schmidt-Hunter global estimation procedure. *Organizational Behavior and Human Decision Processes, 59,* 428–451.

Russell, C. J., Colella, A., & Bobko, P. (1993). Expanding the context of utility: The strategic impact on personnel selection. *Personnel Psychology, 46,* 781–801.

Saal, F. E., & Knight, P. A. (1988). *Industrial/organizational psychology: Science and practice.* Pacific Grove, CA: Brooks/Cole.

Sackett, P. R., & Wilk, S. L. (1994). Within-group norming and other forms of score adjustment in preemployment testing. *American Psychologist, 49,* 929–954.

Schmidt, F. L., & Hunter, J. E. (1981). Employment testing: Old theories and new research findings. *American Psychologist, 36,* 1128–1137.

Schmidt, F. L., & Hunter, J. E. (1982). The money test. *Across the Board, 19,* 35–37.

Schmit, M. J., & Ryan, A. M. (1993). The Big Five in personnel selection: Factor structure in applicant and nonapplicant populations. *Journal of Applied Psychology, 78,* 966–974.

Schmit, M. J., Ryan, A. M., Stierwalt, S. L., & Powell, A. B. (1995). Frame-of-reference effects on personality scale scores and criterion-related validity. *Journal of Applied Psychology, 80,* 607–620.

Schmitt, N., & Ostroff, C. (1986). Operationalizing the "behavioral consistency" approach: Selection test development based on a content-oriented strategy. *Personnel Psychology, 39,* 91–108.

Smith, M., & George, D. (1994). Selection methods. In C. L. Cooper & I. T. Robertson (Eds.), *Key reviews in managerial psychology: Concepts and research for practice.* Chichester, England: Wiley.

Society for Industrial and Organizational Psychology (1987). *Principles for the validation and use of personnel selection procedures* (3rd ed.). College Park, MD: Author.

Spearman, C. (1904). "General Intelligence" objectively determined and measured. *American Journal of Psychology, 15,* 210–293.

Sternberg, R. J., & Wagner, R. K. (1993). The g-ocentric view of intelligence and job performance is wrong. *Current Directions in Psychological Science, 2,* 1–5.

Sternberg, R. J., Wagner, R. K., Williams, W. M., & Horvath, J. A. (1995). Testing common sense. *American Psychologist, 50,* 912–927.

Taylor, H. C., & Russell, J. T. (1939). The relationship of validity coefficients to the practical effectiveness of tests in selection: Discussion and tables. *Journal of Applied Psychology, 23,* 565–578.

Van de Vijver, F. J. R., & Harsveld, M. (1994). The incomplete equivalence of the paper-and-pencil and computerized versions of the General Aptitude Test Battery. *Journal of Applied Psychology, 79,* 852–859.

The Individual

Part II focuses on the individuals in organizations. Chapter 4 examines the processes of recruiting job applicants, screening them for the purpose of making a selection decision, and placing new employees in appropriate jobs. The focus in Chapter 5 is on job training and socialization—the processes by which these newcomers to an organization become productive "insiders." Employee motivation and job satisfaction are discussed in Chapter 6. The primary non-performance aspects of employee behavior that are of interest to I/O psychologists, including absenteeism and turnover, are the subjects of Chapter 7.

4

Recruiting, Selecting, and Placing Employees

PSYCHOLOGY AT WORK

Big Brother Takes a Closer Look

Excerpted from A. Bennett, "Big Brother Takes a Closer Look." *Wall Street Journal,* May 10, 1989, p. B1. Reprinted by permission of *Wall St. Journal,* © 1989 Dow Jones & Company, Inc. All Rights Reserved Worldwide.

When adults volunteer to help out as role models for underprivileged children, it's vital to make sure they'll set a good example.

To weed out potential problems, Big Brothers–Big Sisters of Metropolitan Chicago plans to use a structured interview designed by London House, Inc., a Park Ridge, Ill. human-resources consulting company. The 21-question interview tests motivation, responsibility and emotional maturity, and also checks for drinking, drug abuse or physical violence.

Such interviews are increasingly used to test corporate employees. But most are designed for businesses, and Big Brother found that it needed questions tailored specifically for volunteers. . . .

A sample question in the London House interview: "Tell us about the last time you got angry and how you handled it." Good answers include taking a walk to cool off. . . .

The interview also turns up traits like cooperativeness and responsibility—or the opposite. . . .

THE EMPLOYMENT interview has always been the single most commonly used employment screening method. It seems likely to remain so, but not necessarily in the familiar open-ended form. As described in the excerpt in Psychology at Work, the Chicago Big Brothers–Big Sisters organization decided to use a modified format called a structured interview in which the questions interviewers ask are specified in advance and tailored to the particular screening situation. As a result, collecting the appropriate information, analyzing it, and comparing interview results for different applicants is considerably easier.

The strengths and weaknesses of the interview as an employment screening method are examined in this chapter's discussion of recruiting, selecting, and placing employees. An overview of current thinking in I/O psychology about the desirable end result of these activities sets the stage.

Matching Individuals to Organizations and Jobs

Matching individual abilities and skills to job requirements is at the heart of traditional screening, selection, and placement in organizations. Current thinking in I/O psychology also emphasizes matching individual needs, values, and expectations to what organizations and jobs can offer, to the extent possible. A well-known theoretical statement of this concept of "fit" is the Theory of Work Adjustment (Dawis, England, & Lofquist, 1964; Lofquist & Dawis, 1991).

The Theory of Work Adjustment is a systematic attempt to describe the dynamic ongoing adjustment of an individual and his or her work environment to one another in terms of basic principles from psychology. The core of the theory is the concept of person-environment fit; to the extent that individual (person) abilities fit the ability requirements of the work situation (environment), the individual should be a *satisfactory* employee. To the extent that the rewards the job situation (environment) offers fit his or her needs (person), the individual should be a *satisfied* employee.

The Theory of Work Adjustment was not developed for I/O psychology, but the basic concept is expressed in a **matching model** for organizations (Wanous, 1980). Central to this model is the role that recruiting and screening methods play in bringing about a match between individual and jobs. The following pieces of information are required by this process:

- the skills and abilities required by the job
- the rewards and opportunities offered by the job and by the organization
- the abilities, skills, and experience of the applicant or new employee
- the needs, values, and expectations of the applicant or new employee

Information about job requirements and rewards comes from the process of job analysis, discussed in Chapter 11. The assessment of individual abilities, skills, and experience is examined in the current chapter. Information as to employee needs, values, and expectations must be obtained from the individuals involved, something that sounds easier than it may be in practice. A possible tool for incorporating this information into the formal selection process is the realistic job preview.

Realistic Job Previews

The intent of a **realistic job preview (RJP)** is to provide a job applicant with important information (negative as well as positive) about the organization and the job for which he or she is applying in a straightforward, nonselling manner. The information may be conveyed through interviews, films, a day on the job, work samples, or group discussions with current employees. Sears Roebuck & Company uses a combination of methods in its realistic job preview program. The emphasis is on employee flexibility. Sears wants to make sure that prospective associates understand up front that they will be expected to pitch in and do whatever needs doing, even if it is not what they were hired to do.

The idea of the realistic job preview grew out of I/O psychology research findings that jobs frequently fail to meet expectations set up during traditional recruiting and screening where everyone is putting the best foot forward. If the discrepancy is too large, it may create enough dissatisfaction to cause a promising employee to leave the company soon after joining it. Realistic job previews allow applicants who think it is unlikely that a job will meet their needs and desires to "select themselves out." The applicants who do accept jobs experience fewer disillusionments. Either way, voluntary turnover should decline and employee job satisfaction should increase, and this is exactly what Premack and Wanous (1985) found in a detailed examination of the early realistic job preview research.

Considered together, investigations of realistic job previews in the years since the Premack and Wanous review have yielded mixed results. Sometimes RJPs seem to have the expected effects, but sometimes they don't. At least part of the explanation for these findings undoubtedly lies with the subjects of the studies. Even if those doing recruiting and screening are presenting relevant information in a completely open manner, there is no guarantee that an individual applicant will be equally candid. People take jobs for many reasons, and some accept positions they know are likely to be dissatisfying because other considerations are more important at the time.

Research subjects
See page 27

Another explanation for contradictory results in the realistic job preview literature is that the matter is not quite so simple as originally envisioned; specifically, there seem to be some important moderator variables. Meglino, DeNisi, and Ravlin (1993) found that RJPs had different effects on both job acceptance and job tenure depending on whether applicants for the position of correctional officer knew anything about the job in advance. A similar finding was reported by Vandenberg and Scarpello (1990) with subjects in the insurance industry.

Moderator variable
See page 39

Variation in the extent to which realistic job previews conform to the nonselling ideal is probably relevant to mixed RJP findings as well. In addition, some RJPs may not provide the information that job applicants believe is most important. In this context, work values (achievement, honesty, concern for others, and so on) seem to be gaining in importance (e.g., Meglino, Ravlin, & Adkins, 1989). Organizational values as such have received little attention in the recruiting literature, but there is some evidence that they affect both applicant job choices (e.g., Judge & Bretz, 1992) and the ease with which new hires adjust to the organization (e.g., Chatman, 1991).

Matching in Perspective

Evidence to date supports the conclusion that realistic job previews are effective in certain situations if they are used as intended, but they are not a foolproof method for matching individuals to jobs. There are multiple considerations in getting the right people into the right jobs, and some of the considerations can work at cross-purposes to one another. Doing it right is time-consuming and expensive and the outcome is not guaranteed. The complexities are increased by expanding computer and communication capabilities that change job descriptions almost faster than they can be put into print, and by the increasing use of work teams that share tasks and often manage themselves, redefining old ideas of "the job" (e.g., Bowen, Ledford, & Nathan, 1991). A different approach to matching offers one way to deal with this dynamic situation.

A few companies have begun hiring permanent employees for the organization rather than for a particular job. Because an organization's overall philosophy and values are likely to be relatively stable, a basic compatibility with these characteristics may be more important in some companies than a fit with a particular job at a particular time.

Many I/O psychologists believe that a good match between individual needs, values, and expectations, and what organizations and jobs can offer makes for more satisfied employees.

Sun Microsystems, the fastest-growing U.S. company in the first half of the 1990s, looks for people who like and are good at one thing—solving problems.

These changes and others described in future chapters require related changes in many of the traditional industrial/organizational psychology methods, including those for employee screening and selection. There is no evidence, however, that such adaptation will involve starting over. Rather, it seems likely that what is called for is modification, extension, and reevaluation of existing theories and methods (Cascio, 1995). In screening, for example, there is already a significant revival of personality testing, a source of information that may be particularly useful for matching individuals to organizations rather than to particular jobs.

The discussion of recruiting, selection, and placement in this chapter is organized along traditional lines for two reasons. First, the roughly 100 years of research and practice in these areas of study is the foundation, or baseline, for creating modifications to meet new situations. Second, many (perhaps most) organizations still carry out the basic human resource function of finding people to fill the permanent positions in their companies more or less in the traditional fashion.

Recruiting Job Applicants

Recruiting job applicants is the process of finding and attracting people to fill the positions in an organization. The aim of this activity is to find some number of qualified job applicants who will take a position if it is offered. In most cases, several applicants per opening are preferred, because the more applicants it has (the higher the selection ratio), the more selective an organization can be.

Selection ratio
See page 68

From one perspective, it might seem as if organizations should be able to be as selective as they want to be. By the latter half of the 1990s, the United States had experienced nearly a decade of highly publicized massive job cuts ("downsizing") resulting from corporate mergers, buyouts, and reorganizations; major changes in job design and production methods to increase profitability by accomplishing more work with fewer employees ("reengineering"); and/or the relocation of production facilities to other countries ("exporting jobs"). With so many positions gone, it might seem as if filling jobs in organizations would not be much of a challenge. In fact, something like the opposite is true.

Labor Shortages in the 21st Century

For some time, researchers who track social statistics have been predicting the development of widespread labor shortages that will persist well into the 21st century (e.g., Johnston & Packer, 1987). Many industries are already having difficulties finding and hiring the employees they need. The apparent paradox of a simultaneous reduction in positions and increasing difficulty filling jobs is created by several interrelated factors.

One of the more important reasons for this country's developing labor shortage is the so-called baby bust, a decline in the birthrate in the latter part of the 20th century. The Bureau of Labor Statistics projects that almost 40% of the labor pool will be 45 or older within the next decade. There are simply going to be fewer young people available to work, and many companies draw most of their entry-level employees from this age group. Changing social values also play a role in the situation. As more people assign a higher priority to active parenting, leisure time, and advanced education, options such as working for a temporary agency, job sharing, working part- time, and self-employment become more popular. All of these personal choices reduce the number of people available for permanent full-time employment.

Job skills are a critical part of the picture. The labor shortage expected or already experienced by many organizations is not an across-the-board one. The supply of individuals who are unskilled, minimally skilled, or formerly skilled (possess skills that were once valued but are no longer needed) is plentiful. The labor shortage that is developing is not about numbers as such. It is about the kinds of employees organizations are looking for.

Changes in technology are increasing, not decreasing, the demands on employees in many organizations. One result is that high tech experience or formal qualifications such as a degree in engineering are becoming essential in many industries. Increasing numbers of employers also need employees who have multiple or cross-functional skills, such as computer systems specialists who are familiar with hospital administration. In addition, there is a growing demand for what management scholar Peter Drucker (1994) named "technocrats," people who work both with their hands and with specialized technical knowledge (such as x-ray technicians).

Last but by no means least in the list of skills today's organizations are seeking in their employees is the ability to be effective in "people work." One reason for this requirement is increasing emphasis on teamwork in organizations of all kinds. More fundamental is the far-reaching shift in the U.S. economy from an industrial to a service base. Unfortunately, service jobs, at least at the entry level, usually pay less than the manufacturing jobs they replace, so many displaced industrial workers must accept less pay as well as learn new skills if they are to keep working.

With a closer look at the kinds of employees who are in demand, it is clear that recruiting will continue to be an important human resources function in the foreseeable future. The most effective screening system is of no use if there are no qualified job applicants to screen. This fact has obviously impressed itself already on some companies; the president of Kraft USA gave the 1994 recruiting presentation at the University of Michigan in person.

Establishing Personnel Requirements

Recruiting begins with establishing personnel requirements—the number and type of new employees needed in a defined time period. Ideally this process begins with an overall organizational statement of personnel needs based on formal human resources planning. This planning includes a variety of activities, such as job analysis, current personnel inventory, succession planning, and forecasting, all of which should be coordinated with an organization's short-term and long-term business plans and objectives (Jackson & Schuler, 1990).

Formal human resources planning is a desirable baseline for recruiting, but it is not always feasible to make a systematic connection between these two activities. Much recruiting starts with unexpected terminations or sudden expansion, as when a firm acquires a large contract that cannot be completed with its present work force. Many large companies recruit almost continuously, either to offset turnover or to be prepared for future personnel demands.

*Internal recruiting
offers many advan-
tages to organiza-
tions, including the
motivational ad-
vantages that may
go along with a
company's commit-
ment to expanding
career opportunities
for its current em-
ployees.*

Minnesota Mining and Manufacturing (3M) Company's designated requisition program is an example of planned ongoing recruitment tied to formal human resource planning. 3M maintains an ongoing presence at 25 to 30 carefully selected universities for the
purpose of recruiting college graduates to fill a specified number of entry-level positions
each year. This number (the "designated requisition") is determined by the number of approved requests for new hires that is made formally once each year by company managers
in the context of their business planning.

Sources of Job Applicants

Minnesota Mining and Manufacturing Company recruits a number of new employees
each year from universities, one of its external sources of job applicants. But 3M is also
committed to promotion from within and to helping qualified unassigned employees
(people whose jobs have been or soon will be eliminated) find jobs in other parts of the
organization. These current employees are an internal source of job applicants for the
company. Both internal recruiting and external recruiting have advantages and disadvantages, and like 3M, most organizations use a combination of strategies.

Internal Recruiting

Seeking job applicants from within the ranks of current personnel is less costly than external recruiting. In addition, both the organization and the job applicants have firsthand
knowledge of one another. A policy of recruiting from within can have motivational

advantages as well. Individual employment opportunities are expanded, and there is some protection against automatic unemployment if a job is eliminated. Internal recruiting also conveys an organization's commitment to employee development and career advancement, and both factors may have positive effects on employee work motivation.

Job posting for actual or anticipated vacancies in an organization has been around for a long time, but today's internal recruiting procedures are a far cry from pinning index cards to a bulletin board. Inova Health System in Virginia maintains a 24-hour job line, puts a job vacancy listing on employee e-mail weekly, and conducts internal job fairs. A number of large corporations with facilities and employees all over the country distribute regular newspapers with the pertinent details of current or upcoming vacancies in all locations, including information about applicant requirements and how to apply for the positions.

Internal recruiting can be used to fill jobs at any level in a company, but for many years most internal recruiting was for the purpose of promoting current employees. This policy is still common, but there is also a movement toward large formal internal recruiting programs for other kinds of jobs. Some of the momentum behind this shift may be attributed to the corporate downsizing mentioned earlier; many of the firms that eliminated large numbers of jobs instituted a policy of giving displaced employees first opportunity to fill other vacancies. An interesting variation on this theme occurred in mid-1995 when hundreds of General Motors employees were required to go through a formal application and screening process—for the jobs they already had. Those who did not make the cut retired or were reassigned.

External Recruiting

All of the ways by which people who do not already work for an organization are brought in to apply for positions are referred to collectively as external recruiting. The oldest and least expensive of these methods is the "Now Hiring" sign on an organization's physical premises. The familiar "Help Wanted" advertisement in newspapers and trade publications requires a greater expenditure but often generates significantly more applicants. Screening the replies can be a long and tedious process, however, and the final tally of viable candidates may be small. An alternative is to work through public employment agencies, which do some prescreening, or private employment agencies, which do more but can be expensive. Another option is to send recruiters to one of the increasing number of job fairs.

Job fairs bring large numbers of recruiters and job applicants together in one location, usually for only one or two days. Some people find that they have something of a "meat market" atmosphere, but they do offer an opportunity to see and talk personally with many job applicants at no cost to the recruiting organization save the recruiter's personal expenses. These events vary considerably; some are highly specialized, while others are more generalized come-one-come-all affairs. In a class by itself is the Spring Break Job Fair in Daytona Beach, Florida. In 1995, recruiters from 15 companies interviewed about 400 students, most of whom came straight from the beach "dressed" in bathing suits. The 1996 fair drew even more recruiters and candidates, and the event is expected to be held annually.

More traditional recruiting efforts usually involve visits to professional association meetings and educational institutions. In 1994, NationsBank Corporation's 16 recruiters visited 75 college campuses with an eye to filling 800 jobs. This kind of college tour has a long tradition in recruiting, but some organizations looking for college graduates are beginning to spend more time at fewer, select schools. Alarmed by this trend, college and university placement centers are launching efforts to recruit recruiters. Duke University's aggressive campaign has doubled the number of companies that visit its campus annually.

A growing number of educational institutions, including Rensselaer Polytechnic and the University of Cincinnati, are attacking the problem of fewer on-site campus recruiters with technology; their interactive-video networks make it possible for recruiters to interview job-hunting students without leaving their home offices. Proctor & Gamble found video interviewing so attractive that it is subsidizing the costs of equipment installation at a number of universities.

From video interviewing it is but a short step to the new frontier of external recruiting—the Internet. This worldwide connection of individuals and organizations has enormous potential for bringing about fundamental changes in recruiting methods, but it isn't happening overnight. The Walt Disney organization accepts résumés on "the Net," and a few companies mount direct electronic recruiting efforts. The evidence available to date, however, suggests that most organizations are not quite ready to leap into recruiting cyberspace.

Recruiting Research

Traditionally, I/O psychologists were not involved as actively in external recruiting for organizations as they were in internal recruiting. Some professional recruiters had been trained as psychologists, but in general the interest of those in the field stopped at the door of the company. This situation has changed as the legal aspects and rising costs of screening and selection have led more organizations to ask for help in improving their

Both women and blacks are underrepresented in upper management positions in this country.

external recruiting. Affirmative action programs also stimulated applied psychologists to take more interest in the external sources that produce job applicants.

As their involvement in external recruiting increased, I/O psychologists, together with other researchers interested in this area, began to examine some interesting questions. Here is a sample of some of the answers.

- Former employees (rehires) were the single best source of applicants in a packing plant (Taylor & Schmidt, 1983).

- Employees recruited through informal sources, such as word of mouth, reported receiving more accurate job information from their recruitment source than did employees recruited through formal sources, such as employment agencies (Saks, 1994; Williams, Labig, & Stone, 1993).

- Recruiting source was not related to the length of subsequent employment for college business majors (Swaroff, Barclay, & Bass, 1985) or nurses (Williams, Labig, & Stone, 1993).

- Females and blacks used formal recruiting sources more frequently than did Hispanics, nonminorities, and males (Kirnan, Farley, & Geisinger, 1989).

- A significant number of job applicants use multiple recruiting sources (Vecchio, 1995).

Research such as that represented by these samples reveals that different groupings of job applicants tend to use different recruiting sources, and many use several sources. It also suggests that accurate job information is a more important factor in subsequent job tenure and performance than is recruiting source. Such findings offer indirect support to the realistic job previews discussed earlier, as well as providing guidelines for organizations trying to get the most from their recruiting dollars.

Hypothesis
See page 25

A different line of recruiting research begins with the premise that recruiting is not the one-way street long assumed, but a process that involves two parties—job applicants as well as organizational personnel. Available research supports the hypothesis that job applicants notice and are influenced by the behavior and characteristics of recruiters (e.g., Taylor & Bergmann, 1987). Among the recruiter characteristics found to influence perceptions of organization and job attractiveness are friendliness (Goltz & Giannantonio, 1995), interest shown in the candidate (Turban & Dougherty, 1992), and aggressiveness (with greater aggressiveness being associated with lower job attractiveness; Harris & Fink, 1987).

It appears obvious that disinterested, hard-sell individuals are likely to be less successful recruiters than their friendly, low-key counterparts who show an interest in the people they are recruiting. In addition, there is some evidence that applicants respond more favorably to recruiters perceived as similar to themselves in terms of such attributes as gender and education (e.g., Maurer, Howe, & Lee, 1992). In general, then, organizations might do well to be selective in their choice of recruiting personnel as regards individual characteristics. They might also find it advantageous to do more formal training for the recruiting function. It must be noted, however, that most of the research in this area has focused on attitudes rather than on behavior; the question of the extent to which recruiter characteristics influence an applicant's actual acceptance or rejection of a job offer remains open (Rynes & Barber, 1990).

As appreciation for the complex nature of the recruiting process has grown, I/O psychologists have begun reaching out in new directions. Barber and Roehling (1993), among others, are backing the recruiting process up a step to investigate the factors that influence individuals' decisions as to whether to apply for a particular job at all. Other researchers are interested in the relationship between characteristics of the job and recruiting success (e.g., Turban, Eyring, & Campion, 1993; Williams & Dreher, 1992). Finally, applicant reactions to various screening procedures are being investigated more often than formerly (Landy, Shankster, & Kohler, 1994), although reliable data in this area are still scarce.

Recruiting and the Law

Title VII of the Civil Rights Act of 1964 is the cornerstone of the equal employment opportunity (EEO) laws in this country. This act and some of the subsequent legislation having a direct effect on organizational staffing practices are summarized in Exhibit 4–1. Together, they prohibit employment discrimination based on the nonjob-related characteristics of race, color, sex, religion, country of national origin, age, and, most recently, physical or mental disabilities. The objective is to ensure fair employment practices that allow individuals who are equally qualified on the basis of *job-related requirements* equal access to employment, promotion, and other opportunities.

EEO laws and associated court rulings are concerned first of all with preventing future unfair discrimination, but there also has been substantial pressure on organizations to make up for past shortcomings in this respect. Specifically, they are encouraged in a

---

Civil Rights Act of 1964 and Title VII (amended by Equal Employment Opportunity Act of 1972)

Prohibits discrimination on the basis of race, sex, color, religion, or country of national origin. Establishes the Equal Employment Opportunity Commission (EEOC). Affects all employers (including educational institutions and state and local governments) with 15 or more employees, labor unions, and employment agencies.

Age Discrimination in Employment Act of 1967 (as revised in 1978 and 1986)

Prohibits discrimination against people 40 years of age or older and regulates automatic age-related employment policies (some organizations may have such a policy; most cannot). Affects all employers with more than 25 employees.

Americans with Disabilities Act of 1990

Prohibits discrimination against individuals with physical or mental disabilities, provided reasonable accommodation to the disability can be made. Affects all employers with 15 or more employees.

Civil Rights Act of 1991

Extends Civil Rights Act of 1964 to United States citizens working abroad for an American employer (or working for a foreign corporation controlled by an American employer). Provides for jury trials and punitive damages in discrimination suits found to have merit.

Exhibit 4–1
A Summary of Major Federal Legislation Affecting Hiring Practices in Organizations

variety of ways to find qualified members of certain groups underrepresented in many jobs. In this context, the term **underrepresentation** refers to a significant discrepancy between the number of people in the labor force who are available for a job (or occupation) and the number who are actually employed. One of the most prevalent examples in this country is the very small number of women and blacks in top management positions. A formal plan for reducing such underrepresentation is called an **affirmative action plan** (AAP).

Affirmative Action

Adherence to general fair employment practices is a basic responsibility of all organizations regardless of size. A written affirmative action plan is not required by law unless a firm has at least 50 employees and government contracts worth $50,000 or more a year (making it a federal contractor). In these organizations, affirmative action plans must contain utilization and availability analyses to determine if women, minority group members, or individuals with disabilities are underrepresented; goals for balancing representation; and timetables for correcting the situation. An affirmative action plan may also be ordered by a court as part of an EEO-related settlement against organizations determined to have engaged in past employment discrimination, but many are voluntary. The guidelines provided by the **Equal Employment Opportunity Commission** (EEOC; the enforcement body for fair employment practices) for an effective AAP are summarized in Exhibit 4–2.

Both informal affirmative action and formal AAPs depend on vigorous recruiting efforts for success. Underrepresentation is perpetuated largely by a shortage of applicants from certain groups for certain jobs and occupations. The philosophy behind affirmative action is that this shortage has been caused by two interacting factors. First, social norms and organizational hiring practices for many years directed women and minorities into occupations and jobs considered appropriate for them. Second, these practices led many women and minorities to expect to be turned down if they trained for and/or sought nontraditional jobs or occupations, so they did not bother to do so.

Social conditions have changed and discrimination on a personal basis is now illegal, but changes in expectations often lag behind. Commitment to affirmative action is commitment to active efforts to overcome the perceived obstacles to employment opportunity on the parts of underrepresented groups. Carrying out this commitment requires two special recruiting activities. The first is to develop the potential of current employees for promotion to jobs in which their groups are underrepresented (internal recruiting).

The second special recruiting effort required if a commitment to affirmative action is to be realized is to explore nontraditional sources of job applicants in underrepresented groups in an active fashion (external recruiting). This strategy is illustrated in Exhibit 4–3, which reproduces a notice taken from an American Psychological Association–published I/O psychology research journal. APA is concerned that underrepresentation in journal article reviewing could possibly lead to systematic bias in the kinds of articles recommended for publication.

Affirmative action has been in place for more than a generation now, but it seems to be becoming more rather than less controversial as time goes on. There is more on this subject in this chapter's At Issue. Here, the discussion of recruiting is closed with a look at what may become a new kind of affirmative action—workforce diversity.

A. Issue written equal employment policy and affirmative action commitment.

B. Appoint a top official with responsibility and authority to direct and implement your program.

   1. Specify responsibilities of program manager.
   2. Specify responsibilities and accountability of all managers and supervisors.

C. Publicize your policy and affirmative action commitment.

   1. Internally: to managers, supervisors, all employees, and unions.
   2. Externally: to sources and potential sources of recruitment, potential minority and female applicants, to those with whom you do business, and to the community at large.

D. Survey present minority and female employment by department and job classification.

   1. Identify present areas and levels of employment.
   2. Identify areas of concentration and underutilization.
   3. Determine extent of underutilization.

E. Develop goals and timetables to improve utilization of minorities, males, and females in each area where underutilization has been identified.

F. Develop and implement specific programs to achieve goals.

   This is the heart of your program. Review your entire employment system to identify barriers to equal employment opportunity; make needed changes to increase employment and advancement opportunities of minorities and females. These areas need review and action:

   1. Recruitment: all personnel procedures.
   2. Selection process: job requirements; job descriptions, standards and procedures. Pre-employment inquiries; application forms; testing; interviewing.
   3. Upward mobility system: assignments; job progressions; transfers; seniority; promotions; training.
   4. Wage and salary structure.
   5. Benefits and conditions of employment.
   6. Layoff; recall; termination; demotion; discharge; disciplinary action.
   7. Union contract provisions affecting above procedures.

G. Establish internal audit and reporting system to monitor and evaluate progress in each aspect of the program.

H. Develop supportive in-house and community programs.

Exhibit 4–2
Steps to an Affirmative Action Plan

From Equal Employment Opportunity Commission, *Affirmative Action and Equal Employment: A Guidebook for Employers.* Washington, DC: U.S. Government Printing Office, January 1974, pp. 16–17.

Workforce Diversity

Unlike affirmative action, workforce diversity is not about a moral or legal obligation to give minorities and women preference over white males in hiring and promotion, nor is it about numbers that demonstrate appropriate representation. What workforce diversity *is* about is the desirability of a mix of sexes, races, ages, cultural backgrounds, personalities, and lifestyles within an organization's total workforce. This is neither a legal issue nor a social issue; it is a business issue. **Workforce diversity** means having employees who are able to relate to a broad spectrum of people, a growing necessity in the environment in which contemporary organizations must operate.

There are several converging trends behind the drive toward diversity that is taking place in many contemporary American organizations. One is simply the increasing diversity in the country itself—that is, in the source of employees. Personnel of the Marriott hotel chain speak more than 70 different languages. A second trend is the increasing diversity of customers and clients; Mariott's guest register is as diverse as its personnel. And 61% of the firms responding to one survey said they had more employees overseas than they had five years ago, and that they expected this growth to continue. Finally, there is a growing reluctance among some employees to give up what makes them unique in order to fit in to a particular organization. Silver (1995) sums up the effect on business of ignoring these trends:

> Missed marketing opportunities. Difficulty building rapport with a diverse base of customers. The loss of talented employees who feel excluded or limited in a com-

---

Exhibit 4–3
An Example of Active Recruiting for Members of Underrepresented Groups

Members of underrepresented groups: Reviewers for journal manuscripts wanted

If you are interested in reviewing manuscripts for APA journals, the APA Publications and Communications Board would like to invite your participation. Manuscript reviewers are vital to the publication process. As a reviewer, you would gain valuable experience in publishing. The P&C Board is particularly interested in encouraging members of underrepresented groups to participate more in this process.

If you are interested in reviewing manuscripts, please write to Leslie Cameron at the address below. Please note the following important points:

- To be selected as a reviewer, you must have published articles in peer-reviewed journals. The experience of publishing provides a reviewer with the basis for preparing a thorough, objective review.

- To select the appropriate reviewers for each manuscript, the editor needs detailed information. Please include with your letter your vita. In your letter, please identify which APA journal you are interested in and describe your area of expertise. Be as specific as possible. For example, "social psychology" is not sufficient—you would need to specify "social cognition" or "attitude change" as well.

- Reviewing a manuscript takes time. If you are selected to review a manuscript, be prepared to invest the necessary time to evaluate the manuscript thoroughly.

Write to Leslie Cameron, Journals Office, American Psychological Association, 750 First Street, NE, Washington, DC 20002-4242.

---

pany's culture or organizational hierarchy. All costs of a culture of exclusion rather than inclusion, costs diversity experts say American companies can no longer afford. (p. 5)

The forces pushing and pulling in the direction of workforce diversity are strong, but a commitment to this concept requires more than a memo or a slogan. For most organizations, it requires educating the existing work force on the need for diversity and the factors, such as insensitivity to cultural bias, that can reduce its effectiveness. Mariott's managers attend mandatory diversity training classes where they are taught to deal with conflict by focusing as narrowly as possible on performance and to avoid reference to race, gender, or culture. The classes also cover topics such as religious customs, "personal space," and norms about body language and eye contact in other cultures.

Rynes and Rosen (1995), who surveyed nearly 800 human resources professionals about diversity training in their organizations, found that the adoption and success of diversity training were associated with a number of variables. Larger organizations with top management committed to diversity and specific personnel responsible for diversity issues were more likely to have such programs. Mandatory attendance for all managers and incentives for increasing diversity were among the factors found to affect the success of the training.

Variables
See pages 25–26

Screening Job Applicants

The purpose of recruiting is to find people to apply for jobs in organizations. In most cases, companies like to have several applicants for a job in order to select the one (or more, if needed) they believe will best fit the job. To make this selection decision, they use a variety of methods for **screening**—that is, for separating individuals most likely to be successful in a job (and fit into the organization) from other individuals in the pool of job applicants. If this process reduces that pool to one applicant, screening becomes synonymous with selection, but this is by no means always the case; conceptually, screening and selection are two different processes, with the former preceding the latter.

In the review in Chapter 3 of the major categories of employment screening tests used by organizations, the word *test* was used in the traditional way, and this use is continued in the current chapter. In reality, however, the EEOC has long taken the position that *any* source of information used to make an employment selection decision is to be considered a test in any legal context. For practical purposes, organizations should regard all screening methods as tests, whatever their actual form (see Bersoff, 1988).

Test
See page 84

Application Blank Information

The first screening information collected by almost every organization comes from an application blank, a sample of which is shown in Exhibit 4–4. (A résumé or portfolio is substituted for this form in some instances.) An application blank provides general information about an individual and his or her background, but the EEOC places constraints on the kinds of questions that may be asked. The purpose of these constraints is to block the use of application blanks as a means of unfair (nonjob-related) employment discrimination. Examples of questions that should be *avoided* altogether on an application blank include:

- questions about an individual's arrest record (it is permissible to ask about convictions)
- questions about membership in organizations (unless related to the job)
- questions about disabilities (which may be considered only after a job offer is made)

Questions about marital status, spouse's job, or child care arrangements should not be asked unless they are asked of both sexes and weighed equally in making an employment decision.

Examples of *suspect* questions, questions it is usually better to avoid on application blanks, are questions about race (unless the organization is under a mandated affirmative

---

Exhibit 4–4
A Sample
Application
Blank

Last name_____ First name and middle initial_____ Date_____

Soc. Sec. No._____ Applying for_____

Telephone No._____ Minimum acceptable wage_____

Present address_____ Previous U.S._____

_____ Address Only_____

How Long?_____ How Long?_____

How did you happen to apply for work here?

Newspaper advertisement_____ Agency sent me_____

Friend's recommendation_____ Name of agency_____

Relative's recommendation_____ Other_____

Have you worked for us before?_____ When?_____

Name at that time_____

Are you under age 18?_____

If yes, do you have a current work permit?_____

Date issued_____ Date of expiration_____

If you are not a U.S. citizen, do you have: A permanent visa_____

A temporary visa_____

Do you have any obligations that would prevent you from:_____

Working consistently?_____ Working overtime?_____

Performing job functions?_____ If yes to any, explain_____

action plan), religion, gender, country of national origin, age, and citizenship. (An employee may be required to present proof of age and citizenship after hiring.) The general rule about suspect questions is that they may be asked only if they are used for the purpose of record keeping and do not influence selection decisions, something that can be difficult to prove.

An important exception to the general rule about suspect questions occurs if it can be demonstrated that the answer to such a question has a relationship to some aspect of job behavior for employees at the company. In other words, if there is evidence of criterion-related validity, the application blank may be used for selection decisions as well as for information or research purposes as long as there is no systematic bias against any group of applicants.

Criterion-related validity
See pages 63–66

A well-established and researched method for using validated application blank information for screening is the biodata approach (Owens, 1976), which scores a biographic application blank somewhat like a test. Certain key questions have "credit" and "no credit" answers, because these answers have been found to be correlated with either desirable or undesirable criterion work behaviors (including tenure, performance, or absenteeism). The assumption underlying biodata is that the behavioral patterns revealed by an applicant's personal history are useful in predicting future behavior.

Correlation
See pages 37–39

Biographic information blanks (BIB) are scored with a special key that assigns appropriate weights to various answers to the key questions. (The other items are not scored.) The weights are determined empirically by the degree of correlation between the answers to the questions and a criterion. Job tenure was the criterion in the early study of biodata that is summarized in this chapter's Spotlight on Research.

Criterion
See page 63

In the Cascio (1976) investigation, a weighted biographical application blank was used to predict job tenure. The replies to 16 questions that had been established by previous research to correlate significantly with job tenure were scored. The questions that had negative correlations with tenure were given minus weights; those with positive correlations, positive weights. The 16 item scoring weights were combined to yield one score for each subject; this is the number that was used to calculate the averages shown in the results section of Spotlight on Research.

The items used in the investigation included questions on age, education, home ownership, marital status, children's ages, previous salary, location of residence, tenure on previous job, time at previous address, and number of friends and/or relatives in the company. Many of these questions fall into the EEOC's suspect group, but their use in selection is justified when it is based on research results like those obtained by Cascio. In that study there was a significant difference between the biodata scores of long- and short-tenure employees and there was no evidence of bias; the difference existed for minority as well as nonminority subjects.

Statistical significance
See pages 35–36

Biographic information blanks enjoyed considerable initial popularity but they soon came under attack for being a form of what Dunnette (1962) called "dust bowl empiricism." This term refers to purely statistical prediction that does not advance knowledge (in this case, knowledge of the factors underlying successful screening and selection). Despite such criticism, research continued to show that biodata work and often work better than alternative screening methods for predicting certain employee behaviors. One early review of the relevant literature found the average criterion-related validity coefficients of biodata to range from $r = .32$ to $r = .46$ (Reilly & Chao, 1982). Given that .50 long has been the apparent upper limit for criterion-related validity, these figures compare quite favorably with more traditional types of tests.

SPOTLIGHT ON RESEARCH

Turnover, Biographical Data, and Fair Employment Practice

Research question Can selected application blank information be used to predict turnover? Is there a difference in this relationship between minority and nonminority employees?

Type of study Historical.

Subjects One hundred sixty clerical employees from a large insurance company located in the Southeast. All were hired within the same 14-month period.

Variables

■ Application blank score. Operational definition: One score from summing scores on 16 positive and negative items.

■ Job tenure. Operational definition: Long tenure equals more than one year; short tenure, less than one year.

General procedure Application blank information and job tenure data were acquired from company records. Application blanks were scored according to the predetermined system.

Analysis Correlation.

Results In validation and cross-validation, the same 10 items predicted tenure for both minority and nonminority subjects.

Tenure	Minority Subjects		Nonminority Subjects	
	Long	**Short**	**Long**	**Short**
Average score	-1.53	-10.85	-1.72	-10.54
Cross-validation	-3.41	-14.73	-3.24	-14.22

Conclusion "In summary, even after satisfying the legal requirements for using biographical data, turnover can still be predicted with an appreciable degree of accuracy. Moreover, the same scoring key can be used for both majority and minority groups, although this must be empirically demonstrated in each instance" (p. 579).

Summarized from W. F. Cascio, "Turnover, Biographical Data, and Fair Employment Practice." *Journal of Applied Psychology*, 1976, *61*, 576–580.

Historical study
See page 51

Operational definition
See page 26

In the years since the Reilly and Chao review, evidence for the usefulness of biodata in predicting training success, absenteeism, and measures of job performance and career success as well as turnover has continued to accumulate (e.g., Childs & Klimoski, 1986; Drakeley, Herriot, & Jones, 1988; Mael & Ashforth, 1995; Smith & George, 1994). This record has been impressive enough to convince the federal government's Office of Personnel Management to devise, field test, and implement a biographical data test called the Individual Achievement Record (IAR). The IAR is designed to measure how well a given person has used his or her educational, employment, and personal opportunities, whatever they may have been. It replaces the Professional and Administrative Career Examination (PACE), which was abandoned after being ruled racially discriminatory.

The applied success of biodata has also stimulated considerable interest in the measurement and theoretical issues surrounding it. Mael and his colleagues (Mael, 1991; Mael & Hirsch, 1993) are investigating methods of biographical information blank keying that keep the predictive advantages of statistically derived scoring but put them in a rational framework; a biodata item is retained if it has a logical basis in selection theory *and* predictive ability. The new approach is dubbed "rainforest empiricism" to signify that it is oriented toward both prediction (empiricism) and advancing knowledge about human behavior (unlike a dustbowl, a rainforest is productive). A complete summary of biodata research and application can be found in Stokes, Mumford, and Owens (1993).

Validity generalization
See pages 72–74

Before leaving the subject, a final important point about biodata should be mentioned: this screening method produced the first large-sample evidence of validity generalization outside the area of tests of mental abilities. The I/O psychologist who pioneered the biodata research (Owens, 1968) has always maintained that appropriately developed biographical information blanks could be used in different organizations. In practice, however, it has long been assumed that biodata are situationally specific (see Hunter & Hunter, 1984). Using data from approximately 11,000 first-line supervisors in 79 organizations and the technique of meta-analysis, Rothstein and her colleagues (1990) found that biodata validities are not only generalizable from one organization to another but are also stable across time.

Preemployment Inquiries

The term *preemployment inquiries* refers to the activity of seeking out information about a job applicant from an independent source before making an offer of employment. In most organizations, there are two main parts to preemployment inquiries. One is verifying that the information a job applicant provides on a résumé or application blank is accurate. A 1985 congressional committee estimated that to that time more than 30 million men and women had obtained jobs with the help of a false résumé. These days the most frequent misrepresentation, according to the president of one executive search firm, is an inflation of current or previous salary. One response to such problems is the rise of companies, such as Avert in Colorado, that specialize in verifying previous employment claims.

The second major aspect of preemployment inquiries is verbal or written recommendations from one or more persons (references) familiar with the job applicant (including current or previous employers and teachers). Job applicants may be asked to supply the reference information or to have letters sent directly to the organization. Either way, recommendations are looked upon with scepticism by many people who participate in hiring for organizations. A basic issue is that job applicants are unlikely to offer as references people whom they do not expect to give them a good recommendation.

A second problem with references is that many people asked to provide recommendations are very careful to avoid actually saying much of anything, especially if the individual involved was not a satisfactory employee or student. In early 1997, this practice was given new reinforcement by the state of California. In a controversial decision, the California Supreme Court ruled that employers may face monetary damages for giving positive job recommendations regarding employees whom they know or suspect to present potential safety risks. Under this rule, the only sure way to avoid a lawsuit appears to be either to reveal everything about an employee or to reveal nothing. The former choice opens employers to charges of defaming a departing employee; the latter robs good employees of the positive job references they have earned. (A state-by-state review of current regulations governing preemployment inquiries is offered by Ash, 1991).

A final drawback to employee recommendations is that it is difficult to know how to interpret them even if the information is accurate. Different people have different standards for the words they use, such as *satisfactory, outstanding, reliable,* and so on. This problem, along with the others noted, suggests that letters of recommendation are minimally useful at best; nevertheless, most organizations continue to collect them. I/O psychologists could make a contribution in this area with research aimed toward finding ways to make this information a useful part of the selection process. Peres and Garcia (1962) offer one possibility in a technique for scoring letters of recommendation.

Based on the adjectives used in thousands of letters of recommendation, Peres and Garcia identified five basic categories into which these adjectives could be placed. These

Reliability
See pages 86–91

Validity
See pages 93–108

investigators did not attempt to validate the technique, and it was some years later that Aamodt, Bryan, and Whitcomb (1993) investigated its possible utility. Using psychology instructors as subjects, these authors found the Peres and Garcia technique to be both reliable (as regards the scoring of letters of recommendation) and valid (as a predictor of performance). They concluded that the approach shows promise as a screening device, but to date no significant follow-up has been done on this procedure.

Interviews

The oldest and still most frequently used source of information about job applicants is the familiar one-on-one job interview (e.g., Keenan, 1995). Many companies have job candidates interviewed several times or even by groups (a panel interview). These interviews may take place during the screening process, after applicants have been through other screening procedures, or both. Flight attendant applicants at Southwest Airlines must pass a group interview before progressing on to three one-on-one interviews conducted by a recruiter, a current attendant, and a flight attendant supervisor. When all interviews are completed, the interviewers discuss their separate impressions and either drop or recommend the candidate.

The interview procedure used by Southwest Airlines helps the company choose employees who will fit in with its "community culture." The use of multiple interviewers may also give it more strength than the usual employment interview, which consistently falls short of accepted measurement standards. Study after study has found that neither the reliability (e.g., Kinicki & Lockwood, 1985; McDonald & Hakel, 1985) nor the criterion-related validity (e.g., Hunter & Hunter, 1984; Reilly & Chao, 1982) of the interview justifies the great reliance placed on this screening method in applied situations.

Recently, more sophisticated measurement and analytical techniques have led some investigators to conclude that the validity of the job interview is not as low as has been assumed, although it is still modest (Harris, 1989). Format modifications can change the picture rather dramatically, but before these are considered, it will be useful to take a look at some of the problems with the standard approach to job interviewing.

Sources of Interview Weakness

The typical employment interview is a dynamic interactive process between two people, each with his or her own individual characteristics. Each person brings biases and stereotypes to the situation, which itself has certain characteristics. There is a difference between the situation in which a company must fill an empty position immediately, for instance, and one in which there is not this pressure.

Various personal and situational components of a typical employment interview are shown in the model in Figure 4–1. Of these factors, I/O psychologists have the most information about the way that certain interviewee characteristics (such as age and sex) and behaviors (such as mode of dress and verbal assertiveness) may bias interviewers and affect the outcome of the interview process either positively or negatively.

In an early review of the interviewer bias literature, Arvey (1979) concluded that both women and older applicants tended to be evaluated less favorably than their similarly qualified young male counterparts. This bias was particularly strong when females were applying for traditionally "male" jobs, a finding consistent with Schmitt's (1976)

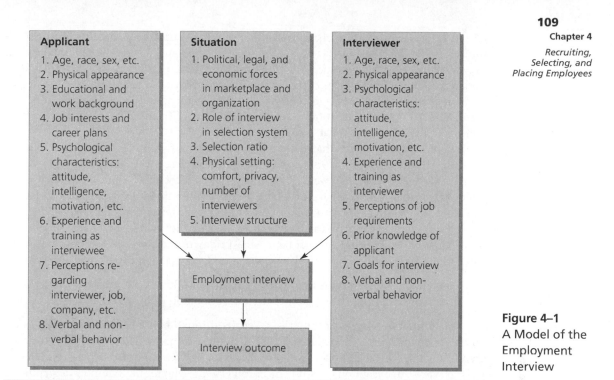

Figure 4–1
A Model of the Employment Interview

From R. D. Arvey and J. E. Campion, "The Employment Interview: A Summary and Review
of Recent Research." *Personnel Psychology,* 1982, *35,* 281–322. Copyright © 1982
Personnel Psychology, Inc. Reprinted by permission.

contention that interviewers tend to measure job applicants against a stereotype of an
ideal applicant. Many of these stereotypes have disappeared; men sell women's makeup
in department stores, senior citizens take the burger and fries order at the fast food restaurant, and women cut the deal at the car agency.

Despite social changes, I/O psychologists continue to find bias against certain categories of job applicants in a variety of job situations. Two of these categories are older applicants and nonwhite applicants, although results of this research are not always consistent (e.g., Finkelstein, Burke, & Raju, 1995; Harris, 1989). Stronger evidence for bias
in the typical job interview is found in research that examines the role of applicant sex
and physical appearance. Other qualifications being more or less equal, males (e.g., Perry,
Davis-Blake, & Kulik, 1994; Sheets & Bushardt, 1994; Van Vianen & Willemsen, 1992)
and physically more attractive job candidates (e.g., Morrow, 1990; Pingitore, Dugoni,
Tindale, & Spring, 1994) are often preferred over female or less attractive candidates.

The consistency of the findings of interview bias research as to interviewers' preferences for more attractive job applicants raises a new cause for concern now that the
Americans with Disabilities Act is in place. Larwood (1995) reports that overweight job
candidates (a category covered by the act) were viewed as less desirable job candidates
than others, because of a perception that they had brought their disability on themselves.
On the other side of the table, Hayes and his co-investigators (1995) report that disabled
job applicants worry about interviewers focusing on their disabilities in the interview
process. These and related problems constitute an important research agenda for the beginning of the new century.

In addition to applicant characteristics, a variety of applicant behaviors during a job interview can affect the interview outcome. Applicants are rated more favorably when they use good grammar and speak clearly (Parsons & Liden, 1984), are assertive (Gallois, Callan, & Palmer, 1992), smile and maintain eye contact (Rasmussen, 1984), use gestures and other body language (Gifford, Ng, & Wilkinson, 1985; Howard & Ferris, 1996), and keep the conversation focused on themselves (Kacmar, Delery, & Ferris, 1992; Stevens & Kristof, 1995; Tullar, 1989).

There is also evidence that female interviewees may be judged by their clothing; Forsythe, Drake, and Cox (1985) found that women were given higher ratings by personnel managers when they were dressed in a more "masculine" dark tailored suit and white blouse than when they were dressed in a "feminine" light beige dress of soft fabric. This topic has not received much subsequent attention from I/O psychologists, but evidence from the field confirms the basic premise in a new form. Many women in positions of responsibility are unhappy with the casual-Friday or business-casual dress codes organizations are adopting. In response to one survey, a female financial executive wrote:

> Women are assumed to be in lower-level positions. Business clothing can override that impression, but casual clothes do not. (quoted in Callender, 1996, p. 11)

When interviewers distort interview results through bias and stereotyping, it is interviewee characteristics and behavior that elicit these responses. Relatively less is known about how *interviewer* characteristics and behavior as such may affect the outcome of a job interview. An exception is a study by Baron (1993), who found that interviewer mood (positive or negative) significantly affected interview ratings of job applicants who appeared to be unqualified for the job (negative mood, poorer evaluation; positive mood, no effect).

There is also a line of research suggesting that interviewers' preinterview expectations about a job candidate may have considerable influence on their conduct and evaluation of the interview (e.g., Macan, & Dipboye, 1994; Phillips & Dipboye, 1989). In

Field study
See page 49

one field study, for example, researchers found that interviewers gave more information, did more selling of the company, and asked for less information from applicants whose paper credentials were perceived to be more favorable (Dougherty, Turban, & Callender, 1994). Finally, Snyder, Berscheid, and Matwychuk (1988) report that people who are highly conscious of their own behavior when they are around other people place greater importance on the appearance of job candidates than do other interviewers.

The biases described do not affect all interviewers all the time. The impact of such variables often depends on the amount and kind of other information about the interviewee that is available (e.g., Gifford, Ng, & Wilkinson, 1985; Huffcutt, McDaniel, & Roth, 1996; Rasmussen, 1984). Characteristics of the situation as listed in Figure 4–1 also play a role. If there is only one qualified candidate for an important job (a selection ratio of 1:1) and the interviewer knows that his or her superior recommended this individual (a political factor), the candidate may receive a favorable interview report whatever the interviewer's personal opinion of him or her.

The possibility of bias on the other side of the job interview table has been given far less attention than interviewer bias and stereotypes. It seems likely, however, that this factor also reduces the validity of the interview as a predictor of job success. Information about "what turns job interviewers on or off" is now widely available to job seekers (see Exhibit 4–5). Also available are interview-training workshops that teach participants the ins and outs of making a favorable impression. With the help of such information, job applicants have become increasingly sophisticated as regards understanding the behaviors and question responses that impress recruiters and interviewers.

Improving the Interview

The weaknesses of employment interviews have been recognized for many years (Wagner, 1949). Still, organizations have not given them up, nor will they; they believe there is no acceptable substitute for seeing and talking to job applicants. It is fortunate, then, that many people are much better at performing this function than the research findings sampled might suggest. Training interviewers sometimes helps them become more effective also (Dougherty, Ebert, & Callender, 1986), but the research in this area remains inconclusive (Harris, 1989). An alternative strategy is to change the form of the interview itself.

One of the very first strategies tried for improving the interview was to change it from the typical free-flowing, open-ended, conversational form to a structured interaction. McMurry's (1947) patterned interview required interviewers to use a printed form detailing specific items to be covered, how information was to be recorded, and how

---

Exhibit 4–5
What Turns Job Interviewers On—or Off?

A . . . nation-wide survey of leading personnel executives should interest anyone about to interview for a job. The study, designed to reveal factors which can determine whether an interview will be successful, was conceived by Robert Half, Inc., the world's largest financial executive, accounting and data processing recruiters. Burke Marketing Research, Inc., an international research firm, conducted the study for the Half organization.

Of the 100 personnel directors and managers surveyed, half worked for Fortune 500 companies, and half were selected from the "Who's Who in the American Society for Personnel Administration" directory. The study revealed the following points:

- Interviewers attach great importance to good grooming and appropriate dress. . . .
- Interviewers like candidates who are enthusiastic and responsive. . . .
- Ask questions about the job. . . .
- Don't ask direct questions about salary or fringe benefits at the beginning of the interview. . . .
- Even if you need the job desperately, don't convey it.
- Don't exaggerate your skills or accomplishments. . . .
- Interviewers are more favorably impressed by candidates who look them in the eye. . . .
- Interviewers prefer the candidate to know about the company. . . .
- Candidates who appear to be overconfident are much more likely to favorably impress interviewers than those who act shy. . . .

Excerpted from American Society for Training and Development, "What Turns Job Interviewers On—or Off?" [FYI: For Your Information]. *Training and Development Journal,* January 1982, p. 7. Copyright © 1982 American Society for Training and Development. Reprinted with permission. All rights reserved.

interviewee qualifications were to be rated. Since that time, I/O psychologists have developed a number of variations on the **structured interview** procedure. The simplest consists of collecting the same information in the same order from each interviewee and recording it on a standard form called an interview guide.

More sophisticated structured interviews begin with job descriptions to ensure that questions and evaluation procedures are job-specific. With the Behavior Description Interview (BDI) (Janz, Hellervik, & Gilmore, 1986) interviewees are asked to describe what they have done in the past when they encountered certain current job-relevant situations. An applicant for a sales position might be asked: "Tell me about a time you had a problem with a customer and how it was resolved," for example.

The Situational Interview (SI) (Latham, Saari, Pursell, & Campion, 1980) poses questions of the same general type as those in the Behavior Description Interview, but they are hypothetical and future-oriented. "Our customers can be difficult sometimes. How would you handle it if you had a problem with _____?" The same general approach is used in the more detailed Comprehensive Structured Interview (CSI) (Pursell, Campion, & Gaylord, 1980).

Results of early investigations into the reliability and validity of structured interviews were consistently favorable, regardless of format. Structured interviews also enjoy the advantage of discouraging interviewers from asking job applicants the kinds of inappropriate questions discussed previously. Nevertheless, it was not until relatively recently that structured interviewing came into its own.

Meta-analysis

See page 43

Some time in the early 1980s, I/O psychologists began focusing more closely on the type of interview used in reported studies of interview evaluation. When investigations involving structured interviews were analyzed separately from those in which the traditional interview had been used, the validity of "the interview" improved dramatically (Wright, Lichtenfels, & Pursell, 1989). One meta-analysis of more than 150 studies carried out worldwide led Wiesner and Cronshaw (1988) to the conclusion that structured interviews have a criterion-related validity roughly twice that of traditional interviews.

The authors of a more recent review of the employment interview literature (McDaniel, Whetzel, Schmidt, & Maurer, 1994) do not find the difference in validity to be quite so great as did Wiesner and Cronshaw, but they agree that structured interviews are more valid than unstructured interviews for predicting job performance. Despite such differences regarding the specifics, there seems little doubt that the structured interview is generally superior to the traditional open-ended interview as a job screening method (Baker & Spier, 1990). With its measurement credentials established, the structured interview is being investigated as such by I/O psychologists, rather than being compared to regular interviews. Here is a sample of findings.

- Police officer candidates who participated in structured interviews expressed a strong belief that the process was a fair one (Lowry, 1994).

- Same-race effects (interviewer preference for job candidates of the same race as himself or herself) were weaker with structured interviews than with conventional interviews (Lin, Dobbins, & Farh, 1992).

- A situational interview format increased interviewer agreement about applicant suitability for employment more effectively than rater training (Maurer & Fay, 1988).

- The situational interview successfully predicted both job performance and potential in a financial services organization (Robertson, Gratton, & Rout, 1990).

Why are structured interviews superior in a variety of ways to the usual approach to job interviewing? Part of the answer lies in the fact that collecting and reporting information are controlled. To the extent that interview unreliability stems from differences in what interviewers do or do not ask (or report), standardization by itself should bring about an improvement. (Low reliability reduces validity.) If the structured interview is based specifically on job analysis, there is a direct correspondence between interview performance and job performance that also helps increase validity.

Training interviewers and structuring interviews are the methods most often mentioned today for improving the job interview's reliability and validity, but other suggestions have been made. Some time ago, Grant and Bray (1969) suggested separating the information-gathering stage of the interview from the evaluation stage. The interviewer would make neither recommendations nor decisions, but merely report interview results as one more piece of information to help the person(s) making the selection decision.

Grant and Bray's suggestion has been largely ignored in the I/O psychology literature, but the structured interview format may give it new life. Indeed, the computer interviewers used by a few organizations, such as Great Western Bank, already make use of the idea. Computers can use a structured format to record what people say, but they can't "understand" it; a person must evaluate the information. Great Western's computer "interviewer" quickly selects out applicants who are clearly unsuited, saving time and, bank officials believe, reducing turnover among new employees.

Tests

The use of tests to screen applicants for employment has a long history in I/O psychology, going back at least to World War I, but the situation is different in important ways today. For one, the Equal Employment Opportunity Commission (EEOC) has been shining a strong spotlight on testing in organizations for some time. If employment decisions are to be made on the basis of tests, the tests must have demonstrated reliability and validity if they show adverse impact against a group protected by law. For another, the federal government has the power to eliminate whole classes of tests from use. The most striking example is the 1988 federal law forbidding the use of lie detector tests on prospective or current employees excepting certain specified government, security, and defense organizations.

Most employment testing did not include lie detector testing even before the 1988 law, but the scope of testing programs *has* expanded considerably since the early days of paper-and-pencil tests of mental ability. Modern organizations have available a wide variety of tests and administrative procedures that have already been subjected to reliability and validity studies. The most common types in use today were reviewed in Chapter 3.

Each of the tests discussed may be given by a human administrator, although computerized testing is a rapidly advancing field and many screening tests now could be so administered. The equivalence of these two modes of administration is by no means guaranteed, however, and it will probably be some time before automated testing is standard procedure. A number of reviews of the issues and research in this new field are available (e.g., Drasgow, Olson, Keenan, Moberg, & Mead, 1993).

Test Batteries

The major categories of screening tests used by organizations today—ability, personality, integrity, and work sample—were reviewed separately in Chapter 3, and they are often administered this way. Some job applicants may be given only one; others may be given several, but at different times. In other instances, job applicants spend a half or a full day taking a **test battery**, a group of tests given one after the other. A typical test battery for screening management trainees might include tests of judgment, personality, and intelligence combined with work sample tests and a biographical inventory.

Multiple tests are often (but not always) administered in a special facility called an **assessment center**, where participants come for assessment stays lasting from one day up to a week. This procedure was first used extensively in industry by psychologists at the original American Telephone and Telegraph Company (AT&T) to generate information for employee development and internal promotion decisions.

Since the early work by psychologists at AT&T, the assessment center idea has been extended to screening as well as evaluation. Among other professions, it is used to select managers, school administrators (Schmitt, Schneider, & Cohen, 1990), and police officers (Coulton & Feild, 1995). Characteristics that are often evaluated include career orientation, work motivation, leadership ability, interpersonal skills, administrative skills, and the ability to perform under stress. Personality tests may also be useful in combination with other measures (e.g., Goffin, Rothstein, & Johnston, 1996). These qualities may be evaluated with assessment center techniques in other settings, but the Task Force on Assessment Center Guidelines (1989) has made it clear that an "assessment center" and "assessment center techniques" are not the same.

A review of the considerable body of research into the effectiveness of assessment centers to that time found substantial evidence for the reliability and criterion-related validity of this approach (Gaugler, Rosenthal, Thornton, & Bentson, 1987). Still, the authors advised organizations to use assessment center results conservatively because there also was evidence that the performance being measured there can be situation-specific (occur only in an assessment center) rather than general (e.g., Bycio, Alvares, & Hahn, 1987).

Some years later, little has changed. As assessment centers have grown in popularity in applied situations, they have been even more widely researched. The evidence for criterion-related validity with little evidence of adverse impact has been consistent. Nevertheless, construct-related evidence of validity for the assessment center procedure continues to elude investigators, and this is the problem that currently occupies center stage of this area of research. As Landy, Shankster, and Kohler express it: "Assessment centers remain an enigma. They seem to 'work' but why?" (1994, p. 277).

**Construct
validity**
See pages 95–97

The Responsible Use of Tests

Many employment screening tests are commercially available and are sold with administration instructions, technical reports, updates of relevant data and research, optional scoring services, and information to assist the user in score interpretation. Comprehensive single sources of information about such tests are available in many public and university libraries. These include *Test Critiques* (published by Pro-Ed, Inc., of Austin, Texas) and *Tests in Print* and the *Mental Measurements Yearbook* (both published by the Buros Institute of Mental Measurements in Lincoln, Nebraska). All are updated regularly.

There are also a number of published guidelines for the appropriate use of tests in industrial, educational, and social settings. A broad-range general guide is the American Psychological Association's *Standards for Educational and Psychological Testing* developed in conjunction with the American Educational Research Association and the National Council on Measurement in Education.

References specific to the use of tests in organizations include the *Standards for Providers of Industrial and Organizational Psychological Services* and *Principles for the Validation and Use of Personnel Selection Procedures.* Both are produced wholly or in part by the Society for Industrial and Organizational Psychology (Division 14 of the American Psychological Association) and, like the *Standards for Educational and Psychological Testing,* both are updated at intervals.

Not all tests used for organizational personnel decisions are developed by commercial test publishers. Organizations also use the services of I/O psychologists or test specialists to develop and validate their own tests. Whatever the source of a test, however, it is only as good as those who use it. Test publishers have long relied on professional credentials and job titles to screen test users, but these have proved inadequate to the task of ensuring that those who purchase tests really are qualified to use and interpret them (Anastasi, 1989).

The problem described was addressed in the late 1980s by a special working group of the Joint Committee on Testing Practices (sponsored by the American Psychological Association and four other national associations concerned with testing issues). The Test User Qualifications Working Group concentrated on identifying competencies that should be possessed by test users (such as following scoring directions), rather than on their credentials (see Moreland, Eyde, Robertson, Primorr, & Most, 1995 for full report). It will take some time before this new approach to qualifications has impact on the sale and use of employment screening tests, but it is a move in the right direction.

In addition to the matter of competency, the use of tests also raises certain ethical considerations for professional psychologists. A good introduction to these issues can be found in a classic article by London and Bray (1980), which is summarized in Exhibit 4–6. These I/O psychologists describe the nature of the various ethical responsibilities that psychologists assume when they use tests in applied settings. Not only can these responsibilities conflict with one another, but also the matter is complicated by a need to balance these responsibilities and compliance with legal requirements and constraints.

Screening and the Law

The aim of equal employment legislation is to ensure that employment decisions, including hiring, promotion, special training, and educational opportunities, are based on job-related factors and not on irrelevant personal factors. There are many inputs to such decisions in organizations, but the EEOC has long focused its attention on the role of testing. (A brief review of some of the landmark cases in this history can be found in Bersoff, 1981.) And, as mentioned, this commission now extends the definition of testing to any procedure used to make discriminations among job applicants or personnel.

The standard reference for the use of tests in making personnel decisions is the EEOC's *Uniform Guidelines on Employee Selection Procedures* (EEOC, 1978). The gist of these guidelines is as follows: Any procedure used to make an employment decision must have demonstrated evidence of validity *if its use results in adverse impact.* **Adverse impact** occurs when a selection procedure results in a selection rate for any protected group that is less than 80% (or four-fifths) of the rate for the highest group. An example should clarify this rather confusing statement, known as the four-fifths rule.

If 6 out of every 10 white applicants are hired for a job on the basis of scores on a particular test, the selection rate is 60%. If using this same test results in hiring 2 out of every 10 nonwhite applicants, the selection rate is 20%. Since 20% is well below 48% (which is four-fifths of 60%), the use of this test results in adverse impact on nonwhite applicants. There are a number of score adjustment techniques that will "correct" this problem and produce comparable selection rates (see Sackett & Wilk, 1994), but the Civil Rights Act of 1991 has banned their use (see Greenlaw & Jensen, 1996).

It is no longer legal to use different scoring standards for different groups of applicants in order to circumvent adverse impact, but a process called banding so far has withstood court challenges. In banding, the individuals within a specified score range (a band) are regarded as having equivalent scores. This means that for selection purposes they are interchangeable. Therefore, a member of a minority group legitimately can be selected over a white male in the same band (or a female over a male) for purposes of enhancing opportunities for protected groups of applicants (see also Cascio, Outtz, Zedeck, & Goldstein, 1991).

The 1991 Civil Rights Act, which was intended to clarify a number of issues arising from Supreme Court rulings on a range of civil rights topics, ended up as a legal compromise that is vague in many important areas (Varca & Pattison, 1993). It is not vague on the point that a screening procedure that violates the four-fifths rule is a prima facie

---

Exhibit 4–6
Ethical Responsibilities of I/O Psychologists Using Tests in Applied Settings

I. **Responsibilities to the profession.**

   A. Keep informed of relevant advances in the field.

   B. Report unethical practices.

   C. Educate others to ethical issues.

II. **Responsibilities to those tested.**

   A. Guard against invasion of privacy.

   B. Keep promised confidentiality.

   C. Explain nature of testing and possible uses to which information might be put.

   D. Impose time limits on organization's use of test data.

   E. Treat all those tested with respect and consideration.

III. **Responsibilities to the organization.**

   A. Convey accurate expectations about costs and benefits of testing program.

   B. Collect the best test data available within the constraints set by the situation.

   C. Monitor the continuing use of testing and revise where necessary (including tests for training administrators).

   D. Recognize the rights of the organization to ownership of methods and procedures it has funded.

Summarized from M. London and D. W. Bray, "Ethical Issues in Testing and Evaluation for Personnel Decisions." *American Psychologist*, 1980, 35, 890–901.

case of adverse impact. If the procedure is challenged, the burden of proof regarding its business necessity now lies squarely with the employer. (In the past it lay mainly with the person or persons bringing the suit.) In addition, the law now allows for damages up to $300,000 to persons who can prove that they were unfairly discriminated against.

Despite all of the regulations and difficulties surrounding screening testing, the results of employment screening research remain clear: properly developed and used, tests are as good as or better than many alternative screening methods as regards reliability, validity, and lack of adverse impact. Furthermore, evaluating abilities or skills across a wide cross-section of job requirements (rather than depending on one or two tests, such as a test of mental ability) helps reduce the adverse impact of the screening process as a whole (Wollack, 1994). Finally, validity generalization research offers organizations the opportunity to use one validated test for a number of jobs, thus preserving the utility of testing for selection purposes while conserving the resources available for testing research.

Whatever the particulars of their employment screening programs, organizations collect all of this information to help them make selection decisions. For this reason, screening methods are often referred to as selection methods. This term is avoided here to emphasize the point that, conceptually, selection is a decision that follows the process of screening. The major vehicles for this screening have been reviewed. Other sources of information about job applicants—including drug testing, genetic testing, English competency tests, height/weight standards, and the "If you smoke at all, you can't work here" rule—have not been discussed because their use is relatively infrequent and/or their legal status is ambiguous.

Selecting Employees

Employee selection is a matter of answering the question: To which job applicant(s) should a job be offered? Many people who make hiring decisions believe that the more information they have, the less likely they are to make one of the major selection errors— hiring someone who does not work out (false positive) or rejecting someone who would have been a successful employee (false negative). The actual extent to which more information will reduce these errors and increase the success rate for hiring depends on whether these three conditions hold:

**False
negative/positive
selection errors**
See pages 67–68

1. The various sources yield different kinds of information. Grades in high school or college math courses are unneccessary if the applicant's record in a computer training course is available and computerized billing is the job in question.

2. The information is relevant to some aspect of job performance. Putting all applicants for jobs in a new shopping mall department store through the same standardized battery of tests will generate a lot of information that will never be used.

3. The costs of getting the information do not exceed its usefulness. Information that is not used at all is not worth the cost of acquiring it, and the same is true for information that is of questionable value. If a large number of applicants is involved, for example, soliciting letters of recommendation probably is not worth the time it takes until the number has been reduced to a short list of candidates.

Today, there is virtually no kind of job, from accountant to zookeeper, that cannot be filled through a general or specialized temporary help agency.

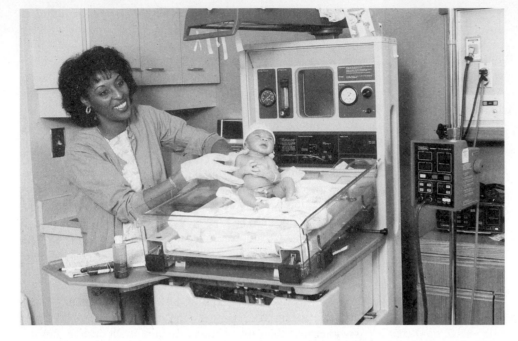

Assuming that the conditions outlined hold, using screening information to make a selection decision becomes a matter of combining various pieces of information about job applicants. How does a person sitting there with application blanks, test scores, interviewer remarks, and letters of recommendation put it all together to mean something?

The Clinical Approach to Selection

When people use their own knowledge, skills, experience, and values to make a judgment about an individual's likely job success, given the information available, the process is called **clinical prediction**. This method originates in the practice of medicine and clinical psychology, where the judgment of trained and experienced professionals is the traditional basis for diagnosis and treatment.

Clinical prediction in organizational selection is also a tradition, as conversations with experienced job interviewers will make clear. Many will tell you flatly that there is no substitute for knowing human nature. These individuals are often very good indeed at identifying people who will be successful employees, but available research evidence does not support the conviction that clinical prediction is superior. From the beginning, reviews of the relevant literature have favored quantitative approaches rather strongly (Wiggins, 1973).

An easy way to appreciate the difficulties of the clinical approach to selection is to compare the situation with that of the unstructured interview. In the same way that irrelevant factors can affect interviewer assessments of applicant suitability for employment, so can they affect the clinical selection process. Evidence continues to accumulate, for instance, that less attractive female applicants are at a disadvantage, even when they are clearly qualified and an experienced manager is making the hiring decision (e.g., Marlowe, Schneider, & Nelson, 1996).

A sample of other research findings in this area reveals a variety of factors unrelated to the outcome of the screening process that affect employee selection. These include the number of job openings available (Huber, Northcraft, & Neale, 1990), the expectations and preferences of current employees (Ito, 1994), whether the candidate has other job offers (Williams, Radefeld, Binning, & Sudak, 1993), and the extent to which a candidate possesses certain generally desirable (as opposed to job-specific) personal attributes (Bretz, Rynes, & Gerhart, 1993).

Research leaves little doubt that there are difficulties with the clinical approach to selection, but it is unlikely to disappear from the organizational scene. Nevertheless, it can be a risky strategy in these days of "failure-to-hire" discriminatory employment practice suits. In addition, the processes by which organizations make their personnel selection decisions send messages to rejected applicants, new hires, and current employees. There are a number of possible reasons, then, for preferring quantitative approaches to selection in many situations.

The Quantitative Approach to Selection

When information about an individual's likely job success is evaluated according to a predetermined numerical decision rule, the process can be called **quantitative prediction**. Clinical prediction rests on a case-by-case judgment; the quantitative approach is based on rules about using numbers. The simplest of these rules for making use of multiple pieces of information about a job applicant is to use each piece of information once in a stepwise fashion that screens out more applicants at each step. This process is called a multiple-hurdle strategy. There are two important conditions for using this decision rule.

First, it must be possible to order the applicant abilities and characteristics assessed in the screening process. One basis for this ordering is from the basic abilities possessed by most people, sometimes called universals, up through successively less common and more particularly job-related abilities (Smith, 1994). A more rigorous ordering would be based on the validity coefficients of the screening methods being used, beginning with the highest.

The second condition for using the multiple-hurdle decision rule is that each hurdle must have a clear and validated accept-reject standard called a cutoff score. A **cutoff score** is a test score or other ranking of some sort that "cuts off" those below it from further consideration for the job, training, school, or other opportunity. Procedures for establishing these scores are currently the focus of a very active line of research, but the mathematical details of these studies place them beyond the scope of the present discussion. It will serve the present purpose well enough to think of cutoff scores in terms of established statistical probabilities for job success.

In testing for organizational selection, statistical probabilities for success are obtained by the same process used to establish criterion-related evidence of validity. One way of displaying the relationship between test scores and the probability of job success is the individual expectancy chart shown in Figure 4–2. This chart provides information about the expected job or training performance of individuals with different scores on a particular test. For example, this expectation is about 50:50 for job applicants with a test score between 50 and 60 (out a possible 100). In the past, approximately half of the

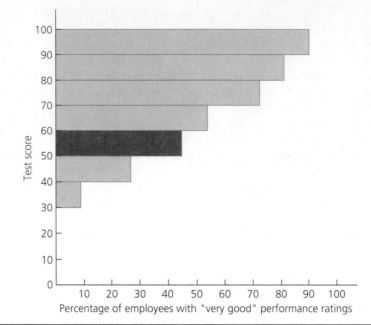

Figure 4–2
Sample
Individual
Expectancy
Chart:
Probability of
Job Success for
Different Test
Score Ranges

employees whose test scores at the time of hiring were in this range subsequently received "very good" performance ratings.

It takes time to develop an individual expectancy chart, and in multiple-hurdle decision making such a chart is the basis for only one cutoff score for one hurdle. Extensive preparation is involved in setting up and validating several hurdles and their respective accept-reject criteria (cutoff scores), but this process is the very factor that tends to make quantitative approaches to selection more successful than clinical approaches.

The multiple-hurdle approach is not the only type of decision-making rule used to evaluate screening information for selection decisions. A variation is the multiple-cutoff method, whereby all applicants go through all screening methods and those who pass *all* cutoffs become candidates. These candidates then can be ranked from most to least preferred according to relative standing and a selection choice made accordingly.

Quantitative methods for making employment decisions have several advantages over clinical prediction. They are validated, they are perceived as fairer by most of the individuals affected, and they stand up to fair employment practices criteria. Nevertheless, many people object to going so strictly by the numbers in selecting new employees. They believe that some human judgment is important, even if the basic method is quantitative. As in all organizational activities, there are trade-offs involved in choosing among the various approaches to evaluating screening information, and it is simply not possible to label any one strategy as always being "the best."

Whatever screening methods are used, and however this information is processed to make selection decisions in a particular case, it is necessary to keep monitoring selection procedures. One reason for ongoing vigilance is that things change. Jobs change and the characteristics of job applicants change, and at some point, tried-and-true screening methods may no longer be useful or sufficient. Word processors have replaced standard typewriters entirely in most organizations, for example. As a result, old reliable and valid typing tests need to be supplemented or dropped for tests more predictive of the skills required to use the new machines.

A second reason selection procedures must be monitored is related to the issue of restriction of range. Good selection practices should raise the level of performance in an organization gradually as people less likely to be successful employees are screened out. This process restricts the range of job performance measurements (criterion), and old cutoff scores may be inappropriate (Linn, Harnish, & Dunbar, 1981). As is true for all scientific research, the job of validation for organizational selection is never really finished.

**Restriction of
range**
See pages 102–103

Selection and the Law

Changes in laws regarding employment practices would make it vital to monitor existing employee selection procedures even if there were no other reason. The Civil Rights Act of 1964 remains the baseline, but new court rulings and new legislation are produced regularly. In addition to the 1991 Civil Rights Act, employers are subject to the immigration reform law of 1986, which bars hiring discrimination against legal aliens. The year 1986 also produced an amendment to the 1967 Age Discrimination in Employment Act, and mandatory retirement because of age is now considered unfairly discriminatory except in certain specified cases.

The legislation likely to have the greatest impact on selection is the Americans with Disabilities Act passed in 1990, which bars employment discrimination against individuals with physical or mental disabilities and affects all but the very smallest companies (see Exhibit 4–1). In addition to the requirement that organizations make reasonable alterations in the workplace to accommodate disabled workers, there is a requirement that companies must add Americans with disabilities to mandatory affirmative action plans.

The Equal Employment Opportunity Commission (EEOC) received about 15,000 ADA-related complaints in 1993, and the number went up sharply when the number of covered employers was increased in 1994. By mid-1995, the commission had a total case backlog (of ADA plus other cases) in excess of 120,000. To help relieve the pressure, the commission chair instituted a new priority system allowing the EEOC to dismiss alleged discrimination cases that obviously lack merit (or over which the EEOC has no jurisdiction). Guidelines for cases considered a national priority are forthcoming. Both moves may be expected to impact personnel policies in organizations, but it will be some time before the effects are fully realized. The bottom line for the impact of laws on selection procedures might well read: "Watch this space."

Placing New Employees

The discussion of how screening information is used has been directed toward selecting one or more new employees, but this is not necessarily the only decision to be made. If there are several jobs for which a newly hired employee is qualified, where should he or she be placed? This kind of decision might arise in a large company that has a variety of entry-level jobs for which turnover tends to be high. A new employee with basic abilities (the universals) often will be suitable for several of these jobs, even if he or she has no experience.

Placement decisions also arise in banks, hotels, restaurants, and other organizations that do central recruiting to fill jobs in a number of locations or when individuals finish organizational training programs. Many larger companies have general management training programs into which recent college graduates are recruited. Upon completion of this program, someone must decide where to place the new manager.

Circumstances in which there is a placement decision as well as a selection decision to be made have always existed, but there is little placement-oriented research as such in the I/O psychology literature. One exception is an investigation by Lefkowitz (1994) in which he found a statistically significant tendency for new bank employees to be assigned to a supervisor of the same ethnic group. It may be hoped that there will be more such research in the future as a result of increasing interest in the field of I/O psychology in aspects of individual-organization fit.

A fundamental placement research question centers on the consequences of getting it wrong—that is, of failing to place individuals in jobs with a good fit. One hypothesis that has received some research support is that individuals involved in a poor fit correct the situation themselves over time by gravitating toward jobs and organizations that are more in tune with their own interests, values, and abilities (Wilk, Sackett, & Desmarais, 1995). This possibility of a systematic connection between organizational placement decisions and self-correction of poor matches is an intriguing one. Certainly, some approaches to placement would seem to have greater potential for maximizing fit than others. There are basically four alternative strategies that might be followed in making this decision.

1. *Place the individual in the job that has the highest priority of those for which he or she is qualified.* This strategy puts out the immediate fires for the organization, but it can lead to consistent underutilization or overchallenging of employee skills and abilities.

2. *Place the individual in the job for which the probability of his or her success appears to be the highest.* This maximizes the opportunity for individual success, but it may limit opportunities for employee development.

3. *Place the individual in the job that incorporates the potential to which he or she might be expected to grow.* This strategy is the opposite of the one above. It can reap the benefits of challenge, but it may backfire if an individual's potential has been overestimated.

4. *Place the individual in the job that he or she favors among those judged to be suitable.* This may be the strategy preferred by new hires, but it can lead to a chronic shortage of employees in jobs that are important but unattractive for some reason.

The variety of trade-offs in the list suggests a basic question to be asked about placement decisions: Does an organization concentrate on *filling* positions or on *fulfilling* individual expectations and potential? Current thinking and research with respect to both selection and placement is that the greatest good for everyone involved will come from a deliberate and coordinated attempt to accomplish both of these goals. This concept is summarized in Figure 4–3.

Linkage A in the figure is the matching focus of traditional organizational recruiting and selection. Linkage B is the newer focus to which I/O psychologists are giving increasing attention. The realistic job preview is one bridge between these two links, in that it allows job applicants to consider the likelihood that a particular job in a particular organization will give them what they need.

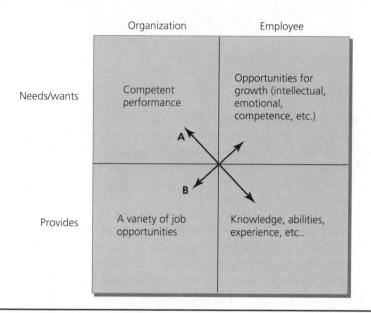

Organization   Employee

Needs/wants

| | Competent performance | Opportunities for growth (intellectual, emotional, competence, etc.) |

A

B

Provides

| A variety of job opportunities | Knowledge, abilities, experience, etc.. |

Figure 4–3
Matching People to Jobs and Organizations Is a Two-Way Street

Figure contributed by John F. Binning, Ph.D., Department of Psychology, Illinois State University, Normal, IL. Reprinted by permission.

Alternative Staffing Strategies

The current discussion is focused on hiring full-time employees for permanent regular positions in organizations (including permanent part-time positions). This is the context in which most of the I/O psychology research into recruiting, screening, selecting, and placing employees has been conducted, and it remains the most common staffing scenario. But there are other arrangements for employing people to perform the work an organization needs done. The two reviewed here are the use of temporary help and outsourcing.

Temporary Help

As a staffing strategy, temporary help is defined by the source of the employee's paycheck, not by how long an individual works for a particular company; many "temps" stay in the same position for a year or longer. Temporary employees are paid by the agency that assigns (or "deploys") them to an organization, not by the organization to which they report for work. As a group they constitute the majority of a small army of contingent (that is, as needed) workers. Retirees called back for temporary work, "loaners" who are borrowed by arrangement between companies, seasonal workers, and contract employees, are also part of this work force.

Since the 1940s, there have been agencies in business to supply temporary employees to companies needing people to fill in for absent permanent employees, to provide extra help for special projects or seasonal upswings in production demands, or to cover emergency situations of various kinds. It wasn't until the 1990s, however, that temporary help agencies suddenly found that they were big business. Organizations that had turned to temps as a way to cut costs during a general downturn in the economy discovered other advantages to this staffing strategy. In particular, temporary help makes it possible to expand or contract a work force as needed without either the expense of recruiting and hiring or the unhappy necessity for laying off permanent employees.

By the late 1990s, there were dozens of temporary help agencies deploying an estimated 2 million temporary employees every day. Some of these companies, like Accountemps, specialize in a particular type of skilled employee. Some do extensive screening; Manpower, Inc., requires candidates to be proficient in 43 special skills before they can be placed as a word processor. Other agencies, like Norell Corporation, will customize training for particular clients.

Most temporary employees work in clerical/office support or industrial/production positions, but there is virtually no job that cannot be filled this way. Organizations can hire accountants, lawyers, salespeople, lab technicians, computer programmers, software writers, chemists, show window designers, artists, writers, engineers, bankers, doctors, nurses, recruiters, cooks, managers, and even chief operating officers by the day, week, month, or year.

Many of the individuals who work for temporary help agencies would prefer permanent employment, and according to the National Association of Temporary and Staffing Services, a substantial percentage (usually quoted at around 40%) receive regular job offers as a direct result of temporary assignments. But for an estimated 50% of agency employees, temping is the career of choice. If asked, permanent temps often say they like the variety of settings and people they meet, the flexibility of choosing (within limits) how much of their time is devoted to work, and the challenge of temporary work assignments. This phenomenon, along with the number and variety of jobs being staffed with temporary workers, has brought this staffing strategy squarely into the mainstream of American organizational life.

The new status of temporary help has brought new challenges with it. If this staffing strategy is to pay off, these employees must become productive quickly even though they have not been through a company's usual training program (and may or may not have received agency training). High turnover among those who do well, many of whom are free to request reassignment at any time, must somehow be circumvented. Companies must also deal with problems that can arise from mixing temps into a regular work force. Pearce (1993) found that the presence of co-workers from this source was associated with lower perceptions of organizational trustworthiness by the regular employees.

On the other side of the equation, Feldman, Doerpinghaus, and Turnley (1994) report that temporary employees can feel they are being treated impersonally, that their skills are not being properly utilized, and that their tenure is insecure because the employer is often allowed to ask for a different employee at any time. These authors recommend that organizations consider providing temps with better orientation and training, clear explanations of the employment contract, and more consistently respectful treatment.

The suggestions of Feldman and his colleagues reinforce the point made by Flynn (1995) that if the use of temporary help is to be effective, close attention must be paid to their ability, training, and performance, just as it would be paid to that of any other employee. To date organizations have had to rely primarily on trial and error to figure out how this might be accomplished without losing the benefits that led them to select this staffing strategy in the first place. This situation will probably change rapidly, however, as I/O psychologists and others respond to this opportunity to explore a new and challenging line of research.

Outsourcing

Outsourcing is a general term for the practice of contracting out organizational functions that traditionally have been performed by regular organizational members "in house." In some cases, the work of an entire established department is sent out and the department is abolished. Among the traditional organizational functions being outsourced in this way are auditing, employee health and benefit plan administration, computer programming, research and development, and payroll.

The outsourcing described takes work currently being done by organizational employees and sends it to individuals or firms specializing in that function. A variation on this theme is for a company to turn its own employees into contractors. Allstate Insurance was following an industrywide trend in the mid-1990s when it terminated the employment contracts it had with its agents and renegotiated independent contractor agreements with the same individuals.

Yet another variation on outsourcing occurs when most (or all) of the work of a company is contracted out. Restoration Company, a small Georgia firm that specializes in dealing with the aftermath of various kinds of catastrophes, has only about 50 permanent employees. Yet within days of being hired to clean up after the 1993 bombing of the World Trade Center parking garage in New York City, it had mobilized a 3,600 worker–strong team. It had also assembled several trailerloads of cleaning supplies and equipment and put together radio communications and security systems tailored to the job. A team of five accountants kept track of this "organization," which was disbanded when the project was completed 16 days later.

Companies that are making use of outsourcing to whatever degree usually cite cost savings, particularly those associated with employee benefits, as the reason behind this staffing strategy. Some human resource managers also mention that outsourcing provides them with the services of talented individuals who would not consider taking a regular full-time job. Despite these advantages, outsourcing is not without its downside.

When it uses outsourcing to any significant degree, an organization gives up a large measure of control over the quality and timeliness of work performance. The relatively common outsourcing of employee health and benefit claims has produced nothing but headaches for many large corporations. Outsourcing can also be a security risk; Microsoft entrusts core product development only to full-time in-house employees, even though the company outsources other aspects of product development. Finally, outsourcing can create organized labor difficulties; the practice of giving union jobs to outside contractors was a factor cited in 1990's strikes at Boeing Company, General Motors Corporation, and McDonnell Douglas Corporation, among others.

In summary, outsourcing is either the wave of the future or the driving force behind the decline of Western industrial competitiveness, depending on who is speaking (e.g., Bettis, Bradley, & Hamel, 1992). It seems unlikely, however, that either of these two extremes is accurate. Outsourcing is made possible in large part by relatively recent technological advances, and the conditions under which it is a viable option for organizational effectiveness are not yet well understood. If this innovation follows the pattern of most, it will lose its faddish image and become a tool that is more or less useful depending on circumstances.

Neither outsourcing nor the use of temps seems likely to replace traditional staffing practices entirely. There will always be organizations whose effectiveness depends on employee loyalty, workforce stability, internal security, and/or hands-on supervision of some or all day-to-day operations. Meeting these conditions requires permanent, full-time employees.

At Issue

Equal Employment Opportunity and Affirmative Action: Catch-22?

There was only one catch and that was Catch-22, which specified that a concern for one's own safety in the face of dangers that were real and immediate was the process of a rational mind. Orr was crazy and could be grounded. All he had to do was ask; and as soon as he did, he would no longer be crazy and would have to fly more missions. Orr would be crazy to fly more missions and sane if he didn't, but if he was sane he had to fly them. (p. 47)

The quotation comes from Joseph Heller's famous novel, *Catch-22*. As many know from personal experience, the unfortunate Orr is not alone in his predicament. Modern life seems full of Catch-22s. One that job applicants have long complained about is the experience requirement for many positions in organizations; applicants must have experience to get jobs, but unless they get jobs, they cannot get experience.

Now organizations themselves are caught in one of the biggest Catch-22s of all. In simple terms, the law says that they must offer equal job opportunities to all qualified applicants and employees. The law also says that under specified conditions, they must give female, minority, and disabled applicants first chance at these opportunities; that is, they must pursue affirmative action policies.

In the mid-1970s, Allan Bakke brought suit against a California university claiming that he had been rejected twice by the university's medical school, not because he was not qualified, but because he was white. The sought-after medical school places, he claimed, were going to people less qualified than he because these people were members of minority groups.

After a protracted legal battle that eventually climbed to the U.S. Supreme Court, Bakke was admitted to the medical school. In a majority decision, the Supreme Court justices ruled that the university was wrong to reject him in order to serve an inflexible quota system biased against white applicants. They also ruled that college admission programs should continue to give minorities special advantages—Catch-22!

Some 20 years after Bakke's successful protest against "reverse discrimination," the regents of the giant nine-school University of California system voted to end affirmative action hiring and student admissions. Nor is the backlash against affirmative action limited to the Golden State; the policy is being assaulted on every front, often by those it is intended to benefit.

Affirmative action policies and programs probably won't be abolished in the near future, but they are undeniably unpopular in many quarters, and reverse discrimination suits are becoming more common as opponents become more vocal. A white high school football coach in Virginia, to cite one of the more interesting examples, filed a suit claiming that black coaches in the system with comparable win-loss records kept their jobs while he was dismissed for his team's poor showing.

The laws of our land state clearly that age, sex, race, religion, and national origin are *irrelevant* employment opportunity criteria. Yet does not affirmative action rest on exactly the opposite premise? The situation appears to be in flux as we leave the 1990s behind, but what kinds of changes might be coming, if they are coming at all, is unclear. For now, organizations, like Orr, must cope as best they can.

Summary

Recruiting is the process of attracting people to consider taking jobs in an organization. Screening is the process of separating qualified and/or promising job applicants from unqualified and/or less promising ones. All methods for obtaining screening information are considered tests by the EEOC.

Selection decisions may use screening information in a judgmental (clinical) way or by means of some decision-making (quantitative) rule. Placement decisions raise the basic dilemma of whether to respond primarily to the individual or primarily to the needs of the organization. The use of temporary help or outsourcing makes this decision unnecessary, although experts do not expect such alternative staffing strategies to replace the traditional model in most organizations.

Questions for Review and Discussion

1. Discuss the relative advantages and disadvantages of internal and external recruiting for private sector versus not-for-profit organizations.

2. Compare and contrast workforce diversity and affirmative action. Do you think diversity will be less controversial than affirmative action? Why or why not?

3. Explain briefly why the reliability and validity of the employment interview are improved with a structured interview format. Suggest several questions for a structured interview for a job with which you are familiar or which you would like to have when you graduate.

4. Outline a screening procedure for a job that you have had or know something about. Indicate how you will make your selection after your candidates have been through the process.

5. Can you see any use for clinical prediction in this age of the EEOC and the documentation that fair employment practices require? Why or why not?

Key Terms

adverse impact	placement
affirmative action	realistic job preview
assessment center	recruiting
clinical prediction	screening
cutoff score	selection
equal employment opportunity	structured interview
matching model	workforce diversity

References

Aamodt, M. G., Bryan, D. A., & Whitcomb, A. J. (1993). Predicting performance with letters of recommendation. *Public Personnel Management, 22,* 81–90.

American Society for Training and Development. (1982, January). What turns job interviewers on—or off? *Training and Development Journal,* p. 7.

Anastasi, A. (1989). Ability testing in the 1980s and beyond: Some major trends. *Public Personnel Management, 18,* 471–484.

Arvey, R. (1979). Unfair discrimination in the employment interview: Legal and psychological aspects. *Psychological Bulletin, 86,* 736–765.

Arvey, R., & Campion, J. E. (1982). The employment interview: A summary and review of recent research. *Personnel Psychology, 35,* 281–322.

Ash, P. (1991). Law and regulation of pre-employment inquiries. *Journal of Business Psychology, 5,* 291–308.

Baker, H. G., & Spier, M. S. (1990). The employment interview: Guaranteed improvement in reliability. *Public Personnel Management, 19,* 85–90.

Barber, A. E., & Roehling, M. V. (1993). Job postings and the decision to interview: A verbal protocol analysis. *Journal of Applied Psychology, 78,* 845–856.

Baron, R. A. (1993). Interviewers' moods and evaluations of job applicants: The role of applicant qualifications. *Journal of Applied Social Psychology, 23,* 253–271.

Bennett, A. (1989, May 10). Big brother takes a closer look. *Wall Street Journal,* p. B1.

Bersoff, D. N. (1981). Testing and the law. *American Psychologist, 3,* 1047–1056.

Bersoff, D. N. (1988). Should subjective employment devices be scrutinized: It's elementary, my dear Ms. Watson. *American Psychologist, 4,* 1016–1018.

Bettis, R. A., Bradley, S. P., & Hamel, G. (1992). Outsourcing and industrial decline. *Academy of Management Executive, 6,* 7–22.

Bowen, D. E., Ledford, G. E. Jr., & Nathan, B. R. (1991). Hiring for the organization, not the job. *Academy of Management Executive, 5,* 35–51.

Bretz, R. D., Rynes, S. L., & Gerhart, B. (1993). Recruiter perceptions of applicant fit: Implications for individual career preparation and job search behavior. *Journal of Vocational Behavior, 43,* 310–327.

Bycio, P., Alvares, K. M., & Hahn, J. (1987). Situational specificity in assessment center ratings: A confirmatory factor analysis. *Journal of Applied Psychology, 72,* 463–474.

Callender, E. (1996, March 25). Casual conflict. *Los Angeles Times,* pp. 11, 19.

Cascio, W. F. (1976). Turnover, biographical data, and fair employment practice. *Journal of Applied Psychology, 61,* 576–580.

Cascio, W. F. (1995). Whither industrial and organizational psychology in a changing world of work? *American Psychologist, 50,* 928–939.

Cascio, W. F., Outtz, J., Zedeck, S., & Goldstein, I. L. (1991). Statistical implications of six months of test score use in personnel selection. *Human Performance, 4,* 233–264.

Chatman, J. A. (1991). Matching people and organizations: Selection and socialization in public accounting firms. *Administrative Science Quarterly, 36,* 459–484.

Childs, A., & Klimoski, R. J. (1986). Successfully predicting career success: An application of the biographical inventory. *Journal of Applied Psychology, 71,* 3–8.

Coulton, G. F., & Feild, H. S. (1995). Using assessment centers in selecting entry-level police officers: Extravagance or justified expense? *Public Personnel Management, 24,* 223–254.

Dawis, R. V., England, G. W., & Lofquist, L. H. (1964) A theory of work adjustment. *Minnesota Studies in Vocational Rehabilitation, 15.*

Dougherty, T. W., Ebert, R. J., & Callender, J. C. (1986). Policy capturing in the employment interview. *Journal of Applied Psychology, 71,* 9–15.

Dougherty, T. W., Turban, D. B., & Callender, J. C. (1994). Confirming first impressions in the employment interview: A field study of interviewer behavior. *Journal of Applied Psychology, 79,* 659–665.

Drakeley, R. J., Herriot, P., & Jones, A. (1988). Biographical data, training success, and turnover. *Journal of Occupational Psychology, 61,* 145–152.

Drasgow, F., Olson, J. B., Keenan, P. A., Moberg, P., & Mead, A. D. (1993). Computerized assessment. In G. R. Ferris & K. M. Rowland (Eds.), *Research in personnel and human resource management.* Greenwich, CT: JAI.

Drucker, P. F. (1994, November). The age of social transformation. *Atlantic Monthly,* pp. 53–80.

Dunnette, M. D. (1962). Personnel management. *Annual Review of Psychology, 13,* 285–313.

Equal Employment Opportunity Commission (1974). *Affirmative action and equal employment: A guidebook for employers.* Washington, DC: U.S. Government Printing Office.

Equal Employment Opportunity Commission (1978). Adoption by four agencies of the "Uniform Guidelines on Employee Selection Procedures." *Federal Register, 43,* 38290–38315.

Feldman, D. C., Doerpinghaus, H. I., & Turnley, W. H. (1994). Managing temporary workers: A permanent HRM challenge. *Organizational Dynamics, 23,* 49–63.

Finkelstein, L. M., Burke, J. J., & Raju, N. S. (1995). Age discrimination in simulated employment contexts: An integrative analysis. *Journal of Applied Psychology, 80,* 652–663.

Flynn, G. (1995). Contingent staffing requires serious strategy. *Personnel Journal, 74,* 50–58.

Forsythe, S., Drake, M. F., & Cox, C. E. (1985). Influence of applicant's dress on interviewer's selection decisions. *Journal of Applied Psychology, 70,* 374–378.

Gallois, C. L., Callan, V. J., & Palmer, J. M. (1992). The influence of applicant communication style and interviewer characteristics on hiring decisions. *Journal of Applied Social Psychology, 22,* 1041–1060.

Gaugler, B. B., Rosenthal, D. B., Thornton, G. C., III., & Bentson, C. (1987). Meta-analysis of assessment center validity. *Journal of Applied Psychology Monograph, 72,* 493–511.

Gifford, R., Ng, C. F., & Wilkinson, M. (1985). Nonverbal cues in the employment interview: Links between applicant qualities and interviewer judgments. *Journal of Applied Psychology, 70,* 729–736.

Goffin, R. D., Rothstein, M. G., & Johnston, N. G. (1996). Personality testing and the assessment center: Incremental validity for managerial selection. *Journal of Applied Psychology, 81,* 746–756.

Goltz, S. M., & Giannantonio, C. M. (1995). Recruiter friendliness and attraction to the job: The mediating role of inferences about the organization. *Journal of Vocational Behavior, 46,* 109–118.

Grant, D. L., & Bray, D. W. (1969). Contributions of the interview to assessment of management potential. *Journal of Applied Psychology, 53,* 24–34.

Greenlaw, P. S., & Jensen, S. S. (1996). Race-norming and the Civil Rights Act of 1991. *Public Personnel Management, 25,* 13–24.

Harris, M. M. (1989). Reconsidering the employment interview: A review of recent literature and suggestions for future research. *Personnel Psychology, 42,* 691–726.

Harris, M. M., & Fink, L. S. (1987). A field study of applicant reactions to employment opportunities: Does the recruiter make a difference? *Personnel Psychology, 40,* 765–784.

Hayes, T. L., Citera, M., Bradey, L. M., & Jenkins, N. M. (1995). Staffing for persons with disabilities: What is "fair" and "job related"? *Public Personnel Management, 24,* 413–427.

Heller, J. (1955). *Catch-22.* New York: Dell.

Howard, J. L., & Ferris, G. R. (1996). The employment interview context: Social and situational influences on interviewer decisions. *Journal of Applied Social Psychology, 26,* 112–136.

Huber, V. L., Northcraft, G. B., & Neale, M. A. (1990). Effects of decision strategy and number of openings on employment selection decisions. *Organizational Behavior and Human Decision Processes, 45,* 276–284.

Huffcutt, A. L., McDaniel, M. A., & Roth, P. L. (1996). A meta-analytic investigation of cognitive ability in employment interview evaluations: Moderating characteristics and implications for incremental validity. *Journal of Applied Psychology, 81,* 459–473.

Hunter, J. E., & Hunter, R. F. (1984). Validity and utility of alternative predictors of job performance. *Psychological Bulletin, 96,* 72–98.

Ito, J. (1994). Current staff development and expectations as criteria in selection decisions. *Public Personnel Management, 23,* 361–372.

Jackson, S. E., & Schuler, R. S. (1990). Human resource planning: Challenges for industrial/organizational psychologists. *American Psychologist, 45,* 223–239.

Janz, T., Hellervik, L., & Gilmore, D. C. (1986). *Behavior description interviewing.* Boston: Allyn & Bacon.

Johnston, W. B., & Packer, A. E. (1987). *Workforce 2000: Work and workers for the 21st century.* Indianapolis: Hudson Institute.

Judge, T. A., & Bretz, R. D. (1992). Effects of work values on job choice decisions. *Journal of Applied Psychology, 77,* 261–271.

Kacmar, K. M., Delery, J. E., & Ferris, G. R. (1992). Differential effectiveness of applicant impression management tactics on employment interview decisions. *Journal of Applied Social Psychology, 22,* 1250–1272.

Keenan, T. (1995). Graduate recruitment in Britain: A survey of selection methods used by organizations. *Journal of Organizational Behavior, 16,* 303–317.

Kinicki, A. J., & Lockwood, C. A. (1985). The interview process: An examination of factors recruiters use in evaluating job applicants. *Journal of Vocational Behavior, 26,* 117–125.

Kirnan, J. P., Farley, J. A., & Geisinger, K. F. (1989).The relationship between recruiting source, applicant quality, and hire performance: An analysis by sex, ethnicity, and age. *Personnel Psychology, 42,* 293–308.

Landy, F. J., Shankster, L. J., & Kohler, S. S. (1994). Personnel selection and placement. *Annual Review of Psychology, 45,* 261–296.

Larwood, L. (1995). Attributional effects of equal employment opportunity: Theory development at the intersection of EEO policy and management practice. *Group and Organization Management, 20,* 391–408.

Latham, G. P., Saari, L. M., Pursell, E. D., & Campion, M. A. (1980). The situational interview. *Journal of Applied Psychology, 65,* 422–427.

Lefkowitz, J. (1994). Race as a factor in job placement: Serendipitous findings of "ethnic drift." *Personnel Psychology, 47,* 497–513.

Lin, T., Dobbins, G. H., & Farh, J. (1992). A field study of race and age similarity effects on interview ratings in conventional and situational interviews. *Journal of Applied Psychology, 77,* 363–371.

Linn, R. L., Harnish, D. L., & Dunbar, S. G. (1981). Corrections for range restriction: An empirical investigation of conditions resulting in conservative corrections. *Journal of Applied Psychology, 66,* 655–663.

Lofquist, L. H., & Dawis, R. V. (1991). *Essentials of person-environment correspondence counseling.* Minneapolis: University of Minnesota Press.

London, M., & Bray, D. W. (1980). Ethical issues in testing and evaluation for personnel decisions. *American Psychologist, 35,* 890–901.

Lowry, P. E. (1994). The structured interview: An alternative to the assessment center? *Public Personnel Management, 23,* 201–215.

Macan, T. H., & Dipboye, R. L. (1994). The effects of the application on processing of information from the employment interview. *Journal of Applied Social Psychology, 24,* 1291–1314.

Mael, F. A. (1991). A conceptual rationale for the domain and attributes of biodata items. *Personnel Psychology, 44,* 763–792.

Mael, F. A., & Ashforth, B. E. (1995). Loyal from day one: Biodata, organizational identification, and turnover among newcomers. *Personnel Psychology, 48,* 309–333.

Mael, F. A., & Hirsch, A. C. (1993). Rainforest empiricism and quasi-rationality: Two approaches to objective biodata. *Personnel Psychology, 46,* 719–738.

Marlowe, C. M., Schneider, S. L., & Nelson, C. E. (1996). Gender and attractiveness biases in hiring decisions: Are more experienced managers less biased? *Journal of Applied Psychology, 81,* 11–21.

Maurer, S. D., & Fay, C. (1988). Effect of situational interviews, conventional structured interviews, and training on interview rating agreement: An experimental analysis. *Personnel Psychology, 41,* 329–344.

Maurer, S. D., Howe, V., & Lee, T. W. (1992). Organizational recruiting as marketing management: An interdisciplinary study of engineering graduates. *Personnel Psychology, 45,* 807–833.

McDaniel, M. A., Whetzel, D. L., Schmidt, F. L., & Maurer, S. D. (1994). The validity of employment interviews: A comprehensive review and meta-analysis. *Journal of Applied Psychology, 79,* 599–616.

McDonald, T., & Hakel, M. D. (1985). Effects of applicant race, sex, suitability, and answers on interviewer's questioning strategy and ratings. *Personnel Psychology, 38,* 321–334.

McMurry, R. N. (1947). Validating the patterned interview. *Personnel, 23,* 263–272.

Meglino, B. M., DeNisi, A. S., & Ravlin, E. C. (1993). Effects of previous job exposure and subsequent job status on the functioning of a realistic job preview. *Personnel Psychology, 46,* 803–822.

Meglino, B. M., Ravlin, E. C., & Adkins, C. L. (1989). A work values approach to corporate culture: A field test of the value congruence process and its relationship to individual outcomes. *Journal of Applied Psychology, 74,* 424–432.

Moreland, K. L., Eyde, L. D., Robertson, G. J., Primorr, E. S., & Most, R. B. (1995). Assessment of test user qualifications: A research-based measurement procedure. *American Psychologist, 50,* 14–23.

Morrow, P. C. (1990). Physical attractiveness and selection decision making. *Journal of Management, 16,* 45–60.

Owens, W. A. (1968). Toward one discipline of scientific psychology. *American Psychologist, 65,* 782–785.

Owens, W. A. (1976). Background data. In M. D. Dunnette (Ed.), *Handbook of industrial and organizational psychology.* Chicago: Rand McNally.

Parsons, C. K., & Liden, R. C. (1984). Interviewer perceptions of applicant qualifications: A multivariate field study of demographic characteristics and nonverbal cues. *Journal of Applied Psychology, 69,* 557–568.

Pearce, J. L. (1993). Toward an organizational behavior of contract laborers: Their psychological involvement and effects on employee co-workers. *Academy of Management Journal, 36,* 1082–1096.

Peres, S. H., & Garcia, J. R. (1962). Validity and dimensions of descriptive adjectives used in reference letters for engineering applicants. *Personnel Psychology, 15,* 279–296.

Perry, E. L., Davis-Blake, A., & Kulik, C. T. (1994). Explaining gender-based selection decisions: A synthesis of contextual and cognitive approaches. *Academy of Management Review, 19,* 786–820.

Phillips, A. P., & Dipboye, R. L. (1989). Correlational tests of predictions from a process model of the interview. *Journal of Applied Psychology, 74,* 41–52.

Pingitore, R., Dugoni, B. L., Tindale, R. S., & Spring, B. (1994). Bias against overweight job applicants in a simulated employment interview. *Journal of Applied Psychology, 79,* 909–917.

Premack, S. L., & Wanous, J. P. (1985). A meta-analysis of realistic job preview experiments. *Journal of Applied Psychology, 70,* 706–719.

Pursell, E. D., Campion, M. A., & Gaylord, S. R. (1980). Structured interviewing: Avoiding selection problems. *Personnel Journal, 59,* 907–912.

Rasmussen, K. G., Jr. (1984). Nonverbal behavior, verbal behavior, resume credentials, and selection interview outcomes. *Journal of Applied Psychology, 69,* 551–556.

Reilly, R. R., & Chao, G. T. (1982). Validity and fairness of some alternative employee selection procedures. *Personnel Psychology, 35,* 1–62.

Robertson, I. T., Gratton, L., & Rout, U. (1990). The validity of situational interviews for administrative jobs. *Journal of Organizational Behavior, 11,* 69–76.

Rothstein, H. R., Schmidt, F. L., Erwin, F. W., Owens, W. A., & Sparks, C. P. (1990). Biographical data in employment selection: Can validities be made generalizable? *Journal of Applied Psychology, 75,* 175–184.

Rynes, S. L., & Barber, A. E. (1990). Applicant attraction strategies: An organizational perspective. *Academy of Management Review, 15,* 286–310.

Rynes, S., & Rosen, B. (1995). A field survey of factors affecting the adoption and perceived success of diversity training. *Personnel Psychology, 48,* 247–270.

Sackett, P. R., & Wilk, S. L. (1994). Within-group norming and other forms of score adjustment in preemployment testing. *American Psychologist, 49,* 929–954.

Saks, A. M. (1994). A psychological process investigation for the effects of recruitment source and organization information on job survival. *Journal of Organizational Behavior, 15,* 225–244.

Schmitt, N. (1976). Social and situational determinants of interview decisions: Implications for the employment interview. *Personnel Psychology, 29,* 79–101.

Schmitt, N., Schneider, J. R., & Cohen, S. A. (1990). Factors affecting validity of a regionally administered assessment center. *Personnel Psychology, 43,* 1–12.

Sheets, T. L., & Bushardt, S. C. (1994). Effects of the applicant's gender-appropriateness and qualifications and rater self-monitoring propensities on hiring decisions. *Public Personnel Management, 23,* 373–382.

Silver, S. (1995, October 15). The bottom line on diversity. *Washington Post,* p. 5.

Smith, M. (1994). A theory of the validity of predictors in selection. *Journal of Occupational and Organizational Psychology, 67,* 13–31.

Smith, M., & George, D. (1994). Selection methods. In C. L. Cooper & I. T. Robertson (Eds.), *Key reviews in managerial psychology: Concepts and research for practice.* Chichester, England: Wiley.

Snyder, M., Berscheid, E., & Matwychuk, A. (1988). Orientations toward personnel selection: Differential reliance on appearance and personality. *Journal of Personality and Social Psychology, 54,* 972–979.

Stevens, C. K., & Kristof, A. L. (1995). Making the right impression: A field study of applicant impression management during job interviews. *Journal of Applied Psychology, 80,* 587–606.

Stokes, G. S., Mumford, M. D., & Owens, W. A. (Eds.). (1993). *The biodata handbook: Theory, research, and application.* Palo Alto, CA: Consulting Psychologists Press.

Swaroff, P. G., Barclay, L. A., & Bass, A. R. (1985). Recruiting sources: Another look. *Journal of Applied Psychology, 70,* 720–728.

Taylor, M. S., & Bergmann, T. J. (1987). Organizational recruitment activities and applicants' reactions at different stages of the recruitment process. *Personnel Psychology, 40,* 261–285.

Taylor, M. S., & Schmidt, D. W. (1983). A process-oriented investigation of recruitment source effectiveness. *Personnel Psychology, 36,* 343–354.

Tullar, W. L. (1989). Relational control in the employment interview. *Journal of Applied Psychology, 74,* 971–977.

Turban, D. B., & Dougherty, T. W. (1992). Influences of campus recruiting on applicant attraction to firms. *Academy of Management Journal, 35,* 739–765.

Turban, D. B., Eyring, A. R., & Campion, J. E. (1993). Job attributes: Preferences compared with reasons given for accepting and rejecting job offers. *Journal of Occupational and Organizational Psychology, 66,* 71–81.

Van Vianen, A. E., & Willemsen, T. M. (1992). The employment interview: The role of sex stereotypes in the evaluation of male and female job applicants in the Netherlands. *Journal of Applied Social Psychology, 22,* 471–491.

Vandenberg, R. J., & Scarpello, V. (1990). The matching model: An examination of the processes underlying realistic job previews. *Journal of Applied Psychology, 75,* 60–67.

Varca, P. E., & Pattison, P. (1993). Evidentiary standards in employment discrimination: A view toward the future. *Personnel Psychology, 46,* 239–258.

Vecchio, R. P. (1995). The impact of referral sources on employee attitudes: Evidence from a national sample. *Journal of Management, 21,* 953–965.

Wagner, R. (1949). The employment interview: A critical summary. *Personnel Psychology, 2,* 17–46.

Wanous, J. P. (1980). *Organizational entry: Recruitment, selection, and socialization of newcomers.* Reading, MA: Addison-Wesley.

Wiesner, W. H., & Cronshaw, S. F. (1988). A meta-analytic investigation of the impact of interview format and degree of structure on the validity of the employment interview. *Journal of Occupational Psychology, 61,* 275–290.

Wiggins, J. S. (1973). *Personality and prediction: Principles of personality assessment.* Reading, MA: Addison-Wesley.

Wilk, S. L., Sackett, P. R., & Desmarais, L. B. (1995). Gravitation to jobs commensurate with ability: Longitudinal and cross-sectional tests. *Journal of Applied Psychology, 80,* 79–85.

Williams, C. R., Labig, C. E. Jr., & Stone, T. H. (1993). Recruitment sources and posthire outcomes for job applicants and new hires: A test of two hypotheses. *Journal of Applied Psychology, 78,* 163–172.

Williams, K. B., Radefeld, P. S., Binning, J. F., & Sudak, J. R. (1993). When job candidates are "hard" versus "easy-to-get": Effects of candidate availability on employment decisions. *Journal of Applied Social Psychology, 23,* 169–198.

Williams, M. L., & Dreher, G. F. (1992). Compensation system attributes and applicant pool characteristics. *Academy of Management Journal, 35,* 571–595.

Wollack, S. (1994). Confronting adverse impact in cognitive examinations. *Public Personnel Management, 23,* 217–224.

Wright, P. M., Lichtenfels, P. A., & Pursell, E. D. (1989). The structured interview: Additional studies and a meta-analysis. *Journal of Occupational Psychology, 62,* 191–199.

Employee Training and Socialization

Rather than respond to the declining earnings of the past three years with companywide layoffs, [IBM Corporation] has shifted 21,500 employees from such areas as manufacturing, development, and administration—where they are not needed—into marketing and programming. . . . The company is dealing with a daunting challenge: How do you teach a plant employee, a lab technician, or a manager to sell?. . .

The training program attacks the problem with a vast amount of role playing. Technology comes to the company's aid here. IBM has developed a self-study system called InfoWindow that combines a personal computer and a laser videodisc so that the computer becomes an interactive TV. Even before attending class in Atlanta, a trainee in a branch office can use a particular InfoWindow program—in finance or hospital administration, say—to practice sales calls with an on-screen actor who portrays a manager in one of these industries. IBM programs the system so that the actor responds differently depending on what the salesperson does.

"We'll always need classrooms," [IBM's director of education] says. "I don't see education going to total technology, but we are learning to expand the limits."

RECRUITING, SCREENING, selection, and placement are the means by which organizations fill positions. Training is the means by which those hired for the jobs learn to perform them. IBM Corporation was able to bypass several of the earlier steps by using training, instead of a more traditional combination of terminations and new hires, to meet its need for more salespeople and fewer employees in other areas. The new IBM salespeople were a diverse group, and they were trained using a diverse set of methods that ranged from traditional classroom instruction to advanced interactive computer simulations. This reallocation of educated, experienced, and loyal employees worked to everyone's advantage: IBM got the salespeople it needed and the "redeploys" acquired valuable new skills.

IBM's innovative approach to changing personnel requirements also had a less obvious effect on organizational functioning. To be successful (and, it is to be hoped, happy), employees must adjust to their work groups and to the company, a process called socialization. The "new" IBM employees already had made this adjustment; they liked the company and wanted to keep working there even though it meant doing work that was completely different from what they had initially been hired and trained to do.

Training people to do their job tasks and socializing them to the procedures, policies, norms, and expectations of the organization are the subjects of this chapter. They are discussed separately for clarity, although they are interrelated processes that are difficult to separate in reality. Training experiences are an important part of the socialization process; in turn, effective socialization is important to the use of skills and to tenure with the organization.

An Overview of Training

A wide variety of activities now comes under the heading of training, but all have the same purpose. **Training** is a structured learning experience intended to develop abilities into specific skills, knowledge, or attitudes. Abilities are physical, mental, or psychological potentials. Skill is a particular application of one or more of these potentials. As people differ with respect to their various abilities, so they differ in the degree of skill they can acquire as a result of training. This difference is the reason that ability tests have long been the most commonly used screening tests in organizations.

The Functions of Training

The training discussed in this chapter is for the purpose of turning abilities, knowledge, and experience into particular job-related skills. This training serves at least three important functions for an organization. One is a maintenance function. Making sure that employees know how to do their jobs the way the organization expects them to be done is a means for maintaining overall employee performance within the limits required for an organization to meet its objectives.

Training also serves a socialization function. Among the features of a training program that send employees messages about the priorities, values, and norms of an organization are its content and structure, the resources put into it, the goals and procedures emphasized, the amount of trainee participation that is possible, and the attitudes and skills of the people doing the training.

Finally, training serves a motivational function. Employees' expectations that they will be able to perform successfully are an important factor in how much effort they exert on the job. To the extent that this confidence is increased by training, there should be an associated increase in motivation. Motivation may also be increased if training serves to heighten an employee's interest in his or her work or if it is seen as helpful to moving up to more challenging positions within the organization.

Ability tests
See pages 74–78

Training as a Learning Experience

As illustrated by the excerpt in Psychology at Work, some very sophisticated instructional methods are available. It is important to remember, however, that it is people who are being trained. Whatever the technology available, changing the behavior of people in a particular way, such as training them for a job, rests on three important principles of human learning—practice, feedback, and reinforcement.

Practice

Some disagreement exists among learning theorists about whether active participation in the form of practice is essential to learning, but practice does *facilitate* learning for most people. This seems to apply to all levels of training and to most training tasks. If actual practice is not possible for some reason (such as time constraints, number of trainees, dangers associated with inexpert practice), mental practice may be an effective alternative (Driskell, Copper, & Moran, 1994). Mental practice is rehearsing a task in the mind rather than with overt physical movement; many athletes routinely undertake this form of practice before competition (Annett, 1994).

It is impossible to state exactly how much practice, be it physical or mental, is optimal for any particular person/task combination, but the relevant literature offers two guidelines that have stood the test of time.

1. *Repetitive practice* appears to be the most effective for motor skills or for any task that requires people to commit material to memory.

2. *Distributed practice* (spread out over time) appears to be more effective than an intensive, one-time practice session for any task.

These are guidelines, not rules. A number of difficulties arise in the process of applying general learning research findings to a training situation. One of the major problems is that the tasks used in learning research often bear little resemblance to real training tasks. Nevertheless, these guidelines are sufficiently well documented to provide a useful benchmark.

Feedback

In the broad sense, **feedback** is information returned, or fed back, about a process, event, or behavior that went before. Feedback may occur automatically; when the battery in a car goes dead, the car won't start (feedback that something has gone wrong in the engine). It also occurs virtually instantaneously in some instances. If a driver presses down suddenly and hard on the car's foot brake while driving on ice, the car will go into a skid. This feedback (the skid) gives the driver the information that his or her behavior in this situation (slamming on the brakes on ice) requires modification.

Feedback is not always automatic or instantaneous. A student who takes an exam may believe that he or she did well, but it isn't possible to be sure until the paper is returned with an *A* (feedback) at the top. To the student, that *A* probably says "well done," but it is very important to keep in mind that feedback is a *neutral* term. Feedback is not praise, it is information.

Learning research in psychology leaves no doubt that feedback, in the neutral sense of information about progress, is vital for the most effective learning to take place, whatever the subject. I/O psychologists have found feedback to increase the effectiveness of training people for such widely diverse tasks as carrying out fire evacuation drills properly (Fox & Sulzer-Azaroff, 1989), predicting the number of wins for major league baseball teams (Balzer, Sulsky, Hammer, & Sumner, 1992), and detecting the presence of weeds within the other growth in a field (Hartley, Higgins, MacLeod, & Arnold, 1990).

Experiment

See pages 29–31

A graph from a well-known field experiment comparing training alone with training plus feedback illustrates the pattern of findings typical of the research into the role that feedback plays in learning (Komaki, Heinzmann, & Lawson, 1980). Figure 5–1 shows a comparison of the percentage of safe work behaviors associated with (a) safety training only and (b) safety training with feedback regarding how trainees were doing on the specified safety criteria.

The graph in the figure shows the performance of employees on four jobs in a large city department of public works at three points in time: before training (baseline), after training with no feedback (training only), and after feedback for safety performance was initiated (training and feedback). The horizontal lines represent the average percentage of work incidents that employees performed to safety standards in each time period. This percentage increased for each job with safety training alone, but it did not rise to the level attained when training was accompanied by feedback.

The feedback in the Komaki, Heinzmann, and Lawson study was delivered in the form of a posted graph based on random, timed observations of trainee behavior. In other cases, training feedback may be built into the training task itself. A student learning a foreign language pronounces a word and the teacher (or a machine) pronounces it correctly for comparison (feedback).

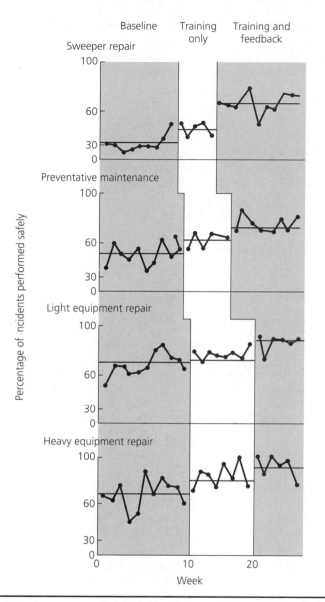

Figure 5–1
The Importance of Feedback in Training

The purpose of giving feedback in a training situation is to give people information about their performance and progress. The nature of the feedback is dictated by the nature of trainee performance; when performance is good, positive feedback helps to reinforce the associated behaviors. When performance is unsatisfactory, negative feedback gives the trainee the information that his or her behavior needs adjusting. To be effective in helping the individual make the necessary changes, this feedback should be as specific as possible. The idea is to help the trainee develop a more effective approach to the learning tasks.

Giving trainees information as they go along on how to adjust their behavior to reach training goals is a form of feedback called *process* feedback. By contrast, the A that the student received on the exam was *outcome* feedback. The person who graded the paper saw only the results of the student's efforts; he or she did not know by what study behaviors the results were achieved. Of course, most students have had a lot of experience taking tests, while the training tasks for most job trainees are new to them.

The experience difference between a college student taking an exam and a trainee learning a new job illustrates an important point about the relationship between feedback and improved performance. Outcome feedback alone may be sufficient to help someone improve his or her performance of a familiar or well-structured task (such as studying for a test). When the situation is new to the individual (as is usually the case in job training), process feedback is equally or more critical (Earley, Northcraft, Lee, & Lituchy, 1990). In either case, to be effective, the feedback should be given as soon as possible after the relevant behavior. Remember how frustrating it is to have to wait weeks for a grade on a test or term paper?

Reinforcement

Positive reinforcement has occurred when a behavior has been strengthened by its consequences; to put it the other way around, a positive outcome of behavior *reinforces,* or strengthens, the behavior. If the student in the example studied in a way that was different from usual for the exam on which he or she got an A, the good grade makes it more likely that the behavior will be repeated; the new way of studying was reinforced by its consequences.

An important aspect of any training program is whether it allows for some reinforcement of desired behavior, be this effort, progress, or skill achievement. Positive feedback is one form of reinforcement; praise and feelings of accomplishment are powerful rewards for many people. For new hires undergoing initial job training, increased training pay as certain standards are met, formal recognition such as a "Trainee of the Week" award, and faster movement out of training and on to the job are frequently used reinforcements.

Practice, feedback, and reinforcement are the Big Three standards that apply to any learning situation, inside organizations or out. They describe the basic conditions necessary for people to learn, but they do not offer much insight about the actual process of learning. Much of the information about *how* people acquire knowledge and skills comes from research in the field of cognitive psychology.

Cognitive Processes and Training

Cognitive psychology is the study of the cognitive, or mental, processes by which people selectively take in, organize, store, remember, and use the stimuli from their environment. These cognitive processes are highly complex, yet most people engage in them continuously and easily.

Without any particularly strenuous effort on your part, you're grasping the meaning of this sentence right now, even as (perhaps) your attention has already begun to wander to an upcoming . . .[meeting], a test tomorrow, hunger pangs, or whatever. (Best, 1989, p. 4)

How can the average person accomplish such mental gymnastics, and many much more complicated feats, without really "thinking" about any of it? Attention, pattern recognition, memory, language, reading and writing skills, reasoning, and problem solving all play a role, and these are among the major subjects of cognitive psychology. Clearly, knowing more about these processes would be useful to people who design, carry out, and conduct research into training in organizations. The following examples are adapted from a discussion by Howell and Cooke (1989).

- *Automatic processing:* Training people for work that includes a mixture of routine and nonroutine tasks can be improved by having trainees practice the routine elements first until they are overlearned (automatic) and do not compete with learning more complex, nonroutine elements. It is easier to train someone to use a word processing program if the actual typing process is automatic. If it is not, learning to use the program is inhibited by the need to "hunt and peck" on the keyboard.

- *Metacognition:* Helping trainees learn to monitor their own progress and evaluate what they know and don't know as they go along can make learning much more efficient. Briggs (1990) gave subjects who had different degrees of word processing experience a simple task to perform with an unfamiliar word processing system. Subjects were given information only if they asked for it. An analysis of these questions revealed an interesting phenomenon: only the most experienced individuals were aware of what *kinds* of knowledge (metacognitions) they needed to complete the task. Less experienced subjects asked questions based on problems that arose as they went along.

Research subjects
See page 27

Feedback is a critical phase of any learning situation; people learn from the results of their efforts.

- *Mental models:* Cognitive research makes it clear that an accurate mental picture of the material to be understood facilitates many training tasks. A study in which inexperienced subjects were trained to operate a plastic extrusion machine illustrates the point (Koubek, Clarkston, & Calvez, 1994). In that investigation, subjects who were given knowledge of abstract relationships relevant to the operation of the machine *before* being given lower-level, specific knowledge performed significantly better than subjects whose training was in the opposite order.

Even if they learn their tasks well initially, individuals trained without "big picture" information (a mental model) may run into trouble later. This out-of-the-loop performance problem is particularly likely to occur with automated jobs. Employees who were trained to use automated equipment without understanding the basic process often are unable to perform their jobs if there is an automation failure (Endsley & Kris, 1995). This problem is familiar to most people who at one time or another have been unable to buy something, get information, or make an appointment because "the system is down."

Most I/O psychologists interested in training in organizations believe that one day it will be standard practice to incorporate cognitive principles into training programs (e.g., Thayer, 1989). Certainly as more and more jobs, even relatively low-paying ones, become increasingly demanding in terms of the skills required to perform them, making use of information about how people learn in the design of training programs should make these programs more efficient as well as more effective.

What Are the Organization's Training Needs?

For many years it was relatively simple to describe a given organization's training needs. New employees had to be trained to do their jobs (or, if they were experienced, trained in the way the new employing organization wanted the jobs done). Upon occasion, it might be necessary to provide refresher training for current employees whose performance was slipping. Retraining might be required by new technology or, as in the example of IBM, by a change in job assignment. Finally, organizations might provide employee development training to help individual employees achieve career potential or goals and to provide a pool of talent from which the organization might draw in the future.

The training needs outlined require relatively separate and distinct activities that take place as needed (or sometimes, in the case of employee development, as the mood strikes). In periods of employee and output stability, some companies might get by with no training activities at all. This simple picture is only a dream for most contemporary organizations where the lines between training, retraining, and development are disappearing rapidly.

There are many reasons for the change. Downsizing often leaves the remaining personnel with expanded job duties and responsibilities that may necessitate their acquiring new skills. Reengineering changes work tools and methods and can make previously acquired work skills insufficient or obsolete. Increased reliance on temporary employees means increased needs for on-the-job training. Difficulty in finding people with adequate basic skills (reading, writing, arithmetic) to fill low-paying jobs puts many organizations into the remedial education training business. (There is more on this subject in At Issue.)

Changes in training needs are not confined to lower organizational levels. Supervisors and line managers can suddenly find themselves needing public speaking skills in order to be able to give talks to civic or school groups in service to business development, recruiting, or community relations. Highly skilled technical employees may move on if not given advanced educational and development opportunities. Mergers and acquisitions can leave members of upper management, who may be experienced and effective at running a company that produces industrial gaskets, scrambling to learn the ins and outs of selling peanut butter. Flatter organizations (fewer layers of management) and operations in other cultures require new management styles.

The changes described make the assessment of training needs both more complex and more critical in contemporary organizations. Beginning in the 1960s with McGehee and Thayer (1963), I/O psychologists have developed some sophisticated methodologies for this assessment (e.g., Ford & Noe, 1987; Goldstein, Braverman, & Goldstein, 1991), and there is more emphasis on coordinating training with organizational strategy (e.g., Carnevale, Gainer, & Villet, 1990; Jackson & Schuler, 1990). An organization planning to expand into the international market should have a different training emphasis from one that is not, for example. Finally, the desirability of forging a link between initial job design and training is also gaining acceptance (Howell, 1993).

The complexity of the training needs described has come upon organizations rather suddenly, compared with the long period of stability that went before. In consequence, the practice of assessing training needs and integrating them with other aspects of organizational functioning lags behind theory. For the sake of clarity, the remainder of the current examination of training is divided into two sections. The first section focuses on initial job training, where this term is understood to include retraining current employees, for whatever reason, as well as training new hires. The second section discusses employee development training.

Initial Job Training

The discussion of initial job training is organized around the four basic questions to be answered in designing any training: What should be taught? Where should it be taught? What instructional method(s) should be used? How should the training be evaluated? The emphasis is on the alternatives and the factors to be considered in choosing among them, because there is no one answer for each question that works in all situations. The same remarks apply to the employee development training discussed later in the chapter.

What Should Trainees Be Taught?

Initial job training needs depend on the size of the discrepancy between what employees can do already and what they are going to need to be able to do. When discrepancies are slight, training may be limited to familiarizing employees with the organization and with the particular work methods, opportunities, and constraints in the job they will be doing. This is often the scenario when new employees are experienced or when the duties of a job to be performed are very simple.

Limited job training also applies if new employees are temporary ones; one reason organizations use temps is to minimize the need for training. Finally, the discrepancy between what employees can do and what they need to be able to do may be relatively small if the new job is essentially a redesigned old job. When discrepancies are larger, as they often are with new hires, training needs are more extensive.

Several factors affect the general ongoing training needs of an organization with respect to new hires. The most important of these is the company's selection policy. Does it hire primarily for potential or for experience? This policy, in turn, is influenced by the size and general skill level of the available work force and by the nature of the jobs for which hiring is done. When the available work force is small or largely unskilled (or both), it may not be possible to find many experienced new employees. The same may be true for organizations that produce highly specialized products or services that require unusual skills. In such cases, hiring is done for potential (ability to be trained) rather than for experience, and training needs are considerable.

As Gagné (1962) noted some time ago, the single most important question in training is: What is to be learned? To answer this question, it is necessary to specify the task requirements of a job. The job of a movie theater concession stand attendant might be described as "to serve customers," but this really is a description of the desired *outcome* of the attendant's work. To bring about this outcome, the individual must perform the tasks of taking and filling orders, adding up charges, and making change. Many attendants also take inventory and keep the stand clean.

For initial job training with inexperienced new hires, it is often useful to break down a general description of job duties into specific individual tasks, a process called **task analysis.** The training tasks that would go with the job duties of a concession stand attendant in a movie theater are described in Exhibit 5–1. Even a job that appears to be as simple as this one reveals many facets when examined from a training standpoint.

The concession stand attendant's job tasks are performed as required by the situation at the time, but in many cases the tasks for a particular job must be accomplished in a particular order. One such fixed-procedure job is described in Exhibit 5–2. Unlike the tasks required of a movie theater concession stand attendant, the basic tasks of putting a

---

Exhibit 5–1

A Training Task Analysis

Job: Attendant at movie theater concession stand.

Training Objective: Employees who can fill customer orders accurately and quickly so as to maximize stand profits in the time available.

Job Duty	Associated Training Tasks
Take customer order	Memorize verbal instructions as given
Fill customer order	Operate beverage dispensers; fill popcorn containers to specified levels; recognize different prepackaged items; use cardboard carrying trays as appropriate
Total customer bill	Memorize stand item prices; calculate sales tax (if appropriate); add customer purchases "in head" or operate equipment provided for addition
Make change	Figure correct change from amount tendered or operate equipment provided
Keep inventory	Fill in inventory control form correctly on basis of day's sales
Clean stand and leave ready for next day	Know required cleaning tasks/standards; deactivate equipment and prepare for next use; remove trash to appropriate location

Exhibit 5–2
Putting a Radar
Set into
Operation

This kind of task is typically what is called a "fixed procedure." That is, the individual is required to push buttons, turn switches, and so on, in a particular sequence. Here, for example, is a set of steps in a procedure used by radar operators to check the transmitter power and frequency of an airborne radar. . . .

1. Turn the radar set to "Stand-by" operation.
2. Connect power cord of the TS-147.
3. Turn power switch on.
4. Turn the test switch to transmit position.
5. Turn DBM dial fully counter-clockwise.
6. Connect an RF cable to the RF jack on the TS-147.

There are 14 more steps in this procedure. Notice that each of the steps by itself is easy enough; the individual is quite capable of turning a switch or connecting a cable. What he [or she] must learn to do, however, is to perform each step in the proper sequence.

From R. M. Gagné, "Military Training and Principles of Learning." *American Psychologist,* 1962, *17,* 83–91.

radar set into operation—flipping switches, turning dials, and connecting cable—are already within the experience of most people. What is critical in this job is the *sequence* of tasks. Doing step 5 before step 4 is not only incorrect but may also be dangerous. The real training objective for this job is teaching trainees to perform the tasks at the right time and in the right order.

The job of a movie theater concession stand attendant is a relatively simple one and modern avionics is largely automated, but the principles of task analysis are the same for all jobs and are not affected by technology. Gagné (1962) describes these steps as follows:

1. Identify the component tasks of final job performance.
2. Make sure that each of these component tasks is learned.
3. Arrange the total learning situation in the appropriate sequence.

In setting up training, task analysis may be supplemented by a description of the human knowledge, skills, and abilities (KSAs) needed to perform these tasks. Such an analysis provides a rational link between selection and training as opposed to the common strategy of gearing training content to the lowest common denominator (Feldman, 1989).

Where Should Training Take Place?

There are three physical locations in which job training might be carried out. One is at the specific location where the work will be performed (on-the-job), the second is at a company's location, but not on the job location (on-site, sometimes called a "vestibule school"), and the third is somewhere other than the organization's premises (off-site). Each of these choices has its advantages and disadvantages.

On-the-Job Training

Much, perhaps most, of initial job training takes place on the job itself. The employee is put to work immediately and is instructed in job tasks by a supervisor, experienced co-worker, or floor training specialist. Most organizations use on-the-job training to some extent because it has several unique advantages. No special personnel or facilities are required, and the relevance of what they are being taught is obvious to trainees. In addition, trainees can begin making some work contribution immediately. Organizations that make a practice of hiring permanent employees from the ranks of temporary workers are getting the maximum use from these advantages while minimizing the risks of hiring people who do not work out.

The success of on-the-job training is less certain than its convenience and its economy. Sometimes there is no designated trainer and new employees are left to their own resources, like the poor hospital administrative aide who knew she wasn't being very efficient but hated to keep bothering her co-workers. Even when there are formal on-the-job trainers, some are disinterested, rushed, or inexperienced and do an inadequate job of instruction. A particular problem occurs when trainers pass on work-method shortcuts that can threaten worker safety or product or service quality instead of training a newcomer in defined procedures.

The problems that may be created by on-the-job training can be reduced by giving people who do this training some training of their own. One approach that has proved effective is the four-step job instruction training (JIT) method developed during World War II to help inexperienced supervisors cope with training thousands of new employees, many of whom had never worked before. The four steps of JIT, as described by Gold (1981), are shown in Exhibit 5–3.

Job instruction training has been used successfully by many people with little or no experience in giving formal job training. It begins with task analysis, dividing the job in question into the tasks for which employee training is necessary. The actual instruction process combines explanation, practice, and feedback. Finally, JIT includes a formal follow-up phase. The employee is not left to feel awkward or embarrassed (like the hospital aide) about asking for help with any problems encountered in early days on the job, as may happen with standard on-the-job training.

On-site Training

On-site job training does not allow trainees to begin making an immediate work contribution; training is carried out in special facilities, not at the location where the job is performed. Offsetting this drawback is the fact that both the trainee and the organization are protected from the consequences of slow or incorrect job performance. In addition, the organization has more control over the quality of training because on-site training is usually carried out by full-time trainers.

The major disadvantage of on-site training is that it can be costly, especially if expensive equipment must be duplicated for training purposes. There can also be a certain artificiality attached to training that takes place in a protected environment away from noise and normal work pressures. Experienced trainers report, however, that if the job is learned well, most trainees adjust to actual working conditions without much difficulty.

The Four Steps in Training

    I. Prepare

        A. Break down the job into tasks

        B. Prepare an instruction plan

        C. Put the trainee at ease

    II. Present

        A. Tell

        B. Show

        C. Demonstrate

        D. Explain

    III. Try Out

        A. Have the trainee describe the job verbally

        B. Have the trainee instruct the supervisor on how to do the job

        C. Let the trainee do the job

        D. Provide the trainee with feedback as to performance

        E. Let the trainee practice

    IV. Follow-Up

        A. Check progress frequently at first

        B. Tell the trainee where to go for help if needed

        C. Gradually taper off progress checks

Exhibit 5–3
Job Instruction Training Method for Supervisors

Summarized from L. Gold, "Job Instruction: Four Steps to Success." *Training and Development Journal*, 1981, *35*, 28–32.

Off-Site Training

Much of the training that takes place somewhere other than on an organization's premises is for employee development, but there is also off-site specific job training. Some organizations staff and run their own off-site training programs solely for their own employees. McDonald's famous Hamburger University and Southwest Airlines' University of People are two such programs. Other organizations take advantage of training programs offered in other settings. One parcel delivery company sends its drivers to a local vocational school to receive training in basic vehicle maintenance and emergency repair. Student nurses in Cleveland pair up with practicing nurses to learn their skills in patients' homes, shelters for the homeless, and community centers.

With the exception of programs like McDonald's, off-site training programs have the advantages of on-site locations without the expense of a permanent facility. The parcel delivery company pays for maintenance training only as it is needed; when driver turnover is low, some time may elapse before any training costs are incurred.

Off-site job training also has its disadvantages. For one, the organization has little control over the quality of training conducted by people outside the organization. In addition, the relevance of off-site training may not be clear to trainees until later when they are on the job, so they may miss some important aspects and require refresher training.

Choosing a Training Site

The preceding brief descriptions of the three main training locations have concentrated on basic advantages and disadvantages because there are no hard-and-fast rules for choosing among these alternatives. Each organization must consider its own situation. If an analysis of training needs shows that even inexperienced individuals need little training to master their jobs, for example, then on-the-job training is the logical choice. Several other factors also need to be considered. A basic one is the average number of employees to receive initial job training in a given time period. If this number is typically small, the expense of a formal on-site training program is not justified. If on-the-job training is not feasible or satisfactory, trainees can be sent to off-site facilities. The resources an organization has available for training also affect the choice of training location. Some organizations use on-the-job training exclusively because they lack the financial resources required by the alternatives.

Finally, choice of a training location may be determined by job factors. In particular, an organization must consider the consequences of trainee mistakes or substandard performance during training. No matter how impeccable the personal driving record of a trainee, no one would seriously consider on-the-job training as the only training for bus or other public transportation drivers. Other organizations must consider sensitive production processes, expensive equipment, or the possibility of employee injury in deciding where to conduct job training. When even a slight error can ruin equipment, compromise employee safety, or require scrapping a day's production, new employees will be trained off the job.

What Instructional Methods Are to Be Used?

The purpose of initial job training is to give employees the skills and knowledge they will need to be successful in day-to-day job performance. Deciding what these skill and knowledge requirements are and where to carry out training are first steps, but the core of a training program is the instructional method, or basic teaching technique, of the learning situation. There are many available; the ones reviewed here are among those used most regularly in job training. For purposes of discussion, they are grouped into three categories—nonparticipative, individual participative, and group participative.

Nonparticipative Instructional Methods

Nonparticipative instructional methods consist of methods in which the trainee's role is that of a passive recipient of information. The information is communicated by means of films, lectures, visual aids, demonstrations, written materials, or some combination of these choices. These methods are relatively inexpensive, provide standardized presentation of material, and may be used with large numbers of trainees at once.

Weighed against the advantages of nonparticipative training methods is the fact that when they are used alone, these methods typically lack all three of the important characteristics of training. There is no practice, the only opportunity for feedback comes from tests if they are given, and the only external reinforcement for learning comes from good test scores if they are achieved.

Despite the fact that they receive poor marks on the basic criteria for effective human learning, nonparticipative instructional methods are necessary or appropriate under certain conditions. When a substantial amount of information must be communicated to a large number of people in a short time, there is little alternative to this approach. This situation may occur when a sudden increase in production or service demands means putting a large number of new employees to work quickly. It also occurs occasionally when managers take over operative jobs during a union walkout.

Nonparticipative training methods may also be necessary when the training information to be communicated is not of a nature that allows for trainee participation. Many jobs have knowledge requirements as well as skill requirements, and a nonparticipative method may be the only way to communicate these during the training stage. Thus, films may be used to demonstrate the dangers of a burning building to firefighter trainees, and written materials explaining the external regulations that affect a company's personnel policies may be given to manager trainees.

Finally, nonparticipative training methods may be appropriate when an overview of training plans and activities is necessary before actual training can take place. This and the other situations described are not uncommon in organizations of all kinds; despite the drawbacks from a purely learning perspective, the place of nonparticipative methods in organizational training programs is secure.

Individual Participative Instructional Methods

A variety of **individual participative instructional methods** allows for both active participation on the part of a trainee and for an individual learning pace. Among the methods most commonly used are programmed instruction, computer-assisted instruction, simulation training, and job rotation.

Programmed Instruction

Programmed instruction (PI) gained fame initially in the form of mechanical devices called teaching machines that presented learning stimuli and feedback to students. Pressey (1926) was the first to conceive of such machines, which subsequently were used extensively to teach children to spell and to perform simple arithmetic computations. They have also been used for training in organizations in the past, but the basic idea has seen wider use in written form. The cornerstones of this method are graduated presentation of material with feedback as to correct or incorrect answers at each step. To illustrate these concepts, a short test of the material from this section is presented in PI form in Exhibit 5–4.

Programmed instruction booklets presenting material in the form shown in the exhibit are a relatively simple and inexpensive way to add elements of practice and feedback to common nonparticipative training methods such as written job instructions. This

Exhibit 5–4
A Programmed
Instruction
Approach to
Training

Instructions: Cover the left side of the page and reveal each answer only after you have filled in the blank space with your own response.

Programmed Instruction	_____ _____ first gained fame in the form of "teaching machines."
Pressey	A teaching machine is a mechanical device for presenting stimuli and feedback to students. It was developed by _____.
graduated	One important aspect of the programmed instruction approach to learning is _____ presentation of material.
feedback	At each stage in a programmed presentation, the learner makes a response and receives immediate _____ as to whether or not the response was correct.

method can also provide positive reinforcement to trainees in the form of feelings of mastery and accomplishment.

The reinforcement potential of programmed instruction is not guaranteed; it depends on whether individuals feel rewarded by getting correct answers and whether they refrain from "cheating" by looking at the correct responses ahead of time. These conditions do not necessarily occur. Nevertheless, programmed instruction adds a participatory element to material that is often presented in lecture form, it allows trainees to move at their own pace, and its cost is a tiny fraction of computer-assisted instructional methods that offer the same basic advantages in more sophisticated form.

Computer-Assisted Instruction

Computer technology has developed rapidly since businesses first began to use computers routinely in the 1950s. This expansion has made computer-assisted instruction (CAI) a logical extension of older teaching machines. CAI has the same advantage of individualized instruction but a considerably wider range of applications. Computers standardize presentation of material and practice (trainees can't skip around as they can with a booklet), and they provide instant, specific feedback that directs the next step.

An early computer-assisted instructional program used at Ford Motor Company to train industrial maintenance electricians and general troubleshooters demonstrates the strengths of this instructional method. As reported by Mallory (1981), trainees in this program learned to locate complex system malfunctions through an analytical process of identifying and then eliminating suspect components until the one causing the malfunction was isolated. With CAI, each step of a trainee's problem-solving process could be analyzed by computer and compared with the optimal solution. This feedback step would considerably increase training time (and cost) were it necessary to accomplish it in a one-on-one dialog between a trainee and a human trainer.

As the use of computers has become commonplace in organizations, the cost of the equipment has come down dramatically, making CAI a more affordable and practical training alternative. Advances in technology, such as the development of multimedia interactive video programs, have broadened the possible applications of computer-assisted instruction. It is now used in many situations that formerly required one-on-one interaction, such as the IBM sales training described in Psychology at Work.

The basis of multimedia interactive video training is a personal computer with a program that may include sound, text, graphics, and animation, as well as a video component. Such a system can be programmed to simulate just about any work situation, to adjust to a particular trainee's learning pattern by modifying the program according to his or her responses as the course progresses, and to provide feedback in a job-related form. When the IBM sales trainee deals correctly with a potential customer on the interactive video training program, for example, he or she "makes a sale."

By the mid-1990s, interactive multimedia training was in use in a wide variety of organizations, including many educational institutions. Students at John Jay High School in New York City use a system designed with the help of Citicorp and the Chemical Banking Corporation to learn banking fundamentals and basic workplace skills. They are also confronted with ethical questions and can be "fired" for making a poor decision. At Norman Thomas High School, students run an imaginary hotel and learn to deal with people as well as with systems.

Back in the world of work, Federal Express has installed a desktop training program in customer service for its more than 35,000 employees who deal directly with customers. J.C. Penney Company uses the technology to train customer service representatives in its credit card division, programming in every type of customer from reasonable to irate. The company reports that this instructional method is both faster and more effective than previous training.

The IBM, Federal Express, and J.C. Penney training programs illustrate one of the greatest strengths of this computer-assisted instructional method—its utility for training employees in the people skills now demanded by so many jobs. In addition to sales and customer service skills, there are programs in use or under development to train people in conflict management, negotiation, crisis hotline counseling, teaching, public speaking, and even questioning suspects in a law-enforcement context. Interacting with digital

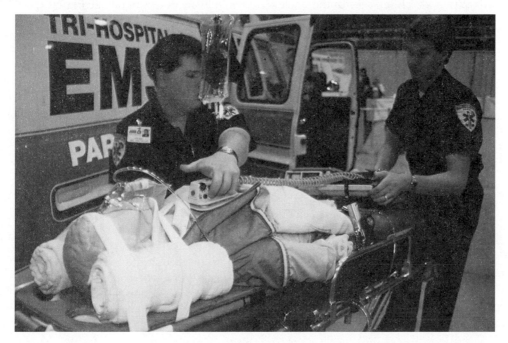

Job simulation training is preferred to on-the-job training when trainee mistakes can have serious consequences.

images rather than with real people gives trainees the opportunity to practice dealing with the kinds of clients or customers their jobs will put them into contact with in an environment that is nonthreatening.

As multimedia interactive video training becomes more sophisticated and more available (much training software can now be purchased off-the-shelf), its potential uses are more widespread. Organizations like it because it often produces better, faster, and cheaper training results than many alternatives. Nevertheless, it is not appropriate in every training situation. There are many jobs for which even the relatively modest cost of such a program is overkill; the training still takes time and the jobs are just not that complicated. There are also jobs at the other end of the spectrum.

Like other computer-assisted training methods, multimedia interactive video is a process in which a person sits in front of a computer pushing keys and watching something happen on a screen. These individual participative training methods provide for practice and feedback, but some jobs require acquiring knowledge as well as skill. An instruction method that retains the advantages of computer-assisted instruction while offering an opportunity to promote understanding of basic principles as well as specific skills, is simulation training (Andrews, 1988).

Simulation Training

Simulation
See page 30

The Riese Organization, which owns more than 200 chain restaurant franchises, has created a full-scale mock-up of a fast-food restaurant that includes a special trainer who plays the role of a hard-charging shift manager. At any given time, some trainees are "customers" while others are "employees." These trainees, all of whom are over 55, are in a special program designed to help older workers enter the service economy.

The simulated restaurant used to train people to work in fast-food restaurants is only a few years old, but **simulation training** itself is far from new. Simulating important aspects of job reality in a controlled setting for training purposes has long been a mainstay in a variety of job settings. In the nuclear power industry, for example, giving inexperienced trainees access to the "real thing" has too many real risks. The aerospace industry and the military also make extensive use of simulation—flight simulators for training pilots and testing aircraft have been in use for many years. Railroads use simulators for training engineers, who must be able to plan their moves more than five miles ahead when they are on the job. After more than a year of observation and classroom instruction, trainees must successfully complete a difficult simulator course before being allowed to drive a train that can weigh in excess of 14 million pounds.

Simulation is also a basic training technique in technical/professional fields, such as medicine, where trainees cannot be given access to the human beings they will work with until they have acquired some skill. Harvey, a medical manikin with lifelike skin and baby blue eyes, can simulate about 30 cardiovascular diseases. Created by the University of Miami School of Medicine, Harvey is connected to a computer that both trains and tests students in recognizing heart-related problems that would take years of on-the-job experience to encounter.

As a training method, simulation has the advantage of giving trainees practice at an individual pace. This feature can be particularly useful in training inexperienced individuals for work that takes place in high pressure and/or chaotic conditions (stockbrokers, fire fighters, and air traffic controllers, to name a few). Many forms of simulation training have built-in feedback as well. When the pilot trainee makes a serious mistake on takeoff, for example, he or she "crashes."

The greatest disadvantage of job simulation training in many cases is the cost of the equipment, although much simulation can be accomplished without the major financial outlay of a flight simulator or a Harvey. Among researchers, however, there have also been some serious disagreements about the effectiveness of a method that approximates, rather than duplicates, reality. A classic experiment in this line of research is summarized in Spotlight on Research.

Weitz and Adler (1973) analyzed the results of their experiment on simulation in a number of ways. They were interested in differences among the various trials on the real task, the different movements used by male and female subjects, and the implications of these findings for different kinds of training. Of particular interest here is the finding that lack of simulator fidelity to the real thing did *not* inhibit subjects' subsequent performance on the actual equipment.

As shown by the graph in Spotlight on Research, the best performance (fewest seconds to task completion) on the first six performance trials was given by subjects trained on the simulator *least* like the real job equipment. The poorest performance (on all but the very early trials) was given by subjects overtrained on the task simulator *most* like the real thing. For the Weitz and Adler subjects who received simulation training, the amount of practice on the simulator was a more important determinant of final job performance than was the degree to which the simulator approximated the real thing.

Determinant
See page 41

One of the most interesting aspects of the Weitz and Adler results is that approximately halfway through the 15 job trials, control subjects began to outperform all other subjects. The only training the controls received was the practice they acquired on the first job trials. Similar results have been reported by other investigators using other tasks (e.g., Gale, Golledge, Pellegrino, & Doherty, 1990; Kozak, Hancock, Arthur, & Chrysler, 1993). These findings lend some weight to the argument that trainees in simulation training may "learn the simulator" rather than the job, but the question remains open.

The task used in the Weitz and Adler experiment was not a difficult one, and simulator fidelity is often critical in contemporary applications. Computer simulation in particular requires a multitude of image decisions (see review by Padmos & Milders, 1992). Kleiss and Hubbard (1993) conducted three studies with pilot subjects solely to determine that the density of the objects in simulator scenes is more important for trainee detection of altitude change than is their complexity and detail.

The cutting edge in simulation training technology is virtual reality, a computer-based experience in which a video screen mounted inside a helmet puts an image directly in front of the viewer's eyes. This technology allows people to view an image from the same perspective as they would in "real reality." On a computer screen, for example, a living room is seen in its entirety and looks like a toy room. With a virtual reality image, the viewer cannot see the floor without actually looking down or see the ceiling without looking up.

Virtual reality was developed for entertainment, but psychologists and others have been quick to see its training potential. The Army has virtual reality simulators that give trainees the sensation of operating tanks and infantry fighting vehicles in the field. Virtual reality also has utility for training in searching tasks, such as those required of air traffic controllers or emergency workers of various types, and as the technology improves, so does its range of application. It is now possible to biopsy a brain tumor or rehearse sophisticated surgical techniques with a device called the Phantom. Developed by an M.I.T. student, the Phantom allows its wearer to "touch" objects, such as a scalpel, that exist only in a nearby computer.

SPOTLIGHT ON RESEARCH

The Optimal Use of Simulation

Research question   What are the effects of (a) simulator fidelity (approximation to the real-job equipment) and (b) amount of practice on (c) performance on the actual job?

Type of study   Laboratory experiment.

Subjects   One hundred males and females with no experience on the task.

Independent variables

- Simulator fidelity. Operational definition: (a) Three-rack collator (less fidelity), (b) Five-rack collator (closer to real eight-rack equipment).

- Practice time. Operational definition: (a) Overtrained (five trials beyond set speed goal), (b) Trained (to set speed goal).

Dependent variable   Performance on job. Operational definition: Time required to collate paper with real-job eight-rack equipment.

General procedure   There were five groups of 10 males and five groups of 10 females: (1) overtrained on three racks, (2) overtrained on five racks, (3) trained on three racks, (4) trained on five racks, and (5) control. Subjects in each group were given 15 trials collating paper with a real collator after training.

Results   The results for male subjects are shown in the following graph. By the end of the 15 performance trials, *overtrained* subjects were performing significantly less well than other subjects, even those with no training (control).

Laboratory experiment
See pages 27–28

Independent variable/dependent variable
See page 29

Operational definition
See page 26

Generalizability
See page 47

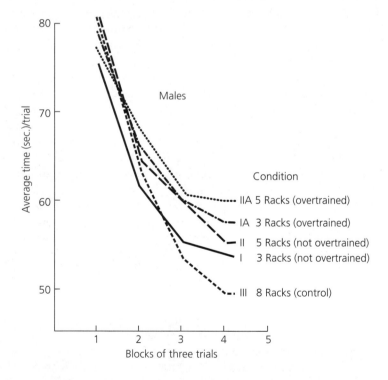

Summarized from J. Weitz and S. Adler, "The Optimal Use of Simulation." *Journal of Applied Psychology*, 1973, *58*, 219–224. Copyright 1973 by the American Psychological Association. Graph reprinted by permission.

Conclusion   "If these . . . results are generalizable, it would mean that in a training situation on a simulator, trainees should not be trained beyond the point at which they have reached some minimal criterion of performance. . . It would also appear that . . . training and overtraining males on a simulator which more nearly approaches the real task . . . leads to greater degradation of performance on the real task than training on a simulator of less fidelity" (p. 223).

As exciting as virtual reality simulation is, in its present state of development it is a technology to be used with care, whether the use is for training or entertainment. Nausea, dizziness, disorientation, loss of balance, reduced eye-hand coordination, flashbacks, and illusory physical sensations (such as a feeling of turning when the body is stationary) are among the effects that can follow immersion (as the experience is called by people who work with this technology). To date, the best way found to reduce the likelihood of such symptoms is to limit both the amount of time spent in and the number of exposures to the virtual world.

Job Rotation

The individual participative methods of training that have been discussed take place off the job. Job rotation provides trainees with firsthand knowledge and experience of a variety of operations on the job. This instructional method does not need virtual reality, it *is* reality. At lower levels in an organization, job rotation strengthens the work force by increasing flexibility. Unless union constraints prohibit the practice, for example, employees so trained can switch jobs to reduce monotony or to perform the work of absent co-workers.

Traditionally, job rotation is a management training technique, and as such its effectiveness varies considerably. The benefits of highly routinized training programs that move all trainees from one job to another in a standard order at preset time intervals are questionable. Everyone involved knows that the time is limited and the trainees will be moving on soon; many of those who have gone through such programs report having been treated more like visitor-observers than trainees.

There are ways to get around the potential problems of job rotation and make it a more effective way to meet training goals for manager trainees. Supervisors on each job may be given some formal coaching and evaluation responsibilities for trainees in order to encourage greater commitment on both parts. It can also be helpful to leave the time to be spent in each position open so that trainees may spend more time where they need it and less where they do not. Research on job rotation is limited, but the authors of one recent study found this training to be related positively to trainees' subsequent career outcomes, including salary increases and promotion (Campion, Cheraskin, & Stevens, 1994).

Group Participative Instructional Methods

The factor unique to **group participative instructional methods** is that trainees interact with and learn from one another as well as from materials and the trainer. This can enhance learning considerably, but it also injects an element of uncertainty into the training. Every group of trainees is different from every other group, and exactly what will happen in any particular group training session cannot be known in advance. To be effective in this situation, trainers must have the ability to work with the dynamics of a group as well as with a method. Considerable skill is required to keep activities and discussions relevant to the training goals without losing the benefits of spontaneous group interaction.

Discussion Techniques

A variety of group instructional techniques center around group discussion of some subject, such as the analysis of a case study. Trainees are given the facts of an organizational problem and they work through the issues and questions together. The problem may be

Plant Democracy at National Foods

Part I

The opening of a new pet food processing plant at Omaha, Nebraska, gave the National Food Company (NF) an opportunity to design its organization structure in a manner that incorporates modern design principles. Utilizing the design principles of (1) *participation,* an attempt to distribute power throughout the organization, and (2) *autonomy,* creation of independent work teams, NF designed a new factory system aimed at overcoming problems that beset other food processing plants. The specific goals of the new factory system, according to T. K. Nunley, manager of organizational development at NF, included maximum machine utilization, minimum waste, low distribution costs, low productivity costs, and low absenteeism and turnover. Many of the functions traditionally the prerogatives of management were designed to be performed by the workers. The aim of the new system was to have workers make job assignments, interview prospective employees, schedule coffee breaks, and decide on pay raises. Having workers perform these duties was NF's way of attempting "to balance the needs of the people with the needs of the business," according to Nunley.

(This case is based largely on an experience of General Foods Corporation as reported in "Stonewalling Plant Democracy," *Business Week,* March 1977, pp. 78–82.)

Analysis Questions

1. If you were asked by Nunley to react to his design ideas and goals, what would you tell him? Why?

2. Do you think a new structure alone will create the behaviors and outcomes that Nunley expects? Discuss.

3. As an organizational development attempt, is the structural design enough, or is more needed to produce the results desired?

a real one or one developed especially for training purposes; the content is far less important than the potential for stimulating thought and discussion to make basic points. An example of an incident (short case) that has been used for training purposes is shown in Exhibit 5–5.

Group discussion of cases and incidents, such as the one in the exhibit, can stimulate the development of trainee analytic and problem-solving skills. Trainees learn not only to examine the facts of a situation as given, but also to identify crucial missing information. In addition, the different opinions and problem-solving approaches of the various group members broaden perspective and help teach an important lesson: there is seldom one solution to a problem that everyone can agree is correct.

Role Playing and Behavior Modeling

Two related training methods extend the learning potential of group discussion to a more realistic level. Instead of talking about issues and problems, trainees become involved with them on a behavioral level. Instead of talking about the need for better communication in a case study, participants communicate with one another as if they were the people in the case (role playing) or watch and imitate effective communication techniques demonstrated by others (behavior modeling).

Role playing was developed originally for use in psychotherapy by J. B. Moreno. This technique, which Moreno called psychodrama, appears to have been applied in a business setting for the first time at Macy's department store in New York City in the 1930s. Its great strength as a training method is that it focuses attention on the human element of dealing with organizational problems.

People involved in real situations have positions to defend and a stake in the way a problem is handled and resolved. Traditional case discussion training techniques make it too easy for everyone concerned to concentrate on the facts of the case and ignore this human element. Role playing is one way to make training in problem solving and interpersonal skills more realistic, and computer-assisted interactive video role playing, such as that described in Psychology at Work, makes this training tool more widely available than when a human trainer was required.

Behavior modeling, based on the social learning theory of Bandura (1969; 1977), is a relatively new training technique. Social learning theory emphasizes the part that watching the behavior of others and observing what happens as a result of this behavior plays in individual learning. Its premise is that some of what people learn is acquired indirectly by imitating behavior they observe to have positive outcomes for others. The four steps to applying this theory to job training are described by Moses (1978).

1. *Modeling.* Trainees observe filmed, videotaped, or live actors performing some task or dealing with some problem or communicating in a desired or effective way. Key behaviors for this successful performance are highlighted.

2. *Rehearsal.* Trainees practice the behaviors as modeled.

3. *Feedback.* Both the trainer and the other participants provide feedback on the rehearsed behavior. The social reinforcement for successful performance that can be provided by other group members is an important part of the process.

4. *Transfer of training.* The new behaviors are followed up on the job, and the trainees are reinforced for using them correctly.

Reviews of the relevant literature consistently support the effectiveness of behavior modeling (e.g., Robertson, 1990), but this instructional method is seldom used for training below the supervisory level. It is also used more for developmental purposes than for initial job training, although there are exceptions. The Philadelphia Retail Council found behavior modeling to be an effective method for teaching new employees the skills needed to be successful in retail sales work, and Simon and Werner (1996) found it to be superior to several alternatives for training naval personnel in computer use. Behavior modeling is also gaining popularity as an instructional method for cross-cultural training intended to help people learn to work effectively in or with cultures other than their own (Harrison, 1992).

Videoconference Training

One of the newer instructional methods being used for both initial job training and development training that can accommodate either one-on-one or group participative instruction is videoconferencing. A two-way live communication tool developed initially to facilitate business meetings between people in different geographic locations, videoconferencing puts together phone lines, desktop computers (or theaterlike big screens), and video cameras for a real-time interaction between the parties.

Videoconference training, or distance learning, can be as simple as an engineer in New York demonstrating the repair of an oil gauge to an air conditioning repair trainee in Nebraska. Or it can be as elaborate as a week-long program of group discussions, games, and simulations guided by a trainer or facilitator with all of the participants being in different locations. The technology for this training has created problems in the past, but state-of-the-art equipment is largely free of such distractions as fuzzy images, jerky movements, sound lagging behind lip movements, and telephone connections breaking at awkward moments.

Investment in good videoconferencing technology has considerable potential for solving a variety of training problems that have been created by a global economy. One dilemma facing increasing numbers of organizations is that of providing certain kinds of training for people at geographically dispersed locations without duplicating the training at each location or incurring the expenses of travel and lost productivity of the trainees. An example is provided by 3M Corporation, whose research and development group conducted an eight-week class on computer imaging involving instructors from Italy and England as well as the United States. If it had been necessary for the participants to get together physically, the cost would have exceeded $100,000; with videoconferencing, it was about one-sixth of that amount.

Concluding Remarks on Instructional Methods

Differences among the three basic training methods with respect to the opportunities they offer for practice, feedback, and reinforcement of desired behavior are summarized in Table 5–1. These differences are differences in potential, and this potential may be altered considerably by the way they are used. A highly skilled trainer can make nonparticipative methods more effective, as can supplementing them with other methods. On the other hand, individual participative training methods can fail to live up to their potential because they guarantee only practice. Unless feedback is built into the training task (as with many applications of CAI), it is up to those who design and carry out the program to add feedback and to reinforce the acquisition of desired behaviors.

The greatest difference between potential and actuality with respect to training effectiveness is likely to occur with group participative methods. These techniques have a very high potential for both feedback and reinforcement, because these can come from other members of the group as well as from the training task and the trainer. This potential will not be realized, however, unless the trainer is skilled enough to keep all group members participating and to handle any problems that may arise in the group interaction.

Table 5–1	Type of Training and Opportunity for Practice, Feedback, and Reinforcement		
	Opportunity for		
Type of Training Method	**Practice**	**Feedback**	**Reinforcement**
Nonparticipative methods	None	Low	Low
Individual participative methods	High	High	High
Group participative methods	Low to high	Very high	Very high

To the extent that training methods allow for practice, feedback, and reinforcement of the desired behaviors, a training program is more likely to be effective. Trainees differ considerably in their training-related abilities, however, and their attitudes and expectations affect the success of a training program as well. Those who do training must accept this individual variation, but they must also attempt to evaluate the general effectiveness of their initial job training program in accomplishing its purpose—providing the organization with employees ready, willing, and able to do the job.

How Will the Success of Training Be Evaluated?

Job training can be an expensive undertaking. Equipment, materials, trainer expenses, wages to trainees who are not yet productive, lost investment in trainees who leave during or shortly after receiving training, and the expense of trainee mistakes, accidents, and slow work are among the costs that may be charged to an organization's training program. Given such an expenditure of resources, some way to evaluate training effectiveness should be part of any program. This evaluation can be made on the basis of internal or external criteria.

Internal criteria for evaluating training are measures of training effectiveness made during the training period. Examples include formal tests of trainee knowledge and skill, and ratings by trainers of trainee progress and performance. External criteria for evaluating training require measuring the extent to which training produces the desired job behaviors in trainees. The degree to which positive evaluations on internal criteria are matched by positive evaluations on external criteria is the degree to which there is successful transfer of training.

Criterion
See page 63

The formal evaluation of training effectiveness is examined here from three different perspectives. First is the question of what trainees think of the training program, an internal criterion approach. Second, training is considered from the standpoint of the organization's investment in the program. Two questions are important. Did trainees learn what they were expected to learn? Was the training method cost effective? To answer these questions, it is necessary to consider both internal and external criteria. Finally, training effectiveness is examined from the perspective of the extent to which training transfers to the job—an external criterion measure.

Trainee Evaluations of Training

Participant evaluations of training are usually made by means of questionnaires. These ask trainees for their *opinions* as to the quality and effectiveness of the training procedures, materials, and methods; their *feelings* of satisfaction or dissatisfaction with the training experience, and their *ratings* of the extent to which they personally gained knowledge or skills from the training.

Anyone who has filled out an evaluation form at the end of a college, university, or other course has taken part in a form of participant evaluation of training. Course evaluation forms usually provide space for written comments as well as asking questions relevant to personal opinions, feelings, and ratings.

In organizations, participant opinions and feelings about training are typically assessed by means of a one-time questionnaire administered at the conclusion of training. Self-ratings of learning may be handled this way also. Alternatively, trainees may be given

**Statistical
Significance**
See pages 35–36

the same questionnaire about the degree of particular skills or knowledge they believe they possess twice—once before and once after training. An example of this approach is seen in the histogram in Figure 5–2. In this instance, participant ratings of their communication skills before and after training were significantly different only with respect to listening skills.

Data like those shown in the figure give a trainer a rough idea of which aspects of the communication program were most effective, but there are some problems with using it to evaluate the training as a whole. Most trainees will rate their skills in a different light before and after training because they know more *about* the skill after training. This tendency, called response-shift bias, gives before and after self-ratings limited utility for evaluating training effectiveness (Howard & Dailey, 1979). They may be useful for counseling or employee development purposes, however; the way people view their own skills and knowledge can have important effects on job performance.

Organization Evaluations of Training

Most of the recognized training methods are effective under the right circumstances, but people in a particular organization want to know if training accomplishes the purpose in *its* circumstances. They also want to know if the benefits of the training are greater than

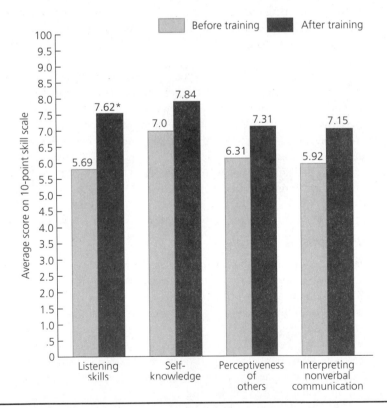

Figure 5–2
Trainee Reports of Communication Training Effectiveness

Data from B. Mezoff, "How to Get Accurate Self-Reports of Training Outcomes." *Training and Development Journal*, 1981, 35, 56–61.

*Difference from pretraining significant at $p < .05$.

the costs. The ultimate answer to the first part of this question lies in whether the job performance of people who have had training leads to improved organizational productivity—that is, in external criteria. A number of factors affect transfer of training to the job, however, so it is usual to check trainee skills and knowledge by means of internal criteria, such as tests or trainer evaluation, as well.

If internal measures show that trainees have indeed learned what a program set out to teach, the question arises as to whether this result was worth the cost. To be cost effective, a training program must yield results that are superior in some way to those that would be achieved without the program. Ideally, these benefits also should outweigh the costs (in either an absolute or a relative sense) of alternative methods of training.

Is Training More Effective Than No Training?

If initial job training is worth what it costs an organization, then new employees who have been through training should be superior (as employees) in some way to those who have not. As a group, employees with formal training should exhibit one or more of the following, as compared with employees who did not have the training:

- They should make fewer work mistakes.

- They should have fewer accidents.

- They should do work of higher quality.

- They should stay with the company longer.

- They should become productive more quickly.

An example of a situation in which employees who received training performed better than those who did not is depicted in Exhibit 5–6. These results come from a training program for senior salespeople at R. R. Donnelley & Sons, a commercial printing firm (Montebello & Haga, 1994). Twenty-six salespeople participated in the training (the experimental group); 26 did not (the control group). As shown in the graph, the sales performance of the subjects in the training group was superior to that of subjects in the control group. A program that cost $125,000 generated a return-on-investment of nearly $13 million.

The corporate sales trainer for R. R. Donnelley & Sons, with the assistance of a psychological consulting firm, followed a basic scientific strategy for finding out if training was more effective than no training. This strategy is a field experiment (or field study) in which some aspect of the job behavior of employees who have formal training is compared with the job behavior of employees who do not have the training. At Donnelly, the basis for comparison was the amount of new business closed by the salespeople. Alternatively, the researchers might have looked at the number of calls, sales volume, or evaluations by managers or customers.

The goal in setting up the investigation is to rule out nontraining explanations for observed differences between trained and untrained subjects. If this goal is to be accomplished, people chosen for the investigation should be assigned randomly to the training (experimental) and no-training (control) groups of subjects. In addition, the control group subjects should have all of the experiences the experimental subjects have *except* the training. They should receive the same orientation to the company and be given the same pretests of job knowledge and skill to establish baselines against which to measure changes.

The Weitz and Adler (1973) study summarized in this chapter's Spotlight on Research demonstrates quite clearly the reason for taking control group precautions

Exhibit 5–6
Trained Group
Outperforms
Control Group

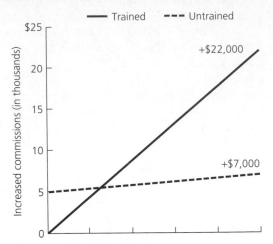

Factors such as gained experience and marketing campaigns contributed to an increase in commissions between two years for a group of sales representatives who received training and a group that didn't. However, commissions for the trained group far exceeded those of the untrained group, indicating that training had an impact.

From A. R. Montebello and M. Haga, "To Justify Training, Test, Test Again." *Personnel Journal,* January 1994, *73,* 83–87. Copyright 1994 ACC Communications. All rights reserved. Reprinted with permission.

when evaluating training effectiveness. Without such a group, these investigators would have missed one of their most important findings: the untrained subjects performed better than trained subjects after only a small amount of job practice.

So important is the control factor in evaluating training effectiveness that some researchers believe one control group is not enough. The experimental design shown in Table 5–2 has three control groups. Control group 1 is the standard control that has been under discussion. The other two groups in this Solomon Design allow the researcher to examine separately the possible effects of pretests on (a) training and (b) posttest or criterion measures. If a significant difference were found on the criterion measure (posttest) between control groups 1 and 3 but not between control group 1 and the experimental

Table 5–2	The Solomon Design for Training Effectiveness Research		
Group	**Pretest**	**Training**	**Posttest***
Experimental group	X	X	X
Control group 1	X	—	X
Control group 2	—	X	X
Control group 3	—	—	X

Summarized from R. L. Solomon, "An Extension of Control Group Design." *Psychological Bulletin,* 1949, *46,* 137–150.

*Posttest is the criterion measure.

group, for example, it would be possible that the pretest was a more powerful teaching tool than the formal training program.

The Solomon Design was first published nearly 50 years ago, and a number of other methodologies for evaluating training effectiveness have been developed since that time (e.g., Arvey & Cole, 1989; Sackett & Mullen, 1993). Detailed discussions of the complexities of training evaluation are found in Kraiger, Ford, and Salas (1993) and Sims (1993).

Is Training Cost Effective?

If careful evaluation by some method supports the conclusion that employees who have had formal training are superior on some work-related criterion to those who have not, there is still an important question left: Was it worth it? An expensive training program that shows only a small gain over no training is not cost effective. If the practice afforded by the job itself closes the gap rather quickly (as in the Weitz and Adler study), the training program may not be earning its way.

Another "Is it worth it?" question about training is whether the results of a particular program might be achieved or exceeded in a different and less costly way, perhaps by setting up training in a graded fashion according to the resources required. Training might begin with lectures and films, move on to behavior modeling, and finally progress to individual, supervised hands-on training. Each step advances the learning process, but each takes greater resources and each is more effective once the earlier steps have been taken. In addition, the more costly resources will not be wasted on trainees who drop out of the program.

As pressures mount for organizational training programs to demonstrate that they produce bottom-line results (Carnevale & Schulz, 1990), I/O psychologists and others are tackling the questions posed from several directions. Mathieu and Leonard (1987) applied standard utility analyses to the evaluation of bank supervisor training. The relative cost effectiveness of training versus equipment expenditures in achieving military force effectiveness was investigated by Deitchman (1990). Taking a broad approach, Cascio (1989) developed a set of guidelines for assessing the economic impact of training on an organization under different sets of assumptions.

Transfer of Training and Training Effectiveness

The term **transfer of training** refers to the generalization of what is learned in training to a real-life setting. The question does not arise when job training is done on the job, and this is one reason many people in industry prefer on-the-job training to other methods. Certainly, off-the-job training raises the possibility that some of what is learned in training will be left behind, but the extent of the problem varies considerably. Exhibit 5–7 presents a summary of Bass and Vaughan's (1966) well-known evaluation of popular off-the-job training methods with regard to transfer-of-training potential. This evaluation is based on the most *likely* degree of similarity between training and job conditions; it is possible to increase the transfer from any method of training.

Feedback and reinforcement are the basic tools for increasing the extent to which skills and knowledge acquired during training are carried to the job setting by newly trained employees, and they are used in exactly the same way as during training. Employees are provided with information (feedback) as to how they are doing, and they are given reinforcement for effort or for what they do well. Any behavior will fail to

Exhibit 5–7
The Transfer-
of-Training
Potential of
Some Popular
Instruction
Methods

I. Methods more likely to facilitate transfer of training

    A. Simulations

    B. Vestibule schools

    C. Role playing

    D. Case studies

    E. Structured group exercises

II. Methods less likely to facilitate transfer of training

    A. Lectures

    B. Special classes

    C. Films and television

    D. Discussion group techniques

    E. Programmed instruction

Summarized from B. M. Bass and J. A. Vaughan, *Training in Industry: The Management of Learning,* Wadsworth Publishing Co., 1966.

persist without feedback and reinforcement, and most will continue if these conditions do hold. In this sense, every kind of job training has an on-the-job component.

Feedback and reinforcement are critical to transfer of training, but many other aspects of the work environment play a role as well. The transfer-of-training climate is defined by Rouiller and Goldstein (1993) as "those situations and consequences which either inhibit or help to facilitate the transfer of what has been learned in training into the job situation" (p. 379). Aspects of a positive transfer climate include frequent opportunity to use the skills acquired in training, co-worker support for doing a job right and well, and the availability of adequate tools, information, and equipment to do the job as trained.

Another aspect of transfer of training that researchers find important is the length of time that specific training skills and behaviors continue to be used on the job (Baldwin & Ford, 1988). If this time is quite short, measuring transfer of training too soon may lead to the incorrect inference that transfer is satisfactory when, in fact, it is not. This often happens in transfer climates that are not supportive of what is taught in training.

Inference
See pages 35–43

A different inference problem can arise if the transfer distance between the training situation and the actual job is too great—that is, if the job situation is very dissimilar (too distant) from the training situation (Laker, 1990). In this case, a conclusion that training does not transfer satisfactorily to the job might be reversed if the training situation were more similar (closer) to the job situation.

In summary, each of the perspectives on evaluating training effectiveness reviewed provides a different kind of information about the training program. All of this information can be valuable. Like most decisions in organizations, however, the decision as to how to evaluate training usually rests on the costs versus the benefits of the alternative evaluation strategies. Full-blown experiments with multiple control groups may yield the most comprehensive and unambiguous information, but the process is time-consuming and expensive and this expenditure of resources is not warranted in many situations.

Trainee questionnaires and skill tests are rougher measures of training effectiveness, but they are inexpensive and may be adequate for many purposes.

At this point, attention turns from initial job training to the continuing education on the job that is usually called employee development. Keep in mind that what is to be learned, where training is to take place, what instructional methods are to be used, and how training is to be evaluated are issues that apply to any kind of training; the same questions, pros and cons apply to employee development as to initial job training.

Employee Development Training

Employee development refers to all of those organizational activities that are for the purpose of helping employees be successful by increasing their career-related knowledge and skills and removing obstacles to their success. These activities may include some training to sharpen skills on the present job, but from an employee development perspective such training would be specifically for the purpose of preparing an individual to move on. By contrast, initial job training is for the purpose of achieving better overall performance for the organization.

While some may argue the point, the position taken here is that true employee development is individual, forward-looking, and specific in nature. In this view, sending all supervisors to a communication workshop on the premise that "everyone could be a better communicator" does not qualify. Such programs undoubtedly are helpful to some participants, but they are not based on an assessment of the development needs of the individuals involved. It would be more accurate to call these activities "human resource development" because their purpose is to upgrade the skill and knowledge level of a segment of an organization's personnel.

For activities to be consistent with the current definition of employee development, they must be based on an analysis of what an individual employee wants or needs to be successful in his or her career. The result of this analysis might reveal obstacles to these

Employee development includes a wide variety of organization-sponsored efforts to help individual employees identify and achieve career goals.

goals in the form of insufficient or outdated work skills and knowledge, personal problems, health problems, or merely a lack of relevant information about career possibilities and how to pursue them. Three broadly defined sets of employee development activities for helping to overcome these obstacles are career development, skill and knowledge enhancement, and personal counseling.

Career Development

In the present context, *career development* refers to organization-sponsored activities designed to assist employees in defining and meeting their career goals. Among these activities are career counseling (as for high-potential employees who are in dead-end jobs), career pathing (as in planning job progression for employees who wish to advance), and career information distribution regarding current or upcoming position vacancies in the company (or even alternative occupational choices for individuals who believe they may have taken a wrong career turn).

Many activities falling into the category of career development are carried out informally through individual relationships, but the number of formal programs is growing. Sun Microsystems has opened career centers where employees discuss career prospects, test their skills, and explore their interests. Intel offers courses that help employees see where opportunities in the company are developing and what skills they need to succeed there. Texas Instruments discusses workers' futures with them as much as a year in advance of any changes that might affect their employment opportunities.

Sun Microsystems, Intel, and Texas Instruments are among the organizations able to appreciate the fact that experienced, capable, loyal employees who are comfortable with an organization make up a superior pool of talent for filling future job vacancies. With the supply of highly skilled employees dwindling and the need growing, formal career planning activities are likely to grow as well.

The multiple objectives an effective employee development program can achieve have been identified by Super and Minor (1987). First, it develops a work force with the skill and experience an organization needs for current and future demands. Second, it prevents individual career plateauing (halted career advancement) and obsolescence (inadequate skills to continue to perform the current job well). The third benefit of a good employee development program is the maintenance of a pool of talented managers and potential managers to meet future goals. It also helps to create an organizational climate that supports and encourages personal growth. Finally, employee development helps an organization comply with affirmative action goals and requirements.

Super and Minor's list incorporates a mixture of individual- and organization-specific goals, but achieving such goals begins with the individual. Driver (1979) believes that effective career development is based on understanding individual differences in career concept. He identifies four such concepts.

1. *Steady state.* Career choice is made early and remains constant—change is not desired.

2. *Transitory.* Career choice is never fixed—major desire is to move on.

3. *Spiral.* Career choice changes at five- to seven-year intervals—emphasis is on creative change.

4. *Linear.* Career choice is made early—emphasis is on upward movement.

According to Driver, effective career planning depends on helping people to identify and follow their own career concepts. In some cases, this may be as simple as providing information. A linear-type engineer would need to know the career paths available to an engineer in his or her organization, for example. Two such paths are illustrated in Figure 5–3. An engineer who has a steady state career concept may not be interested in climbing either of the two ladders shown. One with a spiral concept might be interested in moving from one to the other at some point; clearly, appropriate career development for these two engineers would differ.

Driver believes that the most important application of his idea of career concept lies in its potential for achieving a fit between an individual and the organization in which he or she is employed. This basic idea has been put into practice in a variety of organizations where long-standing "up or out" policies are becoming too rigid for a changed world. The accounting firm of Price Waterhouse has created numerous career ladders in its consulting division for its talented employees who are not interested in the partner track. In this context, as in many others, the idea of matching individuals to job situations to the ultimate benefit of both parties is gaining popularity.

Matching model
See pages 90–91

Skill and Knowledge Enhancement

Training activities in organizations have expanded considerably in recent years, and much of this expansion goes by the name of employee development. Many of these programs are not consistent with the individual approach advocated here; nevertheless, opportunities for skill and knowledge enhancement do appear to be more readily available than in the past. A number of interesting examples have been described recently in various business-related publications.

- Voice lessons to help people make a more favorable first (or telephone) impression
- Clean-desk training courses for employees who meet with customers and clients on a regular basis

Job Level	Managerial Ladder	Professional Ladder
6	Manager of Engineering	Research Engineer
	↑	↑
5	Senior Engineering Manager	Senior Engineer
	↑	↑
4	Engineering Manager	Advisory Engineer
	↑	↑
3	Supervisory Engineer	Staff Engineer
2	Engineer	
	↑	
1	Associate Engineer	

Figure 5–3
Two Possible
Promotion
Ladders for
Engineers

From K. Davis, *Human Relations and Organizational Behavior* (4th ed.). Copyright 1972 McGraw-Hill. Reprinted by permission.

- Programs to educate bar employees in how to limit alcohol or refuse service in a non-confrontive way when customers are becoming intoxicated

- Desktop publishing courses to help secretaries be of more assistance to their bosses

- Public-speaking training for employees who have new training or briefing responsibilites

- A board game called Zodiac (Paradigm Communications) to teach employees at all organizational levels about business strategy and finance

- A "boot camp" to teach top executives how to use a personal computer (Do they need it? One participant asked how to keep his mouse from covering up the text—he was holding it pressed against the computer screen.)

Not all employee development training takes place outside the organization. Job rotation is an increasingly popular method for expanding both skills and career opportunities. John Hancock, IBM, and Southwest Airlines are among the companies making use of this strategy. Alagasco, an Alabama utility company, also uses job rotation to keep employees from getting stale and reduce the possibility of burnout. Specialty skill and knowledge enhancement programs are also conducted on-site by special training staff or outside management consultants, who often are I/O psychologists. A good source of general information about the kinds of programs in use is the *Training and Development Journal* published by the American Society for Training and Development.

With skill and knowledge enhancement available to many more employees than formerly, I/O psychologists have become interested in who takes advantage of it and why. Maurer and Tarulli (1994) explored the relationship between participation in a variety of development activities available to employees (on their own time) and a number of personal and environmental variables. Among other results, these investigators found that people who are high on self-efficacy (belief in personal ability to do well at something) were more likely to participate in voluntary skill and knowledge enhancement opportunities than those who were not. Social support for such activities from colleagues is also important (Leiter, Dorward, & Cox, 1994).

The oldest, and for many years the most available, form of employee development is the management or leadership development program. Many of these opportunities, like the communication workshop mentioned earlier, are not based on an assessment of individual needs; instead, they are oriented toward a general improvement of the management of an organization. The most comprehensive and coordinated approach to individual management development is to be found in the assessment center. Simulation training, such as the well-known in-basket exercise (Fredericksen, 1962), plays a central role in assessment center activities.

In basic form, an in-basket contains letters, reports, and memos that require action (see Exhibit 5–8). Training participants are given a period of time in which to make decisions, write reply letters, request more information, delegate responsibility to others, or take whatever action they consider appropriate in the context of their assigned position in a hypothetical organization. A review of this and other simulations often used for assessing or developing managerial talent is found in Thornton and Cleveland (1990).

Evaluation by an assessment center is not a prerequisite for effective management development. There are other ways to assess individual strengths and weaknesses in order to identify development needs. Nevertheless, the highly specific reports that typically come out of these evaluations provide good examples of the individual approach to development.

Assessment center

See page 114

Exhibit 5–8
Sample In-
Basket Exercises

Memo To: Vice-President, Marketing
From: Manager, Human Resources

Rumor Pat Jones and Chris Brown interviewing other companies. They are valuable employees. Will you talk to them?

Assessee Name _____

What, if any, action would you take?

_____

_____

_____

_____

General Manager
Assembly Plant
City

Dear _____,

As per our discussion last month, you will be addressing the Executive Council next week on "Leadership for Downsizing." We need your outline by this Friday so as to get it to our members.

As ever,

_____, President and CEO

Assessee Name _____

What, if any, action would you take?

_____

_____

_____

_____

Whatever the specifics, an organization committed to helping its personnel enhance skills and knowledge creates a more interesting and challenging work environment that may increase employee desire to stay with the organization, enhance workforce flexibility, and promote better client or customer service. One firm that has embraced such a continuous learning culture wholeheartedly is giant Andersen Consulting, which requires continuing education of all its employees at an estimated annual cost to the organization of around a quarter of a billion dollars.

Personal Counseling

A group of mixed employee development services falls under the heading of personal employee counseling. The oldest and most extensive of these programs are for employees with alcohol or other substance-abuse problems. Counseling services for legal, marital, and psychological difficulties and financial counseling programs are also available in many organizations. A newer trend is information counseling for groups of employees dealing with specific issues; Lotus Development Corporation offers free lectures on a variety of topics including AIDS. There is also a growing trend to offer preretirement counseling and planning services to all employees.

Some organizations have full- or part-time specialists on the premises for employee counseling. Others use outside professionals on a contract basis or have regular referral arrangements with various agencies or educational institutions. A comprehensive review of the nature and extent of use of counseling in industry, together with relevant research, was undertaken by Cairo (1983). On the basis of this review, he offered the following five conclusions and recommendations:

1. There is no consistent use of the word *counseling* among the studies reported. The term is used to describe anything from a short conversation with a supervisor to extended sessions with a trained professional.

2. The objectives of counseling and how its effectiveness will be evaluated need more careful consideration.

3. There is a need for more studies comparing different counseling approaches and counseling compared with other helping activities.

4. More precise and detailed information about the use of counseling in industry is needed.

An increasing number of companies are offering employees access to personal counseling services if they need them.

5. Much of the counseling literature available is in how-to-do-it form. Program developers in industry should assume greater responsibility for balancing such prescriptions with an evaluation of their effectiveness.

An examination of the literature since 1983 leaves little doubt that Cairo's conclusions still have validity, but organizations and researchers are starting to respond to the issues. In particular, there has been considerable progress in classification and terminology, with "employee assistance program" now the widely accepted term of choice. Employee assistance programs (EAPs) are defined "by policies, procedures, and counseling-oriented services that identify or respond to employees having personal, emotional, or behavioral problems interfering with work performance" (Smith, 1988, p. 8).

By the mid-1990s, an estimated one-half of U.S. workers had access to an EAP of some sort. Key ingredients for the success of these programs include support by both top management and first-line supervisors, staffing by professionals, sensitivity to special populations within the work force, and mechanisms for educating employees about the program (Masi & Friedland, 1988). In particular, familiarity with the program, along with perceptions of support by top management, affect employee confidence in the program. Confidence, in turn, is one of the most important determinants of whether employees actually use a program (Milne, Blum, & Roman, 1994). Among the behaviors likely to lead supervisors to refer employees to an EAP are increased absenteeism, irritability, decreased productivity, and apathy (Bayer & Gerstein, 1990).

The Role of the Individual in Training

This section brings the discussion of training in organizations full circle with a reminder that whatever the specifics of other decisions made about a training program, it is always people who are being trained. As in any other learning situation, the characteristics of the individuals involved play an important role in the success of job or employee development training. Ability is basic (Ackerman, 1992; Ree, Caretta, & Teachout, 1995), but I/O psychologists have found other characteristics to be relevant to successful training outcomes as well.

Among the characteristics found to increase individual benefits from training are motivation to learn (Fishbein & Stasson, 1990; Quiñones, 1995); realistic expectations about training (Hicks & Klimoski, 1987); self-confidence (Tannenbaum, Cannon-Bowers, Salas, & Mathieu, 1993); job commitment (Noe & Schmitt, 1986); self-efficacy (Mitchell, Hopper, Daniels, George-Falvy, & James, 1994); and prior experience on a similar job (Gist, Rosen, & Schwoerer, 1988; Morrison & Brantner, 1992). The characteristics are not independent. Prior related experience may increase self-confidence, which may, in turn, increase motivation to learn, to take one example.

The personal characteristics that play a role in training success are affected by aspects of the training situation as well as by one another. Feedback can increase perceived self-efficacy (Karl, O'Leary-Kelly, & Martocchio, 1993), and motivation may be increased when the training content is clearly relevant to the job (Clark, Dobbins, & Ladd, 1993).

Organizational personnel who select people for training can do much to make sure that ability is adequate, and those who conduct training can be straightforward about what trainees can expect and provide frequent, useful feedback. They can also try to make the actual training as interesting, challenging, relevant, and rewarding as the situation will allow. In the last analysis, however, it is the interaction of the trainee's characteristics with the training situation that determines individual training success. Some people will learn from any program; others are unlikely to learn much under any circumstances.

Socialization

Socialization is the process by which newcomers to any group acquire the attitudes, values, and norms necessary to become accepted members of the group. Organizational socialization refers to learning on the part of an individual who is adjusting to a new (or different) role in a particular organization (Louis, 1980). There are two groups to which most organizational newcomers must be socialized. One is the group of people with whom they work. The other is the "group" of the organization itself. Learning the ropes of this larger social system is called orientation.

The process of orientation acquaints newcomers to an organization with its rules, operating procedures, policies, and performance expectations. Organizations with large, formal new employee training programs often make orientation part of the program. Many others accomplish it by means of written employee handbooks that typically cover such diverse topics as the availability of medical insurance plans and the rules for coffee breaks.

Many organizations give orientation responsibility to a new employee's immediate supervisor. This responsibility is often informal, but not always. A formal supervisory orientation checklist is shown in Exhibit 5–9. As is clear from the topics covered in the list, orientation is an introduction process. In most organizations it is also of very brief duration. One exception is the ongoing three-tier employee orientation used by DuPont Merck Pharmaceutical Company (Klein & Taylor, 1994).

DuPont Merck's orientation program, called "orienteering," begins when an employee is hired. A three-member team consisting of a supervisor, an administrative coordinator, and a sponsor work with the new employee to help his or her transition into the new environment. They are assisted in this first tier of orientation by a written training guide that includes an orientation checklist summarizing the duties of each team member.

The second tier of the orientation is a half day of presentations, including videos, a workbook, and handouts, which is scheduled after the newcomer has been on the job for thirty to ninety days. During this program, employees learn how their work units, their jobs, and they as individuals contribute to meeting DuPont Merck's goals. A similar half-day program at the division (rather than organization) level makes up the third tier of the orientation.

The comprehensive orientation program described, which is coordinated and overseen by a corporate orientation programs manager, is the exception rather than the rule. As noted, most organizations make short work of orientation. Furthermore, it has received very little attention in the I/O psychology literature despite the fact that for most newcomers orientation is the first phase of socialization, a process of recognized importance to organizational functioning.

The Importance of Socialization

Katz (1964) lists three types of behaviors that its members must exhibit for an organization to function most effectively. First, employees must stay with the company. Second,

Employee's Name

Discussion Completed
(please check each
individual item)

Exhibit 5–9
A Formal
Orientation List
for Direct
Supervisors

I. Word of welcome   _____

II. Explain overall departmental organization and its relationship to other activities of the company   _____

III. Explain employee's individual contribution to the objectives of the department and his or her starting assignment in broad terms   _____

IV. Discuss job content with employee and give him or her a copy of job description (if available)   _____

V. Explain departmental training program(s) and salary increase practices and procedures   _____

VI. Discuss where the employee lives and transportation facilities   _____

VII. Explain working conditions:

    a. Hours of work, time sheets
    b. Use of employee entrance and elevators
    c. Lunch hours
    d. Coffee breaks, rest periods
    e. Personal telephone calls and mail
    f. Overtime policy and requirements
    g. Paydays and procedures for being paid
    h. Lockers
    i. Other: _____   _____

VIII. Requirements for continuance of employment—explain company standards as to:

    a. Performance of duties
    b. Attendance and punctuality
    c. Handling confidential information
    d. Behavior
    e. General appearance
    f. Wearing of uniform   _____

IX. Introduce new staff members to manager(s) and other supervisors. Special attention should be paid to the person to whom the new employee will be assigned.   _____

X. Release employee to immediate supervisor who will:

    a. Introduce new staff member to fellow workers
    b. Familiarize the employee with his or her workplace
    c. Begin on-the-job training   _____

If not applicable insert N/A in space provided

_____   _____
Employee's Signature   Supervisor's Signature

_____   _____
Date   Division

Form examined for filing:

_____   _____
Date   Personnel Department

From J. Famularo, *Handbook of Modern Personnel Administration.* Copyright 1972 McGraw-Hill. Reprinted by permission.

they must carry out their job tasks dependably, and finally, they must engage in innovative and cooperative behaviors that go beyond job descriptions. There are many factors that influence the extent to which any particular employee exhibits these behaviors. One is the degree to which he or she feels at home, comfortable with job performance, and motivated to help the organization accomplish its goals—that is, the extent to which he or she is effectively socialized to the organization.

A Model of Socialization

Since the role that socialization plays in organizational effectiveness first began to attract attention, a number of I/O psychologists have formulated models of how this process works. Among the more well-known of these are the three-stage early career model (Buchanan, 1977), the three-stage entry model (Porter, Lawler, & Hackman, 1975), the three-stage socialization model (Schein, 1978), and the socialization tactics model (Van Maanen & Schein, 1979). Drawing on this literature, Feldman (1981) proposes the three-stage model shown in Figure 5–4.

In Feldman's model, the three stages of socialization are labeled anticipatory, encounter, and change and acquisition. Each stage has certain goals called socialization tasks.

- *Anticipatory stage.* The potential new employee gets information about the organization, the job, and the extent to which his or her own skills, abilities, needs, and values will fit in.

- *Encounter stage.* The newcomer learns his or her new job tasks, is included into the work group, defines his or her role within the work group, and deals with any conflicts created by being a member of that particular group (intergroup conflict) and of the organization (outside-life conflict).

- *Change and acquisition stage.* The new employee masters his or her job tasks and work roles and satisfactorily adjusts to the work group and the organizational culture. At this point, the newcomer is an insider.

Feldman postulates various direct and indirect relationships between socialization tasks and the job behaviors described by Katz. Innovation and cooperation, for example, depend on successful task mastery and adjustment to work group norms and values (change and acquisition stage). Socialization also has affective (feeling) outcomes for new employees, including feelings of satisfaction and a stronger tendency toward internal work motivation and job involvement.

Socialization as an Ongoing Process

Stage models, such as that depicted in Figure 5–4, have been the classic framework for understanding socialization. Based on their examination of the many such models to be found in the literature, Chao and her colleagues (1994) identify six basic dimensions of organizational socialization.

1. *Performance proficiency.* Learning the tasks involved on the job.

2. *People.* Establishing satisfying, successful work relationships.

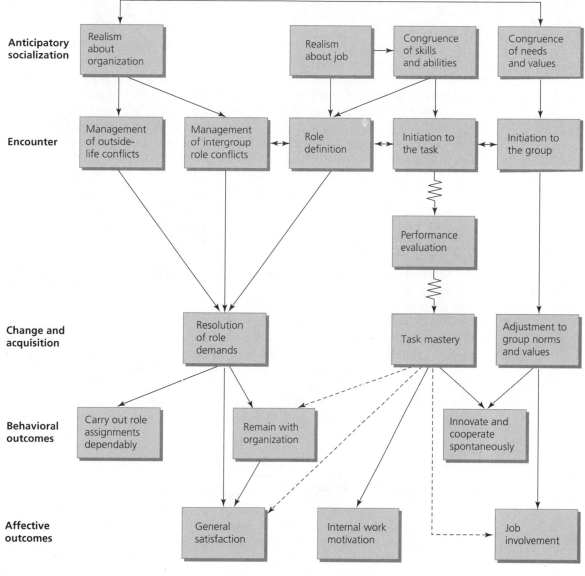

Figure 5–4
A Model of Organizational Socialization

From D. C. Feldman, "The Multiple Socialization of Organization Members." Academy of
Management Review, 1981, 6, 309–318. Copyright 1981 Academy of Management.
Reprinted by permission.

3. *Politics.* Gaining information regarding relationships and power networks
   within the organization.

4. *Language.* Learning the technical language, slang, and jargon unique to the
   organization.

5. *Goals and values.* Understanding the specifics of the organization's particular goals and values.

6. *History.* Learning the traditions, customs, and rituals of the organization.

With one exception (personal relationships), the list is about learning, and much of the current research in the area of socialization is focused on what is learned and how. A general conclusion from these investigations is that organizational newcomers are active seekers of information, not passive sponges soaking up whatever bits and pieces come their way (e.g., Morrison, 1993). Furthermore, important career outcomes seem to be related to the success of various information-seeking strategies (e.g., Ostroff & Kozlowski, 1992).

The idea that people are active participants in their own socialization leads rather naturally to a conceptualization of organizational socialization as a career-long process rather than as an event that either comes to a successful conclusion or does not. In any organization, some people will be exposed to more or different learning opportunities than others. In addition, some people simply learn faster or more efficiently than other people.

Differences in personal characteristics, such as a desire for control over his or her environment, also affect the nature and duration of an employee's search for information about the employing organization (Ashford & Black, 1996). Finally, jobs and organizations change and so do people. Any of these changes can create needs for new learning and resocialization (Louis, 1980).

Looking at socialization as a process rather than an event has stimulated interest in longitudinal studies in which socialization data are collected when employees first enter an organization and then again after some period of time (e.g., Adkins, 1995; Bauer & Green, 1994). One trend to emerge from these investigations is the important role played by insiders, especially supervisors, in socialization (Major, Kozlowski, Chao, & Gardner, 1995).

Mentors and Socialization

The important role current employees play in helping newcomers adjust to an organization is not news. Everyone who has ever worked knows the value of an "old hand," who provides support, information, and assistance and shows a personal interest in the newcomer's job and career success. In I/O psychology, such individuals are called **mentors.** As defined by Wilson and Elman (1990), a mentoring relationship exists when

> . . . an older, more experienced member of an organization takes a junior colleague "under his or her wing," aiding in the organizational socialization of the less experienced person and passing along knowledge gained through years of living within the organization. . . . (p. 88)

Among other findings, research into mentoring suggests that employees (called "protégés") in successful mentoring relationships are able to learn more about practices and issues in the organization than are nonmentored individuals (Ostroff & Kozlowski, 1993). Mentored employees also believe that they have more resources, access to important people, and influence on policy (Fagenson, 1988). Finally, there is evidence that mentored individuals experience greater job satisfaction (Koberg, Boss, Chappell, &

Ringer, 1994) and receive higher salaries (Chao, Walz, & Gardner, 1992) than employees without mentors.

Mentoring has advantages for organizations as well as individuals. In their role as a bridge between insiders and newcomers, mentors can help to strengthen and assure the continuity of organizational culture. They are also in a position to pick up early warning signals of developing problems, such as decreased employee morale, while there is still time to take corrective action. This does not imply that mentors should pass along specific information they receive from protégés in confidence; the idea is mood sensing, not tale bearing.

Although mentoring is clearly important to organizational functioning, it is a fragile process that is difficult to institutionalize. Sears, Roebuck & Company assigns each new sales associate a "buddy," and is pleased so far with the results; such a policy can backfire, however, if the two parties do not hit it off. A formal mentor program can also be less than effective if assigned mentors lack interest or just are not very good in this role (Tannenbaum & Yukl, 1992).

Informal mentoring, in which the participants select one another, is unlikely to suffer the difficulties that can attend formal mentoring, but it often passes by the very employees who might benefit most from having a mentor. Examples of employees who have been found to be left out of mentoring relationships in disproportionate numbers are women (Ragins & Scandura, 1994), individuals with low needs for power and achievement (Fagenson, 1992), and individuals with less favorable performance histories (Olian, Carroll, & Giannantonio, 1993).

The study of mentoring is relatively new, and it is too soon to try to draw firm conclusions about such aspects as formal versus informal mentoring. The matter does raise the more general question, however, of what an organization might do to make the socialization process go more smoothly.

Organizational Activities That Influence Socialization

Three sets of formal organizational activities are known to have particular impact on socialization—screening and selection, training, and performance appraisal. Socialization researchers are moving away from stage models of this process, but in the present context, Feldman's model (Figure 5–4) is a useful frame of reference for illustrating some of these relationships.

Screening, Selection and Socialization

In Chapter 4, the realistic job preview was introduced as one approach to avoiding some of the problems that can go along with individual/organization/job mismatches. The same remarks are relevant to socialization: the more accurate the information given to job applicants, the more effective anticipatory socialization should be.

In Feldman's model, the anticipatory socialization phase is an information-gathering phase; the job applicant must attempt to assess whether he or she will fit into an organization. There seems little doubt that candor on the parts of those doing screening and selection will facilitate this process. To the extent that this candor stimulates unsuited candidates to screen themselves out, fewer problems are likely to occur at later stages of socialization.

Realistic job preview
See pages 91–92

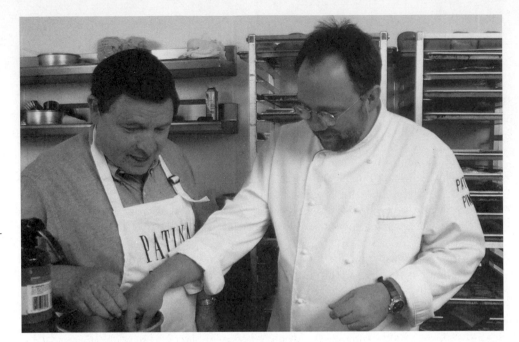

In many organizational settings, a mentor can make it much easier for a new employee to fit in and be successful.

Training and Socialization

Becoming familiar with and mastering job tasks are important parts of the encounter and change/acquisition stages of socialization in Feldman's model, and job training speeds up this process. Training also affects adjustment to the organization (Saks, 1996) and to future co-workers in that it sends messages about the nature of an individual's future work role and the values and standards of the company.

Both anticipatory and encounter socialization are likely to be inhibited if training messages contradict expectations set up earlier. A new employee who is led to expect that his or her value of individualism is supported by the organization may find it more difficult to adjust if the training is routine and "prepackaged." In similar fashion, careless on-the-job training can contradict expectations expressed by supervisors or others for high performance standards.

Performance Appraisal and Socialization

With regard to socialization, the major role of performance appraisal is to help a new employee through to mastery of his or her work role and job; in Feldman's model, this is a task of the change and acquisition stage of socialization. Early and frequent appraisals are important, both to continue the training process and to reinforce performance expectations. Performance appraisal can also affect a new employee's socialization into a work group.

The effect that performance appraisal has on work group socialization depends somewhat on the nature of the group and its informal performance standards. A new employee who receives average evaluations in training may have difficulty finding acceptance in a skilled work group that views itself as elite, for example. On the other hand, a highly motivated performance hotshot may not fit into a group that holds indifferent performance standards.

Screening and selection, training, and performance appraisal have been singled out in the discussion of ways to facilitate effective socialization only because these activities are under the control of formal organizational policy. Other factors that play an important role can be controlled in a limited way or not at all. Among these variables are the behavior of a newcomer's co-workers and the newcomer's own understanding and ability to deal with the issues of socialization (Jones, 1983). Successful socialization, like all behavioral phenomena, must be understood as a complex interaction of individual and environmental factors.

At Issue

Is the Business of American Business Education?

Ask most people what they think the new employees of a particular organization are being taught in that organization's training program and they will probably say something along the lines of "how to do a job." Often this will be the correct answer, but the odds that it will be incorrect, or at least incomplete, are steadily rising.

The U.S. Department of Education estimates that nearly one out of every seven American adults is functionally illiterate. Supposedly, they have learned to read, write, and count, but these skills are so poor as to be virtually useless in practice. An additional 20 million are considered marginally literate, barely getting by as long as tasks are familiar and simple. These dismal figures are reflected in the results of a mid-1990s survey by the American Management Association, which reported that almost half of the job applicants to the companies polled failed to demonstrate basic math skills, and almost one-third lacked the necessary reading skills to do the jobs for which they were applying.

As a result of the many changes that have taken place in the world of work during the past two decades, workers with inadequate educational skills are being pushed downward into ever more poorly paying jobs. At the same time, organizations are becoming increasingly desperate for employees who can do (or be trained for) jobs using today's technologies and/or working directly with customers.

Desperate problems, someone said, call for desperate measures, and more organizations bite the bullet and go into the remedial education business every year.

- Polaroid Corporation spent almost three-quarters of a million dollars providing literacy training for employees.

- Valmont Industries, a maker of steel products, began an ongoing workplace literacy program after it discovered that many of its employees could not read or write well enough to perform their jobs satisfactorily.

- Domino's Pizza teaches the basic arithmetic and reading needed to make pizza dough in conjunction with training in actual dough making.

- Will-Burt, Inc., a machine parts manufacturer, set up classrooms in the plant and hired professors from a nearby university to teach required classes in reading, basic math, and other subjects to its employees.

- Sea-First Bank of Seattle pays for employees to attend English classes.

Some years ago now, Miller (1988) wrote:

> If current . . . trends continue, American business will have to hire a million new workers a year who can't read, write, or count. Teaching them how, and absorbing the lost productivity while they're learning, will cost the industry $25 billion a year for as long as it takes. (p. 47)

The then-current trends did continue and the effects are being felt big time. Organizations are taking on the challenge because they see no choice, but their efforts are only a drop in the bucket and such programs are not a substitute for an adequate basic education. Furthermore, the costs inevitably show up in the cost of the goods and/or services produced by the organizations. How long can we afford it? What will it take to get this enormous social problem attacked head-on, actively, and vigorously by the organizations whose business *is* education?

Summary

Recruiting, screening and selection, and placement bring new employees into an organization. Training and socialization change them from newcomers to insiders. Job training is a structured learning experience intended to transform abilities into specific job skills. Employee development training helps individual employees overcome problems, identify career goals, and progress toward these goals.

Socialization is a broad concept covering all of the ways by which newcomers learn about and adjust to procedures, policies, expectations, norms, values, and attitudes of both the organization itself and particular work groups in it. It is a multidimensional, long-term process that is accomplished through a variety of channels, including mentoring relationships with established organizational insiders.

Questions for Review and Discussion

1. Evaluate a class you are currently taking in terms of the Big Three basic criteria for human learning. Your answer should demonstrate that you understand the criteria.

2. Give an example of a course you have taken in high school, college, or elsewhere in which a nonparticipative instructional method would be appropriate, and explain why. Do the same for individual and group participative instructional methods. (The courses in question do not actually have to have been taught in this way.)

3. Outline a plan for evaluating the training in an organization, showing that you understand the issues in making decisions about such evaluation. You may make whatever assumptions you like, but these should be stated.

4. Use the example of an American manager sent to manage a plant in a South American country to demonstrate that you understand the concept of employee socialization and why it is important to organizational effectiveness.

5. Show that you understand the concept and importance of a mentor by describing a personal experience in which you have been either a mentor or a protégé in one of the following settings: work, school, church, club, sports team, or other organization.

Key Terms

employee development

feedback

instructional methods

mentor/mentoring

positive reinforcement

simulation training

socialization

task analysis

training

training evaluation

training sites

References

Ackerman, P. L. (1992). Predicting individual differences in complex skill acquisition: Dynamics of ability determinants. *Journal of Applied Psychology, 77,* 598–614.

Adkins, C. L. (1995). Previous work experience and organizational socialization: A longitudinal examination. *Academy of Management Journal, 38,* 839–862.

Andrews, D. H. (1988). The relationship between simulators, training devices, and learning: A behavioral view. *Educational Technology, 1,* 48–53.

Annett, J. (1994). The learning of motor skills: Sports science and ergonomics perspectives. *Ergonomics, 37,* 5–16.

Arvey, R. D., & Cole, D. A. (1989). Evaluating change due to training. In I. L. Goldstein (Ed.), *Training and development in organizations.* San Francisco: Jossey-Bass.

Ashford, S. J., & Black, J. S. (1996). Proactivity during organizational entry: The role of desire for control. *Journal of Applied Psychology, 81,* 199–214.

Baldwin, T. T., & Ford, J. K. (1988). Transfer of training: A review and directions for future research. *Personnel Psychology, 41,* 63–105.

Balzer, W. K., Sulsky, L. M., Hammer, L. B., & Sumner, K. E. (1992). Task information, cognitive information, or functional validity information: Which components of cognitive feedback affect performance? *Organizational Behavior and Human Decision Processes, 53,* 35–54.

Bandura, A. (1969). *Principles of behavior modification.* New York: Holt, Rinehart & Winston.

Bandura, A. (1977). *Social learning theory.* Englewood Cliffs, NJ: Prentice-Hall.

Bass, B. M., & Vaughan, J. A. (1966). *Training in industry: The management of learning.* Belmont, CA: Wadsworth.

Bauer, T. N., & Green, S. G. (1994). Effect of newcomer involvement in work-related activities: A longitudinal study of socialization. *Journal of Applied Psychology, 79,* 211–223.

Bayer, G. A., & Gerstein, L. H. (1990). EAP referrals and troubled employees: An analogue study of supervisors' decisions. *Journal of Vocational Behavior, 36,* 304–319.

Best, J. B. (1989). *Cognitive psychology.* St. Paul: West.

Briggs, P. (1990). Do they know what they're doing? An evaluation of word-processor users' implicit and explicit task-relevant knowledge and its role in self-directed learning. *International Journal of Man-Machine Studies, 32,* 385–398.

Buchanan, B. (1977). Building organizational commitment: The socialization of managers in work organizations. *Administrative Science Quarterly, 19,* 533–546.

Cairo, P. C. (1983). Counseling in industry: A selected review of the literature. *Personnel Psychology, 36,* 1–18.

Campion, M. A., Cheraskin, L., & Stevens, M. J. (1994). Career-related antecedents and outcomes of job rotation. *Academy of Management Journal, 37,* 1518–1542.

Carnevale, A. P., Gainer, L. J., & Villet, J. (1990). *Training in America: The organization and strategic role of training.* San Francisco: Jossey-Bass.

Carnevale, A. P., & Schulz, E. R. (1990). Evaluation practices. *Training and Development Journal, 44,* 23, 29.

Cascio, W. F. (1989). Using utility analysis to assess training outcomes. In I. L. Goldstein (Ed.), *Training and development in organizations.* San Francisco: Jossey-Bass.

Chao, G. T., O'Leary-Kelly, A. M., Wolf, S., Klein, H. J., & Gardner, P. D. (1994). Organizational socialization: Its content and consequences. *Journal of Applied Psychology, 79,* 730–743.

Chao, G. T., Walz, P. M., & Gardner, P. D. (1992). Formal and informal mentorships: A comparison on mentoring functions and contrast with nonmentored counterparts. *Personnel Psychology, 45,* 619–636.

Clark, C. S., Dobbins, G. H., & Ladd, R. T. (1993). Exploratory field study of training motivation: Influence of involvement, credibility, and transfer climate. *Group and Organization Management, 18,* 292–307.

Davis, K. (1972). *Human relations and organizational behavior* (4th ed.). New York: McGraw-Hill.

Deitchman, S. J. (1990). Further explorations in estimating the military value of training. *IDA Paper P-2317.* Alexandria, VA: Institute for Defense Analysis.

Driskell, J. E., Copper, C., & Moran, A. (1994). Does mental practice enhance performance? *Journal of Applied Psychology, 79,* 481–492.

Driver, M. J. (1979). Career concepts and career management in organizations. In C. L. Cooper (Ed.), *Behavioral problems in organizations.* Englewood Cliffs, NJ: Prentice-Hall.

Earley, P. C., Northcraft, G. B., Lee, C., & Lituchy, T. R. (1990). Impact of process and outcome feedback on the relation of goal setting to task performance. *Academy of Management Journal, 33,* 87–105.

Endsley, M. R., & Kris, E. O. (1995). The out-of-the-loop performance problem and level of control in automation. *Human Factors, 37,* 381–394.

Fagenson, E. A. (1988). The power of a mentor: Protégés' and nonprotégés' perceptions of their own power in organizations. *Group and Organization Studies, 13,* 182–194.

Fagenson, E. A. (1992). Mentoring: Who needs it? A comparison of protégés' and nonprotégés' needs for power, achievement, affiliation, and autonomy. *Journal of Vocational Behavior, 41,* 48–60.

Famularo, J. (1972). *Handbook of modern personnel administration.* New York: McGraw-Hill.

Feldman, D. C. (1981). The multiple socialization of organization members. *Academy of Management Review, 6,* 309–318.

Feldman, D. C. (1989). Socialization, resocialization, and training: Reframing the research agenda. In I. L. Goldstein (Ed.), *Training and development in organizations.* San Francisco: Jossey-Bass.

Fishbein, M., & Stasson, M. (1990). The role of desires, self-perceptions, and perceived control in the prediction of training session attendance. *Journal of Applied Social Psychology, 20,* 173–198.

Ford, J. K., & Noe, R. A. (1987). Self-assessed training needs: The effects of attitudes toward training, managerial level, and function. *Personnel Psychology, 40,* 39–54.

Fox, C. J., & Sulzer-Azaroff, B. (1989). The effectiveness of two different sources of feedback on staff teaching of fire evacuation skills. *Journal of Organizational Behavior Management, 10,* 19–35.

Fredericksen, N. (1962). Factors in in-basket performance. *Psychological Monographs, 76* (Whole No. 541).

Gagné, R. M. (1962). Military training and principles of learning. *American Psychologist, 17,* 83–91.

Gale, N., Golledge, R. G., Pellegrino, J. W., & Doherty, S. (1990). The acquisition and integration of route knowledge in an unfamiliar neighborhood. *Journal of Environmental Psychology, 10,* 3–25.

Gist, M., Rosen, B., & Schwoerer, C. (1988). The influence of training method and trainee age on the acquisition of computer skills. *Personnel Psychology, 41,* 255–265.

Gold, L. (1981). Job instruction: Four steps to success. *Training and Development Journal, 35,* 28–32.

Goldstein, I. L., Braverman, E. P., & Goldstein, H. W. (1991). The use of needs assessment in training systems design. In K. Wexley (Ed.), *ASPA/BNA handbook of human resource management: Vol. 5. Developing human resources.* Washington, DC: BNA Books.

Harrison, J. K. (1992). Individual and combined effects of behavior modeling and the cultural assimilator in cross-cultural management training. *Journal of Applied Psychology, 77,* 952–962.

Hartley, L. R., Higgins, T., MacLeod, C., & Arnold, P. K. (1990). Training for an agricultural discrimination task. *Applied Ergonomics, 21,* 152–156.

Hicks, W. D., & Klimoski, R. J. (1987). Entry into training programs and its effects on training outcomes: A field experiment. *Academy of Management Journal, 30,* 542–552.

Howard, G. S., & Dailey, P. R. (1979). Response-shift bias: A source of contamination of self-report measures. *Journal of Applied Psychological Measurement, 64,* 144–150.

Howell, W. C. (1993). Engineering psychology in a changing world. *Annual Review of Psychology, 44,* 231–263.

Howell, W. C., & Cooke, N. J. (1989). Training the human information processor: A review of cognitive models. In I. L. Goldstein (Ed.), *Training and development in organizations.* San Francisco: Jossey-Bass.

Jackson, S. E., & Schuler, R. S. (1990). Human resource planning: Challenges for industrial/organizational psychologists. *American Psychologist, 45,* 223–239.

Jones, G. R. (1983). Psychological orientation and the process of organizational socialization: An interactionist perspective. *Academy of Management Review, 8,* 464–474.

Karl, K. A., O'Leary-Kelly, A. M., & Martocchio, J. J. (1993). The impact of feedback and self-efficacy on performance in training. *Journal of Organizational Behavior, 14,* 379–394.

Katz, D. (1964). The motivational basis of organizational behavior. *Behavioral Science, 9,* 131–146.

Klein, C. S., & Taylor, J. (1994). Employee orientation is an ongoing process at the DuPont Merck Pharmaceutical Co. *Personnel Journal, 73,* 67.

Kleiss, J. A., & Hubbard, D. C. (1993). Effects of three types of flight simulator visual scene detail on detection of altitude change. *Human Factors, 35,* 653–671.

Koberg, C. S., Boss, R. W., Chappell, D., & Ringer, R. C. (1994). Correlates and consequences of protégé mentoring in a large hospital. *Group and Organization Management, 19,* 219–239.

Komaki, J., Heinzmann, T., & Lawson, L. (1980). Effect of training and feedback: Component analysis of a behavioral safety program. *Journal of Applied Psychology, 65,* 261–270.

Koubek, R. J., Clarkston, T. P., & Calvez, V. (1994). The training of knowledge structures for manufacturing tasks: An empirical study. *Ergonomics, 37,* 765–780.

Kozak, J. J., Hancock, P. A., Arthur, E. J., & Chrysler, S. T. (1993). Transfer of training from virtual reality. *Ergonomics, 36,* 777–784.

Kraiger, K., Ford, J. K., & Salas, E. (1993). Application of cognitive, skill-based, and affective theories of learning to new methods of training evaluation. *Journal of Applied Psychology, 78,* 311–328.

Laker, D. R. (1990). Dual dimensionality of training transfer. *Human Resource Development Quarterly, 1,* 209–223.

Leiter, M. P., Dorward, A. L., & Cox, T. (1994). The social context of skill enhancement: Training decisions of occupational health nurses. *Human Relations, 47,* 1233–1249.

Louis, M. R. (1980). Surprise and sense-making: What newcomers experience in entering unfamiliar organizational settings. *Administrative Science Quarterly, 25*, 226–251.

Major, D. A., Kozlowski, S. W. J., Chao, G. T, & Gardner, P. D. (1995). A longitudinal investigation of newcomer expectations, early socialization outcomes, and the moderating effects of role development factors. *Journal of Applied Psychology, 80*, 418–431.

Mallory, W. J. (1981). Simulation for task practice in technical training. *Training and Development Journal, 35*, 12–20.

Masi, D. A., & Friedland, S. J. (1988). EAP actions and options. *Personnel Journal, 67*, 60–67.

Mathieu, J. E., & Leonard, R. L., Jr. (1987). Applying utility concepts to a training program in supervisory skills: A time-based approach. *Academy of Management Journal, 30*, 316–335.

Maurer, T. J., & Tarulli, B. A. (1994). Investigation of perceived environment, perceived outcome, and person variables in relationship to voluntary development activity by employees. *Journal of Applied Psychology, 79*, 3–14.

McGehee, W., & Thayer, P. W. (1963). *Training in business and industry.* New York: Wiley.

Mezoff, B. (1981). How to get accurate self-reports of training outcomes. *Training and Development Journal, 35*, 56–61.

Miller, W. H. (1988, July 4). Employers wrestle with "dumb" kids. *Industry Week,* p. 47.

Milne, S. H., Blum, T. C., & Roman, P. M. (1994). Factors influencing employees' propensity to use an employee assistance program. *Personnel Psychology, 47*, 123–145.

Mitchell, T. R., Hopper, H., Daniels, D., George-Falvy, J., & James, L. R. (1994). Predicting self-efficacy and performance during skill acquisition. *Journal of Applied Psychology, 79*, 506–517.

Montebello, A. R., & Haga, M. (1994). To justify training, test, test again. *Personnel Journal, 73*, 83–87.

Morrison, E. W. (1993). Longitudinal study of the effects of information seeking on newcomer socialization. *Journal of Applied Psychology, 78*, 173–183.

Morrison, R. F., & Brantner, T. M. (1992). What enhances or inhibits learning a new job: A basic career issue. *Journal of Applied Psychology, 77*, 926–940.

Moses, J. L. (1978). Behavior modeling for managers. *Human Factors, 20*, 225–232.

Noe, R. A., & Schmitt, N. (1986). The influence of trainee attitudes on training effectiveness: Test of a model. *Personnel Psychology, 39*, 497–523.

Olian, J. D., Carroll, S. J., & Giannantonio, C. M. (1993). Mentor reactions to protégés: An experiment with managers. *Journal of Vocational Behavior, 43*, 266–278.

Ostroff, C., & Kozlowski, S. W. (1992). Organizational socialization as a learning process: The role of information acquisition. *Personnel Psychology, 45*, 849–874.

Ostroff, C., & Kozlowski, S. W. (1993). The role of mentoring in the information gathering processes of newcomers during early organizational socialization. *Journal of Vocational Behavior, 42*, 170–183.

Padmos, P., & Milders, M. V. (1992). Quality criteria for simulator images: A literature review. *Human Factors, 34*, 727–748.

Porter, L. W., Lawler, E. E., III., & Hackman, J. R. (1975). *Behavior in organizations.* New York: McGraw-Hill.

Pressey, S. L. (1926). A simple apparatus which gives tests and scores—and teaches. *School Sociology, 23*, 323–376.

Quiñones, M. A. (1995). Pretraining context effects: Training assignment as feedback. *Journal of Applied Psychology, 80*, 226–238.

Ragins, B. R., & Scandura, T. A. (1994). Gender differences in expected outcomes of mentoring relationships. *Academy of Management Journal, 37*, 957–971.

Ree, M. J., Caretta, T. R., & Teachout, M. S. (1995). Role of ability and prior job knowledge in complex training performance. *Journal of Applied Psychology, 80*, 721–730.

Robertson, I. T. (1990). Behavior modeling: Its record and potential in training and development. *British Journal of Management, 1,* 117–125.

Rouiller, J. Z., & Goldstein, I. L. (1993). The relationship between organizational transfer climate and positive transfer of training. *Human Resource Development Quarterly, 4,* 377–390.

Sackett, P. R., & Mullen, E. J. (1993). Beyond formal experimental design: Towards an expanded view of the training evaluation process. *Personnel Psychology, 46,* 613–627.

Saks, A. M. (1996). The relationship between the amount and helpfulness of entry training and work outcomes. *Human Relations, 49,* 429–451.

Schein, E. H. (1978). *Career dynamics: Matching individual and organization needs.* Reading, MA: Addison-Wesley.

Sellers, P. (1988). How IBM teaches techies to sell. *Fortune, 117,* 141–146.

Simon, S. J., & Werner, J. M. (1996). Computer training through behavior modeling, self-paced, and instructional approaches: A field experiment. *Journal of Applied Psychology, 81,* 648–659.

Sims, R. R. (1993). Evaluating public sector training programs. *Public Personnel Management, 22,* 591–615.

Smith, M. L. (1988). Social work in the workplace: An overview. In G. M. Gould and M. L. Smith (Eds.), *Social work in the workplace: Practice and principles.* New York: Springer.

Solomon, R. L. (1949). An extension of control group design. *Psychological Bulletin, 46,* 137–150.

Super, D., & Minor, F. J. (1987). Career development and planning in organizations. In B. M. Bass and P. J. D. Drenth (Eds.), *Advances in organizational psychology: An international review.* Newbury Park, CA: Sage.

Tannenbaum, S. I., Cannon-Bowers, J. A., Salas, E., & Mathieu, J. E. (1993). Factors that influence training effectiveness: A conceptual model and longitudinal analysis. *U.S. Naval Training Systems Center Technical Reports,* Technical Report 93-011.

Tannenbaum, S. I., & Yukl, G. (1992). Training and development in work organizations. *Annual Review of Psychology, 43,* 399–441.

Thayer, P. W. (1989). A historical perspective on training. In I. L. Goldstein (Ed.), *Training and development in organzations.* San Francisco: Jossey-Bass.

Thornton, G. C., III, & Cleveland, J. N. (1990). Developing managerial talent through simulation. *American Psychologist, 45,* 190–199.

Van Maanen, J., & Schein, E. H. (1979). Toward a theory of organizational socialization. In B. M. Staw (Ed.), *Research in organizational behavior* (Vol. 1). Greenwich, CT: JAI.

Veiga, J. F., & Yanouzas, J. N. (1979). *The dynamics of organization theory: Gaining a macro perspective.* St. Paul: West.

Weitz, J., & Adler, S. (1973). The optimal use of simulation. *Journal of Applied Psychology, 58,* 219–224.

Wilson, J. A., & Elman, N. S. (1990). Organizational benefits of mentoring. *Academy of Management Executive, 4,* 88–94.

6

Employee Motivation and Job Satisfaction

PSYCHOLOGY AT WORK—*PepsiCo Shares Power and Wealth with Workers*

PSYCHOLOGY AT WORK

PepsiCo Shares Power and Wealth with Workers

Excerpted from D. Anfuso, "PepsiCo Shares Power and Wealth with Workers." *Personnel Journal*, June 1995, *74*, 42–49. Copyright 1995 ACC Communications. All rights reserved. Reprinted with permission.

When truck driver Buck Robuck set out to deliver pizza ingredients, he deliberately ignored the computer-generated map his company had supplied him, bypassing the map's highlighted interstates for back roads and side streets. Rather than disciplining Robuck for insubordination, however, his employer, PepsiCo Inc., praised him. Robuck, in choosing the route he knew would save him time and his company money, acted just the way the Purchase, New York–based company wants each of its nearly 500,000 workers in 195 countries to act—like a business owner.

"The ownership mentality is critical to the success of our business," says J. Roger King, senior vice president of personnel for PepsiCo. . . . And for [employees] to take ownership, the company must "trust them to do that and have a way of motivating them to do that."

The motivation comes in the form of SharePower, the first broad-based stock-option program to be offered by a large company. . . .

. . . the concept works. King says that . . . workers tell the HR [human relations] staff that they like their jobs. "When we ask them why they like their jobs, they say it's because they have responsibility and a chance to do their job on their own."

BY GOING the extra mile for giant PepsiCo, Buck Robuck and his fellow employees help save the company money and increase its profits—and their own if they are participants in the employee stock option program called SharePower. As a bonus, most employees also enjoy their work; the "ownership culture" created by PepsiCo gives them a feeling of being part of the company as well as an unusual opportunity to exercise their own judgment and be creative on even the most routine of jobs.

Organizations often use incentives to increase employee effort, or work motivation. This strategy works best when the incentives are valued by the employees concerned, but different people have different ideas about what is rewarding. The PepsiCo program is a mix of monetary incentives (the stock-option plan), a work environment that emphasizes team spirit, and the opportunity for employees to exercise their own judgments and make their work more interesting. This something-for-everyone approach appears to be increasing job satisfaction as well as work motivation.

The recruiting, screening, selecting, and training examined in other chapters are activities designed to produce "can do" employees, but job performance also has a "will do," or motivational, component. The role of job satisfaction in this picture is still a matter for debate, but most theories of job satisfaction are drawn directly from theories of motivation and the convention of treating these topics together is followed here.

The Role of Work Motivation in Performance

The various forces that produce, direct, and maintain effort expended in behavior are known collectively as **motivation**. These forces cannot be seen directly; only the behavioral results are observable. If someone takes a job in sales and works very hard at selling, a co-worker might say that this individual is motivated to become a successful salesperson. In this case, the co-worker is inferring something about an internal state (motivation) on the basis of behavior (hard work).

Inference
See pages 35–43

When people work hard and perform their jobs well, it often is inferred that their work motivation is high. When people do not perform well or do not seem to be trying very hard, the assumption is the opposite—they are not motivated. Such inferences are only partially correct at best. Motivation is but one of the variables that determine work behavior. In many cases, it is not even the most important one.

One of the more obvious situations in which motivation is relatively unimportant as a determinant of job performance occurs when an individual lacks the basic ability to do the task at hand. A high level of motivation may compensate somewhat for limited ability, but it cannot make up for it entirely. Empirical data collected by I/O psychologists over the years have never left much room for doubt that (speaking generally about people who work) ability is the *single* most important factor explaining differences in job performance.

Motivation can also be less important than environmental factors in determining job performance. Some work is designed deliberately so as to minimize the role of employee effort. Some effort is required, but more effort can improve performance only up to the limit set by the technical aspects of job design. In other cases, employee effort may be of little consequence as a determinant of performance because work objectives are not clear or because there are obstacles to good performance, such as insufficient information or outdated work aids.

None of this is to say that motivation is unimportant, only that it is seldom *the* most important determinant of work performance. Nevertheless, it is important enough to be of great concern to those who have managerial positions in organizations. Interest in "how to motivate people" is always high, as evidenced by the continuing popularity of seminars, workshops, books, tapes, and films on the subject.

The practical problems of motivation are of interest to I/O psychologists as well, but they look for solutions in a different way. They believe that understanding how to cope with motivation problems begins with understanding the forces that produce, direct, and maintain effort—that is, with developing a viable theory of motivation. There are many such theories. There are also many ways to group, or classify, them (Katzell & Thompson, 1990). The grouping used here is simple and suits the purpose better than alternatives, but to date no one method of classification has gained general acceptance.

One of the oldest and most enduring approaches to the study of motivation rests on the premise that behavior is driven (motivated) by basic human needs. A related hypothesis is that certain personality traits are important determinants of work effort. Both needs and personality characteristics are individual difference variables that cannot be observed directly; as with motivation itself, they are inferred from observed behavior.

Despite the fact that needs and personality traits cannot be observed directly, most psychologists believe that both constructs are stable enough to be measured by tests developed for the purpose. They also believe that people with particular score patterns on such tests are inclined, or disposed, to behave in predictable ways. Ideas about motivation that focus on needs or personality characteristics, then, are discussed here as *dispositional* theories of motivation.

To focus on needs or personality in the search for the forces that produce, direct, and maintain effort is to focus on person rather than environment variables. The person is also at the center of another group of theories about motivation that emphasize decision-making processes and the associated factors that affect decisions to put forth effort (or not) at work. These *cognitive* theories of motivation are quite different from dispositional theories in emphasis, complexity, and implications. In turn, both groups of theories are quite different from the third major theoretical approach.

Variable
See pages 25–26

Determinant
See page 41

The reinforcement model of motivation is based on the premise that effort (motivation) is determined by whether effort in a similar situation has been rewarded (reinforced) in the past. To put it another way, behavior is shaped by its consequences. In a work setting, most of the consequences of behavior originate in the work environment, especially the social environment of co-workers, supervisors, and subordinates. The *reinforcement* model of work motivation, then, places emphasis on environment rather than person variables.

Dispositional Theories of Work Motivation

Dispositional theories of motivation identify individual characteristics as the source of the forces that produce, direct, and maintain effort expended in particular behaviors. **Need theories,** based on the premise that people exert effort in behaviors that allow them to fill deficiencies in their lives, make up the largest number of these theories. By far the best-known theoretical statement falling into this category is that of Abraham Maslow (1943).

Maslow's Need Hierarchy

Maslow was a clinical psychologist. On the basis of his experience as a practicing clinician, he postulated that people have a common set of five needs that can be arranged in a hierarchy of importance, as shown in Figure 6–1. The most basic needs, the ones that people must satisfy first, are the physiological needs; these are followed in importance by safety, social, and esteem needs. At the top of the hierarchy is a postulated need for self-fulfillment.

According to Maslow's theory, each of the needs shown in Figure 6–1 must be satisfied before the next motivates behavior; in a work setting, this means that people are exerting effort in order to fill the lowest unsatisfied needs. Someone just starting out may be working for money to pay off educational debts and to provide food and shelter (meet physiological and safety needs). He or she would be expected to work hard for a raise in pay because this would help meet these needs more fully. Someone else may be working primarily for companionship and a sense of belonging (social needs), and a raise would not be as motivating.

Maslow's theory allows for considerable variation in where people stand on the hierarchy, but attempts to apply the theory in work settings have focused almost exclusively on upper-level need fulfillment (self-actualization). The belief is that people will expend more effort on jobs that are interesting and challenging and allow them more personal control. The excerpt in Psychology at Work that opens this chapter would seem to lend support to this proposition. Care must be exercised in making such an inference, however.

PepsiCo does provide employees with the opportunity to be innovative and to exercise more control over their work. It also offers them substantial monetary incentives for helping to make the company more profitable through this innovation and control. As is often the case where motivation is concerned, it is difficult to draw any conclusions about the relative importance of these factors to the results achieved without much more information.

Maslow's theory was published well over a half century ago. It excited considerable research interest at the time, but this interest died out almost entirely some years ago due

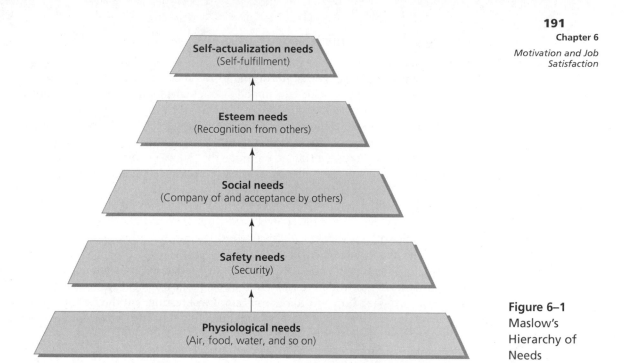

Figure 6–1
Maslow's Hierarchy of Needs

to persistent nonsupport for its basic propositions (see Wahba & Bridwell, 1976). Among practicing managers, students, and many management consultants, however, "Maslow's triangle" has been very influential.

Alderfer's ERG Theory

A theory of work motivation based on Maslow's need hierarchy, but incorporating an important change, was proposed by Alderfer (1969, 1972). ERG theory hypothesizes three sets of needs ranging from most to least concrete (basic). These needs—existence (E), relatedness (R), and growth (G)—are essentially a rearrangement of Maslow's hierarchy, but the rigid ordering of that hierarchy is not part of ERG theory.

In Maslow's conception, an individual's primary effort is expended in behaviors that satisfy the lowest level of unsatisfied needs. Once these have been fulfilled, they no longer motivate the individual; until then, they are the major driving force behind his or her behavior. According to ERG theory, if efforts to satisfy needs at one level are continually frustrated, the individual may regress (fall back) to behavior that meets more concrete needs. An employee unable to meet personal growth needs on his or her job might settle for performing it just well enough to stay employed and meet lower social (relatedness) needs.

It is still possible to find reports of research investigations originating in Alderfer's theory of work motivation in the I/O psychology literature (e.g., Fox, Scott, & Donohue, 1993). Speaking generally, however, ERG theory has suffered the fate of other theories based on Maslow's hierarchy of needs; evidence supporting them is just too difficult to come by. Another theory with the same problem is Herzberg's two-factor theory.

Herzberg's Two-Factor Theory

Herzberg's (1966) two-factor theory of motivation is based on a division of Maslow's hierarchy into upper and lower needs. According to Herzberg, only conditions that allow people to fill upper-level needs for esteem and self-actualization increase work motivation. An organization must make it possible for employees to meet lower-level needs through work so as to keep them from leaving the organization, but being able to meet these needs does not influence their work motivation.

In the two-factor theory, working conditions that allow people to meet upper-level needs are called *motivators.* Among the motivator factors identified by Herzberg are achievement, recognition, responsibility, opportunity to advance, and interesting work. These factors, according to the theory, affect job satisfaction and lead to greater work motivation. Conditions relevant to lower-level needs include type of supervision, company policies, relations with co-workers, physical working conditions, and pay. These *hygiene factors* affect job dissatisfaction (not satisfaction).

Like Maslow's hierarchy of needs, Herzberg's two-factor theory stimulated a significant amount of work motivation research in the years following its appearance. The theory as such has not stood up well to rigorous empirical testing, but the basic motivator-hygiene dichotomy is the foundation of what is currently the most important theoretical statement of a psychological or motivational approach to job design.

A motivational approach to job design emphasizes the importance of design decisions that create meaningful and satisfactory work. Drawing on a line of research extending back some 15 years (Hackman & Lawler, 1971; Herzberg, Mausner, & Snyderman, 1959; Turner & Lawrence, 1965), Hackman and Oldham (1976) identified what they believe are the five basic characteristics (called core dimensions) of such work.

1. *Skill variety.* Jobs that require a variety of different skills are more meaningful than those that require only one or a few skills.

2. *Task identity.* Jobs that constitute a whole piece of work are more meaningful than those that consist of some portion of the whole job.

3. *Task significance.* Jobs that have an identifiable importance to others are more meaningful than those that do not.

4. *Autonomy.* Jobs that allow a person independence, freedom, and decision-making authority with respect to job performance are more meaningful than those that do not.

5. *Job feedback.* Jobs that provide built-in feedback about employee performance are more meaningful than those that do not.

The five core job dimensions (motivator factors in Herzberg's theory) are theorized to affect employee behaviors and attitudes by creating three critical psychological states in the mind of the job holder. Skill variety, task identity, and task significance contribute to experienced meaningfulness of the job, the belief that one's work is important and worthwhile. Autonomy is believed to lead to responsibility for work outcomes, and feedback to knowledge of results for the individual concerned. These relationships are seen in the job characteristics model, shown in Figure 6–2.

The three critical psychological states in the job characteristics model are believed to be necessary to bring about the desired personal and work outcomes of increased motivation, work quality, job satisfaction, and decreased absenteeism and turnover. These relationships, as well as those between the job dimensions and the psychological states, are

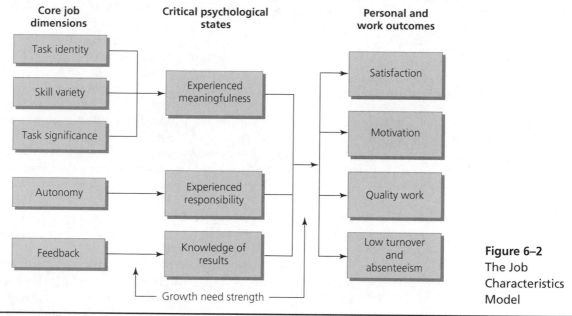

Figure 6–2
The Job Characteristics Model

Core job dimensions | Critical psychological states | Personal and work outcomes

Task identity
Skill variety
Task significance
Autonomy
Feedback

Experienced meaningfulness
Experienced responsibility
Knowledge of results

Satisfaction
Motivation
Quality work
Low turnover and absenteeism

Growth need strength

Based on the discussion by J. R. Hackman and G. R. Oldham, "Motivation Through the Design of Work: A Test of a Theory." *Organizational Behavior and Human Performance,* 1976, *16,* 250–279.

moderated by growth need strength (GNS). GNS is an individual difference variable reflecting the extent to which a person wants to be able to learn and grow on the job.

According to the job characteristics model, a job high on the five motivating core dimensions is more likely to generate positive effects for employees who are high in GNS than for people who see work primarily as a way to make a living. Environmental variables are also important. If the desirable outcomes are to occur, the context of the job must be satisfactory (Hackman & Oldham, 1980). Context is made up of the elements that surround a job and the employee but are not related directly to getting a job done. These elements include amount of pay, level of benefits, and quality of supervision (hygiene factors in Herzberg's theory).

Considered as a whole, research evidence related to the job characteristics model does not contradict the model's basic predictions, even if it does not strongly confirm them. Part of this ambiguity stems from problems with measuring the extent to which jobs have the motivating characteristics. This issue is examined in Chapter 8, along with a broader examination of the tenets of the motivational approach to job design.

McClelland's Need for Achievement Theory

The need for achievement (n'Ach) is hypothesized to be a learned need that either is or is not developed in childhood. According to McClelland (1961), people with a need for achievement will put more effort into work than people without this need (other things being equal). This motivating desire for achievement is balanced against a desire to avoid

Hypothesis
See page 25

failure, however, so behavior may be directed at goals of intermediate, rather than high, difficulty (Atkinson & Feather, 1966).

A unique feature of the n'Ach theory of work motivation is the hypothesis that people who have a low level of this need can be trained to develop it (McClelland & Winter, 1969). Alternatively, it may develop in a work context as people experience the benefits of achievement firsthand. In one well-known study of airline telephone reservation representatives, for example, achievement motivation was found to be related to performance four to eight months after training, but not within the first three months on the job (Helmreich, Sawin, & Carsrud, 1986).

The need for achievement theory of work motivation has been more successful from an empirical standpoint than need theories based on Maslow's hypothesis. There does seem to be a relationship between measures of this need and certain work behaviors, and this remains a moderately active area of I/O psychology research (e.g., Cassidy & Lynn, 1989; Johnson & Perlow, 1992; Medcof & Wegener, 1992). In fairness, however, it should be mentioned that despite its label, this approach is not truly representative of need theories of motivation.

The idea that people exercise some selectivity of activity based on the perceived probability of success in any given situation sets McClelland's theory apart from other need theories, as does the idea that people can be trained to have a higher level of this need. Together, these aspects of need for achievement remove much of the deterministic flavor of other need theories of motivation from McClelland's statement.

Personality and Motivation

Validity
See pages 93–108

Correlation
See pages 37–39

Conceptual and empirical advances in the study of personality have returned personality tests to the mainstream of screening and selection in I/O psychology after an absence of some years. If these tests are valid for selection in some situations, it follows that personality is related in some way to job performance in those situations. Several lines of research suggest some interesting possibilities. First, specific traits such as conscientiousness (e.g., Barrick & Mount, 1991) and personal discipline (e.g., McHenry, Hough, Toquam, Hanson, & Ashworth, 1990) have been found to correlate positively with job performance across measures and across occupations.

Second, researchers have found that some personality-type individual difference variables (such as high self-awareness) are associated with greater self-regulation, which, in turn, facilitates task accomplishment (e.g., Campion & Lord, 1982; Kuhl, 1985). Third, the difficulty of goals that individuals set for themselves may be related to certain personality traits (e.g., Gellatly, 1996). Finally, as described by Kanfer (1994), some investigators are beginning to explore the link between personality variables and cognitive information processing as it affects the performance of complex tasks.

It is premature to speak of an actual personality theory of motivation, but the literature on the subject makes it clear that personality can add something new to the ability of I/O psychologists to predict differences in the effort that people exert in effective job behaviors. Many questions remain to be answered, however. A basic one is: How does this process work? Do particular personality characteristics drive people to work hard, rather like needs are thought to drive behavior? Or is the influence more conscious, part of a cognitive decision to exert effort? This cognitive approach to work motivation is considered next.

Cognitive Theories of Work Motivation

Dispositional theories of motivation postulate that the forces that initiate, direct, and maintain behavior lie in inner states (needs) or those characteristic tendencies to behave in certain ways described as personality. From a cognitive perspective, motivation is a conscious choice made on the basis of a complex decision-making process of weighing alternatives, costs, benefits, and the likelihood of achieving desired outcomes. This thinking perspective on motivation predates Maslow by at least a decade (Tolman, 1932), but cognitive theories of work motivation did not achieve a place of significance in the I/O psychology literature until the 1960s. Three such theoretical approaches are discussed here—expectancy, balance, and goal-setting theories.

General Expectancy Theory

Of the several cognitive approaches to work motivation, a group variously called perceptual theories, VIE theories, E x V theories, and expectancy theories has been the most influential. The first such theory was proposed by Vroom (1964) and modified by a number of later researchers including Campbell and his colleagues (1970) and Porter and Lawler (1968). The term **general expectancy theory** is used here to refer to this theoretical approach to work motivation, with its multiple influences.

General expectancy theory is based on the premise that it is an *expectation* that effort exerted in particular activities will lead to desired outcomes that determines motivation. There are four variables that interact in a multiplicative fashion to produce a particular level of effort.

People whose jobs help them meet what they perceive to be their own needs may work harder and be more satisfied than people who are not well matched to their jobs.

1. *Effort-performance expectancy.* This expectancy is a belief that effort will pay off in a desired level of performance. It is expressed in formal statements as a probability ranging from zero to 1.00. This probability is heavily influenced by a person's perception of his or her job-related skills and knowledge, by the expectations of others, and by the support provided by working conditions, co-workers, and other environmental variables.

2. *Performance-outcome expectancy.* This is a probability concept similar to the effort-performance expectancy, but it reflects the belief that performance will be followed by certain direct, or first-level, outcomes. These outcomes include everything from raises, promotions, and a sense of accomplishment to recognition, more work, and longer hours. Expectancies as to which of these outcomes are likely to follow particular levels of performance depend to a considerable degree on what has happened to the individual and to others in the past.

3. *Instrumentality.* Instrumentality refers to the usefulness of one behavior or outcome for achieving something else that is valued; it reflects a belief that there is a connection (correlation) between two things. An individual who believes that there is a strong connection between the extent of his or her efforts at work and the amount of money he or she can make perceives personal effort to have high instrumentality (usefulness) for achieving a valued first-level outcome of work (money).

Instrumentality is particularly relevant to second-level outcomes of work—desired conditions that do not come directly from work but are made possible by direct (first-level) outcomes of work behavior. A bonus (a first-level outcome) may be the means by which an executive can raise his or her status in the home community (a second-level outcome) by joining a prestigious country club, for instance. Because getting the bonus is contingent upon excellent performance and joining the country club is contingent upon getting the bonus, effort has instrumentality for more than its immediate outcomes.

4. *Value.* Both first- and second-level outcomes have associated values (sometimes called valences), a variable that reflects how attractive the outcome is to the individual. The raise (first-level outcome) that goes with a promotion may have a high positive value because it is instrumental in achieving positively valued second-level outcomes for the employee, such as a better standard of living. The promotion has other outcomes for the employee, however, such as longer working hours, and these may be valued negatively.

Together, the effort-performance expectancy, the performance-outcome expectancy, and the values placed on first-level outcomes and the second-level outcomes for which effort is instrumental determine motivation. Table 6-1 shows the predicted level of effort under different combinations of these variables. (The probabilities are hypothetical.) The second-level outcome used for illustration is the recognition that first-rate job performance can bring.

Table 6-1			General Expectancy Model Predictions of Work Motivation		
Person	Second-Level Outcome	Value or Valence	Performance-Outcome Expectancy	Effort-Performance Expectancy	Predicted Effort
A	Recognition	High	+.6	+.9	High
B	Recognition	Medium	+.8	+.5	Medium
C	Recognition	None	+1.0	+1.0	None

Table 6–1 clarifies the general expectancy theory premise that a change in any one of the relevant variables can create a substantial increase or decrease in work effort (motivation). In other words, "motivation problems" are not all alike. Individual B in the table is not too confident that his or her hard work will pay off in the performance level necessary to achieve recognition and, in any event, does not value this outcome as highly as A. Individual C, on the other hand, has perfect confidence that he or she can do what is required and that doing so will lead to recognition, but recognition is not valued.

A number of hypotheses derived from the general expectancy theory of motivation have been supported by various investigations, but evidence for this model in its entirety is lacking. In the words of Campbell and Pritchard (1979), this model is "a simple appearing formulation that encompasses a highly complex and poorly understood set of variables and variable dynamics" (p. 243).

The complexity of traditional expectancy theories creates measurement difficulties that have so far resisted solution. Adding to the problems is the fact that even if methodologies were available for using them, these theories are predicting *intention* to act, not actual behavior. (The role of intentions in work motivation is discussed in detail by Tubbs and Ekeberg, 1991.)

Meta-analysis
See page 43

Construct validity
See pages 95–97

The authors of a recent meta-analysis of more than 75 studies conclude that the conceptual and measurement problems of general expectancy theory are not trivial and new research designs may be needed to reveal more about the validity of its constructs (Van Eerde & Thierry, 1996). Currently there is little research for the purpose of trying to validate general expectancy theory, but some of its basic concepts are thriving in other forms. A very good example is the concept of self-efficacy. **Self-efficacy** is defined by Bandura (1986) as a person's judgment about his or her capability "to organize and execute courses of action required to attain designated types of performances" (p. 391). In organizations, the information that forms the basis of this judgment comes from the individual (including his or her intentions and perceptions of ability), the task (including how difficult it appears to be and whether the necessary work aids are available), and other people (including their expectations, support, feedback) in the organization (Gist & Mitchell, 1992).

Sound familiar? Take a look back at the description of general expectancy theory's effort-performance expectancy. The fundamental difference is that in current I/O psychology research, self-efficacy is treated as a general individual-difference variable rather than as one component of a complex decision to exert effort in a particular situation (as in general expectancy theory).

As a variable on its own, the idea that self-efficacy has important implications for job performance has stimulated considerable research (e.g., Stern & Kipnis, 1993; Waldersee, 1994). One of the more interesting findings is that experimental boosting of self-efficacy can increase performance without any separate increase in work skills (e.g., Eden & Aviram, 1993), a phenomenon called the Galatea effect.

If higher self-efficacy can increase performance by itself, what role might this variable play in job training effectiveness? Among other results of investigations into the question, measures of self-efficacy have been found to predict training motivation, training performance, and subsequent job attendance (Martocchio, 1994; Mitchell, Hopper, Daniels, George-Falvy, & James, 1994; Quiñones, 1995; Saks, 1995). On the flip side of the coin, training appears to be an important vehicle for increasing individual self-efficacy. To the extent that people with greater self-efficacy have greater work motivation, this finding may be a significant advance for the practice of management.

Balance Theory: Adams's Equity Theory

The basic premise behind the cognitive theories of work motivation called balance theories is that most people try to keep a balance between the effort they put into work and what they get out of it. The most well-established version of this approach to motivation is Adams's (1963, 1965) **equity theory.** According to Adams, people compare the things they get out of their work situation (their outcomes) relative to the contributions they make to it (their inputs) with the outcomes and inputs of other people. Outcomes include pay, status, and job level. Among the important inputs are skills, knowledge, experience, time on the job, and education. The comparison process looks like this:

$$\frac{\text{Self-outcomes}}{\text{Self-inputs}} \quad \text{versus} \quad \frac{\text{Others' outcomes}}{\text{Others' inputs}}$$

If an employee can replace *versus* in the equation above with *equals,* there is equity, and the theory predicts that this individual will continue his or her current level of work effort and performance. Inequity occurs when the two ratios are unequal. According to Adams, inequality that favors the individual making the comparison will affect effort, just as will inequality that favors the relevant other or others.

The term "relevant other" in balance theory is an individual, psychological concept. For many people, relevant others are co-workers in the same organization known (or believed) to have about the same qualifications and experience. These distinctions may be quite precise. In one study, for example, part-time employees were found to use only other part-timers, not full-time employees of the same company, as their relevant others for comparison purposes (Feldman & Doerpinghaus, 1992).

Not everyone uses other employees of the same organization in the equity comparison process. Some people compare themselves with members of a professional group, with what they believe is an industry standard, or even with friends who do entirely different work. Others may use a previous personal job situation as the relevant other, rather than another person in the current situation.

According to equity theory, a perceived imbalance of self-outcomes and inputs relative to others (whoever they may be) leads to attempts to restore balance. One way to do this is to make a change in the amount of work effort (input) expended. Table 6–2 shows the effort adjustments predicted by the theory under inequitable conditions defined in terms of amount of payment for work.

Table 6–2	Equity Theory Predictions of Employee Responses to Inequitable Payment	
	Underpayment	**Overpayment**
Hourly Payment	Subjects underpaid by the hour will produce less or poorer-quality output than equitably paid subjects	Subjects overpaid by the hour will produce more or higher-quality output than equitably paid subjects.
Piece-Rate Payment	Subjects underpaid by piece rate will produce a large number of low-quality units in comparison with equitably paid subjects	Subjects overpaid by piece rate will produce fewer units of higher quality than equitably paid subjects

From R. T. Mowday, "Equity Theory Predictions of Behavior in Organizations." In R. M. Steers and L. W. Porter (Eds.), *Motivation and Work Behavior* (2nd ed.), p. 129. Copyright 1979 McGraw-Hill. Reprinted by permission.

Two unbalanced conditions appear in the table. Underpayment is a condition in which outcomes (payment) are perceived to be less than inputs (productivity). Equity theory predicts that work quantity or quality (or both) will go down in this case, depending on the basis for payment. By contrast, overpayment is an unbalanced situation in which outcomes are perceived to outweigh contributions. In this case, the theory predicts that the quality or quantity (or both) of work will be increased.

Predictions about the effects on effort of overpayment and underpayment have been supported in many contexts (e.g., Dornstein, 1989; Griffeth, Vecchio, & Logan, 1989; Harder, 1992). It should be noted, however, that Adams's theory also allows for other ways to correct the imbalance. Instead of adjusting effort, an employee may adjust his or her cognitive evaluation of the balance. Self-outcomes may be revised upward or self-inputs revised downward.

An alternative adjustment for imbalance is to reevaluate the outcomes and inputs of others. An employee paid less than a co-worker perceived to have the same skills may give more weight to the co-worker's seniority. In this way, the co-worker gets credit for greater input and is entitled to more money (greater outcome) for the same work. Extreme imbalances that cannot be handled by cognitive restructuring, or by adjustments in effort, may lead the individual to leave the job or profession (Adams, 1965).

Not everyone who is unable to justify a perceived compensation inequity in a work situation leaves his or her job. Some are not able to, and people also seem to vary in their sensitivities to inequity. While many people will say they prefer a world where everyone is treated equally, there are some who believe that they should have relatively more than other people. A third group prefers to have relatively less if someone must have less (Huseman, Hatfield, & Miles, 1987). Which situation would make you more uncomfortable, receiving two dollars an hour less than your co-workers for performing exactly the same job or two dollars an hour more?

A likely answer to the question posed is "it depends." Someone who knows he or she is paid less than others because of a supervisor's personal dislike probably would express a preference for making more than co-workers if a choice had to be made. On the other hand, someone who is earning more than co-workers because of the exceptionally high quality of his or her work probably would be more uncomfortable making less than co-workers. In other words, the *process* by which the over- or underpayment is arrived at would make a difference in reactions to it.

Procedural justice is a term used to describe the fairness of the process by which a decision or course of action is arrived at. Perceptions of unfair procedures (or unfair application of fair procedures) often make people feel hostile and resentful, as demonstrated dramatically by the National Basketball Association (NBA) referees' strike of 1983. The substitute referees were operating under the same rules as the regular referees, but they were unable to apply them consistently and impartially. There were so many fights among the players (and in the stands) that one sportswriter called the NBA the "National Boxing Association." (See Mark and Greenberg, 1987, for more on sports and concepts of justice.)

Basketball players and other sports teams play by a common set of rules. These are subject to change, but during any particular game the participants understand and agree to the rules existing at the time and they expect these rules to be applied fairly. Work organizations are not fundamentally different. In very general terms, a just procedure in an organization is one that is applied consistently and without bias, solicits and takes the opinions of affected employees into consideration, and is explained sufficiently for employees to understand how it works.

If the conditions described hold, people may accept decisions even if they believe them to be unfair (Leung & Li, 1990), just as most athletes accept the rulings of referees whom they believe to be competent even if they disagree with them. Miller and Hoppe (1994) found psychological distress to be much higher among workers who believed they had been fired or laid off unjustly because of personal shortcomings or other deficiencies than among workers fired or laid off for other reasons.

There are many organizational activities to which the procedural justice principle may be applied (see Folger & Greenberg, 1985). Among the more important are selection (including selection for promotion), performance appraisal, determining raises and bonuses, and setting performance standards. Such standards, in the form of goals, are the focus of the next section.

Locke's Goal-Setting Theory

The idea that human behavior has purpose is the central tenet of goal-setting approaches to motivation: people set goals for themselves and they are motivated to work toward these goals because achieving them is rewarding. The best-known application of this idea to work motivation is that of Locke (1968), who postulates that people who set themselves higher goals (or accept such goals set by others) exert more effort and perform better.

Laboratory experiment
See pages 27–28

Field research
See page 49

There are many laboratory experiments to support the hypothesis that harder goals are more likely to be associated with better performance than are easier goals. Field research is also supportive, especially of the proposition that goals themselves are critical to motivation and that specific and moderately difficult goals are more effective than vague "do your best" instructions. On the basis of this body of research, it is possible to identify a number of components of the successful use of goals for raising the level of employee motivation. Five such principles are reviewed, together with examples of recent work in each area.

1. *The goal should be specific.* Research has long supported the proposition that specific goals (for example, the number of telephone calls to make in one hour) allow people a better understanding of what is required. Other things being equal, better understanding increases the likelihood that desired performance will be achieved (e.g., Koch, 1979; Smith, Locke, & Barry, 1990). More recent investigations suggest that this effect may be weaker when the task is novel and/or complex than when it is familiar and/or relatively simple (see review by Kanfer, 1990).

2. *The goal should be of an intermediate-to-high level of difficulty.* Taken as a whole, the goal-setting research supports the proposition that difficult goals result in better performance than easy or "do your best" goals (e.g., Garland, 1983). Under certain conditions, however, there may be exceptions to this premise. Staw and Bottger (1990) found that "do your best" goals can facilitate task revision behavior (taking action to correct a problem), whereas more specific goals can inhibit it. Mowen, Middlemist, and Luther (1981) conducted a laboratory study to demonstrate that the type of incentive system in operation can also be important. As Figure 6–3 illustrates, the performance of the subjects in the experiment who were working under a piece-rate reward system (each additional correct response increases the payoff) conformed to predictions about the efficacy of higher goals. For the subjects who were working under a bonus system (meeting a standard earns a bonus), however, the pattern was exactly the opposite.

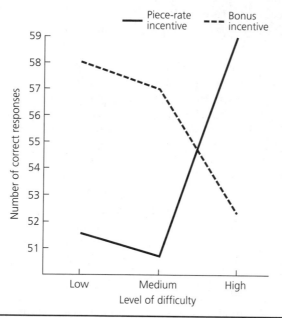

Figure 6–3
Goal Difficulty and Task Performance Under Two Different Incentive Systems

3. *The employee must accept the goal;* that is, he or she must agree to try to achieve it. According to Locke and his colleagues (1988), goal acceptance is determined by many factors, including the authority of the person setting the goal, peer influence, rewards, competition, and the belief that the goal can be attained. It can also be affected by the extent to which the individual is involved in setting the goal(s).

Attempts to verify the premise that employees must accept goals for the goals to be associated with better performance have not been very successful, but it is not clear whether the fault lies in the assumption, the research, or both (Tubbs, 1993). Some I/O psychologists believe that a necessary first step toward clarifying the situation is finding a reliable measure of goal commitment that is generally accepted (e.g., Wright, O'Leary-Kelly, Cortina, Klein, & Hollenbeck, 1994). It may also be important to examine the means by which goals are communicated to people, a variable that has received little attention in this line of research (Bobko & Colella, 1994).

Reliability
See pages 86–91

Feedback
See pages 138–140

4. *The employee must receive feedback about his or her progress toward the goal.* Feedback helps an individual progress toward a goal by indicating that more effort or a different strategy is needed or merely by indicating that the individual is on track and should keep doing whatever he or she is doing. In a work context, there are many ways this feedback can be delivered. It can come directly from the job itself, from employee self-monitoring, or from a supervisor, co-workers, or a mechanized or electronic performance monitor.

The role of feedback in using goals to increase employee effort is not different from the role of feedback in learning. Feedback is necessary no matter who sets the goals or how difficult they are (e.g., Das & Shikdar, 1989), and the relative importance of process versus output feedback will vary according to the situation (e.g., Earley, Northcraft, Lee, & Lituchy, 1990).

5. *Goals that are set participatively may be superior to assigned goals.* In all but the simplest work situations, participating in the goal-setting process should help an individual better understand what is expected of him or her. Better understanding, in turn, makes it more likely that the goal can be achieved and probably more likely that it will be accepted. This does not imply that the goal will be easier; some people assign themselves goals that are more difficult than those that would have been assigned to them by someone else (Latham, Mitchell, & Dossett, 1978; Mento, Locke, & Klein, 1992; Vance & Colella, 1990).

The premise that goals are more effective when people participate in setting their own is the basis for Management by Objectives (MBO, Drucker, 1954), one well-known applied use of goal-setting theory in organizations. As explained by its author in Exhibit 6–1, the core of this process is an up-and-down-the-line mutual understanding of specific goals and performance expectations. Research into the application of MBO finds that the process often increases job satisfaction for those involved, but the perceived support of top management appears to be critical to success (see the meta-analysis by Rodgers, Hunter, & Rodgers, 1993).

I/O psychologists and others continue to pursue an active interest in goal setting as it affects motivation, unlike some of the other cognitive theories reviewed. The five basic principles undoubtedly will continue to be refined, but current research in this area is focusing more on how and why goal setting works than on if it does (e.g., Audia, Kristof-Brown, Brown, & Locke, 1996; DeShon, Brown, & Greenis, 1996).

The Reinforcement Model of Work Motivation

The reinforcement approach to motivation was not developed as a theory of work motivation. In fact, it is not a theory at all, but a set of principles relating behavior to its outcomes. These principles have been drawn from behavioral data accumulated originally in learning laboratory settings. As an approach to work motivation, the **reinforcement model** consists of an extrapolation of these learning principles to the behavior of people at work. Three of these principles are of primary importance.

1. *People keep doing things that have rewarding outcomes.* Rewards strengthen (*reinforce*) the likelihood that the behavior they follow will occur again in similar circumstances.

2. *People avoid doing things that have punishing outcomes.* Punishment reduces the likelihood that the behavior it follows will occur again (at least in the presence of the punishing conditions or agent).

3. *People eventually stop doing things that have neither rewarding nor punishing outcomes.* Behavior that has outcomes that are neutral will be extinguished sooner or later.

Applied to work motivation, reinforcement principles state that effort at work is a direct function of the extent to which connections between work behaviors and rewards have been built up and strengthened. If working hard and doing what was expected have

Exhibit 6–1
Peter Drucker
on
Management
by Objectives

Abridged and adapted from Peter F. Drucker, *The Practice of Management*, pp. 129–130. Copyright 1954 by Peter F. Drucker. Reprinted by permission of Harper & Row Publishers, Inc.

been rewarded more than they have been punished or ignored, an individual will continue these behaviors. If, on the other hand, the outcomes of work effort have been punishing in some way to an individual, effort will be reduced. Work effort will also be reduced, but more gradually, when it seems to have been neither rewarded nor punished.

Where do these rewards that are so central to work effort come from? A pure reinforcement approach to motivation is based on the effects that reinforcement from the environment has on work effort—that is, on *extrinsic* reinforcement. This reinforcement is provided by informal rewards, such as praise or recognition, as well as by formal organizational rewards, such as bonuses, attractive work assignments, a bigger office, or a promotion.

Most I/O psychologists believe that *intrinsic* reinforcement (rewards that a person "gives" himself or herself, such as pride and feelings of accomplishment) is also important to work motivation; some believe it is relatively more important. Deci's (1972) suggestion that extrinsic rewards actually could reduce intrinsic reinforcement stimulated an active line of research that continues more than 20 years later.

Some investigators still believe that under certain conditions, external rewards undermine intrinsically motivated behavior (e.g., Hitt, Marriott, & Esser, 1992), but the bulk of the evidence does not support the proposition (Eisenberger & Cameron, 1996). At this time, it seems more likely that the two types of reinforcement are additive (e.g., Davis, Bagozzi, & Warshaw, 1992; Scott, Farh, & Podsakoff, 1988; Wiersma, 1992). Whatever the relationship, however, intrinsic rewards do not play any formal role in the reinforcement model; in this model, increasing work motivation is a matter of other people observing and rewarding desired behavior so as to build up a positive reinforcement history.

Schedules of Reinforcement

It is not practical to reward every show of effort and every desired behavior on the part of every employee in an organization every time it occurs, and neither is it necessary. Studies of the timing of rewards (of *reinforcement schedules,* in the language of psychology) show that most behavior will persist for quite a long time if it is reinforced only occasionally. There are four basic reinforcement schedules. Fixed schedules reward on a consistent basis, either after a certain period of time, in which case the schedule is called a *fixed interval* (such as a weekly paycheck), or after a certain number of behaviors, in which case it is called a *fixed ratio* (after every 100 units of production, for example).

Under variable schedules of reinforcement, rewards are given at varying intervals. If the interval is independent of behavior (an employee receives a "well done" whenever the boss happens to think of it), the schedule is called *variable interval.* If the reward comes after a varying number of behaviors, the schedule is called a *variable ratio* (this is the programmed payoff schedule of most ordinary coin-operated slot machines).

Data from thousands of experiments leave no doubt that the highest level of performance of any behavior over the long term is obtained through the use of a variable ratio schedule, more usually referred to in this context as *intermittent reinforcement.* This pattern of occasional reinforcement at unpredictable intervals conveniently fits the constraints of busy modern organizations, at least as far as informal reinforcement of behavior is concerned.

An organization's formal reward system is a different matter altogether. A company in which paychecks sometimes appeared days apart and sometimes months apart and employees never knew when to expect one (intermittent reinforcement) would be unlikely to exist for long. This practical problem is not the concern of the reinforcement model, however; the critical point is that there must be some reinforcement of desired work behavior if it is to continue. A review of research on schedules of reinforcement and a discussion of some of the major issues involved is found in Latham and Huber (1992).

The Reinforcement Model and Research

A simple picture of the reinforcement model of work motivation is shown in Figure 6–4. Notice that it is a backward-looking model; it is not incentives as such that produce effort, but the fact that these incentives have been delivered (or not) as promised in the past. By contrast, the general expectancy model is a forward-looking model. The importance of what has happened in the past is recognized only as one of the factors affecting beliefs about what will happen in the future.

Generalizability

See page 45

The reinforcement model diagrammed in Figure 6–4 uses work performance as an example, but it bears repeating that this model was established in quite a different context. To get evidence for its validity as a model of work motivation, it is necessary to determine whether these principles of behavior generalize to behavior in organizations. The most famous example of such a test is probably the Emery Air Freight case ("At Emery Air Freight," 1973). Among other applications of the principles, a positive reinforcement program to encourage employees to make full use of containers on each shipment saved Emery well over a half million dollars a year (a significant savings at that time).

Much of the field research on the reinforcement model has used salespeople as subjects. Luthans, Paul, and Baker (1981) report a significant improvement in three aspects

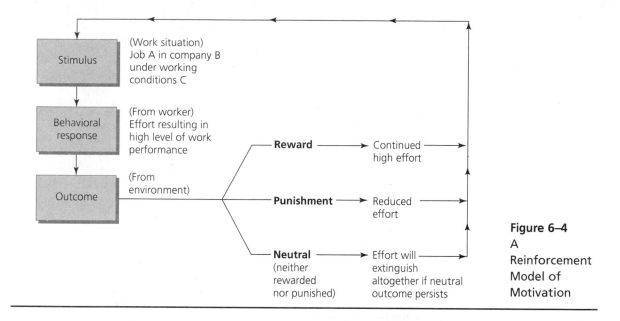

Stimulus	(Work situation) Job A in company B under working conditions C
Behavioral response	(From worker) Effort resulting in high level of work performance
Outcome	(From environment)

Reward → Continued high effort

Punishment → Reduced effort

Neutral (neither rewarded nor punished) → Effort will extinguish altogether if neutral outcome persists

Figure 6–4
A Reinforcement Model of Motivation

Statistical significance
See pages 35–36

of the sales performance of retail clerk subjects when paid time off and other rewards were made dependent on their work performance. A significant drop in absenteeism among these subjects was also observed. Similar conclusions were reached by Casey (1989), who reviewed 18 such experiments in the sales field.

Another work setting often used in studies of the reinforcement model is the food service industry (e.g., Welsh, Berstein, & Luthans, 1992). In one study of three traditional restaurants, changing the method of paying servers from an hourly wage to a system dependent on dollar value of food sold increased both productivity and earnings per hours of work (George & Hopkins, 1989).

The basic experimental paradigm for investigating the predicted effects of a program of positive reinforcement on a particular target behavior is shown in Figure 6–5. There are four steps. The first is to establish a *baseline* by observing the frequency of A, the target behavior of interest (work attendance, for example), under current conditions. In step 2, rewards are offered for this behavior and its frequency again is recorded.

If, as predicted by the model, the desired behavior change occurs (attendance increases) at step 2, it is tempting to pronounce the program a success and stop. But was it really the new reward system that produced the increase in attendance? Without following through with steps 3 and 4 as shown in the figure, there is room for doubt. If the reward really brought about the change, attendance should return to near baseline level when the reward for attendance is removed and then increase again when it is reinstated.

The pattern of the graph in Figure 6–5 is typical of the results in many, but not all, studies of the application of reinforcement principles to behavior in organizations. Not every study achieves positive and significant results, nor is it always practical (or even advisable) to take this route to increasing motivation in an organization. There is no doubt, however, that these principles taken from the learning laboratory apply to the behavior of people in a work setting.

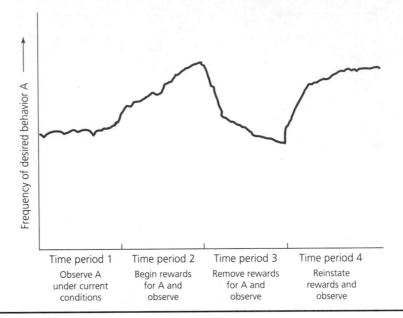

Figure 6–5
Predicted
Results of
Implementing a
Positive
Reinforcement
Program

Note: A is the behavior of interest (such as work attendance).

Much of contemporary positive reinforcement research in organizational settings is directed more toward discovering what kinds of incentives (promised rewards) are most effective with particular categories of workers than with demonstrating that rewards work (e.g., Bergmann, Bergmann, & Grahn, 1994; Gomez-Mejia, Balkin, & Milkovich, 1990; Popper & McCloskey, 1993). I/O psychologists are also addressing questions and problems associated with the effective use of positive reinforcement principles for groups as the use of work teams becomes increasingly popular (e.g., Latham & Huber, 1992). The evolution of thinking about incentives in the workplace is reviewed by Peach and Wren (1992).

I/O psychologists and others who study the behavior of people at work know that positive reinforcement can increase work effort. A great many managers (with or without the help of I/O psychologists) also appreciate the value of rewards, but the problem of providing effective incentives in a tight financial climate can be vexing. What can a manager offer that does not wreck the budget? The following examples of creative alternatives were described in a variety of business-oriented publications.

- A parking space in front of the door for a month

- Free movie tickets

- The loan of a vice president's prestige automobile for a weekend

- Free services of a home handyman if the employee pays for the materials

- A paid leave of absence for up to one month to work for a nonprofit organization of the employee's choice

With the reinforcement model, the review of the leading theoretical statements of the forces that initiate, direct, and maintain behavior at work is complete. Conceptually, these theories of motivation are not mutually exclusive; they are merely different. The likelihood is that all are relevant to work motivation.

In the absence of any clear-cut superiority for one theory, many I/O psychologists and others interested in work motivation are directing their energies toward coordinating and integrating existing approaches (Ilgen & Klein, 1989; Katzell & Thompson, 1990). Consistent with this spirit, a nonpartisan presentation of some practical implications of the various motivation theories for organizational application brings the discussion of motivation theory as such to a close.

The Applied Implications of Motivation Theories

Theory often seems a useless intellectual exercise to people who are concerned with making things work, but for I/O psychologists theory is the basis for practice. The topic of motivation provides an excellent opportunity to illustrate this premise. The applied implications of the leading theories of motivation presented are not put forth as motivation techniques, but as a set of integrated hypotheses about raising the overall motivation level of organizational employees through coordinated human resource and management policies. No technique-based approach for solving motivation problems will be successful in the long run unless the system as a whole is directed toward, and supportive of, increased employee effort on the job.

Hypotheses Based on Dispositional Theories

There is no escaping the fact that need theories of motivation fare poorly as theories, and personality theories of motivation are not yet well developed. Nevertheless, dispositional theories of motivation as a group still have at least three important implications for increasing employee effort.

1. *Selection, placement, and promotion practices that include self-diagnosed needs of applicants and employees in the decision-making process will have a positive effect on the overall level of employee effort in an organization.*

Whatever their specific premises, need theories as a group offer clues about what people will find rewarding enough to direct effort toward. To the extent that people can appreciate in advance the likelihood that a particular job will give them an opportunity to meet what they see as their own needs, some individual/job/organization mismatches may be avoided. The overall level of effort in the organization may be expected to rise as the number of such mismatches falls.

2. *Job design and redesign strategies to make work more interesting and challenging will have a positive effect on the overall level of employee effort in an organization.*

Trying to design jobs to meet postulated upper-level needs is not always practical, nor is it always necessary. People differ considerably in what they want out of a work situation. Nevertheless, a policy of designing or redesigning appropriate jobs to be more interesting and challenging as the opportunity to do so arises will offer more scope for the employees who want such jobs.

3. *The use of validated employment screening tests that measure personality factors correlated with desired work behaviors will have a positive effect on the overall level of employee effort in an organization.*

**Criterion
validity**
See pages 63–66

Personality approaches to motivation are relatively new as a formal area of study and have not to date produced any startling findings. Most people would guess that a person who typically is highly conscientious would work harder than someone who isn't, for example. What is new is the validation of tests of such traits. Where such validity is established, using a personality test as one screening device should make a useful contribution to the process of selecting "motivated employees."

Hypotheses Based on General Expectancy Theories

The research difficulties presented by an expectancy theory of work motivation do not alter the fact that this approach is rich in practical implications for influencing employee effort.

4. *Selection, placement, and promotion practices that match ability (in the form of basic ability to be trained) or experience, knowledge, and skills to job requirements will have a positive effect on the overall level of employee effort in an organization.*

Clarification of the role that ability plays in motivation is one of the more important contributions made by expectancy theories. The key lies in the effort-performance expectancy. A low expectancy means in effect: "Even if I exert substantial effort, it is unlikely that I can perform to the standard necessary to receive the outcomes I value." In many cases, then, "lack of motivation" may reflect a belief that effort will not compensate for perceived inadequacies in ability. This possibility leads directly to the next hypothesis.

5. *A formal job training program will have a positive effect on the overall level of employee effort in an organization.*

Training is related to motivation in several ways. New employee motivation is often high at first, and the quality of training may either strengthen or reduce this motivation. Furthermore, the effort-performance expectancy concept from expectancy theories of motivation suggests that confidence (or, in contemporary terminology, increased self-efficacy) acquired during training may be an important influence on the effort that is put into job tasks.

An employee's lack of confidence in being able to do a job well may affect his or her effort in the same "What's the use?" fashion described earlier. No one likes to look incompetent to others, and lack of effort is one way people can defend themselves against this possibility. The attitude conveyed is: "I could do it if I tried, but who cares?"

6. *Comfortable and appropriate physical working conditions and adequate tools, work aids, information, and other resources will have a positive effect on the overall level of employee effort in an organization.*

If there is one set of variables that tends to be ignored consistently by people interested in motivation, it is those found in the physical environment. The effort-performance expectancy concept from general expectancy theory points up the importance of making sure that this environment *supports* employee effort. A "What's the use?" attitude can be fostered by the realization that conditions make achieving desired performance impossible as well as by the lack of ability or training. Among these conditions are unrealistic time pressures, lack of space or privacy, inadequate or outdated work aids, and insufficient information, workers, raw materials, or other resources to do the job right.

7. *A good performance appraisal system will have a positive effect on the overall level of employee effort in an organization.*

Performance appraisal, like training, has a number of links with motivation. The most obvious is that the possibility of getting a good evaluation can serve as an incentive to perform well, and receiving a good evaluation can be positive reinforcement for the effort by which it was achieved. Expectancy theories of motivation also suggest that performance appraisal is an important source of information relative to the effort-performance expectancy component of the theory. If all-out effort is followed regularly by average performance evaluations, for example, the individual's effort-performance expectancy and level of motivation may be lowered.

In addition to providing information about the effort-performance expectancy, performance appraisal also provides information about the instrumentality of job performance for attaining valued outcomes. Performance appraisal results are often the basis on which organizations allocate such rewards as raises, promotions, and desirable career opportunities. If, for some reason, the performance appraisal method in use does not make meaningful distinctions between individual job performance levels, an important link is broken.

For good performance to be perceived as instrumental to achieving organizational rewards (the case in which motivation will be higher), it must be noticed and recognized as good performance. If it is not, then general expectancy theory predicts work motivation will be reduced accordingly. This prediction is supported by cognitive balance theories of motivation as well. Employees who see that others who work less hard or less effectively receive the same (or greater) rewards may deal with this perceived inequity by reducing their own effort.

Hypotheses Based on Goal Setting

One implication of goal-setting approaches to work motivation has already been discussed.

8. *Clear goals that can be measured are more effective than vague do-your-best instructions in raising the overall level of employee effort in an organization.*

Clear goals stated in such a way that people can know when they have been met help to organize and direct their efforts; most people just find it easier to buckle down when they know what they are trying to accomplish. But clarity is not the only issue; the difficulty of the goal also plays a role in motivation.

9. *Work objectives that are sufficiently difficult to be challenging will have a positive effect on the overall level of employee effort in an organization.*

Hypothesis 9 is not precise, because there is at least one major theoretical disagreement about the relationship between goal difficulty and motivation. Many investigations have found that difficult goals tend to be more effective for increasing work effort. On the other hand, research on the need for achievement suggests that greater effort will be put into goals that are neither too easy nor so hard as to be perceived as unattainable. Both theories and relevant research, however, are in agreement that very easy goals do not stimulate increased effort.

Hypothesis Based on the Reinforcement Model

Because the basic tenet of the reinforcement model is that people exert effort in behaviors that have been rewarded, the implications of this model for motivation have to do exclusively with rewards.

10. *Rewards for desired behavior will have a positive effect on the overall level of employee effort in an organization.*

The principle of rewarding desired work behaviors seems almost too obvious to need stating, but I/O psychologists who are trying to help organizations solve work effort problems are often struck by the extent to which the work behaviors desired by management are ignored. This is true of behaviors such as punctuality, helping others, creative behavior, reliable attendance, and compliance with rules, regulations, and standard operating procedures, as well as job performance.

Ignoring desired work behaviors is not the only way in which organizations often fail to follow the most basic principles of reinforcement. It is also not uncommon to find employees being rewarded for *undesired* behaviors. The excerpt in Exhibit 6–2

Exhibit 6–2
Backfiring
Reward Systems

Whether dealing with monkeys, rats, or human beings, it is hardly controversial to state that most organisms seek information concerning what activities are rewarded, and then seek to do . . . those things, often to the virtual exclusion of activities not rewarded. The extent to which this occurs of course will depend on the perceived attractiveness of the rewards offered, but neither operant nor expectancy theorists would quarrel with the essence of this notion.

Nevertheless, numerous examples exist of reward systems that are fouled up in that behaviors which are rewarded are those which the rewarder is trying to *discourage,* while the behavior he desires is not being rewarded at all. . . .

Business-Related Examples
An Insurance Firm

I. Attempting to measure and reward accuracy in paying surgical claims [a large eastern insurance company]. . . systematically keeps track of the number of returned checks and letters of complaint received from policyholders. However, underpayments are likely to provoke cries of outrage from the insured, while overpayments often are accepted in courteous silence. . . . the new hire in more than one claims section is soon acquainted with the informal norm: "When in doubt, pay it out!"

II. Annual "merit" increases are given to all employees in one of the following three amounts:

1. If the worker is "outstanding" (a select category, into which no more than two employees per section may be placed): 5 percent.

2. If the worker is "above average" (normally all workers not "outstanding" are so rated): 4 percent.

3. If the worker commits gross acts of negligence and irresponsibility for which he might be discharged in many other companies: 3 percent.

III. [There is a] rule which states that, should absences or latenesses total three or more in any six-month period, the entire 4 or 5 percent due at the next "merit" review must be forfeited.

Excerpted from S. Kerr, "On the Folly of Rewarding A, While Hoping for B." *Academy of Management Journal,* 1975, *18,* 769–783. Copyright 1975 Academy of Management. Reprinted by permission.

from a well-known article on the misunderstanding and misuse of rewards in organizations illustrates this point. Three examples of rewarding undesired behavior and discouraging desired behavior can be seen in the policies of the insurance firm described by Kerr (1975).

In section I, the desired behavior is described as accuracy in making insurance claim payments, but the *measure* of accuracy is the number of complaint letters received. Because overpaid clients seldom complain, a claims clerk actually is rewarded for inaccuracy in cases of overpayment. In section II, the desired behavior for a worker is to be rated as "outstanding." Notice, however, that the odds of receiving such an evaluation are very slim, and the difference between the merit increase for this category and the next one down the line is only 1%. Effectively, the rewarded behavior is average performance. (It is called "above average," a misnomer given that almost all employees are put into this category.)

Adding insult to injury in the so-called merit increase plan of the insurance company is the fact that employees who commit "gross acts of negligence and "irresponsibility" *still* get a merit increase of only 2% less than those who are rated as "outstanding." In fact, about the only way an employee can fail to get a "merit" increase in this company is to fail to meet the specified absenteeism and lateness standards. Thus, the rewarded behaviors become (1) coming to work on time every day and (2) doing whatever is necessary to minimize the number of letters of customer complaint.

Ignoring desired behavior and rewarding undesired behavior are two of the major ways organizations misuse basic principles of positive reinforcement. In addition, it is by no means unheard of for employees to be punished for behavior that is desirable (usually by the overenthusiastic enforcement of rules and policies). A Massachusetts postal clerk received a disciplinary letter from her supervisor threatening suspension or dismissal if the behavior complained of was repeated. The great offense? She came to work early and clocked in one minute before her shift was due to start.

Concluding Remarks

The hypotheses about increasing employee effort, or motivation, that are set forth here are drawn in a straightforward manner from the theoretical and research literature on work motivation. At the applied level, they can be seen as strategies for taking a long-term, proactive approach to motivation by incorporating what is known about this subject into the ongoing functions of an organization.

The motivational impact of the strategies outlined may be gradual, but it also will be cumulative. The greater the coordination and integration of the relevant activities with respect to their motivational implications, the greater the impact should be. By way of summarizing this discussion of motivation, the various links in this chain are diagrammed in Figure 6–6.

Job Satisfaction

Job satisfaction is an attitude, and therefore it is an hypothetical construct—like motivation and needs, it is something that cannot be seen, but whose presence or absence is believed to be associated with certain behavior patterns. In simple terms, a person who is satisfied finds more to like than to dislike about his or her job. Where does this job satisfaction come from and how should it be measured? Are there predictable relationships

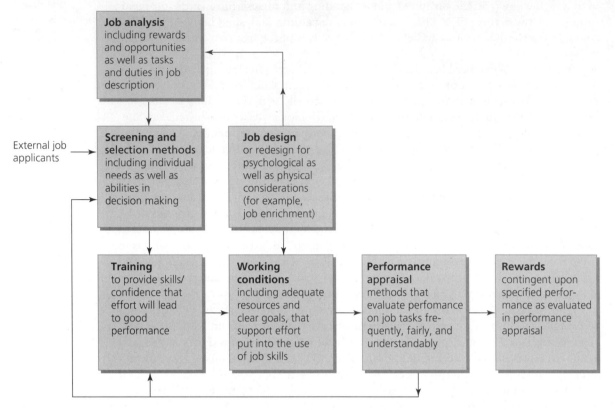

Figure 6–6
An Integrated Model of Influencing Employee Work Effort

between job satisfaction and certain personal variables, such as sex, age, and education? What does job satisfaction mean for an individual's job behavior and other aspects of his or her life?

The Meaning and Measurement of Job Satisfaction

I/O psychologists have been investigating job satisfaction for at least 60 years; it is one of the single most extensively researched topics in the field. Despite the volume of research, theories of job satisfaction—what causes it and how the causal process works—remain inadequately developed. The majority of theoretical statements are offshoots of the motivation theories discussed earlier. Table 6–3 provides a summary of the basic tenets of the major job satisfaction theories and their motivation theory sources.

Operational definition
See page 26

In the absence of an adequate theoretical foundation for their job satisfaction research, I/O psychologists rely more on operational definitions of this concept. For practical purposes, *job satisfaction* is defined by the way it is measured. There are differences of opinion about this measurement, but most instruments fit into one of a few basic categories. Three of these are reviewed—job satisfaction as (1) a global concept, (2) a faceted

Table 6–3 A Summary of Theories of Job Satisfaction

Name/Description	Basic Tenet	Related Theory of Work Motivation
Two-factor or motivation/hygiene (Herzberg, Mausner, & Snyderman, 1959)	Job satisfaction and job dissatisfaction are separate issues; satisfaction comes only from factors intrinsic to work itself.	Need theory
Facet satisfaction (Lawler, 1973)	Satisfaction depends on perception of job inputs, job characteristics, and job outputs relative to other people.	Cognitive theories
Value theory (Locke, 1976)	Satisfaction comes from being able to achieve things one values by means of job.	Need theory
Opponent process (Landy, 1978)	Satisfaction varies over time; forces always acting to reduce it.	None directly related
Need-discrepancy (Porter, 1961)	Satisfaction results from low discrepancy between what person needs and what job gives.	Need theory
Instrumentality (Porter & Lawler, 1968)	Satisfaction depends on match between expected and obtained rewards.	Expectancy theory

concept, and (3) a function of fulfilled needs. In all cases, job satisfaction is measured by means of self-report questionnaires.

There are difficulties associated with any self-report data, and in the case of job satisfaction these difficulties are magnified by the fact that there is no way at all to check the measurement. In I/O psychology research, a person's level of job satisfaction is what he or she reports it to be. This reported, or *expressed,* job satisfaction may or may not be how a respondent truly feels, but there is no way to test its accuracy. However tempting it might be to think that a particular employee's poor attendance record at work "shows" his or her lack of job satisfaction, for example, this conclusion is unfounded. This problem should be kept firmly in mind in the remainder of this chapter. Any conclusion about research that reads "Job satisfaction was found to be correlated with . . . " *always* means "Scores on the measure of job satisfaction used in this study were found to be correlated with . . . "

Job Satisfaction as a Global Concept

Job satisfaction was described as a positive evaluation of a particular job situation. This implies a sort of psychological summary of all of the liked and disliked aspects of a job, and this, in fact, has long been a common approach to measuring job satisfaction. The following question is typical: "On the whole, how satisfied are you with the work you do—would you say that you are very satisfied, moderately satisfied, a little dissatisfied, or very dissatisfied?" (Vecchio, 1980, p. 481).

The single-item job satisfaction questionnaire has both advantages and disadvantages. There are no development costs, and it is quick and easy to administer and score. It also makes sense to subjects, because it allows them to do what comes naturally—combine aspects of their job situation as they ordinarily think of them (Ironson, Smith, Brannick, & Gibson, 1989). However, single-item questionnaire measures leave considerable room for individual interpretation of the question. Some respondents may reply on the basis of pay, some on the basis of the nature of the work, some on the basis of the social climate of the organization, and so on.

One way to increase confidence that subjects are answering a question about job satisfaction from a similar frame of reference is to give them a little guidance. A job satisfaction questionnaire developed by Andrews and Withey (1976) combines the scores from (a) one global response to the job and (b) four questions about specific aspects (coworkers, the work itself, physical working conditions, and work tools) into (c) one job satisfaction score. Scores on this questionnaire have been found to have significant correlations with a number of job behaviors as well as with scores from longer job satisfaction measures (e.g., Rentsch & Steel, 1992).

Job Satisfaction as a Faceted Concept

An alternative to the single-dimension concept of job satisfaction is a faceted, or component, concept based on the assumption that employee satisfaction with different aspects of a job situation can vary independently and should be measured separately. Taken to the limit, the faceted approach would call for measuring satisfaction with individual tasks performed on a job (Taber & Alliger, 1995), but to date this very narrow approach to the assessment of job satisfaction has found little acceptance (Roznowski & Hanisch, 1990).

Most researchers who view job satisfaction as a faceted concept are interested in aspects of a job (facets) that cut across tasks and jobs. Examples of such aspects include work load, job security, compensation, working conditions, status and prestige of job, congeniality of co-workers, company performance evaluation policies, general management practices, supervisor-subordinate relations, autonomy and responsibility on job, opportunity to use knowledge and skills, and opportunity for growth and development.

All of the many components listed have been used in I/O psychology research at one time or another; it is quite usual for the measurement of job satisfaction to vary from one investigation to another. The number of facets measured varies as well; the specific choice of number and kind of facets to measure usually depends on the research question. If an I/O psychologist is interested only in the relationship between turnover and employee satisfaction with supervision in the organization, for example, there is little need to ask employees about satisfaction with pay or co-workers. Even if research interests are fairly specific, it is not necessary for each investigator to construct a specific component scale for each job satisfaction study. Rather, it is common practice in such cases to use only part (one or more subscales) of an established scale. One of the most popular of the multifaceted measures available is the Job Descriptive Index (Smith, Kendall, & Hulin, 1969).

The original Job Descriptive Index (JDI) is a five-facet scale used to measure satisfaction or dissatisfaction with work, supervision, pay, promotional opportunities, and coworkers. The instrument consists of a series of descriptive adjectives or phrases relevant to each of the five job facets. (The Andrews and Withey scale also measures five facets, but only one question is asked about each.) The respondent is asked to reply yes, no, or don't know/can't decide to each. Two items from each of the five scales are shown in Exhibit 6–3.

The JDI currently has some 35 years of development and use behind it. Considered as a whole, the research results support its reliability and its applicability to different demographic groups (such as blacks/whites, males/females, managers/nonmanagers) sufficiently to justify its broad usage. The instrument is not without its problems, however.

Some researchers have questioned scoring procedures (e.g., Hanisch, 1992), and others have identified statistical weaknesses (e.g., Buckley, Carraher, & Cote, 1992; Jung, Dalessio, & Johnson, 1986). An expanded form of the scale has been developed in response to these measurement criticisms, but a more basic issue is whether the JDI measures what it is intended to measure.

The Job Descriptive Index is a *description* of a job situation. A person's *feelings* about that description—that is, the extent to which it is evaluated as personally satisfying or dissatisfying—must be inferred from this description. Can this inference be made with confidence? Consider the description "dead-end job" under "promotional opportunities" in Exhibit 6–3. In the scoring of the JDI, it is assumed that a reply of yes to the question of whether a job is a dead end indicates some job dissatisfaction. Such may not be the case at all, however. The job may be indisputably a dead end, but the current person in this position may not feel negative about this feature. Thus, to the extent that it actually measures job satisfaction, the JDI is dependent on the assumption that people are alike in their evaluations of certain characteristics of work situations.

A faceted measure of job satisfaction that is more obviously evaluative than the JDI is the Index of Organizational Reactions (Smith, 1976). This questionnaire asks for personal reactions to eight facets of work, the five covered by the JDI (with work broken into two facets—kind and amount) plus physical working conditions and the company itself. The following sample question is from the co-workers scale.

How do you generally feel about the employees you work with?

1. Very dissatisfied

2. Somewhat dissatisfied

3. Neither satisfied nor dissatisfied

4. Somewhat satisfied

5. Very satisfied

Work

_____Useful

_____Frustrating

Supervision

_____Impolite

_____Intelligent

Promotional opportunities

_____Dead-end job

_____Regular promotions

Pay

_____Bad

_____Highly paid

Coworkers

_____Smart

_____Hard to meet

Exhibit 6–3

Sample Items from the Job Descriptive Index

From *The Job Descriptive Index* © 1975, Bowling Green State University. Information concerning this instrument can be obtained by writing to Dr. Patricia C. Smith, Department of Psychology, Bowling Green State University, Bowling Green, OH 43403. Reprinted by permission.

If this question is compared with the adjectives used in the Job Descriptive Index (Exhibit 6–3) for co-workers, it is obvious that there is more opportunity for a person to indicate how he or she feels about a job facet with the Index of Organizational Reactions. At the same time, there is still no way to know how important this facet of job satisfaction is to the individual.

Job Satisfaction as Fulfilled Needs

An approach to measuring job satisfaction that does not rely on the assumption that all people feel the same way about the various aspects of a job was developed by Porter and reported in a series of studies beginning in 1961. Porter's original questionnaire, based on a need theory of motivation, consists of 15 statements related to security, esteem, autonomy, social, and self-actualization needs. Based on his or her *own* needs and perceptions of the job, each respondent answers three questions about each statement.

1. How much is there now?

2. How much should there be?

3. How important is this to me?

A sample item from this questionnaire appears in Exhibit 6–4.

On the basis of responses to the questions about need fulfillment at work, job satisfaction is measured by the discrepancy between "How much is there now?" and "How much should there be?" The smaller this discrepancy, the greater the satisfaction. Separate scores are calculated for each of the five need categories. The question "How important is this to me?" gives the investigator a measure of the relative strength of each need for each individual respondent. To return to the earlier example, a person may find co-workers less than satisfying, but this aspect of working conditions may be so unimportant to him or her that it has no effect on job satisfaction.

Porter's questionnaire is difficult to score relative to other measures, and this may be one of the reasons that the need-discrepancy approach to measuring job satisfaction disappeared almost entirely from the I/O psychology literature for some years.

Exhibit 6–4
A Need Discrepancy Approach to Measuring Job Satisfaction

Security Needs: The *feeling of security* in my management position

1. How much is there now?

   (min) 1   2   3   4   5   6   7   (max)

2. How much should there be?

   (min) 1   2   3   4   5   6   7   (max)

3. How important is this to me?

   (min) 1   2   3   4   5   6   7   (max)

From L. W. Porter, "A Study of Perceived Need Satisfaction in Bottom and Middle Management Jobs." *Journal of Applied Psychology,* 1961, *45,* 1–10.

Nevertheless, the individuality of this approach, along with the idea that job satisfaction is a relative rather than an absolute matter, has much to recommend it. Rice, McFarlin, and Bennett (1989) agree. On the basis of their own research as well as the literature in this area, these authors conclude that have-want discrepancies add so significantly to the measurement and understanding of job satisfaction that "it would be difficult to justify any theory of satisfaction that did not have some mechanism for incorporating the discrepancy concept" (p. 598).

Problems in Measuring Job Satisfaction

Virtually all job satisfaction research is based on questionnaire measures of job satisfaction. Given that job satisfaction is an individual, subjective phenomenon, this probably is the most appropriate measure. It is important, nonetheless, to be reminded of certain limitations this method of obtaining data places on job satisfaction research. One set of problems has to do with the accuracy of the responses.

Even if respondents do not give misleading answers intentionally, a host of situational variables can affect both the extent to which they understand the questions and the extent to which they are willing to be frank in their replies to a job satisfaction questionnaire. Among the relevant factors reviewed by Giles and Feild (1978) are the form taken by the cover letter and/or directions, whether the respondents are asked to identify themselves, and where the questionnaire is administered (at home, on the job, in the human resource office).

In their own study of this problem, Giles and Feild found that job satisfaction scores were also influenced significantly by item sensitivity. In this context, item sensitivity refers to the degree of concern respondents have that others might learn how they answered the question. Items about working conditions were generally of low sensitivity, for example, whereas those concerning supervision had high sensitivity. On the basis of their analysis, the authors conclude that questionnaires with depersonalized questions are more likely to elicit candid responses than are questions with a particular person (such as a supervisor) as the focus.

The factors listed by Giles and Feild add error to the measurement of job satisfaction in that they increase the discrepancy between the "true" degree of job satisfaction and the estimate that is obtained by means of the questionnaire. When individual responses are combined or compared in some way, error is multiplied.

**Measurement
error**
See pages 84–85

The problems described are not specific to the measurement of job satisfaction; to a greater or lesser degree they plague all questionnaire-based investigations. The measurement error associated with this form of research cannot be eliminated, but there are certain steps that can be taken to reduce it. These include using a questionnaire with established reliability, pretesting directions for clarity, guaranteeing subject anonymity, and using a sample size sufficiently large to assume that response bias is distributed randomly.

**Research
subjects/sample**
See page 27

The Incidence and Parameters of Job Satisfaction

The extent to which organizational employees in general are satisfied or dissatisfied with their jobs is a question that has been addressed by local and national surveys at regular intervals for many years. Most of the surveys rely on a single-item global measure of job satisfaction, and most find people relatively more satisfied than dissatisfied. But these figures are averages based (typically) on a few hundred to, perhaps, a few thousand subjects. The question of whether such figures obscure important differences in job satisfaction among different subgroups of employed people is a valid one.

Who Is Satisfied?

The question of possible differences in job satisfaction among various subgroups of employees (such as male/female, older/younger, and full-time/part-time) has been investigated many times. One of the more stable findings in this body of research is a positive correlation between age and reported job satisfaction; that is, reported job satisfaction tends to increase with the age of the employee (e.g., Dalessio, Silverman, & Schuck, 1986; Quinn, Staines, & McCollough, 1974). More recent investigations open up the possibility that this inference is oversimplified, however. An example is provided by the data in Figure 6–7.

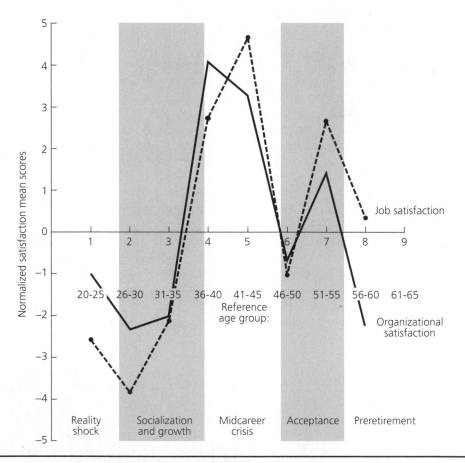

Figure 6–7
Job Satisfaction Variation with Age

From M. F. R. Kets de Vries, D. Miller, J-M Toulouse, P. Friesen, M. Boivert, and R. Theriault, "Using the Life Cycle to Anticipate Satisfaction at Work." *Journal of Forecasting,* 1984, *3,* 161–172. Copyright 1984 John Wiley and Sons. Reprinted by permission.

The figure presents the results from one study that found job satisfaction to vary, both up and down, over the course of an individual's work life (Kets de Vries et al., 1984). Satisfaction in the 20s age group declines as discrepancies between ideals and realities ("reality shock") regarding work and a particular job make themselves felt. As the individual adjusts to these realities and begins to accomplish career goals, satisfaction improves and eventually peaks sometime in the late 30s to early 40s. There follows a "midcareer crisis" that often occurs in the middle to late 40s. Satisfaction is revived as this crisis is resolved, but it begins to decline again as the individual prepares for retirement ("preretirement").

The data in the figure offer an excellent example of the cautions that apply to drawing inferences from correlational data. If the graph is an accurate picture of reality, quite different conclusions could be drawn about job satisfaction and age depending on the actual age distribution of a sample. Indeed, later research supports the hypothesis that the relationship between age and job satisfaction is not a straightforward linear one but may be moderated by any number of variables (e.g., Kacmar & Ferris, 1989; Zeitz, 1990).

Moderator variable
See page 39

Basic differences in job satisfaction between males and females is another possibility that has long interested I/O psychologists. Some researchers have reported one sex (usually women) to be generally more satisfied than the other, but no reliable differences in job satisfaction due to sex have emerged from this line of investigation when it is examined as a whole (Phelan, 1994). Sources of job satisfaction for both men and women are the work conditions and outcomes they consider personally rewarding. These differ from one individual to the next, but they no longer differ predictably by sex, if they ever did (e.g.,Witt & Nye, 1992).

Personality and Job Satisfaction

The search for differences in job satisfaction between broad groupings of people defined on the basis of some observable descriptive characteristic such as age or sex has not, on the whole, been all that productive, and there is far less research along these lines than formerly. Consistent with the renewed interest in personality variables in other areas, many investigators are turning their attention to the possible role that personality plays in job satisfaction. The fundamental hypothesis of this line of investigation is that people have stable traits that predispose them to be satisfied or dissatisfied with their jobs regardless of the actual work situation.

The idea expressed is as revolutionary as it is simple and obvious to many people. The theme that organizations somehow give (or don't give) people job satisfaction runs through much of the literature on this topic, yet almost everyone knows people who seem to like every job situation in which they find themselves as well as people who seem to like none of them. These tendencies to be positive or negative are also quite often characteristic of these same people in situations other than their jobs.

Psychologists refer to a general tendency to respond to one's environment with positive feelings as "positive affectivity" and the tendency to respond negatively as "negative affectivity." Where do such tendencies come from? Like other personality characteristics, they develop from the interaction of inherited physical and physiological traits with life experiences. And like other personality characteristics, they do not always rule behavior. Most people behave "out of character" from time to time, depending on circumstances.

There are exceptions (Gutek & Winter, 1992), but much of the evidence to date supports a positive correlation between measures of positive affectivity and greater job satisfaction (e.g., Arvey, Bouchard, Segal, & Abraham, 1989; Levin & Stokes, 1989; Watson & Slack, 1993). Judge and Hulin's (1993) comment is representative of this viewpoint.

> Job satisfaction is determined to a significant extent by the individual's general level of happiness and his or her way of looking at the world. This does not suggest that job conditions are unimportant. . . . Nothing in the dispositional approach denies the existence of environmental effects or even minimizes the importance of [other] factors. (p. 413)

If an individual's general level of happiness is an important determinant of job satisfaction, it seems reasonable to wonder if there is also a positive correlation between job satisfaction and general satisfaction with life. Is a happy worker also a happy spouse or parent or son or daughter or neighbor or friend?

Job Satisfaction and Life Satisfaction

Two theories about the relationship between job and life satisfaction have been predominant for some time (Near, Rice, & Hunt, 1980). The compensation hypothesis postulates that people who do not find work satisfying will *compensate* by taking actions to make the rest of life more satisfying. The generalization, or spillover, hypothesis rests on the assumption that job satisfaction (or dissatisfaction) *generalizes* ("spills over") from work to nonwork activities. Somewhat more recently, the possibility that job and life satisfaction are unrelated (the segmentation hypothesis) captured the attention of a number of investigators.

In an early review of the relevant literature, Kabanoff (1980) found support for both the compensation and the generalization views of the job satisfaction–life satisfaction relationship and insufficient evidence to conclude that one or the other is more accurate. Some years later, the question is still open. Researchers find support for both the compensation (Kirkcaldy & Cooper, 1993) and the spillover hypotheses (Liou, Sylvia, & Brunk, 1990; Tait, Padgett, & Baldwin, 1989), but neither is demonstratively the stronger explanation of the job satisfaction–life satisfaction relationship. The segmentation hypothesis appears weaker than these alternatives, but there is insufficient evidence to dismiss it entirely.

Why is it proving so difficult to pin down one generalizable relationship between job satisfaction and life satisfaction? An important reason is that one of the many ways in which people are different is in the extent to which work is a central life interest (Dubin & Champoux, 1977). The reactions to job satisfaction (or lack thereof) of people who do not place much importance on work may be quite different from those of people whose work is vitally important to them.

Research into the role that personality plays in job satisfaction suggests that in addition to their basic attitude toward work, people differ in the extent to which they are naturally disposed to feel good about their jobs, and these dispositions may generalize to all of life. The end result of mixing these and other individual differences may be that all three hypotheses about the relationship between job and life satisfaction are correct as far as they go (Judge & Watanabe, 1994).

A second reason for the continuing ambiguity about the relationship between job satisfaction and life satisfaction may be that it just is not as simple as formerly believed.

*The belief that the
work they are doing
is important is a
major source of job
satisfaction for
many people.*

Recent research suggests that there is a *reciprocal* relationship between the two, such that each influences the other, rather than the one-way relationship often assumed (Judge & Watanabe, 1993). Compensation, spillover, and segmentation may be merely three of the processes by which work life and nonwork life can be linked (Lambert, 1990). With both work and home/family life becoming more demanding and complicated for many organizational employees, the relationship between the two offers an exciting research opportunity for "people who understand family and people who understand work" to collaborate (Zedeck, 1995).

Job Satisfaction and Work Performance

The job satisfaction literature is vast and characterized by a belief that people who are more satisfied with their jobs will stay with them longer, be absent less, and perform better. Absenteeism and turnover, reviewed in detail in another chapter, both have modest but well-established negative correlations with job satisfaction. I/O psychologists have been wrestling with the question of the relationship between job satisfaction and job performance for well over 50 years. For much of that time, considerable effort was put into attempts to demonstrate that the two are positively related.

"A happy worker is a good worker" is a very appealing idea to a great many people, but it does not hold up empirically. The results of the many investigations of the hypothesis that job satisfaction causes better job performance offer little evidence of such a relationship or even for a reliable positive correlation between these two variables (Ostroff, 1992). On the other hand, some researchers argue that the results are equally inconclusive with respect to the hypothesis that there is *no* such relationship.

There are those who disagree, but it probably is accurate to say that current mainstream belief in I/O psychology is that there is no significant, straightforward causal relationship between individual job satisfaction and job performance. This conclusion was first reached at least 30 years ago (Vroom, 1964), but the question continues to intrigue researchers (e.g., Cropanzano, James, & Konovsky, 1993; Das & Mital, 1994).

The early job satisfaction–job performance research was almost exclusively a search for a simple positive correlation between these variables. Later investigations moved into a search for relevant moderator variables, such as job level, job commitment, time pressures, and nature of the work performed. The rationale behind this line of inquiry is that failure to identify and control variables that affect the nature of the job satisfaction–job performance relationship in a systematic way may be the reason there appears to be no relationship between satisfaction and performance.

The moderator variable research has produced stronger correlations between measures of job satisfaction and measures of work performance than those found in the older research. Cause-effect inferences cannot be made on the basis of ordinary correlational analysis, however, and as far as this evidence is concerned, the causality in this matter might very well go the other way: "A good worker is a happy worker."

Porter and Lawler (1968) appear to have been the first formally to include job performance as a cause, rather than an effect, of job satisfaction in a model of work performance. The idea was explored by Cherrington, Reitz, and Scott (1971) in an experiment that has become a classic in this line of research. These investigators found evidence to suggest that the nature of the relationship between job satisfaction and job performance depends on a third variable—rewards. This study is summarized in Spotlight on Research.

**Independent/
dependent
variable**
See page 29

Cherrington and his colleagues produced *both* positive *and* negative correlations between job satisfaction and job performance in their laboratory experiment by manipulating the connection between job performance (dependent variable) and the formal reward of a financial bonus (independent variable) for that performance. Under the hypothesis of an inherent causal relationship between job satisfaction and performance, the subjects in the study who reported the greatest satisfaction at the end of the first hour should have been the subjects whose performance improved most during the second hour. Contrary to expectation, better second-hour performance in the experiment was achieved by those subjects who "learned" from the bonuses paid at the end of the first hour that there was a connection between what they did and whether they received a bonus.

What the finding means is that a positive correlation between job satisfaction and job performance depends on the degree to which the same rewards are involved in both. If employee satisfaction depends considerably on being rewarded at a level that seems consistent with performance, satisfaction and performance will be related positively under appropriate reward systems. As mentioned before, however, some people do not define job satisfaction in terms of rewards that depend on their good job performance.

A number of the conditions that have been identified as possible sources of job satisfaction for different people are listed in the left column of Table 6–4. When it is necessary to perform a job well in order to achieve these conditions (the first five on the list), a positive correlation between job satisfaction and job performance will be observed. When conditions that produce job satisfaction have nothing to do with job performance (the second five items on the list), no relationship between the two variables will be observed in a correlational study. Finally, when the primary sources of job satisfaction actually can interfere with performance (the last three items), an inverse relationship will be observed; that is, employees reporting greater job satisfaction will be among the poorer performers.

Research question Is there a causal relationship between job satisfaction and job performance?

Research hypothesis By selective manipulation of reward conditions, any empirical relationship between reported satisfaction and performance may be produced.

Type of study Laboratory experiment.

Subjects Ninety volunteer male and female junior-level business students.

Independent variables Performance-reward contingency. Operational definition: (a) Appropriately rewarded—good performers got a bonus, poor performers did not; (b) Inappropriately rewarded—good performers did not get bonus, poor performers did. One half of good and poor performers were in each condition.

Dependent variable Performance on experimental task. Operational definition: Total number of rows of figures scored as per instructions.

General procedure Subjects were paid $1.00/hour to score tests they believed were taken by paper mill employees. They were told they had a 50:50 chance of receiving a bonus for performance quantity and quality, but these bonuses actually were distributed on a random basis to half of the high performers and half of the low performers.

Subjects worked for two hours. At the end of each hour they (a) answered questions about their performance and the perceived likelihood that they would receive a bonus, (b) were paid according to the experimental plan, and (c) answered a job satisfaction questionnaire.

Results The hypothesis was supported. There was a positive correlation between performance and satisfaction for appropriately rewarded subjects and a negative correlation for inappropriately rewarded subjects. The performance of the appropriately rewarded subjects also improved from the first hour to the next, while that of the other subjects did not.

Conclusion "The results of this study support the hypothesis that the nature and magnitude of the relationship between satisfaction and performance depend heavily upon the performance reward contingencies that have been arranged" (p. 535).

SPOTLIGHT ON RESEARCH

Effects of Contingent and Non-contingent Reward on the Relationship Between Satisfaction and Task Performance

Summarized from D. J. Cherrington, H. J. Reitz, and W. E. Scott, Jr., "Effects of Contingent and Noncontingent Reward on the Relationship Between Satisfaction and Task Performance." *Journal of Applied Psychology*, 1971, 55, 531–536.

Table 6–4	Conditions Under Which Different Job Satisfaction–Job Performance Relationships May Be Observed	
Possible Source of Job Satisfaction	**Relationship of This Source to Job Performance**	**Observed Job Satisfaction–Job Performance Correlation**
Pride Accomplishment Recognition Advancement Challenge	Depends on performance	Positive
Location of company Prestige of company Hours worked Benefits Working conditions	Irrelevant to performance	None
Opportunity to socialize Light work load Job security	Interferes with performance	Negative

Antecedents
See page 40

Contemporary Job Satisfaction Research

General acknowledgment of the important role played by rewards in the job satisfaction–performance relationship has not brought the search for the antecedents and consequences of job satisfaction to a halt, but it has changed it considerably. At least three trends can be identified. The first centers around interest in the role that personality may play in job satisfaction. It is much too early to draw any conclusions from this research, but the basic idea is simple: perhaps happy people are more productive employees as well as more satisfied ones (Staw & Barsade, 1993).

The second trend is a reexamination of the performance side of the satisfaction-performance relationship. A study by Ostroff (1992) investigates the possibility that the traditional level of analysis may be wrong; it may not be individuals whose performance is enhanced by job satisfaction, but organizations. Her data, collected from more than 13,000 teachers in almost 300 schools, support the idea that organizations with more satisfied employees tend to be more effective. Or is it the other way around?

Organ (1977, 1988) takes a different tack, putting forth the proposition that the performance affected by job satisfaction is not productivity in the traditional sense at all; rather, it is what Bateman and Organ (1983) term **citizenship behavior.** In a work organization, citizenship behavior is "helpful, constructive gestures exhibited by organization members and valued or appreciated by officials, but not related directly to individual productivity nor inhering in the enforceable requirements of the individual's role" (Organ, 1988, p. 548).

Examples of citizenship behavior include staying late so that a co-worker can leave early to visit a friend in the hospital, volunteering to be the department representative for a company-sponsored charity drive, or devising a better way to perform a job duty. Social psychologists Katz and Kahn (1966) refer to such behaviors as "spontaneous." Related concepts found in the I/O psychology literature include off-task behavior, prosocial behavior, and extra-role behavior. Some fine distinctions are made among the definitions of these concepts, but the term *citizenship behavior* is adequate here.

There is research support for the hypothesis that people who are more satisfied with their jobs are more likely to make nonrequired contributions at work (Organ, 1988; Organ & Konovsky, 1989; Organ & Ryan, 1995), and the idea seems to be taking on a new life as I/O psychologists in general move away from attempts to prove that job satisfaction is essential to good on-task or in-role behavior (e.g., Moorman, 1993).

Finally, there seems to be a trend in the job satisfaction research to improve the predictive power of attitudes—that is, to increase correlations between observed behavior and measured attitudes. Guagnano, Stern, and Dietz's (1995) study of attitudes and behaviors regarding curbside recycling is an interesting example. These investigators found that attitudes about curbside recycling only predicted recycling behavior in households that had been given collection bins. They suggest that models linking attitudes to behavior could be improved by incorporating the context in which people act (having or not having bins, in the current case).

Concluding Remarks About Job Satisfaction

Job satisfaction is an affective, or feeling, response to a job situation. There is some disagreement as to what brings it about and how the process works. For practical purposes, job satisfaction is as it is measured and there are a number of alternative approaches to this measurement. Many years of research have yielded modest correlations between such measurements and a variety of work behaviors. In no case, however, has job satisfaction been found to be a *major* determinant of work behavior. This conclusion is entirely consistent with investigations and reviews of the general relationship between attitudes and behavior (Bagozzi & Warshaw, 1992). Erlich's (1969) statement is representative: "Studies on the relation of attitudes and behavior have almost consistently resulted in the conclusion that attitudes are a poor predictor of behavior" (p. 29).

What does all of this mean? Perhaps the lesson is simply that the implications of job satisfaction (or lack of it) are more important to an individual than to the organization employing him or her. This is not to say that everyone who works puts satisfaction high on the list of personal priorities. Observation as well as results from research into the ways people perceive the roles of work and nonwork activities in their need and value systems make it plain that this is not true.

To some people, work is a necessity that they accept without any particular expectations of deriving satisfaction from it. Nevertheless, it seems safe to assume that, other things being equal, they would prefer the experience to be positive. To the extent that efforts by I/O psychologists and others to understand job satisfaction can make a contribution to this aspect of the quality of work life, the efforts seem well worthwhile.

Note on a Special At Issue

This chapter's At Issue consists entirely of excerpts from one of the most famous debates in the history of psychology. The protagonists, Carl R. Rogers, the late theorist and practicing psychotherapist and B. F. Skinner, the late learning theorist and philosopher, are two of psychology's giant figures. The debate, which took place more than 40 years ago, centers around an issue that is timeless—the control of human behavior.

Control is an emotionally laden word and its negative connotations seem to arise frequently in discussions of motivation. There is no doubt that making decisions and taking actions for the express purpose of getting people to put more effort into their work (to "motivate" them) is a deliberate attempt to exercise some control over the behavior of those people. As Skinner points out, however, many people find it uncomfortable to confront this fact; thus, the closer a theory of motivation comes to being explicit about control, the more controversy it seems to generate.

Of the theories of motivation discussed, dispositional theories (especially need theories) appear to be the least controlling, and the reinforcement model makes the least attempt to disguise the control element. Thus, these two approaches tend to draw the lines in debates about the ethics of deliberate efforts to motivate people at work. Skinner, the most famous and outspoken proponent of the reinforcement model, and Rogers, a lifelong proponent of the human need for and right to self-actualization, are uniquely qualified to speak to the control issues that lie behind these lines.

At Issue

 The Control of Human Behavior

I (Skinner)

Science is steadily increasing our power to influence, change, mold—in a word, control—human behavior. It has extended our "understanding"... so that we deal more successfully with people in non-scientific ways, but it has also identified conditions or variables which can be used to predict and control behavior in a new, and increasingly rigorous, technology....

Now, the control of human behavior has always been unpopular. Any undisguised effort to control usually arouses emotional reactions. We hesitate to admit, even to ourselves, that we are engaged in control, and we may refuse to control, even when this would be helpful, for fear of criticism....

The dangers inherent in the control of human behavior are very real. The possibility of the misuse of scientific knowledge must always be faced. We cannot escape by denying the power of the science of behavior or by arresting its development. It is no help to cling to familiar philosophies of human behavior simply because they are more reassuring....

If the advent of a powerful science of behavior causes trouble, it will not be because science itself is inimical to human welfare but because older conceptions have not yielded easily or gracefully. We expect resistance to new techniques of control from those who have heavy investments in the old, but we have no reason to help them preserve a series of principles that are not ends in themselves but rather outmoded means to an end. What is needed is a new conception of human behavior which is compatible with the implications of a scientific analysis. All [people] control and are controlled. The question of government in the broadest possible sense is not how freedom is to be preserved but what kinds of control are to be used and to what ends. Control must be analyzed and considered in its proper proportions.

II (Rogers)

I believe that in Skinner's presentation . . . there is a serious underestimation of the problem of power.

To hope that the power which is being made available by the behavioral sciences will be exercised by the scientists, or by a benevolent group, seems to me like a hope little supported by either recent or distant history. . . . If behavioral scientists are concerned solely with advancing their science, it seems most probable that they will serve the purposes of whatever individual or group has the power.

But the major flaw I see in this review of what is involved in the scientific control of human behavior is the denial, misunderstanding, or gross underestimation of the place of ends, goals, or values in their relationship to science. . . .

I would point out . . . that to choose to experiment is a value choice. Even to move in the direction of perfectly random experimentation is a value choice. To test the consequences of an experiment is possible only if we have first made a subjective choice of a criterion value. . . . So even when trying to avoid such choice, it seems inescapable that a prior subjective value choice is necessary for any scientific endeavor, or for any application of scientific knowledge. . . .

It is my contention that science cannot come into being without a personal choice of the values we wish to achieve. And these values we choose to implement will forever lie outside of the science which implements them; the goals we select, the purposes we wish to follow, must always be outside of the science which achieves them. To me this has the encouraging meaning that the human person, with his [or her] capacity of subjective choice, can and will always exist separate from and prior to any of his [or her] scientific undertakings. Unless as individuals and groups we choose to relinquish our capacity of subjective choice, we will always remain persons, not simply pawns of a self-created science.

II (Skinner)

If we are worthy of our democratic heritage, we shall, of course, be ready to resist any tyrannical use of science for immediate or selfish purposes. But if we value the achievements and goals of democracy, we must not refuse to apply science . . . even though we may then find ourselves in the position of controllers. Fear of control, generalized beyond any warrant, has led to a misinterpretation of valid practices and the blind rejection of intelligent planning for a better way of life. In terms which I trust Rogers will approve, in conquering this fear we shall become more mature and better organized and shall, thus, more fully actualize ourselves as human beings.

Summary

Motivation is a construct used to explain observed differences in what people do and how much effort they put into these behaviors. Work motivation is of great interest to organizations because generally the more effort that is put into a job, the better the performance (provided ability is adequate). The current mainstream approaches to understanding work motivation are dispositional theories, cognitive theories, and the reinforcement model. All make contributions to theory and practice, but none is adequate alone.

Job satisfaction is an attitude determined by an individual's affective evaluation of a work situation. There are small but well-established negative correlations between measures of this attitude and absenteeism and turnover. Evidence regarding the relationship between job satisfaction and individual work performance is mixed, with rewards playing a central moderating role. The concept of job satisfaction may be more useful in predicting individual off-task work behavior and/or work performance at the organization level, but much more research is needed before reaching any conclusions.

Questions for Review and Discussion

1. Discuss the role of work motivation in determining work performance. Why do you think many people are so certain that motivation must be the problem when employees do not put much effort into their work?

2. Use the general expectancy theory of work motivation to examine the effort (motivation) that you put into (a) this course, *or* (b) school in general, *or* (c) your present job if you are employed.

3. Discuss one example from your own experience at work, school, home, or in a social situation of each of the following: (a) a desired behavior that is ignored, (b) a desired behavior that is punished, (c) an undesired behavior that is rewarded.

4. Why is there no "objective" measure of job satisfaction? Of the measurement approaches discussed, which comes closest to capturing what job satisfaction means to you? Explain briefly.

5. Discuss briefly the hypothesis that "a good worker is a happy worker" in the light of a work experience of your own (use the job of student if you have not worked).

Key Terms

citizenship behavior

dispositional theories of motivation

equity theory

general expectancy theory

goal-setting theory

job characteristics model

job satisfaction

motivation

need theories of motivation

procedural justice

reinforcement model of motivation

schedules of reinforcement

self-efficacy

work performance determinants

References

Adams, J. S. (1963). Toward an understanding of equity. *Journal of Abnormal and Social Psychology, 67,* 422–436.

Adams, J. S. (1965). Inequity in social exchange. In L. Berkowitz (Ed.), *Advances in experimental social psychology* (Vol. 2). New York: Academic Press.

Alderfer, C. P. (1969). An empirical test of a new theory of human needs. *Organizational Behavior and Human Performance, 4,* 142–175.

Alderfer, C. P. (1972). *Existence, relatedness, and growth: Human needs in organizational settings.* New York: Free Press.

Andrews, F. M., & Withey, S. G. (1976). *Social indicators of well being: Americans' perceptions of life quality.* New York: Plenum Press.

Anfuso, D. (1995). PepsiCo shares power and wealth with workers. *Personnel Journal, 74,* 42–49.

Arvey, R. D., Bouchard, T. J., Segal, N. L., & Abraham, L. M. (1989). Job satisfaction: Environmental and genetic components. *Journal of Applied Psychology, 74,* 187–192.

At Emery Air Freight: Positive reinforcement boosts performance. (1973). *Organizational Dynamics, 1,* 41–50.

Atkinson, J. W., & Feather, N. T. (1966). *A theory of achievement motivation.* New York: Wiley.

Audia, G., Kristof-Brown, A., Brown, K, G., & Locke, E. A. (1996). Relationship of goals and microlevel work processes to performance on a multipath manual task. *Journal of Applied Psychology, 81,* 483–497.

Bagozzi, R. P., & Warshaw, P. R. (1992). An examination of the etiology of the attitude-behavior relation for goal-directed behaviors. *Multivariate Behavioral Research, 27,* 601–634.

Bandura, A. (1986). *Social foundations of thought and action: A social cognitive theory.* Englewood Cliffs, NJ: Prentice-Hall.

Barrick, M. R., & Mount, M. K. (1991). The Big Five personality dimensions and job performance. *Personnel Psychology, 44,* 1–26.

Bateman, T. S., & Organ, D. W. (1983). Job satisfaction and the good soldier: The relationship between affect and employee "citizenship." *Academy of Management Journal, 26,* 587–595.

Bergmann, T. J., Bergmann, M. A., & Grahn, J. L. (1994). How important are employee benefits to public sector employees? *Public Personnel Management, 23,* 397–406.

Bobko, P., & Colella, A. (1994). Employee reactions to performance standards: A review and research propositions. *Personnel Psychology, 47,* 1–29.

Buckley, M. R., Carraher, S. M., & Cote, J. A. (1992). Measurement issues concerning the use of inventories of job satisfaction. *Educational and Psychological Measurement, 52,* 529–543.

Campbell, J. P., Dunnette, M. D., Lawler, E. E., III, & Weick, K. E., Jr. (1970). *Managerial behavior, performance, and effectiveness.* New York: McGraw-Hill.

Campbell, J. P., & Pritchard, R. D. (1979). Research evidence pertaining to expectancy-instrumentality-valence theory. In R. M. Steers and L. W. Porter (Eds.), *Motivation and work behavior* (2nd ed.). New York: McGraw-Hill.

Campion, M. A., & Lord, R. G. (1982). A control systems conceptualization of the goal-setting and changing process. *Organizational Behavior and Human Performance, 30,* 265–287.

Casey, W. W. (1989). Review of applied behavior analytic research on sales performance improvement. *Journal of Organizational Behavior Management, 10,* 53–76.

Cassidy, T., & Lynn, R. (1989). A multifactorial approach to achievement motivation: The development of a comprehensive measure. *Journal of Occupational Psychology, 62,* 301–312.

Cherrington, D. J., Reitz, H. J., & Scott, W. E., Jr. (1971). Effects of contingent and noncontingent reward on the relationship between satisfaction and task performance. *Journal of Applied Psychology, 55,* 531–536.

Cropanzano, R., James, K., & Konovsky, M. A. (1993). Dispositional affectivity as a predictor of work attitudes and job performance. *Journal of Organizational Behavior, 14,* 595–606.

Dalessio, A., Silverman, W. H., & Schuck, J. R. (1986). Paths to turnover: A re-analysis and review of existing data on the Mobley, Horner, and Hollingsworth turnover model. *Human Relations, 39,* 245–263.

Das, B., & Mital, A. (1994). Production feedback and standards as moderators of the worker satisfaction–productivity relationship. *Ergonomics, 37,* 1185–1194.

Das, B., & Shikdar, A. A. (1989). Assigned and participative production standards and feedback affecting worker productivity in a repetitive production task. *Journal of Human Ergology, 18,* 3–12.

Davis, F. D., Bagozzi, R. P., & Warshaw, P. R. (1992). Extrinsic and intrinsic motivation to use computers in the workplace. *Journal of Applied Social Psychology, 22,* 1111–1132.

Deci, E. L. (1972). The effects of contingent and noncontingent rewards and controls on intrinsic motivation. *Organizational Behavior and Human Performance, 8,* 217–229.

DeShon, R. P., Brown, K. G., & Greenis, J. L (1996). Does self-regulation require cognitive resources? Evaluation of resource allocation models of goal setting. *Journal of Applied Psychology, 81,* 595–608.

Dornstein, M. (1989). The fairness judgements of received pay and their determinants. *Journal of Occupational Psychology, 62,* 287–299.

Drucker, P. F. (1954). *The practice of management.* New York: Harper & Row.

Dubin, R., & Champoux, J. E. (1977). Central life interests and job satisfaction. *Organizational Behavior and Human Performance, 18,* 366–377.

Earley, P. C., Northcraft, G. B., Lee, C., & Lituchy, T. R. (1990). Impact of process and outcome feedback on the relation of goal setting to task performance. *Academy of Management Journal, 33,* 87–105.

Eden, D., & Aviram, A. (1993). Self-efficacy training to seed reemployment: Helping people to help themselves. *Journal of Applied Psychology, 78,* 352–360.

Eisenberger, R., & Cameron, J. (1996). Detrimental effects of reward: Reality or myth? *American Psychologist, 51,* 1153–1166.

Erlich, J. J. (1969). Attitudes, behavior, and the intervening variables. *American Sociologist, 4,* 29–34.

Feldman, D. C., & Doerpinghaus, H. I. (1992). Patterns of part-time employment. *Journal of Vocational Behavior, 41,* 282–294.

Folger, R., & Greenberg, J. (1985). Procedural justice: An interpretative analysis of personnel systems. *Research in Personnel and Human Resource Management, 3,* 141–183.

Fox, J. B., Scott, K. D., & Donohue, J. M. (1993). An investigation into pay valence and performance in a pay-for-performance field setting. *Journal of Organizational Behavior, 14,* 687–693.

Garland, H. (1983). Influence of ability, assigned goals, and normative information on personal goals and performance: A challenge to the goal attainability assumption. *Journal of Applied Psychology, 68,* 20–30.

Gellatly, I. R. (1996). Conscientiousness and task performance: Test of a cognitive process model. *Journal of Applied Psychology, 81,* 474–482.

George, J. T., & Hopkins, B. L. (1989). Multiple effects of performance-contingent pay for waitpersons. *Journal of Applied Behavior Analysis, 22,* 131–141.

Giles, W. F., & Feild, H. S. (1978). The relationship of satisfaction level and content of job satisfaction questionnaire items to item sensitivity. *Academy of Management Journal, 21,* 295–301.

Gist, M. E., & Mitchell, T. R. (1992). Self-efficacy: A theoretical analysis of its determinants and malleability. *Academy of Management Review, 17,* 183–211.

Gomez-Mejia, L. R., Balkin, D. B., & Milkovich, G. T. (1990). Rethinking rewards for technical employees. *Organizational Dynamics, 18,* 62–75.

Griffeth, R. W., Vecchio, R. P., & Logan, J. W. (1989). Equity theory and interpersonal attraction. *Journal of Applied Psychology, 74,* 394–401.

Guagnano, G. A., Stern, P. C., & Dietz, T. (1995). Influences of attitude-behavior relationships: A natural experiment with curbside recycling. *Environment and Behavior, 27,* 699–718.

Gutek, B. A., & Winter, S. J. (1992). Consistency of job satisfaction across situations: Fact or framing artifact? *Journal of Vocational Behavior, 41,* 61–78.

Hackman, J. R., & Lawler, E. E. (1971). Employee reactions to job characteristics. *Journal of Applied Psychology, 60,* 159–170.

Hackman, J. R., & Oldham, G. R. (1976). Motivation through the design of work: A test of a theory. *Organizational Behavior and Human Performance, 16,* 250–279.

Hackman, J. R., & Oldham, G. R. (1980). *Work redesign.* Reading, MA: Addison-Wesley.

Hanisch, K. A. (1992). The Job Descriptive Index revisited: Questions about the question mark. *Journal of Applied Psychology, 77,* 377–382.

Harder, J. W. (1992). Play for pay: Effects of inequity in a pay-for-performance context. *Administrative Science Quarterly, 37,* 321–335.

Helmreich, R. L., Sawin, L. L., & Carsrud, A. L (1986). The honeymoon effect in job performance: Temporal increases in predictive power of achievement motivation. *Journal of Applied Psychology, 71,* 185–188.

Herzberg, F. (1966). *Work and the nature of man.* Cleveland: World.

Herzberg, F., Mausner, B., & Snyderman, B. B. (1959). *The motivation to work.* New York: Wiley.

Hitt, D. D., Marriott, R. G., & Esser, J. K. (1992). Effects of delayed rewards and task interest on intrinsic motivation. *Basic and Applied Social Psychology, 13,* 405–414.

Huseman, R. C., Hatfield, J. D., & Miles, E. W. (1987). A new perspective on equity theory: The equity sensitivity construct. *Academy of Management Review, 12,* 222–234.

Ilgen, D. R., & Klein, H. J. (1989). Organizational behavior. *Annual Review of Psychology, 40,* 327–352.

Ironson, G. H., Smith, P. C., Brannick, M. T., Gibson, W. M. (1989). Construction of a Job in General scale: A comparison of global, composite, and specific measures. *Journal of Applied Psychology, 74,* 193–200.

Johnson, D. S., & Perlow, R. (1992). The impact of need for achievement components on goal commitment and performance. *Journal of Applied Social Psychology, 22,* 1711–1720.

Judge, T. A., & Hulin, C. L. (1993). Job satisfaction as a reflection of disposition: A multiple source causal analysis. *Organizational Behavior and Human Decision Processes, 56,* 388–421.

Judge, T. A., & Watanabe, S. (1993). Another look at the job satisfaction–life satisfaction relationship. *Journal of Applied Psychology, 78,* 939–948.

Judge, T. A., & Watanabe, S. (1994). Individual differences in the nature of the relationship between job and life satisfaction. *Journal of Occupational and Organizational Psychology, 67,* 101–107.

Jung, K. G., Dalessio, A., & Johnson, S. M. (1986). Stability of the factor structure of the Job Descriptive Index. *Academy of Management Journal, 29,* 609–616.

Kabanoff, B. (1980). Work and nonwork: A review of models, methods, and findings. *Psychological Bulletin, 88,* 60–77.

Kacmar, K. M., & Ferris, G. R. (1989). Theoretical and methodological considerations in the age–job satisfaction relationship. *Journal of Applied Psychology, 74,* 201–207.

Kanfer, R. (1990). Motivation theory and industrial/organizational psychology. In M. D. Dunnette & L. Hough (Eds.), *Handbook of industrial and organizational psychology: Vol 1. Theory in industrial and organizational psychology.* Palo Alto, CA: Consulting Psychologists Press.

Kanfer, R. (1994). Work motivation: New directions in theory and research. In C. L. Cooper & I. T. Robertson (Eds.), *Key reviews in managerial psychology: Concepts and research for practice.* Chichester, England: Wiley.

Katz, D., & Kahn, R. L. (1966). *The social psychology of organizations.* New York: Wiley.

Katzell, R. A., & Thompson, D. E. (1990). Work motivation: Theory and practice. *American Psychologist, 45,* 144–153.

Kerr, S. (1975). On the folly of rewarding A, while hoping for B. *Academy of Management Journal, 18,* 769–783.

Kets de Vries, M. F. R., Miller, D., Toulouse, J-M., Friesen, P., Boivert, M., & Theriault, R. (1984). Using the life cycle to anticipate satisfaction with work. *Journal of Forecasting, 3,* 161–172.

Kirkcaldy, B. D., & Cooper, C. L. (1993). The relationship between work stress and leisure style: British and German managers. *Human Relations, 46,* 669–680.

Koch, J. L. (1979). Effects of goal specificity and performance feedback to work groups on peer leadership, performance, and attitudes. *Human Relations, 32,* 819–840.

Kuhl, J. (1985). Volitional mediators of cognition-behavior consistency: Self-regulatory processes and action versus state orientation. In J. Kuhl & J. Beckmann (Eds.), *Action control: From cognition to behavior.* Berlin: Springer-Verlag.

Lambert, S. J. (1990). Processes linking work and family: A critical review and research agenda. *Human Relations, 43,* 239–257.

Landy, F. J. (1978). An opponent process theory of job satisfaction. *Journal of Applied Psychology, 63,* 533–547.

Latham, G. P., & Huber, V. L (1992). Schedules of reinforcement: Lessons from the past and issues for the future. *Journal of Organizational Behavior Management, 12,* 125–149.

Latham, G. P., Mitchell, T. R., & Dossett, D. L. (1978). Importance of participative goal setting and anticipated rewards on goal difficulty and job performance. *Journal of Applied Psychology, 63,* 163–171.

Lawler, E. E. (1973). *Motivation in work organizations.* Monterey, CA: Brooks/Cole.

Leung, K., & Li, W. (1990). Psychological mechanisms of process-control effects. *Journal of Applied Psychology, 75,* 613–620.

Levin, I., & Stokes, J. P. (1989). Dispositional approach to job satisfaction: Role of negative affectivity. *Journal of Applied Psychology, 74,* 752–758.

Liou, K., Sylvia, R. D., & Brunk, G. (1990). Non-work factors and job satisfaction revisited. *Human Relations, 43,* 77–86.

Locke, E. A. (1968). Toward a theory of task motivation and incentives. *Organizational Behavior and Human Performance, 3,* 157–189.

Locke, E. A. (1976). The nature and causes of job satisfaction. In M. D. Dunnette (Ed.), *Handbook of Industrial and Organizational Psychology.* Chicago: Rand McNally.

Locke, E. A., Latham, G. P., & Erez, M. (1988). The determinants of goal commitment. *Academy of Management Review, 13,* 23–39.

Luthans, F., Paul, R., & Baker, D. (1981). An experimental analysis of the impact of contingent reinforcement intervention on salespersons' performance behavior. *Journal of Applied Psychology, 66,* 314–323.

Mark, M. M., & Greenberg, J. (1987, January). Evening the score. *Psychology Today,* pp. 44–50.

Martocchio, J. J. (1994). Effects of conceptions of ability on anxiety, self-efficacy, and learning in training. *Journal of Applied Psychology, 79,* 819–825.

Maslow, A. H. (1943). A theory of motivation. *Psychological Review, 50,* 370–396.

McClelland, D. C. (1961). *The achieving society.* Princeton, NJ: D. Van Nostrand.

McClelland, D. C., & Winter, D. C. (1969). *Motivating economic achievement.* New York: Free Press.

McHenry, J. J., Hough, L. M., Toquam, J. L., Hanson, M. A., & Ashworth, S. (1990). Project A validity result: The relationship between predictor and criterion domains. *Personnel Psychology, 43,* 335–354.

Medcof, J. W., & Wegener, J. G. (1992). Work technology and the needs for achievement and nurturance among nurses. *Journal of Organizational Behavior, 13,* 413–423.

Mento, A. J., Locke, E. A., & Klein, H. J. (1992). Relationship of goal level to valence and instrumentality. *Journal of Applied Psychology, 77,* 395–405.

Miller, M. V., & Hoppe, S. K. (1994). Attributions for job termination and psychological distress. *Human Relations, 47,* 307–327.

Mitchell, T. R., Hopper, H., Daniels, D., George-Falvy, J., & James, L. R. (1994). Predicting self-efficacy and performance during skill acquisition. *Journal of Applied Psychology, 79,* 506–517.

Moorman, R. H. (1993). The influence of cognitive and affective based job satisfaction on measures of the relationship between satisfaction and organizational citizenship behavior. *Human Relations, 46,* 759–776.

Mowday, R. T. (1979). Equity theory predictions of behavior in organizations. In R. M. Steers & L. W. Porter (Eds.), *Motivation and work behavior* (2nd ed.). New York: McGraw-Hill.

Mowen, J., Middlemist, R., & Luther, D. (1981). Joint effects of assigned goal level and incentive structure on task performance: A laboratory study. *Journal of Applied Psychology, 66,* 598–603.

Near, J. P., Rice, R. W., & Hunt, R. G. (1980). The relationship between work and nonwork domains: A review of empirical research. *Academy of Management Review, 5,* 415–429.

Organ, D. W. (1977). A reappraisal and reinterpretation of the satisfaction-causes-performance hypothesis. *Academy of Management Review, 2,* 46–53.

Organ, D. W. (1988). A restatement of the satisfaction-performance hypothesis. *Journal of Management, 14,* 547–557.

Organ, D. W., & Konovsky, M. (1989). Cognitive versus affective determinants of organizational citizenship behavior. *Journal of Applied Psychology, 74,* 157–164.

Organ, D. W., & Ryan, K. (1995). A meta-analytic review of attitudinal and dispositional predictors of organizational citizenship behavior. *Personnel Psychology, 48,* 775–802.

Ostroff, C. (1992). The relationship between satisfaction, attitudes, and performance: An organizational level analysis. *Journal of Applied Psychology, 77,* 963–974.

Peach, E. B., & Wren, D. A. (1992). Pay for performance from antiquity to the 1950s. *Journal of Organizational Behavior Management, 12,* 5–26.

Phelan, J. (1994). The paradox of the contented female worker: An assessment of alternative explanations. *Social Psychology Quarterly, 57,* 95–107.

Popper, S. E., & McCloskey, K. (1993). Individual differences and subgroups within populations: The shopping bag approach. *Aviation, Space, and Environmental Medicine, 64,* 74–77.

Porter, L. W. (1961). A study of perceived need satisfaction in bottom and middle management jobs. *Journal of Applied Psychology, 45,* 1–10.

Porter, L. W., & Lawler, E. E. (1968). *Managerial attitudes and performance.* Homewood, IL: Dorsey Press.

Quinn, R. P., Staines, G. L., & McCollough, M. R. (1974). *Job satisfaction: Is there a trend?* Washington, DC: U.S. Department of Labor.

Quiñones, M. A. (1995). Pretraining context effects: Training assignment as feedback. *Journal of Applied Psychology, 80,* 226–238.

Rentsch, J. R., & Steel, R. P. (1992). Construct and concurrent validation of the Andrews and Withey job satisfaction questionnaire. *Educational and Psychological Measurement, 52,* 357–367.

Rice, R. W., McFarlin, D. B., & Bennett, D. E. (1989). Standards of comparison and job satisfaction. *Journal of Applied Psychology, 74,* 591–598.

Rodgers, R., Hunter, J. E., & Rodgers, D. L. (1993). Influence of top management commitment on management program success. *Journal of Applied Psychology, 78,* 151–155.

Rogers, C. R., & Skinner, B. F. (1956). Some issues concerning control of human behavior: A symposium. *Science, 124,* 1057–1066.

Roznowski, M., & Hanisch, K. A. (1990). Building systematic heterogeneity into work attitudes and behavior measures. *Journal of Vocational Behavior, 36,* 361–375.

Saks, A. M. (1995). Longitudinal field investigation of the moderating and mediating effects of self-efficacy on the relationship between training and newcomer adjustment. *Journal of Applied Psychology, 80,* 211–225.

Scott, W. E., Farh, J., & Podsakoff, P. M. (1988). The effects of "intrinsic" and "extrinsic" reinforcement contingencies on task behavior. *Organizational Behavior and Human Decision Processes, 41,* 405–425.

Smith, F. J. (1976). Index of Organizational Reactions (IOR). *JSAS Catalog of Selected Documents in Psychology, 6,* No. 1265.

Smith, K. G., Locke, E. A., & Barry, D. (1990). Goal setting, planning, and organizational performance: An experimental simulation. *Organizational Behavior and Human Decision Processes, 46,* 118–134.

Smith, P. C., Kendall, L. M., & Hulin, C. L. (1969). *The measurement of satisfaction in work and retirement.* Chicago: Rand-McNally.

Staw, B. M., & Barsade, S. G. (1993). Affect and managerial performance: A test of the sadder-but-wiser vs. happier-and-smarter hypotheses. *Administrative Science Quarterly, 38,* 304–331.

Staw, B. M., & Bottger, R. D. (1990). Task revision: A neglected form of work performance. *Academy of Management Journal, 33,* 534–559.

Stern, S. E., & Kipnis, D. (1993). Technology in everyday life and perceptions of competence. *Journal of Applied Social Psychology, 23,* 1892–1902.

Taber, T. D., & Alliger, G. M. (1995). A task-level assessment of job satisfaction. *Journal of Organizational Behavior, 16,* 101–121.

Tait, M., Padgett, M. Y., & Baldwin, T. T. (1989). Job and life satisfaction: A reevaluation of the strength of the relationship and gender effects as a function of the date of the study. *Journal of Applied Psychology, 74,* 502–507.

Tolman, E. C. (1932). *Purposive behavior in animals and men.* New York: Century.

Tubbs, M. E. (1993). Commitment as a moderator of the goal-performance relation: A case for clearer construct definition. *Journal of Applied Psychology, 78,* 86–97.

Tubbs, M. E., & Ekeberg, S. E. (1991). The role of intentions in work motivation: Implications for goal-setting theory and research. *Academy of Management Review, 16,* 180–199.

Turner, A. N., & Lawrence, P. R. (1965). *Individual jobs and the worker.* Cambridge, MA: Harvard University Press.

Van Eerde, W., & Thierry, H. (1996). Vroom's expectancy models and work-related criteria: A meta-analysis. *Journal of Applied Psychology, 81,* 575–586.

Vance, R. J., & Colella, A. (1990). Effects of two types of feedback on goal acceptance and personal goals. *Journal of Applied Psychology, 75,* 68–76.

Vecchio, R. P. (1980). Worker alienation as a moderator of the job quality–job satisfaction relationship: The case of racial differences. *Academy of Management Journal, 23,* 479–486.

Vroom, V. H. (1964). *Work and motivation.* New York: Wiley.

Wahba, M. A., & Bridwell, L. G. (1976). Maslow reconsidered: A review of research on the need hierarchy theory. *Organizational Behavior and Human Performance, 15,* 212–240.

Waldersee, R. (1994). Self-efficacy and performance as a function of feedback sign and anxiety: A service experiment. *Journal of Applied Behavioral Science, 30,* 346–356.

Watson, D., & Slack, A. K. (1993). General factors of affective temperament and their relation to job satisfaction over time. *Organizational Behavior and Human Decision Processes, 54,* 181–202.

Welsh, D. H., Berstein, D. J., & Luthans, F. (1992). Application of the Premack principle of reinforcement to the quality performance of service employees. *Journal of Organizational Behavior Management, 13,* 9–32.

Wiersma, U. J. (1992). The effects of extrinsic rewards in intrinsic motivation: A meta-analysis. *Journal of Occupational and Organizational Psychology, 65,* 101–114.

Witt, L. A., & Nye, L. G. (1992). Gender and the relationship between perceived fairness of pay or promotion and job satisfaction. *Journal of Applied Psychology, 77,* 910–917.

Wright, P. M., O'Leary-Kelly, A. M., Cortina, J. M., Klein, H. J., & Hollenbeck, J. R. (1994). On the meaning and measurement of goal commitment. *Journal of Applied Psychology, 79,* 795–803.

Zedeck, S. (1995). Quoted in "The spillover between work and family life" by R. A. Clay, *APA Monitor, 26,* 44–45.

Zeitz, G. (1990). Age and work satisfaction in a government agency: A situational perspective. *Human Relations, 43,* 419–438.

7

Employee Absenteeism, Turnover, and Organizational Commitment

PSYCHOLOGY AT WORK

When Companies Give, Employees Give Back

Excerpted from D. C. Calabria, "When Companies Give, Employees Give Back." *Personnel Journal*, April 1995, *73*, 75–83. Copyright 1995 ACC Communications. All rights reserved. Reprinted with permission.

You leave for work, your briefcase, your lunch and your family's laundry in hand. But instead of making a delaying detour to the neighborhood dry cleaner, you drive directly to work and drop your soiled clothes at the company's laundry center. At the end of the workday, you pick up your clean clothes, pay a nominal fee to cover the cost of soap and head straight home.

For 450 office professionals and production workers at Charlotte, North Carolina-based Wilton Connor Packaging Inc., this is a familiar scenario. The firm, which designs, produces, fulfills, and distributes point-of-purchase packaging materials, started the employee service in 1989. . . .

[The company also] surveyed the need for transportation service and . . . obtained two vans from the city and recruited some drivers from among the people who would be using the service. The vans provide door-to-door transportation to employees and even stop at day-care centers on the way to and from work. Riders pay $7 a week to the city for the use of the vans.

These services are just two of many at Wilton Connor designed to help workers simplify their lives. . . .

. . . the cost for the additional employee services is fifteen cents per employee per hour, or $540 a day. But in return, the company receives the rewards of turnover well below the industry average, high quality rankings and a productive work force free from some of life's everyday pressures.

EMPLOYEE LATENESS, absenteeism, and turnover are problems for many companies, and some of them have initiated elaborate programs to reduce them. The programs often involve efforts to increase employee job satisfaction, on the premise that more satisfied employees will be more *willing* to come to work. The management at Wilton Connor Packaging takes an ability rather than a motivational approach, doing what it can to make it easier for people to be *able* to get to work regularly and on time. In so doing, they help employees reduce the hassles of balancing their work and personal lives and lose far fewer people to this conflict than previously.

Turnover is one of the two most frequently used nonperformance behavioral criteria in I/O psychology research. The other is absenteeism. Both responses to work are used as measures of the success of recruiting, screening, selection, training, and other personnel activities designed to increase the fit between individuals, jobs, and organizations. In this chapter, the meaning and measurement of absenteeism and turnover are examined, and some of the major lines of research into the determinants of these behaviors are reviewed. Commitment, the psychological state associated with regular work attendance and staying with an organization, is also explored.

Absenteeism

Estimates of the cost of absenteeism to American organizations vary considerably, but fully loaded costs are believed to be well over $25 billion a year. Fully loaded estimates include indirect costs as well as direct pay and benefits to employees who are not productive because they are not at work. Among the indirect costs of absenteeism are the

237

Chapter 7

*Absenteeism,
Turnover, and
Organizational
Commitment*

costs of temporary replacement employees, the costs of administrative time to reorganize around an absent employee, and productivity losses due to a shorthanded staff or to employees who are not as well trained or as familiar with standard procedures as those who are absent.

Not only are the financial costs of absenteeism in American organizations high, but also absenteeism is one of the most common reasons for dismissing employees (Cascio, 1995). Therefore, it benefits individuals as well as organizations when absenteeism is reduced. I/O psychologists have been studying the problem for many years, but until relatively recently that research had taken a rather narrow focus. There has long been widespread acceptance of the view that absenteeism is a withdrawal response to job dissatisfaction (Nicholson, Brown, & Chadwick-Jones, 1976). This premise is based primarily on a large number of studies in which questionnaire measures of job satisfaction have been found to have a modest negative correlation with measures of absenteeism.

The negative correlation between absenteeism and job satisfaction is a stable one; nevertheless, measures of job satisfaction account for only a small amount of the variance in absenteeism. Other factors are clearly involved. It is also possible that the causality might go the other way; perhaps absenteeism has aversive consequences that promote dissatisfaction with the job (Clegg, 1983). Alternatively, perhaps some people need to justify their absenteeism to themselves by expressing job dissatisfaction. Such questioning of long-held assumptions about absenteeism has served to open up the study of this behavior considerably.

Three directions in which the absenteeism research has been moving in recent years can be identified. First, there are investigations of absenteeism itself, its meaning and its measurement. Second, there are investigations of the correlates of absenteeism, including, but not limited to, job satisfaction. Finally, I/O psychologists are investigating ways to control absenteeism that go beyond attempts to increase job satisfaction. Representative research from each of these three categories is discussed here.

Correlation
See pages 37–39

Variance
See pages 40–42

Correlates
See page 40

The Meaning and Measurement of Absenteeism

Absenteeism may seem to be a self-evident variable, but there are actually a number of ways in which it may be operationally defined. The definitions that are used most frequently are total days (or sometimes hours) lost and frequency of absence occurrences, but there are a number of other possibilities (see Kohler & Mathieu, 1993). Further complicating the matter is the question of excused versus unexcused absences. If no such distinction is made, an absence for mandatory jury duty will be given the same weight as an absence to attend a sporting event. If such a distinction is made, someone must make the decision concerning which absences are excused and which are not.

Organizations differ in their policies about excused versus unexcused absences and whether anyone records absence reasons at all. Today, many simply allow employees some number of personal days per month or year and do not question reasons for absence unless the number taken exceeds the allowance. Nike Inc. uses the increasingly popular option of a time-off bank in which employees accrue time-off hours according to how long they have been with the company. These hours are printed on each paycheck and employees can "spend" them in increments of hours, weeks, or days, no questions asked.

In addition to variation in absence policies, there is also considerable variation in the accuracy with which absence information is recorded. As Hammer and Landau (1981)

Variable
See pages 25–26

**Operational
definition**
See page 26

Criterion

See page 63

Measurement error

See page 53–54

Normal curve

See pages 36–37

Statistical significance

See page 35–36

Research subjects

See page 27

Predictor variables

See pages 41–42

note, "...criterion contamination can occur during the initial classification of absences, before a researcher ever touches the raw data" (p. 578).

Potential data contamination, along with differences in organizational absence policies and operational definitions of absenteeism itself, casts some doubt on the wisdom of drawing firm conclusions from the absenteeism research as a whole. Both the amount and the kind of measurement error are likely to differ from one study to the next. The problem is illustrated by the histograms in Figure 7–1 that show the differences in obtained data distributions when six different measures of absenteeism were applied to the same data (Hammer & Landau, 1981). Three of the measures were based on unexcused absences (voluntary) and three on excused absences (involuntary). Not only do these distributions differ from one another, but also every one has a significant deviation from the normal curve.

Most statistical analysis techniques can be used when there are mild deviations from normality, but Hammer and Landau's data are a very useful illustration of the inherent problems faced in using absenteeism as a research variable. A study by Scott and McClellan (1990), for example, found that absence *occurrences* were not significantly different for male and female subjects, but women took significantly *longer* periods off (more days) than did men. Quite different conclusions would have been reached had these investigators used one or the other operational definition of absenteeism rather than both.

One solution to the problem of absenteeism as a variable in research is to use more than one measure, as Scott and McClellan did. Popp and Belohlav (1982) took this approach further by using multiple measures and comparing their relative utility for research purposes (much as Hammer and Landau compared their statistical properties). Subjects were the all male and predominantly black employees of the city of Cincinnati's Solid Waste Collection Division.

Popp and Belohlav used 19 predictor variables in their study of absenteeism; of the 19, only 2—time with the Waste Collection Division and service in the armed forces— had significant correlations (negative) with absenteeism as measured by total days lost. Three additional variables—job satisfaction, marital status, and perceived supervisory attitude toward absenteeism—were significantly correlated with absence frequency. In this organization, it appears that more could be learned about the correlates of absenteeism if it were defined in terms of absence frequency rather than in terms of total days absent.

A different kind of problem in measuring absenteeism is pointed out by researchers who note that global measures fail to address time-trends in the data, such as differences in absenteeism over the five standard work days. The long-standing typical pattern, as illustrated by the graph in Figure 7–2, is characterized by somewhat higher absenteeism on Mondays than on Tuesdays through Thursdays and much higher absenteeism on Fridays than on other days.

The study from which the graph in Figure 7–2 is taken is an investigation into the possible differences between male and female absence patterns in a large manufacturing plant (Markham, Dansereau, & Alutto, 1982a). These daily trends in absenteeism may be circumvented by collecting data for longer time periods, but Markham and his colleagues also found strong seasonal trends. As Figure 7–3 illustrates, very different conclusions might be drawn from January to June data as opposed to July to December data.

The variety of complex problems and issues regarding the meaning and measurement of absenteeism continues to interest researchers. A previously ignored facet is discussed by Johns (1994a, 1994b), who located some 50 published studies in which self-report absenteeism data were used instead of the usual records-based data (raising all of the issues associated with self-report information).

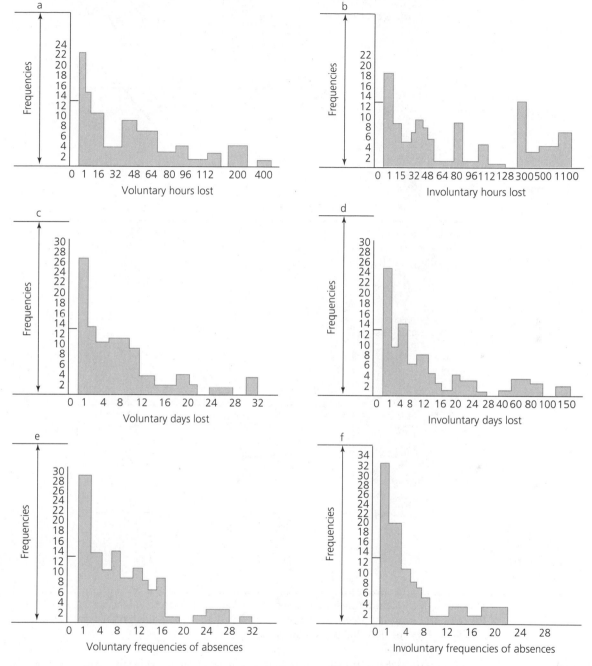

Figure 7–1
Differences in Data Distributions Using Different Absenteeism Measures

From T. H. Hammer and J. Landau, "Methodological Issues in the Use of Absence Data."
Journal of Applied Psychology, 1981, *66*, 574–581. Copyright 1981 by the American
Psychological Association. Reprinted by permission.

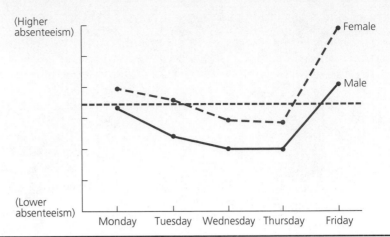

Figure 7–2
Daily Trends in
Absenteeism

From S. E. Markham, F. Dansereau, Jr., and J. A. Alutto, "Female vs. Male Absence Rates: A Temporal Analysis." *Personnel Psychology,* 1982, *35,* 371–382. Copyright 1982 Personnel Psychology, Inc. Reprinted by permission.

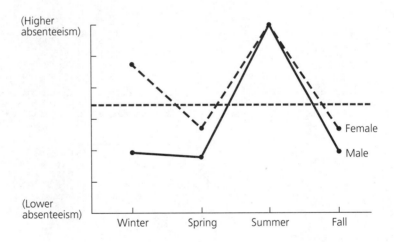

Figure 7–3
Seasonal Trends
in Absenteeism

From S. E. Markham, F. Dansereau, Jr., and J. A. Alutto, "Female vs. Male Absence Rates: A Temporal Analysis." *Personnel Psychology,* 1982, *35,* 371–382. Copyright 1982 Personnel Psychology, Inc. Reprinted by permission.

Inference
See pages 35–43

Meta-analysis
See page 43

Taken as a whole, this line of research suggests that considerable caution should be taken when drawing inferences from the absenteeism literature. Different ways of measuring absenteeism yield different results, and these different results can lead to different conclusions. Particular care should be taken when applying meta-analysis techniques; detailed analysis of absenteeism studies as a group should be undertaken only if the studies are similar as regards subjects, measures of absenteeism, and time periods of data collection.

Determinants of Absenteeism

The search for personal characteristics and organizational variables that are associated with absenteeism has developed partially out of the realization that job dissatisfaction alone is an insufficient explanation. It must be noted, however, that proponents of the "job dissatisfaction causes absenteeism" hypothesis have made significant contributions to this research through their attempts to identify characteristics and variables associated with dissatisfaction (and so with greater absenteeism).

Efforts to prove that job dissatisfaction is a major determinant of absenteeism have largely been abandoned, but newer job satisfaction research offers some provocative hints to those searching for the determinants of absenteeism. George (1989) reports that the dispositional traits of positive and negative affectivity (now believed by many to be important determinants of job satisfaction) had significant effects on the extent to which a sample of more than 200 salespeople experienced positive and negative moods at work. Positive mood at work, in turn, was significantly and negatively correlated with absenteeism—better mood, less absenteeism.

George's investigation is but one in a large body of research into the determinants of absenteeism in organizations. A useful framework for organizing and understanding this literature is provided by Steers and Rhodes (1984). As seen in Figure 7–4, many different kinds of relationships are investigated. In this section, those relationships are reviewed under the two broad categories of personal variables and organizational (or situational) variables. Other topics from this book relevant to the model include motivation ("organizational control systems" in Figure 7–4), group membership ("absence culture and work-group norms"), and job satisfaction ("work-related attitudes").

Determinants
See page 41

Hypothesis
See page 25

Research sample
See page 27

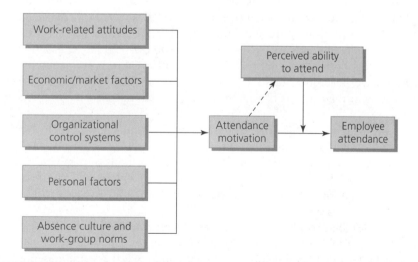

Figure 7–4
A Framework for Organizing Absenteeism Research

From R. M. Steers and S. R. Rhodes, "Knowledge and Speculation About Absenteeism." In P. S. Goodman and R. S. Atkins (Eds.), *Absenteeism: New Approaches to Understanding, Measuring, and Managing Employee Absence.* Copyright 1984 Jossey-Bass. Reprinted with permission.

Personal Variables and Absenteeism

Among the personal characteristics most frequently investigated in connection with absenteeism are age, sex, race, education, off-work responsibilities, income, and marital status. Some researchers consider job tenure and level of position within an organization to fall into this category as well. All of these variables have been found to be correlated with absenteeism, but the trend of the findings is not consistent.

The least ambiguous relationship to emerge from research into the relationship between personal variables and absenteeism is that with sex. As illustrated in Figures 7–2 and 7–3, the results of most studies show women to have a higher rate of absenteeism than men (see also Fitzgibbons & Moch, 1980; Leigh, 1986; Rogers & Herting, 1993). A variety of explanations have been advanced for this finding.

Most of the explanations for the relatively greater absenteeism rates of women focus on the conflict that can be generated by special demands placed on women who work and who also have families relying on them. The fact that women in general hold lower-level jobs than men in general also is believed to be a relevant factor. Whatever the specifics, the consensus among researchers at this time seems to be that the sex of employees must be taken into consideration when developing explanations for absenteeism (e.g., VandenHeuvel & Wooden, 1995), and that accurate explanations are likely to be more complicated for women than for men (e.g., Hendrix, Spencer, & Gibson, 1994).

Hendrix, Spencer, and Gibson's conclusion that the determinants of absenteeism are more complicated for women than for men receives additional support from research into the relationship between age and absenteeism. A large-scale meta-analysis of this literature found that age has a moderately strong negative correlation with voluntary or avoidable absenteeism (as age increases, absenteeism decreases) for men but not for women (Hackett, 1990).

The explanation most usually offered for the fact that, unlike men, women are not absent from work less as their chronological age increases is that women have more domestic responsibilities in middle years than men. Other research throws the adequacy of this explanation into question, however. Hackett (1989) analyzed three separate meta-analyses of the relevant literature and concluded that the greater the proportion of females in the sample, the more negative the association between job satisfaction and absence. Putting this finding together with the fact that (speaking very generally) women tend to have lower-level jobs than men, raises the possibility that the dissatisfaction of many women with their jobs is canceling out any overall decrease in absenteeism with age.

A second "for instance" possibility is raised by the results of a study by Martocchio and Judge (1994), which suggests that the people who can least afford financially to be absent from work are absent less. To a point, financial responsibilities tend to increase with age (mortgage, children in college, and so on) for many people. Would a different age-absenteeism pattern emerge if wage earner status (primary vs. secondary) were taken into account in this research?

The examples are speculative. Perhaps, as Lawrence (1987) suggests, age is only a proxy (stand-in) variable for multiple physiological, psychological, and social processes that must be better undersood before the association between age and absenteeism can be clarified. It seems clear that this is an area in which more research (or perhaps different research) is called for; regardless of what I/O psychologists or their research may say, managers often find older employees of either sex to be more reliable. When a very large British hardware chain experimented with staffing one store entirely with clerks over the

243

Chapter 7

*Absenteeism,
Turnover, and
Organizational
Commitment*

age of 50, for example, absenteeism was almost 40% lower than the average for the chain. In addition, inventory damage and theft dropped almost 60%.

Organizational Variables and Absenteeism

A number of different aspects of the job situation have been investigated in the search for the determinants of absenteeism. The nature of the work that an individual performs has been the focus of much of this research, which usually is based on the hypothesis that boring, unfulfilling work leads to job dissatisfaction. The dissatisfaction, in turn, leads to increased absenteeism. Some of the findings support this hypothesis; some do not. Individual differences appear to be substantial.

A second organizational variable whose possible relationship to absenteeism has interested researchers is size, both of an individual's work group (e.g., Markham, Dansereau, & Alutto, 1982b) and of the organization (e.g., Allen, 1982). These studies are usually conducted at a particular point in time, but Markham and McKee (1991) took a longitudinal approach. These investigators examined absenteeism rates over a five-year period in 17 plants whose size (as determined by a measure of total number of employees) was declining. As predicted, they found that absenteeism declined as plant size declined.

Considered overall, a trend toward less absenteeism in smaller organizations and groups is observed in this line of research. Inferences based on these findings should be made cautiously, however. Differences in operational definitions of size, in the time period involved, and in other variables examined at the same time, make different studies on this question particularly difficult to compare directly.

Despite possible problems with the research, the logic of a decline in absenteeism with a decline in size of group or organization is compelling for at least two reasons. For one, the absence of any particular individual is more noticeable when a group is smaller. For another, when the work force in an organization is being reduced, the remaining employees may be concerned that being absent will place their own jobs in jeopardy.

Other organizational variables whose possible correlation with absenteeism have been investigated include work shift, leader behavior, company ownership, and the extent to which a job is hazardous. Studies reporting statistically significant correlations between absenteeism and all of these variables are to be found in the literature. However, it cannot be said that any one of them alone is an important determinant of absenteeism. A social environmental variable called the "absence culture" (Nicholson & Johns, 1985) is more promising.

An organization's absence culture is probably best explained by an example. Johns (1994a) describes the *anti*-absence culture of a large utility firm as follows:

> The company . . . was actively concerned with good attendance. It kept fairly meticulous attendance records. . . . A senior manager in the health and safety department was charged with overseeing an attendance management program. . . . Managers were required to counsel excessive absentees . . . and a doctor's note was required for absences of 3 days or more. Employees and their managers alike were actively aware that the company emphasized individual (for employees) and work-group (for managers) attendance as a critical variable in performance evaluations. (p. 230)

It isn't difficult to appreciate that working for a company such as the one described might have an important influence on an employee's decision to attend work, and absence culture research has generated considerable support both for the existence of an absence culture in organizations (e.g., Haccoun & Jeanrie, 1995; Martocchio, 1994) and for the influence of this culture on individual absence behavior (e.g., Markham & McKee, 1995).

To review, investigators have found a number of personal and organizational variables that have modest correlations with absenteeism. A number of I/O psychologists have combined those into models that depict the determinants of employee attendance and the relationships among them. One of these is the well-known Steers and Rhodes (1978) model shown in Figure 7–5. It may look complex, but its basic framework is simple: attendance at work depends on an interaction of motivation to attend and ability to attend. Motivation is seen as playing the more important role, and job satisfaction is hypothesized to play a central role in motivation to attend. Today, many I/O psychologists would not agree with these particular assumptions, but the basic framework described is not controversial.

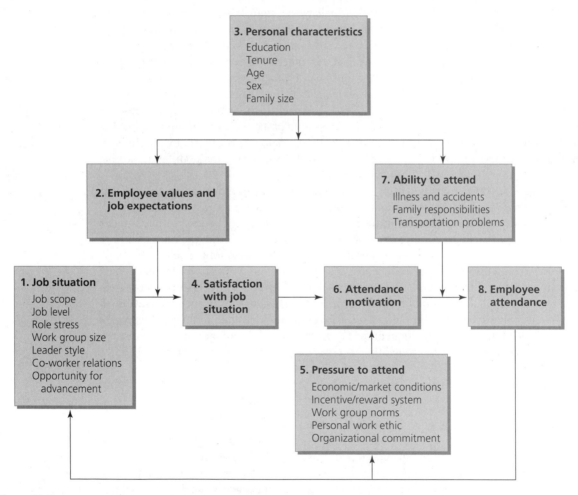

Figure 7–5
A Model of the Major Influences on Employee Attendance

245

Chapter 7

*Absenteeism,
Turnover, and
Organizational
Commitment*

Job Satisfaction and Absenteeism

In his analysis of three independent meta-analyses of the relationship between job satisfaction and absenteeism, Hackett (1989) found consistent negative correlations. The strongest were between (a) absence duration and (b) overall job satisfaction and (a) absence frequency and (b) satisfaction with the work performed. Such negative relationships are well established; the same evidence offers little support for the conclusion that job dissatisfaction accounts for a *major* portion of the variance in absenteeism, however. Breaugh (1981) found that none of the three attitude measures in his longitudinal study of absenteeism among research scientists added anything to the prediction made possible by knowing their attendance records in former positions. Watson (1981) reached a similar conclusion, as did Popp and Belohlav (1982).

One of the more interesting attempts to account for the persistently limited power of job satisfaction to predict absenteeism is offered by Clegg (1983). In his review of some 17 relevant investigations, Clegg points out that the obvious alternative hypothesis to "job dissatisfaction causes more absenteeism" was never investigated at all. This is the idea that the causality may work the other way: more absenteeism may lead to greater job dissatisfaction. The suggestion makes sense at the intuitive level. If absenteeism is followed by unattractive consequences, such as supervisory (or peer) disapproval, wage docking, or having to work late or put in unpaid overtime to catch up, job satisfaction may be reduced accordingly.

In his own study involving some 2,500 employees, Clegg found support for the reverse causality and made a strong case for additional investigations. More recently, Tharenou (1993) investigated both hypotheses in a longitudinal investigation of unexcused absenteeism among apprentices in a utility company. Her conclusion was that the "absenteeism causes dissatisfaction" hypothesis was a better predictor than the traditional view. It is hoped that more I/O psychologists will turn their attention to this interesting and potentially enlightening possibility.

Controlling Absenteeism

One reason that absenteeism receives so much research attention is the expectation that with better understanding will come guidelines for corrective action. The most obvious use of such research is to help organizations "select out" at the beginning those job applicants who have characteristics known to be associated with greater absenteeism. The idea is sound as far as it goes in that a relatively small percentage of the work force in most organizations accounts for a disproportionately high percentage of absenteeism. Despite the logic, the practicality of refusing to hire people who are absence-prone (statistically more likely to be absent from work) is limited.

Sex is the most stable personal correlate of absenteeism, but discrimination in hiring on the basis of sex is prohibited by law. Breaugh's (1981) finding, confirmed by Ivancevich (1985), that the best predictor of future absenteeism is past absenteeism is more promising because this is a behavior and not a personal characteristic. Unfortunately, it is a *past* behavior; refusing to hire someone because he or she had poor attendance on a previous job could be viewed by our courts as unfair discrimination.

A more practical way that knowledge of personal variables might help control absenteeism is illustrated by the Psychology at Work excerpt that opened this chapter. Wilton Connor Packaging focused its attention on ability-to-attend variables. There was nothing

SPOTLIGHT ON RESEARCH

The Impact of Flexible Scheduling on Employee Attendance and Turnover

Research question   What is the effect of flexible scheduling on employee attendance?

Type of study   Naturally occurring field experiment.

Subjects   134 (experimental group) and 140 (control group) hourly employees in nontechnical, white-collar, service-oriented jobs in a large public utility company.

Independent variable   Flexible scheduling or not.

Dependent variable   Rate of unexcused absence as measured by total number of days absent per month divided by total number of employees.

General procedure   With agreement of the labor union, a flexible scheduling program was adopted on an experimental basis in a large subunit of the utility company. Employees were required to be present during core times of 9:30 A.M. to 11 A.M. and 2 P.M. to 3:30 P.M. Balance of hours could be distributed in any way between 7 A.M. and 6 P.M. Absenteeism data were collected during this year.

Analysis   Autoregressive integrated moving average (ARIMA), a class of techniques designed to assess the impact of discrete events on a time series intervention analysis.

Results   The relative absenteeism rates for the experimental and control groups are shown in the histogram below.

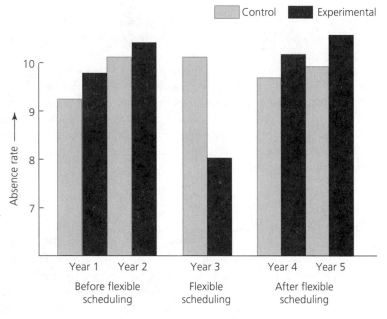

Summarized from D. R. Dalton and D. J. Mesch, "The Impact of Flexible Scheduling on Employee Attendance and Turnover." *Administrative Science Quarterly*, 1990, *35*, 370–387. Histogram developed from data provided in report.

Conclusion   "The results . . . demonstrate large reductions in the absence rate for the experimental group receiving the flexible-scheduling intervention . . . there are obvious practical effects that may increase employees' ability to attend." (p. 381)

they could do about such factors as accidents and illness or family size, but they were able to ease some scheduling problems. They also solved transportation problems for many employees, some of whom had been taking two buses each way going to and from work.

The Wilton Connor experience makes an important point—when it comes to controlling absenteeism, an organization has far more control over environmental variables than over personal ones such as job satisfaction. An interesting field experiment making use of this fact is summarized in Spotlight on Research. In that investigation (Dalton & Mesch, 1990), work hour scheduling (independent variable) was the targeted environmental vari-

Field experiment
See pages 29–31

247

Chapter 7

*Absenteeism,
Turnover, and
Organizational
Commitment*

able. The flexible scheduling that was implemented gives employees some discretion in arranging their work hours to mesh more easily with their life situations. An employee with a long commute, for example, might choose to begin work at 7:30 A.M. and leave at 3:30 P.M. so as to miss the worst of the traffic. One who is trying to coordinate a schedule with a working spouse might choose a different pattern.

The drop in absenteeism (dependent variable) among employees at the utility company who were given a flexible scheduling option was dramatic and turnover also decreased; nevertheless, the program was dropped after one year and absenteeism rates gradually returned to preexperimental levels. As the authors of the study note, flexible scheduling can be difficult to implement and manage in a complex work environment. The attendance control strategy of positive reinforcement for regular work attendance is usually simpler to manage.

**Independent/
dependent
variable**
See page 29

The basic design of a positive reinforcement program for attendance is simple: an incentive is offered for a defined attendance record over a specified time period (often, but not always, perfect attendance). Incentives used in past research include paid time off, eligibility for a drawing for a new television or other prize, and a free two-month membership in a local health club. In a study reported by Landau (1993), the incentive was plain hard cash. It worked. Analysis of changes in attendance over a 204-week period (controlling for season and holidays) showed absenteeism decreased when the incentive system was implemented.

**Positive
reinforcement
program**
See pages 204–206

Positive reinforcement for attendance is not new. It has been recognized for some time and used successfully in a variety of settings (e.g., Brown & Redmon, 1989; Carlson & Hill, 1982). Nevertheless, it would not be accurate to say that the problem of absenteeism is solved. Positive reinforcement techniques do not always fit a particular situation. Even when such a program is successful it may have unintended and undesirable side effects (Miners, Moore, Champous, & Martocchio, 1995). The vice-president of Northwest Airlines' flight-attendants union worries that passenger health and safety could be compromised if legitimately ill employees come to work so as to be able to participate in Northwest's attendance incentive program.

Turnover

For a long time, the study of absenteeism and the study of turnover were linked together quite firmly. These simultaneous investigations were based on a belief that absenteeism is a safety valve for people who are unhappy with their jobs; turnover is the last resort when dissatisfaction becomes too great. This view is supported by the number of studies reporting a positive correlation between absenteeism and turnover. One meta-analysis of 17 of these investigations yielded a corrected average correlation of .33 (a little less than 11% common variance) between the two variables (Mitra, Jenkins, & Gupta, 1992).

**Correlation
coefficient**
See pages 37–38

General recognition that absenteeism and turnover are separate behaviors warranting separate analyses seems to have begun in the mid-1970s. I/O psychologists noticed that many of the coefficients of correlation between absenteeism and turnover were quite small, and many studies found no relationship at all. This is not really all that surprising. As illustrated by the examples in Exhibit 7–1, quite a number of factors might separate a person's decision to be absent from work from his or her decision to leave a job (Mobley, 1982).

There are undoubtedly many cases in which absenteeism and turnover are positively related—that is, cases in which frequent absenteeism is followed by an exit from the organization. This withdrawal hypothesis is still considered by some investigators to be the most appropriate framework for understanding these behaviors. The intent behind Exhibit 7–1 is not to suggest that this never happens; such a position would not be consistent with data in this line of research. On the other hand, the position that it is the only correct explanation is not supported either. For cases in which no relationship between absenteeism and turnover are found, one of the alternative explanations described in Exhibit 7–1 may be more accurate.

The Classification of Turnover

There are at least two different uses of the term *turnover* in the I/O literature. In the generic sense, it refers to a change in the membership of an organization; a position turns over with an outgoing incumbent being replaced by a newcomer. In the specific sense, the term refers to outgoing organizational members. When the term is used in this way, it is common to divide turnover further into voluntary and involuntary categories. This division separates employees who leave of their own accord from those who are terminated involuntarily.

The voluntary-involuntary turnover distinction has been a basic one for some time. As turnover research has expanded, however, it has become apparent that this distinction may be oversimplified. Some voluntary turnover occurs with employees an organization does not mind losing; in other cases, it would prefer to retain the services of the people who leave. From an organization's point of view then, some voluntary turnover is functional and some is dysfunctional.

Exhibit 7–1
Conditions
Under Which
No Correlation
Between
Absenteeism
and Turnover
Would Be
Expected

a. when turnover is a function of the positive attraction of an alternative job rather than escape, avoidance, or "withdrawal" from an unsatisfying or stressful current job;

b. when absenteeism is a function of the need to attend to nonjob role demands (for example, parent, sports person);

c. when the consequences of quitting relative to the consequences of being absent have little in common;

d. when absenteeism or turnover is constrained; for example, a monetarily enforced absenteeism control policy and no job alternatives, respectively;

e. when absenteeism or turnover is a spontaneous or impulsive act;

f. when the work role is structured so as to permit discretionary, nonrecorded time away from the job; for example, professional, managerial positions;

g. when nonused days of absence are "vested" and can be taken with pay at the time of termination;

h. when absenteeism serves as a "safety valve" to dissipate work pressures that otherwise might precipitate turnover.

From W. H. Mobley, "Some Unanswered Questions in Turnover and Withdrawal Research." *Academy of Management Review*, 1982, 7, 111–116. Copyright 1982 Academy of Management. Reprinted by permission.

249

Chapter 7

*Absenteeism,
Turnover, and
Organizational
Commitment*

A case of dysfunctional turnover occurs when an employee who leaves an organization is one it would prefer to keep. There are any number of reasons this might occur, including illness, a decision to make a change in lifestyle, a decision to resume an interrupted education, or a spouse's job opportunity in another location. These reasons have nothing to do with the organization, and there is little that can be done to reduce voluntary turnover in such cases. Accordingly, this turnover may be called unavoidable dysfunctional turnover. The remainder of the dysfunctional turnover group, employees who leave for reasons that are related to the organization or to the job, is the avoidable dysfunctional turnover.

Increasingly refined classifications of turnover are useful both for understanding this behavior and for applied efforts to reduce it. The turnover problem of an organization can be separated into a number of distinct groups; to the extent that there are different dynamics within these groups, I/O psychologists can better understand turnover by making such distinctions. Separating out the unavoidable voluntary turnover group, to take one example, should allow researchers greater success in identifying organizational variables associated with turnover. As can be seen in the diagram in Figure 7–6, these variables have little relevance for the avoidable group.

The practical utility of a more detailed analysis of turnover is illustrated in an investigation by Abelson (1987), who found that nursing employees who were "stayers" and those who were "unavoidable leavers" did not differ from one another in terms of stress, commitment, and job satisfaction. Both groups were significantly different from "avoidable leavers," however. Efforts to reduce turnover among the unavoidable leavers in such a context would probably be wasted.

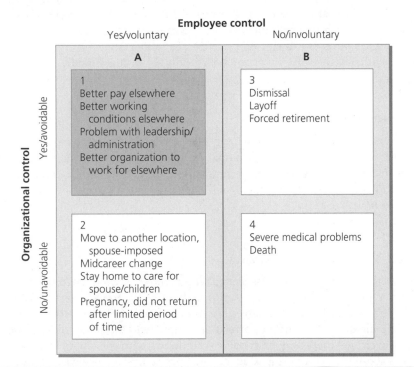

Figure 7–6
Avoidable and
Unavoidable
Turnover

Turnover and Turnover Intentions

In the specific sense of the term, turnover occurs when an individual exits an organization. Much of the literature on turnover is based on recorded information about how many and what kind of employees (sex, age, tenure, and so on) have left. In some research, these statistics are supplemented by information about the reason for the termination. There is also a substantial body of literature in which self-reported intentions to leave an organization, rather than the behavior of leaving, is the dependent variable.

Do people who say they intend to quit a job actually do so? The answer is yes, sometimes. The average correlation coefficient between intention to quit and turnover is in the neighborhood of .25 (Hom, Caranikas-Walker, Prussia, & Griffeth, 1992). This relationship has led most authors to include intentions in models of turnover (e.g., Bannister & Griffeth, 1986; Jackofsky & Peters, 1983; Mobley, Horner, & Hollingsworth, 1978). At the same time, the correlation is not strong enough to assume that intention always leads to termination.

There are many possible explanations for a limited relationship between turnover intentions and turnover. One is simply the weaknesses of self-report data that have been discussed. A second is that turnover intentions probably fluctuate depending on job or other circumstances and data collected at different time points might yield quite different results. More basically, however, is the fact that intentions, like attitudes, are only *one* of the determinants of behavior. An employee may say with all sincerity that he or she has no intention of leaving an organization, then subsequently find an unsolicited offer for a better job from another firm too attractive to turn down.

The fact that turnover intentions are related to, but not the same as, actual turnover gives this variable a dual role in I/O psychology research. As mentioned, it is often investigated as one of the antecedents or determinants of actual turnover. There is also a related body of research in which turnover intention itself is the dependent variable of interest (e.g., Carlopio & Gardner, 1995; Gaertner & Nollen, 1992; George & Jones, 1996). In the current discussion, turnover as a behavior is the primary focus.

Determinants of Turnover

As in the absenteeism research, there has been considerable emphasis in the turnover literature on the personal and organizational variables that are associated with voluntary turnover. Trends from this research are summarized here. It should be noted that in most of these studies the relative percentages of functional versus dysfunctional turnover cases are unknown.

Personal Variables and Turnover

Research into personal variables associated with turnover is dominated by investigations of employee job satisfaction. Findings mirror those of the job satisfaction–absenteeism research. Job satisfaction and turnover are usually found to be negatively related (e.g., Wright & Bonnett, 1993), but the correlation is not large. A number of investigators believe, however, that there may be variables interfering with the ability to make accurate inferences about this relationship. Carsten and Spector (1987) reviewed 47 studies in the job satisfaction–turnover area and found that the correlation between the two varied by the unemployment rate that had existed at the time of the study.

It seems to make sense that if people are less likely to find other jobs, they should be less likely to leave a current one even if they are dissatisfied with it. In this case, a measure of job satisfaction would have a low correlation with turnover. Despite the apparent logic of this proposition, the results of other studies have not been encouraging (e.g., Hui, 1988; Steel & Griffeth, 1989). Further investigation may prove useful, however, as the effects of the major downsizings of the 1990s on employment opportunity continue to accumulate.

A potential moderator of the job satisfaction–job turnover relationship that is new to this line of research is an individual's disposition to be satisfied in general. Some support for this possibility is found in a study reported by Gupta, Jenkins, and Beehr (1992). These investigators found that people who changed jobs tended to retain the same kinds of attitudes toward the new job as toward the old even when the jobs were substantially different. In another investigation, Judge (1993) found that the more positive was the general disposition of individuals within a sample of nurses, the stronger was the relationship observed between turnover and job dissatisfaction. The nurses most likely to quit were those who were generally satisfied with life but dissatisfied with their jobs. Both this study and that of Gupta used actual turnover rather than expressed intention to leave a job as the criterion.

Moderator variable
See page 39

Despite its dominance in the turnover literature, job satisfaction is not the only individual characteristic that has been investigated. Others include age, sex, education level, job tenure, expressed needs for personal growth on the job, past employment history, the degree to which a job meets expectations, turnover intentions, and level of job performance. Level of job performance (good, average, poor) is a personal variable whose relationship to turnover has been of particular interest to I/O psychologists. Job performance might be expected to have direct effects on turnover because it supplies information relevant to both the ease and the desirability of changing jobs.

In a 15-year study of turnover in a large national oil company, Dreher (1982) found no evidence that it was better performers who left the company over the time period studied. Multiple measures of performance, aptitude, potential, and promotional success supported the opposite hypothesis for the 500-plus employees who voluntarily left the company.

The stayers and the leavers in Dreher's study all entered the company at about the same time, but stayers received significantly more promotions per year and significantly higher performance evaluations than leavers. Keller (1984) found a similar pattern with respect to performance and turnover in a medium-sized manufacturing plant (see also McEvoy & Cascio, 1987). Additional support is offered, if less directly, by Werbel and Bedeian (1989), who found that among a group of accountant subjects, the greatest intentions to quit were expressed by older and more poorly performing individuals.

Not all research supports the conclusion that poorer performers are more likely to leave an organization voluntarily. A number of investigators have found just the opposite—the better performers are more likely to leave (e.g., Bassett, 1967; Martin, Price, & Mueller, 1981). There is also evidence that performers at *both* ends of the performance continuum (higher and lower than average) are more likely to quit than are the average performers in the middle (e.g., Jackofsky, Ferris, & Breckenridge, 1986; Zenger, 1992). In this case, a graph of the relationship between performance and turnover would not be a straight line, but a U-shape. More support for a curvilinear relationship was found in a recent meta-analysis of 55 studies (Williams & Livingstone, 1994).

Curvilinearity
See pages 38–39

The matter is by no means settled, but research such as that described makes the conclusion inescapable that an individual's level of performance is relevant to his or her decision to leave a job under some conditions. The influence may not always be direct; another possibility is that level of performance may have indirect effects on turnover by acting as a moderator of the satisfaction-turnover relationship. As shown in Figure 7–7, Spencer and Steers (1981) found that turnover decreased as satisfaction increased, but only for poor performers (dotted line). Turnover rates for good performers (solid line) changed little as job satisfaction increased.

One possible interpretation of the Spencer and Steers data lies in the fact that people want different things from work. In most organizations, poor performers usually get fewer of the formal rewards (a promotion to a higher pay grade, for example) that come with acceptable or superior performance. If these rewards are very important to a person, his or her reported job satisfaction will be lower than that of equally poor performers who find their job satisfaction in other aspects of the work situation (such as compatible co-workers). People in the first low-performing group may move on to search for greener pastures, whereas those in the second may have no interest in leaving the organization.

A few other examples from the research into possible relationships between turnover and individual variables will close this section.

- *Age.* The results of individual investigations vary, but the authors of a recent large-scale (more than 42,000 subjects) meta-analysis of the literature spanning the years 1959–1993 conclude that age is not related in a meaningful way to an individual's decision to leave an organization (Healy, Lehman, & McDaniel, 1995).

- *Job search behavior.* Active job search behavior is an event that frequently occurs between turnover intention and actual turnover. Blau (1993) reports that knowledge of this behavior contributes to the ability to predict turnover above and beyond that of attitudes and intentions.

- *Past employment history.* An analysis of more than 1,500 subjects revealed that a history of job hopping (the "hobo syndrome") predicts present turnover even after controlling for possibly confounding variables (Judge & Watanabe, 1995).

Figure 7–7
Job
Performance,
Job
Satisfaction,
and Turnover

From D. G. Spencer and R. M. Steers, "Performance as a Moderator of the Job Satisfaction–Turnover Relationship." *Journal of Applied Psychology,* 1981, *66,* 511–514. Copyright 1981 by the American Psychological Association. Reprinted by permission.

253

Chapter 7

*Absenteeism,
Turnover, and
Organizational
Commitment*

Organizational Variables and Turnover

The reward system of an organization is an organizational, or situational, influence on turnover. Other situational variables that have been studied in this context include pay/benefits, opportunity for advancement, and the extent to which the work in a job is routine. Pay and benefits have been found to have negative correlations with turnover, as has opportunity for advancement. Routinization usually has a positive correlation with turnover; the more routine the work, the greater the turnover.

The search for organizational variables related to turnover, like the search for personal variables, has yielded a number of simple relationships that account for a modest amount of the variance in turnover. Cotton and Tuttle (1986) summarize this research in terms of the confidence it provides for these relationships. As shown in Table 7–1, relatively greater confidence is to be found in relationships between personal variables and turnover. With the possible exception of pay and benefits, the search for significant relationships between turnover and organizational variables has been less successful.

Table 7–1		A Summary of Turnover Correlates by Confidence		
Strong Confidence $(p < .0005)$	**Moderate Confidence** $(.0005 < p < .005)$	**Weak to Moderate Confidence** $(.005 < p < .01)$	**Weak Confidence** $(.01 < p < .05)$	**No Confidence** $(p > .05)$
Employment perceptions	Unemployment rate	Marital status	Accession rate	Intelligence
Union presence	Job performance	Aptitudes and abilities	Task repetitiveness	
Pay				
Overall job satisfaction	Satisfaction with co-workers			
Satisfaction with work itself	Satisfaction with promo-			
Pay satisfaction	tional opportunity			
Satisfaction with supervision	Role clarity			
Age				
Tenure				
Gender				
Education				
Number of dependents				
Biographical information				
Organizational commitment				
Met expectations				
Behavioral intentions				

From J. L. Cotton and J. M. Tuttle, "Employee Turnover: A Meta-Analysis and Review with Implications for Research." *Academy of Management Review,* 1986, *11,* 55–70. Copyright 1986 Academy of Management. Reprinted by permission.

Turnover as a Process

McCain, O'Reilly, and Pfeffer (1983) believe that the relatively unspectacular results in the search for organizational variables that affect turnover probably reflect the fact that correlational analysis is too limited to capture the dynamic relationship between turnover and an organizational system. Perhaps turnover is not an event that occurs at one point in time (as it is usually conceptualized) but a *process* involving time, change, and individual-organization interactions. A study by Dickter, Roznowski, and Harrison (1996) illustrates the idea. Using a sample of more than 1,000 employed individuals from a wide range of occupations, these investigators found the usual negative correlation between initial job satisfaction and voluntary turnover. Over time, however, job satisfaction clearly became less important than other variables as a determinant of turnover.

Equity theory
See pages 198–200

One of the earlier process views of turnover is an investment model somewhat similar in dynamics to the equity theory of motivation. Farrell and Rusbult (1981; Rusbult & Farrell, 1983) take the position that turnover stems from low job commitment. Job commitment, in turn, is believed to be a function of an individual's perceptions of his or her relative investments in the job, the rewards and costs of staying with the company, and the perceived viable employment alternatives. The process aspect of the model lies in the fact that the relevant variables and the relationships between them are not static in a correlational sense, but change over time. Voluntary turnover is most likely to occur when

- investments in the job are perceived to be low, *and*
- costs of staying in the organization are perceived to be high, *and*
- rewards for staying in the organization are perceived to be low, *and*
- there are attractive viable alternative employment opportunities.

The investment model hypothesizes that a person's intention to quit a job develops over time, and any number of factors may intervene to increase his or her job commitment before the act of leaving is carried out. It is not uncommon, for example, for a company to offer an employee who plans to leave inducements to stay (more money, promotion, better working hours, and so on). In terms of the investment model, such inducements may increase the value of the reward term and shift the balance away from turnover and back toward job commitment.

Lee and his colleagues (Lee & Mitchell, 1994; Lee, Mitchell, Wise, & Fireman, 1996) propose a different kind of process model of turnover, one that is based on concepts from decision-making theory.

> Our unfolding model portrays employee turnover as a complex process whereby individuals assess their feelings, personal situation, and work environment and, over time, make decisions about staying or leaving an organization. (1994, p. 84)

Neither the investment model nor the unfolding model of turnover has been subjected to rigorous research as yet, but the approach holds promise as a means for taking I/O psychologists' understanding of turnover to a level higher than that afforded by static correlational analysis.

Turnover in Perspective

Turnover, like absenteeism, can be expensive with direct and indirect costs estimated to be about one-and-a-half times the annual salary of the position in question. Direct costs

255

Chapter 7

Absenteeism,
Turnover, and
Organizational
Commitment

include recruiting, selecting, and training new employees; many of the indirect costs are hidden in the form of inefficiencies associated with short-timers (outgoing employees), a vacant position, and a new employee (see Darmon, 1990, for more on identifying sources of turnover costs).

Interventions into organizational systems for the purpose of reducing operational costs by reducing turnover have a long tradition in I/O psychology. The idea that not all turnover is created equal, in that some has benefits instead of costs, did not come along until fairly recently. Much of this work has been done by Dalton and his colleagues, who argue that turnover can have economic, sociological, and psychological benefits to organizations. The last two are difficult to define in the abstract, but a few examples convey the idea.

- The departure of a disruptive employee who likes to "keep things stirred up" may make for a more productive work group even if the departed member was a good worker.

- An overbearing supervisor's leaving for a better job opportunity may reduce feelings of stress on the part of his or her former subordinates.

- An employee with seniority whose work standards are minimum can cause hard feelings among those who have to work harder to compensate, so his or her exit may increase job satisfaction for those co-workers.

Most organizations of any size have some employees like those in the examples. Their behavior does not fall into any legitimate category for terminating them, but it affects work group cohesiveness, employee morale, and work efficiency in a negative way. Whatever their strengths as individuals, they are dysfunctional members of a social system who engender negative psychological reactions in some co-workers. When such an individual leaves voluntarily, the organization and those in it benefit.

Evidence for the economic benefits of turnover under certain conditions is easier to document. One of the first of these investigations found that a 15% turnover rate in one subunit of a large western public utility led to a one-year savings of more than $375,000 (Dalton & Todor, 1982). These savings stemmed primarily from the fact that the employees hired to replace the ones who left were paid at lower entry-level salaries with associated lower benefit plan costs. (Replacing employees who leave with employees of temporary agencies may result in an even greater savings.) This is not always the case, but such figures do undermine the conventional wisdom that turnover always costs money.

Dalton and Todor also have some interesting ideas for controlling the turnover level in an organization—not through elaborate, costly programs, but by paying closer attention to absenteeism and transfer policies. Employees who want to transfer and are allowed to are much less likely to quit (Dalton & Todor, 1987). Likewise, these authors believe, there are occasions when absenteeism should be largely ignored for the same reason (Dalton & Todor, 1993).

Liberal transfer and absenteeism policies do not make sense if the jobs in question have minimal requirements and can easily be refilled. Nor will these policies always solve a turnover problem. Absenteeism may be too disruptive to the work of the organization or transfer may not be possible for one reason or another. Nevertheless, there is ample research to support the basic assumption that absenteeism and turnover rates are manageable, not dictated or predetermined in some way. Much of that research has been reviewed in this chapter; for greater detail see Dalton and Todor (1993).

Organizational Commitment

The behavioral opposite of leaving an organization is staying with it. The psychological state believed to be associated with staying is attachment or commitment, but commitment to what? To a job? To the employing organization? To an occupation? To a career? To work in general? All of these concepts appear in the I/O psychology literature, but are they distinct forms of commitment (Blau, Paul, & St. John, 1993; Koslowsky, 1990), separate but interdependent forms of commitment (Vandenberg & Scarpello, 1994), or redundant terms for the same concept (Morrow, 1983)?

Organizational commitment is the focus of much of the research involving the commitment variable at the present time. This concept suits the purpose of the current chapter, in which the focus is on absenteeism and turnover from an organization's point of view. Occupational and career commitment may be partial determinants of organizational commitment as some I/O psychologists believe, they may be entirely independent of it, or the relationship may vary from individual to individual.

It is not difficult to think of people who are very attached to their employing organizations without any particular attachment to a definable occupation or career. Likewise, work commitment (a value placed on work for its own sake) may be part of organizational commitment for some people and irrelevant for others. Job commitment is a narrower focus yet. Jobs change, people are promoted or asked to transfer or even retrained to do something entirely different from that which they were hired to do (like the "techies" retrained to be IBM salespeople). Do they still want to work for this organization?

The Meaning and Measurement of Organizational Commitment

Organizational commitment is a variable reflecting the degree of connection an individual perceives himself or herself to have with the particular organization in which he or she is employed. At one end of the continuum is alienation, a condition under which there is no perceived connection. At the other end is identification; the individual's feeling of connection is so strong that self-descriptions tend to be primarily in terms of work role in a particular organization (Guion, 1958). Most people fall somewhere between these extremes.

How is the degree to which a person feels connected to a particular organization to be measured? In an interesting investigation of this question, Randall, Fedor, and Longnecker (1990) asked the employees of a manufacturing plant how *they* recognized organizational commitment in fellow employees. These subjects believed that coming to work regularly, showing a concern for work quality, and being willing to share knowledge and help others were typical of their more committed co-workers. This result suggests that greater organizational commitment, like greater job satisfaction, may be related to organizational citizenship behaviors.

Another way to assess the degree of an individual's organizational commitment is simply to ask a question along the lines of "Would you continue to work for this company if a somewhat better alternative were offered to you?" This global approach has been taken by some researchers, but it incorporates the same risk that is taken when measuring job satisfaction in this way: different people will use different standards to answer the question. As a result, it is difficult to know how to interpret the results of a study or to compare them to the results of other investigations.

An alternative measure of organizational commitment is to ask a series of specific questions. One such questionnaire is the Organizational Commitment Scale (Allen & Meyer, 1990), which is based on the authors' three-dimensional concept of organizational commitment. Sample questions from this instrument are shown in Exhibit 7–2.

The first two questions in the exhibit are samples of questions designed to assess an individual's emotional attachment to an organization. Allen and Meyer call this the affective dimension of organizational commitment. The next two questions are from the continuance dimension, which is based on an individual's assessment of the costs associated with leaving the organization. Normative commitment, an individual's feelings of obligation to remain with the organization, is reflected in the last two questions.

The three-dimensional model of organizational commitment is widely used in I/O psychology research, and its theoretical and measurement properties have been examined in a number of studies. The three dimensions, or factors, of the scale have been confirmed by some researchers (e.g., Hackett, Bycio, & Hausdorf, 1994; Meyer, Allen, & Smith, 1993). Others have concluded that in its present form the questionnaire primarily measures the affective (feeling) component of commitment (e.g., Dunham, Grube, & Castanèda, 1994). This conclusion is consistent with that of McCaul, Hinsz, and McCaul (1995), who found that scores were highly correlated with a single measure of overall attitude toward the employing organization.

A different approach to the meaning and measurement of organizational commitment is based on the premise that people become committed to actions (such as accepting a job offer from a particular company) to the extent that the action (1) is perceived to have been a free choice, (2) has been made public, and (3) is perceived to be difficult or costly to reverse (Salancik, 1977). The more strongly these conditions hold, the more

---

From affective commitment scale

- I really feel as if this organization's problems are my own.

- I think that I could easily become as attached to another organization as I am to this one.

From continuance commitment scale

- Too much in my life would be disrupted if I decided I wanted to leave my organization now.

- I am not afraid of what might happen if I quit my job without having another one lined up.

From normative commitment scale

- I was taught to believe in the value of remaining loyal to one organization.

- I do not think that wanting to be a "company man" or a "company woman" is sensible anymore.

Exhibit 7–2
Sample Items from a Measure of Organizational Commitment

From N. J. Allen and J. P. Meyer, "The Measurement and Antecedents of Affective, Continuance and Normative Commitment to the Organization." *Journal of Occupational Psychology,* 1990, *63,* 1–18. Copyright 1990 British Psychological Society. Reprinted with permission.

committed is the individual to behaving in a way consistent with the action—that is, the higher is the behavioral commitment (in this case, to staying with the organization).

The position described is usually called a behavioral commitment model (Staw, 1977) to distinguish it from attitude models, such as that of Allen and Meyer. To date, there have been relatively fewer investigations of commitment based on this model than on the attitude model, and most measures of behavioral commitment require more research. Kline and Peters (1991) developed their own 14-item questionnaire for use in their work; subjects indicate the extent of their agreement with such statements as "I felt pressured into accepting this job" (low free-choice perception).

The subjects in Kline and Peters's study (new employees observed over an 18-month period) who were high on behavioral commitment stayed with the company almost three times as long as subjects who were low. As shown in the graph in Figure 7–8, this significant difference began to appear as early as the second month of employment, implying that new employees may differ from the beginning in their commitment to their job choices. Whether this commitment continues or grows over a longer period of time is an interesting question, as is the matter of the conditions under which employees who enter with low commitment might develop it over time.

In summary, there is still some conceptual confusion and theoretical disagreement about the concept of commitment, so there is not yet strong consensus regarding how to measure this variable. Research findings are influenced by the kind of commitment measure used (Cohen, 1993a; Tett & Meyer, 1993), just as they are by different operational definitions of absenteeism. With this caution in mind, some representative research into the relationship between organizational commitment and work behavior is reviewed.

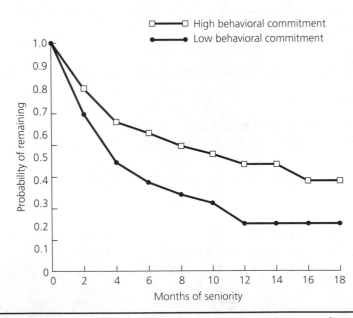

Figure 7–8
Survival Rates for Employees with High and Low Behavioral Commitment

From C. J. Kline and L. H. Peters, "Behavioral Commitment and Tenure of New Employees: A Replication and Extension." *Academy of Management Journal*, 1991, *34*, 194–204. Copyright 1991 Academy of Management. Reprinted by permission.

Organizational Commitment and Work Behavior

Interest in organizational commitment has been stimulated by reports of some relatively strong negative correlations between this variable and absenteeism (e.g., Cheloa & Farr, 1980; Mathieu & Kohler, 1990), tardiness (e.g., Blau, 1986), and turnover or turnover intentions (e.g., Farrell & Rusbult, 1981; Martin & Hafer, 1995; Shore, Newton, & Thornton, 1990). The relevant literature also offers hints of a relationship with work performance (e.g., Brett, Cron, & Slocum, 1995). Finally, there is some evidence that greater organizational commitment helps to protect people somewhat from the negative effects of stress, perhaps because it gives their work more meaning (e.g., Begley & Czajka, 1993).

I/O psychology researchers agree that organizational commitment comes about through an interaction of individual difference variables (such as age and sex), personal psychological variables (such as needs and values), and aspects of the specific work situation (such as the nature of work). With the possible exception of leadership behavior, investigations of organizational variables related to commitment have not, to date, revealed any strong patterns. The following findings are representative.

- Gaertner and Nollen (1989) report that the strongest predictor of commitment among employees of a manufacturing firm was perceptions of the company's career-oriented employment practices (such as internal recruiting and training and development opportunities).

- Glisson and Durick (1988) found a positive correlation between leadership behavior and commitment, as did Morris and Sherman (1981).

- Mottaz (1988) reports a relationship between organizational commitment and the nature of work performed, with commitment being greater for work whose tasks are perceived to be more autonomous and more significant.

More of the recent research into the determinants of organizational commitment focuses on personal variables. Age continues to show up as an important factor, although the nature of the relationship needs clarification. Morris and Sherman (1981) report that older employees had more commitment, for example, while meta-analysis by Cohen (1993b) suggests that the age-commitment relationship is stronger for younger employees.

Level of education is another personal variable that appears to be related to organizational commitment (Glisson & Durick, 1988), but the relationship probably is not direct. In general, people with greater education are more likely to identify with a particular profession than are those with less education, and professional commitment has been found to have a moderately strong positive correlation with organizational commitment (e.g., Wallace, 1993). Employees with more education are also more likely to have white-collar jobs, another variable that seems to be associated with stronger organizational commitment (see meta-analysis by Cohen and Hudecek, 1993).

A review of the organizational commitment research is offered by Mathieu and Zajac (1990). This research offers hints but few practical strategies for increasing commitment. Many of the relevant variables that have been identified are simply outside an organization's control. Others seem to vary considerably from one individual to the next. One very important exception is the degree of commitment an organization has *to* its employees (Eisenberger, Huntington, Hutchinson, & Sowa, 1986).

On-site child care pays off for organizations in the form of greater employee commitment, less absenteeism, and, some believe, greater work efficiency.

The Shoe on the Other Foot

When an individual accepts a job position with a particular organization, an unwritten psychological contract is established between the parties consisting of mutual understandings regarding expectations and obligations. In general, both sides expect loyalty, honesty, and fair treatment in their dealings with one another. This includes keeping any verbal promises made during employment negotiations, such as the potential employee saying he/she would finish college at night school or the potential employer saying that a better job would be available when the degree was in hand.

The failure of an organization to hold up its end of what is perceived to be the bargain has a negative effect on employee evaluations of their own obligations (e.g., Robinson, Kraatz, & Rousseau, 1994), as well as on their commitment to the organization (e.g., Brockner, Tyler, & Cooper-Schneider, 1992). Research in this area also indicates that increasing numbers of people believe their employers are violating these understandings (Robinson & Rousseau, 1994). One obvious way an organization can encourage and maintain commitment, therefore, is to make sure that the expectations with which people begin work are realistic and then live up to these expectations.

The second major arena for demonstrating commitment to employees goes by a variety of labels in the scientific and popular literature. Of these, the broadest is **workplace flexibility**, a term that refers to the establishment of policies to help employees manage conflicts between their work and their personal lives, whether or not they have children or other dependent care responsibilities (Hall & Parker, 1993).

Balancing work and personal life is emerging as one of the dominant employment-related issues of the new century. (See Zedeck and Mosier, 1990, for a review of the issues and a suggested research agenda in this area.) Cambridge Reports/Research International and Stephen Zimney, a New York consultant, conducted surveys in 1992 and again in

1994 to identify areas in which workers felt their needs were not being met by their employers. The number of respondents who focused on the need to integrate work and personal demands doubled in that time period, as did the number who said their employers did not have policies that supported this need. According to Zimney (1994),

> Employers increasingly depend on commitment as they stress teamwork in their efforts to raise productivity. But [they] may unwittingly risk eroding employee commitment by making it harder, in a post-downsizing environment, for them to take care of personal needs. . . . In focus groups, people are saying [things like], "Sometimes I have to go to the doctor and he isn't open after 5 p.m., or I have to go to school to pick up the kids. I don't need my boss to manage all of this for me. I just need him to understand." (p. 1)

The essence of workplace flexibility is providing resources and avenues that enable employees to handle conflicting personal-work demands and priorities without threatening their jobs, jeopardizing their careers, or shortchanging their families or the quality of their off-job lives. With flexibility, be it a boss who understands, a formal flexible work scheduling policy, or an on-site day-care center, comes a sense of control, and with a sense of control comes greater psychological availability for work (Hall & Parker, 1993; Thomas & Ganster, 1995).

Most research to date supports the positive impact of workplace flexibility practices on employee commitment (e.g., Grover & Crooker, 1995), provided that the organizational culture is perceived to be supportive. This kind of commitment must be a genuine reflection of management's appreciation of the mutual benefits of workplace flexibilty; if experience to date is representative, it cannot be legislated.

The Family and Medical Leave Act of 1993 requires employers of 50 or more employees to grant unpaid leaves of up to 12 weeks to individuals who are ill or who are needed at home to care for a family member. In the only major study of compliance to date, 40% of the 300 companies surveyed were not granting the 12 weeks leave or guaranteeing jobs and continuing benefits if leave were taken ("Many Employers Flout," 1994).

On the other side of the desk, only a very small percentage of the employees who are eligible for this benefit (no more than 4% by most estimates) have taken advantage of it in organizations where it is offered. Some people don't need to take the leave, and some who do just can't afford to be without the income. But the biggest problem, according to most experts in work/family issues, is fear that career opportunities or job security will be jeopardized if time off is taken to help an elderly parent through surgery or spend time with a new baby.

Hard data on the extent to which such fears are justified are lacking, but many people who work have a story to tell. Companies that are genuinely committed to helping employees integrate their work and personal lives can overcome such fears only by letting it be seen that the playing field is really level. Promoting qualified "jugglers" as well as single-minded careerists to leadership positions is particularly crucial. Judith Sprieser, chief financial officer for Sara Lee and mother of two young children, makes a point of being seen leaving the office in time to have dinner with her family (and works from home in off hours).

By most accounts, Sara Lee is not a typical organization. Rather, it is part of a leading-edge change in the American work culture, a culture whose very foundation is the premise that people who are serious about their work and their careers leave their family problems at home.

Millions of employees still break into a sweat when their children have a fever or school is closed because of snow. People still prefer to say they have car trouble rather than child-care problems. (Solomon, 1994, p. 73)

The report card on workplace flexibility options and their use in American organizations of the mid-1990s that has been assembled by the panel of experts in Solomon's (1994) article is not overly impressive. At the same time, it is clear from this and other sources that workplace flexibility is on its way to mainstream. Job recruiters note that increasing numbers of candidates are raising questions about work-life balance early in the recruitment process. In the past, this issue might have been mentioned after a candidate believed there definitely was going to be a job offer; more likely, it was not raised at all for fear of appearing to be less committed than other applicants. Increasingly, organizations that do not offer flexibility to their employees are losing them to those that do. There is more on child care—the driving core issue of this movement—in At Issue.

At Issue:

Who's Minding the Kids?

The work force in this country has changed enormously in the last generation. In the 1980s, the fastest-growing segment of the labor force was mothers of children younger than 3 years old. The conflict that can occur when these women strive to integrate the roles of career person and mother has been publicized widely. More recently, men have begun experiencing similar problems. Many are single parents, but increasing numbers are the primary child-care givers in a two-parent family. Still other men are trying to be breadwinners and modern nurturing fathers simultaneously. As one member of DuPont Corporation's Corporate Work and Family Committee notes:

> What we found three years ago was that child care was still a female issue. Clearly, that is no longer the case. (Saltzman & Barry, 1988, p. 68)

What is this issue that is no longer a "female issue"? Basically, it is a question of who should provide, and pay for, child care for working parents. Until recently, there was no question; parents were on their own. If they could not afford private day-care, they prevailed upon a relative or a neighbor. If no one could be found, one parent stayed home, even if it meant giving up a career or accepting a reduced lifestyle. If there was only one parent, welfare

checks often took the place of paychecks. The situation is changing. More organizations are offering flextime working hours, paternity as well as maternity leave, job sharing, and work-at-home programs to make it easier for employees to juggle their responsibilities successfully.

Today, an estimated one in ten U.S. firms provides some form of child-care assistance. Programs vary widely from distributing lists of community services to helping offset the cost of child care; some programs allow employees to pay for child care in installments with pretax dollars. A leader in this arena is IBM, which maintains a multi-million-dollar fund to expand and improve child and elder care for its employees in the towns where it operates.

But what about the obvious solution—day-care programs operated and funded by employing organizations? In 1978, about 100 companies offered on-site day-care services to their employees. Twenty years later, the number has increased to an estimated 10% of the larger firms, including John Hancock Insurance Company, California's Union Bank, Marquette Electronics, Lancaster Laboratories, and Mariott International. Mariott executives estimate that before the day-care centers were opened, child care and other personal problems were fueling a turnover rate approaching 300% in some of the chain's hotels.

Solid data in this area are scarce, but by all reports, on-site day-care centers pay their way and then some by increasing employee attendance, work efficiency, and organizational commitment. The turnover rate at SAS Institute, a North Carolina computer software firm, fell to around 4% after the company established its day-care center in 1981 (the industry average is 25–35%). Despite such success stories, the overwhelming majority of work organizations do not have any form of on-site child care.

For some companies, failure to help employees with child care is a question of economics. Decision makers in other organizations simply don't believe that it is their responsibility to get involved with this particular employee problem. But is this a moral issue? Many managers complain that good employees are hard to find today. If this is the case, the issue is as practical as they come. This is not a problem that is going to go away; if you have good employees and want to keep them, don't make them choose between their children and their jobs.

Summary

Although they are separate behaviors, absenteeism and turnover have long been linked in the I/O psychology literature. The assumption that both are caused by job dissatisfaction, with turnover being the final resolution of the problem, was accepted by most researchers as valid. The inadequacy of this conceptualization has now become clear, and research on both behaviors has begun to progress independently.

Organizational commitment can be defined as the degree of connection an individual perceives himself or herself to have with a particular organization. Less commitment has been found to be correlated with greater absenteeism and higher rates of turnover. In general, commitment can be increased by fair treatment of employees and by management behavior and policies that help individuals deal with conflicts between their work and personal lives.

Questions for Review and Discussion

1. Discuss absenteeism as a particular example of some of the general problems that can arise in defining and measuring research variables in I/O psychology. Would measuring attendance instead of absenteeism reduce these problems? Why or why not?

2. What employee and situational characteristics would you examine for the purpose of dividing the turnover in an organization into "functional" and "dysfunctional" categories, and why?

3. Based on the discussion in this chapter, develop a short questionnaire to measure organizational commitment and outline a very short research study for trying it out.

4. If you work at an outside job, list and discuss briefly several ways your employer might make it easier for you to work, go to school, and meet your other obligations. (If you do not hold an outside job, answer this question on the basis of a previous job or interview a friend or fellow student who is employed.)

Key Terms

absence culture

absenteeism measurement

classification of turnover

controlling absenteeism

determinants of absenteeism

determinants of turnover

organizational commitment

psychological contract

process models of turnover

workplace flexibility

References

Abelson, M. A. (1987). Examination of avoidable and unavoidable turnover. *Journal of Applied Psychology, 72*, 382–386.

Allen, N. J., & Meyer, J. P. (1990). The measurement and antecedents of affective, continuance and normative commitment to the organization. *Journal of Occupational Psychology, 63*, 1–18.

Allen, P. T. (1982). Size of workforce, morale, and absenteeism: A re-examination. *British Journal of Industrial Relations, 20*, 83–100.

Bannister, B. D., & Griffeth, R. W. (1986). Applying a causal analytic framework to the Mobley, Horner, and Hollingsworth (1978) turnover model: A useful reexamination. *Journal of Management, 12*, 433–443.

Bassett, G. A. (1967). *A study of factors associated with turnover of exempt personnel.* Crotonville, NY: Personnel and Industrial Relations Service, General Electric.

Begley, T. M., & Czajka, J. M. (1993). Panel analysis of the moderating effects of commitment on job satisfaction, intent to quit, and health following organizational change. *Journal of Applied Psychology, 78*, 552–556.

Blau, G. J. (1986). Job involvement and organizational commitment as interactive predictors of tardiness and absenteeism. *Journal of Management, 12*, 577–584.

Blau, G. (1993). Further exploring the relationship between job search and voluntary individual turnover. *Personnel Psychology, 46*, 313–330.

Blau, G., Paul, A., & St. John, N. (1993). On developing a general index of work commitment. *Journal of Vocational Behavior, 42*, 298–314.

Breaugh, J. A. (1981). Predicting absenteeism from prior absenteeism and work attitudes. *Journal of Applied Psychology, 66*, 555–560.

Brett, J. F., Cron, W. L., & Slocum, J. W. (1995). Economic dependency on work: A moderator of the relationship between organizational commitment and performance. *Academy of Management Journal, 38*, 261–271.

Brockner, J., Tyler, T. R., & Cooper-Schneider, R. (1992). The influence of prior commitment to an institution on reactions to perceived unfairness: The higher they are, the harder they fall. *Administrative Science Quarterly, 37*, 241–261.

Brown, N., & Redmon, W. K. (1989). The effects of a group reinforcement contingency on staff use of unscheduled sick leave. *Journal of Organizational Behavior Management, 10*, 3–17.

Calabria, D. C. (1995). When companies give, employees give back. *Personnel Journal, 73*, 75–83.

Carlopio, J., & Gardner, D. (1995). Perceptions of work and workplace: Mediators of the relationship between job level and employee reactions. *Journal of Occupational and Organizational Psychology, 68*, 321–326.

Carlson, J. G., & Hill, K. D. (1982). The effect of gaming on attendance and attitude. *Personnel Psychology, 35*, 63–73.

Carsten, J. M., & Spector, P. E. (1987). Unemployment, job satisfaction, and employee turnover: A meta-analytic test of the Muchinsky model. *Journal of Applied Psychology, 72*, 374–381.

Cascio, W. F. (1995). Whither industrial and organizational psychology in a changing world of work? *American Psychologist, 50*, 928–939.

Cheloa, R. S., & Farr, J. L. (1980). Absenteeism, job involvement, and job satisfaction in an organizational setting. *Journal of Applied Psychology, 65*, 467–473.

Clegg, C. W. (1983). Psychology of employee lateness, absence, and turnover: A methodological critique and an empirical study. *Journal of Applied Psychology, 68*, 88–101.

Cohen, A. (1993a). Organizational commitment and turnover: A meta-analysis. *Academy of Management Journal, 36*, 1140–1157.

Cohen, A. (1993b). Age and tenure in relation to organizational commitment: A meta-analysis. *Basic and Applied Social Psychology, 14*, 143–159.

Cohen, A., & Hudecek, N. (1993). Organizational commitment–turnover relationship across occupational groups: A meta-analysis. *Group and Organization Management, 18*, 188–213.

Cotton, J. L., & Tuttle, J. M. (1986). Employee turnover: A meta-analysis and review with implications for research. *Academy of Management Review, 11*, 55–70.

Dalton, D. R., & Mesch, D. J. (1990). The impact of flexible scheduling on employee attendance and turnover. *Administrative Science Quarterly, 35*, 370–387.

Dalton, D. R., & Todor, W. D. (1982). Turnover: A lucrative hard dollar phenomenon. *Academy of Management Review, 7*, 212–218.

Dalton, D. R., & Todor, W. D. (1987). The attenuating effects of internal mobility on employee turnover: Multiple field assessments. *Journal of Management, 13*, 705–711.

Dalton, D. R., & Todor, W. D. (1993). Turnover, transfer, absenteeism: An interdependent perspective. *Journal of Management, 19*, 193–219.

Darmon, R. Y. (1990). Identifying sources of turnover costs: A segmental approach. *Journal of Marketing, 54*, 46–56.

Dickter, D. N., Roznowski, M., & Harrison, D. A. (1996). Temporal tempering: An event history analysis of the process of voluntary turnover. *Journal of Applied Psychology, 81*, 705–716.

Dreher, G. F. (1982). The role of performance in the turnover process. *Academy of Management Journal, 25*, 137–147.

Dunham, R. B., Grube, J. A., & Castanèda, M. B. (1994). Organizational commitment: The utility of an integrative definition. *Journal of Applied Psychology, 79*, 370–380.

Eisenberger, R., Huntington, R., Hutchison, S., & Sowa, D. (1986). Perceived organizational support. *Journal of Applied Psychology, 71*, 500–507.

Farrell, D., & Rusbult, C. E. (1981). Exchange variables as predictors of job satisfaction, job commitment, and turnover: The impact of rewards, costs, alternatives, and investments. *Organizational Behavior and Human Performance, 28*, 78–95.

Fitzgibbons, D., & Moch, M. (1980). Employee absenteeism: A multivariate analysis with replication. *Organizational Behavior and Human Performance, 26*, 349–372.

Gaertner, K. N., & Nollen, S. D. (1989). Career experiences, perceptions of employment practices, and psychological commitment to the organization. *Human Relations, 42*, 975–991.

Gaertner, K. N., & Nollen, S. D. (1992). Turnover intentions and desire among executives. *Human Relations, 45*, 447–465.

George, J. M. (1989). Mood and absence. *Journal of Applied Psychology, 74*, 317–324.

George, J. M., & Jones, G. R. (1996). The experience of work and turnover intentions: Interactive effects of value attainment, job satisfaction, and positive mood. *Journal of Applied Psychology, 81*, 318–325.

Glisson, C., & Durick, M. (1988). Predictors of job satisfaction and organizational commitment in human service organizations. *Administrative Science Quarterly, 33*, 61–81.

Grover, S. L. & Crooker, K. J. (1995). Who appreciates family-responsive human resource policies: The impact of family-friendly policies on the organizational attachment of parents and non-parents. *Personnel Psychology, 48*, 271–288.

Guion, R. M. (1958). Industrial morale: The problem of terminology. *Personnel Psychology, 11*, 59–64.

Gupta, N., Jenkins, G. D., & Beehr, T. A. (1992). The effects of turnover on perceived job quality: Does the grass look greener? *Group and Organization Management, 17,* 431–445.

Haccoun, R. R., & Jeanrie, C. (1995). Self-reports of work absence as a function of personal attitudes toward absence and perceptions of the organisation. *Applied Psychology: An International Review, 44,* 155–170.

Hackett, R. D. (1989). Work attitudes and employee absenteeism: A synthesis of the literature. *Journal of Occupational Psychology, 62,* 235–248.

Hackett, R. D. (1990). Age, tenure, and employee absenteeism. *Human Relations, 43,* 601–619.

Hackett, R. D., Bycio, P., & Hausdorf, P. A. (1994). Further assessments of Meyer and Allen's (1991) three-component model of organizational commitment. *Journal of Applied Psychology, 79,* 15–23.

Hall, D. T., & Parker, V. A. (1993). The role of workplace flexibility in managing diversity. *Organizational Dynamics, 22,* 5–18.

Hammer, T. H., & Landau, J. (1981). Methodological issues in the use of absence data. *Journal of Applied Psychology, 66,* 574–581.

Healy, M. C., Lehman, M., & McDaniel, M. A. (1995). Age and voluntary turnover: A quantitative review. *Personnel Psychology, 48,* 335–345.

Hendrix, W. H., Spencer, B. A., & Gibson, G. S. (1994). Organizational and extraorganizational factors affecting stress, employee well-being, and absenteeism for males and females. *Journal of Business and Psychology, 9,* 103–128.

Hom, P. W., Caranikas-Walker, F., Prussia, G. E., & Griffeth, R. W. (1992). A meta-analytic structural equations analysis of a model of employee turnover. *Journal of Applied Psychology, 77,* 890–909.

Hui, C. H. (1988). Impacts of objective and subjective labour market conditions on employee turnover. *Journal of Occupational Psychology, 61,* 211–219.

Ivancevich, J. M. (1985). Predicting absenteeism from prior absence and work attitudes. *Academy of Management Journal, 28,* 219–228.

Jackofsky, E. F., Ferris, K. R., & Breckenridge, B. G. (1986). Evidence for a curvilinear relationship between job performance and turnover. *Journal of Management, 12,* 105–111.

Jackofsky, E. F., & Peters, L. H. (1983). The hypothesized effects of ability in the turnover process. *Academy of Management Review, 8,* 46–49.

Johns, G. (1994a). Absenteeism estimates by employees and managers: Divergent perspectives and self-serving perceptions. *Journal of Applied Psychology, 79,* 229–239.

Johns, G. (1994b). How often were you absent? A review of the use of self-reported absence data. *Journal of Applied Psychology, 79,* 574–591.

Judge, T. A. (1993). Does affective disposition moderate the relationship between job satisfaction and voluntary turnover? *Journal of Applied Psychology, 78,* 395–401.

Judge, T. A., & Watanabe, S. (1995). Is the past prologue? A test of Ghiselli's hobo syndrome. *Journal of Management, 21,* 211–229.

Keller, R. T. (1984). The role of performance and absenteeism in the prediction of turnover. *Academy of Management Journal, 27,* 176–183.

Kline, C. J., & Peters, L. H. (1991). Behavioral commitment and tenure of new employees: A replication and extension. *Academy of Management Journal, 34,* 194–204.

Kohler, S. S., & Mathieu, J. E. (1993). Individual characteristics, work perceptions, and affective reactions influences on differentiated absence criteria. *Journal of Organizational Behavior, 14,* 515–530.

Koslowski, M. (1990). Staff/line distinctions in job and organizational commitment. *Journal of Occupational Psychology, 63,* 167–173.

Landau, J. C. (1993). The impact of a change in an attendance control system on absenteeism and tardiness. *Journal of Organizational Behavior Management, 13,* 51–70.

Lawrence, B. S. (1987). An organizational theory of age effects. *Research in the Sociology of Organizations, 5,* 37–71.

Lee, T. W., & Mitchell, T. R. (1994). An alternative approach: The unfolding model of voluntary employee turnover. *Academy of Management Review, 19,* 51–89.

Lee, T. W., Mitchell, T. R., Wise, L., & Fireman, S. (1996). An unfolding model of voluntary employee turnover. *Academy of Management Journal, 39,* 5–36.

Leigh, J. P. (1986). Correlates of absence from work due to illness. *Human Relations, 39,* 81–100.

Many employers flout family and medical leave law. (1994, July 26). *Wall Street Journal,* pp. B-1, 5.

Markham, S. E., Dansereau, F., Jr., & Alutto, J. A. (1982a). Female vs. male absence rates: A temporal analysis. *Personnel Psychology, 35,* 371–382.

Markham, S. E., Dansereau, F., Jr., & Alutto, J. A. (1982b). Group size and absenteeism rates: A longitudinal analysis. *Academy of Management Journal, 25,* 921–927.

Markham, S. E., & McKee, G. H. (1991). Declining organizational size and increasing unemployment rates: Predicting employee absenteeism from within- and between-plant perspectives. *Academy of Management Journal, 34,* 952–965.

Markham, S. E., & McKee, G. H. (1995). Group absence behavior and standards: A multilevel analysis. *Academy of Management Journal, 38,* 1174–1190.

Martin, T. N., & Hafer, J. C. (1995). The multiplicative interaction effects of job involvement and organizational commitment on the turnover intentions of full- and part-time employees. *Journal of Vocational Behavior, 46,* 310–331.

Martin, T. N., Price, J. J., & Mueller, C. W. (1981). Research note on job performance and turnover. *Journal of Applied Psychology, 66,* 116–119.

Martocchio, J. J. (1994). The effects of absence culture on individual absence. *Human Relations, 47,* 243–262.

Martocchio, J. J., & Judge, T. A. (1994). A policy-capturing approach to individuals' decisions to be absent. *Organizational Behavior and Human Decision Processes, 57,* 358–386.

Mathieu, J. E., & Kohler, S. S. (1990). A test of the interactive effects of organizational commitment and job involvement on various types of absence. *Journal of Vocational Behavior, 36,* 33–44.

Mathieu, J. E., & Zajac, D. M. (1990). A review and meta-analysis of the antecedents, correlates, and consequences of organizational commitment. *Psychological Bulletin, 108,* 171–194.

McCain, B. E., O'Reilly, C., & Pfeffer, J. (1983). The effects of departmental demography on turnover: The case of a university. *Academy of Management Journal, 26,* 626–641.

McCaul, H. S., Hinsz, V. B., & McCaul, K. D. (1995). Assessing organizational commitment: An employee's global attitude toward the organization. *Journal of Applied Behavioral Science, 31,* 80–90.

McEvoy, G. M., & Cascio, W. F. (1987). Do good or poor performers leave? A meta-analysis of the relationship between performance and turnover. *Academy of Management Journal, 30,* 744–762.

Meyer, J. P., Allen, N. J., & Smith, C. A. (1993). Commitment to organizations and occupations: Extension and test of a three-component conceptualization. *Journal of Applied Psychology, 78,* 538–551.

Miners, I. A., Moore, M. L., Champous, J. E., & Martocchio, J. J. (1995). Time-serial substitution effects of absence control on employee time-use. *Human Relations, 48,* 307–326.

Mitra, A., Jenkins, G. D., Jr., & Gupta, N. (1992). A meta-analytic review of the relationship between absence and turnover. *Journal of Applied Psychology, 77,* 879–889.

Mobley, W. H. (1982). Some unanswered questions in turnover and withdrawal research. *Academy of Management Review, 7,* 111–116.

Mobley, W. H., Horner, S. O., & Hollingsworth, A. T. (1978). An evaluation of precursors of hospital employee turnover. *Journal of Applied Psychology, 63,* 408–414.

Morris, J. H., & Sherman, J. D. (1981). Generalizability of an organizational commitment model. *Academy of Management Journal, 24,* 512–526.

Morrow, P. (1983). Concept redundancy in organizational research: The case of work commitment. *Academy of Management Review, 8,* 486–500.

Mottaz, C. J. (1988). Determinants of organizational commitment. *Human Relations, 41,* 467–482.

Nicholson, N., Brown, C. A., & Chadwick-Jones, J. K. (1976). Absence from work and job satisfaction. *Journal of Applied Psychology, 61,* 728–737.

Nicholson, N., & Johns, G. (1985). The absence culture and the psychological contract—Who's in control of absence? *Academy of Management Review, 10,* 397–407.

Popp, P. O., & Belohlav, J. A. (1982). Absenteeism in a low status work environment. *Academy of Management Journal, 25,* 677–683.

Randall, D. M., Fedor, D. B., & Longnecker, C. O. (1990). The behavioral expression of organizational commitment. *Journal of Vocational Behavior, 36,* 210–224.

Robinson, S. L., Kraatz, M. S., & Rousseau, D. M. (1994). Changing obligations and the psychological contract: A longitudinal study. *Academy of Management Journal, 37,* 137–152.

Robinson, S. L., & Rousseau, D. M. (1994). Violating the psychological contract: Not the exception but the norm. *Journal of Organizational Behavior, 15,* 245–259.

Rogers, R. E., & Herting, S. R. (1993). Patterns of absenteeism among government employees. *Public Personnel Management, 22,* 215–235.

Rusbult, C. E., & Farrell, D. (1983). A longitudinal test of the investment model: The impact on job satisfaction, job commitment, and turnover of variations in rewards, costs, alternatives, and investments. *Journal of Applied Psychology, 68,* 429–438.

Salancik, G. R. (1977). Commitment is too easy! *Organizational Dynamics, 5,* 62–80.

Saltzman, A., & Barry, P. (1988, June 20). The superdad juggling act. *U.S. News & World Report,* pp. 67–70.

Scott, K. D., & McClellan, E. L. (1990). Gender differences in absenteeism. *Public Personnel Management, 19,* 229–253.

Shore, L. M., Newton, L. A., & Thornton, G. C. (1990). Job and organizational attitudes in relation to employee behavioral intentions. *Journal of Organizational Behavior, 11,* 57–67.

Solomon, C. M. (1994). Work/family's failing grade: Why today's initiatives aren't enough. *Personnel Journal, 73,* 72–87.

Spencer, D. G., & Steers, R. M. (1981). Performance as a moderator of the job satisfaction-turnover relationship. *Journal of Applied Psychology, 66,* 511–514.

Staw, B. M. (1977). Two sides of commitment. Paper presented at the annual meeting of the Academy of Management, Atlanta.

Steel, R. P., & Griffeth, R. W. (1989). The elusive relationship between perceived employment opportunity and turnover behavior: A methodological or conceptual artifact? *Journal of Applied Psychology, 74,* 846–854.

Steers, R. M., & Rhodes, S. R. (1978). Major influences on employee attendance: A process model. *Journal of Applied Psychology, 63,* 391–407.

Steers, R. M., & Rhodes, S. R. (1984). Knowledge and speculation about absenteeism. In P. S. Goodman & R. S. Atkins (Eds.), *Absenteeism: New approaches to understanding, measuring, and managing employee absence.* San Francisco: Jossey-Bass.

Tett, R. P., & Meyer, J. P. (1993). Job satisfaction, organizational commitment, turnover intention, and turnover: Path analyses based on meta-analytic findings. *Personnel Psychology, 46,* 259–293.

Tharenou, P. (1993). A test of reciprocal causality for absenteeism. *Journal of Organizational Behavior, 14,* 269–287.

Thomas, L. T., & Ganster, D. C. (1995). Impact of family-supportive work variables on work-family conflict and strain: A control perspective. *Journal of Applied Psychology, 80,* 6–15.

Vandenberg, R. J., & Scarpello, V. (1994). A longitudinal assessment of the determinant relationship between employee commitments to the occupation and the organization. *Journal of Organizational Behavior, 15,* 535–547.

VandenHeuvel, A., & Wooden, M. (1995). Do explanations of absenteeism differ for men and women? *Human Relations, 48,* 1309–1329.

Wallace, J. E. (1993). Professional and organizational commitment: Compatible or incompatible? *Journal of Vocational Behavior, 42,* 333–349.

Watson, C. J. (1981). An evaluation of some aspects of the Steers and Rhodes model of employee attendance. *Journal of Applied Psychology, 66,* 385–389.

Werbel, J. D., & Bedeian, A. G. (1989). Intended turnover as a function of age and job performance. *Journal of Organizational Behavior, 10,* 275–281.

Williams, C. R., & Livingstone, L. P. (1994). Another look at the relationship between performance and voluntary turnover. *Academy of Management Journal, 37,* 269–298.

Wright, T. A., & Bonnett, D. G. (1993). Role of employee coping and performance in voluntary employee withdrawal: A research refinement and elaboration. *Journal of Management, 19,* 147–161.

Zedeck, S., & Mosier, K. L. (1990). Work in the family and the employing organization. *American Psychologist, 45,* 240–251.

Zenger, T. R. (1992). Why do employers only reward extreme performance? Examining the relationships among performance, pay, and turnover. *Administrative Science Quarterly, 37,* 198–219.

Zimney, S. (1994, August 31). Quoted in S. Shellenbarger, "Work and Family." *Wall Street Journal,* p. B-1.

The Job

In Part III, the focus shifts from employee to job. Chapter 8 presents an overview of general physical working conditions and of job design from both physical and psychological perspectives. In Chapter 9, employee health and safety are examined, with particular focus on the psychological aspects of working conditions and the issue of work-related stress. The determinants and assessment of work performance is the subject of Chapter 10. Job analysis, a process requiring information about job design, working conditions and hazards, and performance appraisal, brings Part III to a close in Chapter 11.

Job Design and Working Conditions

Human Factors Lessons from Three Mile Island

After the automatic shutdown system of a New Jersey nuclear reactor failed twice in February [1983]—the most significant nuclear incidents since the Three Mile Island scare—two psychologists were there, helping the government to probe the scene. . . .

At TMI [Three Mile Island], there were no NRC [Nuclear Regulatory Commission] engineering psychologists to turn to as government and utility officials struggled to explain how a series of mechanical and human errors—at a plant in commercial operation just three months—was doused just an hour before igniting a major nuclear tragedy.

In fact, before TMI there were almost no human factors professionals, psychologists or otherwise, on the staffs at [the] NRC, the firms designing and building nuclear plants, or the utilities operating them.

Consequently, human factors engineers' special expertise—the science of how best to integrate people into systems—was all but absent from an industry confronting one of the most complex and potentially hazardous systems in the world.

Humans Ignored

"Before Three Mile Island [the NRC] wasn't even aware of the fact that there were any humans in that plant," says Robert Mackie, an experimental psychologist who directs Human Factors Research, a subsidiary of the Essex Corporation. . . .

The NRC has hired about 30 psychologists since TMI. It has issued a series of new regulations and guidelines for the nation's 76 nuclear plants licensed for full power to address human factor problems identified by TMI investigators, particularly those of faulty control room design, inadequate training of operators, and emergency operating procedures.

Excerpted from C. Cordes, "Human Factors and Nuclear Safety: Grudging Respect for a Growing Field." *APA Monitor,* April 1983, *14*(5), pp. 1, 13–14.

THE NUCLEAR Regulatory Commission hired 30 psychologists to deal with a variety of complex issues raised by the March 1979 events at Three Mile Island near Harrisburg, Pennsylvania, events whose effects on this industry are being felt to this day. Many of these issues concerned training people to work effectively and safely in one of the most technologically advanced and controversial industries in this country. Other matters were more basic, having to do with the design of jobs, equipment, and work space at the site.

The evidence that has been accumulating since the initial Three Mile Island investigations reveals that the most elementary principles of human factors engineering had often been overlooked. Here are examples of just a few of the problems found with respect to the use of control and display panels for the operation of the plant.

- Display methods for critical information (such as that indicating the stuck valve for the automatic shutdown system) were not designed to stand out and get operator attention.

- The same colors had opposite meanings on different control panels used by the same operators (such as, "everything okay" versus "there's a problem!").

- Almost 30% of the displays were so high that operators could not read them at all.

The problems described are typical of those addressed by people who work in the field of human factors engineering (called ergonomics outside of the United States). These experts come from a variety of disciplines, including engineering, biology, medicine, and psychology, and they specialize in designing jobs, equipment, and work environments to be compatible with human capabilities and limitations.

Human factors psychologists often have experimental or I/O psychology backgrounds. In common with their colleagues from other disciplines, their professional interest in job design lies in its physical aspects, which for convenience are summarized here under the heading of the **human factors approach to job design**. Other psychologists focus on the psychological aspects of job design. Some of the basic issues of both approaches are addressed in this chapter.

The Human Factors Approach to Job Design

As it exists today, human factors engineering came into its own around the time of World War II. Before that, the physical aspects of job and workplace design had largely been the province of industrial engineers, such as Frederick Taylor and the husband-wife team of Frank and Lillian Gilbreth. Between them, Taylor (1911) and the Gilbreths (1921) developed the basic principles of time analysis and motion study that are used today.

Time analysis and motion study are complementary strategies for developing the most efficient way to perform a job. Both technologies involve studying employee movements to find a way to maximize speed and minimize wasted movement. Should a person who packs books into boxes for shipping use one hand or two? Should the books to be packed be located to the right, the left, or in front of the box? Should the packer be seated or standing?

Time analysis and motion study are still important tools in job design. United Parcel Service (UPS) drivers are trained to carry packages under their left arm, step from the vehicle with their right foot, walk at a pace of three feet per second, hold their keys teeth up on the third finger, and fold their money face up. Such attention to detail has made UPS the largest and most successful parcel delivery service in the country by a factor of two.

In modern form, time analysis and motion study are also used to uncover difficulties with the design of job tools, machines, and other work aids. One large consulting firm sends teams into offices to record (via camcorder) and take notes while employees use new software. The films and the notes go "back to the drawing board" to assist in making these work aids (software programs) easier for the people who use them. This new use of traditional industrial engineering tools reflects a new conceptualization of the relationship between person and job.

In the day of Taylor and the Gilbreths, time analysis and motion study were used to come up with the best way to do a job; it was left to I/O psychologists to fit people into the picture through appropriate selection and training. Today, employee, machine, tools, and work space are viewed as components of a system. As in any system, these components must be compatible if the whole is to work effectively and efficiently. Human factors engineers, unlike the early industrial engineers, are charged with fitting the job to the person as well as the person to the job.

Operator-Machine Systems

In an **operator-machine system**, a human and a machine work together to accomplish a job. They work together, but they perform different tasks and the allocation of these tasks between the two components of the system is a critical job design decision. In an ideal system, the operator is assigned the tasks that humans do better and the machine is assigned the tasks that machines do better. Basic guidelines for this assignment are outlined in Exhibit 8–1.

Exhibit 8–1
Operator-
Machine Task
Allocation
Guidelines

People Are Usually Better At

- Detecting unexpected/unusual (unprogrammed) events in the environment
- Recognizing patterns of complex stimuli that are not always consistent (such as human speech)
- Remembering large amounts of unrelated information over long periods of time
- Applying principles to solutions of novel problems
- Drawing upon experience to modify actions to meet changing situational requirements
- Developing creative solutions to problems
- Generalizing from observations (inductive reasoning)

Machines Are Usually Better At

- Making rapid and consistent responses to input signals
- Counting or measuring physical quantities
- Performing repetitive actions reliably to a specified standard
- Maintaining a specified level of performance over long periods of time
- Sensing stimuli outside of the capabilities of most humans
- Retrieving specified information quickly and accurately upon demand (with appropriate coding and instructions)
- Exerting considerable force in a controlled manner for long periods of time
- Grouping stimuli into specified classes (deductive reasoning)

Advances in technology have moved a great many job tasks that once had to be accomplished by humans (not because humans did them better, but because there were no machines to do them) to the machine side of operator-machine systems. Many more tasks have been shifted over into an area that is somewhere in between; they could be done either by person or by machine. The question job designers face is how to allocate such tasks to fit a particular situation; in this gray area, *could* (be done by machine) does not necessarily mean *should*.

Despite impressive progress on the technological front, the fundamentals in Exhibit 8–1 have not been altered significantly to date. A machine can answer a telephone. It can even answer a question by the caller. But it cannot answer a question that it has never "heard" before, nor can it give an answer that is outside of the preprogrammed choices. At present, the very best it can do in such a circumstance is to switch the caller to a human being.

Within the framework outlined, there are many possible variations for the relative mix of tasks in any particular operator-machine system. Often, the human operates the controls and the machine does the work. An ordinary household sewing machine is a system of this sort. So are many industrial robots These "workers" can use tools, do the same tasks over and over again without getting tired or bored, and work in conditions that are

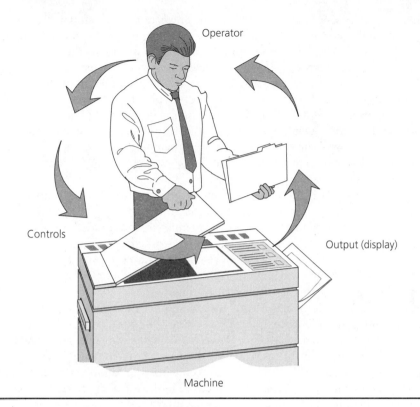

Operator

Controls

Output (display)

Machine

Figure 8–1
An Operator-
Machine
System

unpleasant or dangerous to humans. But they are still machines and they must be programmed and operated by the human half of the system.

Once their programs are set and their controls have been activated, many industrial robots may be left to get on with the job under minimal supervision to monitor for malfunctions. Other operator-machine systems require the operators to feed the machine in some way and to watch various forms of displays, taking actions or making adjustments based on what they see. A simple and familiar example is the ordinary photocopier machine shown in Figure 8–1.

A photocopier has visual displays that tell the operator when to begin input, when paper must be added, when the toner cartridge must be replaced, when paper is jammed, and when service is required. In addition, the quality of the output provides information about making other adjustments, such as the placement of material to be copied and changes in the light contrast of the copies.

The photocopier operator-machine system has counterparts in many industrial jobs. The employee operates controls and makes adjustments based on information provided by various displays or machine output (or both). But today's organizations also have machines that are far more complex. The work that they do is primarily the organizing, processing, and display of information. The human component of the system is a passive observer, using the information provided by the machine to make decisions and take actions as appropriate.

The equipment used by an air traffic controller provides a picture of the skies in a given area, but it is the controller who must make the correct decisions about aircraft movement on the basis of the information. The crews of the aircraft combine the information communicated from the control tower with information provided by their own cockpit displays to make numerous split-second decisions about their aircraft movements. In a big-picture sense, this operator-machine system consists of the interface of the flight crew/equipment system with the air traffic controller/equipment system.

It seems something of a paradox that the more sophisticated and complex machines become, the greater are the demands they place on the human component—demands on perceptual and cognitive abilities and on the ability to maintain sustained attention, or vigilance. These demands, in turn, put more pressure on human factors psychologists to help industrial designers develop control and display mechanisms that are compatible with human abilities.

The impact that poorly designed control and display mechanisms can have on human operation is often seen in the average person's contact with everyday objects. Televisions and VCRs with rows of tiny identical buttons whose functions have to be discovered with a magnifying glass and a flashlight (or worked out from elaborate and complex diagrams in the accompanying manual) are frustrating to use. Modern buildings with sleek glass doors that have no knobs, push plates, or other clues as to how to open them can be dangerous to use as well as frustrating.

Psychologist D. A. Norman describes these and other examples of emphasis on sleek design without regard to function in his best-selling 1988 book called *The Psychology of Everyday Things.* With a master's degree in electrical engineering and a doctorate in psychology, Norman still couldn't figure out how to operate a watch that he was considering buying for his young son. Nor could the high tech whiz who founded Digital Equipment Corporation figure out how to heat a cup of coffee in the office microwave oven.

Norman and others are taking American manufacturers to task for ignoring a basic premise of human engineering psychology: the first criterion for the design of controls and displays is that they work well and be easy to understand. Appearance and the convenience of those who manufacture and install the equipment should always be secondary. These principles apply to any equipment used in a work setting, as well as to consumer goods, such as watches and microwave ovens.

The Design of Controls

Machine controls are the means by which a machine is activated and operated, the first interface between human and machine in an operator-machine system. Familiar examples of controls include keys, levers, pedals, wheels, buttons, and switches. Many machines, such as the photocopier shown in Figure 8–1, have very simple controls. Others, such as those needed to fly an airplane or to make a studio musical recording, have banks of dozens or more controls. In every case, designing the controls requires making multiple decisions as to shape, form, and location relative to (1) purpose, (2) other controls and/or displays, and (3) human capacities.

Criterion

See page 63

The human capacities of relevance in designing controls are both general (such as average human range-of-motion limitations) and specific. An important question, for example, is whether the control can be operated as effectively and efficiently by a left-handed person as by a right-handed one (Garonzik, 1989). Five simple and frequently used controls are compared on four human operation criteria in Table 8–1. The criteria are (1) the speed with which an operator can use the control to make necessary adjustments; (2) the accuracy with which an operator can use the control; (3) the physical ef-

Table 8–1			A Comparison of Five Common Controls	
Component	**Speed**	**Accuracy**	**Effort Required**	**Working Range**
Handwheel	Poor	Good	Moderate	Moderate
Knob (continuous) Small	Poor	Good	Very Poor	Moderate
Large	Very Poor	Moderate	Poor	Moderate
Knob (clock stops)	Good	Good	Very Poor	Very Poor
Push button	Good	Very Poor	Very Poor	Very Poor
Pedal	Good	Poor	Good	Very Poor

Adapted from E. Grandjean, *Fitting the Task to the Man: An Ergonomic Approach* (3rd ed.). New York: International Publications Service, and London: Taylor & Francis, Ltd., 1982. Adapted by permission of the author and the publishers.

fort required to use the control; and (4) the range of responses that the control will accommodate.

An examination of the table reveals numerous trade-offs among the criteria that apply to controls. The pedal allows for good speed, but it is not very accurate; the handwheel has the opposite characteristics. If a machine has multiple controls, the situation becomes more complex. Each control must be compatible with the others as well as with its own purpose and with operator capabilities. In addition, each control must be readily distinguishable from the others, particularly if operator speed is important or if the operator cannot see all of the controls.

The various issues involved in designing multiple machine controls can be illustrated by taking a look at the control requirements of an ordinary standard-shift automobile. The basic controls required are for activation (starting the car), steering, accelerating, braking, and changing gears. These controls must be consistent with a number of constraints.

- Starting the car is an independent operation.
- It must be possible to steer and accelerate simultaneously.
- It must be possible to change gears simultaneously with steering and accelerating as required.
- It must be possible to brake while simultaneously steering and changing (or disengaging) gears.

The constraints mean that an automobile operator is often called upon to operate several controls at the same time. All controls, therefore, must be within easy reach and easily distinguishable from one another. The designer of the controls must also consider the fact that driving a car requires close visual attention to the road and that the operator can look only occasionally at the controls he or she is using.

Today, most automobiles are operated by means of the fairly standard control layout shown in Figure 8–2. Steering is accomplished with a large wheel (for accuracy) placed directly in front of the operator. Gear shifting is done by means of a lever usually located to the right of the operator around sitting waist level. Braking, accelerating, and gear disengagement are controlled by foot pedals (good speed) placed in a standard position on the floorboard in easy reach of the feet. Automobiles with automatic transmissions are somewhat simpler in that one of the requirements for hand-foot coordination has been eliminated.

The control design of the modern automobile fairly approximates the requirements of this operator-machine system, but it has not been developed in any systematic way and there are some flaws from a human factors perspective. For example, braking is a function that frequently is used in an emergency fashion. Because eye-hand reaction time for humans is faster than eye-foot reaction time, braking ideally should be accomplished by hand, as it is in automobiles modified for use by handicapped drivers.

Brake pedals were put on the floor of automobiles in the days before power-assisted braking. The average person at that time was more likely to be able to apply the force needed by foot. Unfortunately for good human factors design, it would be very difficult to change this arrangement now. Machine operators become control dependent over time, as any driver used to a gear shift lever between the seats finds when switching to an automobile with the shift lever located on the steering column (or vice versa).

The fact that experienced machine operators become dependent on a particular configuration of controls highlights the importance of the initial human factors research behind the design of these controls. An interesting example of what can happen when this research is inadequate is provided by the case of the familiar typewriter or computer key-

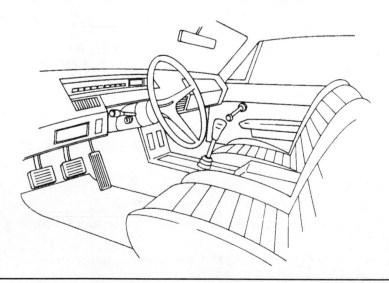

Figure 8–2
An Automobile
Control System

board. Figure 8–3 shows two such keyboards; the one at the top is the standard control layout.

The keyboard on the bottom was designed from a human factors perspective, and it makes more efficient use of the movements and the relative finger strengths of the normal human hand. Although it was developed some time ago, this keyboard is not in general use. Experienced typists simply cannot make the switch, and new typists are taught by experienced typists. As a result, the improved keyboard design shown in Figure 8–3 (Dvorak, 1943), remains a little-known and seldom-seen alternative to the standard arrangement.

Control dependency is not limited to machines that have been around for generations. The same issue arises when people who are accustomed to controlling a computer with a mouse try to switch to keyboard controls (or vice versa), and newer efforts to develop effective voice-activated commands are encountering related problems (Karl, Pettey, & Schneiderman, 1993). Computers and computer-controlled machines and office equipment in general have created a host of challenges for human factors engineers. Here are but a few of the specific recommendations that have come out of this research about using the controls of these machines.

- Position the keyboards about an inch from the top of the legs at the lowest point to reduce shoulder shrugging, elbow problems, and neck tension.

- Tilt the keyboard platforms about 12 degrees away from the operator to minimize wrist bending.

- Locate the mouse platform higher than the operator's elbow (and operator, please don't squeeze the mouse!).

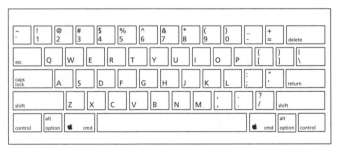

Standard design

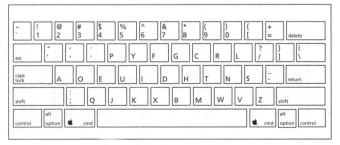

Improved design

Figure 8–3
Keyboard
Control Designs

The Design of Displays

Machine displays provide the operator of a machine with work-related information. This information may be dynamic (fluctuating, as a pressure gauge) or static (steady, such as an on-off light) in nature. It may pertain to the machine's operation, or it may be the actual output (work) of the machine. Many machines have displays for both purposes. In all cases, displays are subject to the same design decisions—size, shape, location, form, and compatibility—as controls, but they also add new considerations.

Most machine displays are video or audio in form, and designing them requires knowledge of human visual and hearing processes as well as knowledge of human physical attributes. Displays also provide information that must be used in some fashion by the operator, and so their design must incorporate human capacities and limitations in information processing as well. Cognitive engineering is an applied science that draws from cognitive psychology and related disciplines to help in the development of guidelines for this specialized integration of human and machine (Woods & Roth, 1988).

Cognitive psychology
See pages 140–142

The relationship between human perceptual and information-processing abilities and the design of displays is not self-evident. Insufficient research can lead to serious flaws, such as those at Three Mile Island. Another example is found in the results of a study by Momtahan, Hétu, and Tansley (1993). These investigators discovered that operating room and intensive care unit personnel in a large hospital could identify (on average) only about half of the emergency auditory alarms in use in their work areas. Similar problems have been found in many other work environments where auditory warnings are often too loud, too numerous, and too indistinguishable from one another (Edworthy, 1994).

Not all problems with displays stem from inadequate research. Computer screen display design has been investigated in detail, but certain issues are still unresolved. The question of whether people read faster from paper than from computer screens is a simple example. Many researchers have concluded that paper has a clear superiority (e.g., Gould et al., 1987), whereas Oborne and Holton (1988) find no difference, and Dillon (1992) states that a review of the literature to that time provides no evidence for the superiority of one mode over the other.

Computer screen displays are not in use to enable readers to read faster, but whether people read them more slowly than print is relevant to many jobs. The issue in designing any display is how best to represent and present information to the human component of an operator-machine system. The basic question in evaluating display design according to this criterion is: Can the machine operator take in (perceive) the information that the display presents as quickly as the job requires? Technology offers many more options than were once available, but basic human perceptual and cognitive abilities and limitations are much the same as they have always been. A simple illustration of some good and poor visual display designs with respect to these abilities is presented in Figure 8–4.

There are five types of visual display dials shown in the figure. In each case, the preferred design makes reading quicker and easier than the poor design. When a fixed dial with a moving pointer (similar to an ordinary wall clock) is used, for example, an operator can read it more quickly and easily if the numbers are printed horizontally to his or her line of sight. Most operators *could* read the other dial (with the numbers askew), but they would take longer, make more errors, or both (Coury & Boulette, 1992).

Another factor that affects the ease and speed with which visual display information is perceived is the display label. There is some consensus that a combination of symbols and words is more effective than either alone (e.g., Baber & Wankling, 1992; Kline &

Design	Preferred	Poor

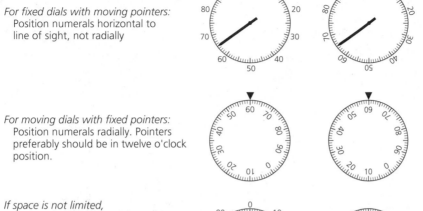

For fixed dials with moving pointers:
Position numerals horizontal to
line of sight, not radially

For moving dials with fixed pointers:
Position numerals radially. Pointers
preferably should be in twelve o'clock
position.

If space is not limited,
It is desirable to place the numerals
beyond the scale markers to avoid
having numerals obscured by pointer.
(If there is any restriction at all on
space, however, it is usually desirable
to place the numerals inside the markers
in order to have the scale as large as
possible.)

For open-window dials:
Window should show numbered scale
markers at either side, to indicate
direction of scale.

Numerals should be placed to appear
right side up when exposed.

Figure 8–4
Visual Display
Designs

From E. J. McCormick, *Human Factors Engineering* (2nd ed.). Copyright 1964 McGraw-Hill.
Reprinted by permission.

Beitel, 1994), but less agreement about color and word combinations. Chapanis (1994)
examined the perceptions of hazard associated with three words (*caution, warning,* and
danger) and four colors (white, yellow, orange, and red). Subjects agreed significantly
with one another only as regards the meaning of the red danger sign ("extremely hazardous").

The actual placement of displays is also important. Remember the displays that were
too high for operators to read at Three Mile Island? This is a mistake repeated on a regular basis in modern organizations where computer screens almost invariably are placed
too high. They also are usually too close to the operator. Experts recommend that the display be placed about 26 inches from the eyes and positioned so that the operator has to
look slightly down to see it.

**Research
subjects**
See page 27

**Statistical
significance**
See pages 35–36

SPOTLIGHT ON
RESEARCH

A
Reaction-
Time Study
of Four
Control-
Display
Linkages

Research question   What is the nature of the relationship between stove control/burner (display) arrangements and subject reaction time and errors in operating the appropriate control?

Type of study   Laboratory experiment.

Subjects   Not described. (This classic experiment predates the current emphasis on describing subjects.)

Independent variable   Arrangement of the stove control/display unit. The four arrangements are shown below.

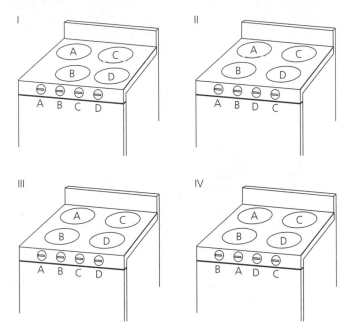

Dependent variables

- Speed of subject response. Operational definition: Number of seconds between illumination of two lights.
- Errors made by subjects. Operational definition: Number of mismatches between illuminated lights.

General Procedure   When a ready signal was given, the upper light on one of the wooden stove model burners shown was illuminated by the experimenter. The subject's task was to illuminate the matching lower light by pressing the appropriate burner control button (A, B, C, or D). Each subject was tested individually for 80 trials. The order of burner illumination for each subject was random.

Results   Reaction times were significantly faster for stove I. No errors were made on stove I. There was no significant difference in the rate of error on the other three stoves.

Conclusion   "The results of the experiment show that a control-display arrangement like that in the upper-left corner . . . is clearly superior to the other three. Linkage pattern II is next best, while III and IV are about equally bad" (p. 6).

The extent to which a display stands out from its surroundings is relevant, whatever its height. Again, Three Mile Island provides an example of what *not* to do; the malfunction of one critical operation was displayed to the operator at the control panel only as the absence or presence of a single red light among hundreds of displays.

**Independent/
dependent
variable**
See page 29

**Operational
definition**
See page 26

Summarized from
A. Chapanis and
L. E. Lindenbaum,
"A Reaction-Time
Study of Four
Control-Display
Linkages." *Human
Factors*, 1959, *1*,
1–7. Copyright
1959 by the
Human Factors
Society, Inc.
Reprinted by permission.

A detailed list of the principles involved in designing and placing machine displays can be found in any basic human factors engineering textbook. These principles are based on accumulated findings from many individual human factors engineering studies. A classic investigation into the placement of displays vis-à-vis their relevant controls is summarized in Spotlight on Research. Chapanis and Lindenbaum (1959) performed a laboratory experiment to determine which of the four stove control-display (knob-burner) combinations in common home use was superior in terms of human capacity for processing information. Interestingly, many stoves continue to look like design II, although the superiority of design I is quite clear.

Laboratory experiment
See pages 27–28

Work Methods

Whether the machine used by an individual is a stove, a computer, a punch press, or a backhoe, decisions about **work methods**, the actual movements by which people carry out job tasks, are an important part of job design. Work methods were studied extensively by the early industrial engineers whose analytical techniques are still in use. This analysis is not always appreciated by the employees who do the job; when a more efficient way to perform a task is discovered, people can do it faster so management may expect higher production for the same pay. On the other hand, management may follow the example of UPS, where the considerable increase in wealth that has been generated by more efficient work methods is shared with the drivers through a generous profit-sharing plan.

The behavior of UPS drivers looks a bit stilted to many people, but a basic principle in work method design is that the most efficient way to perform a job is also the least tiring way. Promoting work efficiency is only one goal of those who study work methods, and it cannot be separated from the other goal—reducing employee fatigue and increasing employee safety. To meet these goals, it is necessary to work with the human body rather than against it. The pushing power of the average male is substantially greater than his pulling power, for example. Both the work and the man whose job requires shifting heavy loads benefit from work specifications based on pushing rather than pulling the loads.

Sometimes the design of work from a human standpoint is focused on increased efficiency and reduced fatigue, as in the example of pushing power. In other cases, injury may result from poor work method specifications or from the failure of the operator to follow them. How many keyboard operators follow the recommendation to rest their hands in their laps in short, frequent breaks (totaling about 10 minutes per hour) and to close their eyes briefly every half hour?

The study of work methods incorporates a variety of physiological measures including energy consumption, heart rate, and the type of muscular effort involved. There are two types of such effort. One is dynamic effort, in which the muscles alternately contract and relax. The other is static effort, in which there is a prolonged state of muscular contraction. Figure 8–5 illustrates the critical difference between the two. Static effort produces an imbalance between the amount of blood needed to make the effort and the actual flow of blood to the muscles. By contrast, although dynamic effort requires a greater flow of blood than no effort (resting), these greater requirements are met by the supply.

The physiological difference between dynamic and static effort means that tasks calling for dynamic effort approximate a natural condition, whereas tasks requiring static effort lead to higher energy consumption and a raised heart rate. As a result, people

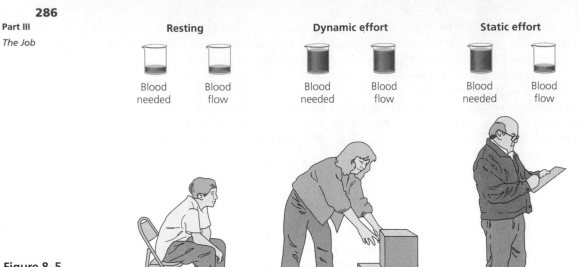

Figure 8–5
Blood Use and
Blood Flow at
Rest and at
Work

performing static effort tasks need longer and more frequent rest periods. They are also more subject to joint, ligament, and tendon deterioration. A good rule of thumb to follow in the work methods phase of job design is: Reduce the amount of static effort required to perform work tasks as much as possible.

Some familiar work activities requiring substantial static effort are standing in one place, sitting with no back support, holding and carrying objects, and keeping the head turned in one direction for extended periods of time. Even a casual glance around most workplaces will reveal employees in one or more of these poses. In many cases, the increased strain that is created is probably unnecessary; it could be reduced or eliminated by redesigning work methods, work space, tools, or work aids as appropriate, and by training people to recognize and avoid unnecessary static effort.

Taxing static effort in many jobs could be reduced or eliminated, but other jobs with such components are not changed so easily. Ambulance drivers and medics can spend up to a third of a work shift in strenuous and harmful positions (Doormaal, Driessen, Landeweerd, & Drost, 1995), but most of this exertion is made necessary by the emergency situations that are central to this job. Working at a computer also creates static effort problems. Most people who use computers all day do not sit with back support. In addition, a great many keep their heads turned toward material being entered into the computer for long periods of time.

People who perform work in which prolonged static effort or harmful posture cannot be "designed out" of the job or "trained out" of the employee should be given shorter shifts or longer rest periods to offset the negative effects. This recommendation raises an interesting question. Unless people complain, how is it possible to know if a job is poorly designed from an effort standpoint or too hard in some way on those who perform it?

The Measurement of Workload

For present purposes, workload can be defined in terms of the overall demands that a job makes on an individual. Objective measures of physical workload vary, but the basic idea is to compare the physical requirements of job tasks with the physical capacities and limitations of the "average" man or woman. With such an analysis, it is obvious that lifting and loading 30-pound cartons for eight hours a day is more demanding than, for instance, lifting and loading 20-pound cartons. Or is it?

Lifting and loading 20-pound cartons is only less physically demanding if the physical capabilities of the individual doing the lifting and loading are average, and obviously this is by no means always the case (Karwowski, Shumate, Yates, & Pongpatana, 1992). For practical purposes, a carton is as heavy as it feels to the person lifting it. People who do physical work rate the workload subjectively; they do not measure it objectively.

The subjective measurement of workload is a very active line of ergonomic research. In many studies a formal rating scale is used (e.g., Hendy, Hamilton, & Landry, 1993). Other investigators use the "perceived exertion" assessment familiar to anyone who has participated in aerobic exercise instruction. Ulin and her colleagues (1993) conducted a study in which subjects used air-powered tools to drive screws into perforated sheet metal. Combinations of five different work locations (three vertical and two horizontal) and three different work paces (8, 10, and 12 screws per minute) created the experimental conditions.

**Experimental
conditions**
See page 29

After the subjects in the study had driven screws under each of the different conditions, they were asked to assess how hard the work was at each location. They also ranked seven body areas for discomfort at each location. The smallest exertion and discomfort were associated with driving the screws at elbow height on a vertical surface or with the lower arm close to the body on a horizontal surface.

A variation on the procedure for assessing workload in the study described, which was a laboratory study, is to collect perceived exertion data under the circumstances in which the work is actually performed. In one such study, 92 adult computer users kept diaries in which they recorded any physical signs of discomfort and the types of work tasks being performed at the time (Collins, Brown, Bowman, & Carkeet, 1990).

Data from investigations such as those described are of great value in helping human factors engineers develop physical work methods that are more human friendly—easier to perform, less fatiguing, creating fewer work-related injuries, and so on. A review of the concept of physical workload and the development of guidelines is presented by Westgaard and Winkel (1996). The measurement of mental workload is more complex (see review by Howell, 1993), but as the number of jobs that are nonphysical in nature continues to increase, research efforts in this area become more vital.

The Workspace Envelope

From a job design viewpoint, the portion of the work environment that is of the greatest interest is the part used by a single employee in performing his or her job. This space is called the **workspace envelope** to convey a sense of a three-dimensional physical space that surrounds and is unique to an individual employee. Some people, such as traveling sales representatives, have no actual workspace envelope in the sense that it is defined. For others, such as grounds maintenance employees, the workspace envelope is the great outdoors. The workspace envelope for an airline pilot is an airplane cockpit. More typically, however, a workspace envelope is an office, private or shared, a partially walled cubicle (or "cube"), or simply a space on a larger floor area. Among the questions that must be answered in designing this space for effective work performance are the following:

- How high should the work surfaces be?
- What kind of chair is best for an individual who is seated most of the time?
- Where should tools and supplies used regularly, but not constantly, be stored?
- Where should desks and chairs be located relative to shelves, files, doors, and so on?
- How compact can a workspace envelope be without the occupant feeling confined or closed off?

The list includes only a very small number of the relevant considerations in designing a workspace envelope. It is possible to find precise recommendations for almost every aspect of design for virtually any situation. Grandjean (1982) lists 10 specific criteria for chair seat designs for office workers; the chair itself involves another whole set of considerations. It seems that the optimal solution for workspace envelope design would be to tailor each space to the individual occupant, but this seldom is practical. As a compromise, the following two principles serve as general guidelines.

1. To the extent possible, furnish workspace envelopes with chairs, drawing tables, and other elements that are designed to be adjustable. More of these items are being developed all the time. The Trakker Adjustable Table (Haworth Incorporated) includes a memory that will return the desk station to one employee's preferred adjustment after another has used the same space.

2. Elements that are not adjustable should be designed for the individual who would incur the greatest discomfort or inconvenience from alternative arrangements. Permanent shelves should be placed to give shorter people easy access, whereas nonadjustable work surfaces should be at a height comfortable for taller people. Stooping over for any length of time frequently produces severe back and neck ache; shorter employees can be provided with a raised platform to stand on while working at such surfaces.

Flexiplace: Alternative Work Sites

Most organizations cannot afford to tailor workspace envelopes specifically to each and every employee, but there are growing alternatives to working in an office, known collectively as **flexiplace.** Of these, the last word in individual design is the employee's own home. In some cases, this arrangement is merely an option to be taken up or not. Other companies actively encourage eligible employees to work from home by reducing the amount of traditional office and desk space available for use. Account executives and consultants below the senior level at the accounting firm of Ernst and Young must reserve an office a day in advance (a procedure known as "hoteling"). Compaq turned all of its computer salespeople into "road warriors" by closing its sales offices completely. Employees communicate with one another and with the home office through a computer network—how else?

Working at home is not new, but large numbers of regular organizational employees performing full-time jobs at home is a relatively recent phenomenon.

Technology has made it possible for clerical employees to take dictation, type copy, and transmit results directly back to their offices without ever leaving home. Stockbrokers, newspaper reporters, market analysts, computer programmers, service personnel, and salespeople, among others, can do most or all of their work from home and/or their automobiles.

These employees are telecommuters—they use computers and other communications technology rather than wheels to commute to their employer's premises. Estimates of their numbers vary from 5 to 20 million (Ford & McLaughlin, 1995), but whatever the actual number, it is growing and expected to continue to do so. The plan saves organizations money and expands their labor pool to skilled people who might otherwise not be available, such as parents of young children, employees with physical disabilities, and people who live too far away for a reasonable commute.

Despite its growth, there is very little empirical research on telecommuting; most of the information available comes from interviews with participants. Some people like it and some do not. Many miss the social interaction of the office or fear that lack of visibility will cause their careers to suffer. Yet others find they have exchanged one set of workplace problems for another (see Figure 8–6).

In terms of productivity, telecommuting seems to be paying off (Turnage, 1990). Compaq road warriors sell six times as many computers as under the old system, for instance. But managers and employees alike emphasize that this arrangement is not for everyone. Finding effective ways to select employees who will be comfortable with telecommuting

Figure 8–6
The Problems of Flexiplace

From *Across the Board,* July–August 1982, *19,* 68. Reprinted by permission of The Conference Board and R. Doty.

and productive without the supporting structure of a formal workplace is one of the major contributions I/O psychologists can make to the emerging new world of work.

Considered overall, telecommuting potentially offers many desirable outcomes to employees (such as control of own schedule), employing organizations (an expanded labor pool), and society in general (less traffic, less smog, fewer children left alone or in substandard day care). It also holds potential for exploitation on both sides, and it raises concerns about the effects of isolating employees from co-workers and possibly from advancement opportunities (especially when it is enforced, rather than voluntary).

Challenges to Human Factors Job Design

The core of the human factors approach to job design is achieving harmony among human perceptual, cognitive, and physical abilities; work methods; tools, machines, and other work aids; and the area in which the work is performed. These elements have been reviewed separately, but in practice they should work together. Unfortunately, this objective very often is not met. In particular, aspects of the workspace envelope often do not support sophisticated work methods and equipment. People who work with computers are especially vulnerable to "ergonomically incorrect" work spaces, which often feature poor lighting, awkward placement of computer displays and controls, and chairs almost guaranteed to cause muscle strain.

Telecommuting is not helping the problems described. Most people lack the knowledge to configure their work spaces appropriately, although the development of a new computer program to help people understand proper workstation set-up and adjustment principles may help (Hochanadel, 1995). Traveling telecommuters have more problems; to date the majority of hotel rooms are still not computer friendly. After practically rewiring the room, the jet-lagged road warrior finds himself or herself kneeling on the floor in the dubious illumination of a 30-watt "reading lamp" operating a laptop computer that is perched precariously on the side of the bed.

There is little human factors engineers can do about problems that an organization's employees face at home or on the road, but there is much they could do on-site if given the opportunity. There may be more of these opportunities soon in response to both the general aging of the work force and the passage of the Americans with Disabilities Act in 1990. The issues and concerns raised by the need to accommodate disabled and older employees offer an opportunity for organizations to upgrade job design for everyone (Haigh, 1993).

There will be exceptions, but many of the changes required to accommodate the special needs of employees who are not average do not have to be specific. Machine displays that are too high are hard on anyone, not just people in a wheelchair. Large, clearly marked controls are used more effectively and comfortably than tiny ones with same-color braille-like markings by 25-year-olds as well as by 65-year-olds. It isn't necessary to be either older or disabled to appreciate wider corridors and doorways.

Changes like those suggested would make work safer, less tiring, and more efficient for everyone, but human factors engineering applications often meet with resistance from those who should benefit from them (as well as from those who must pay for them). I/O psychologists know that, in general, such resistance is reduced and implementation of changes goes better when time is taken to understand the work processes involved in detail and to consider how the employees who will be affected view their work. May and Schwoerer (1994) made use of these principles to create a participatory ergonomics job redesign program in a large midwestern organization.

Assembly-line jobs usually lack all of the elements that many I/O psychologists believe are critical to a satisfactory work experience.

After they had received training in team-building and ergonomic principles, management-labor teams from each department in the organization set priorities and developed and implemented job redesigns. The changes were based on observations, videotapes, employee surveys, and interviews with employees about their jobs. When the program was complete, there were significant reductions in lost production time, restricted duty days, and physical symptoms of cumulative trauma disorders (such as carpel tunnel syndrome).

Participatory ergonomics is a method consistent with both the value I/O psychologists place on the individual and what they have learned about effective organization change efforts. It also is consistent with a basic belief of human factors psychologists that much of the job satisfaction of many people depends on being able to do their jobs effectively. A job that is well designed from a human factors viewpoint supports rather than hinders this achievement (Eklund, 1995). Participatory ergonomics could prove to be a much-needed bridge between the human factors approach to job design and the psychological approach.

The Psychological Approach to Job Design

The **psychological approach to job design** is characterized by the assumption that effectiveness and efficiency are correlates of satisfaction with the work that is being performed. Many psychologists believe that this satisfaction is the key to allowing people to meet needs for self-actualization (Maslow, 1943) and that meeting these needs is crucial to work motivation.

Correlates
See page 40

Three psychological job design techniques are examined here—job enlargement, job enrichment, and sociotechnical job design. These methods are applied to initial job design less often than to the redesign of traditional efficiency-oriented jobs when problems surface in an organization. Among the symptoms that many I/O psychologists believe call for examination of the psychological aspects of jobs are wasted time, chronic lateness, employee theft, poor work quality, high turnover rate, chronic absenteeism, and excess waste of materials.

Job Enlargement

A basic decision in job design is how many tasks to include within the definition of a job. At the ends of the continuum of possibilities lie performance of one task over and over and performance of all tasks that make up a complete job. In some restaurants, for example, the task of serving customers is divided up among a host or hostess, a wine steward, a server who takes the food order, a kitchen server who brings the food to the table, and yet another person who clears everything away. In other restaurants, a single individual performs all of these functions for his or her assigned tables.

In the early 1800s, an Englishman demonstrated that ten people, each performing only one task, could produce a pound of straight pins for about one-quarter of the cost incurred when the pound was produced by one person performing all of the tasks (Babbage, 1835). This **specialization approach to job design** was promoted and used with great success in the United States by industrial engineers, and it became the basis for virtually all industrial job design in this country.

It is not surprising that limiting the number of job tasks to be performed by one person works well from the standpoint of effectiveness and efficiency. Specialization allows each employee to concentrate on getting very good at one or a few tasks. But doing the same task(s) over and over again, eight hours a day, five days a week, is also monotonous, and many people find such work boring and meaningless. A job design strategy that attempts to reduce or eliminate these potential problems is called job enlargement.

Job enlargement is a plan to make jobs "bigger," or larger, by adding to the number of work tasks each person performs. Typically, these tasks are at about the same level of skill or difficulty as those performed originally (a horizontal loading of tasks). Job enlargement became quite popular in the 1950s and 1960s as an offshoot of interest in the causes and effects of employee boredom and alienation from work (see Fisher, 1993, for a recent review). Psychologists hypothesized that task specialization frustrates people's needs for variety, for challenge, and for a sense of making a meaningful contribution to group goals. To the extent that this is true, job enlargement should help alleviate the problem.

Reports of the early research into the effects of job enlargement are almost all glowing. The classic success story is reported by Kilbridge (1960). In that study, enlarging the job of water pump assembler from one task to assembling, checking, and approving the entire pump produced significant savings for the company involved. When job satisfaction, rather than performance, was the criterion, results were even more favorable.

A bibliography and brief review of the early job enlargement research can be found in the 1979 book by Aldag and Brief, who discuss a number of methodological problems with these investigations. As applied job enlargement was subjected to closer examination, a number of practical problems emerged as well. Not all jobs can be enlarged, and not all people want their jobs enlarged even if it is possible to do so. In addition, the ability and skill requirements of an enlarged job may be beyond the capabilities of the present job holder; some of these employees will have to be given more training and some will have to be replaced.

Even when no obstacles to job enlargement are apparent, problems in the application of this strategy remain because there are no guidelines. Should jobs always be enlarged to the maximum (as in the case of the water pump assembly), or is there some other standard by which to determine the optimal degree of enlargement in a particular case? Are there different types as well as different degrees of job enlargement? Is enlargement more relevant to certain occupations than to others?

Answers to these and other questions about job enlargement are slow in developing. With some exceptions, most notably a continuing line of research by Campion and his colleagues (e.g., Campion & McClelland, 1993; Campion & Thayer, 1987; Wong & Campion, 1991), job enlargement research as such had all but vanished from the literature by the end of the 1970s. This is not to say that the concept vanished; rather, that the distinction once made between job enlargement and job enrichment has not been maintained by most I/O psychologists.

Job Enrichment

As a psychological approach to job design, job enrichment has much in common with job enlargement. The premise underlying both is that job design should be based on appreciating human needs for meaningful work. The distinction between the two strategies lies in concepts of how this is to be accomplished. Job enlargement works on the assumption that meaningfulness is dependent on the number and variety of tasks that are performed relative to the whole job. By contrast, the basic premise of **job enrichment** is that it is the kind, not the number, of tasks performed that is important.

In practical application, job enrichment usually means giving people more responsibility and decision-making authority with respect to planning, scheduling, and controlling their own work. These management-type tasks represent vertical loading of job tasks, as opposed to the horizontal loading of job enlargement. Some general questions that are helpful in conceptualizing how such redesign is accomplished are shown in Exhibit 8–2.

As illustrated by questions in the exhibit, the element of increased individual control is central to the motivational effects of job enrichment. Greater perceived control over work is associated with higher job satisfaction, higher work motivation, better job performance, more involvement with the job, greater commitment to the organization, and reduced job stress, absenteeism, and turnover (Orpen, 1994; Spector, 1986). The importance of some measure of control over their jobs to employees appears to be general, extending even to assembly line work (Wall, Jackson, & Davids, 1992).

The early job enrichment literature, like the early job enlargement literature, contains many success stories (e.g., Ford, 1973; Paul, Robertson, & Herzberg, 1969), and in a similar parallel fashion practical problems began to emerge. Unlike job enlargement, however, job enrichment has remained very much in the mainstream of I/O psychology research. In part, this is because enlargement is part of enrichment. The tasks that are added to enrich jobs usually are management-type tasks, but job enrichment, like job enlargement, always makes jobs "bigger."

Exhibit 8–2
Some
Questions to
Guide Job
Enrichment

- Are there steps from earlier work stages that might be incorporated into this job to form a more complete unit of work?

- Are there steps from later work stages (for example, inspection) that might be incorporated into this job to form a more complete unit of work?

- Are there tasks that could be automated or pushed down to a job at a lower skill level to increase the meaningfulness of this job?

- Are there tasks or responsibilities that employees in this job perform in an emergency or in the absence of a supervisor that they could do on a regular basis?

- Are there supervisory tasks that could be performed as effectively by employees who have demonstrated job competency?

- Are there supervisory controls on this job that could be reduced or eliminated?

- Is it feasible to let employees do more of their own work planning and scheduling?

- What training might employees in this job provide for co-workers?

Summarized from the discussion by E. F. Huse and T. G. Cummings, *Organization Development and Change* (3rd ed.), 1985, West Publishing (copyright now held by South-Western Publishing).

Job characteristics model
See pages 192–193

Another part of the explanation for the continuing popularity of job enrichment lies in the better-developed theoretical underpinnings of job enrichment, specifically in the work of Hackman and Oldham (1975, 1976). These authors' job characteristics model was examined in detail in the context of its motivational theory origins in Chapter 6. To recapitulate briefly, the model postulates five basic characteristics (called core dimensions) of jobs—task identity and significance, skill variety, feedback, and work autonomy.

According to the job characteristics model, the core dimensions increase employee motivation, job satisfaction, and work quality, and decrease absenteeism and turnover through their effects on three internal psychological states—experienced meaningfulness, responsibility, and knowledge of results. The effects are stronger for employees who have higher needs for growth and development on the job (growth need strength), and they also depend to some extent on a satisfactory job context (working conditions, pay, and so forth).

Hypothesis
See page 25

Moderator variable
See page 39

Empirical investigations of the various aspects of the job characteristics model have yielded mixed results. Some employees perceive the five core job dimensions to be separate from one another, but others do not make the hypothesized distinction between skill variety, task significance, and autonomy (e.g., Fried & Ferris, 1986). Growth need strength is found to have the hypothesized moderating effects in some studies (e.g., Das, 1991; Graen, Scandura, & Graen, 1986), but these relationships are not supported in others (e.g., Tiegs, Tetrick, & Fried, 1992).

The research record is similar when it comes to the critical psychological states in the job characteristics model. There is evidence both for (e.g., Renn & Vandenberg, 1995) and against (e.g., Johns, Xie, & Fang, 1992) the links between (a) these states, (b) the core dimensions, and (c) the attitudinal outcomes. The extent to which the job characteristics model dominates the field of motivational job design makes stronger evidence for the hypothesized variables and relationships among them desirable. The consensus among I/O psychologists, however, seems to be that there is sufficient evidence for the model's viability to warrant continuing research efforts (Wall & Martin, 1994).

Turning from investigations of job enrichment theory to investigations of job enrichment outcomes, I/O psychologists often find a positive relationship between "richer" jobs (defined differently in different studies) and increased employee job satisfaction (e.g., Campion & McClelland, 1993; Long, 1993; Zeffane, 1994). To that conclusion must be added the vital proviso that the employees involved must have both interest in and skills for expanded job responsibilities (e.g., Ferguson & Cheyne, 1995; Wichman, 1994; Xie & Johns, 1995).

On the basis of research to date, a positive relationship between job enrichment and employee performance is more speculative, but it is possible that this state of affairs is at least partially a result of research methodology. In particular, the very few published long-term studies of motivational job design application in the field have been consistent in their findings that job enrichment outcomes change over time. A two-year investigation by Griffin (1991) illustrates the point.

In the Griffin study, results of an organizational change intervention to enrich the jobs of 526 bank tellers showed that both satisfaction and organizational commitment increased quickly following the intervention, then declined to their original levels. On the other hand, performance, which was originally unchanged, improved significantly by the end of the research period. Had Griffin followed the more common procedure of taking his measures only twice (once before and once shortly after the change), he would have reached the usual conclusion: job enrichment has a positive effect on job satisfaction and no effect on performance.

Another measurement problem that creates confusion in job enrichment research is the by-now familiar one stemming from individual differences. To conduct research into the effects associated with job enrichment (or lack of it), a researcher must have a way to measure job characteristics. It is not enough just to look at the job and form an opinion as to its quality.

Perceived Versus Objective Task Characteristics

Hackman and Oldham (1974) developed a questionnaire instrument called the Job Diagnostic Survey (JDS) to measure the degree to which a job possesses the five characteristics in their model. The assumption underlying the scale is that the more of each of these characteristics people doing a job say it has, the richer the job. The Job Characteristics Inventory, or JCI (Sims, Szilagyi, & Keller, 1976), is a different instrument created for the same purpose, and Breaugh (1985, 1989) developed a separate questionnaire to measure work autonomy.

Of the instruments mentioned, the JDS has been used most often as an operational definition of job richness, and numerous investigations of the measurement properties of this scale have been carried out. In the course of this research, it was discovered that the mixture of positively and negatively worded items on the original JDS was introducing significant error into the score (Harvey, Nilan, & Billings, 1985).

As anyone who has taken a true-false test probably knows, it is easy to miss a *not* when reading a question and give an answer quite different from the one that would be given if the question had been read correctly. This situation is an example of the kind of problem discovered with Hackman and Oldham's original questionnaire. A revised

**Measurement
error**
See pages 53–54

version (Idaszak & Drasgow, 1987) is proving more satisfactory (e.g., Cordery & Sevastos, 1993), although additional work appears to be needed (e.g., Renn, Swiercz, & Icenogle, 1993). In any case, the best of such questionnaires from a measurement standpoint would not really be measuring a job's richness (or lack thereof). What the JDS and JCI and similar questionnaires actually measure is the degree to which a job is *perceived* by the person answering the questions to possess these characteristics. Another person can see things differently, and research results leave no doubt that they often do.

Perceptions of the characteristics of the same job can vary in a systematic way according to differences in individual preferences, background, age, and degree of identity with one's profession (O'Reilly, Parlette, & Bloom, 1980). Similar effects have been reported for differences in perceptual ability and general mental ability (O'Connor & Barrett, 1980) and for level of expressed job satisfaction (James & Tetrick, 1986). As illustrated by the data in Table 8–2 (Brenner & Tomkiewicz, 1979), the sex of the respondent is relevant as well.

Males and females look for the same general set of characteristics in jobs, but there are some important differences in emphasis, and such differences are likely to affect perceptions of current jobs. Details vary, but similar studies confirm most of the statistically significant differences shown in the table, such as the greater importance placed by females on congenial colleagues and the greater importance placed by males on pay (e.g., Bigoness, 1988).

Individual differences in perceptions of job characteristics do not stop with differences in personal characteristics like age, sex, and degree of satisfaction with a job. According to Salancik and Pfeffer's (1978) social information processing model, people pick up clues from fellow employees about the "right" attitudes toward a job. If co-workers keep saying that the work is great, because it provides the opportunity to make a positive contribution to society, employees asked to fill out a questionnaire like the JDS are quite likely to say that the job has high task significance.

Field studies

See pages 27–34

The social information processing model has received research support from both field (e.g., Glick, Jenkins, & Gupta, 1986) and laboratory (e.g., Griffin, Bateman, Wayne, & Head, 1987) studies. This support does not imply that people rely solely on others in their judgments of job characteristics, but it does suggest that social cues should be added to the list of factors that I/O psychologists know influence perceptions of job characteristics.

The significance of the individual and situational variables that affect how people view and describe their work lies in the fact that people react to their jobs based on the way *they* see them, not on how an I/O psychologist sees them. From this viewpoint there is no such thing as "objective" task characteristics, a situation that can confound research efforts and create considerable practical difficulty for the I/O psychologist seeking to help an organization implement job enrichment redesign (O'Connor, Rudolf, & Peters, 1980).

Sociotechnical Job Design

A **sociotechnical view of organizations** is a systems perspective that emphasizes the necessity for fit between the human and the technological components in an organization (Trist & Bamforth, 1951). In this view, job design and social organization depend to some extent on job technology. Some technologies permit or require individuals to work independently. An example of such a job is a telephone customer service position. Other technologies create tasks that require jobholders to work together.

Table 8–2   Male-Female Differences in Job Characteristic Preferences

Characteristic	Rank Males	Rank Females
Provides a feeling of accomplishment	1	1
Provides job security	2	3.5
Provides the opportunity to earn a high income	3	10.5*
Encourages continued development of knowledge and skills	4	2*
Permits advancement to high administrative responsibility	5	10.5
Provides comfortable working conditions	6	3.5*
Provides change and variety in duties and activities	7	6
Is respected by other people	8	8
Rewards good performance with recognition	9	9
Involves working with congenial colleagues	10	5*
Provides ample leisure time off the job	11	15
Permits you to develop your own methods of doing the work	12	13
Is intellectually stimulating	13	7*
Requires originality, creativeness	14	17
Makes use of your specific educational background	15	14
Requires working on problems of central importance to the organization	16	19
Permits working independently	17	16
Requires meeting and speaking with many other people	18	18
Permits you to work for superiors you admire and respect	19	12*
Gives you the responsibility for taking risks	20	22*
Makes a social contribution by the work you do	21	21
Requires supervising others	22	23*
Satisfies your cultural and aesthetic interests	23	20
Permits a regular routine in time and place of work	24	24
Has clear-cut rules and procedures to follow	25	25

*Indicates that difference is statistically significant.

From O. C. Brenner and J. Tomkiewicz, "Job Orientation of Males and Females: Are Sex Differences Declining?" *Personnel Psychology*, 1979, *32*, 741–750. Copyright 1979 Personnel Psychology, Inc. Adapted by permission of the authors and the publisher.

When technology requires synchronization of effort, sociotechnical principles often lead to a group approach to job design rather than an individual one. If the technology is complex, each team member may master only one or a few tasks. In many cases, however, the technology is sufficiently simple that all or most people can perform all or most tasks. Groups, or teams, of employees are given the responsibility for completing a whole unit of work, and they decide among themselves who will perform what tasks at any particular time.

The most famous application of the sociotechnical team strategy is the one that evolved out of a series of experiments at the Saab-Scania plant in Sweden in the late 1960s. As a result of the experiments, Saab switched from the standard continuous assembly line (specialization) design for assembling automobile engines to a parallel group assembly design similar to that shown in Figure 8–7. Teams of employees were responsible for assembling an entire engine, with each team working at its own rate. Parts and material were delivered by truck, and assembled engines were carried away by a mechanical conveyor belt accessible to each work group.

Saab later gave up the sociotechnical design, but the success of this and similar programs led a number of other companies to adopt the principles. At the Volvo plant in Uddevalla, Sweden, prepainted car frames sit on individually rotating holders called tilts. The stands can raise, lower, or rotate the frame by as much as 90 degrees while assembly crews of eight to ten workers attach the parts that come from a central warehouse on a computer-guided ferry system. Employees take turns managing the shop floor and acting as liaisons with management.

Sociotechnical team job design is often cited as a form of job enrichment, but it also embodies the basic principles of job enlargement—task variety and individual involvement with the job to be done on a level that is meaningful. No one person is responsible for the whole job, but each can see how his or her effort fits into the accomplishment of that job. Equally important, no one person is confined to the monotonous repetition of single tasks unless by choice. Fox (1995) traces the development of this job design approach in manufacturing organizations.

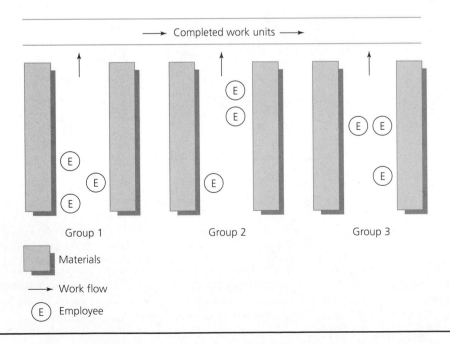

Figure 8–7
Parallel Group
Assembly Job
Design

There are a few empirical investigations of sociotechnical job design in the I/O psychology literature, but data lag behind case studies and general accounts describing how such programs have been implemented. Considered as a whole, this literature provides support for the proposition that this form of job design has performance and attitudinal benefits, but there are also costs (Wall, Kemp, Clegg, & Jackson, 1986). In an experiment in a minerals processing plant, there was both higher absenteeism and greater turnover in autonomous work groups (Cordery, Mueller, & Smith, 1991). At Volvo, some workers have had difficulty adjusting to their new freedom and managerial responsibilities, and there has been friction and disagreement within teams.

Challenges to Psychological Job Design

For some time now, motivational job design research and application have been dominated by the job characteristics model and its associated measures. This concentration has added substantially to I/O psychologists' acquisition of knowledge about psychological job design. At the same time, it has so focused attention on a particular set of variables that other features of jobs have been largely ignored (Wall & Martin, 1987).

The job characteristics model was developed more than 20 years ago. During that period, jobs have changed more in basic character than at any time since the Industrial Revolution. While there is no reason to believe that the job characteristics specified by the model are outdated, there is every possibility that they are no longer inclusive. A major challenge facing those who work in this area is to broaden their outlook to examine new-technology jobs for different characteristics that have important effects on employee performance and well-being (Jackson, Wall, Martin, & Davids, 1993).

A second challenge facing I/O psychologists who work with psychological approaches to job design is better integration of research and application. This is an active area of research, but only a small percentage of published reports are based on field interventions. The results of many of these investigations suggest that the effects of job enrichment, job enlargement, or sociotechnical job design are not as easily described as a difference between before and after measures of job satisfaction or performance. As the study by Griffin (1991) described earlier illustrates, the observed effects of psychological job redesign may be different depending on when observations are made. Other research makes it clear that this approach to job design also affects more than just the way one person does his or her job.

When a group of employees is given new skills and more responsibility for making decisions and detecting and correcting errors, the nature of the job that their supervisor performs is changed. Changing this job affects the manager's activities, and so on up and down the line. Psychological job design is not alone in creating such systems effects in organizations, but the issues involved tend to be more emotional, political, and philosophical than do those involved in the human factors approach.

Concluding Remarks on Job Design

Two very different views of job design have been discussed. The goals of human factors engineers and psychologists are to design jobs in such a way as to help people perform them effectively, efficiently, and safely with a minimum of strain and fatigue. The goal of I/O psychologists who take a psychological approach to job design is to make work more satisfying. These goals are entirely complementary to one another in theory, but it is un-usual to find them applied in an integrated fashion.

There are exceptions, certainly, but in general I/O psychologists and human factors psychologists have a long tradition of ignoring one another's existence. A more produc-tive view suggests taking both human and psychological factors into consideration from the beginning.

> . . . different approaches to job design influence different outcomes, each approach has costs as well as benefits, trade-offs may be needed, and both theory and prac-tice must be interdisciplinary in perspective. (Campion, 1988, p. 467)

Working Conditions

Hawthorne studies
See pages 4–5

Job design is one component of a person's work situation. Working conditions make up the other component. I/O psychologists have studied the physical work environment throughout the entire history of their discipline. It is often forgotten now, but the famous Hawthorne experiments were originally designed to investigate the effects of changes made in various aspects of the physical environment on employee work performance. It is these traditional aspects of working conditions that are reviewed here. Included are the variables of temperature, lighting, noise, the arrangement and architecture of the work-place, and the distribution of employee work hours. Psychological aspects of the work environment are examined in the following chapter.

Temperature of the Workplace

Psychologists and others who study the effects of temperature on work behavior are try-ing to establish limits within which most people doing a job can work effectively and comfortably. This is not quite as easy as it might sound because there is no simple one-to-one relationship between thermometer reading and perceived human comfort. Humidity, air flow, and the number, size, and temperature of objects and materials in a work space affect air temperature. Clothing and the nature of the work being performed affect perceptions of temperature. Finally, individual differences in physiology can have large effects on comfort. Some people do not feel cold until the mercury gets into the 40-to-50°F range. Others start to shiver as soon as it dips below 70°F.

Because so many variables affect human perception of temperature, one line of re-search into this aspect of working conditions is directed toward finding reliable ways of measuring "effective temperature," the perceived, or experienced, temperature as distinct from a thermometer reading (e.g., Vogt, Candas, & Libert, 1982). The development of computer simulations to predict human reactions to temperature under a range of envi-ronmental conditions is recent, but holds promise for helping find an answer to office temperature wars (Thellier, Cordier, & Monchoux, 1994).

Scientists who are investigating ways to measure effective temperature are doing ba-sic research. In this particular area, however, most I/O psychologists are more interested in applied research, specifically in the relationship between effective temperature and work performance. They find that extremes of both heat and cold lead to physiological changes that can have undesirable effects on work performance. The nature of the work performed and the length of exposure are the two factors that usually have the greatest impact on how extreme temperatures in the workplace affect people.

Most studies of complex cognitive tasks that require sustained attention indicate that subjects performing this work under prolonged exposure to high temperatures make significantly more errors than subjects working in lower temperatures (e.g., Fine & Kobrick, 1978; Razmjou & Kjellberg, 1992). The results reported in one laboratory investigation of the relationship between (a) room temperature and (b) the amount of time subjects could continue to perform cognitive tasks to a defined accuracy standard are shown in Figure 8–8. The time decreases quite sharply when the temperature rises above 80° F; at temperatures above 100° F, subjects could not meet performance standards for as long as one hour.

The performance of perceptual motor tasks also tends to deteriorate in higher temperatures (e.g., Ramsey, 1995). In this kind of task, a person must take in a stimulus (perception) and then make some response (motor reaction) based on what is seen or heard or smelled or felt. Cold temperatures have adverse effects on certain kinds of cognitive and perceptual motor tasks (e.g., Ellis, Wilcock, & Zamon, 1985; Thomas, Ahlers, House, & Schrot, 1989), but the physiological changes that accompany extremes of cold (such as numb fingers) usually have a greater effect on the performance of manual work (e.g., Lockhart, 1966). When *very* heavy manual labor is performed, however, most people seem to be both more efficient and more comfortable with temperatures below those in which cognitive or perceptual-motor tasks can be performed effectively.

The implications of temperature research for controlling the temperature in a work environment are relatively straightforward. Most people perform office work and light manual labor most efficiently and comfortably with an effective temperature no higher than 80°F. Cooler temperatures generally are better for heavy manual work. Specific recommendations for various work tasks are offered by the American Society of Heating,

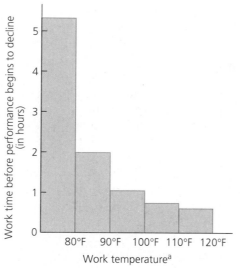

Figure 8–8
Temperature and the Performance of Cognitive Tasks

[a]Conversion from Celsius to Fahrenheit scale is approximate.

Data from J. F. Wing, "Upper Tolerance Limits for Unimpaired Mental Performance." *Aerospace Medicine,* 1965, *36,* 960–964.

Refrigerating, and Air Conditioning Engineers (ASHRAE) in their *Fundamentals Handbook,* which is revised periodically.

The recommendations of ASHRAE are based on the assumption that workplace temperature can be controlled, but there are many people who work out-of-doors. Construction crews, landscape gardeners, and fire fighters are among those who work in whatever temperatures prevail. If these temperatures are extreme, both employee health and performance may be jeopardized unless the debilitating physiological effects are offset by job rotation or regular rest periods.

Illumination of the Workplace

Just as researchers who study the effects of temperature on work performance and comfort want to specify ideal temperature ranges for various work environments, those who study illumination want to prescribe the best level of lighting for a workplace. Related questions concern the number of light sources (called *luminaries*), their type, and their placement in the work area. Perceptions of illumination, like perceptions of temperature, can vary with individual visual ability and with room conditions, but this variation is less dramatic. Therefore, the measurement of illumination, at least in the physical sense, is less of a problem than the measurement of effective temperature.

Professional lighting specifications are almost always given in a standard measure of illumination called footcandles. Developing these specifications is a highly technical process, but it is possible to note some of the factors that must be taken into account. A primary consideration is the nature of the task. Reading, assembling, monitoring, and inspection all have large visual components, for example, while answering a telephone, conducting meetings, and many manual tasks (such as shifting cartons) do not.

A second variable in determining illumination needs is the visually related attributes (such as size and color) of the materials, tools, or other work aids used on a job. Reading has a large visual component, but all reading tasks do not require high illumination. More light is needed to read the small print in a telephone directory than to read the large letters on a packing carton. Similarly, certain colors, such as yellow, orange, and red, can be seen more easily under lower illumination than other colors, such as gray, brown, and many shades of blue and green.

A third variable of relevance in determining appropriate illumination is contrast, the extent to which details stand out from a background. In general, the lower the level of illumination, the more contrast is required for accuracy in task performance (Gilbert & Hopkinson, 1949). Even when the parts are large, more light is required to fit gray screws into gray metal than to fit orange screws into gray metal.

A modern example of the need to consider contrast when specifying illumination is provided by the increased use of electronic visual display units. The contrast between material on the screen and the screen itself can usually be controlled by the operator, but reading the material can still be difficult if there is insufficient contrast between the light on the screen and the light in the room. An ironic instance of this problem was discovered when office employees of an electric power company were found to be turning off the room lights in order to read the screens on their personal computers.

The solution the power company employees found to their illumination problem will create problems of its own in time. Watching cathode ray tubes in the dark, be they computer screens or television screens, creates eyestrain for many people. So does prolonged exposure to bright lights, which also causes headaches if accompanied by glare. In general, an indirect, uplighting system (similar in concept to an ordinary torchier-style home floor lamp) seems to minimize the vision problems often experienced in computer-intensive work (e.g., Hedge, Sims, & Becker, 1995). A basic sourcebook for lighting specifications that meet visual task requirements in different work environments is the *Lighting Handbook,* revised periodically by the Illuminating Engineering Society.

Lighting specifications are important in designing workplace illumination, but this is not the only research being conducted in this area. Some investigators are more interested in nonperformance aspects of lighting, such as the impressions created by the way a room is illuminated. As shown in Exhibit 8–3, feelings of privacy, for example, are associated with lighting that is not too bright and comes from a variety of luminaries in a space. (This arrangement is rare in modern offices, where the visual clarity mode tends to be the rule.) Lighting also affects mood. Knez (1995) found that cool light was associated with less negative moods for men; for women, the same effect was achieved with warm light. All subjects performed the experimental long-term memory and problem-solving tasks better under the lighting that induced the least negative mood for their sex.

Noise in the Workplace

The number of noise sources in a work environment can be surprising. Some manufacturing employees work in conditions so noisy that a normal conversation is impossible.

To create an impression of spaciousness
Uniform (even) lighting

Peripheral (wall) light sources

Relatively bright lighting

To create an impression of privacy or intimacy
Nonuniform lighting

Peripheral (wall) light sources

Low intensity lighting near user(s)

Brighter lighting at distance from user(s)

To create an impression of pleasantness
Nonuniform lighting

Peripheral (wall) light sources

To create an impression of visual clarity
Uniform lighting

Some peripheral emphasis, such as highly reflective wall surfaces

Bright lighting

Exhibit 8–3
Impressions,
Mood, and
Lighting

Data from J. E. Flynn, "A Study of Subjective Responses to Low Energy and Nonuniform Lighting Systems." *Lighting and Design Application,* 1977, 7, 6–15.

Many office workers must contend with the persistent clatter of office machines, the insistent ringing of telephones, conversations among people in the office, and sometimes with piped music or public address systems as well.

Workplace noise, such as that found in manufacturing plants and offices, comes from tools, machinery, and people performing job tasks. Such noise has always been part of work in most organizations, and reducing it has long been a priority of industrial engineers and I/O psychologists interested in the problem. Today, however, it is common to find sound, in the form of music, introduced into work settings that would be relatively quiet if left alone. The fact that sound is being introduced deliberately into some work environments simultaneously with efforts to reduce noise in others reflects the complexity of this aspect of physical working conditions. Specifically, sound, or the lack of it, seems to have two distinct kinds of effects on individuals. One effect is physical; the other effect is psychological and depends on employee preferences for noisy or quiet working conditions.

After more than 50 years of research, the question of the physical effects of noise on work performance is still open. Some investigators have found that long-term exposure to noise is detrimental to performing cognitive tasks (e.g., Loewen & Suedfeld, 1992) and that noise can hinder the learning of other kinds of tasks (e.g., Key & Payne, 1981). Other researchers have come to the conclusion that noise, as such, does not have any predictable negative effects on performance (e.g., Davies & Jones, 1985).

What appears to be confusion in the research into relationships between noise and work performance suggests that individual differences, both physical and psychological, play a large part in such investigations. In fact, some scientists believe that the noise itself may account for less of the variation in reactions to it than do the other factors (Staples, 1996). There is also evidence that reactions to noise change over time, with some people getting used to it and some becoming more sensitive to it (Evans & Tafalla, 1987). Taken together, all of these potentially confounding variables are sufficient to make drawing general inferences from the noise-performance literature difficult.

The confounding effects of individual and situational variables on noise research are substantially reduced when it is physical well-being rather than employee work performance that is under examination. In their study of earth-moving equipment operators, LaBenz, Cohen, and Pearson (1967) found that substantial hearing loss was experienced by long-term operators of these kinds of machines. Their findings, shown in the graph in Figure 8–9, have been repeated many times in other work settings; hearing loss is the most common occupational disease in the United States.

There is no doubt at all that prolonged exposure to high levels of noise leads to hearing loss. Some people have hearing receptors that are more sensitive to noise than others, but the primary determinants of hearing loss are situational. The National Institute for Occupational Safety and Health (NIOSH) estimates that more than 30 million people are exposed to hazardous noise in the workplace. To help protect them, the U.S. Department of Labor established ceilings on the amount of noise employees may be subjected to without protection.

As a result of the Department of Labor regulations, employees in many lines of work are now issued "earmuffs" to guard against excess noise. Unfortunately, many people refuse to wear them (e.g., Melamed, Rabinowitz, & Green, 1994). This problem can be overcome in some settings with the use of newly developed noise-cancellation devices that produce equal but opposite sound waves ("antinoise") that block noise more effectively than protective ear coverings.

Variance
See pages 40–42

Confounding variables
See page 28

Inference
See pages 35–43

Determinants
See page 41

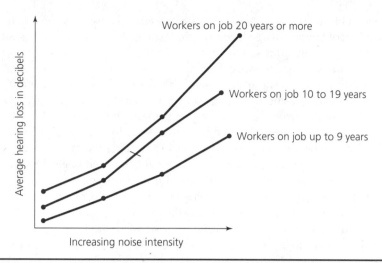

Figure 8–9
Hearing Loss
Among Earth-
Moving
Equipment
Operators

Data from P. LaBenz, A. Cohen, and B. Pearson, "A Noise and Hearing Study of Earth-
Moving Equipment Operators." *American Industrial Hygiene Association Journal,* 1967,
28, 117–128.

The general trend of research into the effects of noise on people dictates that all possible steps be taken to reduce noise in the workplace. Findings do not support the hypothesis that noise is always detrimental to work performance, but they leave no doubt
that reducing the level and duration of noise creates a more healthful work environment.
The problem with this strategy from a practical standpoint is that it ignores individual
preferences.

The well-known fact that people do not always prefer what is good for them is illustrated
yet again in attraction to noise. The manager of one teen-oriented clothing shop reports that
he is unable to hire and retain the younger assistants he prefers for his business unless he allows them to work with a background of loud rock music from a local radio station. The
same problem faces the manager of a popular hair salon, who says that she receives dozens
of complaints per month from clients about the piped-in music her stylists insist upon.

As the world gets noisier, the problem of individual differences in preferences for
noisy or quiet working environments may become more pressing; the relative rights of
music/no-music employees could become an issue just as the rights of smokers and non-
smokers once was. Undesired noise creates stress, but people who prefer music say they
find quiet stressful. Some organizations are letting employees who want to listen to music do so over individual headphones where it will not disturb those who prefer quiet, but
this is not always a practical solution. In addition, headsets at typical volume are known
to be a major factor in premature hearing loss among younger people.

"Mom, They've Squashed My Cube!": Workplace Layout

There are many possible ways in which the physical space available for office-type work
(as contrasted with manufacturing activities, warehouses, and so on) may be configured.
The individual employee office is a long-standing tradition. A modern variant is division
of the available space into cubicle offices. "Cubes" typically have no door and no ceiling
and they tend to be just large enough to accommodate one employee, one desk, one chair,

and whatever additional work equipment is required. Because they are erected of movable walls, cubicles can be enlarged, contracted ("squashed"), or removed as is necessary.

So-called open-plan offices, like those typically found in contemporary branch banks, have no walls, movable or otherwise. Work stations are simply placed here and there in the space available. The arrangement is flexible and economical and it allows co-workers easy access to one another, but employee reactions to this workplace layout have been less than favorable from the beginning (e.g., Oldham & Brass, 1979). In a series of three early studies, Sundstrom, Burt, and Kamp (1980) found that all of their subjects, regardless of the type of job they had, preferred the privacy of enclosed offices. Specifically, the investigators found that the physical and psychological privacy afforded by individual offices was correlated positively with job satisfaction and satisfaction with the work environment, and, to a limited extent, with job performance.

Correlation

See pages 37–39

Conclusions based on correlational analyses must be made with caution, but the findings of Sundstrom and his colleagues do not stand alone. Investigators continue to report positive relationships between the existence of office walls and feelings of privacy and satisfaction with the office setting (e.g., Duvall-Early & Benedict, 1992; Mazumdar, 1992). Employees who work in partitioned spaces also are more likely to spend their breaks in the office (Oldham & Fried, 1987) and to interact with one another on a voluntary basis (Hatch, 1987).

Evidence that the open-plan office idea may have more drawbacks than advantages as far as both productivity and employee satisfaction are concerned is unambiguous, but this arrangement is still to be found in many organizations. New trends, such as "hoteling," encourage the practice. At one IBM location, some 400 desks are set in rows on a huge warehouse floor. The desks are numbered and assigned by computer to the employees who request one on any given day.

Los Angeles ad agency Chiat/Day Incorporated has no offices or desks at all in the usual sense. Employees report each morning to a *concierge* where they pick up a portable computer and a mobile telephone and then set to work in one of several open areas containing chairs and tables. The only space these employees can call their own is a high school–type locker. The rationale behind this workspace layout (called "neighborhooding"), variations of which are being tried in a number of companies, is that it emphasizes and facilitates the teamwork believed to be necessary to good performance in these enterprises.

Will new open approaches to office layout along the lines of the illustration in Figure 8–10 be successful where older open-plan arrangements have often had results exactly the opposite of those intended? As in many other areas, it may turn out that the answer is "it depends." Individual differences in preferences, the ability to work in the midst of distractions, and the nature of the work performed are some of the factors that are probably most relevant (e.g., Oldham, Kulik, & Stepina, 1991).

Work-Hour Distribution

Responding to a range of influences, the work-hour distribution pattern in this country has evolved into a standard eight-hour-a-day, five-day-a-week arrangement. Organizations that must operate for more than eight consecutive hours a day usually have two or more eight-hour shifts, but a number of variations on the standard pattern have been devised and implemented. Two of these—the compressed work week and flexible working hours—are discussed here, along with some conclusions from research into standard shift-work patterns.

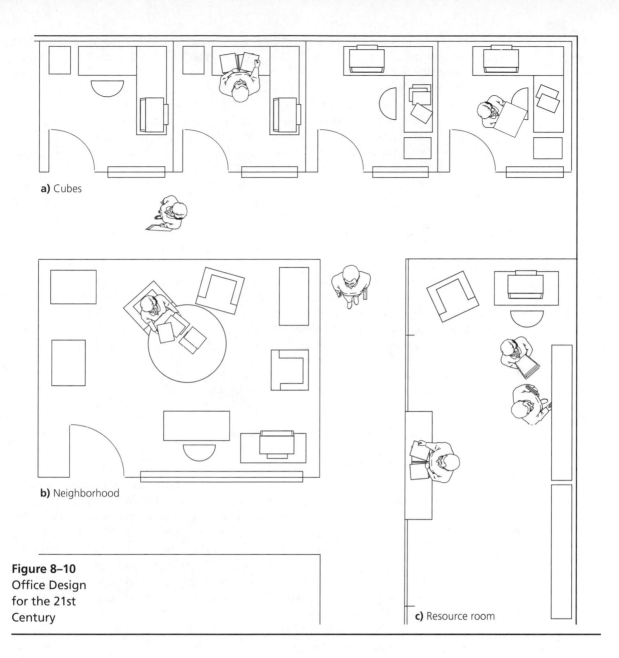

a) Cubes

b) Neighborhood

Figure 8–10
Office Design
for the 21st
Century

c) Resource room

The Compressed Work Week

A **compressed work week** (CWW) is a redistribution of the standard 40 hours of work. In its most common form, people work four days a week and still put in 40 hours because they work 10 hours a day. Some industries and professions have developed other plans. A few offer three-day, 12-hour-a-day work "weeks." The World Bank in Washington, D.C. is experimenting with a 9/1 plan, which gives employees who work nine extended-hour days the tenth day off.

The compressed work week offers employees a greater block of personal time than the standard work hour arrangement. Among the benefits believed to be associated with this change are reduced anxiety and stress and an improved home life. It is expected that these benefits in turn will be associated with less absenteeism from work, better attitudes toward the organization, greater job satisfaction, and higher job productivity.

Research into the expectations mentioned has generally lagged behind adoption of various forms of the plan. One early review of the literature on work scheduling (Ronen & Primps, 1981) turned up only 14 reports that were clearly relevant to CWW issues. This research supported the assumption that CWW schedules are associated with improvements in the perceived quality of home life and leisure time. In slightly more than half of the studies reviewed, there was also a positive change in attendance and reported job satisfaction. Employee fatigue, however, tended to increase under CWW.

Research since the review by Ronen and Primps generally supports the association between implementation of CWW and increased satisfaction with work schedules (e.g., Cunningham, 1989; Dunham, Pierce, & Castanèda, 1987). There is less evidence for productivity improvements, but some evidence that performance does not *decline* under CWW scheduling (e.g., Duchon, Keran, & Smith, 1994). On the down side, fatigue remains a problem, and there is concern that it may lead to more accidents and injuries.

Despite some potential disadvantages, the compressed work week appears to be on its way to the mainstream. By the mid-1990s, about 25% of larger organizations were using this schedule for some or all of their employees. Many reasons lie behind this trend, among them the fact that CWW provides a way of responding to increased employee demands for workplace flexibility that is considerably easier to administer than its most common alternative, flextime.

Flexible Working Hours

The term **flexible working hours** (abbreviated as **flextime** or flexitime) refers to a range of variations in the distribution of work time. All are characterized by some number of core hours during which all organizational employees must be at work, together with some flexibility in the starting and stopping times on either side of this core. The basic concept is illustrated in Figure 8–11. In this diagram, all employees must be at work between the hours of 9:15 A.M.–12 noon and 2 P.M.–4:15 P.M. (core time), but they have considerable flexibility in when they arrive, take a lunch break, and leave. One person may come in to work as early as 7:30 A.M. and leave as early as 4:15 P.M.; another may come in as late as 9:15 A.M. and stay until 6 P.M.

Flextime has been around for more than 60 years. The federal government began to experiment with staggered work hours in the 1930s, when traffic in the District of Columbia increased far more rapidly than road building, and employee lateness and absenteeism from work were rampant. The city of Los Angeles used the strategy to great effect to clear the freeways (and the air) during the 1984 summer Olympic Games. Marquette Electronics, a producer of medical devices, allows *all* of its 2,000-plus employees, production workers included, to adjust their own schedules.

Having employees come and go at different times is not a feasible situation for every organization, but for those that can handle it, the potential advantages of flextime to employees are considerable. They can avoid rush-hour traffic, take care of personal business during normal business hours instead of trying to fit it in at lunch or on weekends, be

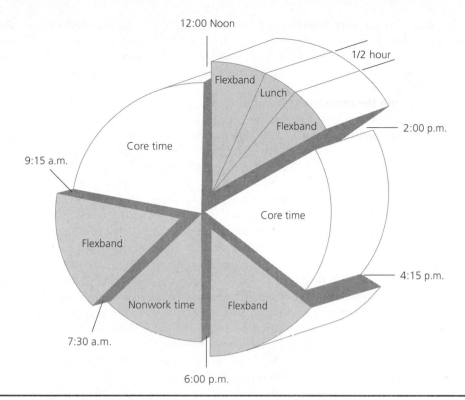

12:00 Noon

1/2 hour

Flexband

Lunch

Flexband

2:00 p.m.

Core time

9:15 a.m.

Core time

Flexband

4:15 p.m.

Nonwork time

Flexband

7:30 a.m.

6:00 p.m.

Figure 8–11
The Concept of
Flextime

From S. Ronen, *Flexible Working Hours: An Innovation in the Quality of Work Life.*
Copyright 1981 McGraw-Hill. Reprinted by permission.

home when children get out of school, or sleep late—whatever suits their particular needs and situations.

The research on flextime is somewhat more comprehensive than that on compressed work weeks. There have been a number of field experiments on this work arrangement, such as that carried out by Narayanan and Nath (1982). Subjects in that study were employees of a large multinational corporation. Experimental (flextime) and control (standard work hour) groups were matched on age, tenure, education, salary, and absenteeism history. No significant differences were found between these groups on production measures or reported job satisfaction, but the experimental subjects showed greater work flexibility, better work group relations, better supervisor-subordinate relations, and less absenteeism than did the control group.

Narayanan and Nath's finding that flextime is associated with less absenteeism is consistent with other studies in this line of research. In their review of 24 flextime studies, Ralston and Flanagan (1985) report that absenteeism and turnover were reduced in almost all of the organizations that measured these variables. In their own research on computer programmers in two state agencies, Ralston and Flanagan and their colleagues found that absenteeism went down and stayed down one year after the introduction of flextime (Ralston, Anthony, & Gustafson, 1985; Ralston & Flanagan, 1985).

The association between the implementation of flextime and reduced absenteeism is considerably more reliable than any relationship between flextime and increased

Field experiment
See pages 29–31

productivity. The evidence available is sufficiently mixed to suggest that the most valid inference is that old friend "it depends" (e.g., Dunham, Pierce, & Castanèda, 1987). An interesting study by Ralston, Anthony, and Gustafson (1985) identified the shared use (or not) of physical work resources as one of the variables upon which increased productivity under flextime depends.

Figure 8–12 compares the productivity of a computer programming (experimental) group of employees of a large state agency with that of a control group of subjects in the same agency. Data were collected at three points in time: 0–6 months before flextime was implemented (pretest), 0–6 months after flextime (posttest), and 12–18 months after flextime (long posttest). By the time of the long posttest measure, the computer programmers had a productivity gain under flextime of almost 25% compared with their control group. No such increase was found for a group of data entry clerks. The difference between the programmers and the data entry operators is that the former had to share work equipment while the latter did not. Flextime made it possible to reduce considerably the amount of time programmers formerly had been wasting waiting for access to a machine.

The number of work situations in which co-workers must share equipment is relatively small, and the productivity benefits of flextime in other situations have yet to be demonstrated in any convincing way. Like the compressed work week, however, flextime does seem to be associated with increased job satisfaction (e.g., Ralston, 1989), as well as with decreased absenteeism for employees who participate in these programs voluntarily. In these facts lies a useful illustration of the caution repeated at various points in this book against jumping to conclusions on the basis of simple correlational analysis.

An I/O psychologist who hypothesized a negative relationship between job satisfaction and absenteeism and who happened to conduct his or her study in a company with a well-established and successful compressed work week or flextime work-scheduling

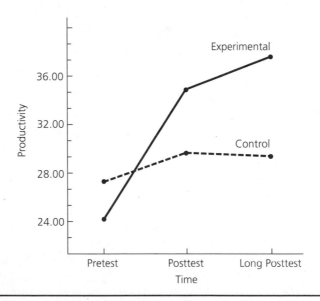

Figure 8–12
Flextime and Productivity Among Computer Programmers

From D. A. Ralston, W. P. Anthony, and D. J. Gustafson, "Employees May Love Flextime, but What Does It Do to the Organization's Productivity?" *Journal of Applied Psychology,* 1985, *70,* 272–279. Copyright 1985 the American Psychological Association. Reprinted by permission of the authors and the publisher.

policy in place might very well collect data that supported the hypothesis. (As discussed, job satisfaction tends to go up and absenteeism tends to go down under both of these work-hour distributions.) Are job satisfaction and absenteeism related to each other in this organization? Without more information, there is no way to be certain. Two variables (job satisfaction and absenteeism) that are each related to a third variable (nontraditional work schedule) are not necessarily related to one another. If much of the prior absenteeism in this company had been the result of failed employee efforts to juggle personal and work life, the I/O psychologist's observed relationship between absenteeism and job satisfaction could be a spurious (accidental) correlation.

Shift Work

Shift work is a long-standing work-hour scheduling strategy in which different groups of full-time employees perform the same job duties in different blocks of time during a 24-hour period. It is the rule in many public-sector organizations, including hospitals, fire departments, and police departments, and it is relatively common in the private sector. At any given time, approximately 20% of the labor force in North America is on night or rotation shift-work schedules.

Shift work is an established method of work-hour distribution, but the actual pattern of this scheduling varies. There are differences in shift starting and stopping times, in the number of hours a shift lasts, and in arrangements for individual assignments to shifts and days off (permanent or rotating shifts). Most investigators who study shift work use a simple division of three shifts—day, afternoon (swing), and night (graveyard)—along with a basic distinction between permanent shift assignment and rotating shifts (day one month, night the next, for example). These researchers are interested in systematic differences in employee responses associated with each of these shifts and with schedules that require employees to change shifts at intervals.

Shift Work and Attitudes

Many employees on shift work express a preference for permanent day work. Disturbances to sleeping and eating habits and disruption of family and social life are the most common objections to deviations from this pattern. People are different, however, and most studies of shift work also report a percentage of employees (sometimes as high as a third) who prefer a permanent night-shift arrangement. Other research in this area suggests that whether night shift assignment is voluntary also makes a difference (e.g., Barton, Smith, Totterdell, Spelten, & Folkard, 1993; Dirkx, 1993). Among the advantages to working nights that are frequently mentioned are less work supervision, lower performance expectations, and freedom to shop or take care of personal matters during normal business hours.

More surprising, perhaps, than the fact that some people prefer a permanent night-shift arrangement is the fact that a few express a preference for rotating shift work. Rotating shifts are characterized by changes in shift assignment following days off; for example, four days on night shift, three days off, and five days on day shift. Wedderburn, whose 1975 studies of shift work in the steel industry are still influential, refers to the various preferences outlined as shift types. Insofar as there are shift types and it is practical to do so, it makes sense to give people their choice of shift arrangements on a

Shift work is a way of life for an estimated 20% of American workers.

permanent basis. A review of individual differences in tolerance for shift work is provided by Härmä (1993).

Shift Work and Job Performance

There are not many reports by I/O psychologists on differences in employee performance on the various standard shifts, but those available suggest a tendency for employee output to be somewhat lower, and errors, scrap, and so on to be somewhat higher on night shifts (e.g., Jamal & Jamal, 1982). The following are among the possible explanations for such a pattern:

- Employees who do not want to work nights but must to keep their jobs may indeed work less hard, make more mistakes, or both.

- Many support services in an organization shut down or have skeletal crews at night, even though other operations are fully staffed. Thus, some decisions and activities may of necessity be put off or carried out with less than complete or accurate information.

- There may be less direct supervision on the night shift in some organizations.

- People who work nights as part of a rotating shift schedule may be inadequately adapted to the change (in the physical sense) and unable to work up to par (Totterdell, Spelten, Smith, Barton, & Folkard, 1995).

A recent review of the safety and performance issues related to shift work is found in Monk, Folkard, and Wedderburn (1996).

Shift Work and Employee Health

Both afternoon and night work shifts are deviations from long-established life patterns for most adults. As such, they are potential stressors, and it may be expected that they would have adverse effects on the health and well-being of some employees. Much of the evidence available supports this expectation; night shift work is frequently found to be associated with more reported health disorders, including fatigue, than day shift work (Costa, 1996). A rotating shift schedule appears to be even more detrimental to health because as it is usually implemented, it does not allow employees to adapt to unfamiliar patterns of working, sleeping, and eating before there is a change.

The conclusions are general. Many factors, including the speed of rotation (how often the individual moves from one shift to another), the direction of rotation (day to night or vice-versa), the type of work, and the amount of sleep the employee gets on off days, affect responses to shift work (Knauth, 1996). In addition, not everyone is negatively affected by deviations from routine, and the role of certain individual employee characteristics may be substantial (e.g., Härmä, 1996).

Work Scheduling and Work-Related Fatigue

The need for 24-hour operation creates work schedules that often lead to cumulative sleep loss and increasing fatigue for many employees. As measured by the quality of work performance, fatigue quickly revealed itself as the biggest single drawback to compressed work week and flextime schedules. It is also a major problem for people who work overtime on a regular basis, something that is happening more often as increasing numbers of the organizations that went through extensive downsizing now find themselves short-staffed. Rather than hire more people, many are meeting demands for greater production with overtime. In 1994, for example, auto-parts manufacturer Gentex Corporation increased overtime by 40%.

Overtime is a cost-effective strategy under certain conditions and many employees are happy to have the extra money, but both sides can pay a substantial price. Overtime-related fatigue is a major safety concern in many occupations, such as nuclear power plant operation and the various transportation industries. Among other examples, operator fatigue has been cited as a contributing factor in the 1989 *Exxon Valdez* grounding, the 1994 crash of a DC-8 at a U.S. Navy base, and the 1996 crash of a New Jersey commuter train. At the time of the DC-8 crash, the navigator had been awake for 21 straight hours, the first officer for 21 hours, and the pilot for almost 24 hours.

Long hours and/or irregular schedules are not the only cause of fatigue at work, nor is all fatigue physical (e.g., Okogbaa, Shell, & Filipusic, 1994). A variety of other factors in the work situation are also associated with the experience of fatigue. Finkelman (1994) reports that, other things being equal, employees who have low job control, low pay rates, poor supervision, and low job challenge are more likely than others to experience non-schedule-related fatigue. Personal factors, such as poor sleeping, eating, and general health habits also play a role in lower resistance to fatigue.

In some instances, employee fatigue is related to working conditions only marginally or not at all. Some people have extensive nonwork obligations or work two jobs. For a variety of reasons, others drive themselves to excessively long hours, refusing to go home at a reasonable hour, stay away from the office on weekends, or take a vacation. But whatever the source of fatigue at work, there is no doubt that it can affect employee health, safety, and job performance negatively (e.g., Baker, Olson, & Morisseau, 1994; Bohnen & Gaillard, 1994; Rogers, Spencer, Stone, & Nicholson, 1989). The longer the condition persists, the more likely it is to have these effects.

There is little organizations can do about employee fatigue that results from decisions individuals make about their lives. Fatigue stemming from organizational factors, such as work scheduling, can be offset in the short run by giving affected employees more rest periods, including short naps (e.g., Bonnet & Arand, 1994; Kopardekar & Mital, 1994). The results to date of nap studies conducted by the National Aeronautics and Space Administration's Fatigue Countermeasures Program team, under the leadership of psychologist Mark Rosekind, have been very encouraging. The "Z Team" has found that air crew members who take a 40-minute in-flight nap are measurably more alert than their unrested colleagues and are able to maintain consistently good performance throughout long flights, night flights, and a sequence of several flights.

At this time, the Federal Aviation Authority does not sanction in-flight sleep for crew members, nor are employee naps a practical solution in many work settings. Substantial reductions in work-related fatigue await the time when this becomes one of the criteria by which job design and working conditions are evaluated. I/O psychologists could make a significant contribution to this goal, especially through research to demonstrate the relationship between fatigue and the traditional criteria of job performance, absenteeism, turnover, and job satisfaction.

At Issue

Computer Phobia

Just the other day in the *Washington Post*, a columnist named Tony Kornheiser wrote that he went out and bought a home computer but can't use it. "I sit there staring at a blank screen," he wrote, "waiting for it to do something magical on its own. . . . The only thing I can do on that screen is Windex it. (quoted in Mossberg, 1994, p. B-1)

An estimated three-quarters of the work force now need (or at least could use) computer skills to perform their jobs. This requirement holds no terror for people under 40, most of whom seem to have been born wearing headsets and playing video games. But what about their elders? Incredible as it may seem, the average adult who was 50 years old in 1990 got through childhood without benefit of television. As for computers, most had not even seen one by college graduation. Personal computers as we know them today didn't arrive on the scene until these people were well into their 30s.

Many of the individuals described have taken to computer use like a duck to water. Others are uncomfortable at best, and fearful at worst, at the prospect of "interfacing" with a computer. Some of them, especially those at upper organizational levels, reject the whole idea; if computers are necessary, let someone else deal with them. (They can't type anyway!) But age is not the only, or even the primary, reason for "computer phobia" (Parasuraman & Igbaria, 1990). Many people, like newspaper columnist Kornheiser, are willing but they just haven't got a clue as to how to use the thing.

The inability to use a machine that virtually everyone else in the world seems to master with ease (or so it appears) can make people feel frustrated and inadequate, but the truth is that computers and people are not a natural match. Computers don't do things the way people do, and some of them (or at least their programs) are downright unfriendly. Anxiety at the prospect of mastering and memorizing the complicated operating details of a machine that can bring you to a dead halt for hitting the wrong key, wipe out an hour's work at the touch of another wrong key, or simply freeze up and refuse to do anything at all is a perfectly understandable reaction.

People who do not know how to use a computer are by no means the only ones who have computer phobia. Many others believe that too much reliance on machines is detrimental to both personal and professional growth and development. "Word processing is not the same as writing," says one prominent author. "How can students gain any understanding of mathematics when they can push a few keys and get the answer without doing any thinking at all?" asks an educator. "Working out plans, elevations, and perspective sketches on pieces of paper gets the architect into the fundamentals of the craft," says architect and historian Robert A. M. Stern, who believes computer-assisted design has assumed too large a role in his profession.

Finally, there are the legions of people whose computer phobia is based not on a fear of computers but on a fear of how they restructure the workplace. Computer-based work methods sever human communication links to a far greater degree than any work method revolution in recent history. The information that used to be acquired after a nice chat with Pat about the kids is now available at the touch of a few keys. With e-mail and voice mail, secretaries go for days or longer without actually seeing their bosses, even when they are in the same facility. Increasing numbers of employees, especially in financial services, have clients they have *never* seen. For many of today's workers, these are not attractive scenarios. Computers don't need each other; people do.

Summary

The human factors approach to job design focuses on specifying the work methods, tools and machines, and workspace arrangements that are compatible with human physical, perceptual, and cognitive abilities. The goals of this approach are to allow work to be carried out more effectively, efficiently, and safely. The psychological approach to job design rests on the assumptions that people have a need for interesting and meaningful work and that meeting this need increases job satisfaction, which, in turn, leads to better job performance.

Working conditions include physical environmental variables such as temperature, lighting, sound, workplace layout, and work-hour distribution. The fact that these variables affect work behavior and attitudes is well established. The factors to be considered in applying the relevant research to a particular organization include the nature of the work performed, the preferences of the work force, and the relevant external standards and regulations.

Questions for Review and Discussion

1. What is the basic premise behind the human factors approach to job design? What are the major issues that must be considered in designing jobs to meet human factors goals?

2. Identify an object you use in your daily life that is more difficult to use than it needs to be because of its design. Describe several control and/or display improvements.

3. The three techniques for psychological job design or redesign discussed in this chapter were all developed at least 30 years ago. Which do you see as having the greatest relevance for the organizations of today, and why?

4. Compare and contrast the relative advantages and disadvantages of the compressed work week and flextime from the viewpoint of (a) a single parent or employee with a dependent parent at home and (b) the community in which the employing organization is located.

5. Using what you know about how physical work environments affect behavior and attitudes at work, design an "ideal work environment" (classroom) for students and professors during class hours.

Key Terms

compressed work week/flextime

human factors job design

job enlargement/job enrichment

machine controls

machine displays

operator-machine system

perceived task characteristics

physical working conditions

shift work

sociotechnical job design

telecommuter

work methods

workspace envelope

References

Aldag, R. J., & Brief, A. P. (1979). *Task design and employee motivation.* Glenview, IL: Scott, Foresman.

Babbage, C. (1835). *On the economy of machinery and manufacture* (4th ed.). London: Charles Knight.

Baber, C., & Wankling, J. (1992). An experimental comparison of text and symbols for in-car reconfigurable displays. *Applied Ergonomics, 23,* 255–262.

Baker, K., Olson, J., & Morisseau, D. (1994). Work practices, fatigue, and nuclear power plant safety performance. *Human Factors, 36,* 244–257.

Barton, J., Smith, L. R., Totterdell, P. A., Spelten, E. R., & Folkard, S. (1993). Does individual choice determine shift system acceptability? *Ergonomics, 36,* 93–100.

Bigoness, W. J. (1988). Sex differences in job attribute preferences. *Journal of Organizational Behavior, 9,* 139–147.

Bohnen, H. G. M., & Gaillard, A. W. K. (1994). The effects of sleep loss in a combined tracking and time estimation task. *Ergonomics, 37,* 1021–1030.

Bonnet, M. H., & Arand, D. J. (1994). The use of prophylactic naps and caffeine to maintain performance during a continuous operation. *Ergonomics, 37,* 1009–1020.

Breaugh, J. A. (1985). The measurement of work autonomy. *Human Relations, 38,* 551–570.

Breaugh, J. A. (1989). The work autonomy scales: Additional validity evidence. *Human Relations, 42,* 1033–1056.

Brenner, O. C., & Tomkiewicz, J. (1979). Job orientation of males and females: Are sex differences declining? *Personnel Psychology, 32,* 741–750.

Campion, M. A. (1988). Interdisciplinary approaches to job design: A constructive replication with extensions. *Journal of Applied Psychology, 73,* 467–481.

Campion, M. A., & McClelland, C. L. (1993). Follow-up and extension of the interdisciplinary costs and benefits of enlarged jobs. *Journal of Applied Psychology, 78,* 339–351.

Campion, M. A., & Thayer, P. W. (1987). Job design: Approaches, outcomes, and trade-offs. *Organizational Dynamics, 15,* 66–79.

Chapanis, A. (1994). Hazards associated with three signal words and four colours on warning signs. *Ergonomics, 37,* 265–275.

Chapanis, A., & Lindenbaum, L. E. (1959). A reaction-time study of four control-display linkages. *Human Factors, 1,* 1–7.

Collins, M., Brown, B., Bowman, K., & Carkeet, A. (1990). Workstation variables and visual discomfort associated with VDTs. *Applied Ergonomics, 21,* 157–161.

Cordery, J. L., Mueller, W. S., & Smith, L. M. (1991). Attitudinal and behavioral effects of autonomous group working: A longitudinal field study. *Academy of Management Journal, 34,* 464–476.

Cordery, J. L., & Sevastos, P. P. (1993). Responses to the original and revised Job Diagnostic Survey: Is education a factor in responses to negatively worded items? *Journal of Applied Psychology, 78,* 141–143.

Cordes, C. (1983, April). Human factors and nuclear safety: Grudging respect for a growing field. *APA Monitor,* pp. 1, 13–14.

Costa, G. (1996). The impact of shift and night work on health. *Applied Ergonomics, 27,* 9–16.

Coury, B. G., & Boulette, M. D. (1992). Time stress and the processing of visual displays. *Human Factors, 34,* 707–725.

Cunningham, J. B. (1989). A compressed shift schedule: Dealing with some of the problems of shift-work. *Journal of Organizational Behavior, 10,* 231–245.

Das, B. (1991). Individual growth need strength as a moderator of the relationship of worker satisfaction and job attitudes to worker productivity. *Journal of Human Ergology, 20,* 89–94.

Davies, D. R., & Jones, D. M. (1985). Noise and efficiency. In W. Tempest (Ed.), *The noise handbook.* London: Academic Press.

Dillon, A. (1992). Reading from paper versus screens: A critical review of the empirical literature. *Ergonomics, 35,* 1297–1326.

Dirkx, J. (1993). Adaptation to permanent night work: The number of consecutive work nights and motivated choice. *Ergonomics, 36,* 29–36.

Doormaal, M. T. A. J., Driessen, A. P. A., Landeweerd, J. A. L., & Drost, M. R. (1995). Physical workload of ambulance assistants. *Ergonomics, 38,* 361–376.

Duchon, J. C., Keran, C. M., & Smith, T. J. (1994). Extended workdays in an underground mine: A work performance analysis. *Human Factors, 36,* 258–268.

Dunham, R. B., Pierce, J. L., & Castanèda, M. B. (1987). Alternative work schedules: Two field quasi-experiments. *Personnel Psychology, 40,* 215–242.

Duvall-Early, K., & Benedict, J. O. (1992). The relationships between privacy and different components of job satisfaction. *Environment and Behavior, 24,* 670–679.

Dvorak, A. (1943). There is a better typewriter keyboard. *National Business Education Quarterly, 11,* 58–66.

Edworthy, J.(1994). The design and implementation of non-verbal auditory warnings. *Applied Ergonomics, 25,* 202–210.

Eklund, J. A. E. (1995). Relationships between ergonomics and quality in assembly work. *Applied Ergonomics, 26,* 15–20.

Ellis, H. D., Wilcock, S. E., & Zamon, S. A. (1985). Cold and performance: The effects of information load, analgesics and the rate of cooling. *Aviation, Space, and Environmental Medicine, 56,* 233–237.

Evans, G. W., & Tafalla, R. (1987). Measurement of environmental annoyance. In H. S. Koelega (Ed.), *Environmental annoyance: Characterization, measurement, and control.* New York: Elsevier Science.

Ferguson, E., & Cheyne, A. (1995). Organizational change: Main and interactive effects. *Journal of Occupational and Organizational Psychology, 68,* 101–107.

Fine, B. J., & Kobrick, J. L. (1978). Effects of altitude and heat on complex cognitive tasks. *Human Factors, 20,* 115–122.

Finkelman, J. M. (1994). A large database study of the factors associated with work-induced fatigue. *Human Factors, 36,* 232–243.

Fisher, C. D. (1993). Boredom at work: A neglected concept. *Human Relations, 46,* 395–417.

Flynn, J. E. (1977). A study of subjective responses to low energy and nonuniform lighting systems. *Lighting and Design Application, 7,* 6–15.

Ford, R. C., & McLaughlin, F. (1995, May–June). Questions and answers about telecommuting programs. *Business Horizons,* pp. 66–72.

Ford, R. N. (1973). Job enrichment lessons from AT&T. *Harvard Business Review, 51,* 96–106.

Fox, W. M. (1995). Sociotechnical system principles and guidelines: Past and present. *Journal of Applied Behavioral Science, 31,* 91–105.

Fried, Y., & Ferris, G. R. (1986). The dimensionality of job characteristics: Some neglected issues. *Journal of Applied Psychology, 71,* 419–426.

Garonzik, R. (1989). Hand dominance and implications for left-handed operation of controls. *Ergonomics, 32,* 1185–1192.

Gilbert, M., & Hopkinson, R. G. (1949). The illumination of the Snellen chart. *British Journal of Ophthalmology, 33,* 305–310.

Gilbreth, F. B., & Gilbreth, L. M. (1921). *First steps in finding the one best way to do work.* Paper presented at the annual meeting of the American Society of Mechanical Engineers, New York.

Glick, W. H., Jenkins, G. D., Jr., & Gupta, N. (1986). Method versus substance: How strong are underlying relationships between job characteristics and attitudinal outcomes? *Academy of Management Journal, 29,* 441–464.

Gould, J. D., Alfaro, L., Barnes, V., Finn, R., Grischkowsky, N., & Minuto, A. (1987). Reading is slower from CRT displays than from paper: Attempts to isolate a single-variable explanation. *Human Factors, 29,* 269–299.

Graen, G. B., Scandura, T. A., & Graen, M. R. (1986). A field experimental test of the moderating effects of Growth Need Strength on productivity. *Journal of Applied Psychology, 71,* 484–491.

Grandjean, E. (1982). *Fitting the task to the man: An ergonomic approach* (3rd ed.). New York: International Publications Service. London: Taylor & Francis, Ltd.

Griffin, R. W. (1991). Effects of work redesign on employee perceptions, attitudes, and behaviors: A long-term investigation. *Academy of Management Journal, 34,* 425–435.

Griffin, R. W., Bateman, T. S., Wayne, S. J., & Head, T. C. (1987). Objective and social factors as determinants of task perceptions and responses: An integrated perspective and empirical investigation. *Academy of Management Journal, 30,* 501–523.

Hackman, J. R., & Oldham, G. R. (1974). *The Job Diagnostic Survey: An instrument for the diagnosis of jobs and the evaluation of job redesign projects* (Tech. Rep. No. 4). New Haven, CT: Yale University, Department of Administrative Sciences.

Hackman, J. R., & Oldham, G. R. (1975). Development of the Job Diagnostic Survey. *Journal of Applied Psychology, 60,* 159–170.

Hackman, J. R., & Oldham, G. R. (1976). Motivation through the design of work: Test of a theory. *Organizational Behavior and Human Performance, 16,* 250–279.

Haigh, R. (1993). The ageing process: A challenge for design. *Applied Ergonomics, 24,* 9–14.

Härmä, M. (1993). Individual differences in tolerance to shiftwork: A review. *Ergonomics, 36,* 101–109.

Härmä, M. (1996). Ageing, physical fitness and shiftwork tolerance. *Applied Ergonomics, 27,* 25–29.

Harvey, R. J., Nilan, K. J., & Billings, R. S. (1985). Confirmatory factor analysis of the Job Diagnostic Survey: Good news and bad news. *Journal of Applied Psychology, 70,* 461–468.

Hatch, M. J. (1987). Physical barriers, task characteristics, and interaction activity in research and development firms. *Administrative Science Quarterly, 32,* 387–399.

Hedge, A., Sims, W. R., & Becker, F. D. (1995). Effects of lensed-indirect and parabolic lighting on the satisfaction, visual health, and productivity of office workers. *Ergonomics, 38,* 260–280.

Hendy, K. C., Hamilton, K. M., & Landry, L. N. (1993). Measuring subjective workload: When is one scale better than many? *Human Factors, 35,* 579–601.

Hochanadel, C. D. (1995). Computer workstation adjustment: A novel process and large sample study. *Applied Ergonomics, 26,* 315–326.

Howell, W. C. (1993). Engineering psychology in a changing world. *Annual Review of Psychology, 44,* 231–263.

Huse, E. F., & Cummings, T. G. (1985). *Organization development and change* (3rd ed.). St. Paul: West.

Idaszak, J. R., & Drasgow, F. (1987). A revision of the Job Diagnostic Survey: Elimination of a measurement artifact. *Journal of Applied Psychology, 72,* 69–74.

Jackson, P. R., Wall, T. D., Martin, R., & Davids, K. (1993). New measures of job control, cognitive demand, and production responsibility. *Journal of Applied Psychology, 78,* 753–762.

Jamal, M., & Jamal, S. M. (1982). Work and nonwork experiences of employees on fixed and rotating shifts: An empirical assessment. *Journal of Vocational Behavior, 20,* 282–293.

James, L. R., & Tetrick, L. E. (1986). Confirmatory analytic tests of three causal models relating job perceptions to job satisfaction. *Journal of Applied Psychology, 71,* 77–82.

Johns, G., Xie, J. L., & Fang, Y. (1992). Mediating and moderating effects in job design. *Journal of Management, 18,* 657–676.

Karl, L. R., Pettey, M., & Shneiderman, B. (1993). Speech versus mouse commands for word processing: An empirical evaluation. *International Journal of Man-Machine Studies, 39,* 667–687.

Karwowski, W., Shumate, C., Yates, J. W., & Pongpatana, N. (1992). Discriminability of load heaviness: Implications for the psychophysical approach to manual lifting. *Ergonomics, 35,* 729–744.

Key, K. F., & Payne, M. C., Jr. (1981). Effects of noise frequency on performance and annoyance for women and men. *Perceptual Motor Skills, 52,* 435–441.

Kilbridge, M. D. (1960). Reduced costs through job enrichment: A case. *Journal of Business, 33,* 357–362.

Kline, T. J. B., & Beitel, G. A. (1994). Assessment of push/pull door signs: A laboratory and field study. *Human Factors, 36,* 684–699.

Knauth, P. (1996). Designing better shift systems. *Applied Ergonomics, 27,* 39–44.

Knez, I. (1995). Effects of indoor lighting on mood and cognition. *Journal of Environmental Psychology, 15,* 39–51.

Kopardekar, P., & Mital, A. (1994). The effect of different work-rest schedules on fatigue and performance of a simulated directory assistance operator's task. *Ergonomics, 37,* 1697–1707.

LaBenz, P., Cohen, A., & Pearson, B. (1967). A noise and hearing survey of earth-moving equipment operators. *American Industrial Hygiene Association Journal, 28,* 117–128.

Lockhart, J. M. (1966). Effects of body and hand cooling on complex manual performance. *Journal of Applied Psychology, 50,* 57–59.

Loewen, L. J., & Suedfeld, P. (1992). Cognitive and arousal effects of masking office noise. *Environment and Behavior, 24,* 381–395.

Long, R. J. (1993). The impact of new office information technology on job quality of female and male employees. *Human Relations, 46,* 939–961.

Maslow, A. H. (1943). A theory of human motivation. *Psychological Review, 50,* 370–396.

May, D. R., & Schwoerer, C. E. (1994). Employee health by design: Using employee involvement teams in ergonomic job redesign. *Personnel Psychology, 47,* 861–876.

Mazumdar, S. (1992). "Sir, please do not take away my cubicle": The phenomenon of environmental deprivation. *Environment and Behavior, 24,* 691–722.

McCormick, E. J. (1964). *Human factors engineering* (2nd ed.). New York: McGraw-Hill.

Melamed, S., Rabinowitz, S., & Green, M. S. (1994). Noise exposure, noise annoyance, use of hearing protection devices and distress among blue-collar workers. *Scandinavian Journal of Work, Environment, and Health, 20,* 294–300.

Momtahan, K., Hétu, R., & Tansley, B. (1993). Audibility and identification of auditory alarms in the operating room and intensive care unit. *Ergonomics, 36,* 1159–1176.

Monk, T. H., Folkard, S., & Wedderburn, A. (1996). Maintaining safety and high performance on shiftwork. *Applied Ergonomics, 27,* 17–23.

Mossberg, W. S. (1994, Oct. 20). Personal computing is too dumb to know easy is smart. *Wall Street Journal,* p. B-1.

Narayanan, V. K., & Nath, R. (1982). A field test of some attitudinal and behavioral consequences of flexitime. *Journal of Applied Psychology, 67,* 214–218.

Norman, D. A. (1988). *The psychology of everyday things.* New York: Basic Books.

Oborne, D. J., & Holton, D. (1988). Reading from screen versus paper: There is no difference. *International Journal of Man-Machine Studies, 28,* 1–9.

O'Connor, E. J., & Barrett, G. V. (1980). Informational cues and individual differences as determinants of subjective perceptions of task enrichment. *Academy of Management Journal, 23,* 697–716.

O'Connor, E. J., Rudolf, C. J., & Peters, L. H. (1980). Individual differences and job design reconsidered: Where do we go from here? *Academy of Management Review, 5,* 249–254.

Okogbaa, O. G., Shell, R. L., & Filipusic, D. (1994). On the investigation of the neurophysiological correlates of knowledge worker mental fatigue using the EEG signal. *Applied Ergonomics, 25,* 355–365.

Oldham, G. R., & Brass, D. J. (1979). Employee reactions to an open-plan office: A naturally occurring quasi-experiment. *Administrative Science Quarterly, 24,* 267–284.

Oldham, G. R., & Fried, Y. (1987). Employee reactions to work space characteristics. *Journal of Applied Psychology, 72,* 75–80.

Oldham, G. R., Kulik, C. T., & Stepina, L. P. (1991). Physical environments and employee reactions: Effects of stimulus-screening skills and job complexity. *Academy of Management Journal, 34,* 929–938.

O'Reilly, C. A., III, Parlette, G. N., & Bloom, J. R. (1980). Perceptual measures of task characteristics: The biasing effects of differing frames of reference and job attitudes. *Academy of Management Journal, 23,* 118–131.

Orpen, C. (1994). Interactive effects of work motivation and personal control on employee job performance and satisfaction. *Journal of Social Psychology, 134,* 855–856.

Parasuraman, S., & Igbaria, M. (1990). An examination of gender differences in the determinants of computer anxiety and attitudes toward microcomputers among managers. *International Journal of Man-Machine Studies, 32,* 327–340.

Paul, W. J., Jr., Robertson, K. B., & Herzberg, F. (1969). Job enrichment pays off. *Harvard Business Review, 41,* 61–78.

Ralston, D. A. (1989). The benefits of flextime: Real or imagined? *Journal of Organizational Behavior, 10,* 369–373.

Ralston, D. A., Anthony, W. P., & Gustafson, D. J. (1985). Employees may love flextime, but what does it do to the organization's productivity? *Journal of Applied Psychology, 70,* 272–279.

Ralston, D. A. & Flanagan, M. F. (1985). The effect of flextime on absenteeism and turnover for male and female employees. *Journal of Vocational Behavior, 26,* 206–217.

Ramsey, J. D. (1995). Task performance in heat: A review. *Ergonomics, 38,* 154–165.

Razmjou, S., & Kjellberg, A. (1992). Sustained attention and serial responding in heat: Mental effort in the control of performance. *Aviation, Space, and Environmental Medicine, 63,* 594–601.

Renn, R. W., Swiercz, P. M., & Icenogle, M. L. (1993). Measurement properties of the revised Job Diagnostic Survey: More promising news from the public sector. *Educational and Psychological Measurement, 53,* 1011–1021.

Renn, R. W., & Vandenberg, R. J. (1995). The critical psychological states: An underrepresented component in job characteristics model research. *Journal of Management, 21,* 279–303.

Rogers, A. S., Spencer, M. B., Stone, B. M., & Nicholson, A. N. (1989). The influence of a 1 hour nap on performance overnight. *Ergonomics, 32,* 1193–1205.

Ronen, S. (1981). *Flexible working hours: An innovation in the quality of work life.* New York: McGraw-Hill.

Ronen, S., & Primps, S. B. (1981). The compressed work week as organizational change: Behavioral and attitudinal outcomes. *Academy of Management Review, 6,* 61–74.

Salancik, G. R., & Pfeffer, J. (1978). A social information processing approach to job attitudes and task design. *Administrative Science Quarterly, 23,* 224–253.

Sims, H. P., Jr., Szilagyi, A. D., & Keller, R. T. (1976). The measurement of job characteristics. *Academy of Management Journal, 19,* 195–212.

Spector, P. E. (1986). Perceived control by employees: A meta-analysis of studies concerning autonomy and participation at work. *Human Relations, 39,* 1005–1016.

Staples, S. L. (1996). Human response to environmental noise: Psychological research and public policy. *American Psychologist, 51,* 143–150.

Sundstrom, E., Burt, R. E., & Kamp, D. (1980). Privacy at work: Architectural correlates of job satisfaction and job performance. *Academy of Management Journal, 23,* 101–117.

Taylor, F. W. (1911). *The principles of scientific management.* New York: Harper.

Thellier, F., Cordier, A., & Monchoux, F. (1994). The analysis of thermal comfort requirements through the simulation of an occupied building. *Ergonomics, 37,* 817–825.

Thomas, J. R., Ahlers, S. T., House, J. F., & Schrot, J. (1989). Repeated exposure to moderate cold impairs matching-to-sample performance. *Aviation, Space, and Environmental Medicine, 60,* 1063–1067.

Tiegs, R. B., Tetrick, L. E., & Fried, Y. (1992). Growth need strength and context satisfactions as moderators of the relations of the job characteristics model. *Journal of Management, 18,* 575–593.

Totterdell, P., Spelten, E., Smith, L., Barton, J., & Folkard, S. (1995). Recovery from work shifts: How long does it take? *Journal of Applied Psychology, 80,* 4–57.

Trist, E., & Bamforth, K. (1951). Some social and psychological consequences of the long-wall method of coal getting. *Human Relations, 4,* 3–38.

Turnage, J. J. (1990). The challenge of new workplace technology for psychology. *American Psychologist, 45,* 171–178.

Ulin, S. S., Armstrong, T. J., Snook, S. H., & Keyserling, W. M. (1993). Perceived exertion and discomfort associated with driving screws at various work locations and at different work frequencies. *Ergonomics, 36,* 833–846.

Vogt, J. J., Candas, V., & Libert, J. P. (1982). Graphic determination of heat tolerance limits. *Ergonomics, 25,* 285–294.

Wall, T. D., Jackson, P. R., & Davids, K. (1992). Operator work design and robotics system performance: A serendipitous field study. *Journal of Applied Psychology, 77,* 353–362.

Wall, T. D., Kemp, N. J., Clegg, C. W., & Jackson, P. R. (1986). An outcome evaluation of autonomous work groups: A long-term field experiment. *Academy of Management Journal, 29,* 280–304.

Wall, T. D., & Martin, R. (1987). Job and work design. In C. L. Cooper and I. T. Robertson (Eds.), *International review of industrial and organizational psychology.* New York: Wiley.

Wall, T. D., & Martin, R. (1994). Job and work design. In C. L. Cooper and I. T. Robertson (Eds.), *Key reviews in managerial psychology: Concepts and research for practice.* Chichester, England: Wiley.

Wedderburn, A. A. I. (1975). *Studies of shiftwork in the steel industry.* Edinburgh: Heriot-Watt University.

Westgaard, R. H., & Winkel, J. (1996). Guidelines for occupational musculoskeletal load as a basis for intervention: A critical review. *Applied Ergonomics, 27,* 79–88.

Wichman, A. (1994). Occupational differences in involvement with ownership in an airline ownership program. *Human Relations, 47,* 829–846.

Wing, J. F. (1965). Upper tolerance limits for unimpaired mental performance. *Aerospace Medicine, 36,* 960–964.

Wong, C. S., & Campion, M. A. (1991). Development and test of a task level model of motivational job design. *Journal of Applied Psychology, 76,* 825–837.

Woods, D. D., & Roth, E. M. (1988). Cognitive engineering: Human problem solving with tools. *Human Factors, 30,* 415–430.

Xie, J. L., & Johns, G. (1995). Job scope and stress: Can job scope be too high? *Academy of Management Journal, 38,* 1288–1309.

Zeffane, R. M. (1994). Correlates of job satisfaction and their implications for work redesign: A focus on the Australian telecommunications industry. *Public Personnel Management, 23,* 61–76.

Employee Health, Safety, and Well-Being

PSYCHOLOGY
AT WORK

**Cool Cures
for
Burnout**

Excerpted from B.
Dumaine, "Cool
Cures for
Burnout." *Fortune*,
1988, *117*, 78–84.
© 1988 Time Inc.
All rights reserved.
Reprinted with
permission.

Burnout is a growing problem in business everywhere. Increasing numbers of [employees] are plain worn out, complaining of fatigue, [and] anxiety. . . .

Burnout has no precise medical definition, but the commonly accepted symptoms include fatigue, low morale, absenteeism, increased health problems, and drug or alcohol abuse. Says Herbert Freudenberger, a New York psychologist who has written two books on burnout and treats executives in major corporations: "It is a process that happens over time. There's a wearing down of our hopes and ideals." . . .

A recent survey of some 200 Fortune 500 companies revealed that 70% offer some kind of anti-burnout training. . . . A sensible approach used by Hay Associates' Dubnicki brings executives together for a weekend retreat at which managers can mingle in an environment away from the office. . . .

Flexitime programs are becoming more popular, allowing at least one member of a harried, dual-career couple to leave work, say, an hour earlier to pick up junior at the dentist. . . .

Sometimes burnout prevention can be as simple as making sure managers take their vacations each year or occasionally giving them a surprise three-day weekend. . . . Several companies, including Time, Intel, Apple Computer, and IBM believe that a sabbatical is the best way to keep their best people from burning out.

THEIR DESIRES to do good work and to make major contributions to their organizations lead many people to push themselves too hard for too long. Psychologists and others interested in employee health have investigated a variety of strategies for coping with that generally debilitated state called burnout. As described in the excerpt in Psychology at Work, many of these approaches involve removing the individual from the work environment for a period of time or altering that environment in some way, as in the use of flexible working hours or sabbaticals.

The health, safety, and general well-being of people in organizations is the focus of this chapter. The topics examined include accidents and injuries on the job site and how they might be reduced or prevented, workplace health hazards, and the antecedents and consequences of work-related stress. The chapter concludes with a look at fitness and wellness programs to enhance the quality of work life.

Antecedents
See page 40

Safety at Work

The **Occupational Safety and Health Administration (OSHA)**, brought into being in 1970 by the Occupational Safety and Health Act, is the primary regulatory agency for the safety and health of American workers. Among other provisions, OSHA requires organizations to supply the U.S. Department of Labor with annual reports of certain work-related illnesses, accidents, and deaths. Decision guidelines from OSHA for recording any particular incident are shown in Figure 9–1.

Data collected and sent to OSHA through the process shown in the figure, together with information from other sources, leads to estimates of some 56,000 people killed by work-related accidents and illnesses every year. Many more are injured, some too seriously to work again. Still more suffer from work-related health impairments that affect

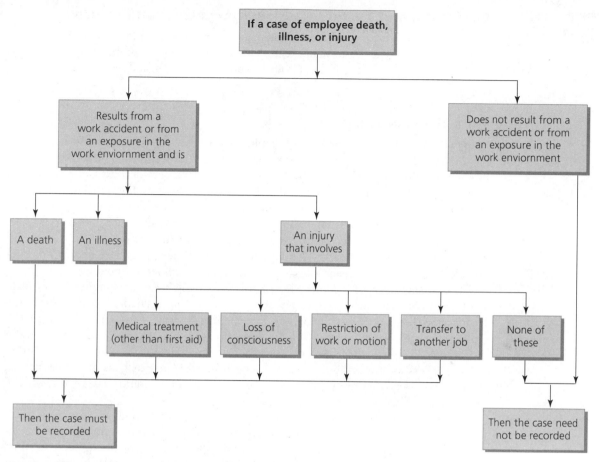

Figure 9–1
Occupational Safety and Health Administration Guide to Records

From *Personnel and Human Resource Management*, Third Edition, by R.S. Shuler. Copyright
© 1987 West Publishing Company. Reprinted by permission of South-Western College
Publishing, a division of International Thomson Publishing, Inc., Cincinnati, Ohio
45227.

them for the rest of their lives. The human costs of these occurrences are incalculable; the
financial costs to society are estimated to exceed 10% of the U.S. gross national product
in any given year.

Accidents and illnesses, whatever the context in which they originate or occur, are
the product of an interaction of individual and situational factors. A "careless person"
working in a hazardous job is more likely to have an accident, for example, than is someone else in the same job or even a careless person in a safer job. Certain individual-difference characteristics, such as age and race, make some people more likely to contract
certain kinds of work-related illnesses than others. To emphasize this interaction, some
of the research into the people who have accidents or become ill on the job follows an
examination of situational factors to be found in working conditions, methods, and
equipment.

Environmental Factors and Work Accidents and Injuries

Efforts by industrial safety engineers and others to reduce hazards in the work environment have been going on for many years. The majority of these efforts have centered on work tools and equipment, general housekeeping procedures, and work practices.

Work Tools and Equipment

Many people today take it for granted that in most working environments electrical coils have replaced dangerous trailing cords, machines shut down automatically if a dangerous malfunction occurs or a foreign object (such as a finger) becomes enmeshed, and moving parts of machines are shielded from employee hands and limbs. But basic safety could not always be taken so much for granted. OSHA reinforces progress by publishing safety standards for most tools, machinery, and other work aids (OSHA, 1984). Stepladders must be labeled as to the maximum weight they can bear, for instance. In many work environments, safety equipment, such as helmets, goggles, earplugs, and special clothing is required in addition to conformity to equipment standards.

OSHA standards, along with state regulations, which can be tougher, have made work safer for most people, but they are not always appreciated. In late 1995, home builders, roofers, and construction contractors won a battle to loosen up a new OSHA regulation requiring construction employees who were working more than 6 feet off the ground to use protective equipment. The group claimed that low-rise workers were filing more workers' compensation claims as a result of accidents that occurred when they tripped over gear they were not used to using (the old standard was 16 feet off the ground).

There are no figures pinpointing the number of employee accidents that are actually caused by inappropriate, unsafe, or defective equipment. When they do occur, these accidents are often spectacular, as when a scaffold collapses or a boiler explodes. In some of these cases, the safety standards specified by OSHA or state regulatory agencies are found to have been disregarded. In 1995, OSHA cited 17 companies for egregious violations (a category of serious offenses that carries high penalties) of safety regulations, such as not providing safety rails on high-rise girders and not equipping dangerous industrial machines with safety guards.

The failure of some organizations to conform to basic safety standards is an exception to the observation that absent or defective work equipment probably causes fewer accidents than misuse, abuse, faulty maintenance, or failure to use the safety devices provided. In the experience of OSHA officials, the great majority of industrial accidents are caused not by equipment but, as in "The Case of the Clumsy Construction Workers" referred to above, by people.

Despite the fact that not all of the results are successful, there is no reduction in efforts by safety engineers, human factors psychologists, and others to make work and work environments safer. In recent years, a particular challenge has been raised by the very large number of people who now work with computers all or part of each workday. Some recommendations for reducing eye strain and muscle problems (such as neck tension) were discussed in the chapter on job design, but computer work has brought with it a potential for employee injury that is not remedied by tilting displays or lowering keyboards.

Repetitive stress injuries (properly called musculoskeletal disorders) afflict people engaged in repetitive manual tasks. The problem begins with a sore wrist or a numb finger or a tingling hand, and it can end up on the operating table (although this is relatively rare). Once limited almost entirely to assembly workers, injuries in this category account for up to half of the work-related physical injuries reported each year—thanks largely to computers.

Of the various forms of musculoskeletal disorders, a condition called carpal tunnel syndrome accounts for the majority of the debilitating cases. The condition occurs when repetitive tasks injure any of the nine tendons to the hand, causing them to swell and fill with fluid. The fluid places pressure on the median nerve and the result is weakened hand muscles, numb fingers, and pain that can radiate up the arm through the carpal tunnel (see Figure 9–2). The afflicted individual can be out of commission for 6 weeks or more, and the condition often flares up again after he or she returns to the task that caused it.

A full-time keyboard operator makes more than 100,000 keystrokes in a typical workday, and in the process can press up to 25 tons of weight through the fingertips. This is not all that different from the work done by people in former times who used typewriters all day, so why didn't they suffer from repetitive stress injuries? Most likely, some of them did. Unlike the modern computer operator, however, those typists had to change hand positions frequently so as to insert and change paper or to grasp and operate a return lever. The result was less efficiency—and less strain.

Human factors engineers emphasize that adjustable office furniture and equipment are basic weapons in making computer operation less of a strain, and that keyboard operators can help themselves by taking frequent breaks (even just dropping the hands to

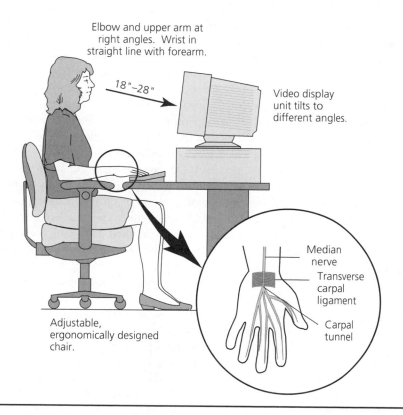

Elbow and upper arm at right angles. Wrist in straight line with forearm.

18"–28"

Video display unit tilts to different angles.

Adjustable, ergonomically designed chair.

Median nerve

Transverse carpal ligament

Carpal tunnel

Figure 9–2
Reducing Repetitive Stress Injuries

**Dvorak
Keyboard**
See page 281

the lap for a few seconds helps) and using a support for the lower arm. The Dvorak keyboard, which is estimated to cut finger movements by almost 40%, remains an option as yet unexploited. Conditioning exercises to increase the strength of fingers, hands, and arms may be useful as well. The only really effective measure for preventing repetitive stress injuries associated with the use of computers, however, is to limit the time people spend pounding the keys.

Changing the nature of jobs so that no one employee spends most or all of his or her time at a computer keyboard is a matter of job redesign, with emphasis on task or job rotation. Many organizations would prefer not to go through the inevitable disruptions this would entail, but they may have no choice. Requiring organizations to locate and correct the causes of repetitive stress injuries has become a top priority of the Occupational Safety and Health Administration. In November 1996, the state of California approved the nation's first ergonomics standard aimed at preventing repetitive motion injuries in the workplace. Later that year, in the first jury verdict against a computer keyboard manufacturer, a former executive secretary who is disabled due to carpal tunnel syndrome was awarded $5.3 million in damages.

Housekeeping and Work Practices

Solutions to some threats to employee safety may be controversial, but no such problems are attached to housekeeping issues. Both common sense and OSHA dictate that an organization must be responsible for seeing that the work environment is clean and free from obvious physical hazards, including trash piles, puddles of oil or water, and blocked safety exits. Despite the obviousness of this precaution, however, and the fact that businesses with fewer than 250 employees are eligible for a free OSHA consultation service, at least 5% to 10% of recorded safety violations each year fall into this category.

Another safety problem in work environments is the use of shortcuts and unsafe work practices, such as failure to follow work method specifications (e.g., Stager & Hameluck, 1990). The reasons for this behavior are varied; in some cases they originate with the individual, while in other instances they stem from management pressures to meet deadlines or co-worker pressures to achieve bonus production levels.

Reluctance or refusal to wear the protective devices and/or clothing provided is one of the more common unsafe work practices. Occasionally, this behavior seems justified. Unless they have to do so in order to keep their jobs, for example, many employees who are issued one of the weightlifting belts that were developed to reduce or prevent back injuries do not wear them. Some of these employees believe the belts are not helpful; others are concerned that their own muscles will be weakened by relying on this aid.

The early research comparing back support belt use with non–belt use failed to yield consistent evidence that wearing such a belt prevented injury (e.g., Reddell, Congleton, Huchingson, & Montgomery, 1992). In addition, some physicians warned that the belts could do more harm than good, by giving some people a false sense of security when lifting heavy weights. The results of a large-scale five-year study released in late 1996 by researchers at the University of California at Los Angeles sharply contradict these opinions. Back injuries were reduced by one-third when Home Depot, Incorporated, made the belts mandatory for its 36,000 employees in 1989. Low-back injuries account for one-fourth of workers' compensation claims, and officials at the National Institute for Occupational Safety and Health (NIOSH), which previously had concluded that the evidence did not support mandatory belt use, are reviewing that policy.

Weightlifting belts are still viewed by many people as ineffective and/or counterproductive, but in other instances, a safety device or protective clothing is rejected because it is uncomfortable to wear and/or makes it more difficult to perform the job effectively (e.g., Akbar-Khanzadeh, Bisesi, & Rivas, 1995). The solution to these problems is to make this equipment more effective and more comfortable. When the failure to wear protective clothing, eye wear, ear coverings, or other safety equipment stems from social pressures of the "only wimps wear that stuff" type, or from shared co-worker perceptions that risk taking is part of the job (e.g., Niskanen, 1994), making work safer goes beyond the bounds of safety engineering solutions. I/O psychologists concentrate their efforts to deal with this problem in two areas—safety education and training, and safety incentive programs.

Safety Education and Training

Education and training are means to increase workplace safety that focus on employee knowledge. Training people in basic problem-solving and stress-management skills, for example, may be relevant to safer working conditions in some jobs (Spettell & Liebert, 1986). Problem-solving skills can help people handle novel emergency situations more effectively. Stress-management skills may eliminate some of these situations entirely because stress can lead to carelessness and a reduced ability to cope with job demands.

There are alternatives, like those described, but most safety training programs are focused more directly on transmitting information about safe working methods and housekeeping practices. The means employed to distribute this information range from posters and placards carrying safety slogans to job-specific training courses. Most organizations have always made some use of the former; Exhibit 9–1 contains excerpts from a safety poster for supervisors published in the early 1950s. Specific training programs have been less widespread than such written reminders, but they have gained in popularity as the problem has escalated.

Observation, interviews, and accident records are useful sources of data about the kind of safety training that is needed in any particular situation (Cooper & Newbold, 1994). Once the specific areas in which improvement is required have been identified, the next step is to set goals for the safety training. Some investigators have found it useful to make this process a participative one that includes the employees involved as well as managers, supervisors, safety experts, or I/O psychologists (e.g., Cooper, Phillips, Sutherland, & Makin, 1994).

Consistent with basic training principles, any program for increasing workplace safety is more likely to bring about a significant change in employee behavior when the safe behavior is practiced (as well as described), the individuals concerned receive feedback about this practice, and some form of reinforcement for effective practice is provided. In one program, for example, vehicle maintenance employees participated in a 45-minute discussion session in which slides depicting unsafe conditions and practices were contrasted with slides showing the corresponding safe conditions and practices (Komaki, Heinzmann, & Lawson, 1980). After the desired safety behavior information was described to the employees, they were encouraged to adopt (practice) them through a safety incentive plan (reinforcement). Little improvement was recorded, however, until feedback was incorporated into the program. The lesson is a very important one: people have to know how they are doing for incentives to be effective.

Feedback
See pages 138–140

Exhibit 9–1
Ten Command-
ments of Safety
for Supervisors

ONE. Be sure each of your . . . [employees] understands and accepts . . . personal responsibility for safety.

TWO. Know the rules of safety that apply to the work you supervise. . . .

THREE. Anticipate the risks that may arise from changes in equipment or methods. . . .

FOUR. Encourage your . . . [employees] to discuss with you the hazards of their work . . .

FIVE. Instruct your . . . [employees] to work safely. . . .

SIX. Follow up your instructions consistently. See to it that workers make use of the safeguards provided them. . . .

SEVEN. Set a good example. Demonstrate safety in your own work habits and personal conduct. . . .

EIGHT. Investigate and analyze every accident—however slight—that befalls any of your . . . [employees]. . . .

NINE. Cooperate fully with those in the organization who are actively concerned with employee safety. . . .

TEN. Remember: Not only does accident prevention reduce human suffering and loss; from the practical viewpoint, it is no more than good business. Safety, therefore, is one of your prime obligations—to your company, your fellow managers, and your fellow . . . [human beings].

Adapted from the "Ten Commandments of Safety for Supervisors" by the American Management Association, 1953.

Safety Incentive Programs

Although protecting oneself from injury, illness, or death would seem to be sufficient reinforcement for safe work practices, the observation that it is not is almost universal. Among the reasons that have been advanced to explain this phenomenon are employees' beliefs that accidents only happen to other people; a desire on the parts of some employees to be considered tough by disregarding safety precautions; and conflicting work demands, such as those created by simultaneous pressures for high production and observance of time-consuming safe work practices.

**Positive
reinforcement**
See pages 202–207

The most effective way to deal with such problems is to provide incentives for compliance with safety rules and safe work practices. This approach, which focuses on employee motivation rather than knowledge, is not new; safety incentive programs have been around for many years. In traditional form, the incentives were group ones consisting of some form of recognition for the team, unit, department, or plant that had the fewest accidents in a period of time.

Evidence as to the effectiveness of traditional safety incentive programs was mixed, and conclusions were confused by the possibility (confirmed in many cases) that accident data were being manipulated to avoid making individual employees, supervisors, or plants look bad. Some believed the problem lay in the fact that group recognition was not a sufficiently powerful incentive. J. Parsons, owner of a company whose incentive programs for promoting health and reducing accidents were widely publicized, expressed it thus: "No matter what you do, it doesn't really make a dent until the people themselves see that they are going to lose a dollar by not being safe" ("How to Earn 'Well Pay,'" 1978).

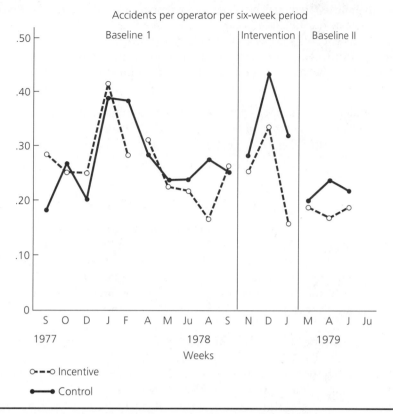

Accidents per operator per six-week period

Figure 9–3
Employee
Safety
Incentives and
Accident Rates

From R. S. Haynes, R. C. Pine, and H. G. Fitch, "Reducing Accident Rates with
Organizational Behavior Modification." *Academy of Management Journal*, 1982, *25*,
407–416. Copyright 1982 Academy of Management. Reprinted by permission.

Parsons's plan was as simple as it was effective. His company had an unusually high
accident rate and it paid correspondingly high premiums to the state's industrial accident
fund. By distributing any retroactive refunds the firm got from the state when accidents
were reduced, Parsons cut his company's accident bill more than 90% in one year and employees gained by almost a thousand dollars per individual. The success of this program
is not an isolated occurrence. Field experiments utilizing the same principle consistently
confirm the effectiveness of this approach. The data in Figure 9–3, taken from a safety behavior modification experiment with bus drivers in a large midwestern city, are typical
(Haynes, Pine, & Fitch, 1982).

The figure shows average six-week accident rates per bus driver over a 17-month period. Significant differences in accident rates between experimental and control groups
appear in the 18-week intervention (experimental) period. During this time, the experimental subjects were divided into teams. Every two weeks, members of the team with the
lowest accident rate received monetary rewards ranging from cash to free gasoline.
Members of any team that was accident free in any two-week period received a double
bonus.

During the intervention period, the accident rate for the experimental group of bus
drivers fell by almost 25%. To complete the experiment, the researchers discontinued the

**Field
experiment**
See pages 29–31

**Statistical
significance**
See pages 35–36

**Research
subjects**
See page 27

incentive program; as predicted, significant differences in accident rates between the experimental and control subjects disappeared (baseline II).

Experiments such as that by Haynes and his colleagues emphasize the basic truth that when it comes to employee health and safety, the bottom line is the behavior of the individual. Safe and healthful working conditions are a prerequisite and an obligation of every employer, but no environment can protect people against themselves.

It is difficult to provide a safe work environment solely through safety engineering. Workers must also be aware of the hazards in their workplace and adjust their behavior to avoid risk. (Hoyos & Ruppert, 1995, p. 107)

Individual Factors and Work Accidents and Injuries

For many years, federal and state governments (along with any unions involved) put responsibility for the health and safety of employees squarely on the employing organization. This emphasis led to substantial progress in making working conditions safer and healthier for all employees, but it has its limits. Individual characteristics and behavior are an important component of workplace safety. A long line of research suggests that employee abilities, skills, and experience are particularly critical (Fell, 1976).

One way of looking at how accidents are produced by the interaction of work environment factors and individual abilities, skills, and knowledge factors is illustrated in Figure 9–4. The fluctuating demands of a work environment are shown by the lower wavy line; the upper line represents employee capacities relative to these demands. Accidents occur when the work environment (which includes task, tools, machines, noise, and co-workers) demands more of an employee than he or she is able to give at that moment (Oborne, 1982). For instance, the environment requires a fairly high level of coordinating skill for an employee to operate controls and guide material through an industrial sewing machine according to a pattern. If the individual operating the sewing

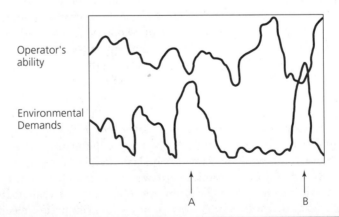

Figure 9–4
A Model of Accident Causation

From D. J. Oborne, *Ergonomics at Work.* Copyright 1982 John Wiley & Sons, Ltd. Reprinted by permission of John Wiley & Sons, Ltd.

machine is experienced, he or she is capable of meeting the demands of the work situation, although wandering attention (not using skills fully) brings demands and capabilities very close at point A. At point B, an accident occurs. In the current example, perhaps the operator gets a finger under the machine needle.

. According to Oborne's model, an accident happened because the demands of the work environment exceeded the employee's capabilities at that moment. There are any number of ways this might have happened, even with an experienced operator. Perhaps he or she continued to operate the machine while trying to explain to a co-worker how to deal with a problem. The combined environmental demands of request for help from another employee plus normal work requirements momentarily exceeded the capacities of the operator.

Oborne's model is a useful framework for understanding that accidents in any job are the product of varying patterns of interactions between individuals and their environments. More than 60 years of research leave no doubt, however, that accidents are not distributed evenly throughout employee populations; some people definitely have more than others. The implied possibility of an "accident-prone personality" has captured the interest of many I/O psychologists.

Over the years, certain individual traits (as measured by particular tests) have been found to be correlated with the number of work accidents in particular research investigations. Among these traits are pessimism, low level of trust in others, an external locus of control (belief that much of what happens to a person is out of his or her control), general social maladjustment, and a depressed temperament (e.g., Davids & Mahoney, 1957; Hansen, 1989; Holcom, Lehman, & Simpson, 1993; Salminen & Klen, 1994). These findings are interesting in themselves, but it cannot be said that the search for the accident-prone personality has been very successful.

Correlation
See pages 37–39

To some extent, the failure of researchers to identify a stable pattern of personality characteristics associated with accident proneness may be due to the fact that chance factors alone will produce an uneven distribution of accidents regardless of the individuals involved. Investigators are also hampered by a certain ambiguity of definition. There is a difference between accidents precipitated by individuals and accidents that occur when individuals fail to take appropriate action in a hazardous situation (Maier & Verser, 1982). This distinction can be illustrated by the difference between a traffic accident that occurs when a driver attempts to pass another car on a hill and runs into an oncoming driver, and a traffic accident that occurs because a driver did not know what to do when the automobile began to skid on an icy road.

If Maier and Verser's line of reasoning is accepted, it follows that no one set of personal characteristics is likely to define both (1) accident repeaters who *cause* accidents to themselves and others and (2) accident repeaters who lack the skills or experience (or both) to *avoid* accidents in the workplace. To date, the characteristics that have been identified by researchers as reliably associated with more work accidents are more descriptive of the second group than of the first.

Reliability
See pages 54–58

Among the characteristics that reliably describe accident-prone individuals are inexperience on the job, subnormal reaction times, and basic perceptual skill deficiencies including a tendency to be easily distracted. Age also plays a role in that people over 55 have a disproportionate number of fatal accidents, particularly falls (Agnew & Suruda, 1993). It is likely that this statistic reflects common (but not inevitable) age-related declines in hearing, vision, reaction time, and other physical variables rather than age as such, however.

Employee personal characteristics are not the only factors associated with more accidents at work; behavior plays an important role as well. As mentioned, ignoring safety regulations, refusing to wear safety equipment, and using unsafe work practices to demonstrate one's toughness are all behaviors that put the employee and his or her co-workers at risk, as does the excessive use of alcohol (Dawson, 1994). Another interesting possibility is suggested by research in the coal mining industry.

Goodman and Garber (1988) found that underground coal miners who were frequently absent from work had more accidents than those who were not. One explanation for this finding is that increased absenteeism reduces a miner's familiarity with the hazards of the work environment. Investigations of this hypothesis in other occupations characterized by dangerous working conditions (such as high-rise construction) are required to determine if this is a more general phenomenon, but the possibility is intriguing.

Hypothesis
See page 25

Violence in the Workplace

In the summer of 1994, the U.S. Labor Department released statistics from its second national census of fatal occupational injuries. In the report were figures on murder in the workplace, and within a very short time a national crisis had been manufactured. Some executives were reported to be wearing bulletproof vests to work, the security guard and equipment business boomed, and safety consultants could not keep up with the demand for advice on protecting employees from the human time bombs walking among them.

As often is the case in such matters, the truth is both more and less disturbing than the media hype suggests. More than 80% of the reported workplace murders were com-

Many organizations post safety information to remind employees to be safety conscious.

mitted during the course of robberies or other crimes. Another 10% were police officers killed in the line of duty or employees killed at their place of work by people who had nothing to do with their employment (such as an ex-husband or a girlfriend). The chances of any one individual being murdered by a disgruntled or "deranged" co-worker, former co-worker, or other work-related associate—the scenario that attracts the greatest share of media attention to this issue—are remote.

The slant given to the Bureau of Labor statistics by the news media was often inappropriate, but the furor did put a spotlight on the general problem of violence in the workplace. This threat to the safety of people at work had received little formal attention previously, even though investigations by I/O psychologists and surveys by interested groups, such as the American Management Association and the National Education Association, confirm that workplace aggression is on the rise.

Threats and verbal abuse are the most common expressions of aggression in the workplace. Actual physical attacks usually take the form of hitting, kicking, beating, pinching, scratching, or twisting an arm or a leg. Women are far more likely to be attacked physically than are men (Younger, 1994), and teachers, health care workers, and government employees in general are especially vulnerable (e.g., Goodman, Jenkins, & Mercy, 1994).

The threat to employee safety posed by workplace violence is a threat that lies squarely at the intersection of environmental and personal factors. Most psychologists would agree that anyone is capable of violence; at the same time, they know that some people are more likely than others to behave violently. In either case, the actual exhibition of violent behavior at work usually (if not always) depends on whether or not something in the work setting, be it real or imagined, triggers it.

Not all work environmental triggers can be anticipated or avoided. An individual who is very upset about rumored company downsizing, for example, may lash out when a co-worker makes a remark that seems slighting. On the other hand, in almost every incident of dramatic workplace violence reported by the press, the individual responsible had a major grievance with the organization or particular people in it over some aspect of the way he or she was treated. There is no reason to assume that such problems are not equally relevant to lesser acts of violence.

Among the environmental factors identified by Johnson and Indvik (1994) as triggers of workplace violence of all kinds are poor quality of supervision or mistreatment of the employee by a supervisor; threats to feelings of job security from downsizing or work restructuring; and actual termination. To this list, Elliot and Jarrett (1994) add hiring, retention, reward, and incentive practices that are perceived to be unfair, and inadequate (or nonexistent) formal grievance procedures.

Most of the factors listed are under some control by an organization and its managers. Playing fair seems to be particularly critical. Procedural justice and standing by the psychological employment contract are important elements of this fair play, both for individual employees and for the work force in general. Formal grievance procedures for employees who feel that they have *not* received fair treatment should be made available and their use encouraged and explained to all.

**Procedural
justice**
See page 199

Not everyone who feels ill-treated will make a formal complaint, even if there are formal channels for doing so. Nor does everyone who exhibits violent behavior at work *have* such a complaint. Therefore, it is also vital to make managers aware of their responsibilities in dealing with the problem. A portion of one company's memorandum on this subject is shown in Exhibit 9–2.

Exhibit 9–2
Management
Announcement:
Workplace
Violence

Managers and supervisors play a key role in preventing violent acts by identifying situations which hold the potential for workplace violence. Use this bulletin to remind you of the actions you must take if and when you identify a potentially threatening situation. You should brief your employees on the content of this bulletin, encourage them to report to you any threatening behaviors they witness, and assure them that procedures are in place for their protection.

Workplace violence refers to threatening and potentially threatening behavior on or about the job. It includes everything in the following spectrum of behavior:

- Actual physical assault and battery on a person, armed or unarmed.

- Verbal or written threats of assault (either direct or implied).

- General expressions of intent to seek revenge over some issue.

- Acts or threats of damage to products, property, or company data.

- Any angry or aberrant behavior which goes beyond the bounds of what would be considered normal or expected in a particular stress situation.

Managers must be alert for and deal with such situations promptly and effectively. It is important to understand that you are not alone in this task. In fact, your primary role is to identify threatening situations and report them. Once a threatening situation is recognized and reported, it will be evaluated by professionals, put in a proper perspective, coordinated back with the manager, and dealt with on its merits.

As managers, you have several reporting channels available:

- For immediate response to actual incidents of violence, either those in progress or about to occur, call Plant Protection.

- For less immediate physical threats, you should promptly consult with an Employee Relations representative, who will involve appropriate professional and security staff.

- Other resources include Investigations and Employee Assistance.

Workplace violence causes human pain and emotional distress, and courts and regulatory agencies are increasingly holding employing organizations responsible when it erupts. Written notices, such as that in the exhibit, are not substitutes for training programs to make sure that managers and supervisors know how to recognize and deal with potentially explosive situations. Educational programs that help employees protect themselves by teaching them how to avoid or manage interpersonal conflict can also help to make the workplace safer. Various community service agencies provide such training if a company is unable to offer it.

The workplace violence problem also reinforces the need for employee assistance programs of various kinds. Not everyone who explodes at work is a violent person; the majority most likely are not. Some are frustrated by work they don't like or by conditions that make it difficult for them to perform well work they do like. Some have been pushed to the wall by personal problems that have nothing to do with work. Some have substance abuse problems, some have serious financial problems, and some have been overtired for so long that they can't remember when things were otherwise. Bashing a co-worker in the face won't solve these problems. Access to professional help might.

Health at Work

The list of hazardous materials and substances in common use in many work environments is a long one. Arsenic, asbestos, cyanide, lead, and benzene are only a few of the substances to which an estimated half-million or more American workers are exposed on a daily basis. Among the associated health dangers of these substances are cancer, anemia, kidney disease, birth defects, and various forms of skin disease.

An estimated ten million people are exposed to workplace health hazards of a different sort. Health care workers and employees of other kinds of organizations whose work brings them into contact with infected individuals or objects may be exposed directly to the viruses that cause hepatitis B and AIDS. Examples of such organizations include linen services, funeral homes, medical equipment repair services, and emergency-response and law-enforcement agencies.

Yet another large number of organizational employees are exposed daily to poor lighting and air quality in offices and possible, if controversial, hazards from computer display units. Headaches, nausea, drowsiness, difficulty concentrating, eyestrain, itchy eyes, scratchy throat, upper-respiratory tract infections (such as bronchitis), and painfully dry skin are but a few of the physical symptoms that may be experienced by people who work in inadequately ventilated or poorly designed work areas.

Not everyone who works in any of the physically unhealthful conditions described becomes ill. For those who do, it can often be difficult to sort out the relative contributions made to the illness by working conditions, outside-work factors, and any predisposing physical factors the individual might have. The health of a person with allergies is more likely to be negatively affected by mold spores growing in the ventilation system, for example, than is that of a co-worker with no such condition. When it comes to taking action to reduce physical health hazards in the workplace, however, individual differences are for once not very important. Cleaning the ventilation system will create a healthier work environment for everyone. In so doing, it will also help to reduce the health care costs that are of such concern to so many organizations. The same two objectives are accomplished by other measures to reduce health hazards in the workplace.

There are several alternative strategies for protecting employees from unnecessary health hazards at work. First, the hazard can be reduced or removed entirely. The most publicized example of this approach is cleaning up the air by prohibiting the use of tobacco in the workplace except in designated areas. Restrictive smoking policies are controversial (Greenberg, 1994), but it is unlikely that there will be any reversal in this trend. A number of companies go further, refusing to hire people who smoke at all. To date, this policy has not been challenged successfully in the courts.

It usually is the most obvious, but cigarette smoke is by no means the only indoor pollutant reducing the quality of air in workplaces. Many of the materials used in the construction and decoration of work areas give off unhealthful fumes, as do a number of common work aids, such as correcting fluid. Then there are overheating office machines and the chemicals used by the cleaning crew or the pest control service. The list is very long and it would be impossible to remove every item on it from every workplace.

An alternative to reducing or removing indoor pollution is better ventilation. This is hardly a new discovery, but organizations have been slow to make voluntarily the expensive changes better ventilation systems require. In 1994 the federal government weighed in as OSHA began public hearings on a controversial set of proposed regulations (referred to by some skeptics as "the wind tunnel legislation").

Not all potential health hazards in a work environment can be removed or even reduced. Doctors, nurses, dentists, and other health care workers are exposed to patient blood and other bodily fluids, and some of these patients have infectious diseases. In other work environments, potentially dangerous substances are essential to production processes. Even though it is not possible to remove such hazards, in many cases it is possible to protect workers to an appreciable extent.

In 1991, OSHA announced its first health regulations (as opposed to safety regulations). These rules, designed to protect employees from AIDS and hepatitis, require employing organizations to provide and pay for protective clothing, puncture-proof containers for contaminated needles and medical wastes, vaccinations (for hepatitis), and employee training. Many of these measures had been adopted voluntarily, but the new legislation makes them mandatory and levies heavy fines against violators.

The discussion of strategies for making workplaces healthier has focused on the environment to this point. An alternative that works in some situations is to restrict employee exposure to health risks to a specified time limit. Occasionally, exposure may be forbidden entirely for individuals at particular risk (such as pregnant women who work in nuclear power plants). This solution, while practical, offends people who are concerned with individual freedom of action, and it does not satisfy those who believe that organizations have a moral obligation to protect the people who work for them (e.g., Angelini, 1987). In short, there are a number of dilemmas involved in protecting people from work-related illness that still await satisfactory solutions.

Ilgen (1990) suggests that I/O psychologists can make valuable contributions to the problem of making workplaces healthier. This is not an aspect of organizational activity in which they traditionally have been involved, but the associated lack of commitment to a particular solution to the problem may be an advantage. In particular, Ilgen sees I/O psychologists as capable of shedding light on this important work concern through the basic tenets of the scientific method.

Scientific method
See pages 23–24

1. Conduct an analysis of the problem.

2. Evaluate a wide variety of measures that could be taken to improve the situation.

3. Carry out an intervention based on the analysis and possible solutions.

Cleaner air in the workplace is a priority of the Occupational Safety and Health Administration.

4. Gather data to evaluate the intervention.

5. Repeat the steps as necessary.

The ultimate aim of these activities would be to find ways to make the work environment less likely to provoke ill health. An important component of any such effort would be to reduce those negative physical and psychological reactions to work called stress, an area in which I/O psychologists have been very much involved for some time.

Stress at Work

Stress is commonly used to refer to both conditions of the environment ("there is a lot of stress at work right now") and an individual's reaction to his or her environment ("I am really stressed out"). Often, it is used interchangeably to mean either of these (e.g., Jex, Beehr, & Roberts, 1992).

At this time, most I/O psychologists who conduct research in this area use the term *stressor* to refer to events and conditions in the environment that have the potential to create stress, reserving the term **stress** for this reaction to these events and conditions. This distinction serves to separate cause (stressor) from effect (stress), allowing for individual differences in reactions to this aspect of the environment.

Stressors in the Work Environment

The causes of job-related stress have been under investigation for some time and the list of potential culprits is a long one. On it will be found physical factors that make the workplace a hostile environment (too hot, too noisy, too crowded, and so on), as well as a host of psychosocial factors arising from the particular mixture of the job, organizational, and social environmental features of a workplace. A summary of the more firmly established psychosocial workplace stressors is presented here. The more recent recognition of sexual harassment as a workplace stressor is discussed separately.

• *Job insecurity.* Fear of losing one's job—whether through downsizing, inadequate performance, age, or any other reason—is an ongoing stressor for many organizational employees (e.g., Kuhnert, Sims, & Lahey, 1989).

• *Lack of control over work.* The extent to which an individual has control over his or her own work has been found by many investigators to be related to the experience of stress (e.g., Lennon, 1994). Monotonous machine-paced work and responsibility for things that are outside of their control are particularly stressful for some people (e.g., Barnett & Brennan, 1995).

• *Role ambiguity and role conflict.* Uncertainty about just what is expected from a person in a particular job role creates role ambiguity, whereas different and incompatible expectations from important others in the work environment create role conflict (Kahn, Wolfe, Quinn, Snoek, & Rosenthal, 1964). Some problems with measuring these concepts for research purposes have been identified (e.g., King & King, 1990), but there seems little doubt that both conditions can be perceived as stressors.

• *Work scheduling pressures.* Shift work, particularly rotating shift work, creates the need for a number of physiological and off-work life adjustments that are potential stressors (e.g., Jamal & Baba, 1992). At the other end of the spectrum, rigid work schedules that make it difficult or impossible to coordinate work and personal life demands constitute a major stressor for people in every kind of job situation.

It bears repeating that the conditions described are *potential* stressors, rather than factors that automatically create stress. Some people will react to them, some won't. Others will react at some times and not at others. Sensitivity, or stress tolerance, is affected by a number of situational and personal variables.

The *nature* of a stressor is one of the more important situational factors influencing peoples' reactions; fear of job loss is probably more stressful than is assignment to a non-preferred work shift, for example. But it doesn't take a major threat to produce stress; sheer numbers can do it as well. When it comes to stressors, little daily hassles add up and the result can be every bit as stressful as a major event (Savery & Wooden, 1994).

The *pattern* of stressors present and stressors absent is also important in determining individual reactions. Poor relationships with co-workers and other people at work is a potential source of stress, for example, but the finding that *good* relationships can help reduce negative reactions to other stressors has been repeated many times (e.g., Beehr, King, & King, 1990; Daniels & Guppy, 1994; Koeske & Koeske, 1991; Revicki, Whitley, & Gallery, 1993; Singh, 1990).

The *duration* of exposure to the stressor is yet another situational factor that affects individual sensitivity. Daily lack of control over job demands is more likely to be stressful than is a temporary work overload created by an ill co-worker, for example. Finally, as the study summarized in Spotlight on Research illustrates, the *predictability* of the stressor is important, with unpredictable stressors more likely to elicit negative reactions. In this laboratory investigation of performance under high-stress conditions (Inzana, Driskell, Salas, & Johnston, 1996), subjects who were given information in advance about what to expect reported less anxiety and greater confidence, and made fewer performance errors under stress than other subjects.

Laboratory experiment
See pages 27–28

Sexual Harassment in the Work Environment

According to guidelines issued by the U.S. Equal Employment Opportunity Commission (1980), there are two broad classes of behavior that constitute sexual harassment in the workplace (made illegal by the Civil Rights Act of 1964). One is using subtle or explicit threats of job-related consequences to attempt to achieve sexual cooperation (called quid pro quo harassment). The other is sex-related verbal or physical behavior that is unwelcome or offensive and creates a hostile environment.

Like violence in the workplace, sexual harassment is not a new phenomenon; published accounts of this behavior date back to colonial times (Fitzgerald, 1993). What is new is the formal prohibition of such behavior by law. This change has brought about a number of consequences, the most visible of which is the number of highly publicized harassment suits (mostly, but not all, by women) that have been filed with the Equal Employment Opportunity Commission.

One outcome of the harassment litigation to date is that sexual harassment has been recognized by the courts as a work-related stressor that can have a wide range of negative effects on the mental health of its victims. In 1993, the Supreme Court ruled that plaintiffs in harassment cases no longer have to prove psychological damage to prove harassment. The problem of whose opinion of the behaviors in question counts, however, remains, especially as regards the hostile environment standard.

SPOTLIGHT ON
RESEARCH

Effects of Preparatory Information on Enhancing Performance Under Stress

Summarized from C. M. Inzana, J. E. Driskell, E. Salas, and J. H. Johnston, "Effects of Preparatory Information on Enhancing Performance Under Stress." *Journal of Applied Psychology*, 1996, *81*, 429–435.

Research question: Does advance information about what to expect reduce stress and help task performance?

Type of study: Laboratory experiment.

Subjects: 92 Navy enlisted personnel.

Independent variables: (1) High stress/normal work conditions and (2) general/stress preparatory information.

Dependent variables: (1) Speed and (2) accuracy on a radar monitoring task.

General procedure: Subjects were assigned randomly to one of the 4 experimental conditions created by combining the 2 levels of each independent variable. All subjects received general instructions on performing the task; preparatory information subjects also received detailed information on task stressors, common reactions to stress, and effects of stress. High stress subjects (a) performed a more difficult form of the task, (b) worked under greater time pressures, and (c) experienced greater distractions than subjects in the normal conditions.

Analysis: Analysis of variance.

Results: Preparatory information subjects performing under the high-stress condition reported less anxiety and greater confidence and made fewer errors than other subjects performing under high stress. Speed was not affected by the experimental manipulations.

Conclusion: "The results of this study suggest that the saying, 'What you don't know can't hurt you' may be more appropriately rephrased, 'What you do know can help you,' especially when one is faced with a novel, stressful environment" (p. 434).

I/O psychologists and others have created a substantial body of literature on perceptions of sexual harassment in the workplace. Some of this research is methodologically weak (Lengnick-Hall, 1995), but when the results are considered as a whole they reveal substantial consensus regarding the evaluation of questionable behavior (Frazier, Cochran, & Olson, 1995). The following examples are representative.

ANOVA
See page 42

- Both males and females consider sexist jokes aimed toward women to be more offensive than sexist jokes aimed at men (Hemmasi, Graf, & Russ, 1994).

- Ambiguous behaviors are more likely to be perceived as sexually harassing in mixed or male-dominated work settings than in female-dominated work settings (Sheffey & Tindale, 1992).

- The organizational hierarchy relationship of the parties has a strong influence on perceptions of harassment. Incidents directed toward a subordinate by a superior are far more likely to be considered harassing than are incidents in which the parties are of equal status (Hemmasi, Graf, & Russ; 1994; Tata, 1993).

- Questionable behaviors are more likely to be considered harassing when they are public and occur in a strongly traditional work setting (Rhodes & Stern, 1995).

- The aspects given the most weight in evaluating the seriousness of a sexual harassment incident are evidence of coercion, the reaction of the victim, and negative job consequences (York, 1989).

- Under certain conditions, women and men differ in their definitions of sexual ha-rassment, but the difference is not large (Gutek, 1995).

If organizations are to reduce or eliminate sexual harassment in the workplace, they must understand what their employees consider harassing. Research results such as those cited can be of considerable practical value in defining the parameters, especially when the way a behavior is perceived depends on its context. Nevertheless, such investigations are only the first step on a long road to a fundamental social change, and both more and better research is needed in this area (Pryor & McKinney, 1995). A review of the basic is-sues can be found in the 1993 article by Robinson and his colleagues.

Responses to Stressors

Despite the voluminous literature on the subject, the meaning of stress is often misun-derstood. What exactly happens when a person is "under stress"? A simple way to think of the situation is in terms of mobilization. Stress brings about chemical and other changes in a person's usual physical, mental, or emotional state. These reactions gener-ate energy to help the person combat a perceived threat (stressor) to well-being. So far so good, but if the stressor is not removed and the energy is not dissipated some other way (as in physical exercise), it simply wears the person down. Eventually it produces exhaustion and/or physical illness.

In a work setting, operating in a state of continual readiness for action (stress) that never takes place can lead to "inefficient behavior, over-reactivity, and the incapacity to re-cover from work"(Gaillard, 1993, p. 991). Gaillard's simple phrase summarizes a very large body of literature in which investigators have found that too much stress at work (how-ever that is defined for a particular individual) can lead to decreased performance, more accidents, difficulty getting along with people, greater absenteeism, lower job satisfaction, and more health-related complaints (and claims). A review of the stress–job performance and stress–job satisfaction literature can be found in Sullivan and Bhagat (1992). Levi (1994) presents a general overview of the way stress can affect employee health.

Given the high cost of stress, many I/O psychologists have directed their attention to the detection of this problem. Some behavioral signals that may mean someone is past the limit of his or her individual tolerance for stressors are listed in Exhibit 9–3. In isola-tion, most of these warning signs could have other explanations. But when a number oc-cur together, and when they represent a rather sudden change from an individual's usual personality and behavior, excessive stress may be the culprit.

Why are some people debilitated by stress responses to workplace stressors while co-workers in the same work environment show no such signs? Part of the answer has been mentioned; for many people, stressors seem to be additive, and the total load is always greater for some than for others. Another factor is that some people are simply better at dealing with the situation than others.

Among the personal characteristics researchers have found to affect reactions to stressors in a helpful way are good physical condition, high self-esteem, past experience in coping with stress successfully, and a positive, goal-oriented, and independent ap-proach to life. A great deal of research in this area has also been devoted to exploring the possible connection between reactions to stressors and personality factors, especially the two opposing behavior pattern types called Type A and Type B (Rosenman et al., 1966).

The qualities of a Type A person, as described by Cox (1978), are listed in Exhibit 9–4. The Type B person is described in opposite terms. Research into this behavior

On the job

- Has more accidents than usual
- Misses deadlines, meetings, or other appointments
- Makes careless errors
- Has difficulty making decisions
- Quantity and/or quality of work decreases
- Works late or more "obsessively" than usual
- Speech and/or written reports have a vague, disconnected quality

With co-workers

- Seems to have lost sense of humor
- Displays anger, hostility, or outbursts of temper
- Has sudden difficulty in communicating and getting along with others
- Displays irrational or excessive mistrust of co-workers

Personal

- Is usually tired, cannot seem to "rest up"
- Apathetic toward life; not very interested in anything
- Feels ill or on the verge of being ill often

From a variety of sources, including J. M. Ivancevich and M. T. Matteson, "Employee Claims for Damages Add to the High Cost of Job Stress." *Management Review,* 1983, 72, 9–13.

Exhibit 9–3
Some Stress Warning Signals

- An intense and sustained drive to achieve self-selected, but usually poorly defined, goals
- A profound inclination and eagerness to compete
- A persistent desire for recognition and advancement
- A continuous involvement in multiple and diverse functions constantly subject to time restrictions
- An habitual propensity to accelerate the rate of execution of many physical and mental functions
- An extraordinary mental and physical alertness

As described by T. Cox, *Stress,* University Park Press, 1978.

Exhibit 9–4
Personality and Behavioral Characteristics of the Type A Individual

pattern suggests that Type A individuals are likely to seek out stressful and challenging situations and to see their worlds in a way that poses continual personal challenge. As a result of this orientation, they tend to be high-level performers in demanding tasks (e.g., Lee, Earley, & Hanson, 1988) and to have high job commitment (e.g., Chusmir & Hood, 1988).

Type A behavior may have some positive aspects from an organization's viewpoint, but these individuals are more likely than their Type B co-workers to be workaholics. In addition, they find certain kinds of stress, such as that created by lack of control over elements of the job, particularly difficult to handle (e.g., Ivancevich, Matteson, & Preston, 1982; Pace & Suojanen, 1988). A fairly substantial body of research also suggests a connection between Type A behavior and coronary heart disease (e.g., Schaubroeck, Ganster, & Kemmerer, 1994; Wright, 1988).

Three specific behavioral tendencies of the Type A pattern seem to put such people more at risk of heart disease. The first tendency (time urgency) is turning every situation into a race with the clock—constantly changing lanes in traffic to save a few minutes over a long commute to work, for example. The second is staying keyed up most of the time every day (chronic activation), and the third tendency is doing more than one thing at a time most of the time (multiphasia). In effect, the Type A individual is manufacturing stressors to add to whatever ones are already present in his or her life.

In considering the implications of a Type A or Type B behavior pattern, it is important to keep in mind that the distinction is a relative one. Most people exhibit a mixture of these behavioral characteristics, and this fact affects researchers' abilities to make valid generalizations based on this variable. Individuals who exhibit obviously extreme or dysfunctional Type A tendencies, however, may benefit from two techniques that have been developed for self-modification of Type A behavior.

Generalizability
See page 45

Variable
See pages 25–26

1. Training people to monitor their own behavior and identify the times when they need to practice specific relaxation techniques. For example, the woman who knows that swinging her foot while sitting in a meeting signals impatience (and mounting frustration) can be taught unobtrusive physical relaxation techniques to be used whenever she catches herself in this behavior.

2. Teaching people to use Type A characteristics to sabotage Type A behavior. For example, the Type A's obsessiveness might be turned toward an obsession with *not* acting like a Type A. Thus, a man who wanted to change some of this behavior might "force" himself to go to the longest line in the grocery store or stay in one lane on the freeway all the way to work.

Burnout: "The Smell of Psychological Wiring on Fire"

Burnout is a response to chronic stress that is characterized by lowered levels of accomplishment (including job productivity), physical or emotional exhaustion (or both), and a tendency to think in impersonal terms, even of oneself (Leiter & Maslach, 1988). Among the identified consequences of burnout for an organization are low-quality services for clients, decreased job commitment on the parts of those affected, and increased turnover. Individual consequences include deterioration of the quality of home life, health problems, and poor relationships with co-workers.

There is doubt as to whether burnout is something new, but no question that the trendy label has served to call attention to the plight of those who suffer from this syndrome. (The colorful description in the heading is from Morrow, 1981.) There are many self-help articles and books on the subject, as well as formal training courses to teach people how to deal with burnout. On the research side, there are a number of scales for measuring burnout, of which the Maslach Burnout Inventory is the most widely used and researched (Maslach & Jackson, 1981).

Much of the research by I/O psychologists and others on burnout has been focused on identifying risk factors associated with this syndrome. These investigations have revealed a tendency for women to be more vulnerable than men (e.g., Pretty, McCarthy, & Catano, 1992), especially if the work environment is one into which women have been introduced relatively recently (Leiter, Clark, & Durup, 1994). Two factors go some way toward explaining the apparent sex difference. One is the greater number of stressors many working women are subject to, especially those arising from work-family conflict or employment in a "man's world." The second is the lack of social support systems for women in many contexts (such as upper management).

Finally, it must be noted that the majority of employees in many people-oriented service organizations are women, and employees in these professions seem to be at particular risk of burnout. Included in this group are teachers (Firedman, 1993), child protective service workers (Savicki & Cooley, 1994), social welfare workers (Matthews, 1990), nurses (Kandolin, 1993), and police officers (Hurrell, 1995). The most effective countermeasure for these and other people who cannot remove stressors from their work is to get away from the work. To the extent that the problem is aggravated by a poor physical condition and health habits, steps to increase fitness and wellness should also be helpful.

Psychologists who deal with burnout victims recommend that people who work under continual stress talk to a counselor or friend rather than bottling up the frustrations. As indicated by the excerpt in Psychology at Work, they should also take advantage of vacations, holidays, and days off and, if possible, do something entirely different from their work activities during this time. A review of the burnout research can be found in Cordes and Dougherty (1993).

The Organization's Role in Reducing Stress

Stress is a response to events and conditions called stressors that can lead to a variety of negative physical, psychological, and behavioral consequences. As illustrated in the model of work-related stress in Figure 9–5 (Ivancevich, Matteson, Freedman, & Phillips, 1990), stressors outside the workplace may add to or interact with workplace stressors. Individual differences affect both the experience (assessment) of stress and reactions to it (outcomes).

The decade of the 1990s has seen job stress become one of the most pervasive occupational health problems in the workplace. As the problem grows, creating healthier workplaces is becoming a priority for many I/O psychologists (Cooper & Cartwright, 1994). The basic options available as far as combatting the negative effects of work-related stress are concerned are indicated by the numbered arrows in Figure 9–5.

First, the intensity or number of stressors in the work environment can be reduced. This is the strategy that will have the greatest impact on the greatest number of employees, as well being the easiest for organizations to implement. Many workplace stressors have their origins in decisions that have been made about selection and placement, training, job design, and the arrangement of working conditions, and these decisions are subject to alteration.

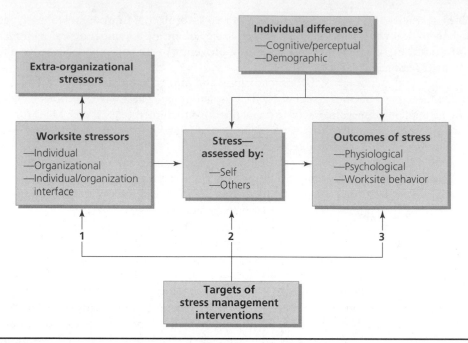

Figure 9–5
Stress in the
Workplace

From J. M. Ivancevich, M. T. Matteson, S. M. Freedman, and J. S. Phillips, "Worksite Stress Management Interventions." *American Psychologist*, 1990, *45*, 252–261. Copyright 1990 by the American Psychological Association. Reprinted by permission.

Second, actions can be taken to change the assessment of the situation by the individuals exposed to stressors. Organizational change can be a major stressor, to take one example, but much of its power arises out of fear of the unknown. Giving employees advance warning, along with as much detail as possible about how the changes will affect them, may remove or reduce this fear. It is also possible to use employee assistance programs to make books, courses, or counselors available to help employees learn to evaluate potentially stressful situations more objectively.

Third, actions can be taken to increase the ability of individuals to cope effectively with the consequences of stress. This is the most common approach, and the one that most people think of when they hear the phrase "stress management." Some organizations are very creative in their use of this strategy. Cigna Corporation offers a group break time called recess in which workers stretch, dance, or listen to music. When accountants at Lipschultz, Levin, and Gray start feeling the pressure they can play darts or miniature golf or twirl a hula hoop—all right in the office. Other firms provide showers, nap rooms, and even masseuses to give employees a few minutes of relaxation.

The informal stress management techniques described interrupt work and are not practical in many settings. As far as formal programs for helping individual employees cope with stress go, a more practical approach for most organizations is to make resources available through employee assistance programs. Exercise, relaxation, and meditation classes, and instruction in time management, goal setting, and the realistic appraisal of stressors are among the possibilities. A review of the research literature on coping with work-related stress is offered by Latack and Havlovic (1992). The guidelines in Exhibit

EAP
See page 171

Workload and Work Pace
- Physical and mental job demands should be in the range of individual resources and capabilities.
- Allow time to recover from demanding tasks.
- Increase individual control over work pace.

Work Schedule
- Demands and responsibilities off the job should be considered in setting individual work schedules.
- Rotating shift schedules should be stable, predictable, and in a forward (day-to-night) direction.

Work Roles
- Job duties should be clearly defined and explained.
- Conflicts as to job expectations should be avoided.

Job Future
- Employees should be made aware of avenues for growth and promotion opportunities within the organization.
- Employees should be informed in a timely manner of impending changes that may affect their employment.

Social Environment
- Job design should not isolate employees from opportunities for support and/or assistance from others.

Job Content
- Meaning, stimulation, and opportunity to use skills on the job are desirable.

Participation and Control
- Employees should be able to make input to decisions or actions affecting their jobs or the performance of their tasks.

Summarized from the discussion by S. L. Sauter, L. R. Murphy, and J. J. Hurrell, Jr., "Prevention of Work-Related Psychological Disorders." *American Psychologist,* 1990, *45,* 1146–1158.

Exhibit 9–5
Guidelines for Reducing Stressors in the Workplace

9–5 are aimed at decreasing this stress. They were created by a National Institute for Occupational Safety and Health (NIOSH) working group charged with developing a comprehensive strategy to protect and promote worker psychological health. I/O psychologists are well qualified to help organizations apply the NIOSH guidelines, but such enviromental strategies for reducing worker-related stress receive little attention.

Stress in Perspective

The clear implication of most of what is said and written about stress is that it is bad for people and should be eliminated to every extent possible. This is not entirely accurate, however. The stress response that is referred to in that literature as well as in this chapter is *distress,* but this is not an inevitable reaction to the presence of stressors.

Little is known about it, but there is a positive reaction to stressors called *eustress* (pronounced "you-stress"). The energy generated by stress helps some people get up for their work instead of getting them down, but it is rare to find any discussion of this response to stressors (one exception is an article by Bruhn, 1989). The question of why some people don't just cope or manage stress, but actually seem to thrive on the very conditions that threaten the well-being of others is an area wide open to investigation. Answers might be of considerable use in developing effective stress management techniques.

The Quality of Work Life and Employee Well-Being

Quality of work life refers to the impact of the entire work situation on an individual. Is it a force for good in his or her life, or not? Among the components that make up the quality of work life that are discussed in this and other chapters are the following:

- work that suits individual needs and abilities
- jobs designed so as to be performed with a minimum of stress and strain
- an opportunity for personal growth and development on the job if desired
- safe and comfortable working conditions
- appropriate rewards for good job performance
- good working relationships
- assistance with balancing job and personal life demands
- a degree of job satisfaction (as an individual defines it for himself or herself)

Work-related accidents, illness, excess stress, and burnout reduce the quality of work life. A proactive approach aimed at preventing these problems, rather than dealing with them in a reactive fashion once they occur, pays dividends for all concerned. One component of this approach is removal of stressors to the extent possible. Another is organization-sponsored fitness and wellness programs for employees.

Organizational Fitness Programs

In the early 1970s, doctors told the chairman and CEO of Kimberly-Clark Corporation that he had throat cancer. The diagnosis changed his life and led to the creation of one of the first extensive organization-sponsored employee fitness programs in this country. The idea caught on. Northwestern Mutual Life Insurance Company began by offering em-

*Physical exercise is
a powerful weapon
against job-related
stress as well as a
means for helping
people look and feel
good.*

ployees reimbursements of fees if they would join the YMCA. Today, they have their own on-site fitness center offering aerobic exercise, weight training, and fitness consultation 24 hours a day (as do a number of other large organizations).

At least 50 years' worth of research has demonstrated that participation in fitness programs decreases body fat and increases strength, aerobic capacity, and flexibility (Astrand & Rodahl, 1977). It also reduces risk factors associated with heart disease (Paffenbarger, Hyde, Wing, & Hsiech, 1986), long the number one cause of death in this country. These benefits are directly reflected in the hundreds of dollars a year per employee in insurance premiums that organizations save when employees start to exercise regularly and/or to lose weight. If they stop smoking as well (a not-uncommon side benefit of regular exercise), the savings increase substantially.

The benefits of fitness programs are not limited to slimmer employees and lower insurance premiums. Exercise is one of the most effective stress management tools available, providing a natural physical outlet for that excess physiological and mental energy (e.g., Kiely & Hodgson, 1990). Because people who exercise feel better, they can work better, and there is often a reduction in absenteeism and turnover as well (e.g., Cox, Shephard, & Corey, 1981; Shephard, 1988).

Specific job-related fitness programs for employees in physically demanding occupations can make a significant difference in their ability to perform effectively and to protect themselves from accidents and injuries (e.g., Cady, Thomas, & Karwasky, 1985). Contrary to what might seem to be common sense, the effort demanded in much of this work is counterproductive to physical fitness. Frequent bending, lifting of heavy objects, static effort (such as holding heavy objects or uncomfortable postures for extended periods of time), exertion of body force against outside force (such as operating a jackhammer), and extended periods of inactivity followed by sudden bursts of high energy activity (as with fire fighters) characterize such work.

Exercise has many unquestioned benefits, but putting in a fitness center does not a fitness program make. Employees have to use the facilities, and this can be a problem; there is a tendency for the individuals who need them most to stay away. Based on the experience of many employers, however, incentives are useful in getting people moving, and results keep many of them participating. For example, the fitness program at Sara Lee Knit Products grew 125% in one year after the company started giving points that can be turned in for prizes for attendance at exercise classes and related activities.

Organizational Wellness Programs

The movement that started with a little exercise during the lunch hour has progressed to comprehensive programs that focus on the whole person with heavy emphasis on the early detection and/or prevention of health problems. Across the country, "companies are teaching, cajoling, coaching, and scolding their way to a hidden treasure—the rewards of keeping employees healthy" (Tully, 1995, p. 106).

By the mid-1990s, at least two out of three employers with more than 50 employees were offering some form of wellness program, and almost 2,500 employers, representing some two million employees, were members of the Wellness Council of America. The Health Project, a nonprofit group dedicated to the promotion of healthier employees, awards an "Oscar" (called the C. Everett Koop National Health Award) to outstanding programs. Among the past winners are L.L. Bean, Dow Chemical, and the Union Pacific Railroad.

A wellness program differs from a fitness program in its focus on the whole person. Physical fitness is a necessary part of this focus, as are weight loss, giving up smoking, and stress management. Some organizations, such as Perdue Farms in North Carolina, have set up on-site health centers to encourage employees to take care of any other health problems promptly. As health costs have skyrocketed, detection and prevention have joined remedial measures. Examples include free medical screening tests for body fat, high blood pressure, high cholesterol, breast and other cancers; diet, nutrition, and healthful cooking classes; and a full range of services for women who are pregnant.

As with fitness programs, participation in wellness plans is a necessary element for them to be successful. One effective way to encourage employees to get on the band-wagon is similar to the Parsons' safety incentive program discussed previously. A well-known example is the Quaker Oats Company plan in which a medical expense account is budgeted for each employee each year. Individuals who stay well and do not use their full sickness-related benefits get a refund, just as Parsons employees get a refund for accident benefits not used.

Financially, the health promotion stakes are high. Appliance maker Sunbeam Corporation cut the medical costs associated with employee pregnancies by 90% after it started a mandatory prenatal course. Johnson & Johnson, whose Live for Life program has been so successful that it sells the plan to other firms, estimates the associated reduction in medical bills to be $13 million (15%) a year. The cost of the Union Pacific Railroad's program to motivate "stubborn, secretive workers to talk about their health risks and change their habits" generates a three-to-one return on investment (Tully, 1995).

The experience of the organizations mentioned, along with that of many others and more than 20 years' worth of related research, supports the general conclusion that healthier employees are happier employees who come to work more regularly, perform better, and stay with the company longer. In a review of this area, Gebhardt and Crump (1990) identify four activities associated with the more successful wellness programs.

1. *Plan.* Identify the needs of the organization and its employees and set goals that are congruent with these needs.

2. *Commit.* Make wellness an organizational mission and allocate adequate resources to support a long-term commitment to this mission.

3. *Recruit.* Promote the program in an aggressive manner and use incentives as necessary to encourage participation with special emphasis on at-risk employees.

4. *Evaluate.* Develop an ongoing testing program of multiple measures to determine if the wellness program is enhancing organizational performance, reducing health care costs, and improving the quality of work life for employees.

I/O psychologists have the training and the scientific orientation to help organizations implement the steps listed. They also have long-standing research interests in particular areas of importance to the success of such programs. For example, wellness participation rates are typically between 15 and 30% of the eligible employees, with white-collar workers making up a sizeable majority. I/O psychologists' knowledge of motivation could be used to help recruit more participants, especially blue-collar and special-risk employees. As employee wellness programs go mainstream, nonparticipants who have health problems related to poor life and health habits may increasingly be viewed as having inflicted these problems on themselves (Brody, 1995).

Concluding Remarks on Employee Health and Safety

Efforts to identify individual variables that reliably identify people who are more likely to have accidents at work or to become ill because of work are consistent with I/O psychology's focus on the individual. If such patterns could be reliably identified and measured, hiring, placement, and training activities might be modified so as to reduce potential problems. That stage has not been reached; in addition, many problems result from the *interaction* of employees with their work environments.

For now, a practical approach to improving employee health and safety rests on three strategies. First, make the physical work environment as healthy and free from safety hazards as possible. Second, be sure employees understand and have the skills and knowledge to do their jobs in ways that protect their health and safety. Finally, reinforce safety and health-oriented behaviors, such as wearing the safety equipment provided, taking advantage of company-paid medical screening tests and general check-ups, and participating in organizational fitness and wellness programs.

At Issue

Drug Testing in the Workplace

A number of dramatic and highly publicized incidents have stimulated ongoing and widespread concern about drug use and abuse on the job. In one, engineers of a northeastern railroad failed to heed a warning signal that another train was headed toward them. The trains collided head on, causing the injury or death of scores of people. At least one of the engineers has admitted that he was using an illegal substance on the job just before the accident.

The use of illegal drugs may not affect a person's work performance if such drug use is confined to the person's living room, and if the drug is metabolized before he or she arrives for work. In some jobs, drug use may not adversely affect performance even if the drug is still active while the person is working. In most jobs, however, the use of illegal substances (and the abuse of some legal substances) is likely to lower the quantity of work, the quality of work, or both. And in some situations, an employee who goes to work under the influence of such a substance (or uses it at work) creates a safety hazard for himself or herself, co-workers, and the public.

In 1990, railroad workers joined the half-million-plus private-sector employees subject to Department of Transportation rules requiring random drug testing. Other organizations have undertaken these programs on their own in hopes of protecting themselves, their employees, and the public. Many more have made drug testing part of the screening and selection process. A sign in the window of one large retail outlet in southern California proclaims in giant red letters: "If you do drugs, you can't work here."

To say that drug testing programs are controversial would be understating the matter considerably (Cavanaugh & Prasad, 1994; Comer, 1994; Tepper & Braun, 1995). Invasion of privacy is a central issue. Drug testing also smacks of guilty-until-proved-innocent to some people, making it counter to the most basic tenet of our legal system. Complicating the issue is the fact that a variety of factors can raise the false-positive rate of the standard urine test to scientifically unsound levels. A new hair sample test is more accurate, but this procedure is little used because it costs nearly twice as much. In any event, a positive test does not determine impairment, only that a drug may have been used as much as several weeks before the test.

The issue of random drug testing is but one of many forms of a delicate balancing act that organizations today must try to perform. On the one side is what is best for the organization as a whole, its personnel, and those who consume its products or services. On the other side is the individual with all of his or her rights as guaranteed by the Constitution and reinforced by a wide variety of laws and court decisions relating to fair employment practices.

Unlike some problems facing today's organizations, the drug issue has the potential to affect us all. People working under the influence of many of the substances in question have impaired physical ability, and, like the railway engineers, impaired judgment. As consumers of the products and services that they make, provide, or maintain, each of us is potentially at risk if illegal drug use in organizations is not controlled. But where is the line between our protection and unwarranted organizational interference in the personal lives of employees?

Summary

Employee health and safety is only partially a function of working conditions, but these conditions remain a basic focus for those concerned with this issue. The Occupational Safety and Health Administration, along with state agencies, has regulations for work equipment and materials, work methods, and general housekeeping practices. Industrial/organizational psychologists emphasize the importance of safety education and training coupled with positive reinforcement for safe work practices.

Work-related stress, an energized physical and mental response to the presence of work-related stressors, can affect both the health and the safety of employees in a negative way. A variety of situational and individual characteristics affect individual stress tolerance at any point in time. Organizational fitness and wellness programs are one weapon for combatting excess stress as well as a way for employees to take charge of their own health and for organizations to save money on insurance and medical costs.

Questions for Review and Discussion

1. If you work, describe one example of a health or safety hazard at your job and make at least one practical suggestion for reducing it based on what you have learned about safety education, training, and incentives. Alternatively, use an example you have observed in a restaurant, store, service station, or other place of business.

2. Discuss the relative merits of individual versus institutional (employing organization or OSHA) regulation of employee health and safety. How do the "accident-prone personality" and "Type A personality" fit into this discussion?

3. List several stressors that exist in your school, home, or work environment and briefly discuss your response to these. If that response is distress, how might you reduce or cope with it? If it is not, what personal and environmental factors do you believe have increased your stress tolerance?

4. Assume that you have just accepted the newly created position of employee wellness administrator for (a) a mall department store in a major city, *or* (b) a manufacturer of heavy equipment, *or* (c) a large banking firm. Outline your new wellness program for this organization, being sure to address the issues of participation and evaluation. You may make any assumptions you wish about general work force characteristics, but these should be stated.

Key Terms

burnout

individual role in health and safety

Occupational Safety and Health Administration

organizational stressor reduction

organizational fitness programs

organizational wellness programs

quality of work life

safety incentive programs

sexual harassment

stress

stressor

workplace health hazards

workplace violence

References

Agnew, J., & Suruda, A. J. (1993). Age and work-related falls. *Human Factors, 35,* 731–736.

Akbar-Khanzadeh, F., Bisesi, M. S., & Rivas, R. D. (1995). Comfort of personal protective equipment. *Applied Ergonomics, 26,* 195–198.

Angelini, F. (1987). Ethical behaviour for the prevention of injuries in the workplace. *Ergonomics, 30,* 231–237.

Astrand, P., & Rodahl, K. (1977). *Textbook of work physiology.* New York: McGraw-Hill.

Barnett, R. C., & Brennan, R. T. (1995). The relationship between job experiences and psychological distress: A structural equation approach. *Journal of Organizational Behavior, 16,* 259–276.

Beehr, T. A., King, L. A., & King, D. W. (1990). Social support and occupational stress: Talking to supervisors. *Journal of Vocational Behavior, 36,* 61–81.

Brody, J. (1995, October). Quoted in T. DeAngelis, Eat well, keep fit and let go of stress. *APA Monitor,* p. 20.

Bruhn, J. G. (1989). Job stress: An opportunity for professional growth. *Career Development Quarterly, 37,* 306–315.

Cady, L. D., Thomas, P. C., & Karwasky, R. J. (1985). Program for increasing health and physical fitness of fire fighters. *Journal of Occupational Medicine, 27,* 110–114.

Cavanaugh, J. M., & Prasad, P. (1994). Drug testing as symbolic managerial action: In response to "A case against workplace drug testing." *Organization Science, 5,* 267–271.

Chusmir, L. H., & Hood, J. N. (1988). Predictive characteristics of Type A behavior among working men and women. *Journal of Applied Social Psychology, 18,* 688–698.

Comer, D. R. (1994). A case against workplace drug testing. *Organization Science, 5,* 259–267.

Cooper, C. L., & Cartwright, S. (1994). Healthy mind; healthy organization: A proactive approach to occupational stress. *Human Relations, 47,* 455–471.

Cooper, M. D., Phillips, R. A., Sutherland, V. J., & Makin, P. J. (1994). Reducing accidents using goal setting and feedback: A field study. *Journal of Occupational and Organizational Psychology, 67,* 219–240.

Cooper, S. E., & Newbold, R. C. (1994). Combining external and internal behavioral system consultation to enhance plant safety. *Consulting Psychology Journal: Practice and Research, 46,* 32–41.

Cordes, C. L., & Dougherty, T. W. (1993). A review and an integration of research on job burnout. *Academy of Management Review, 18,* 621–656.

Cox, M. H., Shephard, R. J., & Corey, P. (1981). Influence of an employee fitness programme upon fitness, productivity, and absenteeism. *Ergonomics, 24,* 795–806.

Cox, T. (1978). *Stress.* Baltimore: University Park Press.

Daniels, K., & Guppy, A. (1994). Occupational stress, social support, job control, and psychological well-being. *Human Relations, 47,* 1523–1544.

Davids, A., & Mahoney, J. T. (1957). Personality dynamics and accident proneness in an industrial setting. *Journal of Applied Psychology, 41,* 303–306.

Dawson, D. (1994). Heavy drinking and the risk of occupational injury. *Accident Analysis and Prevention, 26,* 655–665.

Dumaine, B. (1988). Cool cures for burnout. *Fortune, 117,* 78–84.

Elliot, R. H., & Jarrett, D. T. (1994). Violence in the workplace: The role of human resource management. *Public Personnel Management, 23,* 287–299.

Equal Employment Opportunity Commission. (1980). Discrimination because of sex under Title VII of the 1964 Civil Rights Act as amended: Adoption of interim guidelines— Sexual harassment. *Federal Register, 45,* 25024–25025.

Fell, S. C. (1976). A motor vehicle accident causal system: The human element. *Human Factors, 18,* 85–94.

Firedman, I. A. (1993). Burnout in teachers: The concept and its unique core meaning. *Educational and Psychological Measurement, 53,* 1035–1044.

Fitzgerald, L. F. (1993). Sexual harassment: Violence against women in the workplace. *American Psychologist, 48,* 1070–1076.

Frazier, P. A., Cochran, C. C., & Olson, A. M. (1995). Social science research on lay definitions of sexual harassment. *Journal of Social Issues, 51,* 21–37.

Gaillard, A. W. (1993). Comparing the concepts of mental load and stress. *Ergonomics, 36,* 991–1005.

Gebhardt, D. L., & Crump, C. E. (1990). Employee fitness and wellness programs in the workplace. *American Psychologist, 45,* 262–272.

Goodman, P. S., & Garber, S. (1988). Absenteeism and accidents in a dangerous environment: Empirical analysis of underground coal mines. *Journal of Applied Psychology, 73,* 81–86.

Goodman, R. A., Jenkins, E. L., & Mercy, J. A. (1994). Workplace-related homicide among health care workers in the United States, 1980 through 1990. *Journal of the American Medical Association, 27,* 1686–1688.

Greenberg, J. (1994). Using socially fair treatment to promote acceptance of a work site smoking ban. *Journal of Applied Psychology, 79,* 288–297.

Gutek, B. A. (1995). How subjective is sexual harassment? An examination of rater effects. *Basic and Applied Social Psychology, 17,* 447–467.

Hansen, C. P. (1989). A causal model of the relationship among accidents, biodata, personality, and cognitive factors. *Journal of Applied Psychology, 74,* 81–90.

Haynes, R. S., Pine, R. C., & Fitch, H. G. (1982). Reducing accident rates with organizational behavior modification. *Academy of Management Journal, 25,* 407–416.

Hemmasi, M., Graf, L. A., & Russ, G. S. (1994). Gender-related jokes in the workplace: Sexual humor or sexual harassment? *Journal of Applied Social Psychology, 24,* 1114–1128.

Holcom, M. L., Lehman, W. E., & Simpson, D. D. (1993). Employee accidents: Influences of personal characteristics, job characteristics, and substance use in jobs differing in accident potential. *Journal of Safety Research, 24,* 205–221.

How to earn "well pay." (1978, June 12). *Business Week,* pp. 148–149.

Hoyos, C. G., & Ruppert, F. (1995). Safety diagnosis in industrial work settings: The Safety Diagnosis Questionnaire. *Journal of Safety Research, 26,* 107–117.

Hurrell, J. J. (1995). Police work, occupational stress and individual coping. *Journal of Organizational Behavior, 16,* 27–28.

Ilgen, D. R. (1990). Health issues at work: Opportunities for industrial/organizational psychology. *American Psychologist, 45,* 273–283.

Inzana, C. M., Driskell, J. E., Salas, E., & Johnston, J. H. (1996). Effects of preparatory information on enhancing performance under stress. *Journal of Applied Psychology, 81,* 429–435.

Ivancevich, J. M., & Matteson, M. T. (1983). Employee claims for damages add to the high cost of job stress. *Management Review, 72,* 9–13.

Ivancevich, J. M., Matteson, M. T., Freedman, S. M., & Phillips, J. S. (1990). Worksite stress management interventions. *American Psychologist, 45,* 252–261.

Ivancevich, J. M., Matteson, M. T., & Preston, C. (1982). Occupational stress, Type A behavior, and physical well being. *Academy of Management Journal, 25,* 373–391.

Jamal, M., & Baba, V. V. (1992). Shiftwork and department-type related to job stress, work attitudes and behavioral intentions: A study of nurses. *Journal of Organizational Behavior, 13,* 449–464.

Jex, S. M., Beehr, T. A., & Roberts, C. K. (1992). The meaning of occupational stress items to survey respondents. *Journal of Applied Psychology, 77,* 623–628.

Johnson, P. R., & Indvik, J. (1994). Workplace violence: An issue of the nineties. *Public Personnel Management, 23,* 515–523.

Kahn, R. L., Wolfe, D. M., Quinn, R. P., Snoek, J. D., & Rosenthal, R. A. (1964). *Occupational stress: Studies in role conflict and ambiguity.* New York: Wiley.

Kandolin, I. (1993). Burnout of female and male nurses in shiftwork. *Ergonomics, 36,* 141–147.

Kiely, J., & Hodgson, G. (1990). Stress in the prison service: The benefits of exercise programs. *Human Relations, 43,* 551–572.

King, L. A., & King, D. W. (1990). Role conflict and role ambiguity: A critical assessment of construct validity. *Psychological Bulletin, 107,* 48–64.

Koeske, G. F., & Koeske, R. D. (1991). Underestimation of social support buffering. *Journal of Applied Behavioral Science, 27,* 475–489.

Komaki, J., Heinzmann, A. T., & Lawson, L. (1980). Effects of training and feedback: Component analysis of a behavioral safety program. *Journal of Applied Psychology, 65,* 261–270.

Kuhnert, K. W., Sims, R. R., & Lahey, M. A. (1989). The relationship between job security and employee health. *Group and Organization Studies, 14,* 399–410.

Latack, J. C., & Havlovic, S. J. (1992). Coping with job stress: A conceptual evaluation framework for coping measures. *Journal of Organizational Behavior, 13,* 479–508.

Lee, C., Earley, P. C., & Hanson, L. A. (1988). Are Type As better performers? *Journal of Organizational Behavior, 9,* 263–269.

Leiter, M. P., Clark, D., & Durup, J. (1994). Distinct models of burnout and commitment among men and women in the military. *Journal of Applied Behavioral Science, 30,* 63–82.

Leiter, M. P., & Maslach, C. (1988). The impact of interpersonal environment on burnout and organizational commitment. *Journal of Organizational Behavior, 9,* 297–308.

Lengnick-Hall, M. L. (1995). Sexual harassment research: A methodological critique. *Personnel Psychology, 48,* 841–864.

Lennon, M. C. (1994). Women, work, and well-being: The importance of work conditions. *Journal of Health and Social Behavior, 35,* 235–247.

Levi, L. (1994). Work, worker and wellbeing: An overview. *Work and Stress, 8,* 79–83.

Maier, N. R. F., & Verser, G. C. (1982). *Psychology in industrial organizations.* Boston: Houghton-Mifflin.

Maslach, C., & Jackson, S. E. (1981). The measurement of experienced burnout. *Journal of Occupational Behavior, 2,* 99–113.

Matthews, D. B. (1990). A comparison of burnout in selected occupational fields. *Career Development Quarterly, 38,* 230–239.

Morrow, L. (1981, Sept. 21). The burnout of almost everyone. *Time,* p. 84.

Niskanen, T. (1994). Assessing the safety environment in work organization of road maintenance jobs. *Accident Analysis and Prevention, 26,* 27–39.

Oborne, D. J. (1982). *Ergonomics at work.* Chichester, England: Wiley.

Occupational Safety and Health Administration. (1984). *General industry: OSHA safety and health standards* (29 CFR 1910), revised 7/1/84. Washington, DC: U.S. Department of Labor.

Pace, L. A., & Suojanen, W. W. (1988). Addictive type A behavior undermines employee involvement. *Personnel Journal, 67,* 36–42.

Paffenbarger, R. S., Hyde, R. T., Wing, A. L., & Hsiech, C. (1986). Physical activity, all cause mortality, and longevity of college alumni. *New England Journal of Medicine, 314,* 605–614.

Pretty, G. M., McCarthy, M. E., & Catano, V. M. (1992). Psychological environments and burnout: Gender considerations within the corporation. *Journal of Organizational Behavior, 13,* 701–711.

Pryor, J. B., & McKinney, K. (1995). Research on sexual harassment: Lingering issues and future directions. *Basic and Applied Social Psychology, 17,* 605–611.

Reddell, C. R., Congleton, J. J., Huchingson, R. D., & Montgomery, J. F. (1992). An evaluation of a weightlifting belt and back injury prevention training class for airline baggage handlers. *Applied Ergonomics, 23,* 319–329.

Revicki, D. A., Whitley, T. W., & Gallery, M. E. (1993). Organizational characteristics, perceived work stress, and depression in emergency medicine residents. *Behavioral Medicine, 19,* 74–81.

Rhodes, A. K., & Stern, S. E. (1995). Ranking harassment: A multidimensional scaling of sexual harassment scenarios. *Journal of Psychology, 129,* 29–39.

Robinson, R. K., Allen, B. M., Franklin, G. M., & Duhon, D. L. (1993). Sexual harassment in the workplace: A review of the legal rights and responsibilities of all parties. *Public Personnel Management, 22,* 123–135.

Rosenman, R. H., Hahn, W., Werthesseu, N., Jenkins, C., Messinger, H., Kositchek, R., Wurm, M., Friedman, M., & Straus, R. (1966). Coronary heart disease in the western collaborative group study. *Journal of the American Medical Association, 195,* 86–92.

Salminen, S., & Klen, T. (1994). Accident locus of control and risk taking among forestry and construction workers. *Perceptual and Motor Skills, 78,* 852–854.

Sauter, S. L., Murphy, L. R., & Hurrell, J. J., Jr. (1990). Prevention of work-related psychological disorders: A national strategy proposed by the National Institute for Occupational Safety and Health (NIOSH). *American Psychologist, 45,* 1146–1158.

Savery, L. K., & Wooden, M. (1994). The relative influence of life events and hassles on work-related injuries: Some Australian evidence. *Human Relations, 47,* 283–305.

Savicki, V., & Cooley, E. J. (1994). Burnout in child protective service workers: A longitudinal study. *Journal of Organizational Behavior, 15,* 655–666.

Schaubroeck, J., Ganster, D. C., & Kemmerer, B. E. (1994). Job complexity, "type A" behavior, and cardiovascular disorder: A prospective study. *Academy of Management Journal, 37,* 426–439.

Schuler, R. S. (1987). *Personnel and human resource management* (3rd ed.). St. Paul: West.

Shephard, R. J. (1988). Sport, leisure and well-being: An ergonomics perspective. *Ergonomics, 31,* 1501–1517.

Sheffey, S., & Tindale, R. S. (1992). Perceptions of sexual harassment in the workplace. *Journal of Applied Social Psychology, 22,* 1502–1520.

Singh, R. G. (1990). Relationship between occupational stress and social support in flight nurses. *Space and Environmental Medicine, 61,* 349–352.

Spettell, C. M., & Liebert, R. M. (1986). Training for safety in automated person-machine systems. *American Psychologist, 41,* 545–550.

Stager, P., & Hameluck, D. (1990). Ergonomics in air traffic control. *Ergonomics, 33,* 493–499.

Sullivan, S. E., & Bhagat, R. S. (1992). Organizational stress, job satisfaction and job performance: Where do we go from here? *Journal of Management, 18,* 353–374.

Tata, J. (1993). The structure and phenomenon of sexual harassment: Impact of category of sexually harassing behavior, gender, and hierarchical level. *Journal of Applied Social Psychology, 23,* 199–211.

Tepper, B. J., & Braun, C. K. (1995). Does the experience of organizational justice mitigate the invasion of privacy engendered by random drug testing? An empirical investigation. *Basic and Applied Social Psychology, 16,* 211–225.

Tully, S. (1995, June 12). America's healthiest companies. *Fortune,* pp. 98–106.

Wright, L. (1988). The Type A behavior pattern and coronary artery disease. *American Psychologist, 43,* 2–14.

York, K. M. (1989). Defining sexual harassment in workplaces: A policy-capturing approach. *Academy of Management Journal, 32,* 830–850.

Younger, B. (1994). Violence against women in the workplace. *Employee Assistance Quarterly, 9,* 113–133.

10

Work Performance and Its Measurement

PSYCHOLOGY AT WORK

Partner-ships Help a Company Manage Perfor-mance

Excerpted from M. Moravec, R. Julitt, and K. Hesler, "Partnerships Help a Company Manage Performance." *Personnel Journal,* January 1995, *75,* 104–108. Copyright, 1995 ACC Communications. All rights reserved. Reprinted by permission.

Most managers and employees consider the performance review to be, at best, a necessary evil. Everyone anticipates it with dread. . . .

The managers and staff of Rosemead, California-based Southern California Edison wanted . . . to change this dismal scenario. . . .

The first step was to call for volunteers to participate in a consultant-facilitated task force. Surprisingly, 40 people of the 335-person department—managers and non-managers from the various functions—offered their services, even though everyone in the organization was overwhelmed with work. . . .

Assisted by the consultant, who provided process guidance and information . . . , the task force maintained their enthusiasm during the six months or so it took to implement the new system. . . . What they needed, they concluded, was a process in which:

- Employees as well as supervisors assume responsibility,

- Both supervisors and employees learn new skills so that they can work better,

- The steps are "doable" for both,

- The focus is on values and future growth, not past problems,

- Both parties are honest and candid,

- The discussion is not a control tool, but rather supports a partnership between employee and supervisor.

THE EXCERPT in Psychology at Work illustrates a trend—involving employees in the evaluation of their own work. California Edison has taken the process further than most companies by using a system that was designed by employees, but the basic premise of performance appraisal as a partnership activity is catching on as more companies move away from organizational hierarchies and toward team orientations.

The new Cal Ed performance appraisal system focuses on development and future behavior, rather than on evaluation and past behavior. This performance management, or performance targeting, requires setting individual employee performance objectives that help achieve company goals, monitoring progress, evaluating results, and revising goals or devising plans for performance improvement if needed.

The majority of organizations still carry out performance appraisal in a more traditional way, but the questions of what aspects of performance to emphasize, how to evaluate them, and how to use the information so acquired remain basic. The appraisal of work performance and I/O psychologists' efforts to improve this important organizational activity are the subjects of this chapter. As a preface to these issues, the factors that determine individual work performance are reviewed.

The Determinants of Work Performance

Determinants
See page 41

Work performance is defined by McCloy, Campbell, and Cudeck as "behaviors or actions that are relevant to the goals of the organization in question" (1994, p. 493). I/O psychologists and others who study organizations and the behavior of people in them are concerned with a host of issues, but job performance remains the bottom line. Unless employees do their jobs, the organization will ultimately fail. As with all other human be-haviors, the level and quality of work performance are determined by a host of personal and environmental variables.

Blumberg and Pringle (1982) propose a model of work performance that attempts to incorporate the full range of individual and environmental variables that interact to pro-duce level and quality of individual work performance. This model, shown in Figure 10–1, consists of three components that the authors call capacity, willingness, and op-portunity to perform. Together, capacity (C), willingness (W), and opportunity (O) com-bine to produce observed work performance (P): $P = f(O \times C \times W)$.

Variables
See pages 25–26

A basic assumption of the Blumberg-Pringle model is that the variables within each of the components are additive. Of two people with equal ability (a capacity variable), the one with the greater energy would have the greater capacity to perform. The components themselves interact multiplicatively; a change in any of the component variables will pro-duce a change in observed performance. A favorable environment (O) may increase em-ployee willingness (W), which, in turn, gives him or her performance experience. Over time, this experience is likely to increase the employee's skills and knowledge (C).

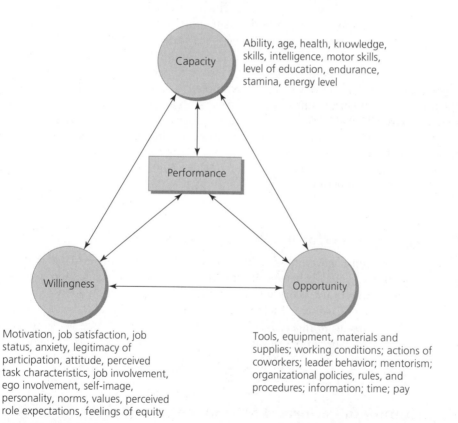

Capacity

Ability, age, health, knowledge, skills, intelligence, motor skills, level of education, endurance, stamina, energy level

Performance

Willingness

Opportunity

Motivation, job satisfaction, job status, anxiety, legitimacy of participation, attitude, perceived task characteristics, job involvement, ego involvement, self-image, personality, norms, values, perceived role expectations, feelings of equity

Tools, equipment, materials and supplies; working conditions; actions of coworkers; leader behavior; mentorism; organizational policies, rules, and procedures; information; time; pay

Figure 10–1
The Blumberg-Pringle Model of Work Performance Determinants

From M. Blumberg and C. D. Pringle, "The Missing Opportunity in Organizational Research: Some Implications for a Theory of Work Performance." *Academy of Management Review*, 1982, 7, 560–567. Copyright 1982 Academy of Management. Adapted by permission.

Blumberg and Pringle's model of the determinants of work performance is an attempt to organize and integrate what I/O psychologists and others interested in this field know about relationships between work performance and its correlates. Its basic components provide a useful framework for a brief review of these relationships.

Capacity to Perform: "Can Do" Variables

Capacity to perform is determined by a class of variables made up of relevant physical, physiological, knowledge, and skill attributes. As confirmed by many researchers over the years, job-related ability is basic (e.g., Coward & Sackett, 1990; O'Reilly & Chatman, 1994; Varca & James-Valutis, 1993). The degree to which a significant lack of ability may be compensated for by other characteristics and behaviors (such as effort or dependability) is limited.

The extent to which an organization's employees have the ability to perform their jobs satisfactorily depends considerably on the way in which it carries out its recruiting, selection, placement, and training activities. Other variables in this category, such as endurance, stamina, health, and energy, may be boosted by the organization-sponsored fitness and wellness programs discussed in Chapter 9. Many of the aspects of aging that might depress performance in physically demanding jobs can be reversed or delayed by participation in such programs as well (Shepherd, 1995).

Does job performance deteriorate with age unless steps are taken to prevent it? Stereotypes about older workers still exist to some degree (e.g., Hassell & Perrewe, 1995; Lawrence, 1988), but many years of I/O psychology research have made it very clear that it is not possible to answer the question posed with a simple yes or no. For jobs that do not have extreme physical demands (the vast majority), individual differences in the way people age overwhelm generalizations (Sterns & Miklos, 1995). In addition, older employees usually have more job experience, and experience is an important predictor of job performance (e.g., Avolio, Waldman, & McDaniel, 1990; Quiñones, Ford, & Teachout, 1995).

Willingness to Perform: "Will Do" Variables

Willingness variables encompass a host of individual psychological characteristics, among which are values, beliefs, attitudes, certain personality traits, and perceptions. Most of these variables are incorporated into the various motivation and job satisfaction theories discussed in Chapter 6. Included in the list are perceptions of reward equity, personal values relevant to work and its outcomes, beliefs in self-efficacy, perceptions of job characteristics, and expectations of various kinds (such as that good performance will be rewarded).

Opportunity to Perform: Environmental Variables

Environmental variables are included in the opportunity component of Blumberg and Pringle's model. Peters and O'Connor (1980) review many examples of the kinds of environmental factors that I/O psychologists have discovered are relevant to performance variation among employees. Among them are task preparation, budgetary support, time availability, tools and equipment, materials and supplies, job-related information, and required services and help from others. Research continues to support the position that such variables operate as constraining variables in the work environment, and that they affect performance independently of ability or motivation (e.g., Steel, Mento, & Hendrix, 1987). Hall (1994) puts the case strongly:

> It is argued that the true productivity problem comes from the environmental gap between what American workers need and what they have, and that this gap could be closed by adopting policies and practices that encourage and facilitate competence. (p. 33)

Not all I/O psychologists agree with Hall or with others who take the more moderate position that the influence of environmental variables on work performance is often dismissed too lightly. Campbell (1990) sets out a model that omits these factors entirely except as they affect an individual's position on the proposed performance determinants of individual motivation, declarative knowledge (knowledge of what to do), and procedural knowledge (knowledge of how and when to do it).

In the Campbell model, environmental constraints on behavior (for example, not getting materials in a timely fashion) are considered sources of contamination in measuring work performance rather than as determinants of work performance. The utility of making this distinction would seem to lie more in the research domain than in the applied domain, however. Whatever the actual processes in action, environmental variables affect job performance and they should not be ignored.

The Appraisal of Work Performance

Models of the determinants of work performance, such as that shown in Figure 10–1, are complex, but then, so is human behavior. Understanding the large number of variables that interact to produce work performance makes it easier to appreciate the difficulty that I/O psychologists have in evaluating that performance. Consider a manager whose performance is partially evaluated by keeping operational expenses within a defined budget. This manager will receive a low rating if his or her department goes 20% over the budget in the evaluation period. Yet, a careful examination of the situation might reveal that it took considerable knowledge and skill to keep expenditures even *that* low under the conditions prevailing in the organization at that time.

Depending on perspective, the manager's performance might be evaluated as either unsatisfactory or outstanding. Which is fair? Which is accurate? The answer is very important to the individual concerned, but it also has a broader significance. From the standpoint of effective human resource utilization, performance appraisal is one of the most critical organizational activities.

Performance appraisal is the process used by an organization to evaluate the degree to which its members are doing their work satisfactorily. As Glen (1990) describes it, it is "an unnerving yet useful process" involving social, situational, affective, and cognitive elements (Ferris, Judge, Rowland, & Fitzgibbons, 1994). The end product is information that serves a major coordinating function for personnel-related activities in an organization. As shown in Figure 10–2, performance appraisal is a control system with both feedback and feedforward aspects.

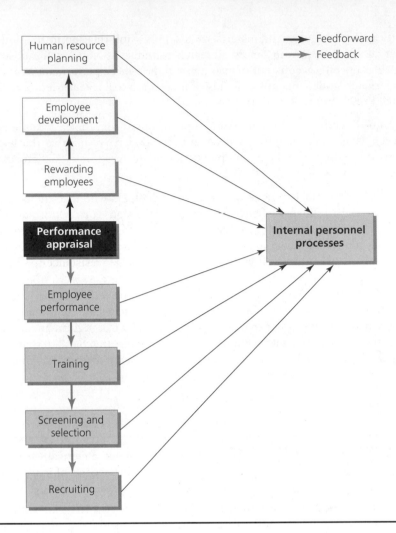

Figure 10–2
The Feedback and Feedforward Functions of Performance Appraisal Information

As a feedback mechanism, performance appraisal provides information to individual employees about the way their job performance is perceived. It also feeds back important information to those who were involved in recruiting, screening, selecting, and training an organization's current employees. For example, a consistent pattern of poor evaluations among new employees might suggest that the processes by which these individuals were brought to the job need reexamining.

As a feedforward mechanism, performance appraisal provides information for making administrative decisions about rewarding organizational employees. These formal work-related rewards include raises, bonuses, promotions, and desirable work assignments (or in some instances, just retention of the job). This administrative application remains the single most common use (e.g., Cleveland, Murphy, & Williams, 1989), but performance appraisal information has other feedforward functions. A major one is developmental.

Potentially, performance appraisal is a very important source of information about individual employee development needs and opportunities. Working together, employees and their supervisors and/or managers can use this information to help assess personal strengths and weaknesses and to make plans to achieve better performance and future career opportunities and goals. At the organization level, performance appraisal information paints a picture of overall work force strengths and weaknesses that can be used for more effective human resource planning. In particular, performance appraisal information can help determine future recruiting, training, and development needs and by so doing can assist in creating a pool of internal talent for filling future job openings.

The feedback and feedforward functions mentioned are specific to the individual employees of an organization. Performance appraisal information is also useful for (and, in some cases, critical to) a variety of purposes that have little or nothing to do with particular individuals. These internal personnel purposes include job design and redesign, screening test validation, training method design or redesign, and documentation of fair employment practices.

Effective performance appraisal gives very good value for the resources put into it, but the key word is *effective.* Poor systems almost always create resistance from raters and resentment from ratees, and the information they generate is suspect at best and useless at worst. As illustrated by the excerpt in Psychology at Work, many organizations are working with I/O psychologists to improve their performance appraisal methods. In general however, this is an area in which existing knowledge is not being applied as well as it might be (Fisher, 1989; Maroney & Buckley, 1992).

In the next section, the issues involved in making performance appraisal effective are examined closely. The discussion is centered around the major questions to be asked in setting up any performance appraisal program, rather than on the appraisal of particular kinds of job performance. There are differences in the specifics of evaluating the performance of people in professional, production, managerial, sales, and staff jobs, but as with training, the basic questions remain the same. Whether the individual to be appraised is an aircraft assembly line worker, a middle manager in a bank, a clerical employee, or a vice-president of marketing, someone must still decide what aspects of job performance to appraise, who is going to do it, how often it is going to be done, and what method is going to be used.

What Should Be Appraised?

Just as the fundamental decision in setting up a training program is what is to be taught, the fundamental decision in setting up a performance appraisal program is what is to be appraised. Conceptually, there are only three choices—the person, some result of the person's work behavior, or the behavior itself.

Appraising the Person

The oldest type of performance appraisal instrument asks raters to evaluate ratee personal characteristics, or traits, such as those shown in the example in Exhibit 10–1. An individual's evaluation on such a scale is very dependent on the rater's *perception* of traits, and such perceptions are affected considerably by opinions, biases, and experiences that have nothing to do with the particular ratee. One rater's idea of a "likeable personality" may differ significantly from another's, for example. In consequence, trait instruments tend to have poor interrater reliability.

	Excellent	Good	Average	Fair	Poor
Personality The external mannerisms consciously adopted in meeting situations	☐ Radiant, confident, poised, courteous	☐ Pleasant, forceful	☐ Likeable	☐ Ill at ease, not too forceful	☐ Negative, colorless person
Appearance Outward impressions made by a person	☐ Superior style, grooming, taste, and a sense of the fitness of things	☐ Well-dressed and neat	☐ Neat, but not particularly striking	☐ Intermittently careless	☐ Slovenly and untidy
Character Integrity of an individual	☐ Has the courage of his or her convictions and unquestioned habits	☐ Morally sound, tolerant	☐ An average human being possessing average personal weaknesses	☐ A person whose behavior harms no one but himself or herself	☐ A person who is a bad influence on the behavior of the group
Mentality Quality of mind, mental power, and creative intellectual ability of a person	☐ Superior ability to think clearly and arrive at sound conclusions	☐ Worthwhile ideas of his or her own, and ability to make useful decisions	☐ Well-informed on certain subjects useful in his or her daily work	☐ Little ability to comprehend, interpret, or grasp new ideas	☐ Unable to reason logically
Sociability Sense of mutual relationship, and friendliness with others	☐ A genuine interest in people and extremely well liked by others	☐ A friendly, pleasant person, happy in a group	☐ Willing to be a part of a group but makes little contribution	☐ Poorly adjusted to the group	☐ Unwilling to be a part of any group activities

Exhibit 10–1
Example of a Trait Performance Appraisal Instrument

The validity of trait performance appraisal is also highly questionable. A close look at Exhibit 10–1 reveals something very interesting. It would be quite possible for an individual being evaluated on this scale to get a rating of excellent on every item and still be a *poor* worker, because these items are irrelevant to performance on most jobs. About the only real advantage of the trait approach to performance appraisal is an economic one; such an instrument can be used to evaluate any individual on any job. From a measurement standpoint, its reliability and validity weaknesses more than offset this advantage, but trait-based performance appraisal instruments are still in common use. Werner (1994) suggests that one reason for this durability is that such instruments reflect aspects of employee behavior that managers consider important even though they are not related directly to productivity. "Character" and "sociability," for example, may be stand-ins for the voluntary, cooperative, helping behavior called organizational citizenship.

Appraising Results

An alternative to appraising an individual's personal characteristics is to evaluate the results of what he or she does on the job. A salesperson might be evaluated in terms of dollar volume of sales perhaps, or profit made on sales. Lawyers are often evaluated on the number of hours they bill clients for services. The number of articles published in scholarly journals is an important component of performance appraisal for many college and university professors. Other examples of results criteria include number of units produced per hour, percentage of waste materials, and number of customers served in a period of time.

Criterion
See page 63

At first glance, measuring performance by its results appears to be an attractive solution to the problem of what to evaluate in performance appraisal. After all, aren't results the bottom line? The answer is yes, but results come in all flavors, not just plain production vanilla. A given supervisor may get only average productivity from subordinates but have such a good relationship with them that absenteeism and turnover in that department are almost zero. This dimension of the supervisor's work behavior would be bypassed altogether in a typical results-oriented appraisal.

A second difficulty with appraisal by results is that it depends on accurate records, and records may be neither accurate nor complete or even available at all. Complicating the problem is the fact that results in organizations are seldom dependent solely on the performance of one individual. The low volume of sales for one salesperson may be due partially to quality control problems with the product, for example, or to price or delivery schedules that are not competitive in that individual's territory.

Despite the problems with results performance appraisal for individuals, it may turn out to be the method of choice for evaluating the performance of work teams. Not only is it difficult (or impossible) to evaluate individual performance in this context, it often is counterproductive to try to do so (Saavedra & Kwun, 1993). A group usually functions more effectively as a team when its members work together cooperatively toward a common goal, whether that goal is assembling an automobile, writing an advertising jingle, or making a presentation in a college class. Individual appraisal introduces an element of competition, implying, as it does, that some members will get more credit than others. If such appraisal is necessary, it may be useful to take one of the peer evaluation approaches discussed in a later section.

Appraising Behavior

An alternative to appraising people by the final results of their job behaviors is to appraise them on the behaviors themselves. Instead of evaluating a salesperson on "sales personality" (a common item on a trait instrument for salespeople) or profit made on sales (results approach), the evaluation could be based on sales-related behaviors such as number of calls, submission of required paperwork, follow-up activities, and so on.

The behavior approach to performance appraisal is generally more reliable and valid than the trait approach. Behaviors are directly observable, whereas traits must be inferred from behavior. Cutting out the middle step (inference) eliminates some portion of the error introduced into appraisal by the different opinions, biases, values, and experiences of different raters. If this error is reduced, reliability and validity should be increased.

The behavioral approach is also often more realistic than the results approach, and it is almost always more useful from an employee development standpoint. A substandard volume of sales (result) is just a number. To help a salesperson improve this performance, it is necessary to look behind the number at the behaviors that created it.

Generalizations are risky, but it is probably safe to say that more I/O psychologists today would recommend appraising behaviors over traits in all cases and over results in most cases. Exceptions may arise when there is no ambiguity about the direct connection between the behavior of an individual and the results obtained, when an organization insists on a bottom line criterion, or in some group performance appraisal situations.

Operating on the assumption that job behaviors are the best all-around choice of what to evaluate in performance appraisal, the question arises as to what work behaviors should be appraised. The specific answer depends on the nature of the work, but a sample of the many choices available includes the timely and correct execution of job duties, the ability to plan ahead, accurate self-inspection of work, satisfactory relationships with customers or clients, maintenance of discipline, clarity of written and/or oral communication, and cooperation with co-workers.

The addition to the list of prosocial, extrarole, or organizational citizenship behaviors such as volunteering new ideas, helping co-workers, accepting extra work without complaint, or acting as peacemaker in disputes is controversial. Katz (1964) lists innovative and spontaneous behavior that goes beyond a job description as one of the three employee behaviors required for organizations to function effectively. The fact that labor unions are

Quantity of output is a result measure often used in the appraisal of work performance.

able to use working-to-rule tactics (perfect adherence to job requirements and rules and not one action more) to depress performance levels supports this position (McNeely & Meglino, 1994), as does general research into organizational effectiveness (e.g., Posdakoff & MacKenzie, 1994).

Despite an obvious need for employees to go beyond a strict adherence to a job description, inclusion of such behaviors on a performance appraisal instrument creates a dilemma. Once behavior is included in a formal performance evaluation process, it tends to become viewed as a job requirement rather than an option. On the other hand, if such behaviors are not included on a performance appraisal instrument, but their presence or absence influences the evaluation of an employee, they become a source of measurement error (Werner, 1994).

Measurement error
See pages 53–54

The kinds of behaviors under discussion are examples of what Borman and Motowidlo (1993) call contextual performance behaviors as distinct from task performance behaviors. The latter category consists of activities that relate directly to the organization's product or service or its support (such as operating a machine or purchasing raw materials). By contrast, contextual performance behaviors emphasize "interpersonal skills and motivation to interact with others in ways that foster good working relationships and help them perform their tasks effectively" (Van Scotter & Motowidlo, 1996).

When Should Appraisal Take Place?

Formal performance appraisal is done infrequently in most organizations, once a year having long been the norm (e.g., Lazer & Wikstrom, 1977). Moreover, most appraisal systems are fixed-date, such as 6 months after an employee joins the company and every 12 months after that. These infrequent, fixed-date appraisal policies have the effect of separating evaluation from the natural flow of work performance. Most people charged with the appraisal of others' work performance are busy people who do not typically have evaluation in mind on a day-to-day basis (Bernardin & Villanova, 1986). Instead, they process the performance information they have acquired over time when the appraisal instrument is sitting in front of them. As a result, the utility of the evaluation for feedback is limited and an already difficult task is made even more difficult.

A long time span between formal performance evaluations taxes the memory of a rater and can introduce error into the results. In one laboratory experiment, a delay of only three weeks between observation and evaluation of performance led to a significant decrease in rater accuracy (Heneman & Wexley, 1983). The problem is magnified if the time period is a matter of months or a year rather than weeks.

Laboratory experiment
See pages 27–28

One common form of error that results from a long time span between performance appraisals is a tendency to recall only those job behaviors that are consistent with the way the rater generally thinks of an employee (Wyer & Srull, 1981). If a new employee makes an early impression as an especially industrious worker, it may be only behaviors consistent with this impression that come to mind at the next formal evaluation. Alternatively, the most recent performance may be the most important factor.

Recent behavior bias refers to a tendency to bias performance appraisal by giving the greatest weight to work observed immediately prior to formal evaluation. There is also some evidence that the recent level of performance affects the appraiser's recall of previous performance (e.g., Murphy, Gannett, Herr, & Chen, 1986). If more recent performance is good, then the rater may remember the good aspects of earlier performance more readily than any poorer aspects of this performance. Of course, current performance may be typical of usual performance, but it is not necessarily so, especially if employees are aware that the annual performance appraisal is coming up soon (e.g., DuBois, Sackett, Zedeck, & Fogli, 1993; Sackett, Zedeck, & Fogli, 1988).

Possible reduced accuracy is not the only problem that can be created by a long time period between performance appraisals. If results are to be used for developmental purposes, these results constitute feedback to the employee being evaluated. To be consistent with basic learning principles, this feedback should come at relatively frequent intervals so that an individual does not get too far down the wrong path if his or her performance is unsatisfactory in some way. At aerospace manufacturer Northrop Grumman, performance appraisal is a year-round activity. The steps in this process are outlined in Figure 10–3.

Feedback

See pages 138–140

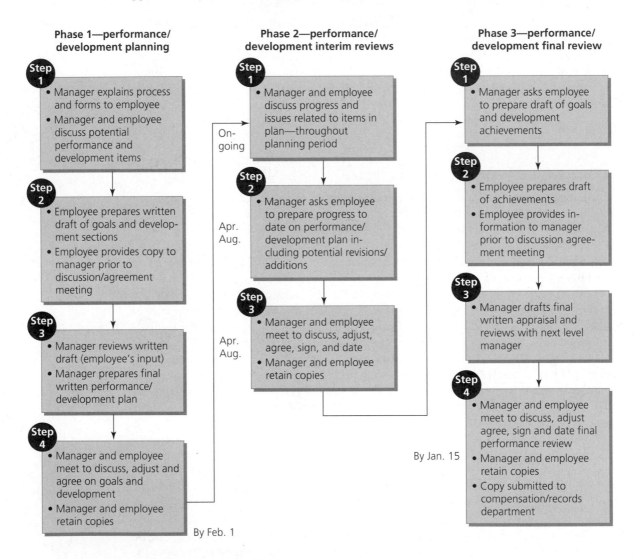

Figure 10–3
A Year-Round Performance Appraisal Process

As illustrated by the figure, performance appraisal at Northrop Grumman is a joint employee-manager process that begins with setting performance and development goals for the employee and continues throughout the year with regular meetings to discuss progress and make any revisions or adjustments to the plan. The process not only keeps the employee on track, it keeps the evaluation of his or her work performance in the front of the manager's mind.

Who Will Make the Appraisal?

There are several alternatives, but the person most commonly chosen to do a performance appraisal has always been the employee's immediate supervisor. The primary rationale for this practice is that this individual understands the job and has the opportunity to observe its performance by subordinates. On the other hand, these same factors often give rise to considerable resistance toward the task. Because they do work closely with those they are asked to evaluate, many supervisors feel unable to perform appraisals objectively or are just uncomfortable in general with evaluating other people (e.g., Bernardin & Villanova, 1986). In addition, many people in this position believe that the task interferes with good superior-subordinate relationships.

Industrial/organizational psychologists have ample evidence that superiors and subordinates often disagree in their evaluations of subordinate performance (see Farh & Werbel, 1986; George & Smith, 1990; Mabe & West, 1982; Shore & Thornton, 1986). Investigations of performance feedback interviews suggest that they do not necessarily even *hear* the same things when evaluations are being discussed. In one study, subordinates persistently overestimated the evaluations of their performance in postappraisal interview questioning even though supervisors were especially careful to give feedback in a straightforward, unambiguous manner during the interview (Ilgen, Peterson, Martin, & Boeschen, 1981).

They are relatively infrequently used, but there are a number of alternatives to the immediate supervisor as an appraiser of employee performance. Self-appraisal has been the focus of considerable I/O psychology research. In general, results of this line of investigation find that self-appraisals are somewhat more lenient than other methods. Some researchers have also found self-appraisals to be lower on discriminant validity—that is, on the extent to which they differentiate between good and poor performance (e.g., Campbell & Lee, 1988; Thornton, 1980).

The differences found between self- and other performance appraisals are not usually large and not always significant, raising the possibility that subordinates' lack of knowledge about the nature of the appraisal task and what is expected of them may be a factor (Williams & Levy, 1992). The kind of measurement scale used may also make a difference (see Schrader & Steiner, 1996). In a study by Fox, Caspy, and Reisler (1994), police officers who rated themselves on an unbalanced scale (the midpoint is called "above average") showed less leniency than did the officers whose self-ratings were done on a conventional balanced scale (the midpoint is called "average").

Statistical significance
See pages 35–36

As the research suggests, self-appraisal might be improved; nevertheless, it is not the best choice if only one source of evaluation information is to be used. The picture changes if multiple rating sources are to be used. Self-ratings measure something different (or the same thing differently) from supervisory or other ratings, and this different vantage point may be a highly useful source of additional relevant information (Kraiger, 1985).

Collaborative employee-supervisor performance appraisal plans, such as the one described in Psychology at Work, are promising variations on this approach.

Other than the employee, his or her immediate supervisors, or some combination of both, possible performance appraisers include peers or co-workers, subordinates, a group or committee, a human resource specialist in performance appraisal, an internal staff consultant, or an external management consultant. In practice, use of these alternatives tends to be concentrated in certain kinds of organizations. Specialists and outsiders are often used in public-sector organizations, such as public school systems. Committee ratings also see limited use in such settings. Performance appraisal by groups would seem to offer some advantages, but research comparing groups with individuals on this task is limited and results are inconclusive (e.g., Martell & Borg, 1993).

Ratings by subordinates have always been relatively rare, although student evaluation of college and university professors might be considered one common instance. Recently, however, upward feedback has popped into the limelight due to interest in 360-degree-feedback performance appraisal. In this multiple source feedback method, data are collected from the employee as well as from all of those "around" him or her—the immediate supervisor, peers, subordinates, and clients or customers if relevant. Among the companies that are experimenting with or have adopted this process are Digital Equipment Corporation, Toyota Motor Sales, U.S.A., and Federal Express.

The 360-degree performance appraisal idea has focused research attention on appraisal by subordinates, an area of I/O psychology in which relatively few empirical studies are available. To date, results suggest that managers (like almost everyone else) tend to rate themselves higher than others, including subordinates, rate them (Furnham & Stringfield, 1994; Riggio & Cole, 1992). Managers in general do not support the use of upward feedback for administrative purposes (such as deciding who will be promoted or get merit raises), but they believe that the feedback is useful for personal development (e.g., Ash, 1994; McEvoy, 1990). The extent to which they actually *use* it to change their behavior, however, is uncertain (Smither, Wohlers, & London, 1995). In any case, unless the anonymity of the subordinates is protected (often very difficult), the ratings are likely to be inflated and therefore of limited developmental utility (Antonioni, 1994).

Feedback from peers is also part of the 360-degree methodology, and I/O psychologists have a long-standing interest in this method of evaluation. There are several ways in which peers—an individual's co-workers, or other members of some group—may be used to evaluate the individual. Peer nominations call for peers to nominate, or vote for, outstanding colleagues. Peer rankings require each member of the group to rank all members on some dimension, whereas peer ratings ask an individual's peers to do the standard performance appraisal.

Most of the research with peer appraisal methods has been with peer nominations, and these generally have been found to be acceptably reliable and valid. There is ample evidence that peers can agree as to who are the top performers in a group (e.g., Flynn, Sipes, Grosenbach, & Ellsworth, 1994). Peer ratings tend to have somewhat lower interrater reliability than supervisory ratings (Viswesvaran, Schmidt, & Ones, 1996), but peer evaluations of all kinds seem to be substantially more in agreement with supervisory ratings than are self-evaluations (e.g., Harris & Schaubroeck, 1988).

Potentially, peer appraisal is a rich source of information, both for performance appraisal and for individual development. However, it is typically not liked by either party to the process (e.g., De Nisi, Randolph, & Blencoe, 1983; McEvoy & Buller, 1987), and its use has largely been confined to upper management levels and professional occupations. It has also been used extensively and successfully in the Peace Corps, an organiza-

Although formalized peer appraisal is not found in many organizations, informal evaluation of an individual's work by his or her peers takes place frequently.

tion distinguished by a noncompetitive reward system and training that gives members an unusual opportunity to observe and get to know one another. To the extent that work groups or teams in other organizations can be organized along similar lines, peer appraisal may prove to be both an acceptable and a very useful alternative to supervisory or leader appraisal.

How Will Appraisal Be Done?

The question of how to appraise is a question of method. There are two broad classifications of performance appraisal methods—comparative and individual. Within each classification are a variety of approaches. The physical means by which the method is implemented is called the performance appraisal instrument. As is true of all measuring instruments, those measuring performance must be evaluated according to whether they yield reliable and valid results. If a performance appraisal instrument is reliable, it should give highly correlated results when used by two different raters (called interrater reliability) or the same rater more than once (called intrarater reliability). If it is valid, there should be evidence that it is appropriate to draw conclusions about work performance from the ratings (measurements) taken with it.

Performance appraisal in general is plagued by both reliability and validity problems. To some extent these problems stem from the difficulty of assessing whether a method meets these standards. The concept of reliability presumes that what is being measured remains constant or "holds still" for measurement, but the work performance of any given individual can vary substantially, even within a short time period. There are work situations in which the degree of this variability is itself a critical aspect of job performance (performance variability is not desirable in air traffic controllers, for example).

Correlation
See pages 37–39

Reliability
See pages 43–44

Validity
See pages 59–70

When this is the case, it should be assessed as such (Steiner, Rain, & Smalley, 1993). In most circumstances, however, variability in performance is more likely to add error to work evaluation than to help it.

Research suggests that ratees exhibiting different patterns of performance variation receive different ratings even when their overall level of performance for the evaluation period is the same (Karl & Wexley, 1989). Ambrose and Kulik (1994) report that typists whose performance was manipulated to improve during an observation period got better ratings from subjects, for example, than did typists whose performance was arranged to deteriorate.

Research subjects
See page 27

The validity of performance appraisal methods creates even more difficulties than its reliability. Conceptually, the problem is this: If there were some standard of true performance good enough to use in assessing the validity of a performance appraisal instrument, the standard, and not the appraisal instrument, would be used. This criterion problem is considered by many to be the most difficult problem in I/O psychology, and it may never be solved except in a "probabilistic, partial, and, conditional" way (Austin & Villanova, 1992, p. 862).

The more common comparative and individual performance appraisal instruments are discussed briefly below. None comes up to ideal standards, although some fare better than others when it comes to reliability and validity. The discussion is general; there are many variations of these methods, and situational differences can be substantial.

Comparative Methods of Performance Appraisal

Performance appraisal methods that require a comparison of all of the people to be appraised (ratees) at a given time are called comparative methods. Most of these are variations of **straight ranking**, in which ratees are ordered from best to poorest on some dimension such as overall quality of work. This method has several advantages. It costs nothing to develop, it is easy for raters and ratees to understand, and it forces raters to make distinctions among ratees.

Along with its advantages, straight ranking has some drawbacks. A fundamental one is the zero-sum basis of the procedure; regardless of the *relative* differences in performance, some individuals *must* be ranked lower merely because others are ranked higher. In addition, rankings provide no information about the absolute level of performance, and so the evaluations of different groups of ratees cannot be compared. The top-ranked individual in one department of an organization might be performing at a level that would rank him or her only in the middle in another department, for instance.

Another problem with straight ranking is that it can be a very difficult task for the rater, especially in the center of the ranks, unless the number of ratees is small. Most people find it relatively easy to distinguish between the top few performers in a group and the bottom few, but a rationale for ranking an employee 9th out of 20th instead of 8th or 10th out of 20th can be difficult to find. Finally, because they are not based on defined aspects of job performance, straight ranking procedures make it very difficult to give ratees the information they need to improve their job performance.

Variations of straight ranking solve some of the problems of using this method. A **forced-distribution ranking** requires raters to assign a certain percentage of ratees to each of a set number of categories. The process yields a distribution of ratings, such as that shown in Exhibit 10–2, that approximates a normal curve. The forced distribution is eas-

Normal curve
See pages 36–37

Directions: Distribute the 26 ratees as shown by the numbers below on the basis of your appraisal of their overall job performance.

Exhibit 10–2 Example of a Forced-Distribution Ranking

Job Dimension	Lowest 10%	Next 20%	Middle 40%	Next 20%	Highest 10%
Overall quality of work	2	6	10	6	2

ier than straight ranking because the distinctions it requires are not as fine, but this format presents no real improvement over straight ranking for developmental purposes.

Yet another variation of straight ranking is the **paired-comparison method,** in which each ratee is compared with every other ratee. Final ranking depends on the number of times each individual is ranked number one. This method makes rankings easier for raters because it breaks the task into components—each ratee is ranked only first or second in each pair. As a result of the decreased demands it makes on the appraiser, the paired-comparison method tends to be more reliable than either straight or forced-distribution ranking. It is likely to encounter rater resistance, however, unless the number of people to be evaluated is very small; if there are as many as 18 ratees, for example, the rater must make more than 150 comparisons.

Rated ranking is a technique for getting around some of the drawbacks of straight ranking by combining ranking with rating (Miner, 1988). An employee is *ranked* on some aspect of performance, such as "learning to perform new tasks," and then *rated* as "outstanding," "good," and so on to "poor" for that aspect. Rated ranking gives some indication of the absolute as well as the relative position of an individual on a job requirement, but empirical data for this variation of straight ranking are lacking.

Individual Methods of Performance Appraisal

Psychologically, comparative methods of performance appraisal are probably closest to a natural approach to this activity. Most people tend to compare individuals with one another when evaluating performance. Nevertheless, such methods create problems and, as a group, have little utility for employee development. An alternative is the use of individual methods, which evaluate performance against defined standards.

The most popular individual performance appraisal method is a **graphic rating scale,** such as that shown in Exhibit 10–3. With this method, a rater assesses the degree to which every ratee exhibits the behaviors and/or traits shown on the scale. Degree usually is indicated by a number, adjective, or descriptive phrase. The scale in the exhibit has two adjectives ("outstanding," "poor") and three descriptive phrases ("exceeds requirements," and so on) to describe the degree to which ratees plan, organize, control costs, and demonstrate technical knowledge. This mixing of standards is relatively common, but it can be confusing. What does "outstanding" mean when "exceeds requirements" is used to define a lower level of performance?

The traditional graphic rating scale is something of an improvement over comparative assessment methods in that it allows both for comparing different groups of ratees

Exhibit 10–3
Example of a
Graphic Rating
Scale

	Outstanding	Exceeds Requirements	Meets Requirements	Meets Minimum Requirements	Poor
Planning and Organizing Consider how this employee plans work and organizes job activity Comments:_____					
Technical, Scientific, Professional Knowledge and Ability Consider how this employee applies technical, scientific, or professional knowledge and ability on the job. Comments:_____					
Control of Costs Consider how this employee utilizes materials, equipment, processes, work time, and services. Comments:_____					

and for more specific feedback to ratees. The improvement may be slight, however. Different raters may use quite different standards in defining terms such as "outstanding" (Exhibit 10–3). A variation of the graphic rating scale widely believed to be a significant improvement is the behaviorally anchored rating scale, or BARS (Smith & Kendall, 1963).

A **behaviorally anchored rating** scale anchors graphic rating scale points with specific behaviors to help raters make their appraisals. The sample behavior anchors are not intended to be used in a checklist fashion; that is, it is not necessary that an employee be observed performing the specific behaviors listed. Rather, the anchors are examples of the kinds of behaviors that might be *expected* of an employee at a particular level of job performance. For this reason, a BARS is sometimes called a behavioral expectation scale (BES). One item from this type of scale is shown in Exhibit 10–4.

Developing a traditional behaviorally anchored rating scale starts with a version of Flanagan's (1954) critical incident technique. The supervisors who will be using the new scale provide examples of important job behaviors (critical incidents), both good and poor, that they have observed at one time or another. The process then proceeds through a number of categorizing and scaling steps to produce an item of the form shown in Exhibit 10–4. (See Latham and Wexley, 1981, for a detailed description.)

Given that cooperative behavior (Exhibit 10–4) is only one item for evaluating one aspect of one job, it is clear that developing a BARS instrument is a time-consuming and expensive process. Some I/O psychologists have argued that the result is not worth this expenditure of resources. In their review of the early studies comparing the BARS with other appraisal instruments, Kingstrom and Bass (1981) conclude that there is little difference with respect to reliability, validity, or rater preference.

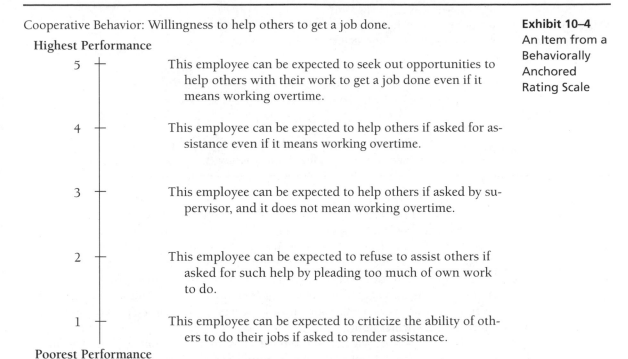

Cooperative Behavior: Willingness to help others to get a job done.

Highest Performance

5 ── This employee can be expected to seek out opportunities to help others with their work to get a job done even if it means working overtime.

4 ── This employee can be expected to help others if asked for assistance even if it means working overtime.

3 ── This employee can be expected to help others if asked by supervisor, and it does not mean working overtime.

2 ── This employee can be expected to refuse to assist others if asked for such help by pleading too much of own work to do.

1 ── This employee can be expected to criticize the ability of others to do their jobs if asked to render assistance.

Poorest Performance

Exhibit 10–4
An Item from a Behaviorally Anchored Rating Scale

Bernardin and Smith (1981) disagree with the conclusions of Kingstrom and Bass and others who continue to question the superiority of behaviorally anchored rating scales to other methods (e.g., Banks & Roberson, 1985; Gomez-Mejia, 1988; Piotrowski, Barnes-Farrell, & Esrig, 1989). Among other points discussed in support of the BARS instrument, they point out that this approach helps to standardize the observation of performance as well as the evaluation of performance. Therefore, they argue, it is a valuable tool for documenting fair employment practices. Given the pressure on organizations to justify the numbers by which decisions about employees are made, the point seems well taken.

Behaviorally anchored rating scales were developed some years ago, and a number of variations on the basic technique have been put forward since. One of the first was the mixed standard scale, or MSS (Blanz & Ghiselli, 1972). The MSS instrument consists of three randomly ordered, behaviorally based performance statements per job dimension. Each statement represents either a high, an average, or a low level of performance. Raters respond by indicating whether the ratee's performance is better than, worse than, or about the same as that described. This approach has its proponents, but the empirical data available are not encouraging (e.g., Benson, Buckley, & Hall, 1988).

Latham, Fay, and Saari (1979) propose what they call a behavioral observation scale (BOS), which, like the BARS, is based on descriptions of actual job behaviors. The major difference is that BOS raters evaluate the extent to which ratees have been observed performing *each* behavior. Tziner and Latham (1989) report that this type of scale was superior to a graphic rating scale on several criteria in a study of airport managers and subordinates, but to date the behavioral observation scale has not seen widespread use.

Exhibit 10–5

Two Items from
a Forced-Choice
Performance
Appraisal
Instrument

Directions: For each item, place a check by the *one* statement that best describes the ratee. You must choose one statement from each pair.

Item One

_____ Is generally at work on time in the mornings.
_____ Gets along well with almost everyone.

Item Two

_____ Usually takes a little longer than the specified deadline to finish work.
_____ Does not make a very good first impression with strangers.

Generalizability
See page 45

The major disadvantages of behavior-based performance appraisal instruments remain development cost and lack of generalizability. A standard old-style graphic rating scale may be used to evaluate performance on a variety of jobs. The usual behavior-based scale is largely or exclusively job specific. Recently, however, Hunt (1996) published the results of a long-term study in which a number of generic work behaviors (behaviors that contribute to the performance of any job independent of specific technical requirements) were identified. More work of this nature may make it possible to develop BARS appraisal instruments with broader utility.

Graphic rating scales, whether standard or behaviorally anchored, do not exhaust the possibilities for individual performance appraisal instruments. At least two other methods should be mentioned. A **forced-choice scale** requires raters to pick one of two (or two of four) statements as most descriptive of a ratee. The statements have been equated ahead of time as to apparent favorableness or unfavorableness (equal degree of social desirability). Despite this apparent equality, only one (or two) of the statements differentiates between good and poor job performance. In the sample items in Exhibit 10–5, the first statement in each pair is the scored item.

Forced-choice appraisal item pairs make it difficult or impossible for a rater to bias results of a performance evaluation deliberately, provided that the items in each set of statements appear equally favorable or unfavorable and the rating key (the list of which items are the real ones) is kept confidential. Unfortunately, this necessity makes forced-choice scales worthless for developmental purposes, and it also can give rise to considerable rater resistance. The logic of having to choose between one of two quite dissimilar statements as a way of evaluating job performance is by no means obvious, and many raters are not prepared to take it on faith.

The last major individual performance appraisal method reviewed is called a **behavior checklist**. This instrument, such as the empirically weighted one shown in Exhibit 10–6, requires that the observer record, but not evaluate, behavior. The question is: Did the behavior described occur or did it not? The primary strength of this purely descriptive instrument is its utility for developmental use; more than any other method, the checklist offers employees very specific feedback as to what they need to do to improve their job performance.

Many years of I/O psychology research have made it clear that there is no ideal performance appraisal instrument, only ones that serve particular purposes better than others. Building a program suited to goals and consistent with resources begins with understanding the issues. The decisions to be made when setting up performance appraisal and the relative strengths and weaknesses of the major alternative choices for each decision

Item	Scale Value
He occasionally buys some of his competitor's products.	6.8
He never consults with his head salesgirl when making out a bake order.	1.4
He belongs to a local merchant's association.	4.9
He criticizes his employees unnecessarily.	0.8
The window display is usually just fair.	3.1
He enjoys contacting customers personally.	7.4
He does not know how to figure costs of products.	0.6
He lacks a long range viewpoint.	3.5
His products are of uniformly high quality.	8.5
He expects too much of his employees.	2.2
His weekly and monthly reports are sometimes inaccurate.	4.2
He does not always give enough thought to his bake orders.	1.6
He occasionally runs a selling contest among his salesgirls.	6.8
Baking in his shop continues until 2 P.M. or later.	8.2
He keeps complaining about employees but doesn't remedy the situation.	0.9
He has originated one or more workable new formulas.	6.4
He sometimes has an unreasonably large inventory of certain items.	3.3
Employees enjoy working for him.	7.6
He does not delegate enough responsibility to others.	2.8
He has accurately figured the costs of most of his products.	7.8
He wishes he were just a baker.	0.8
His shop is about average in cleanliness.	4.4
He is tardy in making minor repairs in his sales room.	1.9
He periodically samples all of his products for quality.	8.1

Exhibit 10–6
Example of a Behavior Checklist

From E. B. Knauft, "Construction and Use of Weighted Checklist Rating Scales for Two Industrial Situations." *Journal of Applied Psychology,* 1948, *32,* 63–70.

Note: This exhibit was selected for its historical value as well as for its illustration of the behavior checklist. Use of the masculine pronoun for the baker and the term *salesgirl* reflect social reality at the time this instrument was developed.

have been outlined. To keep the discussion as clear as possible, the various questions to be answered have been treated as if they were independent, but of course they are not. Decisions concerning what to appraise, to take one case, tend to play a large part in deciding what method to use. Underlying all of these decisions are the basic issues of reliability and validity, and it is now time to turn attention more closely to the subject of error in performance appraisal.

Error in Evaluating Work Performance

Performance appraisal is a measurement question and a complex one. The problem is to find some combination of what, who, when, and how to appraise work performance that will yield acceptably reliable and valid measurements. The errors that can act to reduce the accuracy of these measurements stem from the instrument, the environment in which the appraisal takes place, and the rater.

Instrument Sources of Error

Sample
See page 27

Domain
See page 62

Deficiency
See page 63

The items on a performance appraisal instrument are only a sample of all of the possible items that might be on it; that is, the instrument consists of a sample of the domain of items that describe job performance. To the extent that this sample omits items that represent important aspects of job performance, the instrument is deficient. Deficiency is a major issue when performance is appraised on a single item of overall work effectiveness. It can also be a problem when performance is evaluated by its results if the instrument ignores important nonproduction aspects of job behavior.

To the extent that a performance appraisal instrument contains items that are irrelevant to work performance, it is contaminated. Contamination is often a problem with traditional trait instruments, which tend to include such job-irrelevant items as "sincerity." Items whose evaluation is heavily dependent on nonperformance factors (such as assigned sales territory) are also sources of contamination when job performance is being appraised.

Deficiency and contamination are two major sources of instrument error in performance appraisal. When instruments have these problems (and the same instrument may

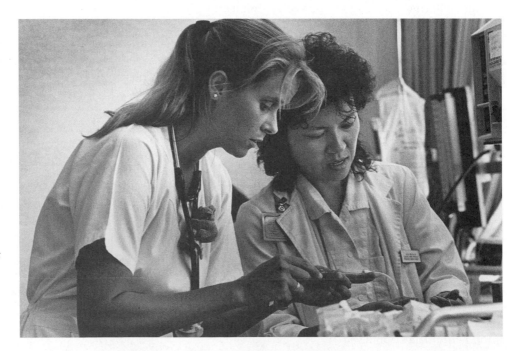

I/O psychologists have found that the social environment of the workplace can influence the appraisal of work performance.

have both), there is less evidence of content-related validity. The most direct route to reducing this source of error is job analysis, a strategy reviewed later in the chapter.

Another possible source of error in performance appraisal instruments is ambiguity in the instructions, format, or terms by which the evaluation is to be made. For example, the word *satisfactory* by itself probably has as many definitions as there are people defining it. Evidence from a 1986 study by Pearce and Porter also suggests that many ratees perceive this term as negative when it is applied to their performance. Reducing variation in the way raters and ratees perceive items on an evaluation instrument is one of the main goals behind behavior-based approaches to performance appraisal.

Content validity
See pages 62–63

Environmental Sources of Error

The situation for a person using a performance appraisal instrument to evaluate the work performance of another individual is complex. The rater must draw on his or her knowledge of behavior observed over some specified time period, but this observation has not taken place in isolation. Work behavior occurs in the context of a particular social environment, and its appraisal can be affected by a number of social factors that introduce error into the appraisal.

The Social Context of Performance Appraisal

One social environmental factor found to affect performance appraisal is a ratee's apparent social standing among his or her peers. This factor is illustrated by a pair of investigations, one carried out in the laboratory and one in the field. In these studies, Mitchell and Liden (1982) found that co-worker perceptions of a ratee affected the rater's appraisal of his or her performance. The effect was stronger in the laboratory, but results of both studies supported the hypothesis that ratees who were more popular with their peers received more favorable work performance evaluations by their supervisors.

Field research
See pages 27–34

Hypothesis
See page 25

The value placed on the outcome of work behavior by the particular environment is another social environmental factor that has been found to influence performance appraisal results. A good illustration is found in an investigation by Mitchell and Kalb (1981) using nurses and their supervisors as subjects. These researchers found that nursing supervisors tended to give different appraisals of the same nursing behavior when they had knowledge of some outcome of that behavior and when they did not. Furthermore, the effect varied systematically with whether the outcome was valued as positive or negative. For example, the competence of a nurse who forgot to change a dressing would be downgraded more if the patient's wound became infected than if it did not.

The perceived advantages and disadvantages of giving certain ratings to certain ratees from the viewpoint of organizational politics also influence performance appraisal outcomes (Gioia & Longnecker, 1994). This is more likely when the rater has considerable latitude in how the evaluations are accomplished and the work performed by the ratee is not highly structured (for example, the job of manager). Greater latitude usually accompanies higher positions in an organization, giving those at the top the greatest freedom to pursue personal agendas in this way.

The amount of error introduced into performance appraisal by the social environmental factors discussed may be substantial; Gandz and Murray (1980) report performance appraisal to be one of the two activities managers cited most frequently as an example of workplace politics in action. Zammuto, London, and Rowland (1982) believe that the social environment of an organization is a sufficiently important independent source of error in performance appraisal results to merit vigorous research efforts. One of the more active lines of this research is that into the influence of particular supervisor-subordinate (or leader–group member) relationships.

Relationships and Performance Appraisal

One of the most consistent social variables that I/O psychologists have found to influence the outcome of performance appraisal is the relationship between the rater and the ratee. Many investigators have confirmed a tendency for supervisors to give higher ratings to the subordinates they like better (e.g., Duarte, Goodson, & Klich, 1993; Judge & Ferris, 1993; Tsui & Barry, 1986; Wayne & Liden, 1995). Many factors affect liking, but in general, subordinates who are perceived to be more similar to the supervisor are liked more and receive higher performance ratings than those who are not (e.g., Thacker & Wayne, 1995; Zalesny, 1990; Zalesny & Kirsch, 1989).

Putting the shoe on the other foot, there is also evidence that some supervisors use deliberately inflated performance ratings to gain the goodwill, liking, or gratitude of subordinates (Fried & Tiegs, 1995). Inflated evaluations may also help raters avoid time wasting or uncomfortable conflict created by the need to confront individual subordinates and defend lower performance ratings.

I/O psychologists have accumulated a considerable body of evidence that rater-ratee conferences do affect actual ratings. In general, there tends to be greater leniency in ratings when raters know that they must meet with ratees about the results than when they do not have to do so (e.g., Benedict & Levine, 1988; Fisher, 1979; Klimoski & Inks, 1990). In short, unfortunate as it may be, deliberate distortion of performance ratings is one way a supervisor can increase his or her control over this aspect of the work environment.

Rater Sources of Error

The effect that the performance appraisal ratings done by one individual can have on the lives of others may be significant. One subordinate may be denied a promotion or even laid off while another gets a large increase in salary as a result of the annual evaluations. Given such possibilities, it is unfortunate that raters, as the source of a variety of measurement errors, are often the weakest link in a performance appraisal program.

Some rater errors arise from unexpected events, states, or circumstances that may never recur simultaneously with the performance appraisal task. Rater A got into a traffic jam on the way to work and arrived in a foul temper 45 minutes late to be faced with a large stack of semiannual performance evaluation forms. On the other hand, rater B just got word that a long-awaited transfer has come through and everything looks rosy. Meanwhile, poor rater C has a bad head cold and is finding it difficult to concentrate.

The error that raters A, B, and C may introduce into their evaluations as the result of their unusual physical and/or psychological states could be considerable, but it cannot be predicted or controlled. The only remedy is for the people concerned to monitor themselves and avoid doing appraisals when they are out of their usual form, if this is possible. Keeping accurate performance data throughout the evaluation period, so that there is less reliance on memory and current mood, may also help minimize this kind of error.

A second kind of error introduced into performance appraisal by the rater is not unpredictable but regular and characteristic of the rater even if he or she is not aware of it. These errors bias performance appraisal in a particular direction, so they are often referred to collectively as rater bias.

Rater Bias

Rater bias may affect all ratees evaluated by a particular rater or only certain ones, depending on whether it is task-based or ratee-based. **Task-based rater bias** in performance appraisal is an oversimplification of the appraisal task. This bias tends to be consistent across evaluation situations because it is a response to the appraisal task itself and not to the particular individuals being appraised. The most common form of rater bias is called **evaluative set**, a characteristic tendency on the part of a rater to use only a narrow range of a performance evaluation scale. That range may be the lower end (a strictness set), the upper end (a leniency set), or the middle (a central tendency set).

Many I/O psychologists have investigated evaluative sets, especially the leniency set. Their research supports the concept of performance appraisal leniency as a stable and predictable response tendency that is not related to the work of particular ratees (e.g., Kane, Bernardin, Villanova, & Peyrefitte, 1995; Villanova, Bernardin, Dahmus, & Sims, 1993). There also appears to be a tendency for all raters to be somewhat more lenient when they believe the outcome of the ratings will be used to make important administrative decisions about the employees involved than when they are used for other purposes (e.g., Harris, Smith, & Champagne, 1995; Ostroff, 1993).

Of the three response sets described, the central tendency set is probably most common in organizational performance appraisal. Going down the middle and labeling everyone average is an easy way out for raters unable or unwilling to identify differences among individual levels of performance. Using a rating scale that has no midpoint forces the issue somewhat, but the central tendency set is strong, and those who take this approach to rating will continue to stick as close to the center as possible.

Evaluative sets are very common, but they can be circumvented by certain types of evaluation methods. Ranking methods, forced-choice scales, and behavior checklists all get around the problem. The common graphic rating scale is the most susceptible to evaluative sets, but scrambling the scale point descriptions (as shown in Exhibit 10–7) can reduce the problem or at least make the fact that a rater has used a particular response set fairly obvious.

Ratee-based rater bias is not a response to the appraisal task, but a response to specific individuals being evaluated. As a result, the performance of some ratees may be overestimated, that of some underestimated, and that of others not affected at all. The most common form of this bias is called **halo error**, the tendency to evaluate all of the behaviors or traits of one ratee in a manner that is consistent with a global impression or evaluation of that person (Thorndike, 1920).

The basis for the impression that casts a "halo" over an employee varies. It may stem from a particular piece of information, such as the knowledge that a new employee made the highest score ever recorded on a certain employment screening test. It may come from some dramatic work performance incident, or it may originate from a simple personal liking or disliking of the ratee.

Halo error may introduce either a positive or a negative bias into performance appraisal. Either way, the result is a general similarity of evaluations for a particular

Exhibit 10–7
Reducing
Evaluative Sets
in Performance
Appraisal:
"Scrambled"
Scale Anchors

NOTE: Two common mistakes in rating are: (1) A tendency to rate nearly everyone as "average" on every trait instead of being more critical in judgment—the rater should use the ends of the scale as well as the middle, and (2) the "halo effect"—that is, a tendency to rate the same individual "excellent" on every trait or "poor" on every trait based on the overall picture one has of the person being rated.

I. **Job Performance**

Volume of Work is the amount of work an individual does in a workday.

☐	☐	☐	☐	☐
Does just enough to get by.	Superior work production record.	Does not meet minimum requirements.	Volume of work is satisfactory.	Very industrious, does more than required.

Comments: _____

_____

Accuracy is the correctness of work duties performed.

☐	☐	☐	☐	☐
Requires absolute minimum of supervision; is almost always accurate.	Usually accurate: Makes only average number of mistakes.	Careless: makes recurrent errors.	Requires little supervision; is exact and precise most of the time.	Makes frequent errors.

Comments: _____

_____

Creativity is talent for having new ideas, for finding new and better ways of doing things, and for being imaginative.

☐	☐	☐	☐	☐
Has average imagination; has reasonable number of new ideas.	Rarely has a new idea; is unimaginative.	Continually seeks new and better ways of doing things; is very imaginative.	Frequently suggests new ways of doing things; is very imaginative.	Occasionally comes up with a new idea.

Comments: _____

_____

individual across all of the items on a rating instrument. An example of this is seen in the behavior of rater l in Table 10–1. Such consistency in marks may be justified by the ratee's behavior (Murphy & Reynolds, 1988), but this is unlikely to be the case for more than a very few ratees (Cummings & Schwab, 1973).

Unlike evaluative sets, halo error cannot be circumvented by the method of evaluation; there is doubt that it can be controlled at all. Even highly specific behaviorally anchored rating scales seem to be vulnerable. In a comprehensive review of the literature on halo error in performance appraisal research, Balzer and Sulsky (1992) conclude that halo

Table 10–1   Halo Error in Performance Appraisal

Both raters are appraising the same employee. Which one is more likely to be making a halo error?

Appraisal Category	Rater 1	Rater 2
Attendance	7	7
Ability to follow orders	7	2
Quantity of units produced	6	4
Ability to get along with others	7	6
Quality of units produced	6	5
Ability to learn new tasks	6	6

error is more appropriately studied as a cognitive information processing method than as a measure of the quality of performance appraisal (see also Murphy, Jako, & Anhalt, 1993).

Halo error is an interesting form of information processing in that the tendency to make this error is predictable, but the direction it takes is not. It seldom is possible to predict accurately which ratees will have a positive bias introduced into their appraisals in this way and which will have a negative bias. A different case is presented by error that stems from rater prejudice or stereotypes.

Many ratee characteristics that seem to attract prejudice or stereotypes in a work situation have been investigated as possible sources of rater bias in performance appraisal. Among those more frequently researched are sex (e.g., Maurer & Taylor, 1994; Sidanius & Crane, 1989), race (e.g., Kraiger & Ford, 1985; Landau, 1995), age (e.g., Finkelstein, Burke, & Raju, 1995; Waldman & Avolio, 1986), and physical attractiveness (e.g., Collins & Zebrowitz, 1995; Ross & Ferris, 1980). Results of these studies vary considerably; systematic performance appraisal bias against females, nonwhites, older employees, and less physically attractive people has been found in some cases and not in others.

To some extent, the inconsistent findings of the research into ratee-based differences in performance appraisal are a reflection of actual differences. As Dunnette and Borman (1979) point out, obtained differences in the appraisals of males and females, whites and nonwhites, and other groups may be due to real differences in performance, rater bias, or a combination of these two factors, and most researchers do not separate out these effects.

Rater Cognitive Processes

In recent years, considerable research effort has been devoted to the way in which people doing performance appraisal process information and make appraisal decisions. I/O psychologists hope that if they can reach a better understanding of the process by which errors occur, they may be able to find ways to structure appraisal situations so as to reduce them (Kinicki, Horn, Trost, & Wade, 1995).

Ilgen and Feldman (1983) examine a considerable body of literature that relates cognitive processes to the performance appraisal process. Among other factors, these authors note that differences in the way that raters pay attention to their environments, the "theories" they hold about people in general, and the particular way in which they go about remembering information all affect how they make appraisals. The amount of information a rater is able to process (called cognitive complexity) is also relevant; people with greater cognitive complexity are less likely to make the rater errors reviewed (Landy & Farr, 1980).

Research into various aspects of the way that people go about noticing, storing, recalling, and using information relevant to performance appraisal has revealed some interesting findings. Schoorman (1988) reports that when supervisors participated in a hiring or promotion decision and *agreed* with the decision, they tended to give high performance ratings to these individuals in subsequent appraisals. Supervisors who had participated in decisions with which they *disagreed,* tended to bias their evaluations of these employees in a downward direction.

Knowledge of past performance appraisal results can also affect the information processing that leads to a performance appraisal. It may be easier to rely on that general information than to try to recall and evaluate more recent performance, for example (Woehr & Feldman, 1993). Alternatively, the presence of information about past performance may create a contrast effect by highlighting differences (either positive or negative) in ratee behavior since that rating was performed (Sumer & Knight, 1996).

In addition to information about the individuals they are evaluating, raters process information about other aspects of the situation in making appraisal decisions. One of these, whether or not there is a necessity for discussing the results of the appraisal with the ratee, has been mentioned. There is also evidence that having to justify ratings to a third party affects the way people collect, recall, and evaluate information (e.g., Simonson & Nye, 1992).

Electronic Performance Monitoring

The factors discussed are potential sources of error when one person evaluates the performance of another. **Electronic performance monitoring** (EPM) is a set of computer-based methods for collecting, storing, and analyzing information about employee work attendance, speed, and accuracy. More than 10 million American workers, mostly in clerical or other jobs in which the work is repetitive and relatively simple, currently are subject to EPM. On the surface, it appears to be a good alternative to the complicated and often-flawed decision processes required to collect this information from human beings, but there are some problems. A primary one is a well-documented increase in employee stress under EPM; monitored employees complain about increases in work load, loss of control over the manner in which they do their jobs, and reduced opportunities to socialize at work (e.g., Amick & Smith, 1992; Gallatin, 1989; Smith, Carayon, Sanders, Lim, & LeGrande, 1992; Stanton & Barnes-Farrell, 1996).

Another drawback to electronic performance monitoring is that it has a direct and ongoing effect on the performance it is measuring. This phenomenon is illustrated in an experiment by Aiello and Kolb (1995), a portion of which is summarized in Spotlight on Research. Note that high-skill subjects in the experiment worked faster when their performance was electronically monitored, but low-skill subjects worked more slowly. In a related study, Aiello and Chomiak (1992) found the same effect when their subjects only *thought* that their performance was being monitored.

SPOTLIGHT ON RESEARCH

Electronic Performance Monitoring and Social Context: Impact on Productivity and Stress

Summarized from J. R. Aiello and K. J. Kolb, "Electronic Performance Monitoring and Social Context: Impact on Productivity and Stress." *Journal of Applied Psychology*, 1995, *80*, 339–353.

Research question   What is the effect of electronic performance monitoring on task performance?

Type of study   Laboratory experiment.

Subjects   202 undergraduate students.

Independent variables

Social context: (1) alone (2) in presence of others (3) as part of a group.

Electronic performance monitoring: (1) individual monitoring (2) group monitoring (3) no monitoring.

Dependent variable   Number of 6-digit entries keyed into a computer (plus others not examined in this Spotlight).

General procedure   After a practice session with the experimental task (and a series of exercises unrelated to this Spotlight), subjects performed the task for 15 minutes using a computer software program designed to record the number of entries.

Analysis   Analysis of variance.

Results   High-skill monitored subjects (as measured by performance during practice session) keyed more entries than high-skill unmonitored subjects. Low-skill subjects exhibited the opposite pattern.

Conclusion   "EPM may lead to productivity improvements among employees who have attained a high level of task mastery. In contrast, EPM may lead to performance debilitation among employees who are still learning the tasks that comprise their jobs" (pp. 348–349).

The results of the experiment summarized are consistent with the principle of **social facilitation** (Zajonc, 1965), which predicts that the performance of simple and/or well-learned behaviors will be enhanced (facilitated) by the presence of an audience. Complex and/or less well learned behaviors, on the other hand, will suffer when someone is watching, apparently even if that "someone" is an electronic keystroke counter.

A way to increase productivity is always attractive to some people, but the possible price tag on this one—increased stress and the possibility of decreased productivity among many employees—may be too high. Both effects may be offset to some degree by monitoring at the work-group level (combining the data so that individual performance is not evaluated). Several countries have passed laws regulating individual monitoring, but the United States is not among them so far. Work-group performance monitoring is not useful for individual performance appraisal, but it is consistent with team-oriented approaches to work and for implementing associated group reward systems.

Electronic performance monitoring is a relatively new phenomenon, and all of its implications have by no means been identified or investigated. As do most other tools, it holds the potential for abuse. Supervisors who dislike doing, explaining, or defending performance appraisals can use EPM as a way out, stressing its "objectivity." Organizations fearful of litigation can use EPM as a way to avoid the risk that is always inherent in "subjective" performance ratings. In both cases, however, important aspects of job performance are likely to be sacrificed to a preoccupation with speed.

The most effective use of electronic performance monitoring is not as a substitute for, but as an aid to, improving traditional performance appraisal (Carayon, 1993). This activity is widely criticized by all parties to it, and many organizations are undertaking modifications (Flynn, 1995). What should they do? How can performance appraisal be improved?

> If less than 10% of your customers judged a product effective and if seven out of 10 said they were more confused than enlightened by it, you would drop it, right? So, why don't more companies drop their annual job-performance reviews? (Schellhardt, 1996)

In virtually every survey ever conducted, both raters and ratees condemn performance appraisal practices in their organizations as resounding failures. The problem is not getting better. As organizations downsize, the number of subordinates that a given manager must evaluate becomes larger and more diverse. The use of work teams can make the evaluation of individuals within them very difficult. Worst of all, perhaps, the frequent reshuffling of personnel can make annual performance reviews useless. Many organizational personnel today have two, three, or more bosses in the course of a year.

So why don't organizations give up performance appraisal? Some, like Hunt Oil Company, have, but lawyers say they do so at their peril. As discussed, performance appraisal information is basic to defense against unfair employment practices charges, to employee development, and to coordinating the human resource functions in an organization. To give up formal performance evaluation because it is unpopular or difficult to do well is to give up a very powerful tool for effective human resource utilization.

Rather than giving up performance appraisal, organizations would be better served by training personnel in how to give and receive performance feedback effectively. Performance appraisal as it is usually carried out is vulnerable to many sources of error that reduce the reliability, validity, acceptability, and usefulness of the evaluation results. Certain decisions about what, when, and how to evaluate reduce some of this error, but there are almost always trade-offs. Straight ranking offsets bias from a central tendency set, but it introduces reliability problems. A central tendency set, on the other hand, produces very reliable ratings—the error it introduces has to do with the validity of the inferences that are made from the evaluations.

Despite the complexity of the situation, the I/O psychology literature offers a number of suggestions for improving performance appraisal. Most of these suggestions have to do with the raters because no method can ever be any better than those who use it. Rater training and the use of multiple raters are discussed here. The use of job analysis for improving performance appraisal is also reviewed.

Training Raters

The recommendation for improving performance appraisal that has been made most frequently is that the people who do the evaluations be given training for the task. I/O psychologists have developed several methods for this training, all of which focus in some way on (1) improving the observation and recall of performance information or (2) improving the understanding and use of the performance appraisal method itself. In their review of the rater training literature, Woehr and Huffcutt (1994) conclude that each of the various rater training strategies is at least moderately effective in bringing about its objective. The extent to which rater training benefits persist without periodic refresher training is open to some question, however (e.g., Ivancevich, 1979; Sulsky & Day, 1994).

The appropriate objective for rater training is also an issue for some I/O psychologists (e.g., Hedge & Kavanagh, 1988). Traditional rater training is oriented toward teaching raters to avoid common errors in performance appraisal. This rater *error* training may well result in substitution of the approach covered in the training, such as using all points of a scale, for the previous approach, such as a leniency set (Bernardin & Pence, 1980). According to Bernardin and Buckley (1981), real improvements in performance appraisal require a training emphasis on appraisal *accuracy*. The basic principles imparted in rater accuracy training are summarized in Exhibit 10–8.

The first principle conveyed in rater accuracy training is standardizing rater observation of ratee behavior in such a way that appraisals are based on a sufficient, accurate, and representative sample of performance-relevant information (not just performance the week before the review, for example). Recall of this information is not the only issue in increasing performance appraisal accuracy (e.g., Sanchez & De La Torre, 1996), but it is a fundamental one. Bernardin and Buckley (1981) suggest that those who do appraisals keep ongoing notes (diaries) about the day-to-day job performance of ratees. They also suggest that the rater's superior monitor this diary to emphasize the organization's commitment to good performance appraisal. (Making good evaluation matter to those who do it is explored in this chapter's At Issue.)

The effect of open-ended ongoing records, such as a performance diary, on the final performance appraisal product depends on a number of factors, especially the diary keeper's choice of information to record (Balzer, 1986; Maurer, Steilberg, & McCoy, 1991). If only behaviors consistent with his or her first or general impressions of the ratee are noted, the performance appraisal will be biased accordingly. For this reason, a behavioral checklist, similar to that shown in Exhibit 10–7, may be preferable for this purpose (e.g., Maurer, Palmer, & Ashe, 1993; Reilly, Henry, & Smither, 1990).

The second principle of rater accuracy training requires educating the raters in an organization to acquire and use a common frame of reference when making evaluations. Frame-of-reference (or FOR) training (Bernardin & Buckley, 1981) includes emphasizing the multiple aspects (dimensions) of job performance, providing examples of each dimension relevant to the rating situation, and giving raters guided practice and feedback in using these standards to evaluate work performance. To date, research on this training indicates that it is very effective at increasing rater accuracy (e.g., Athey & McIntyre, 1987; Pulakos, 1984; Woehr, 1992), but its general superiority for all aspects of rater training has been questioned (e.g., Stamoulis & Hauenstein, 1993).

The third principle of rater accuracy training—reducing the threat in the performance appraisal situation—is one that is often overlooked in general concern with the measurement aspects of performance appraisal. Many people dislike having to "judge" others, especially people with whom they have to work on a daily basis. In addition, the social environment of an organization can create a variety of situations that make performance appraisal an uncomfortable task. Some of the rating strategies people use to defend against this discomfort are leniency (inaccurately inflated ratings), central tendency

---

Standardize the observation of the performance that is the basis for appraisals.

Establish a frame of reference for observing and appraising performance that is shared by all raters in an organization.

Reduce defensive rating by helping raters overcome perceived threats in the appraisal situation.

Exhibit 10–8
SER: The Basic Principles of Rater Accuracy Training

sets, and total reliance on objective performance measures (such as dollar value of sales, number of cases closed, and data from electronic performance monitoring) to the exclusion of other important aspects of performance.

Rater training that increases understanding of the appraisal process in general and teaches skills related to effective use of a particular method should increase a rater's confidence in his or her judgment and reduce defensive rating. Making performance appraisal a year-round affair in the sense of regular joint supervisor-employee feedback meetings to discuss goals and progress should also help; the unpleasant situation in which a supervisor springs bad news on an employee at the annual performance review meeting is avoided.

That meeting is at the heart of the problem for many people who are charged with evaluating the performance of others. Good news presents few problems (making inflated ratings an attractive defensive strategy). Unfortunately, not everyone is a star, and many people find it very difficult to look an employee in the eye and tell him or her that performance on certain criteria (or in general) is mediocre or substandard (e.g., Brewer, Socha, & Potter, 1996).

The ability to deliver criticism in a constructive way is not something a person is either born with or not. It is a skill, and as such it can be taught. The demonstration of good and poor feedback techniques (by means of videotapes, computer software programs, or live actors) followed by imitation, participation in role-playing, and guided practice almost always helps to increase feedback skills. Even limited training can be effective; Apple Computer Inc. offers its managers a three-hour training session in which they practice giving feedback before small and large groups of colleagues, and those who have participated are enthusiastic.

Using Multiple Raters

Second to rater training, the use of more than one rater for each individual being evaluated is the most consistent recommendation in the I/O psychology literature for improving performance appraisal. This practice serves first of all as a check on rater sources of error. The evidence suggests that all raters introduce some error into performance evaluations. The use of multiple raters provides an opportunity for some of these to cancel one another out. One rater's strictness set might be offset by another's leniency set. One rater's lack of information about a particular facet of work behavior could be offset by the relevant observations of the other rater.

The 360-degree performance feedback process is one form of multisource feedback, but to date there is little empirical data available about its effectiveness. In addition, it is a time-consuming process whose practical application is probably limited to certain kinds of occupations and/or to upper levels in an organizational hierarchy. In the majority of organizational settings, the most practical way to get the benefits of multiple performance appraisers is to use two raters with one being the individual evaluated.

Differences between rater and ratee perceptions of performance are common, and they can be substantial. Formalizing ratee perceptions into self-appraisals (on the same instrument used by the other rater) is one way to encourage rater and ratee to confront, rather than to dismiss, one another's evaluations (Campbell & Lee, 1988). In addition, employees have a unique perspective on their own jobs as well as their own job behavior, and this perspective may contribute useful information, both to appraisal and to the identification of factors that may be inhibiting better performance.

A joint self-other performance appraisal method has yet another potential advantage for improving the performance appraisal process. Understanding and being able to make input into decisions that affect them are important components of employee perceptions of procedural justice, and performance appraisal is no exception (e.g., Taylor, Tracy, Renard, Harrison, & Carroll, 1995). To the extent that they are involved in the process, ratees are less likely to be defensive. To the extent that ratees are less defensive, raters feel less defensive.

**Procedural
justice**
See page 199

Basing Performance Appraisal on Job Analysis

Despite some differences of opinion as to the details of performance appraisal methods, I/O psychologists agree that appraisal should be based on behaviors relevant to performing a job. Job descriptions, based on job analysis, are the logical basis for specifying these behaviors, although many organizations still use performance appraisal instruments that have not been developed in this way.

Job analysis is the process of examining a job to determine its component duties and responsibilities, which are then written into a formal statement called a job description. The logic of basing performance appraisal on this description seems self-evident. Certainly, from an employee's point of view, being evaluated on a specific task from a job description makes more sense than being evaluated on "character" (see Exhibit 10–1).

I/O psychologists have ample evidence that people are more receptive to job-relevant performance appraisals, but an instrument based on job descriptions offers other advantages as well. As discussed, most performance appraisal is done by immediate supervisors and managers whose job it is to see that their subordinates are carrying out defined job

Performance evaluation that is based on the job behaviors identified on a job description is more acceptable to raters and ratees alike.

duties. Thus, these are the behaviors they have reason and opportunity to observe and these should be the behaviors they can evaluate most accurately.

Job analysis also offers a possible way out of the considerable time and expense involved in developing and validating individual performance appraisal instruments for the multiplicity of jobs in an organization. Solomon (1990) describes a job-analysis-based method for identifying job-specific performance appraisal factors across a wide range of jobs. Early evidence from a county government with 375 job classifications supports the content validity, reliability, and cost-effectiveness of this approach.

Basing performance appraisal on job analysis offers a number of avenues for improving this important function, and external forces are pushing organizations in the same direction. Both unions and the Equal Employment Opportunity Commission have become increasingly firm about job-related performance appraisal, and job analysis is the means by which this job relatedness is documented. In one well-known review of unfair discrimination charges related to performance appraisal, Feild and Holley (1982) found that defendants (organizations) lost 11 of 14 cases where no job analysis had been used to develop the performance appraisal instrument.

Beginning with job analysis will help build a better performance appraisal program, but it is not a guarantee. A job description is merely a guide as to what to appraise. Developing an instrument from this base does not eliminate the need for rater training, but its specificity should facilitate such training. Nor does this strategy invalidate the suggestion that more than one rater may be useful, especially when it comes time to discuss evaluations with employees.

In closing, it should be noted that the suggestions that have been discussed are for the improvement of performance appraisal in general. Improving any particular program depends on an analysis of existing procedures from the standpoint of the issues relevant to the basic questions of this chapter—what, when, who, and how.

The Performance Appraisal Interview

Throughout the discussion of performance evaluation there has been a tacit assumption that at some point there will be at least one face-to-face interview between rater and ratee at which the results of the performance evaluation will be discussed. This is not always the case. Some organizations do not have such a policy; managers and supervisors are pressed for time, and many dislike the feedback interview process and/or believe that such interviews do little good anyway.

It may be true that feedback sessions are not a sufficient condition for employee performance improvement, but they are a necessary condition if appraisal is to have any developmental utility. Moreover, the Equal Employment Opportunity Commission takes the view that such interviews are necessary if performance appraisal information is to be used for administrative purposes. In the Feild and Holley analysis, organizations won seven out of nine cases in which performance appraisal results had been reviewed formally with employees. All cases in which there had been no such review were lost.

Ideally, the performance appraisal interview should contribute to improved performance on the part of the individual being appraised. The relevant research encompasses a number of issues centering around the question of how such interviews can accomplish this goal in a fashion that is satisfactory to both participants. A review of this literature suggests that a major stumbling block in the usual situation (appraisal has been done by the supervisor and must be discussed with the subordinate) is the very different perspectives of the participants. This difference holds the potential for conflict that can have a variety of negative effects on both the interview and the effectiveness of the feedback.

Conflict is least likely to surface in a performance appraisal interview when the news is good. Things are different when a rater must give negative feedback. As Kay, Meyer, and French (1965) pointed out some years ago, most ratees do not react well to such feedback, even when it is deserved. In another study of ratee reactions to performance feedback, Dipboye and dePontbriand (1981) found a strong positive correlation between (a) favorability of the feedback received in the interview and (b) ratee satisfaction with the interview and the appraisal method. In further analysis, the authors concluded that there was greater acceptance of negative feedback if ratees were allowed to participate in the feedback session, plans and objectives for the future were discussed in addition to evaluations of past performance, and ratees were evaluated on factors they perceived as relevant to their work.

The results of Dipboye and dePontbriand are consistent with subsequent findings in related literature; fairly frequent, mutual problem-solving and goal-setting discussions based on job-relevant factors make for more effective and satisfactory performance appraisal interviews. A two-way exchange of information that addresses the employee's concerns in addition to conveying the supervisor's formal appraisal is the goal. Several items from one organization's checklist for managers' conduct of this type of interview are shown in Exhibit 10–9. Additional considerations and methods for developmental appraisal interviews are discussed by Beer (1987) and Meyer (1991).

Like the suggestions for improving performance appraisal, the implications of the feedback interview research are general. It is not always possible to carry out a fully participative two-way problem-solving and developmentally oriented feedback session with each individual whose performance must be appraised. Cederblom (1982) suggests that knowledge about feedback and feedback interviews be put to use in a manner tailored to the particular employees and job situation. Among the specific suggestions offered for such tailoring are the following:

- Interviews with high performers in jobs that are not routine should be scheduled at flexible intervals and focused on development.

- Interviews with satisfactory employees in routine jobs should be held at relatively infrequent set intervals and focused on evaluation.

- Did I provide clear feedback on my assessment of the employee's performance on major objectives and responsibilities?

- Did I listen to the employee's views on his or her performance in these areas?

- Did I show a willingness to see the merit of the employee's opinions and did I use any new insights to adjust my own opinions?

- Did I ask the employee how I could help in any area that could be improved?

- Did I listen to the employee's assessments of my performance and ask for help in areas that could be improved?

Exhibit 10–9
Performance
Appraisal
Interview
Checklist

• New or poorly performing employees should have frequent feedback interviews with a dual focus on evaluation and feedback.

Meyer (1991) agrees with Cederblom's premise that feedback interviews should be arranged and conducted in a flexible manner. He emphasizes that the traditional interview is inappropriate in many situations, especially when professional and administrative personnel are involved. In such situations, Meyer is a strong advocate of giving the employee the lead in the feedback interview, with the supervisor abandoning the traditional role of judge for the role of counselor or coach.

There are practical difficulties to implementing the suggestions of Cederblom or Meyer in many organizations. Nevertheless, the fundamental message that performance appraisal interviews should not be conducted according to old cut-and-dried formulas is consistent with the current climate of more employee involvement in organizations. If more widely accepted, this view could be an important stimulus to much-needed research and more effective practice in this area.

At Issue

Appraising the Appraisers

Anyone given the opportunity to observe the performance appraisal process over a period of time in a number of organizations must come away impressed with the amount of indifference, resistance, or downright hostility exhibited toward this task by those charged with performing it. A natural reluctance to set themselves up as judges of others may account for some of these reactions. A belief that "nothing is ever done with them anyway" may account for others. Still, these seem inadequate explanations for the frequency with which such reactions are encountered.

A closer look at the administration of performance appraisal programs often reveals a curious phenomenon that may go some way toward explaining common negative rater attitudes about this task. Despite sophisticated instruments, elaborate feedback interview arrangements, and numerous written and verbal statements from top management on the importance of performance appraisal, there seldom are any rewards for doing it well (or any consequences for doing it poorly). Raters understand that they must do it and do it by the date specified, but past that, it often simply does not matter.

Some years ago, Mager and Pipe (1970) wrote a book about analyzing the causes of discrepancies between desired and actual behavior in organizations. Along with many other factors, they discuss the frequency with which such discrepancies occur because doing "it" the desired way does not matter to an employee one way or the other. All too frequently this seems to be the case when "it" is performance appraisal.

To make any work behavior matter, it is necessary for those concerned to recognize the behavior and to reward a person when it is done well. As Mager and Pipe put it: " 'You oughta wanna' does not qualify as a universal incentive . . ." (p. 71), and this applies to performance appraisal as well as to any other behavior. To recognize and reward performance appraisal that is done well, it is necessary to evaluate this behavior; that is, it is necessary to appraise the appraisers.

The I/O psychology literature has much to say about performance appraisal. But it has little to say about differences in (1) the effort raters put into collecting relevant information (making observations) for the appraisal task, (2) the time they take to do the evaluation carefully, or (3) the use they make of the results to help subordinates improve their performance. And it has almost nothing at all to say about rewarding people who take the time to do appraisals well and to work with subordinates on evaluated strengths and weaknesses in the time period between appraisals.

The general lack of attention to appraising the performance appraisal behaviors of raters and to reinforcing those who do it well probably stems in part from the difficulty of differentiating good from poor performance on this complex task. If so, finding ways around this difficulty is a signifi- cant challenge to I/O psychologists. Until this problem is solved, there is no way to make good performance appraisal matter because there is no way to define "good." And until it matters to those who must do it, significant overall improvement in the quality of this critical organizational activity is highly problematical.

Summary

The evaluation of work performance involves finding a combination of what, who, when, and how to measure this performance that produces a measurement sufficiently reliable and valid to be used for a wide variety of organizational and employee-centered purposes. The potential for error in this measurement is substantial because it can originate in the instrument used, the environment in which appraisal takes place, the individual doing the rating, or any combination of these sources. Suggestions for reducing this error in- clude basing the appraisal instrument on job analysis, training the raters, and using more than one rater.

The performance appraisal interview is the usual vehicle for providing feedback to ratees about the evaluation of their work. This process can be hampered considerably by the different perspectives of the participants and by the necessity for giving negative feedback to some ratees. A joint problem-solving approach consistent with the limits of the situation can often improve the effectiveness of, and employee satisfaction with, these interviews.

Questions for Review and Discussion

1. Describe the important factors that affect the level of an individual's performance in the "job" of student in this class, and explain the implications of this discussion for the evaluation of that performance.

2. Describe the strengths and weaknesses of the three major choices of what to evalu- ate when appraising work performance. Give one example of a situation in which each of these choices might be appropriate and briefly explain why.

3. Make what you think is an appropriate checklist (unweighted) for the classroom be- havior of a college professor. Explain briefly (in general terms) how you and your classmates might go about using your checklists to develop a BARS for evaluating this aspect of a professor's job (classroom behavior).

4. Compare and contrast the use of performance appraisal for administrative and de- velopmental purposes. Of the various sources of performance appraisal error dis- cussed, which are more likely to occur when the appraiser knows the results will be used for one purpose or the other? Which sources of error do you think are proba- bly independent of rating purpose, and why?

5. Summarize the major problems that interfere with effective and satisfactory perfor- mance appraisal interviews and outline a practical strategy for reducing them.

Key Terms

comparative performance appraisal

behavior-based performance appraisal

determinants of work performance

electronic performance monitoring

individual performance appraisal

peer appraisal

performance appraisal

performance appraisal interview

performance management

rater bias

rater training

self-appraisal

References

Aiello, J. R., & Chomiak, A. (1992). *The effects of computer monitoring and distraction on task performance.* Unpublished manuscript.

Aiello, J. R., & Kolb, K. J. (1995). Electronic performance monitoring and social context: Impact on productivity and stress. *Journal of Applied Psychology, 80,* 339–353.

Ambrose, M. L., & Kulik, C. T. (1994). The effect of information format and performance pattern on performance appraisal judgments in a computerized performance monitoring context. *Journal of Applied Social Psychology, 24,* 801–823.

Amick, B. C., & Smith, M. J. (1992). Stress, computer-based work monitoring and measurement systems: A conceptual overview. *Applied Ergonomics, 23,* 6–16.

Antonioni, D. (1994). The effects of feedback accountability on upward appraisal ratings. *Personnel Psychology, 47,* 349–356.

Ash, A. (1994). Participants' reaction to subordinate appraisal of managers: Results of a pilot. *Public Personnel Management, 23,* 237–256.

Athey, T. R., & McIntyre, R. M. (1987). Effect of rater training on rater accuracy: Levels of processing theory and social facilitation theory perspectives. *Journal of Applied Psychology, 72,* 567–572.

Austin, J. T., & Villanova, P. (1992). The criterion problem: 1917–1992. *Journal of Applied Psychology, 77,* 836–874.

Avolio, B. J., Waldman, D. A., & McDaniel, M. A. (1990). Age and work performance in nonmanagerial jobs: The effects of experience and occupation type. *Academy of Management Journal, 33,* 407–422.

Balzer, W. K. (1986). Biases in the recording of performance related information: The effects of initial impression and centrality of the appraisal task. *Organizational Behavior and Human Decision Processes, 37,* 329–347.

Balzer, W. K., & Sulsky, L. M. (1992). Halo and performance appraisal research: A critical examination. *Journal of Applied Psychology, 77,* 975–985.

Banks, C. G., & Roberson, L. (1985). Performance appraisers as test developers. *Academy of Management Review, 10,* 128–142.

Beer, M. (1987). Performance appraisal. In J. W. Lorsch (Ed.), *Handbook of organizational behavior.* Englewood Cliffs, NJ: Prentice-Hall.

Benedict, M. E., & Levine, E. L. (1988). Delay and distortion: Tacit influences on performance appraisal effectiveness. *Journal of Applied Psychology, 73,* 507–514.

Benson, P. G., Buckley, M. R., & Hall, S. (1988). The impact of rating scale format on rater accuracy: An evaluation of the mixed standard scale. *Journal of Management, 14,* 415–423.

Bernardin, H. J., & Buckley, M. R. (1981). A consideration of strategies in rater training. *Academy of Management Review, 6,* 205–212.

Bernardin, H. J., & Pence, E. C. (1980). Effects of rater training: Creating new response sets and decreasing accuracy. *Journal of Applied Psychology, 65,* 60–66.

Bernardin, H. J., & Smith, P. C. (1981). A clarification of some issues regarding the development and use of behaviorally anchored rating scales (BARS). *Journal of Applied Psychology, 66,* 458–463.

Bernardin, H. J., & Villanova, P. (1986). Performance appraisal. In E. A. Locke (Ed.), *Generalizing from laboratory to field settings.* Lexington, MA: Lexington.

Blanz, F., & Ghiselli, E. E. (1972). The mixed standard scale: A new rating system. *Personnel Psychology, 2,* 185–199.

Blumberg, M., & Pringle, C. D. (1982). The missing opportunity in organizational research: Some implications for a theory of work performance. *Academy of Management Review, 7,* 560–569.

Borman, W. C., & Motowidlo, S. J. (1993). Expanding the criterion domain to include elements of contextual performance. In N. Schmitt & W. C. Borman (Eds.), *Personnel selection in organizations.* San Francisco: Jossey-Bass.

Brewer, N., Socha, L., & Potter, R. (1996). Gender differences in supervisors' use of performance feedback. *Journal of Applied Social Psychology, 26,* 786–803.

Campbell, D. J., & Lee, C. (1988). Self-appraisal in performance evaluation: Development versus evaluation. *Academy of Management Review, 13,* 302–314.

Campbell, J. P. (1990). Modeling the performance prediction problem in industrial and organizational psychology. In M. D. Dunnette & L. M. Hough (Eds.), *Handbook of industrial and organizational psychology* (Vol. 1, 2nd ed.). Palo Alto, CA: Consulting Psychologists' Press.

Carayon, P. (1993). Effect of electronic performance monitoring on job design and worker stress: Review of the literature and conceptual model. *Human Factors, 35,* 385–395.

Cederblom, D. (1982). The performance appraisal interview: A review, implications, and suggestions. *Academy of Management Review, 7,* 219–227.

Cleveland, J. N., Murphy, K. R., & Williams, R. E. (1989). Multiple uses of performance appraisal: Prevalence and correlates. *Journal of Applied Psychology, 74,* 130–135.

Collins, M. A., & Zebrowitz, L. A. (1995). The contributions of appearance to occupational outcomes in civilian and military settings. *Journal of Applied Social Psychology, 25,* 129–163.

Coward, W. M., & Sackett, P. R. (1990). Linearity of ability-performance relationships: A reconfirmation. *Journal of Applied Psychology, 75,* 297–300.

Cummings, L. L., & Schwab, D. P. (1973). *Performance in organizations: Determinants and appraisals.* Glenview, IL: Scott, Foresman.

De Nisi, A. S., Randolph, W. A., & Blencoe, A. G. (1983). Potential problems with peer ratings. *Academy of Management Journal, 26,* 457–464.

Dipboye, R. L., & dePontbriand, R. (1981). Correlates of employee reactions to performance appraisals and appraisal systems. *Journal of Applied Psychology, 66,* 248–251.

Duarte, N. T., Goodson, J. R., & Klich, N. R. (1993). How do I like thee? Let me appraise the ways. *Journal of Organizational Behavior, 14,* 239–249.

DuBois, C. L. Z., Sackett, P. R., Zedeck, S., & Fogli, L. (1993). Further exploration of typical and maximum performance criteria: Definitional issues, prediction, and white-black differences. *Journal of Applied Psychology, 78,* 205–211.

Dunnette, M. D., & Borman, W. C. (1979). Personnel selection and classification systems. *Annual Review of Psychology, 30,* 477–525.

Farh, J. L., & Werbel, J. D. (1986). Effects of purpose of the appraisal and expectation of validation on self-appraisal leniency. *Journal of Applied Psychology, 71,* 527–529.

Feild, H. S., & Holley, W. H. (1982). The relationship of performance appraisal system characteristics to verdicts in selected employment discrimination cases. *Academy of Management Journal, 25,* 392–406.

Ferris, G. R., Judge, T. A., Rowland, K. M., & Fitzgibbons, D. E. (1994). Subordinate influence and the performance evaluation process: Test of a model. *Organizational Behavior and Human Decision Processes, 58,* 101–135.

Finkelstein, L. M., Burke, M. J., & Raju, N. S. (1995). Age discrimination in simulated employment contexts: An integrative analysis. *Journal of Applied Psychology, 80,* 652–663.

Fisher, C. D. (1979). Transmission of positive and negative feedback to subordinates: A laboratory investigation. *Journal of Applied Psychology, 64,* 533–540.

Fisher, C. D. (1989). Current and recurrent challenges in HRM. *Journal of Management, 15,* 157–180.

Flanagan, J. C. (1954). The critical incident technique. *Psychological Bulletin, 51,* 327–358.

Flynn, C. F., Sipes, W. E., Grosenbach, M. J., & Ellsworth, J. (1994). Top performer survey: Computerized psychological assessment in aircrew. *Aviation, Space, and Environmental Medicine, 65,* A39–A44.

Flynn, G. (1995). Employee evaluations get so-so grades. *Personnel Journal, 74,* 21–22.

Fox, S., Caspy, T., & Reisler, A. (1994). Variables affecting leniency, halo and validity of self-appraisal. *Journal of Occupational and Organizational Psychology, 67,* 45–56.

Fried, Y., & Tiegs, R. B. (1995). Supervisors' role conflict and role ambiguity differential relations with performance ratings of subordinates and the moderating effect of screening ability. *Journal of Applied Psychology, 80,* 282–291.

Furnham, A., & Stringfield, P. (1994). Congruence of self and subordinate ratings of managerial practices as a correlate of supervisor evaluation. *Journal of Occupational and Organizational Psychology, 67,* 57–67.

Gallatin, L. (1989). *Electronic monitoring in the workplace: Supervision or surveillance?* Boston: Massachusetts Coalition on New Office Technology.

Gandz, J., & Murray, V. V. (1980). The experience of workplace politics. *Academy of Management Journal, 23,* 237–251.

George, D. I., & Smith, M. C. (1990). An empirical comparison of self-assessment and organizational assessment in personnel selection. *Public Personnel Management, 19,* 175–190.

Gioia, D. A., & Longnecker, C. O. (1994). Delving into the dark side: The politics of executive appraisal. *Organizational Dynamics, 22,* 47–58.

Glen, R. M. (1990). Performance appraisal: An unnerving yet useful process. *Public Personnel Management, 19,* 1–10.

Gomez-Mejia, L. R. (1988). Evaluating employee performance: Does the appraisal instrument make a difference? *Journal of Organizational Behavior Management, 9,* 155–172.

Hall, J. (1994). Americans know how to be productive if managers will let them. *Organizational Dynamics, 22,* 33–46.

Harris, M. M., & Schaubroeck, J. (1988). A meta-analysis of self-supervisor, self-peer, and peer-supervisor ratings. *Personnel Psychology, 41,* 43–62.

Harris, M. M., Smith, D. E., & Champagne, D. (1995). A field study of performance appraisal purpose: Research versus administrative-based ratings. *Personnel Psychology, 48,* 151–160.

Hassell, B. L., & Perrewe, P. L. (1995). An examination of beliefs about older workers: Do stereotypes still exist? *Journal of Organizational Behavior, 16,* 457–468.

Hedge, J. W., & Kavanagh, M. J. (1988). Improving the accuracy of performance evaluations: Comparison of three methods of performance appraiser training. *Journal of Applied Psychology, 73,* 68–73.

Heneman, R. L., & Wexley, K. N. (1983). The effects of time delay in rating and amount of information observed on performance rating accuracy. *Academy of Management Journal, 26,* 677–686.

Hunt, S. T. (1996). Generic work behavior: An investigation into the dimensions of entry-level, hourly job performance. *Personnel Psychology, 49,* 1–49.

Ilgen, D. R., & Feldman, J. M. (1983). Performance appraisal: A process focus. In L. L. Cummings & B. M. Staw (Eds.), *Research in organizational behavior* (Vol. 5). Greenwich, CT: JAI.

Ilgen, D. R., Peterson, R. B., Martin, B. A., & Boeschen, D. A. (1981). Supervisor and subordinate reactions to performance appraisal sessions. *Organizational Behavior and Human Performance, 28,* 311–330.

Ivancevich, J. M. (1979). Longitudinal study of the effects of rater training on psychometric error in ratings. *Journal of Applied Psychology, 64,* 502–508.

Judge, T. A., & Ferris, G. R. (1993). Social context of performance evaluation decisions. *Academy of Management Journal, 36,* 80–105.

Kane, J. S., Bernardin, H. J., Villanova, P., & Peyrefitte, J. (1995). Stability of rater leniency: Three studies. *Academy of Management Journal, 38,* 1036–1051.

Karl, K. A., & Wexley, K. N. (1989). Patterns of performance and rating frequency: Influence on the assessment of performance. *Journal of Management, 15,* 5–20.

Katz, D. (1964). The motivational basis of organizational behavior. *Behavioral Science, 9,* 131–146.

Kay, E., Meyer, H. H., & French, J. R. P. (1965). Effects of threat in a performance appraisal interview. *Journal of Applied Psychology, 49,* 311–317.

Kingstrom, P. O., & Bass, A. R. (1981). A critical analysis of studies comparing behaviorally anchored rating scales (BARS) and other rating formats. *Personnel Psychology, 34,* 263–289.

Kinicki, A. J., Hom, P. W., Trost, M. R., & Wade, K. J. (1995). Effects of category prototypes on performance-rating accuracy. *Journal of Applied Psychology, 80,* 354–370.

Klimoski, R., & Inks, L. (1990). Accountability forces in performance appraisal. *Organizational Behavior and Human Decision Processes, 45,* 194–208.

Knauft, E. B. (1948). Construction and use of weighted checklist rating scales for two industrial situations. *Journal of Applied Psychology, 32,* 63–70.

Kraiger, K. (1985). Analysis of relationships among self, peer, and supervisory ratings of performance. Prepublication report.

Kraiger, K., & Ford, J. K. (1985). A meta-analysis of ratee race effects in performance ratings. *Journal of Applied Psychology, 70,* 56–65.

Landau, J. (1995). The relationship of race and gender to managers' ratings of promotion potential. *Journal of Organizational Behavior, 16,* 391–400.

Landy, F. J., & Farr, J. L. (1980). Performance rating. *Psychological Bulletin, 87,* 72–107.

Latham, G. P., Fay, C., & Saari, L. M. (1979). The development of behavioral observation scales for appraising the performance of foremen. *Personnel Psychology, 32,* 299–311.

Latham, G. P., & Wexley, K. N. (1981). *Increasing productivity through performance appraisal.* Reading, MA: Addison-Wesley.

Lawrence, B. S. (1988). New wrinkles in the theory of age: Demography, norms, and performance ratings. *Academy of Management Journal, 31,* 309–337.

Lazer, R. I., & Wikstrom, W. S. (1977). *Appraising managerial performance: Current practices and future directions.* New York: The Conference Board.

Mabe, P. A., III., & West, S. G. (1982). Validity of self-evaluation of ability: A review and meta-analysis. *Journal of Applied Psychology, 67,* 280–296.

Mager, R. F., & Pipe, P. (1970). *Analyzing performance problems or "You really oughta wanna!"* Belmont, CA: Fearon.

Maroney, B. P., & Buckley, M. R. (1992). Does research in performance appraisal influence the practice of performance appraisal? Regretfully not! *Public Personnel Management, 21,* 185–196.

Martell, R. F., & Borg, M. R. (1993). A comparison of the behavioral rating accuracy of groups and individuals. *Journal of Applied Psychology, 78,* 43–50.

Maurer, T. J., Palmer, J. K., & Ashe, D. K. (1993). Diaries, checklists, evaluations, and contrast effects in measurement of behavior. *Journal of Applied Psychology, 78,* 226–231.

Maurer, T., Steilberg, C., & McCoy, J. (1991). Effects of reviewing prior performance information immediately before subsequent evaluations. Presented at the 99th convention of the American Psychological Association, San Francisco.

Maurer, T. J., & Taylor, M. A. (1994). Is sex by itself enough? An explanation of gender bias issues in performance appraisal. *Organizational Behavior and Human Decision Processes, 60,* 231–251.

McCloy, R. A., Campbell, J. P., & Cudeck, R. (1994). A confirmatory test of a model of performance determinants. *Journal of Applied Psychology, 79,* 493–505.

McEvoy, G. M. (1990). Public sector managers' reactions to appraisals by subordinates. *Public Personnel Management, 19,* 201–212.

McEvoy, G. M., & Buller, P. F. (1987). User acceptance of peer appraisals in an industrial setting. *Personnel Psychology, 40,* 785–797.

McNeely, B. L., & Meglino, B. M. (1994). The role of dispositional and situational antecedents in prosocial organizational behavior: An examination of the intended beneficiaries of prosocial behavior. *Journal of Applied Psychology, 79,* 836–844.

Meyer, H. H. (1991). A solution to the performance appraisal feedback enigma. *Academy of Management Executive, 5,* 68–76.

Miner, J. B. (1988). Development and application of the rated ranking technique in performance appraisal. *Journal of Occupational Psychology, 61,* 291–305.

Mitchell, T. R., & Kalb, L. S. (1981). Effects of outcome knowledge and outcome valence on supervisors' evaluations. *Journal of Applied Psychology, 66,* 604–612.

Mitchell, T. R., & Liden, R. C. (1982). The effects of social context on performance evaluations. *Organizational Behavior and Human Performance, 29,* 241–256.

Moravec, M., Juliff, R., & Hesler, K. (1995). Partnerships help a company manage performance. *Personnel Journal, 75,* 104–108.

Murphy, K. R., Gannett, B. A., Herr, B. M., & Chen, J. A. (1986). Effects of subsequent performance on evaluations of previous performance. *Journal of Applied Psychology, 71,* 427–431.

Murphy, K. R., Jako, R. A., & Anhalt, R. L. (1993). Nature and consequences of halo error: A critical analysis. *Journal of Applied Psychology, 78,* 218–225.

Murphy, K. R., & Reynolds, D. H. (1988). Does true halo affect observed halo? *Journal of Applied Psychology, 73,* 235–238.

O'Reilly, C., & Chatman, J. A. (1994). Working smarter and harder: A longitudinal study of managerial success. *Administrative Science Quarterly, 39,* 603–627.

Ostroff, C. (1993). Rater perceptions, satisfaction and performance ratings. *Journal of Occupational and Organizational Psychology, 66,* 345–356.

Pearce, J. L., & Porter, L. W. (1986). Employee responses to formal performance appraisal feedback. *Journal of Applied Psychology, 71,* 211–218.

Peters, L. H., & O'Connor, E. J. (1980). Situational constraints and work outcomes: The influence of a frequently overlooked construct. *Academy of Management Review, 5,* 391–397.

Piotrowski, M. J., Barnes-Farrell, J. L., & Esrig, F. H. (1989). Behaviorally anchored bias: A replication and extension of Murphy and Constans. *Journal of Applied Psychology, 74,* 823–826.

Posdakoff, P. M., & MacKenzie, S. B. (1994). Organizational citizenship behaviors and sales unit effectiveness. *Journal of Marketing Research, 31,* 351–363.

Pulakos, E. D. (1984). A comparison of rater training programs: Error training and accuracy training. *Journal of Applied Psychology, 69,* 581–588.

Quiñones, M. A., Ford, J. K., & Teachout, M. S. (1995). The relationship between work experience and job performance: A conceptual and meta-analytic review. *Personnel Psychology, 48,* 887–910.

Reilly, R., Henry, S., & Smither, J. (1990). An examination of the effects of using behavior checklists on the construct validity of assessment center dimensions. *Personnel Psychology, 43,* 71–84.

Riggio, R. E., & Cole, E. J. (1992). Agreement between subordinate and superior ratings of supervisory performance and effects on self and subordinate job satisfaction. *Journal of Occupational and Organizational Psychology, 65,* 151–158.

Ross, J., & Ferris, K. R. (1980). Interpersonal attraction and organizational outcomes: A field examination. *Administrative Science Quarterly, 26,* 617–632.

Saavedra, R., & Kwun, S. K. (1993). Peer evaluation in self-managing work groups. *Journal of Applied Psychology, 78,* 450–462.

Sackett, P. R., Zedeck, S., & Fogli, L. (1988). Relations between measures of typical and maximum job performance. *Journal of Applied Psychology, 73,* 482–486.

Sanchez, J. I., & De La Torre, P. (1996). A second look at the relationship between rating and behavioral accuracy in performance appraisal. *Journal of Applied Psychology, 81,* 3–10.

Schellhardt, T. D. (1996, Nov. 19). It's time to evaluate your work, and all involved are groaning. *Wall Street Journal,* pp. A1, 5.

Schoorman, F. D. (1988). Escalation bias in performance appraisals: An unintended consequence of supervisor participation in hiring decisions. *Journal of Applied Psychology, 73,* 58–62.

Schrader, B. W., & Steiner, D. D. (1996). Common comparison standards: An approach to improving agreement between self and supervisory performance ratings. *Journal of Applied Psychology, 81,* 813–820.

Shepherd, R. J. (1995). A personal perspective on aging and productivity, with particular reference to physically demanding work. *Ergonomics, 38,* 617–636.

Shore, L. N., & Thornton, G. C., III. (1986). Effects of gender on self- and supervisory ratings. *Academy of Management Journal, 29,* 115–129.

Sidanius, J., & Crane, M. (1989). Job evaluation and gender: The case of university faculty. *Journal of Applied Social Psychology, 19,* 174–197.

Simonson, I., & Nye, P. (1992). The effect of accountability on susceptibility to decision errors. *Organizational Behavior and Human Decision Processes, 51,* 416–446.

Smith, M. J., Carayon, P., Sanders, K. J., Lim, S-Y, & LeGrande, D. (1992). Employee stress and health complaints in jobs with and without electronic performance monitoring. *Applied Ergonomics, 23,* 17–28.

Smith, P. C., & Kendall, L. M. (1963). Retranslation of expectations: An approach to the construction of unambiguous anchors for rating scales. *Journal of Applied Psychology, 47,* 149–155.

Smither, J. W., Wohlers, A. J., & London, M. (1995). A field study of reactions to normative versus individualized upward feedback. *Group and Organization Management, 20,* 61–89.

Solomon, R. J. (1990). Developing job specific appraisal factors in large organizations. *Public Personnel Management, 19,* 11–24.

Stamoulis, D. T., & Hauenstein, N. M. A. (1993). Rater training and rating accuracy: Training for dimensional accuracy versus training for ratee differentiation. *Journal of Applied Psychology, 78,* 994–1003.

Stanton, J. M., & Barnes-Farrell, J. L. (1996). Effects of electronic performance monitoring on personal control, task satisfaction, and task performance. *Journal of Applied Psychology, 81,* 738–745.

Steel, R. P., Mento, A. J., & Hendrix, W. H. (1987). Constraining forces and the work performance of finance company cashiers. *Journal of Management, 13,* 473–482.

Steiner, D. D., Rain, J. S., & Smalley, M. M. (1993). Distributional ratings of performance: Further examination of a new rating format. *Journal of Applied Psychology, 78,* 438–442.

Sterns, H. L., & Miklos, S. M. (1995). The aging worker in a changing environment: Organizational and individual issues. *Journal of Vocational Behavior, 47,* 248–268.

Sulsky, L. M., & Day, D. V. (1994). Effects of frame-of-reference training on rater accuracy under alternative time delays. *Journal of Applied Psychology, 79,* 535–543.

Sumer, H. C., & Knight, P. A. (1996). Assimilation and contrast effects in performance ratings: Effects of rating the previous performance on rating subsequent performance. *Journal of Applied Psychology, 81,* 436–442.

Taylor, M. S., Tracy, K. B., Renard, M. K., Harrison, J. K., & Carrol, J. J. (1995). Due process in performance appraisal: A quasi-experiment in procedural justice. *Administrative Science Quarterly, 40,* 495–523.

Thacker, R. A., & Wayne, S. J. (1995). An examination of the relationship between upward influence tactics and assessments of promotability. *Journal of Management, 21,* 739–757.

Thorndike, E. L. (1920). A constant error in psychological ratings. *Journal of Applied Psychology, 4,* 25–29.

Thornton, G. C., III. (1980). Psychometric properties of self-appraisals of job performance. *Personnel Psychology, 33,* 263–271.

Tsui, A. S., & Barry, B. (1986). Interpersonal affect and rating errors. *Academy of Management Journal, 29,* 586–599.

Tziner, A., & Latham, G. P. (1989). The effects of appraisal instrument, feedback, and goal-setting on worker satisfaction and commitment. *Journal of Organizational Behavior, 10,* 145–153.

Van Scotter, J. R., & Motowidlo, S. J. (1996). Interpersonal facilitation and job dedication as separate facets of contextual performance. *Journal of Applied Psychology, 81,* 525–531.

Varca, P. E., & James-Valutis, M. (1993). The relationship of ability and satisfaction to job performance. *Applied Psychology: An International Review, 42,* 265–275.

Villanova, P., Bernardin, H. J., Dahmus, S. A., & Sims, R. L. (1993). Rater leniency and performance appraisal discomfort. *Educational and Psychological Measurement, 53,* 789–799.

Viswesvaran, C., Schmidt, F. L., & Ones, D. S. (1996). Comparative analysis of the reliability of job performance ratings. *Journal of Applied Psychology, 81,* 557–574.

Waldman, D. A., & Avolio, B. J. (1986). A meta-analysis of age differences in job performance. *Journal of Applied Psychology, 71,* 33–38.

Wayne, S. J., & Liden, R. C. (1995). Effects of impression management on performance ratings: A longitudinal study. *Academy of Management Journal, 38,* 232–260.

Werner, J. M. (1994). Dimensions that make a difference: Examining the impact of in-role and extrarole behaviors on supervisory ratings. *Journal of Applied Psychology, 79,* 98–107.

Williams, J. R., & Levy, P. E. (1992). The effects of perceived system knowledge on the agreement between self-ratings and supervisor ratings. *Personnel Psychology, 45,* 835–847.

Woehr, D. J. (1992). Performance dimension accessibility: Implications for rating accuracy. *Journal of Organizational Behavior, 13,* 357–367.

Woehr, D. J., & Feldman, J. (1993). Processing objective and question order effects on the causal relation between memory and judgment in performance appraisal: The tip of the iceberg. *Journal of Applied Psychology, 78,* 232–241.

Woehr, D. J., & Huffcutt, A. I. (1994). Rater training for performance appraisal: A quantitative review. *Journal of Occupational and Organizational Psychology, 67,* 189–205.

Wyer, R. S., Jr., & Srull, T. K. (1981). Category accessibility: Some theoretical and empirical issues concerning the processing of social stimulus information. In E. T. Higgins, C. P. Herman, & M. P. Zanna (Eds.), *Social cognition: The Ontario symposium* (Vol. 1). Hillsdale, NJ: LEA.

Zajonc, R. B. (1965, July 16). Social facilitation. *Science,* pp. 269–274.

Zalesny, M. D. (1990). Rater confidence and social influence in performance appraisal. *Journal of Applied Psychology, 75,* 274–289.

Zalesny, M. D., & Kirsch, M. P. (1989). The effect of similarity on performance ratings and interrater agreement. *Human Relations, 42,* 81–96.

Zammuto, R. F., London, M., & Rowland, K. M. (1982). Organization and rater differences in performance appraisals. *Personnel Psychology, 35,* 643–658.

Job Analysis and Evaluation

The last thing David P. Rogers remembers seeing on that awful night . . . was a car tire flying toward him as he drove down the Harbor Freeway. . . .

It's been a long road back, but today Rogers, 39, enjoys a rich professional life working with several prenatal diagnostic centers as a clinical geneticist. . . .

Rogers uses a Macintosh PowerBook computer and a Macintosh desktop to take notes, write reports and letters, send e-mail and access online medical databases. He can move only his right arm, which he uses to operate his wheelchair, and the computers are controlled with an ultrasound device called a Headmaster. . . .

"Technology has the power to drastically reduce the percentage of people with disabilities who are unemployed in this country," says Mary Lester, associate director of the San Rafael, California–based Alliance for Technology Access.

WITH THE passage of the 1990 Americans with Disabilities Act, the services of consultants from groups like the Alliance for Technology Access, the National Institutes of Health, and others are increasingly in demand by employers as well as by disabled individuals. Among other provisions, the Americans with Disabilities Act requires organizations to make reasonable accommodation to assist disabled employees in performing their job functions.

Accommodating people with disabilities in jobs usually performed by people without disabilities may occasionally require sophisticated technological equipment like that used by Dr. David Rogers. But it can also be as simple as letting an employee sit down to do a job that has always been done in a standing position. The flexibility to adapt jobs to the special needs of employees with disabilities of any kind begins with detailed knowledge of what is to be accomplished on a job. This information is the data collected in the process of job analysis.

In addition to providing the basis for modifying traditional jobs so that they can be carried out by employees with disabilities, the information provided by job analysis can be applied to a wide variety of other purposes. Among these are employee development, collective bargaining, performance appraisal, human resource planning, wage and salary administration, fair employment practices documentation, and employee recruiting, selection, placement, and training. The decision to forego formal job analysis is merely a decision to get the information required to carry out these activities in a less systematic way.

Introduction to Job Analysis

Organizations are social systems brought into being and designed to accomplish things that individuals acting alone cannot accomplish. These things fit into two broad categories—the manufacture of a product, such as a washing machine, and the delivery of a service, such as insurance. Many organizations market both products and services; Sears, Roebuck and Company sells both washing machines and insurance. Mail-order companies provide a service (convenient purchase of goods) and a product (the goods that are purchased).

Products or services (or both) are the output of an organization. They are the end results of the thousands of tasks that are performed by the members of the organization. A

task is an assigned piece of work that is to be finished to some standard within some time period. Some of the tasks performed in organizations relate directly to the production of the product or the delivery of the service; an employee in the appliance section of a Sears retail store helps a customer select a washing machine, conducts the financial transactions, and arranges for the delivery of the machine.

Other tasks in organizations relate to their management. Another Sears employee is responsible for making sure that there is a salesperson in the appliance section to wait on customers and that this person does his or her job in the prescribed manner. Still other tasks are support tasks for members of the organization. The human resource department has hired the salespeople and been instrumental in promoting the appliance manager to his or her current position.

The collection of tasks, responsibilities, and activities that are to be performed by an individual define a **position,** the basic building block of an organization. A position exists whether or not there is a person (incumbent) holding it, and it can be created, abolished, or altered at will by the organization (as happens during a reorganization). Identical or similar positions in an organization make up one **job.** A group of jobs that are sufficiently similar in terms of their work activities to be grouped together for a given purpose (such as payroll or a validity generalization study) is called a **job family.** The relationship between tasks, positions, jobs, and job families is illustrated in Figure 11–1.

Validity generalization
See pages 72–74

The top row of boxes in the figure shows the various tasks that must be performed in the office of a group of physicians. Each employee in this office occupies one position that is defined by primary responsibility for certain of these tasks. The positions defined by the same tasks make up one job. Three jobs (seven positions) are similar enough in terms of their basic duties to be grouped into one job family, here called "front office, clerical."

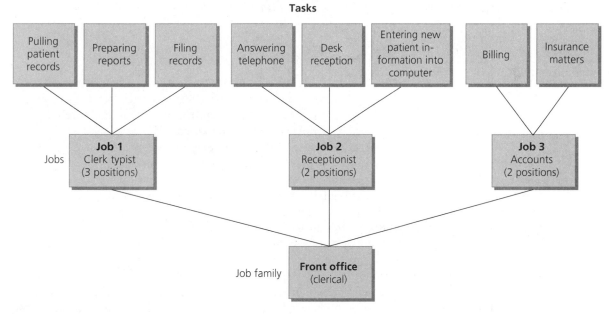

Figure 11–1
Tasks, Positions, Jobs, and Job Families

Inference
See pages 35–43

Groupings like that in Figure 11–1 are created by a process called job classification, one application of job analysis data. Job classification is far from a cut-and-dried process. How similar is similar enough? Is similarity on some aspects of a job more important than similarity on others? The answers to these and other questions are only as good as the data upon which they are based. Some I/O psychologists have taken the position that a holistic approach to job analysis based on inferences regarding job content, rather than on data, is adequate for this and other personnel-related purposes (e.g., Schmidt, Hunter, & Pearlman, 1981). The majority opinion, as well as the position of the courts, however, lies with traditional job analysis.

What Is Job Analysis?

Job analysis is a defined data collection and analysis procedure through which information about job behaviors is obtained. Behaviors in this context must be *observable*; that is, they must be "able to be seen, heard, or otherwise perceived by a person other than the person performing the action" (EEOC, 1978, Section 1607.16N). It is difficult to overemphasize the importance of restricting job analysis to observables. If job analysis data are to be valid, they must be reliable; that is, independent analysts with about the same degree of familiarity with a job should get similar results. To the extent that a job analyst strays from behaviors that can be "seen, heard, or otherwise perceived," reliability is reduced.

Keeping the importance of observable behaviors firmly in mind should help to avoid the confusion that sometimes arises between job analysis and other organizational activities. Job analysis is a process for describing *only* what must be done on a job. By itself it has nothing to say about the best way to do a job (job design), what kind of person is needed to do the job (job specification), how well it is being done currently (performance appraisal), or what it is worth to the organization to have this job done (job evaluation). All of these activities are (or should be) *applications* of job analysis data.

Job Analysis and Equal Employment Opportunity

Job analyis data are also central to an organization's defense against unlawful employment discrimination suits. In one of the first of these cases, which was heard more than 20 years ago, performance evaluations used by the Mississippi Extension Service were ruled invalid because the appraisal instruments were not based on job analysis.

Adverse impact
See pages 115–116

Among other provisions not relevant here, fair employment practice laws and legislation in this country require that organizations use selection procedures that do not have adverse impact on groups protected by law, and that they treat employees who are in similar circumstances as regards job level, tenure, and so on, equally. Should an organization be challenged for violating either of these mandates, the only possible successful defense is to demonstrate the job relatedness of the action. Refusing to promote an employee because he or she is considered unfriendly by co-workers, for example, violates the equal treatment requirement *unless* it can be demonstrated empirically that friendliness is essential to satisfactory performance on the new job.

The ability to demonstrate job relatedness does not guarantee that an organization will win a discrimination suit filed against it, but the organization is almost certain to lose if it cannot make this connection. The crucial role of job analysis in demonstrating job relatedness is laid out quite clearly in the Supreme Court decision in *Albemarle Paper*

Company v. Moody (1975), and the Equal Employment Opportunity Commission publication *Guidelines on Employment Testing Procedures* (EEOC, 1978) states explicitly that organizations are responsible for carrying out such analyses. These guidelines are not laws; they are intended to assist organizations in complying with the laws and with court interpretations of the laws under Title VII of the 1964 Civil Rights Act.

The wisdom of following the uniform guidelines, despite the fact that they have no legal status in and of themselves, does not seem open to question. The analysis of relevant court cases reveals that many judges are reluctant to accept findings that are inconsistent with the guidelines (e.g., Kleiman v. Faley, 1985). Thus, time and money spent on job analysis today may be time and money—and court appearances—saved tomorrow.

Preparing for Job Analysis

Job analysis is a data collection process. If the process is done well, the resulting data have great utility for coordinating the personnel-related functions of an organization. To perform job analysis well requires preparation. Who is to perform the job analysis? What information is to be collected? What source or sources of information will be used?

Who Performs a Job Analysis?

Job analysis traditionally has been carried out by human resource personnel trained in the process. If no trained specialist is available, an I/O psychologist or other outside consultant may do the analyses and/or train someone in the company to perform this function. The emphasis is on training when it comes to deciding who is to undertake job analysis. Most methods require interpersonal skills as well as technical skills. They involve personal interaction with job incumbents, and this situation can be threatening to employees. Many people still confuse job analysis with time and motion study, which, in turn, are often perceived as means to get more work out of people without paying them more money.

The threat that some employees may feel when someone shows up to discuss what they do on the job can lead them to distort the information they provide. Even when no threat is perceived, the information may not be accurate if the employees do not understand what is expected of them. In either case, knowing how to go about getting information, as well as what information to get, is vital in job analysis.

What Information Is to Be Collected?

The specific data yielded by job analysis depend on the method employed, but any or all of the kinds of information listed in Exhibit 11–1 may be collected. As mentioned, this information can be used to help an organization carry out an impressive variety of individual-, organizational-, and research-oriented activities. Information about work procedures (IB) may be used to help develop safety training programs, for example. Information about the place of a job in the organization structure (IIIA) is useful for individual career counseling. Information about work standards (IIB) can help human factors psychologists involved in job design/redesign.

Exhibit 11–1
Information
That May Be
Collected in Job
Analysis

I. Information about the job itself

    A. Work tasks

    B. Work procedures

    C. Machines, tools, equipment, materials used

    D. Responsibilities involved

II. Information about the outcome of worker activities

    A. Products made or services performed

    B. Work standards (time limits, quality, and so on)

III. Information about working conditions

    A. Place of job in organization structure

    B. Work schedule

    C. Physical working conditions

    D. Incentives (financial and other)

A basic choice in deciding what information to collect through job analysis is the level of data specificity. Some job analysis is conducted with no particular application in view, but if there is a particular purpose, the level of specificity is best chosen on this basis. Harvey (1990) identifies three levels of specificity for job analysis information: task, duty, and dimension or construct.

If job analysis information is to be used to set up a basic job training program, high-specificity job analysis information is needed. This information is task-oriented: "Holds animals while veterinarians give injections." A medium-specificity level of job analysis information is duty-based: "Oversees postsurgery recovery of animals." This information is more useful for employee screening or performance appraisal than for training because there is an assumption that an individual knows the basic tasks involved in this duty.

The least specific level of job analysis information is based on job dimensions or basic job constructs. An example might be "carries out defined job duties appropriately without supervision." This statement is relevant to a great many jobs, so it is more useful than task- or duty-based information for grouping jobs. Tannenbaum and Rosenfeld (1994) conducted a job analysis to determine basic skills judged to be important for all entry-level teachers regardless of the subject or grade taught, for example.

Choosing an appropriate level of information specificity is important for making the best use of the data for particular purposes. The choice also has implications for both the method and the source(s) of information to be used. Job analysis methods are examined in a later section; here the choice of data source is reviewed.

What Source Is to Be Used?

Quite a range of different kinds of information may be collected in job analysis. Where does this information come from? Possible human sources, referred to in the job analysis literature as subject matter experts, include job incumbents, supervisors, and outside experts (e.g., Tannenbaum & Wesley, 1993). Records made for other purposes are potentially useful sources of information as well. Each of these sources may be better suited than others to obtaining certain kinds of information.

In general, reasonably experienced job incumbents (as opposed to new employees or very old hands) are good sources for obtaining information about the job itself (I in Exhibit 11–1). The most important criterion to be used in selecting a specific employee is that his or her position be representative of the job being analyzed. If "administrative assistant" is the title of the job to be studied, the employees interviewed should perform typical administrative assistant duties. Interviewing a single company librarian, whose position happens to be classified as administrative assistant for payroll purposes, would not be an appropriate choice.

Observing incumbents at work is probably the best way for job analysts to discover what is actually done on a job (Markowitz, 1981), but this procedure has its drawbacks. For one, it takes a considerable amount of time, and for another, the information may be biased; being observed may affect the employee so that the observer does not see typical performance. An alternative or supplement to observation is an interview, although this process has potential drawbacks as well (Gatewood & Feild, 1987). Some employees lack interest or motivation to participate in a job analysis interview. Others may have difficulty communicating their job activities in a way that is useful to the job analyst.

Interviewing job incumbents also raises the possibility that job activities will not be described accurately for personal reasons, such as making the job seem more important. Supplementing job incumbent information with information from a supervisor provides one check against such problems, although it is not a guarantee. Supervisors may also be better sources of information regarding the outcome of employee activities (II in the exhibit) than the employee. Many people working in large organizations know little of the final product or service to which their jobs contribute.

Organizational employees other than a job incumbent or a supervisor may be more useful sources of information about aspects of working conditions, such as the company's incentive program or the place of a job in the organization structure (III in Exhibit 11–1). Records made by others can be a rich source of relevant data as well. Among the nonhuman sources of information that may be available to a job analyst are filmed records of the job being performed, company records relating to the initial design of the job, and existing job descriptions from another source or organization.

A standard source of existing job analysis information that is available to anyone is the U.S. Department of Labor Employment and Training Administration's *Dictionary of Occupational Titles* (DOT). The DOT classifies some 40,000-plus jobs by means of a nine-digit code developed from the Functional Job Analysis technique discussed later. It also offers narrative descriptions of many jobs, as the sample entry in Exhibit 11–2 illustrates.

The DOT is a useful place for job analysts on unfamiliar ground to begin. It can also help in developing an overall picture of the job structure in a particular organization. For most purposes, however, information from this source is not an acceptable substitute for an in-house analysis. Organizations differ so widely from one another that it is not safe to assume that jobs that have the same title necessarily encompass the same job tasks.

In summary, the various sources of job analysis information are not interchangeable. Each is more useful for acquiring certain kinds of information than others, and none is infallible. Ideally, a job analyst would use a combination of sources, both to get fuller information and to provide a cross-check of information.

Exhibit 11–2
A Sample Entry
from the
*Dictionary of
Occupational
Titles*

Job Analyst: 166-267-018*

Collects, analyzes, and prepares occupational information to facilitate personnel, administration, and management functions of organization. Consults with management to determine type, scope, and purpose of study. Studies current organizational occupational data and compiles distribution reports, organization and flow charts, and other background information required for study. Observes job and interviews workers and supervisory personnel to determine job and worker requirements. Analyzes occupational data, such as physical, mental, and training requirements of jobs and workers, and develops written summaries, such as job descriptions, job specifications, and lines of career movement. Utilizes developed occupational data to evaluate or improve methods and techniques for recruiting, selecting, promoting, evaluating, and training workers, and administration of related personnel programs. May specialize in classifying positions according to regulated guidelines to meet job classification requirements of civil service system and be known as POSITION CLASSIFIER (gov. ser.).

*166-267-018

166	1 indicates a Professional, Technical, or Managerial occupation
	16 indicates that the occupation is in Administration
	166 indicates that the occupation is in Personnel Administration
267	2 indicates that *data* are *analyzed*
	6 indicates that involvement with *people* is on a *speaking-signaling* level
	7 indicates that work with *things* is on a *feeding-offbearing* level
018	This code gives the job being described its unique classification number since other jobs may have the same first six digits. It is based on an alphabetical arrangement of the titles of those other jobs.

From Employment and Training Administration, *Dictionary of Occupational Titles* (4th ed.). Washington, DC: U.S. Department of Labor, 1977, pp. 99–100. A complete explanation of codes and scales used in the DOT is found in the front of the volume.

Collecting Job Analysis Data

Once decisions have been made as to who is to do the analysis, what information is to be collected, and what sources are to be used to get it, the heart of job analysis has been reached—collecting the data. To illustrate this phase, three job analysis methods corresponding to the three levels of job information specificity are reviewed. The correspondence must be considered as approximate, relating to the basic objectives of the method rather than to specific applications.

Task-Based Job Analysis

The foundation of task-based job analysis is a task inventory, which is a list of all of the job tasks likely to be performed in all of the jobs included in the job analysis. Part of a task inventory for jobs in a city government (Harvey, 1990) is shown in Exhibit 11–3. The

Inspecting

Conduct field inspections.

Conduct building inspections.

Perform on-site inspections.

Participate in preplanning.

Inspect and enforce adherence to city codes and specifications.

Check sites for compliance with approved plans and contract documents.

Ensure compliance by contractor.

Check for compliance with traffic codes.

Examine, replace water flow charts.

Read meters.

Check water plant for sanitary conditions.

Collect water samples.

Ensure thorough completion of job activities.

Monitor changing conditions of job site, patrol area, emergency scene.

Patrol streets to control animals.

Check records to ensure that information is in accordance with laws and ordinances.

Examine equipment before purchase.

Inspect food preparation areas to determine degree of cleanliness.

Conduct home safety inspections.

Investigating

Research penal code, traffic code, code of criminal procedure, city ordinances, election code, local government code, etc.

Gather, maintain resource information from public and private sectors.

Research, assemble, and present material for new ordinances.

Gather information for preparation of reports.

Develop cases against suspects leading to arrest.

Conduct searches.

Survey crime scenes for evidence.

Determine crucial events related to emergency situations.

Investigate illegal drugs and controlled substances.

Investigate spills and points of discharge pollution.

Investigate offenses, complaints.

Exhibit 11–3
Sample Task
Inventory Items
and Duties

full inventory contains almost 700 items. Many of these tasks will not apply to a specific job, but all of the tasks performed on all of the jobs to be studied should be on the inventory.

The standard procedure for using a task inventory to conduct a job analysis is to have a job incumbent from each job in the analysis go through a questionnaire (prepared from the task inventory) and mark the tasks performed on his or her job. Ratings of how often the task is performed, how much time is spent on it, and how important (significant or critical) the task is to performance on his or her job are made at the same time. The process can take hours to complete, a fact that may have a significant effect on the reliability of the results.

Test-retest reliability
See page 55

Precisely because the task is so laborious, there is little information in the I/O psychology literature regarding the test-retest reliability of task inventory job analysis (Wilson, Harvey, & Macy, 1990). There is evidence, however, that this method generates results that are very different from those of other methods. In one study, the dissimilarities in results were so great that the organization altered its policy of allowing employees to transfer from one position to another in the same job classification (Clifford, 1996).

The legal climate in which contemporary organizations operate, increasing emphasis on personal employee development as well as on evaluation in performance appraisal, the ever-greater need for training, and the redesign of jobs for teams rather than individuals are all factors supporting high specificity job analysis. Computers can make the task of analyzing and managing the large amounts of data that are generated feasible, although the problem of collecting the data remains. The current status of task analysis and suggestions for improvement are reviewed by Stammers (1995).

Duty-Based Job Analysis

Job analysis that is duty based (also referred to as worker based in the literature) generates information that is less specific than task analysis but more specific than broad job dimensions. This method begins with a **structured questionnaire**, a detailed written list of questions in a set order. In this respect, it is similar to a structured interview; the primary difference between the two is that the response choices (as well as the questions) are specified in a structured questionnaire. The questionnaire is similar to a multiple-choice test, although it is not actually a test but merely a way to collect information.

Of the ready-made structured job analysis questionnaires that are available, the one that has the most extensive research behind it is the Position Analysis Questionnaire (PAQ) developed at Purdue University (McCormick, Jeanneret, & Mecham, 1972). The PAQ has 194 questions that fall into six groupings: job context, work output, mental processes, information input, relationships with other persons, and other job characteristics.

A sample page from the Job Context series of questions from the Position Analysis Questionnaire is shown in Exhibit 11–4. Each of these (and all of the other questions) is rated on one of six scales, according to appropriateness. Two of these scales—possibility of occurrence and importance to this job—are shown in the exhibit. The other four scales are extent of use, degree of detail, amount of time, and applicability.

The end result of rating a job on the Position Analysis Questionnaire's 194 questions is considerable information about the pieces, or elements, of a job. The results of the many investigations into the basic job dimensions (type of duties) underlying these elements vary somewhat according to the form of the PAQ used and the method of analysis.

Job Context

Exhibit 11–4
The PAQ: A
Structured Job
Analysis
Questionnaire
Sample

Code	Possibility of Occurrence (P)
N	Almost no possibility
1	Very limited
2	Limited
3	Moderate
4	Fairly high
5	High

5.2 Physical Hazards (Con't.)

144 P First-aid cases (minor injuries or illnesses which typically result in a day or less of "lost" time and are usually remedied with first-aid procedures)

145 P Temporary disability (temporary injuries or illnesses which prevent the worker from performing the job from one full day up to extended periods of time but which do not result in permanent disability or impairment)

146 P Permanent partial impairment (injuries or illnesses resulting in the amputation or permanent loss of use of any body member or part thereof, or permanent impairment of certain body functions)

147 P Permanent total disability/death (injuries or illnesses which totally disable the worker and permanently prevent further gainful employment, for example, loss of life, sight, limbs, hands, or radiation sickness, etc.)

Code	Importance to This Job (I)
N	Does not apply
1	Very minor
2	Low
3	Average
4	High
5	Extreme

5.3 Personal and Social Aspects

This section includes various personal and social aspects of jobs. Indicate by code the *importance* of these aspects as part of the job.

148 I Civic obligations (because of the job the worker assumes, or is expected to assume, certain civic obligations or responsibilities)

149 I Frustrating situations (job situations in which attempts to deal with problems or to achieve job objectives are obstructed or hindered, and may thus contribute to frustration on the part of the worker)

150 I Strained personal contacts (dealing with individuals or groups in "unpleasant" or "strained" situations, for example, certain aspects of police work, certain types of negotiations, handling certain mental patients, collecting past due bills, etc.)

151 I Personal sacrifice (being willing to make certain personal sacrifices while being of service to other people or the objectives of an organization, for example, in law enforcement, in the ministry, in social work, etc.: do not consider physical hazards here)

152 I Interpersonal conflict situations (job situations in which there are virtually inevitable differences in objectives, opinions, or viewpoints between the worker and other persons or groups of persons, and which may "set the stage" for conflict, for example, persons involved in labor negotiations, supervisors who must enforce an unpopular policy, etc.)

The following 12 dimensions were identified by Mecham (1977), one of the instrument's developers:

1. Engaging in physical activity
2. Operating machines or equipment
3. Public or customer-related contacts
4. Being aware of the work environment
5. Performing service or related activities
6. Performing clerical or related activities
7. Performing technical or related activities
8. Performing routine or repetitive activities
9. Supervising or coordinating other personnel
10. Working regular day versus other work schedules
11. Working in an unpleasant, hazardous, or demanding environment
12. Having decision-making, communicating, or general responsibilities

The PAQ manual provides the information necessary to match each question on the questionnaire with the basic dimension listed above. Questionnaire results can then be used to develop an overall profile of a job in terms of these 12 dimensions, rather than in terms of 194 elements. For example, a telephone operator's job might be described as high on dimensions 2, 3, 5, 8, and 12 and low on dimensions 1, 4, 6, 7, 9, 10, and 11 (although this simplifies the process somewhat).

The PAQ has been used successfully by college students, job incumbents, and supervisors, as well as by professional job analysts, but its relatively high reading level can be a disadvantage in some work settings. The Job Element Inventory, or JEI (Cornelius & Hakel, 1978), covers the same ground with a much lower reading skill requirement. Neither questionnaire is appropriate for all jobs. A large number of "Does not apply" answers (see Exhibit 11–4) signals that another questionnaire or another method is more appropriate for a particular job.

Together with other questionnaires for the same purpose, such as the Management Position Description Questionnaire, or MPDQ (Tornow & Pinto, 1976), and the General Work Inventory, or GWI (Cunningham & Ballentine, 1982), the PAQ focuses on worker-oriented behaviors that could be performed in many jobs. Both the questions and the order in which they are presented are standardized, avoiding the problems that can arise when different people analyze different jobs. As a result, the end product may be compared across different jobs or different organizations.

Dimension-Based Job Analysis

Worker-oriented job analysis methods begin with many specific questions about job tasks and then apply statistical procedures to identify general dimensions of work behavior. By contrast, dimension-based (or construct-based) job analysis methods begin with dimensions that describe jobs in terms of basic constructs. The best-known job analysis technique that falls into this category is the Functional Job Analysis (FJA) procedure developed by the U. S. Employment and Training Administration (1977). The basis of FJA is a conversation between a job analyst and an employee about his or her

Exhibit 11–5

FJA Data
Classification
Code

Data (4th Digit)

0 Synthesizing
1 Coordinating
2 Analyzing
3 Compiling
4 Computing
5 Copying
6 Comparing
7 } No significant
8 } relationship

Data

Information, knowledge, and conceptions, related to data, people, or things, obtained by observation, investigation, interpretation, visualization, mental creation; incapable of being touched; written data take the form of numbers, words, symbols; other data are ideas, concepts, oral verbalization.

0 *Synthesizing:* Integrating analyses of data to discover facts and/or develop knowledge concepts or interpretations.

1 *Coordinating:* Determining time, place, and sequence of operations or action to be taken on the basis of analysis of data; executing determinations and/or reporting on events.

2 *Analyzing:* Examining and evaluating data. Presenting alternative actions in relation to the evaluation is frequently involved.

3 *Compiling:* Gathering, collating, or classifying information about data, people, or things. Reporting and/or carrying out a prescribed action in relation to the information is frequently involved.

4 *Computing:* Performing arithmetic operations and reporting on and/or carrying out a prescribed action in relation to them. Does not include counting.

5 *Copying:* Transcribing, entering, or posting data.

6 *Comparing:* Judging the readily observable functional, structural, or compositional characteristics (whether similar to or divergent from obvious standards) of data, people, or things.

From Employment and Training Administration, *Dictionary of Occupational Titles* (4th ed.). Washington, DC: U.S. Department of Labor, 1977.

job duties, combined with observation of job performance. Notes from both the observation and the interview form the basis for a narrative account of the job (Fine, 1974).

The FJA technique is based on the premise that all jobs may be described in terms of three underlying basic dimensions—interaction with *data, people,* and *things.* The job analyst rates a job on each of these dimensions according to a DOT code. (The code for data is shown in Exhibit 11–5.) As an example of the FJA dimensions, consider an attendant in the fitness equipment room of a sports club (treadmills, stationary bicycles, step machines, and so on). Among other duties, he or she may keep records of attendance at various times of day (data), provide assistance to patrons with questions about equipment use (people), and check equipment periodically for safety and proper functioning (things).

In Exhibit 11–2, the code number for data interaction is 2; as seen in Exhibit 11–5, a 2 means that a job analyst works with data at what is called the analyzing level—examining and evaluating data. The FJA provides similar codes for employee interaction with people and things.

A very important aspect of the FJA technique is the distinction that is made between tasks performed and the purpose (or end result) of the tasks. The employee in the fitness room may have a job title along the lines of "personal fitness counselor," and, indeed, he or she may have a specialized degree or certification in some area of the health or fitness field. Nevertheless, the job title has to do with the purpose of the tasks the employee performs. It does not describe the tasks themselves.

In the FJA, the personal fitness counselor performs quite specific tasks. Different establishments have different requirements for this job, but sample tasks include logging people in, making notes regarding progress on their charts, demonstrating equipment use, watching for any physical problems people may be having as they use the equipment, and so on. The work/purpose distinction is an important one because in many cases the information provided by job analysis is used by people who have never seen anyone performing the job in question.

The most comprehensive use of the FJA has been in developing the *Dictionary of Occupational Titles,* but the method has been employed extensively in this country and abroad by other job analysts. Perhaps partially because it is so well established, there is not a great deal of research into the basic construct validity or measurement properties of the three dimensions. Research lends support to the reliability of this method (e.g., Geyer, Hice, Hawk, Boese, & Brannon, 1989), however, and to the validity of the seven levels of the People scale (McCulloch & Francis, 1989).

Construct validity
See pages 60–61

Marching to a Different Drummer: Organizational Analysis

As mentioned in the chapter on recruiting and selection, a few companies are beginning to experiment with hiring for the organization rather than for a specific job within it. This selection policy focuses on individual characteristics such as personality, values, and learning attitudes rather than on job-specific skills of the type identified in job analysis. The underlying rational is summarized as follows: "A desire to learn new jobs is an attribute that cannot be taught easily to employees, as job skills can. You either hire people who have this attribute, or do without" (Bowen, Ledford, & Nathan, 1991, p. 39).

I/O psychologist Ed Lawler (1994) believes the shift to "competency-based selection" will become essential for many organizations. An interesting case study is described by Bowen, Ledford, and Nathan (1991). The process began with an analysis designed to assess the key norms, values, and characteristics of the organization. Personnel specifications were inferred from this analysis. Appropriate technical skills (as identified through traditional job analysis) were deemed necessary, but insufficient, for good job performance in this organization. Over the course of their employment, employees would be expected to learn various new skills, work in teams, and take on an increasing share of decision-making responsibility. Thus, openness to learning was as important as technical skills, perhaps more so.

The resulting screening and selection process was a long, expensive undertaking. Techniques for organizational analysis are not well established, and the many personality and other individual attribute measures that lie at the heart of this approach are still in the early stages of being validated against job performance. Nevertheless, Bowen and his colleagues believe this new approach to selection is less likely to have adverse impact than traditional methods because the hiring criteria—values, needs, and motives—may be more evenly distributed in the population. It is an empirical question.

Criterion validity
See pages 63–66

Error in Job Analysis

The use of job analysis data has the potential for improving decision making in many aspects of human resource management, but if this potential is to be realized, the data must be as free from error as possible. There are three major sources of error: the data base, the interpretation of the information in the data base, and the environment in which the job analysis is carried out.

Measurement error
See pages 53–54

The Job Analysis Data Base

A job analysis data base consists of all the information that has been collected to help analyze a job. As a general rule, the smaller the job analysis data base, the more likely it is that the information collected is biased or incomplete. A particular job incumbent who is interviewed may not be very experienced and/or may not perform the full range of tasks actually encompassed by the job being analyzed, for example. Alternatively, he or she may not be willing or able to report job duties accurately, or the report may be influenced by irrelevant personal values and biases (Landy & Shankster, 1994). The best protection against all such problems is multiple sources of information.

Data base error can also occur if subject matter experts do not have sufficient time to complete the task (such as fill in a questionnaire) or if the method chosen for the job analysis is not appropriate for the job. An example of this second problem was mentioned in connection with the Position Analysis Questionnaire; a large number of "Does not apply" answers should signal the job analyst that another method should be selected for analyzing this job.

The Interpretation of Job Information

Incomplete or distorted information, whether deliberate or not, is not the exclusive province of job incumbents or others interviewed in the data collection process. A classic example of a distorted *report* of information is presented in Exhibit 11–6. A more accurate description of the job in question can be found in the summary at the end of the chapter. It is unlikely that much of the error in job descriptions comes from such deliberate attempts to mislead, but job analysts do make mistakes. Inexperienced or untrained job analysts also have a tendency to focus on what is, rather than what should be (Grant, 1988a). The person doing a job is only one source of information about it. What he or she does on the job is not necessarily what *should* be done.

The Environment of Job Analysis

The environment in which the process is carried out can be the source of a number of errors in job analysis. Time pressures can rush one or both parties through the process faster

Exhibit 11–6
Can You
Identify This
Job? How Job
Descriptions
Can Mislead

Proposed Job Description

1. Job identification

    a. Title: Director of Industrial and Agrarian Priorities

    b. Dept.: Maintenance

2. Job duties

    a. Directs, controls, and regulates the movement of interstate commerce, representing a cross section of the wealth of the American economy. Exercises a broad latitude for independent judgment and discretion without direct or intermediate supervision.

    b. Integrates the variable factors in an evolving situation utilizing personal judgment, founded on past experience, conditioned by erudition, and disciplined by mental intransigence. Formulates a binding decision relative to the priority of flow of interstate and intrastate commerce, both animate and inanimate, such decisions being irreversible and not subject to appellate review by higher authority or being reversed by the legal determination of any echelon of our judicial complex. Influences the movement, with great finality, of agricultural products, forest products, minerals, manufactured goods, machine tools, construction equipment, military personnel, defense materials, raw materials, end products, finished goods, semifinished products, small business, large business, public utilities, and governmental agencies.

    c. Deals with all types of personalities and all levels of education, from college president and industrial tycoon to truck driver, requiring the exercise of initiative, ingenuity, imagination, intelligence, industry, and discerning versatility. Implements coordinated motivation on the part of the public, which is consistent with the decision of the incumbent, failure of which could create a complex objurgation of personnel and equipment generating a catastrophic loss of mental equilibrium by innumerable personnel of American industry, who are responsible for the formulation of day-to-day policy, and guidance implementation of the conveyances of transportation, both interstate and intrastate.

    d. Appraises the nuances of an unfolding situational development and directs correction thereof commensurate with its seriousness and momentousness.

From E. B. Flippo, *Principles of Personnel Management* (3rd ed.). Copyright 1971 by McGraw-Hill, Inc. Reprinted by permission.

than accuracy demands. Lack of interest or commitment on the parts of managers, supervisors, or job incumbents (or even actual obstruction of job analysis efforts) can also be a problem. The support of top management is critical if this source of error is to be reduced or avoided.

Rapidly changing technology, job redesign, and organizational mergers, acquisitions, and reorganizations are other environmental factors adding error to job analysis. In some cases, the data are rendered obsolete even as they are being put into use by the organization. This kind of error cannot be avoided; it can only be managed by continued monitoring of job analysis information.

A general strategy for dealing with error in job analysis has four parts.

1. Use multiple sources of information about the job.

2. Use more than one trained and experienced analyst if possible.

3. Give the analyst(s) enough time to do the job right.

4. Check and recheck information and results.

The list is a tall order, and many organizations will lack the resources or the commitment to follow it. Industrial/organizational psychologists can help by continuing to research the development of job analysis methods less susceptible to errors stemming from the conditions under which they are used.

Job Analysis Research

I/O psychologists interested in job analysis believe that more research into the way instruments are used, as well as into the instruments themselves, is needed. In this context, Richman and Quiñones (1996) undertook a laboratory experiment to investigate a number of aspects of the job analysis process. The portion of the study relevant to the question of who should do the analysis is summarized in Spotlight on Research. At least as far as making ratings of how often specific tasks are performed goes, results suggest that people who actually do a job (incumbents), are better sources of information than people who merely observe the job being performed.

Laboratory experiment
See pages 29–31

In an aspect of their experiment not summarized, Richman and Quiñones also found that subjects with lower levels of experience were more accurate than people with more experience. This conclusion may seem to run counter to common sense, but it is

Research subjects
See page 27

SPOTLIGHT ON RESEARCH

Task Frequency Rating Accuracy: The Effect of Task Engagement and Experience

Summarized from W. L. Richman and M. Quiñones, "Task Frequency Rating Accuracy: The Effect of Task Engagement and Experience." *Journal of Applied Psychology*, 1996, *81*, 512–524.

Research question   Do people who perform jobs make more accurate ratings of task frequencies than those who observe job tasks being performed?

Type of study   Laboratory experiment.

Subjects   33 female and 31 male undergraduate students.

Independent variable   Performer versus observer status.

Dependent variable   Accuracy of task frequency ratings as measured by deviation from a true score measure.

Hypothesis   Performers will make more accurate task frequency ratings than observers.

General procedure   After appropriate orientation (experiment included elements not described here), one-half of subjects (randomly assigned) watched videotape of toys being assembled and then completed questionnaire on frequency with which various task elements were performed. Remaining subjects completed the same questionnaire after performing the assembly.

Results   Hypothesis supported.

Conclusion   ". . . the present study highlights the need to expand the job analysis research paradigm to investigate psychological processes involved in job analysis" (p. 522).

consistent with memory research suggesting that the more often an event has occurred, the more difficult it is to recall its details (e.g., Bruce & Van Pelt, 1989; Robinson & Swanson, 1990).

In another study of job analysis methods and their use, Levine and his co-investigators (1983) sought the opinions of experienced job analysts regarding the utility and practicality of seven popular job analysis methods. Of the two methods used in the study that are discussed in this chapter, Functional Job Analysis (FJA) fared very well on the effectiveness rating scales, whereas the Position Analysis Questionnaire (PAQ) got high marks for being easy to use. This result is consistent with what might be expected. The FJA technique relies on observation and open interviews, which give the analyst considerable leeway in getting whatever information will be useful. By contrast, the PAQ is a structured questionnaire that takes less time and requires less skill, but also limits the information collected to the specific questions asked. The investigations reviewed have been of traditional job analysis methods that have seen considerable applied use. Other I/O psychologists focus their attention on developing new and better job analysis methods. Among current efforts is a computer software "job analyst" that allows a job incumbent to punch keys in answer to questions about his or her job as they are "asked" by a personal computer (Wilson, 1991). Computers may also make it possible to create comprehensive generic task inventories for general occupational categories. This information would not be a substitute for organization-specific job information, but a basic reference source that would vastly reduce the time and cost of job analysis.

A particular need in contemporary organizations is for sound (from a measurement perspective) general-purpose job analysis methods that require less time and less skill than most of those in current use. At present, job analysis is an enormously expensive and laborious process in organizations of any size; accumulating, managing, and using a comprehensive job analysis data base often is simply not a realistic goal. Making the process more efficient would allow more organizations to exploit the great potential of this information for driving an effective integrated personnel system.

The workhorse of an integrated system, the job description, is considered next. As a prelude to that discussion, it must be acknowledged that not all job descriptions are based on job analysis, by any means. There are many reasons for this fact, of which the time and expense of job analysis is a primary one. Nevertheless, job descriptions are of maximum utility for the many personnel-related functions to which they are relevant when they are created from job analysis data.

Writing a Job Description

Job analysis is a process for collecting information. A **job description** presents the information so collected in the form of a written statement setting forth the tasks, responsibilities, and working conditions of each job analyzed. In scope, a job description can range from the DOT's nine-digit summary to an entire book, such as Mintzberg's *The Nature of Managerial Work* (1980). The more typical job description is a narrative of one to three pages in length, but not just any written information about a job is a job description. There are certain requirements as to both content and style.

A complete job description has two sections. One consists of identifying information and the other is a summary of job tasks and responsibilities. (A third section, consisting of clarifying comments, is optional.) Identifying information consists of (at least) the following items: the name of the company, the job or payroll title, the department and/or division in which job is located, the name of the job analyst, and the date of the report. The sources of information, including the names of anyone interviewed, are optional. The job summary section describes the duties performed, the working conditions, the supervision given or received, the relation of the job to other jobs, and the machines, tools, and methods used.

The purpose of a job description is solely to convey information. It is not intended to entertain, nor is it the appropriate vehicle for demonstrating an elegant writing style. A good job description is complete, direct, and succinct. There are several generally accepted style guidelines to help bring about this result.

- Use the present tense: "opens," not "opened."

- Start each sentence in the job summary with an action verb: "opens mail," not "the mail is opened."

- Use "may" only if some people holding the job *never* perform the task.

- Use "occasionally" only if *every* person holding the job performs the task at one time or another.

Guidelines for writing job descriptions are not the brainstorm of some crank grammarian. They serve both to make communication clearer and to make it easier to compare job descriptions written by different people or for different jobs. One example of a job description written in the appropriate style was presented in Exhibit 11–2. A portion of another is shown in Exhibit 11–7.

The job description shown in the exhibit is a standard one that would be accepted almost anywhere, but the traditional form is not without its critics. Grant (1988b) believes that the usual job description can be misleading because it does not indicate the relative importance of, or the relative amount of time taken for, each job task. The conditions under which job tasks are performed and the standards by which employees doing the job will be evaluated are additions suggested by Klinger (1979). Finally, traditional job descriptions do not usually have anything to say about any group assignments in which a job holder might be involved.

A different kind of inadequacy in traditional job descriptions that concerns many I/O psychologists relates to the utility of the information for screening, selection, and placement. Current thinking in I/O psychology is that a successful individual/job/organization match is more than a matter of matching job duties with employee skills, knowledge, and abilities. It also involves matching what people need or want with those things that the organization and the job can offer. From a complete matching perspective, conventional job descriptions give those involved in screening, selection, and placement only half of the information they need. They know what an individual must be able to do for the job, but not what the job can do for an individual.

Matching model
See pages 90–91

Job rewards (also referred to in this context as *reinforcers*) are personally valued outcomes of doing certain work or being in a particular work environment, or both. The reward potential of a job has often been examined from a motivational perspective; this is the basis of the psychological approach to job design. The systematic description of the rewards offered by a job and an organization as an addition to traditional job descriptions is a newer idea.

One approach to identifying job rewards is offered by an instrument called the Minnesota Job Description Questionnaire, or MJDQ (Dawis, Lofquist, & Weiss, 1968).

This questionnaire asks job supervisors to rank the extent to which 21 potential job rewards (such as ability to use skills, job security, and opportunity to be creative) are present in the jobs they supervise. Results of this structured questionnaire approach can be used both for individual jobs and for making comparisons between jobs. The Job Diagnostic Survey (Hackman & Oldham, 1975) that was discussed in Chapter 8 is also widely used for identifying job rewards. The primary weakness of both instruments is probably that they are based on the perceptions of those who do the rankings, and the perceptions of a new employee may be different. Nevertheless, some variation of this ap-

---

Exhibit 11–7
A Sample Job
Description

Job Title: Financial Aids Technician

Supervisor: Financial Aids Office Manager

Typical Duties [partial]

- Collects and processes student financial aid applications as prescribed by state and federal guidelines.

- Reviews and analyzes financial aid applications and determines financial need.

- Determines type(s) and amount of aid to be recommended in financial aid packages based on state, federal, and local rules, regulations, and guidelines.

- Packages awards, notifies students, and disburses awards.

- Monitors, checks, and evaluates student progress for continued eligibility in financial aid programs.

- Disseminates information related to financial aid programs; assists prospective students in completing applications, ensuring that all necessary information is obtained.

- Advises students regarding money management and their responsibilities as financial aid recipients.

- Conducts interviews with financial aid applicants and suggests counseling when needed.

- Establishes, maintains, and updates confidential student files related to financial aid; performs data entry of all pertinent information related to financial aid and loan recipients.

- Maintains accurate accounts and ledger of awards funded, revised, or cancelled for all campus-based financial aid programs.

- Performs a variety of arithmetical calculations and recalculations related to financial aid and eligibility determination.

- Procedures financial aid warrants and payment schedules.

Excerpted from the Shasta/Tehama/Trinity Joint Community College District job description for financial aids technician.

proach seems worth pursuing as a standard feature of job descriptions. As a way of rounding out the job picture, it offers another potential check against serious individual/job/organization mismatches.

Writing a Job Specification

A job description describes a *job*. By contrast, a **job specification** (also called a person or human specification) describes a *person*. It is a statement of the human characteristics required to perform the duties detailed in a job description. Together, the specifications for a job often are referred to as KSAs (knowledge, skills, and abilities) or KSAOs (knowledge, skills, abilities, and other traits). The experience and education specifications for the financial aids technician job described in Exhibit 11–7 are listed in Exhibit 11–8.

Compared with writing a job description, writing a job specification is a difficult task, even with the help of job analysis information. A major problem is that there can be quite a range in the degree to which equally satisfactory employees exhibit a particular characteristic. Complicating the matter is the fact that this range may be unknown, because organizational policy (or chance) has restricted the actual range in some way. As an example of this problem, consider Company R.

Restriction of range
See pages 65–66

All of the office receptionists in Company R have been to college for one or more years; several have college degrees. Does this mean that an education specification for this job should state that at least one year of college is required? Most likely, it is *not* required.

Knowledge of

- Rules, regulations, and interpretations for determining student eligibility for all state, federal, and local financial aid programs.

- College, community agencies, services, and resources available to students.

- Effective telephone techniques.

- Effective communication techniques, including speaking in front of large groups.

- Office methods, practices, and procedures, including information systems and electronic data processing.

Experience

- Experience in conducting interviews.

Education

- At least two years of college or equivalent; AA degree preferred.

- Directly related practical experience may be substituted for education.

Exhibit 11–8

A Sample Job Specification

Excerpted from the Shasta/Tehama/Trinity Joint Community College District job description for financial aids technician.

If all of the employed receptionists have attended college, however, lower educational limits for learning and performing this job must be estimated. This kind of difficulty is not uncommon when a job specification is developed on a judgmental basis—that is, when the qualities required to do a job are *inferred* from a job description or "common sense."

The judgmental approach to developing a job specification is used by the U.S. Employment and Training Administration in the DOT, and it may work very well in practice. If Company R has a sufficient number of receptionist applicants who have attended at least one year of college, there is no immediate need to know if the educational requirements of the job can be lowered. If the company is challenged for turning down an applicant for a receptionist position because he or she has not been to college at all, however, the situation changes. Now it is essential to know.

The alternative to a judgmental approach to job specifications is an empirical approach. Job performance appraisals of current employees are compared with their scores on employment screening tests, biographical data, interview ratings, and any other relevant information that is available. Once enough data have been collected, the test score ranges and personal characteristics associated with job success may be specified with more accuracy than usually is possible by the judgmental method.

The empirical process has at least four long-term benefits. First, possible sources of good employees are less likely to be overlooked in recruiting if the actual requirements for a job are known in detail. Second, traditional selection criteria that turn out to be unimportant to job success can be eliminated, thus conserving organizational resources. Third, the more effective screening and selection that eventually come from this process should result in better job performance on the part of the organization's personnel as a whole. Finally, this validation process is central to documenting fair employment practices in the United States. As in all areas of personnel decision making, it is necessary for an organization to be able to show that the qualities it looks for in employees are related to the jobs they will do.

The qualities that an organization is looking for in its employees are what job specifications are about. The more emphasis that is placed on the *specific* in *specification*, the more useful the information will be. If post–high school education is required, the type and number of years should be stated, as is done in Exhibit 11–8. If tests are involved, upper and lower score limits should be spelled out unambiguously.

To the extent possible, job specifications should also be behavioral in nature. The judgmental approach to listing requirements frequently produces statements such as "must be dependable" and "must be able to communicate with others," but these qualities cannot be observed. Behavior can. Appropriate behavioral substitutes can be found for most "must be whatever" specifications (Schneier, 1976) by asking the question "How would someone *know* if this person is dependable or can communicate?" In this fashion, "must be dependable" might become "did not miss more than one day of work per month on last job," and "answers interview questions clearly" could replace "must be able to communicate with others."

Job specifications that cannot be translated into behaviors should, at the least, be given a second or third look. The further a job specification requirement strays from observable behavior, the more difficult it is to demonstrate its job relatedness, and this, as discussed, creates problems if a personnel decision is formally challenged. The superiority of behavior-based requirement statements also shows itself when the specification is put to use. A fact of life in many organizations is that some of the people involved in recruiting, hiring, employee development, and related personnel decisions know little or nothing about the jobs in question. In this case, the less left to interpretation or imagination, the better.

425
Chapter 11
*Job Analysis and
Evaluation*

Job Evaluation

The role of the job analysis process as the source of information for a range of organizational activities has been stressed throughout this chapter. One of the activities with which it is most often associated is **job evaluation**, a formal process for determining the financial worth of a job to an organization.

There are many ways in which an individual can be compensated for his or her contribution to an organization. The core of this compensation is usually a paycheck; a variety of bonuses or benefits (or both) may be added for total compensation. To be fair, this compensation should be based on actual job requirements—that is, on a job analysis. This analysis provides the information for someone to determine the value of a job relative to other jobs in the organization.

Compensable Job Factors

Some qualitative methods are available, but most job evaluation methods are quantitative in nature. A common approach involves assigning points to the aspects of work for which employees should be compensated. The physical demands of a job, the amount of responsibility the job carries, the experience and/or training required to do the job, and the working conditions under which the job is performed are among the more frequently used of these aspects, called compensable factors.

In job evaluation, each compensable factor is broken down into degrees from lowest to highest, with points assigned accordingly. An example of a breakdown of points awarded for a training/education compensable factor is presented in Exhibit 11–9. There are four degrees of this factor, and each of the degrees is assigned a different number of points. The same procedure is followed for all of an organization's compensable factors to produce a yardstick. The total number of points from all compensable factors is the worth of any one job relative to other jobs in the organization.

First Degree: 15 points
Definition: A basic high school education is sufficient.
Second Degree: 30 points
Definition: High school plus one year of specialized training is required.
Third Degree: 45 points
Definition: High school plus extensive technical training is required.
Fourth Degree: 60 points
Definition: The job incumbent must have the equivalent of four years of college training.

Exhibit 11–9
Four Degrees of the Job Compensable Factor "Training and/or Education Requirements for the Job"

Wage Trend Lines

A job evaluation yardstick is a measuring instrument. When a job is evaluated with this instrument, the result is one number. Because the same measuring scale is used for all of the jobs in an organization, the numbers can be compared directly with one another. If each of these numbers is placed on a graph relative to a measure of its current compensation (again, the same yardstick must be used to measure compensation for all jobs), the result is a picture of the organization's compensation structure. When compensation is generally consistent with job evaluation, most of the points in the scattergram will fall close to a straight line. An example of such a wage trend line is presented in Figure 11–2.

The wage trend line shown in the figure depicts a compensation program that is well in line with the worth of jobs as determined by job evaluation; that is, in general, the more points a job has, the more the incumbent in that job is paid. Two jobs, A and B, are somewhat underpaid relative to the number of points they have been assigned, and job C is somewhat overpaid. In a formal wage adjustment program, compensation for underpaid jobs should be increased immediately, and instances of overcompensation should be adjusted as the current incumbents vacate the positions.

The wage trend line shown in Figure 11–2 depicts a considerably better fit between job worth and compensation than might be found in some organizations. Many factors other than the nature of the work and the human qualities required to do it play a role in setting compensation. Some people are paid more for the position they hold than for the work they actually do; that is, status acts as a moderator variable in the job worth–compensation relationship. Other nonwork factors that can affect job compensation include the cost of living in the company's location; the going rate for a job in an industry or area; legal constraints (such as minimum wage laws); union agreements that set pay rates for included jobs and not for others; and what had to be offered to induce the current incumbent (or a predecessor) to take the job.

Moderator variable
See page 39

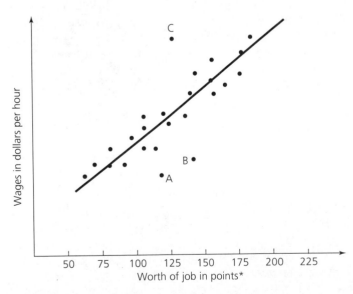

Figure 11–2
A Sample Wage
Trend Line

*Each point on the graph represents one job.

Many people also believe that sex modifies the appropriate job worth–compensation relationship, citing the acknowledged fact that employees in female-dominated occupations earn less money than employees in male-dominated occupations. Are these jobs really worth less? That is the central question in the issue of comparable worth.

Job Evaluation and Comparable Worth

If one person does a job that contributes $5,000 to an organization, and another person does a completely different job that also contributes $5,000, both people should be paid the same regardless of the nature of their actual work. For many of the reasons mentioned, this does not always happen, but this is the essence of the concept of **comparable worth.**

The basic data for determining comparable worth come from job evaluation, which unfortunately is not always equal to the challenge of determining the worth of a job. Error may enter the process in the choice, definition, and scaling of the compensable factors (e.g., Collins & Muchinsky, 1993; Davis & Sauser, 1993) or in the application of the factors to the jobs being evaluated.

In one of the more extensive published field studies of the possible impact of the particular job evaluation method used on the resulting wage trend line, Madigan and Hoover (1986) asked trained job analysts to interview current jobholders in Michigan's civil service. Six different job evaluation methods to determine a wage trend line were applied to the data from these interviews; six different results were achieved.

Even when the same method is used, other factors may affect the evaluation given to a job. Smith, Benson, and Hornsby (1990) report that information placed near the beginning of a job description carries more weight in evaluation than information placed toward the end. If a group or committee of some kind is used to make the evaluations, different group decision-making processes produce different evaluations (Hornsby, Smith, & Gupta, 1994).

The status of a job may also affect the evaluation it is given. Mount and Ellis (1987) conducted a laboratory study in which the sex and the average pay level of a hypothetical jobholder were manipulated. No sex bias appeared, but both male and female subjects (all experienced job analysts) gave higher evaluations to the jobs that had been assigned higher pay levels by the experimenter. In other words, it appears that people's judgments of what a job *should* be paid may be influenced by their knowledge of what it *is* paid.

I/O psychologists have some evidence that training the people who do job evaluation in the method to be used and giving them more information about the jobs in question can lead to greater accuracy in this process (e.g., Hahn & Dipboye, 1988). Nevertheless, problems such as these described have led some authors to conclude that job evaluation methods are simply too unreliable for comparable worth applications (e.g., Madigan, 1985). What is the solution? Should organizational use of job evaluation methods be regulated so that all are using the same or similar ones of known reliability? Would training people to avoid bias in job evaluation be effective? The questions are not likely to go away.

Reliability
See pages 54–58

More than ten years ago, the Equal Employment Opportunity Commission estimated that more than 75% of its pending cases were related to comparable worth issues. One response was a movement by states, counties, cities, and school districts across the country to raise the wage levels of public-sector jobs traditionally held by women (Berstein,

Managerial and executive jobs are among the most difficult for job analysts to break down into component parts.

1988). Accompanying this movement have come challenges by interested parties to the job evaluation methods used to make such adjustments.

I/O psychologists can make a significant contribution to the issues of comparable worth by continuing to explore the difficulties associated with present methods of job evaluation and creating better methods based on this research. Organizations cannot leave the matter entirely up to I/O psychologists, however. Affirmative action applies to pay discrimination as well as to hiring discrimination. Sape (1985) suggests several basic steps that all employers should consider taking, both to help solve the problem and to show good-faith effort in this area.

1. Examine each element of the compensation system for controls on possible discrimination.

2. Review key job evaluation determinations for bias.

3. Audit the impact of pay practices on men's and women's salaries on a regular basis.

4. Work to eliminate job segregation (male- and female-dominated jobs).

5. Take corrective action if pay disparities are identified that might be based on sex discrimination.

These five steps are comprehensive ones, and to date there is a long way to go before they become anything like standard human resource management procedure. Complicating the issue is the fact that the issue of comparable worth does not exist in a vacuum. When it comes to pay, fair play is not wholly a matter of numbers—individual satisfaction with level of income is a more complex matter. A primary determinant of this satisfaction is the absolute amount of pay that is received (Huber, Seybolt, & Venemon, 1992), but satisfaction also has a strong relative component based on perceptions of its fairness.

Researchers have discovered three important factors that have a significant impact on the degree to which a person is relatively satisfied or dissatisfied with his or her pay. The first is the extent to which pay is perceived to be related to level of performance (e.g., Heneman, Greenberger, & Strasser, 1988). The second is the extent to which pay is perceived to be equitable relative to what other people in similar jobs with similar qualifications are making (e.g., Pfeffer & Langton, 1993; Williams, 1995). The third factor in perceptions of pay fairness is beliefs about the absolute amount of pay that is appropriate (in the opinion of the jobholder) to the worth of the job being performed (e.g., Berkowitz, Fraser, Treasure, & Cochran, 1987). In short:

> The ultimate test of job evaluation lies in acceptance of the process by those affected and the compatibility of results with their subjective norms of comparability. Judgments of worth ultimately are based on subjective norms, regardless of the tradition employed. (Mahoney, 1983, p. 21)

At Issue

Does Comparable Worth Obscure the Real Issue?

All societies have occupational differences in wages that have little or nothing to do with relative contribution to an organization or with idealistic notions about contribution to society. Ours is no exception. There are professional basketball players who make more in one year than grade school teachers make in a lifetime. The star of a movie makes many times the salary of a supporting player, although both are essential to the production.

There are also large pay differences between industries and between geographic regions that have nothing to do with the actual work being performed. A secretary for an oil company may get paid more than a secretary for a retail store, and a secretary in Los Angeles, California, may get paid more than one in Anniston, Alabama, even though all do the same work. And all of these secretaries will make less than the people they work for. These differences have nothing to do with sex discrimination; they would be true even if all of the secretaries were male.

It is far more likely that most of the secretaries are female, and it is also very likely that most of their bosses are male. In our society, women are overrepresented in lower-paying jobs (such as secretary) and underrepresented in higher-paying ones (such as executive). The result is a wage gap of varying size depending on the particular study but always favoring men.

Equal employment opportunity laws have been around for more than a generation now, and attitudes toward women in "male jobs" have undergone significant changes. The U.S. Census Bureau lists women as well as men in every one of its occupational categories, although it may still be more difficult for a woman to qualify herself and advance at the same rate as a man in certain settings. But this difficulty is insufficient to explain the continued existence of the pink-collar ghetto, as the concentration of women in lower-paying jobs has been called. Why do they stay there?

In the article from which the title of this **At Issue** is taken, Hoffmann and Hoffmann (1987) describe an Eastern manufacturing firm in which more than half of the employees in the packaging department were female, although only 10% of the better-paid production jobs were held by women. Federal regulatory agencies wanted to know why women were so underrepresented in a department where they could earn much more money for doing work that was no more difficult.

The answer appeared to be that the women were where they wanted to be. When asked if they would take a job in the production department if it were offered, only 9% said yes, compared with 50% of the men who were asked. Why? The answer turned out to be very simple. Employees in the production department worked rotating shifts, and they were often asked to work overtime. These schedules are disruptive for most people but they have a greater negative impact on women, who are still far more likely than men in our society to have family obligations that make irregular work hours impossible.

In the company studied, women were not in the poorly paid jobs because of discrimination or inadequate knowledge of the availability of better jobs or stereotyped views of themselves or any of the other reasons often offered for this phenomenon. They were there so that they could fulfill the responsibilities placed on them in their private lives.

Comparable worth, as the concept is currently understood and applied, will not help these women or the hundreds of thousands like them who work the equivalent of two jobs for less than they would earn in one if they were free to leave the pink-collar ghetto. The real issue in comparable worth may be recognition of the worth of their major contribution to our society.

Summary

Job analysis is a formal data collection process that yields information about the tasks, context, and working conditions of jobs in an organization. This information is the foundation for writing job descriptions (which tell what is done on a job) and job specifications (which list the human qualities needed to do a job). A description of the work done by the individual who regulates traffic flow when highway construction makes one-way traffic temporarily necessary provided an example of how *not* to write a job description.

Job analysis information is basic to such organizational functions as screening, selection, training, performance appraisal, and the documentation of fair employment practices. Job descriptions and job specifications are the basis for job evaluation, a formal process for determining the worth of a job to an organization.

Questions for Review and Discussion

1. In your own words, demonstrate that you understand the differences between the following: job analysis, job evaluation, job description, job specification, job classification.

2. Make a list of up to ten questions you would ask the professor in this class if you were going to conduct a job analysis interview with him or her.

3. Write a job description of the job of "student in this course" that conforms to the standards outlined in the chapter.

4. Describe and give one example of the three major sources of error in job analysis. Which of the basic strategies for reducing error outlined in the chapter is most appropriate in each case?

5. Make a convincing case for *one* of the following positions:

   a. Women make less money than men because they stay home more (that is, enter and leave the work force more often) than men.

   b. Women stay home more than men because they make less money than men when they work.

Key Terms

comparable worth

compensable job factors

Dictionary of Occupational Titles

dimension-based job analysis

duty-based job analysis

job analysis

job description

job evaluation

job information sources

job specification

organizational analysis

task-based job analysis

References

Albemarle Paper Company v. Moody. (1975). 422 U.S. 405.

Berkowitz, L., Fraser, C., Treasure, F. P., & Cochran, S. (1987). Pay equity, job gratifications, and comparisons in pay satisfaction. *Journal of Applied Psychology, 72,* 544–551.

Berstein, A. (1988, May 2). The new federalism hasn't meant less government. *Business Week*, p. 110.

Bowen, D. E., Ledford, G. E., Jr., & Nathan, B. R. (1991). Hiring for the organization, not the job. *Academy of Management Executive, 5,* 35–50.

Bruce, D., & Van Pelt, M. (1989). Memories of a bicycle tour. *Applied Cognitive Psychology, 3,* 137–156.

Clifford, J. P. (1996). Manage work better to better manage human resources: A comparative study of two approaches to job analysis. *Public Personnel Management, 25,* 89–102.

Collins, J. M., & Muchinsky, P. M. (1993). An assessment of the construct validity of three job evaluation methods: A field experiment. *Academy of Management Journal, 36,* 895–904.

Cornelius, E. T., & Hakel, M. D. (1978). *A study to develop an improved enlisted performance evaluation system for the U.S. Coast Guard.* Washington, DC: Department of Transportation, USCG.

Cunningham, J. W., & Ballentine, R. D. (1982). *The general work inventory.* Raleigh, NC: Authors.

Davis, K. R., & Sauser, W. I. (1993). A comparison of factor weighting methods in job evaluation: Implications for compensation systems. *Public Personnel Management, 22,* 91–106.

Dawis, R. V., Lofquist, L. H., & Weiss, D. J. (1968). A theory of work adjustment (A revision). *Minnesota Studies in Vocational Rehabilitation: XXIII.* Minneapolis: University of Minnesota.

Employment and Training Administration. (1977). *Dictionary of occupational titles* (4th ed.). Washington, DC: U.S. Department of Labor.

Equal Employment Opportunity Commission (1978). *Guidelines on employment testing procedures.* Washington, DC: Government Printing Office.

Fine, S. A. (1974). Functional job analysis: An approach to a technology for manpower planning. *Personnel Journal, 53,* 813–818.

Flippo, E. B. (1971). *Principles of personnel administration* (3rd ed.). New York: McGraw-Hill.

Gatewood, R. D., & Feild, H. S. (1987). *Human resource selection.* New York: CBS College Publishing.

Geyer, P. D., Hice, J., Hawk, J., Boese, R., & Brannon, Y. (1989). Reliabilities of ratings available from the Dictionary of Occupational Titles. *Personnel Psychology, 42,* 547–560.

Grant, P. C. (1988a). What use is a job description? *Personnel Journal, 67,* 45–53.

Grant, P. C. (1988b). Why job descriptions don't work. *Personnel Journal, 67,* 52–59.

Hackman, J. R., & Oldham, G. R. (1975). Development of the Job Diagnostic Survey. *Journal of Applied Psychology, 60,* 159–170.

Hahn, D. C., & Dipboye, R. L. (1988). Effects of training and information on the accuracy and reliability of job evaluations. *Journal of Applied Psychology, 73,* 146–153.

Harvey, R. J. (1990). Job analysis. In M. D. Dunnette & L. M. Hough (Eds.), *Handbook of industrial and organizational psychology,* Vol. 2 (2nd ed.). Palo Alto, CA: Consulting Psychologists Press.

Heneman, R. L., Greenberger, D.G., & Strasser, S. (1988). The relationship between pay-for-performance perceptions and pay satisfaction. *Personnel Psychology, 41,* 745–759.

Hoffmann, C. C., & Hoffmann, K. P. (1987). Does comparable worth obscure the real issues? *Personnel Journal, 66,* 83–95.

Hornsby, J. S., Smith, B. N., & Gupta, J. N. D. (1994). The impact of decision-making methodology on job evaluation outcomes: A look at three consensus approaches. *Group and Organization Management, 19,* 112–128.

Huber, V. L., Seybolt, P. M., & Venemon, K. (1992). The relationship between individual inputs, perceptions, and multidimensional pay satisfaction. *Journal of Applied Social Psychology, 22,* 1356–1373.

Kleiman, L. S., & Faley, R. H. (1985). The implications of professional and legal guidelines for court decisions involving criterion-related validity: A review and analysis. *Personnel Psychology, 38,* 803–833.

Klinger, D. E. (1979). When the traditional job description is not enough. *Personnel Journal, 58,* 243–248.

Landy, F. J., & Shankster, L. J. (1994). Personnel selection and placement. *Annual Review of Psychology, 45,* 261–296.

Lawler, E. E. (1994). From job-based to competency-based organizations. *Journal of Organizational Behavior, 15,* 3–15.

Levine, E. L., Ash, R. A., Hall, H., & Sistrunk, F. (1983). Evaluation of job analysis methods by experienced job analysts. *Academy of Management Journal, 26,* 339–348.

Madigan, R. M. (1985). Comparable worth judgments: A measurement properties analysis. *Journal of Applied Psychology, 70,* 137–147.

Madigan, R. M., & Hoover, D. J. (1986). Effects of alternative job evaluation methods on decisions involving pay equity. *Academy of Management Journal, 29,* 84–100.

Mahoney, T. A. (1983). Approaches to the definition of comparable worth. *Academy of Management Review, 8,* 14–22.

Markowitz, J. (1981). Four methods of job analysis. *Training and Development Journal, 35,* 112–118.

McCormick, E. J., Jeanneret, P. R., & Mecham, R. C. (1972). A study of job characteristics and job dimensions as based on the Position Analysis Questionnaire (PAQ). *Journal of Applied Psychology, 56,* 347–368.

McCulloch, M. C., & Francis, D. J. (1989). Analyzing the social content of jobs: Testing the social scale of Functional Job Analysis. In T. W. Mitchell (Chair), *Theory, instrumentation, applications, and consequences in recent job analysis research.* Symposium presented at the annual meeting of the American Psychological Association, New Orleans.

Mecham, R. C. (1977). Unpublished manuscript.

Mintzberg, H. (1980). *The nature of managerial work.* Englewood Cliffs, NJ: Prentice-Hall.

Mount, M. K., & Ellis, R. A. (1987). Investigation of bias in job evaluation ratings of comparable worth study participants. *Personnel Psychology, 40,* 85–96.

Pfeffer, J., & Langton, N. (1993). The effect of wage dispersion on satisfaction, productivity, and working collaboratively: Evidence from college and university faculty. *Administrative Science Quarterly, 38,* 382–407.

Richman, W. L., & Quiñones, M. A. (1996). Task frequency rating accuracy: The effect of task engagement and experience. *Journal of Applied Psychology, 81,* 512–524.

Robinson, J. A., & Swanson, K. L. (1990). Autobiographical memory: The next phase. *Applied Cognitive Psychology, 4,* 321–335.

Sape, G. P. (1985). Coping with comparable worth. *Harvard Business Review, 63,* 145–152.

Schmidt, F. L., Hunter, J., & Pearlman, K. (1981). Task differences as moderators of aptitude test validity in selection: A red herring. *Journal of Applied Psychology, 66,* 166–185.

Schneier, C. (1976). Content validity: The necessity of a behavioral job description. *The Personnel Administrator, 21,* 38–44.

Smith, B. N., Benson, P. G., & Hornsby, J. S. (1990). The effects of job description content on job evaluation judgments. *Journal of Applied Psychology, 75,* 301–309.

Stammers, R. B. (1995). Factors limiting the development of task analysis. *Ergonomics, 38,* 588–594.

Tannenbaum, R. J., & Rosenfeld, M. (1994). Job analysis for teacher competency testing: Identification of basic skills important for all entry-level teachers. *Educational and Psychological Measurement, 54,* 199–211.

Tannenbaum, R. J., & Wesley, S. (1993). Agreement between committee-based and field-based job analyses: A study in the context of licensure testing. *Journal of Applied Psychology, 78,* 975–980.

Tornow, W. W., & Pinto, P. R. (1976). The development of a managerial job taxonomy: A system for describing, classifying, and evaluating executive positions. *Journal of Applied Psychology, 61,* 410–418.

Walford, L. (1996, March 25). Technology helps disabled enrich lives. *Los Angeles Times,* p. D3.

Williams, M. L. (1995). Antecedents of employee benefit level satisfaction: A test of a model. *Journal of Management, 21,* 1097–1128.

Wilson, M. A. (1991). An expert system for abilities-oriented job analysis: Are computers equivalent to paper-and-pencil methods? In R. J. Harvey (Chair), *Measurement issues in job analysis: New approaches to old problems.* Symposium presented at the annual conference of the Society for Industrial and Organizational Psychology, St. Louis.

Wilson, M A., Harvey, R. J., & Macy, B. A. (1990). Repeating items to estimate the test-retest reliability of task inventory ratings. *Journal of Applied Psychology, 75,* 158–163.

Part IV

The Organization

The work that most people do is carried out within the context of an organization of some kind where they are surrounded by other people—co-workers, friends, superiors, and subordinates. I/O psychologists have long understood that the behavior of these others has a considerable impact on individual responses to the work situation.

The organizational context of work is considered in Part IV. Chapter 12 examines the organization as a social system—its components and the communication that maintains it. The groups and groupings within this social system are the focus of Chapter 13, and its leadership is the topic in Chapter 14. The subject matter of Chapter 15 is organization development, bringing about deliberate changes in the organizational social system to make the organization more effective and a better place in which to work.

12

The Organizational Social System and Communication

PSYCHOLOGY AT WORK

Disney Goes in Pursuit of the Perky

Excerpted from K. Swisher, "Disney Goes in Pursuit of the Perky." *Washington Post,* April 23, 1994, pp. C-1, 8. Copyright © 1994, The *Washington Post.* Reprinted with permission.

Whistle while you work?

No, actually, because if you are whistling, you probably can't cheerfully and immediately hear and answer the questions of "guests"—Walt Disney Co's preferred term for customers.

But a lot of perky smiles, only one ring on each hand, no facial hair and no "visible tattoos" are likely to be requirements if you are thinking about working for Disney. . . .

All that, plus lots of "pixie dust," are part of Disney's longtime personnel policies. . . .

They have been attracting good, loyal employees to Disney for decades, and have helped make it the best-known, and one of the most successful theme park and entertainment companies in the world. . . .

Other ways Disney creates and reinforces its corporate culture: Nice landscaping "backstage" (anywhere a guest is present is called "onstage"). Cast member services, such as special discounts. A superfriendly "Casting Castle" where "auditions" (that is, hiring) takes place.

Everyone wears name tags because . . . Disney is a "first-name organization."

And three times a year, top managers work right in the parks, cleaning up ice cream messes and the like in a technique known as "cross-utilization."

CAST MEMBERS (otherwise known as employees) of Disney theme parks must wear costumes or uniforms, and they are required to follow company guidelines for makeup, hairstyle, and jewelry. While on stage, everyone is to wear a smile. These carefully controlled faces of the Disney culture assure a standard show for each guest and a consistent image for the organization. But as described in the excerpt in Psychology at Work, this is no facade merely for show. The Disney organization follows the principles of its "happy place" corporate culture for job applicants and employees as well.

Corporate culture, a concept encompassing the sum total of the traditions, values, and priorities that characterize a company, is a term that appears frequently these days in both the popular and the academic literature on analyzing business operations. Culture provides a shorthand definition of how both employees and outsiders (including competitors) view a company. In addition, analyses from this perspective provide researchers with some interesting insights into such matters as the origin of corporate policies and decisions, the ability of new employees to be successful in an organization, and why certain company mergers are successful and others have been relatively disastrous.

It is more traditional for I/O psychologists to study an organization's climate than its culture, but the two are related aspects of the same thing—the social environment of the organization. It is this environment that is discussed in this chapter. In addition to organizational climate and culture (concepts that relate to how people personally experience their workplaces), communication, the process by which these experiences are created and shared, is examined closely.

The Nature of the Social Environment in Organizations

An individual's **social environment** is created by other people, his or her relationships with them, and the relationships among them. The nature of this environment in organizations is complex; among other factors, it includes the leadership of the organization; its rules and policies; relationships among co-workers, superiors, and subordinates; and norms (unwritten rules) of the organization and of particular subgroups within it.

All of the aspects of an organization's social environment influence the behavior of people in it. Leadership, membership in groups, and the organization's reward policies are three factors that have particular significance for employee performance and satisfaction, and each is examined individually in this book. The purpose of the current chapter is to provide an overview of an organization's social environment and the ways people experience and respond to it. This view is built on the concept of an organization as an open system.

In every area of study there are events that stand out because they dramatically changed the thinking of people in the field. Interestingly, one of the events that has had far-reaching influence on the study of organizations and the people in them occurred in biology, a field that would seem to be totally unrelated to I/O psychology. This event was the publication of a paper by biologist Ludwig von Bertalanffy (1950) on the subject of general systems theory. In his paper, von Bertalanffy proposed that the biological concept of a system is a useful framework for studying the phenomena of all sciences.

As far as the study of organizations was concerned, von Bertalanffy's idea was not a completely new one; the idea had been suggested at various times in the past. But in 1950, it seemed to be an idea whose day had finally arrived. For some time now, both the theory and the application of I/O psychology, organizational behavior, and organization theory have been based on a conceptualization of organizations as systems. More specifically, the conceptualization is that of open systems, systems that interact with their external environments (see also Mayo, Pastor, & Wapner, 1995).

Of the many people who have made contributions to the systems view of organizations, social psychologists Katz and Kahn (1966, 1978) have been especially influential in clarifying its meaning and significance and its relationship to more traditional views of organizations.

> Our thesis, then, is that the study of organizations should take the social system level as its conceptual starting point, but that many of the actual measures will be constructed from observations and reports of individual behavior and attitude. Concepts at the system level tell us what particular individual data to gather and how to use them. (1978, p. 13)

A system of any kind is a whole, made up of parts (subsystems) that function together in an interdependent fashion to meet the goals of the system. An **open system** is a system that affects, and is affected by, its environment; that is, it *interacts* with its environment. The essentials of conceptualizing an organization as an open system include (1) stressing the interrelatedness of the various components and functions of the organization and (2) recognizing the reciprocal dependency between the organization and its external environment (which is both the source of labor and raw materials and the recipient of the organization's product and/or service). From a systems viewpoint, an organization will survive and prosper to the extent that (1) its various internal components function in harmony with one another and (2) the system as a whole maintains a viable relationship with its environment. A pictorial representation of these interdependencies is presented in Figure 12–1.

In the figure, the heavy line that approximates a circle is the boundary of the organization. Outside this boundary, the external environment ("suprasystem") is shown as a shaded area that completely surrounds it. In the suprasystem are all of the external

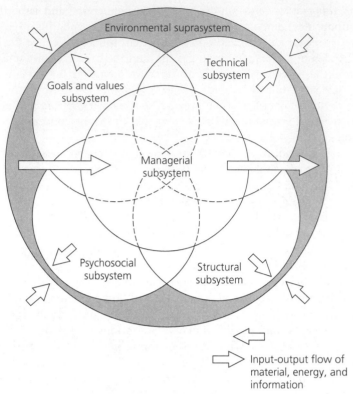

Figure 12–1
The Organization as an Open System

From *Contingency Views of Organization and Management* by James E. Rosenzweig and
   Fremont E. Kast. © 1973, Science Research Associates, Inc. Reproduced by permission
   of the publisher.

factors that affect an organization's functioning. Among these factors may be the labor
pool; suppliers; stockholders; customers or clients; environmentalists; trade associations; local, state, and federal government regulations; and community groups that are
impacted by an organization's activities.

The large arrows in Figure 12–1 represent the interdependency between an organization and external forces. Inputs are what the organization as a whole gets from its environment, including labor, materials, information, financing, customers, and so on.
Products, services, information, and trained employees are among the outputs that an organization sends out into its suprasystem.

Within the boundary of Figure 12–1, there are five subsystems. Each one, except the
management subsystem, has some independent functioning (as indicated by the part of
each circle that stands alone), and each one has functioning that overlaps with other subsystems (as indicated by the part of each circle that overlaps with other circles). The subsystems shown in the exhibit are described by Kast and Rosenzweig (1973).

- *Technical subsystem:* Techniques, equipment, processes, and facilities used in transforming inputs to the organization to outputs to the environment.

- *Goals and values subsystem:* Purpose, strategies, philosophy, and assumptions of the organization.

- *Psychosocial subsystem:* Individual behavior, role and status hierarchies, group dynamics, and influence patterns within the organization.

- *Structural subsystem:* Formal job descriptions, rules and procedures, formal authority and communication relationships, and defined work flows of the organization.

- *Managerial subsystem:* Management objectives, planning, organizing, controlling, and relating the organization to its environment.

The smaller arrows in the figure depict the passing back and forth across organizational boundaries of specific subsystem inputs and outputs. For instance, the technical subsystem takes in relevant technical information and uses technical products and services from the environment in order to play its role in the organization. It also makes contributions to the external environment in the form of shared information and trained individuals who leave the company for employment elsewhere.

The picture of an organizational system in Figure 12–1 is useful in a number of ways. In particular, it provides a concrete reference for the basic premise that behavior at work is the result of a large number of *interacting* factors. In terms of the figure, the behavior of any one individual at work may be seen to be a function of all of his or her personal characteristics interacting with (among other variables) the following:

- The tools and equipment he or she works with (in the technical subsystem)

- The nature of the corporate culture of the organization (in the goals and values subsystem)

- His or her relationships with co-workers (in the psychosocial subsystem)

- The rules and policies of the organization (in the structural subsystem)

- The reward policies of management (in the managerial subsystem)

A concept that describes the sum total of all of these social influences on behavior in organizations is organizational climate.

Organizational Climate

Organizational climate is a term used to describe the consensus of its members about how a particular organization (and/or subsystems within it) deals with its members and its external environment. Because the concept is based on individual perceptions, most measures of climate are self-report questionnaires. These ask the employees of an organization to give their perceptions of its goals and values, leadership policies and behavior, and other aspects of functioning.

Among the climate questionnaires developed specifically for use in business organizations that are used frequently in I/O psychology research are the Organizational Climate Questionnaire (Litwin & Stringer, 1968), the Work Environment Scale (WES; Moos, 1981), and the Business Organization Climate Index (BOCI; Payne & Pheysey, 1971). Some sample items from the 24 scales of the BOCI are shown in Exhibit 12–1.

Respondents to BOCI items reply true or false to each question. The answers for all respondents are then combined to get a measure of organizational climate on each scale.

Exhibit 12–1
Sample Items
from the
Business
Organization
Climate Index

Personal Relations Scales

T   F   Most people here seem to be especially considerate of others.

Sociability

T   F   There is a lot of group spirit.

T   F   Social events get a lot of enthusiasm and support.

Interpersonal Aggression

T   F   There always seem to be a lot of little quarrels going on here.

Homogeneity

T   F   There are many differences in nationality, religion, and social status here.

Routine Scales

Rules orientation

T   F   Formal rules and regulations have a very important place here.

T   F   People ask permission before deviating from common policies or practices.

Administrative efficiency

T   F   Work is well organized and progresses systematically from week to week.

T   F   The flow of information downwards is smooth and efficient.

From R. L. Payne and D. C. Pheysey, "G. G. Stern's Organizational Climate Index: A Reconceptualization and Application to Business Organizations." *Organizational Behavior and Human Performance,* 1971, *6,* 77–98. Copyright 1971 Academic Press, Inc. Reprinted by permission.

Statistical analyses of the 24 scales have shown them to be measuring two basic factors, or dimensions, of climate. Payne and Pheysey call the two BOCI factors "organizational progressiveness" (progressiveness of attitude toward employees and problems concerned with the central task of the company) and "normative control" (extent of rules and formality in the company).

Considerable research has gone into the development of questionnaires such as the BOCI, although some I/O psychologists maintain that the concept is too subtle to be measured in this way (e.g., Katz & Kahn, 1978). The always-sticky issue of whether the questionnaires measure characteristics of the organization or characteristics of the people who answer the questions has long been a particular point of controversy (e.g., Campbell, Dunnette, Lawler, & Weick, 1970). Research with the measurement tools available supports the hypothesis that climate does influence employee behavior and attitudes, however. Furthermore, investigators continue to find substantial agreement among the employees of a given organization as to its climate and/or the climate of certain features or units within it (e.g., James, Joyce, & Slocum, 1988; O'Driscoll & Evans, 1988; Revicki & May, 1989).

Hypothesis
See page 25

Behavioral and Attitudinal Correlates of Organizational Climate

The difficulties I/O psychologists and others have in reaching agreement about the meaning and measurement of organizational climate have created corresponding difficulties in their efforts to investigate the effects of this variable on the behavior of people at work. Therefore the following conclusions, drawn from the literature at this time, are very general ones.

Correlates
See page 40

Variable
See pages 25–26

Determinant
See page 41

First, there are many characteristics of organizations that interact to create its climate. Managerial behavior seems to be the most significant means by which these characteristics are communicated to individual employees (e.g., Kozlowski & Doherty, 1989; Schneider, Gunnarson, & Niles-Jolly, 1994), but it is only one determinant of climate. The size and age of the organization, its physical environment, job design features, and the kinds of rewards it offers to employees are among other important aspects (Field & Abelson, 1982).

The second statement that can be made is that a number of variables, including the nature of an individual's work and work group and his or her personality (e.g., Hershberger, Lichtenstein, & Knox, 1994), affect the way that any individual views the various elements that make up climate. As noted, it is often possible to find substantial agreement about an organization's climate among its employees, but within this consensus there is room for different employees to see the organization quite differently from one another.

The third general conclusion from the climate research is that the individual differences mentioned also affect *responses* to organizational climate, however it may be perceived. This means that even if two employees assess the climate of an organization in a similar fashion, they may react to it quite differently in terms of both job behaviors and job attitudes. This may be one of the reasons, along with measurement difficulties, that investigations into relationships between overall measures of organizational climate and job behavior have not been very successful.

I/O psychologists have had more luck with studies in which specific aspects of climate have been examined. The nature of the "training climate" in an organization has been found to affect successful transfer of training skills from the training environment to the job environment, for example (Rouiller & Goldstein, 1993). On a different level, Scott and Bruce (1994) report that the perceived "innovation climate" of an organization is associated with the extent to which organization members exhibit innovative behavior. It has also been suggested that organizations have a distinctive "cognitive climate" having to do with preferred ways of thinking and working, and that this line of research has potentially important implications for hiring and placement (Kirton & McCarthy, 1988).

Organizational Climate and Job Satisfaction

Much of the organizational climate research in I/O psychology has been focused on the relationship between perceptions of overall climate and the attitude of job satisfaction. Evidence as to a positive correlation between these variables has always been so mixed that one researcher suggested organizational climate and job satisfaction might be two different terms for the same phenomenon (Johannesson, 1973). This hypothesis stimulated considerable research at the time, but it is largely unsupported.

Correlation
See pages 37–39

Today, most I/O psychologists are in agreement that the concepts of organizational climate and job satisfaction are, in fact, different. Schneider and Snyder (1975) suggest that climate is a *descriptive* concept based on perceptions of the organization's social environment. Job satisfaction, by contrast, is an *affective* concept based on feelings about those perceptions. From this perspective, it is easy to see that the two concepts, while clearly related, are not redundant.

Schneider and Snyder's distinction is attractive because it allows for the range of correlational relationships that have been found between organizational climate and job satisfaction. For some people in some situations, perceptions of climate may be an important component of job satisfaction. In this case, a positive correlation would be observed between the two variables (the more positive the perceptions of climate, the greater the job satisfaction). For other people in other situations, climate may not be important to job satisfaction, so no correlation between the two would be found.

The descriptive-affective distinction made by Schneider and Snyder helps explain the weak results mentioned of investigations into relationships between measures of overall climate and job behaviors. In some cases, the factors that affect climate may be relevant to job performance, absenteeism, and turnover, or other behaviors; in other cases, these factors may not be relevant. Again, the result would be a range of reported correlational measures between measures of organizational climate and these job responses.

In summary, organizational climate is a descriptive concept based on individual perceptions of the social environment of an organization. Definitions of this concept are somewhat imprecise, a fact that helps to create and perpetuate measurement difficulties (Payne, 1990). There seems to be sufficient evidence, however, that climate (whatever it is) affects employee behavior to continue research into employee perceptions of characteristics of organizational environments. A different approach to the study of this environment is considered next.

An organization's culture is communicated to people in many ways, including the architecture and appearance of its physical facility.

Organizational Culture

Wilkins (1983) defines culture as the "taken-for-granted and shared meanings that people assign to their social surroundings" (p. 25). The social surroundings in question may be a country, an ethnic group, a rural village, or an organization. The shared meanings are expressed by means of customs (such as rites of passage), slogans, legends (particularly about heroes and heroines), architecture, and symbolic artifacts. The Statue of Liberty has long been a symbol of the American culture's traditional hospitality to people seeking new opportunity, for example.

By simple analogy to Wilkins's definition, the term **organizational culture** refers to the collective meaning of an organization's social environment to the people in the particular organization. There are many more specific and complex views of this concept to be found in the I/O psychology literature (see Allaire & Firsirotu, 1984), but widely shared values and assumptions that create particular behavior patterns in an organization are fundamental. More colorfully, Kilmann (1985) refers to an organization's culture as its soul.

Culture: The Soul of an Organization

The study of organizational culture as such is relatively recent in I/O psychology, and it takes the field further into the territory of sister social sciences anthropology and sociology than it has been before (see Hatch, 1993). In consequence, I/O psychologists "are still operating in the context of discovery" in this area (Schein, 1990, p. 109). The phenomenon that is culture is greater in scope than most I/O psychology topics, requiring consideration of an organization's history, its industry, and the environment in which it operates, as well as many of the more usual variables of interest in the field (Gordon, 1991).

According to Schein (1990), an organization's culture is also multilayered, revealing itself in three successively deeper levels. On the surface are the *artifacts,* which are the observable, physical expressions of the culture. The Disney dress and makeup codes and first-name form of address mentioned in Psychology at Work are examples. To understand why such forms of expression have come about or what they mean to organizational members, however, it is necessary to look below this surface.

At the next level of organizational culture lie the *values* behind cultural artifacts. One of the basic Disney values is that guests be made to feel welcome and totally secure, unmenaced by the dangers, uncertainties, rudeness, or even litter of the real world. A basic *assumption* (the third layer of culture) underlying this value is that friendliness, helpfulness, cleanliness, and a consistent emphasis on the positive ("We are open today until 6 P.M.," not "We close today at 6 P.M.") are among the keys to the Magic Kingdom's success.

All organizations whose members have a history of shared experiences have a culture, although the cultures of some, like Disney, are more easily identified and seem to have more impact (that is, are stronger) on both employees and customers/clients than others. There are no rules about how strong a culture should be for organizational success (Arogyaswamy & Byles, 1987), however, nor does any one particular element of culture so far stand out as critical to an organization's performance.

The Study of Organizational Culture

Much of the research on organizational culture has focused on artifacts, a culture's observable expression or form. Like any other group, organizations have legends: "Did you hear about Jess Smith, who started in the stockroom and became a vice-president?" They have heroes, such as the innovative employee whose production idea made the company millions of dollars. They have rites of passage, such as giving an individual a critical assignment to accomplish successfully before recommending him or her for promotion. Most organizations also have logos, such as Express Mail's flying eagle, that help define their identity for customers and employees. Even the location and architecture of its building say something about the identity of an organization; think of the different images conveyed by a tall, glass city skyscraper versus a low, rambling suburban building surrounded by trees, shrubs, and flowers.

Many investigators who are interested in this area of study believe that expressions of an organization's culture reveal something significant about its people, especially top management. If the major legends and stories are about the founder (or other organizational employees) who made and followed through on risky decisions, for example, this suggests that the organization's management places value on innovation and risk taking. If these stories are about the unpleasant consequences that followed when employees did not take the established company line, it is more likely that the organization and its management value tradition, consistency, and not rocking the boat.

Legends, stories, rites of passage, symbols, and other expressions of culture are difficult phenomena to define operationally, and explorations of cultural artifacts are often based on anecdotal reports and other qualitative methods. With values, I/O psychologists are on more familiar ground, and a number of questionnaire measures of cultural values, such as the Organizational Culture Profile, or OCP (O'Reilly, Chatman, & Caldwell, 1991), are in use. In general, however, the study of organizational culture, like the study of organizational climate, is experiencing both definitional and measurement difficulties (Allaire & Firsirotu, 1984).

If the formal study of organizational culture is in its infancy, it still opens up some interesting and exciting new perspectives on organizations. An examination of the relevant literature suggests two areas for which it might have particular relevance for I/O psychology—selection and placement, and organization change.

Culture widens the lens of the matching model discussed in previous chapters to a perspective that is consistent with cutting-edge competency-based hiring experiments. Empirical data in this area are promising, if skimpy. In one study, Sheridan (1992) found a measure of organizational cultural values to be a better predictor of six-year tenure in six public accounting firms than employee characteristics and the state of the labor market combined.

The second area in which the study of culture can make a major contribution to the field of I/O psychology is in the perspective it offers on organization change. To quote Schein again:

> All of the activities that revolve around recruitment, selection, training, socialization, the design of reward systems, the design and description of jobs, and broader issues of organizational design require an understanding of how organizational culture influences present functioning. Many organizational change programs that failed probably did so because they ignored cultural forces in the organizations in which they were to be installed. (1990, pp. 117, 118)

Operational definition
See page 26

Matching model
See pages 90–91

Is Schein saying that to bring about change in an organization it first is necessary to change its culture? He is not, but it would be easy to get this impression from some of the popular literature on the subject. An organization's culture involves deep-seated values and assumptions that evolve over time in response to many influences. To suggest that it must be altered deliberately and suddenly so as to support a particular change is to fail to appreciate its very nature (Fitzgerald, 1988). The summary of events at International Business Machines (IBM) during the mid-1990s presented in Exhibit 12–2 offers an example of the struggles that can accompany the attempt.

Cultural change is coming to IBM, just as it is coming to a great many other organizations big and small as the century turns. But despite strenuous efforts on the part of a new CEO, it didn't happen overnight. There may be some exceptions, but, in general, changes in organizational culture follow other changes, they do not lead (e.g., Zamanou & Glaser, 1994). An interesting example is to be found in Japan, where new communication technology is beginning to bring about major changes in some organizational cultures. Most Japanese offices have been structured in rigid hierarchies based on seniority for a great many years, but where computers are concerned, age and position mean little. As managers struggle with the mysteries of e-mail, they find themselves turning to much younger subordinates for help, upsetting long-standing traditional work relationships in the process. Eventually, inevitably, new ones will take their place and cultural change will have occurred.

NEW YORK. A few months after International Business Machines Corp. tapped Louis V. Gerstner Jr. as the first outsider to run the 70-year-old company, he imposed a seemingly small change that drew little notice in the outside world.

The new chief executive shelved the three "basic beliefs" that had guided IBM for decades: pursue excellence; provide the best customer service; and, above all, show employees "respect for the individual." In their place came eight [results-oriented] goals. . . .

Longtime IBMers were shocked. Like a mantra, the triad of beliefs had been imbued in the company's employees. . . .

Mr. Gerstner is learning that it is easier to talk about change than it is to dismantle seven decades of culture. . . .

It isn't for lack of trying. The new CEO . . . exhorts IBMers to embrace urgency. He wants them to stop feeling "entitled" to their jobs. . . . Mr. Gerstner makes much ado over his distaste for the white shirts IBMers always wore. . . .

"We're really talking about fundamental values and philosophies," says Ross Williams, an IBM human-resources director. Decision-making is one such process, and if we need to have a greater sense of urgency, we need to change the way people think about it." . . .

Still, interviews with some 30 IBMers . . . show that any revolution could take a while. Thomas Booker, a sales manager in Baltimore, says IBM's future is "a lot brighter with Mr. Gerstner at the helm." But, he says, "it's hard to change when something has been good to you for so long."

**Exhibit 12–2
Cultural
Change at Big
Blue**

Excerpted from L. Hays, "Gerstner Is Struggling as He Tries to Change Ingrained IBM Culture." *Wall Street Journal,* May 13, 1994, pp. A-1, 8. Reprinted by permission of Wall Street Journal, ©1994 Dow Jones & Company, Inc. All Rights Reserved Worldwide.

Communication

I/O psychologists who study organizational culture and climate are attempting to capture certain facets of an organization's social environment. This environment is created by the interaction both of the subsystems within an organizational system and between the organization and the external environment. The means by which these interactions take place, and the means by which the individuals involved are affected by them, is communication.

Communication is the exchange of information, ideas, or feelings between two or more individuals or groups. It is

> a social process of the broadest relevance in the functioning of any group, organization, or society. It is possible to subsume under it such forms of social interaction as the exertion of influence, cooperation . . . imitation, and leadership. (Katz & Kahn, 1978, p. 478)

Given the importance of influence, cooperation, imitation, and leadership, it is clear that communication is the means by which things get done in organizations. However, the focus of this chapter is not the uses to which specific communications are put (to influence, for example), nor is it the skills that are required to make these communications effective. The view here is a broader one. Consistent with the macro (big picture) view of organizations in Part IV, it is the patterns and processes of the communication system of an organization that are of primary interest.

The Communication Process in Organizations

Even in a world in which change is the rule rather than the exception, the changes wrought by technology in the field of communication over the past decade stand out as remarkable. These changes do not alter the basic meaning of communication, however. It remains a process involving at least two individuals or groups, one of whom is initially in the role of sender of the communication while the other is in the role of receiver. As shown in Figure 12–2, communication begins when the sender forms symbols (words, numbers, facial expressions, voice tone, and so on) to convey some meaning into a message that is sent through a channel to the receiver. This process is called encoding.

Communication is effective if the intended meaning of the message is received and understood, or decoded, accurately. The process may stop there or continue via the feedback

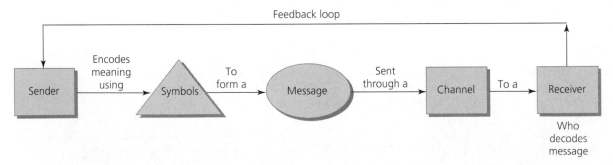

Figure 12–2
The Communication Process

loop until one party or the other breaks it off. Most members of an organization participate in the process depicted in the figure many times a day. In fact, they are often senders and receivers at the same time. An executive may be speaking on the telephone (message sender) and reading a letter (message receiver) at the same time. He or she may interrupt both activities to answer an assistant's question (receiver, then sender, of a message).

The communications of the executive are work related, although much communication in organizations is not. The executive's communications are also formal in nature—he or she is the designated person to make that call, read that letter, and answer the assistant's question. Informal communication in organizations is communication that goes outside of, or around, the formal organizational information exchange policies or authority lines. Often it is gossip or personal, but not all informal communication in organizations is social or nonwork related. If the sales manager asks the boss's assistant to "break the bad news that we lost the Arnold account when it looks like the time is right," the communication is both work related and informal; in everyday language, the sales manager is passing the buck.

The Flow of Organizational Communication

Researchers who study communication in organizations have found it useful to examine the flow in terms of the various routes, or directions, it takes. The characteristics of communication in the three basic directions—upward, downward, and horizontal—are described in Figure 12–3. Arrows indicating the flow of communication are superimposed on a simple and traditional organization hierarchy diagram.

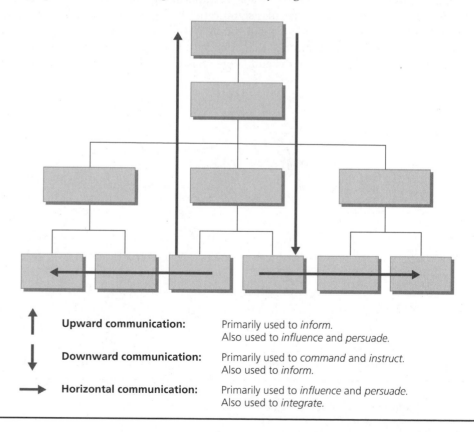

Upward communication:
Primarily used to *inform*.
Also used to *influence* and *persuade*.

Downward communication:
Primarily used to *command* and *instruct*.
Also used to *inform*.

Horizontal communication:
Primarily used to *influence* and *persuade*.
Also used to *integrate*.

Figure 12–3
The Flow of Communication in Organizations

As shown in Figure 12–3, upward communication in an organizational hierarchy flows from subordinate to superior; downward communication is the opposite. Horizontal communication passes between people at the same level of the organization. The overall patterning of the formal upward, downward, and horizontal communication flow in an organization is called a **communication network**. A close examination of an organization's structure and policies would make it possible to draw a rough picture of this network, but informal communication networks, called grapevines, are considerably more complicated.

Field survey
See pages 32-33

In a study that has become a classic, Davis (1953) conducted a field survey investigation of the informal communication patterns among the managers of a medium-sized leather goods factory. The four basic types of grapevine patterns he found are shown and described in Figure 12–4.

- *Cluster:* A communicates to selected receivers (B and E in Figure 12–4) who, in turn, do the same (B to C and D; E to F and G).

- *Probability:* Both A and A's first receiver (B or F in Figure 12–4) pass the message to others in a random fashion.

- *Gossip:* A seeks out and passes the message on to a number of selected receivers—B, C, and so on.

- *Single strand:* The message passes from A to B to C and so on to the ultimate receiver.

Research subjects
See page 27

Davis describes several characteristics of different grapevines as informal communication networks. In the well-known replication of that study summarized in Spotlight on Research, Sutton and Porter (1968) were able to duplicate two of Davis's most interesting findings. This replication is of particular significance because it expanded Davis's study to include all of the employees in an organization, not just the managers, as subjects.

First, Sutton and Porter confirmed that informal communication networks appear to have a relatively small number of disseminators (called "A"s by Davis and "liaisons" by

Cluster

Probability

Figure 12–4
Informal Communication in Organizations: The Grapevine

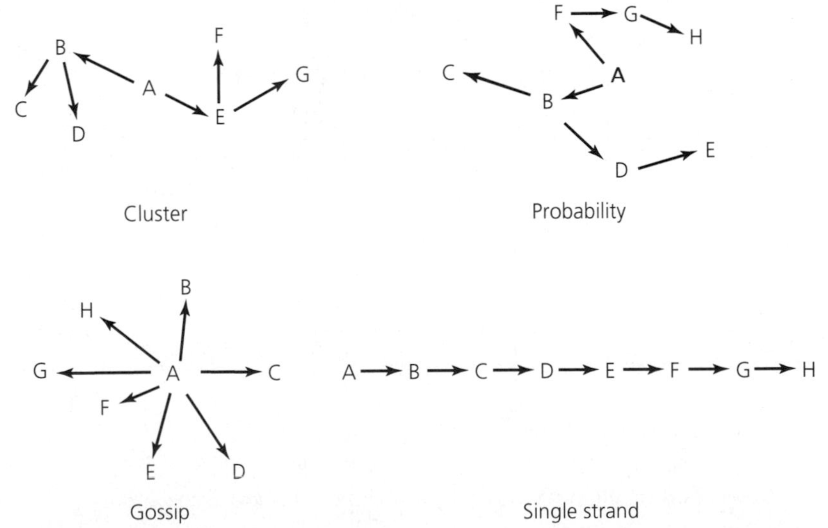

Gossip

Single strand

Note: Letters refer to people, "A" being the individual who originally sends the message. Arrows indicate the direction in which the message flows.

SPOTLIGHT ON RESEARCH

A Study of the Grapevine in a Governmental Organization

Research question   Do grapevine patterns found among managers in a small manufacturing organization hold among all employees of a larger government organization? Are these patterns related to personality characteristics?

Type of study   Field survey research.

Subjects   All 79 employees of a state regional tax office, 8 of whom were managers.

Variables

- Grapevine items (nine selected pieces of information).
- Classification of subjects. Operational definition:
  - ☐ "Isolates" had not heard information more than 50% of the time.
  - ☐ "Liaisons" were nonisolates who had passed on information more than one-third of the time.
  - ☐ "Dead-enders" were nonisolates who had passed on information less than one-third of the time.
- Scores on a personality measure.

General procedure   The progress of nine particular pieces of information ("grapevine items") through the organization was studied over seven months by means of questionnaires asking employees when, where, and how they learned (or did not learn) the information.

Results

- Managers received slightly over 97% of all grapevine information, and all passed it on at least 50% of the time (were "Liaisons").
- Rank-and-file employees received about 56% of the grapevine information, but only about 10% were "Liaisons." Fifty-seven percent were classified as "Dead-enders" and 33% as "Isolates."
- The predominate flow of information for all subjects was within, rather than between, their own functional groups (auditors, clerical, executive, and enforcement).

Conclusion   "The purposes of this investigation were to replicate a classic study of the grapevine reported by Davis in 1953 and to extend the results by obtaining personality data . . . on the subjects. . . . Two of Davis' findings . . . were confirmed. Two other findings of Davis . . . were not confirmed" (p. 230). [The personality data were not significant and are not reported here.]

Summarized from H. Sutton and L. W. Porter, "A Study of the Grapevine in a Governmental Organization." *Personnel Psychology*, 1968, *21*, 223–230.

Sutton and Porter). Second, they confirmed that the higher an individual's level is in an organizational hierarchy, the greater his or her knowledge is of what is going on. Note that the managers in the Sutton and Porter study received virtually all of the grapevine information.

Sutton and Porter caution against overgeneralization of their results, but subsequent research evidence supports the conclusion that a relatively small number of organizational members spread most of the information around. Furthermore, most of this information is accurate. In another classic study, for example, Allen (1967) found that a very few individuals in a research and development organization were named consistently as the most important internal sources of information.

Generalizability
See page 45

Traditional Communication Research

I/O psychologists still investigate informal communication patterns in organizations (e.g., Mishra, 1990), but more of the traditional communication research involves formal networks. Relationships between various aspects of formal communication patterns (independent variables) and the way people in organizations use and react to them (dependent

Independent/ dependent variables
See page 29

variables) have been of particular interest. Four lines of this research are examined briefly: use of communication channels, direction of communication and type of message, direction of communication and accuracy of message, and communication patterns as they relate to employee performance and satisfaction.

Use of Communication Channels

For each of the three directions in which communication in an organization may flow, there are various mechanisms (channels) for sending messages. Open-door policies on the parts of managers and reports sent from subordinate to superior are upward communication channels. The once-popular suggestion box is another, and one that is enjoying a return to favor in updated formats (Mishra, 1994). The Toyota auto plant in Kentucky gets thousands of employee suggestions a year. Office furniture maker Haworth, Inc., saved $8 million in 1994 by using suggestions from its employees.

Plant tours, written newsletters "from your CEO," and superior-instigated meetings with subordinates are examples of downward communication channels. Staff meetings and written memoranda may serve as channels for horizontal communication, as well as for upward or downward message transmission.

In general, organizational communication researchers find upward communication channels in organizations to be the least used on a voluntary basis (e.g., Dubin & Spray, 1964; Luthans & Larsen, 1986). There seem to be certain inhibiting psychological factors that can get in the way of communicating freely with someone in an organization who has greater status or more formal authority. Not everyone is affected; nevertheless, much communication that might be useful if it were sent upward is diverted horizontally to peers.

Failure to make use of formal upward communication channels in organizations is particularly likely when a message would reflect unfavorably on the subordinate (Dansereau & Markam, 1987) or when it is bad news—an unexpected construction problem, expenditures over budget, or customer dissatisfaction, to note a few examples. Instead of communicating this information to superiors so that it may be incorporated into planning and decision making, those involved may discuss it among themselves in an attempt to cover up or correct the situation before it becomes general knowledge.

Direction of Communication and Type of Message

The types of messages most likely to go through the various formal channels in the communication network are described in Figure 12–3. Formal upward communication channels are most often used to inform or to attempt to influence or persuade, for example. But such channels are also useful ways for subordinates to increase their perceptions of job control (e.g., Deluga, 1989) or to manage impressions about their relationship with people higher in the organization. In a study that is cited frequently in the communication literature, Cohen (1958) reports that subordinates with little hope of actual upward career advancement sent more and longer nonwork-related messages upward than their more mobile peers. The author speculates that this behavior might be for the purpose of creating an impression of a personal relationship between the parties that would help compensate for the subordinate's lack of actual upward movement.

Downward communication channels also offer opportunities for uses other than the usual ones. An executive might communicate certain information only to particular subordinates, thereby conveying messages to others about his or her perception of relative subordinate importance. Such communication can also be used as a reward. For some people, being the boss's confidant is a powerful incentive for them to support the superior's plans and goals.

Direction of Communication and Accuracy of Message

One of the more active lines of traditional research in the area of organizational communication concerns the relationship between (a) the direction of communication and (b) the accuracy of the information that flows through the channels. Message inaccuracy occurs in all three directions, but the dynamics differ. Much of the inaccuracy in downward communication, for example, stems from transmission loss, or *filtering*. Each time information moves from one receiver to another, it loses something.

A classic study of message filtering was carried out by Nichols (1962), who tracked the content of messages in much the same way that Davis (1953) and Sutton and Porter (1968) tracked the movement of messages. Nichols found that some 80% of the information in the content of a message had been lost by the time it was passed from the top of the organizational hierarchy down to the level of the average individual employee.

In contrast to the filtering that tends to occur in downward communication, inaccuracies in horizontal communication often stem from adding to, or embroidering, the original message. Thus, Sam's sprained wrist becomes a broken arm, and a minor production flaw becomes the likelihood of a massive recall. How much of this horizontal distortion is deliberate is not known, but deliberate distortion of messages sent through upward communication channels appears to be relatively common. Gaines (1980) found this distortion most often took the form of sending incomplete messages, a result that fits in with conclusions about the use of, and types of messages sent through, upward channels.

Communication Patterns and Employee Performance and Satisfaction

Most of the employees in any organization are part of the informal communication system known as the grapevine. Each is also one link in one or more formal upward, downward, and horizontal channels. On any given day, a head nurse in a hospital might give any unusual information about patients to doctors making their rounds (upward communication), give special instructions for the day to floor nurses (downward communication), and meet with other head nurses to plan for an administrative board tour of inspection (horizontal communication).

Most of the information available about the relationships between (a) place in a communication network and (b) job performance and satisfaction comes from laboratory experiments with small groups. These groups are established to perform experimental tasks of controlled difficulty within the context of communication networks manipulated by the experimenter. These networks are designed to simulate the formal organizational communication channels that are part of an organization's structure. Some of the more common networks used in such studies are shown in Figure 12–5.

Laboratory experiment
See pages 27–28

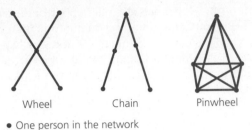

Figure 12–5
Formal
Communication
Networks

Wheel   Chain   Pinwheel

● One person in the network

The networks diagrammed in the figure bear a resemblance to the grapevine patterns shown in Figure 12–4, but there is a fundamental difference. The grapevine is an informal communication network; it develops over time as particular employees interact with one another. The patterns in Figure 12–5 simulate a formal network; it is independent of the personalities of job holders. In the wheel network, for example, the person at the center is designated by organizational policy to deal directly with the other four members of the network. These members, in turn, communicate with one another, at least formally, through the central position (behavior often called "going through channels").

The wheel network of the laboratory may be found approximated in decentralized organizations with geographically dispersed units. The head of each unit reports to a common executive at corporate headquarters. A pattern more typical of many organizations is the chain; formal communication roughly follows the organization's chain of command, or hierarchy. The pinwheel network, in which every member communicates directly with every other member, is usually found only in very small companies or in subunits or teams in larger ones.

Laboratory research with small groups is most clearly relevant to departmental or work group communication in organizations. Therefore, the extent to which the following summary of results from these studies may be generalized to organizations as a whole is speculative. Nevertheless, this research offers insights into the dynamics of group communication patterns that may be quite useful in planning and organizing work at the departmental level or for work teams of various kinds.

• *Centralized* communication networks (such as the wheel) are associated with better job performance when job tasks are relatively simple.

• *Decentralized* communication networks (like the pinwheel) are associated with better job performance when job tasks require more communication of ideas, information, and problem-solving strategies.

• *General* member satisfaction is greatest in communication networks that are less centralized—that is, where members of the network have formal communication links with many other members.

• The greatest *individual* satisfaction is associated with centrality of individual position in the network. Most members of a wheel network report less satisfaction with the communication process than the members of a pinwheel network, for example. The single most satisfied member of either network, however, is likely to be the one in the center of the wheel, the person who has access to (and control over) the maximum amount of information.

These conclusions are summarized from a long line of small-group communication research. For the most part, they are well documented and noncontroversial, and few reports of this type of research are found in contemporary I/O psychology literature. Much the same remarks apply to other traditional communication research, which concentrated on particular elements of the communication process, such as the channel or the direction of communication. There is no sharp line in the sand, but contemporary research in the area of organizational communication has a more dynamic focus.

Contemporary Communication Research

Communication in organizations takes place between people, not between rectangles labeled "sender" and "receiver." Furthermore, this communication may have effects on one or both parties, on the relationship between them, or on outside parties that have little or nothing to do with message content. Finally, communication occurs for a purpose. Work-related information in particular is intended to be used. These are the kinds of issues addressed by more contemporary organizational communication research.

Communication and Job Satisfaction

Much of the communication literature, now as before, focuses on communication between superior and subordinate. The traditional research is characterized by a strong emphasis on the superior's skills as a sender. If the message gets through accurately despite noise (anything that interferes with communication, including receiver defensiveness), the communication attempt is considered a success. More recent investigations in this area focus on communication as an interactive process that has effects on behaviors and attitudes unrelated to the content of a message.

Subordinate job satisfaction is a variable appearing in much of the more recent organizational communication research. Both the openness of the communication lines between supervisor and subordinate (e.g., O'Reilly & Roberts, 1977) and the frequency with which the supervisor uses them (e.g., Schuler, 1979) have been found to affect satisfaction. The extent to which subordinates and supervisors agree about the nature of their communication interactions is also relevant, as a field study by Hatfield and Huseman (1982) demonstrates.

Field study
See pages 27–34

These investigators asked more than 1,200 hourly employees questions about (a) their superior-subordinate communication, (b) their satisfaction with work and with supervision, and (c) their general job satisfaction. A number of relationships emerged from analysis of this data; for example, when supervisors and subordinates agreed that communication encouraged subordinate participation in job-related decisions, white male subordinates reported higher satisfaction with the work situation.

In another study of the relationship between supervisory communication and subordinate satisfaction, Frone and Major (1988) found that the quality of information nurses in managerial positions received from hospital administrators was positively related to their job satisfaction. Alexander, Helms, and Wilkins (1989) also report relationships with the content of supervisor messages. In that study, information about the job and the organization and explanations of supervisor decisions had positive relationships with the reported job satisfaction of professional vocational rehabilitation counselors. Messages about how to do their jobs had a negative relationship; many professionals neither need nor appreciate close supervision or efforts to tell them how to do their jobs.

Contingency Views of Organizational Communication

Some years ago, Tushman and Nadler (1978) hypothesized that organizations will be more effective to the extent that their information-processing *capacities* match their information-processing *requirements*. Tushman (1979) took this a step further, hypothesizing that the best way to structure an organization's formal communication network depends on the nature of the work being performed. Given that different parts of organizations do different work, organizations may need several kinds of communication networks in order to be effective. This "it depends on the work" approach to organizational communication policy is called a contingency approach.

A **contingency approach** to any area of organizational policy is characterized by a rejection of the idea that there is one standard best way to set up and carry out each organizational function. Rather, the best way for an organization to do anything depends on its own particular situation, including type of employees, nature of product or service, extent of external regulation, and financial and market positions. A variety of hypotheses may be generated from a contingency approach to organizational communication networks. It might be speculated, for example, that more complex work requires more communication among the people who perform it. Tushman (1978) investigated this and other hypotheses using a research and development laboratory as a setting. A summary of the findings with respect to the average amount of technical communication over a 15-week period appears in Figure 12–6.

The laboratory in which Tushman made his observations employed some people to do relatively routine service projects and some people to do complex research projects. As expected, employees performing the complex tasks (dotted lines) engaged in significantly more communication within the laboratory and within the project than did those performing the more routine work (solid lines). There was no significant difference between the two groups in the amount of communication outside the organization. Keller (1994) followed up this line of investigation with a longitudinal study of 98 research and development project groups. Ratings of project quality were found to be related to a measure of the correspondence between the nonroutineness of work tasks and information-processing (communication) needs.

O'Reilly (1980) has examined work requirement and communication matching at the individual level, noting a tendency for people to seek more information than is needed for the task at hand. His hypothesis is that the resulting information overload leads to poorer performance than does information underload. (Information underloaded employees believe that they have less information than they need to do their jobs.)

O'Reilly tested his hypothesis in two field studies and confirmed that employees who believed they were working with insufficient information received *higher* performance evaluations. But these employees also reported lower job satisfaction than those working with an information overload. O'Reilly believes this finding suggests greater care should be given to the dissemination of information within organizations, an idea that is explored further later in the chapter.

Finally, Eisenberg and Witten (1987) propose that the amount of communication openness within organizations should be contingent on several factors. For example, openness may not be desirable during an organizational crisis. These authors also note that lower-level employees are risking the power they have if they give out specialized information uniquely in their possession.

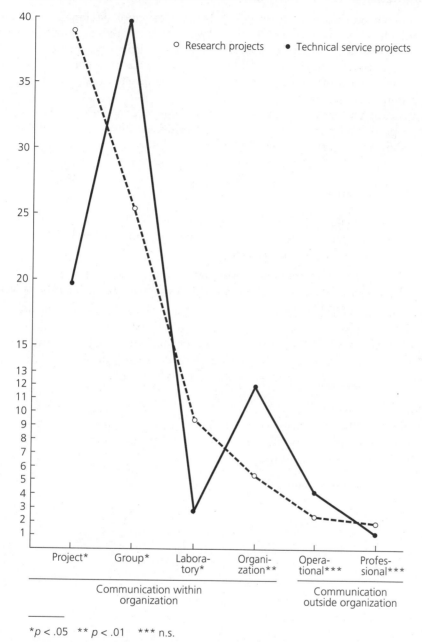

Mean amount of technical communication/15 wks.

○ Research projects   ● Technical service projects

Communication within organization

Communication outside organization

Project* Group* Labora-tory* Organi-zation** Opera-tional*** Profes-sional***

*p < .05   ** p < .01   *** n.s.

Figure 12–6
Communication and Type of Work Tasks

From M. L. Tushman, "Technical Communication in R & D Laboratories: The Impact of Project Work Characteristics." *Academy of Management Journal*, 1978, *21*, 624–645. Copyright 1978 Academy of Management. Reprinted by permission.

Communication and Power

A connection between power and the possession of information has long been recognized at the individual level of analysis (French & Raven, 1959). Within organizations, the balance of power between various groups or individuals is also recognized as an important factor in organizational functioning. More recently, there has been considerable research interest in the impact of computerized management information systems on communication patterns in organizations.

A model that brings together communication, power, and management information systems is proposed by Saunders (1981). The three determinants of power in the model, which is shown in Figure 12–7, may be described as follows:

1. *Coping with uncertainty:* Reduction of unpredictability stemming from lack of information about the future. Up to a point, ability to decrease uncertainty increases power.

2. *Nonsubstitutability:* The extent to which the activities of a department or unit cannot be performed easily by some other department or unit. Greater power is associated with greater nonsubstitutability.

3. *Pervasiveness:* The number of communication or work-flow links with other departments or units. The greater the pervasiveness, the greater the power.

Drawing on a wide base of relevant research, Saunders proposes that the use of management information systems can increase the ability to cope with uncertainty, nonsubstitutability, and pervasiveness in a department or unit whose tasks the system was designed to facilitate. Provided these tasks are critical to the primary activities of the organization, the power of this department or unit will be higher.

Saunders's model is a theoretical link between communication, power, and management information system usage. As such, it is consistent with this chapter's focus on communication as the basic linking mechanism of organizational subsystems. These links are being forged ever tighter as technology changes the way communication occurs in organizations in some very basic ways.

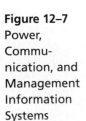

Figure 12–7
Power, Communication, and Management Information Systems

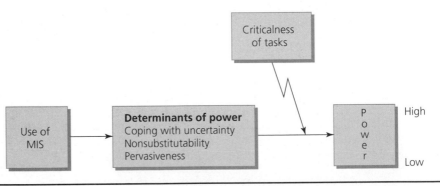

From C. S. Saunders, "Management Information Systems, Communications, and Departmental Power: An Integrative Model." *Academy of Management Review,* 1981, 6, 431–442. Copyright 1981 Academy of Management. Reprinted by permission.

Organizational Communication in the Future

Electronic mail. Voice mail. Fax (facsimile or exact copy) machines. Cellular telephones. Pagers. The Internet. Videoconferencing. The number of ways that people can communicate with one another both on-site and across the miles has expanded beyond the wildest fantasies of science fiction writers a generation ago. Not everyone likes these innovations; voice mail with multiple-option greetings ("Press 1 to leave a message, Press 2 to . . . ") seems to be especially unpopular. Despite some negative reactions, however, there is no prospect of turning back.

Researchers who study communication in contemporary organizations realize that long-held ideas about organizational communication are likely to be altered by the new technology. Even the basic model itself is affected. Many of the new channels are one-way, for example. As regards Figure 12–2, the sender, the message, and the channel are all present and accounted for, but what about the receiver? The voice mail very kindly took the message, but it has not been answered. Is the intended receiver of the message unable or just not interested in returning it? Did someone else take the message and discard it without passing it on? Unless one-way communication is what the situation calls for, the use of such channels can be inefficient and time consuming, particularly if multiple receivers are involved (when setting up a meeting, for example).

On another level, the new ways of communicating may also have a profound effect on the amount and quality of work people accomplish. Electronic mail (e-mail) communication is fast and easy and is done alone. In consequence, it vastly increases the number of messages that can be sent relative to those accommodated by traditional channels. The 13,000-plus employees of Sun Microsystems e-mail 1.5 *million* messages a day. Each of these messages is sent with the expectation that the recipient will read it, but doing so can consume up to a third or more of a workday in some companies. The head of Computer Associates, Inc., a company that sells e-mail software, struck back. The company's e-mail system is shut down for five hours a day to allow employees to get some work done.

Arguably, the most dramatic effect of new ways of communicating will be on the familiar communication pathways and associated relationships that have long existed in many organizations, especially larger ones. Computer-mediated communication "can alter rhythms and patterns of social interactions in ways both powerful and pervasive, neither positive nor negative in themselves, but shaped by local contexts of use" (Mantovani, 1994, p. 45).

Electronic mail systems in organizations illustrate Mantovani's point. Unless it is regulated in some way, e-mail makes it possible for anyone in the system to communicate *directly* and *instantly* up, down, or sideways with any other member of the system. Or with all of them at once—24 hours a day. The phrase "going through channels" ceases to have meaning in this world. More significantly, none of this communication occurs face to face or even voice to voice. It is difficult to imagine anything with more potential for creating basic alterations in the rhythms and patterns of traditional social interactions in organizations than significant reliance on e-mail communication.

Electronic mail channels carry uniformly encoded messages up, down, or horizontally in an organization; the sender does not have to choose a channel or code, but the subtleties that can accompany such choices are lost. There are many situations, for example, in which the decision to write a note or memo on a subject instead of speaking to a receiver face to face carries a message of its own. To the extent that one-channel, one-way communication becomes the norm in organizations, much of the richness of communication will be lost. What is the e-mail equivalent of the magic marker? The voice mail equivalent of an eloquent shrug?

Richer it is, but relevant research also makes no bones about the fact that much of the context or subtext of traditional communication is more confusing than enlightening. Closing the eyes briefly while listening to someone can signal boredom or disgust while meaning nothing more than dry contact lenses. E-mail, and to a lesser extent, voice mail, eliminates the noise originating in such deceptive cues. As direct channels, they, along with fax machines, can also increase communication accuracy by eliminating the filtering and omission problems associated with serial (nondirect) communication channels (Huseman & Miles, 1988). Distortion of messages can also be eliminated, unless the distortion is deliberate.

Neither the potential disruptions nor the potential benefits of the new communication technologies that have been described are anything more than that—potential. What actually happens depends, as Mantovani notes, on the context of use. The same is true for the effects of new ways of communicating on employee job performance and satisfaction. Past research suggests that if e-mail, fax machines, car telephones, and the like make people feel more in control of their work environments and more generally part of the communication loop, many will be more satisfied with their jobs. Some, most notably those who lose the power that was associated with their unique access to (and control of) certain information, are likely to be less satisfied.

To the extent that more and faster communication provides them with timely information that they need to do their jobs right, organizational employees should be able to perform better. For the many people in organizations already laboring under information overload, the idea that more will help them is not unlike a belief in more water as a cure for drowning. The observation that unrestrained communication wastes time, obscures issues, raises problems as well as solves them, and generally creates noise in the system has been made by many communication researchers (e.g., Eisenberg & Witten, 1987; Katz & Kahn, 1978; Kursch, 1971; O'Reilly, 1980).

Communication is the means through which the activities of members of an organization's social systems are coordinated.

The task of I/O psychologists who undertake research in organizational communication in the future will involve reconfirming (or not reconfirming) many of the traditional research findings in a new context. Will e-mail alter the fact that upward communication channels are the least used in most organizations, for example? What effect will new ways of communicating have on supervisor-subordinate relationships, given the research findings that satisfaction with these relationships is enhanced through two-way, face-to-face communication (Young & Post, 1993)?

Future communication research also requires looking into some questions that did not arise prior to the information age. For instance, e-mail is a powerful tool for flattening organizational hierarchies. Will it have this effect or will substitute mechanisms for maintaining power and status distinctions be put into place? And what about privacy? None of the new technology communication methods as commonly used is any more secure than an ordinary telephone. Some are considerably less so. (There is more on this subject in At Issue.)

Finally, it may be suggested that new communication technologies seem almost to cry out for effective contingency research to begin identifying the appropriate functional, situational, and organizational conditions under which various systems can be used to advantage (e.g., Caldwell & Uang, 1995). For an organization to function effectively as a system, it must be *organized*. New communication technologies have a potential for assisting this organization far beyond anything that existed previously.

At Issue

Is Anybody Listening?

Could be. Michael Huffman thought that the steamy romantic messages he exchanged with a co-worker were private, but he was very much mistaken. Another co-worker listened, then played them back to Michael's wife and his boss. Exit Michael from his managerial position at McDonald's Corporation.

Huffman has filed suit, but eavesdropping on voice mail isn't illegal. Nor, apparently, is it uncommon. Up to one-third of the respondents to most surveys admit to monitoring employee voice mail, e-mail, and computer files, often without employee knowledge. It is tempting to divide companies into good guys and bad guys on this basis, but that would be an oversimplification. Hewlett-Packard, longtime poster firm for decentralized, open, flexible, innovative, and team-oriented management, has always maintained a no-secrets work environment. Here is

CIO (chief information officer) Robert Walker on the subject.

> We treat e-mail and probably everything else as if it isn't a private matter, that it's part of the company. We don't assume, and I don't think individuals should ever assume, that what they do is going to be private within the HP context. (quoted in Robin, 1996, p. 136.)

Walker's statement fairly represents the position of many people in organizations today on the subject of workplace privacy. New communication technologies are subject to misuse in an astonishing variety of ways, ranging from faxing pornography to co-workers to running a side business out of the employer's office. A meter reader for a large British utility company was discovered to be staying at home and making up the readings he entered into his hand-held field computer terminal.

Companies can be held liable for such employee misdeeds because the equipment used to commit them is a company asset. If they do not monitor the system, how can they protect themselves? So far at least, the law is on their side. A new state law in Illinois permits employers to eavesdrop on employee work telephones provided they get permission. Judges have ruled for the employer in at least three lawsuits that followed the dismissal of an employee for e-mail messages that were explicitly derogatory of their bosses.

The impersonal nature of e-mail communications seems to lure some people into indiscretions they would not commit face to face. Confidential information, foul language, caustic verbal zingers, or cultural insensitivities wing their way through the company or around the world at the touch of a key. A U.S. District Court ruling against an employee dismissed by Pillsbury Company states that the company's interest in preventing such inappropriate and unprofessional comments outweighs the privacy rights of individual employees.

Does the need to discipline employees for the misuse of employer time or materials extend to the right to know the contents of any message sent or received? A trend toward longer work hours and less leisure time has left growing numbers of people with little choice but to conduct some of their personal business from their place of employment. When telephone calls and e-mail are monitored, there is always the possibility that employers will end up knowing more about employees' marital, credit, medical, or personal situations than they either need to or should know.

Because there currently are no guidelines, information acquired through eavesdropping may be used against an employee directly, as in the case of Michael Huffman, or indirectly and covertly. In one instance, a woman discovered quite accidentally that she had been left off a high-profile project team because a routine telephone audit had revealed the fact that her father had Alzheimer's disease. When confronted, her boss confessed that she assumed the employee would not be able to give full time and attention to the project.

Privacy in the workplace is a sensitive issue, and both employer and employee face dilemmas. Currently, there seems little alternative for many employees but to assume that it is entirely possible that somebody *is* listening.

Summary

If an organization is viewed as a system, its social environment can be seen as created by a complex interaction of the various components of the system. The concept of organizational climate, measured in terms of individual perceptions of organizational policies and practices, appears to be a useful way to describe this environment. The related concept of organizational culture can be thought of rather loosely as the accepted meanings that employees share regarding the social environment of their organization. An increasing number of I/O psychologists believe that the study of culture offers an important new perspective on an organization's social environment.

Communication is the means by which the people in an organization interact; it is the energy of the organization's social system, running continuously in formal and informal channels up, down, and sideways. Traditional research into this process focused on various aspects of the nature and use of these channels and on increased personal communication effectiveness. Later researchers began shifting toward investigations of the process as a whole and of the relationship of this process to organizational functioning. Advanced computer-driven and telecommunication technologies necessitate a reexamination of this research as well as investigations into new questions.

Questions for Review and Discussion

1. Give one example of how an open-systems view of organizations could affect a researcher who wants to conduct a study into some aspect of the behavior of people at work. You may use whatever independent and dependent variables you choose.

2. Compare and contrast the concept of organizational climate with the concept of job satisfaction. Your answer should address measurement issues as well as definitions.

3. Using two organizations of your own choosing, describe the way you view them based on what you know of their cultures (for example, slogans, logos, advertising, buildings, any inside information about legends, and so on).

4. Using Figure 12–2 as a guide, describe two communication links in which you are a participant. Be sure to note if and how feedback occurs.

5. Discuss the statement: There seems to be a danger that communication in organizations is becoming an end in itself rather than a means to an end.

Key Terms

communication

communication direction

communication network

contingency approach

electronic communication

grapevine

open system

organizational climate

organizational culture

organizational subsystems

social environment

References

Alexander, E. R., Helms, M. M., & Wilkins, R. D. (1989). The relationship between supervisory communication and subordinate performance and satisfaction among professionals. *Public Personnel Management, 18,* 415–429.

Allaire, Y., & Firsirotu, M. E. (1984). Theories of organizational culture. *Organization Studies, 5,* 193–226.

Allen, T. J. (1967). Communications in the research and development laboratory. *Technology Review, 70,* 1–8.

Arogyaswamy, B., & Byles, C. M. (1987). Organizational culture: Internal and external fits. *Journal of Management, 13,* 647–659.

Caldwell, B. S., & Uang, S. (1995). Technology usability and utility issues in a state government mail evaluation survey. *Human Factors, 37,* 306–320.

Campbell, J., Dunnette, M. D., Lawler, E. E., & Weick, K. E. (1970). *Managerial behavior, performance, and effectiveness.* New York: McGraw-Hill.

Cohen, A. R. (1958). Upward communication in experimentally created hierarchies. *Human Relations, 11,* 41–53.

Dansereau, F., & Markham, S. E. (1987). Superior-subordinate communication: Multiple levels of analysis. In F. M. Jablin, L. L. Putnam, K. H. Roberts, & L. W. Porter (Eds.), *Handbook of organizational communication: An interdisciplinary perspective.* Newbury Park, CA: Sage.

Davis, K. (1953). Management communication and the grapevine. *Harvard Business Review, 31,* 43–49.

Deluga, R. J. (1989). Employee-influence strategies as possible stress-coping mechanisms for role conflict and role ambiguity. *Basic and Applied Social Psychology, 10,* 329–335.

Dubin, R. S., & Spray, S. L. (1964). Executive behavior and interaction. *Industrial Relations, 3,* 99–108.

Eisenberg, E. M., & Witten, M. G. (1987). Reconsidering openness in organizational communication. *Academy of Management Review, 12,* 418–426.

Field, R. H. G., & Abelson, M. A. (1982). Climate: A reconceptualization and proposed model. *Human Relations, 35,* 181–201.

Fitzgerald, T. H. (1988). Can change in organizational culture really be managed? *Organizational Dynamics, 17,* 5–15.

French, J. R. P., & Raven, B. H. (1959). The bases of social power. In D. Cartwright (Ed.), *Studies in social power.* Ann Arbor, MI: Institute for Social Research.

Frone, M. R., & Major, B. (1988). Communication quality and job satisfaction among managerial nurses: The moderating influence of job involvement. *Group and Organization Studies, 13,* 332–347.

Gaines, J. H. (1980). Upward communication in industry: An experiment. *Human Relations, 33,* 929–942.

Gordon, G. G. (1991). Industry determinants of organizational culture. *Academy of Management Review, 16,* 396–415.

Hatch, M. J. (1993). The dynamics of organizational culture. *Academy of Management Review, 18,* 657–693.

Hatfield, J. D., & Huseman, R. C. (1982). Perceptual congruence about communication as related to satisfaction: Moderating effects of individual characteristics. *Academy of Management Journal, 25,* 349–358.

Hays, L. (1994, May 13). Gerstner is struggling as he tries to change ingrained IBM culture. *Wall Street Journal,* pp. A-1, 8.

Hershberger, S. L., Lichtenstein, P., & Knox, S. S. (1994). Genetic and environmental influences on perceptions of organizational climate. *Journal of Applied Psychology, 79,* 24–33.

Huseman, R. C., & Miles, E. W. (1988). Organizational communication in the information age: Implications of computer-based systems. *Journal of Management, 14,* 181–204.

James, L. R., Joyce, W. F., & Slocum, J. W., Jr. (1988). Comment: Organizations do not cognize. *Academy of Management Review, 13,* 129–132.

Johannesson, R. E. (1973). Some problems in the measurement of organizational climate. *Organizational Behavior and Human Performance, 10,* 118–144.

Kast, F. E., & Rosenzweig, J. E. (1973). Evolution of organization and management theory. In F. E. Kast and J. E. Rosenzweig (Eds.), *Contingency views of organization and management.* Palo Alto, CA: Science Research Associates.

Katz, D., & Kahn, R. L. (1966). *The social psychology of organizations.* New York: Wiley.

Katz, D., & Kahn, R. L. (1978). *The social psychology of organizations* (2nd ed.). New York: Wiley.

Keller, R. T. (1994). Technology-information processing fit and the performance of R & D project groups: A test of contingency theory. *Academy of Management Journal, 37,* 167–179.

Kilmann, R. H. (1985, April). Corporate culture. *Psychology Today,* pp. 62–68.

Kirton, M. J., & McCarthy, R. M. (1988). Cognitive climate and organizations. *Journal of Occupational Psychology, 61,* 175–184.

Kozlowski, S. W., & Doherty, M. L. (1989). Integration of climate and leadership: Examination of a neglected issue. *Journal of Applied Psychology, 74,* 546–553.

Kursh, C. O. (1971). The benefits of poor communication. *The Psychoanalytic Review, 58,* 189–208.

Litwin, G. H., & Stringer, R. A. (1968). *Motivation and organizational climate.* Boston: Harvard University Press.

Luthans, F., & Larsen, J. K. (1986). How managers really communicate. *Human Relations, 39,* 161–178.

Mantovani, G. (1994). Is computer-mediated communication intrinsically apt to enhance democracy in organizations? *Human Relations, 47,* 45–62.

Mayo, M., Pastor, J-C, & Wapner, S. (1995). Linking organizational behavior and environmental psychology. *Environment and Behavior, 27,* 73–89.

Mishra, J. M. (1990). Managing the grapevine. *Public Personnel Management, 19,* 213–228.

Mishra, J. M. (1994). Employee suggestion programs in the health care field: The rewards of involvement. *Public Personnel Management, 23,* 587–592.

Moos, R. (1981). *Work Environment Scale manual.* Palo Alto, CA: Consulting Psychologists Press.

Nichols, R. G. (1962). Listening is good business. *Management of Personnel Quarterly, 4,* 4.

O'Driscoll, M. P., & Evans, R. (1988). Organizational factors and perceptions of climate in three psychiatric units. *Human Relations, 41,* 371–388.

O'Reilly, C. A., III. (1980). Individuals and information overload in organizations: Is more necessarily better? *Academy of Management Journal, 23,* 684–696.

O'Reilly, C. A., III., Chatman, J., & Caldwell, D. F. (1991). People and organizational culture: A profile comparison approach to assessing person-organization fit. *Academy of Management Journal, 34,* 487–516.

O'Reilly, C. A., III., & Roberts, K. H. (1977). Communication and performance in organizations. *Academy of Management Proceedings,* 375–379.

Payne, R. L. (1990). Madness in our method: A comment on Jackofsky and Slocum's paper, "A longitudinal study of climates." *Journal of Organizational Behavior, 11,* 77–80.

Payne, R. L., & Pheysey, D. C. (1971). D. C. Stern's Organizational Climate Index: A reconceptualization and application to business organizations. *Organizational Behavior and Human Performance, 6,* 77–98.

Revicki, D. A., & May, H. J. (1989). Organizational characteristics, occupational stress, and mental health in nurses. *Behavioral Medicine, 15,* 30–36.

Robin, M. (1996, June 26). Managing a global network. *Microtimes,* pp. 132–234.

Rouiller, J. Z., & Goldstein, I. L. (1993). The relationship between organizational transfer climate and positive transfer of training. *Human Resource Development Quarterly, 4,* 377–390.

Saunders, C. S. (1981). Management information systems, communications, and departmental power: An integrative model. *Academy of Management Review, 6,* 431–442.

Schein, E. H. (1990). Organizational culture. *American Psychologist, 45,* 109–119.

Schneider, B., Gunnarson, S. K., & Niles-Jolly, K. (1994). Creating the climate and culture of success. *Organizational Dynamics, 23,* 17–29.

Schneider, B., & Snyder, R. A. (1975). Some relationships between job satisfaction and organizational climate. *Journal of Applied Psychology, 60,* 318–328.

Schuler, R. S. (1979). A role perception transactional process model for organizational communication-outcome relationships. *Organizational Behavior and Human Performance, 23,* 268–291.

Scott, S. G., & Bruce, R. A. (1994). Determinants of innovative behavior: A path model of individual innovation in the workplace. *Academy of Management Journal, 37,* 580–607.

Sheridan, J. E. (1992). Organizational culture and employee retention. *Academy of Management Journal, 35,* 1036–1056.

Sutton, H., & Porter, L. W. (1968). A study of the grapevine in a governmental organization. *Personnel Psychology, 21,* 223–230.

Swisher, K. (1994, April 23). Disney goes in pursuit of the perky. *Washington Post,* pp. C-1, 8.

Tushman, M. L. (1978). Technical communication in R & D laboratories: The impact of project work characteristics. *Academy of Management Journal, 21,* 624–645.

Tushman, M. L. (1979). Work characteristics and subunit communication structure: A contingency analysis. *Administrative Science Quarterly, 24,* 82–98.

Tushman, M. L., & Nadler, D. A. (1978). Information processing as an integrating concept in organizational design. *Academy of Management Review, 3,* 613–624.

von Bertalanffy, L. (1950). The theory of open systems in physics and biology. *Science, 111,* 23–28.

Wilkins, A. L. (1983). The culture audit: A tool for understanding organizations. *Organizational Dynamics, 11,* 24–38.

Young, M. B., & Post, J. E. (1993). Managing to communicate, communicating to manage: How leading companies communicate with employees. *Organizational Dynamics, 22,* 31–43.

Zamanou, S., & Glaser, S. R. (1994). Moving toward participation and involvement: Managing and measuring organizational culture. *Group and Organization Management, 19,* 475–502.

13

Groups in Organizations

Air Force Streamlines Its Fliers' Physicals

Excerpted from J. Schmit, "Air Force Streamlines Its Fliers' Physicals." *USA Today,* May 5, 1995, p. 6B. Copyright 1995, *USA Today.* Reprinted by permission.

Travis Air Force Base, California. Senior airman Mark Redden was stationed in Italy last fall as Iraqi troops were moving toward the Kuwaiti border.

Redden, 27, was one of 16 soldiers sent from Travis to refuel aircraft. The pace was frantic.

Then word came from Travis. Redden hadn't had his annual physical. He would be grounded—unable to fly and do his job—unless he got the checkup before his birthday, three weeks away.

At one time, Redden would have had to fly home immediately—crisis or no crisis. That's because it took Travis' 1,400 fliers an average 13.2 days to get a physical. But changes made by the base's Flight Physical Team had cut the time to one day. So, Redden stayed on the job until the crisis passed. Then, he flew back to Travis for his checkup. . . .

In 1991, the Flight Medicine Clinic formed one of Travis' first quality improvement teams. . . .

The eight people on the team locked themselves in a conference room twice a week for three months. The team included one person from every department involved: labs, X-ray, dental, physical exams, flight medicine and records. It also included a flier. . . .

The team looked at every step of the process for ways to cut the time it took. "We had the walls covered with flow charts," says [one member]. . . .

The changes [the team recommended] . . . met little resistance. The old process was universally disliked. . . .

The hardest part was forming the team. Most members had never met each other. Each department did its own thing. Yet for years, they grumbled about each other. Once they became part of the same team, their focus shifted to the entire process.

THE TRAVIS Air Force Base Flight Physical Team is a form of quality circle—groups of employees who meet to brainstorm problems and their solutions at the production level. Part of production at the Travis Flight Medicine Clinic is giving fliers their annual physicals, and the remarkable improvement in this process described in the excerpt in Psychology at Work earned the Travis quality team the 1995 RIT/*USA Today* Quality Cup for not-for-profit organizations.

The eight-person quality team at the Travis clinic is a formal task group that cuts across functional divisions within the clinic, forming a new communication channel within this organization. After some initial resistance on the parts of some members, the group turned the clinic around. In doing so, it helped to increase efficiency on the base— pilots no longer need be grounded because they are overdue for their physicals nor do they need to waste days of duty time in waiting rooms to get checked out and certified for duty.

Being part of the quality improvement team in the medical clinic added a new dimension to the social environment of these employees. In addition to having friendships with co-workers, identifying with a particular functional specialty at the clinic, and belonging to various informal groups on the air base, these individuals became part of a formal group having a specific purpose outside of normal job duties.

Groups in organizations, their nature, their influence on individual employee behavior, and their behavior as decision-making/problem-solving entities are the focus of this chapter. Among the particular kinds of groups examined are unions and various forms of job and project teams. A complete examination of groups is found in Forsyth (1990). More detail about groups in the workplace is found in Ross (1989).

Groups in Organizations

Organizations are made up of individuals, but few of these individuals work alone. Most are members of some smaller group within an organization's social system. A manager may have a private office, but he or she is still part of the company's management team. In addition, the manager identifies with (and is seen by others as part of) the particular group of employees for whose work he or she is responsible. Employees who are not managers likewise are part of groups; they are members of specific work teams, departments, or divisions. Some are members of unions as well. In other words, organizations are perceived by most people as sets of groups rather than as collections of individuals.

Formal and Informal Work Groups

Every member of an organization is perceived by others as a member of some group within the organization. That group may be as large and as loosely defined as "management," or as specific as "Project Team Delta." Project groups are defined on the basis of the work that is done by the group members. They are formal task groups; like the Flight Physical Team at Travis Air Force Base, they have been created deliberately for some purpose. Other examples of formal groups in organizations include committees, crews of various kinds, and boards of directors.

Informal groups get together on the basis of individual liking or similarity of interests, background, or personal characteristics. In organizations, informal groups may be subsets of a formal work group. Alternatively, they may have no basis in work assignments. Four out of a group of five automobile salespeople may become friends, have lunch together, and share customer leads. A fifth may get along well with the others but not join in these activities. Instead, he or she may be part of another informal group whose members—a mechanic, a bookkeeper, and a lot attendant at the automobile agency—share an interest in racquetball.

Reference Groups

Most people are members of several formal and informal groups, both in and out of organizations, but some of these groups are more important to them than others. A group that is personally important to an individual in a particular way is called a reference group. The upper-level management in an organization may be a reference group for a manager trainee. His or her opinions, attitudes, and beliefs (such as the proper relationship between labor and management) are partially formed by the opinions of those in this group. In addition, career success is measured partly by comparison with these same individuals; if most are in their early 40s, for instance, the trainee will feel that he or she must attain such a position by this age to be successful.

In the example of the manager trainee are found the ways that a group must be important to qualify as a reference group. A **reference group** is any group that an individual uses as a source of personal values, beliefs, or attitudes, and/or as a standard for evaluating his or her own behavior. There is a degree of identification, a perception of sharing characteristics with the group's members and of sharing (or aspiring to share) similar experiences (Mael & Tetrick, 1992).

Group membership is one of the most significant influences on the behavior of individual members who take the group as a reference group.

Identification is an individual psychological response; a group that is a reference group for one person may not be for another, even though the two people seem quite similar. The American Psychological Association is a reference group for many of its members, but not for all. For some people, membership in this group is just a good way to keep up with developments in the field of psychology.

Unions: A Special Case of Group Membership

Much of the research on groups in organizations is centered on small groups that have their origins within a particular company. But employees also belong to groups and groupings that originate outside of organizational boundaries and crosscut formal organizational groups. Foremost among such identity groups (Alderfer & Smith, 1982) are unions.

The number of union members in any particular organization may be large or small, but union membership is a characteristic shared by 12% to 18% (estimates vary) of the employees in this country. Some important norms affecting the workplace behavior of these individuals originate outside the employing organization and are maintained by identification with other union members in the workplace. For those who take their particular union as a reference group, the influence of union membership on performance, attendance, and other work behaviors and attitudes is substantial.

The study of unions—why people join them (e.g., Kelly & Kelly, 1994), their relations with management (e.g., Huszczo & Hoyer, 1994), and the constraints they place on organizational functioning (e.g., Collins, 1995)—is an active area of research. In much of this work, unions are treated as if they are all the same, and a considerable body of knowledge about "union behavior" and individual differences between union and nonunion

Exhibit 13–1
Work Groups Can Help or Hinder Organizations

From L. N. Jewell and H. J. Reitz, *Group Effectiveness in Organizations*. Copyright 1981 Scott, Foresman and Company.

---

employees has accumulated. In fact, unions are not all the same nor are subunits (locals) of the same union all the same. One of the important ways in which they differ is in their strength. Hammer (1978) found that this difference has significant effects on the attitudes, perceptions, and behaviors of members.

In Hammer's study, the stronger union locals were reference groups for their members; these locals had more influence on some aspects of employees' behavior than did their organizational membership. In particular, subjects in these locals perceived their work supervisors to have less power over them (than did members of weaker locals), and they gave little support to company goals. They tended to be lax about showing up for work on time, and they got lower marks for being friendly and cooperative with other workers than did other subjects.

Research subjects
See page 27

The subjects in Hammer's stronger locals exhibited different behavior patterns from those in weaker locals. What makes a union local stronger? The short answer is member commitment and associated member participation in union activities. Commitment and participation, in turn, are related to a variety of individual and situational factors, including the degree to which decision making in the local is shared by officers and members (Mellor, Mathieu, & Swim, 1994), the socialization experiences of new members (Fullagar, Gordon, Gallagher, & Clark, 1995; Kelloway & Barling, 1993), successful union performance (Fryxell & Gordon, 1989; Johnson & Johnson, 1992), and how long an individual has been a member of the union (Barling, Wade, & Fullagar, 1990).

Socialization
See pages 172–179

Member commitment to union local membership and member participation in its activities make a local stronger, and stronger locals have more influence over the behavior of individual members. Employees in the study by Hammer exhibited behavior patterns that are consistent with long-held stereotypes about the us-versus-them mentality of union members. As the incidents described in Exhibit 13–1 illustrate, however, this stereotype, like most, is oversimplified.

The union members at the midwestern food processing plant followed their exhibition of "typical union behavior" (in the minds of many nonunion people) with behavior that was very different. The same group of individuals shut down the food plant to protest a management decision, then saved it from a flood. It takes more than stereotyped ideas about unions to explain such incidents. What the story really illustrates is that groups in organizations sometimes facilitate and sometimes hinder the accomplishment of organizational goals, and the same group may do both at different points in time.

The fact that the group in the story in Exhibit 13–1 was a union group is interesting, given the way many people think of unions, but it is not critical to the point. All groups have the potential to help or hinder organizations; if their members, like many union members, are strongly attracted to the group (that is, if it is a reference group for most members), this potential is more likely to be realized.

To recapitulate, every individual may have several reference groups, both in and out of organizations. The significance of such groups for I/O psychologists is that their personal importance gives them substantial influence over their members. In organizations, this influence is separate from the influence of organizational norms, rules, policies, and leadership. In the next section, the dynamics that make it possible for a group to exert what can be enormous influence on its individual members are reviewed.

Group Influences on Individual Behavior

The fact that group membership can alter the behavior of an individual is a long-established phenomenon in psychology and one that research continues to support (e.g., Baratta & McManus, 1992; Kameda & Davis, 1990; Shepperd, 1993). This group influence can act to make members do things in the company of other group members that they would not do alone. Group membership can also influence the behavior of a member when no other member is around. This influence on individual member behavior is particularly strong in groups with a high degree of cohesiveness.

Group Cohesiveness

Group cohesiveness refers to the extent to which members of a group are attracted to one another and to being in the group; in a highly cohesive group, every member has a strong commitment to keeping the group together. Groups differ in their degree of cohesiveness, and many never reach the stage of mutual attraction and commitment that characterizes strong cohesiveness.

Other things being equal, greater cohesiveness is more likely to develop in groups that are relatively small, that are somewhat difficult to enter, and that are organized in a cooperative, rather than a competitive, fashion. Opportunity for the group members to interact with one another frequently also helps develop greater cohesiveness. In addition, there is evidence that successful group performance helps increase group cohesiveness (e.g., Mullen & Copper, 1994).

Finally, social psychologists have long been aware that group cohesiveness is greater in groups in which there is considerable similarity of attitudes, opinions, values, and behaviors among group members. In the early stages of group development, this similarity reduces the possibility of interpersonal conflict that could split the group into factions or break it up entirely. As the development process continues, the group may tolerate greater differences of opinion on some issues. At the same time, group consensus as to what characterizes this group and, especially, how it is different from other groups will increase.

Differences in perception about one's own group and other groups are illustrated by an interesting study of intergroup relations in a large corporation (Alderfer & Smith, 1982). Opinions about the goals and values of two organizational groups from each group's own members and from members of the other group are shown in Exhibit 13–2. Notice the relative uniformity of member perceptions within each group and the difference between these perceptions and those of members of the other group. For example, 64% of the members of the White Foremen's Club (WFC) agreed that the Black Managers' Association (BMA) was essentially a racist organization; only 16% of the BMA agreed with this statement.

The different racial composition of the two groups in Alderfer and Smith's study may have intensified differences in perceptions, but the groups also had much in common. All members of both groups were employees of the same organization, and all were at a similar level in the management hierarchy of that organization. The Black Managers' Association did not limit its membership to first-level management as did the White Foremen's Club, but most of the black managers were, in fact, at this level.

Researchers following the Alderfer and Smith study have continued to demonstrate the in-group/out-group differences in perception found between the White Foremen's Club and the Black Managers' Association. In a series of four studies of stereotypes, Rettew, Billman, and Davis (1993) found that a variety of groups consistently overestimated the extent to which they (or a third group) were perceived as different by outsiders. The stereotypes investigated included women, business students, and people who had grown up in different parts of the United States.

Item: The White Foremen's Club works to improve working conditions for its members.

%WFC[a] Agreeing: 86   %BMA[b] Agreeing: 75

Item: The Black Managers' Association works with top management to solve racial problems in XYZ.

%WFC Agreeing: 84   %BMA Agreeing: 81

Item: The Foremen's Club is essentially a social organization.

%WFC Agreeing: 85   %BMA Agreeing: 57

Item: The Black Managers' Association is essentially a social organization.

%WFC Agreeing: 43   %BMA Agreeing: 34

Item: The Foremen's Club is essentially a racist organization.

%WFC Agreeing: 23   %BMA Agreeing: 53

Item: The Black Managers' Association is essentially a racist organization.

%WFC Agreeing: 64   %BMA Agreeing: 16

[a]WFC = White Foremen's Club
[b]BMA = Black Managers' Association

Exhibit 13–2
Group Membership and Perception of Self and Others

Reprinted from "Studying Intergroup Relations Embedded in Organizations," by C. P. Alderfer and K. K. Smith published in *ASQ (Administrative Science Quarterly)*, Vol. 27, #1, 1982, by permission of ASQ.

The similarity of expressed opinions about one's own group and another group illustrated in Exhibit 13–2 and by other research is one aspect of group member adherence to group norms. **Norms** are unwritten standards for behavior, values, and attitudes that grow out of the interaction of a group. The more cohesive a group, the stronger its norms and the better the group is able to enforce individual conformity to them.

Norms in Organizational Groups

In a sense, an organization is one big group and as such it has norms that affect the behavior of its members. These norms are a strong component of the organizational culture described in Chapter 12. Most organizations are too large to become highly cohesive groups as such, however, and the most powerful norms for individual employees originate in smaller formal or informal groups. Some of the norms described by various members of one organization are shown in Exhibit 13–3.

The norms listed relate to a variety of different behaviors. They also vary considerably in how specific they are. "Begin closing up 15 minutes before quitting time" is very specific. On the other hand, "Help yourself . . ." leaves substantial room for individual interpretation. For this norm, as for most, there is usually a range of behavior that constitutes acceptable conformity to the group. Taking home the desktop computer lies outside of that range, but this group probably would object to a holier-than-thou reaction from one member when another takes home some copy paper.

Not only is there variation in the behaviors that are considered appropriate conformity to group norms, but there is also variation in the strength of group approval or disapproval that goes along with conformity or nonconformity. A model that incorporates both the range of behavior and the strength of approval associated with group norms was developed by Jackson (1966). An example of this model, called a return potential curve, is shown in Figure 13–1. The norm used to illustrate the concept is about unexcused absences from work.

The diagram in the figure shows that maximum approval (return) from this group is associated with several unexcused absences per year (point a). Group approval changes to disapproval if too few absences are taken (point b) and to extreme disapproval if too many are taken (point c). The logic of this approval-disapproval pattern from the group's point of view is clear. If too few days off are taken by one individual, people who take more will look bad. If too many are taken, other group members will have to take up the work slack.

Exhibit 13–3
Some Work
Group Norms
for Employee
Behavior

- Speak up for the boss if someone outside the group is criticizing him or her.
- Begin closing up shop 15 minutes before quitting time.
- Leave the work area spotlessly clean each night.
- Help yourself to paper, pens, scissors, or whatever you need for home use.
- Do not wear your earplugs; they are for sissies.
- If you need help, ask a co-worker, not the boss.
- Never wear a dirty uniform to work.

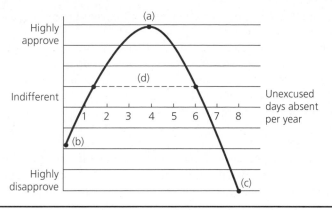

Figure 13–1
The Return
Potential Curve
for an
Unexcused
Absence Norm

From Thomas V. Bonoma and Gerald Zaltman, *Psychology for Management.* Copyright 1981 Kent Publishing Company. Reprinted by permission of the author.

In Figure 13–1, the range of acceptable behavior with regard to the norm governing unexcused absences is between 2 and 6 days per year (dotted line d). In a highly cohesive work group, this standard may be as powerful (or more so) as any organizational policy about attendance; the significant influence of group norms on both the absenteeism and the lateness behavior of their members has been demonstrated in many studies (e.g., Blau, 1995; Mathieu & Kohler, 1990). Conformity by group members to this norm is part of the price they pay for the rewards of being accepted into the group.

Group Influences on Work Behaviors and Attitudes

Norms are the primary mechanism through which groups influence the behavior of their members. Penalties, called sanctions, for violating norms can include teasing, ignoring, scapegoating, physical punishment, or expulsion from the group. Some of the work behaviors and attitudes that are influenced by group membership are reviewed in this section. For a complete discussion of the development and enforcement of work group norms, see Feldman (1984).

Influences on Performance

The ability of a work group to affect the performance of its individual members first gained widespread attention in the Hawthorne experiments (Roethlisberger & Dickson, 1939). The bank wiring room studies from that series of experiments revealed the existence of two sets of production standards. One was set by the company; a second, lower, one represented a norm of the work group that wired the terminals in this phase of production.

Hawthorne studies
See pages 4–5

The Hawthorne researchers collected a great deal of interesting data about the social processes among the bank wiring room employees. Among other things, they found two distinct small groups with two different sets of norms about appropriate behavior at work. They also found that a few individuals belonged to neither group, but all employees conformed to some degree to a general wiring room norm of not doing as much work as engineering standards specified.

The phenomenon observed in the wiring room some 60 years ago is so common that it has its own name. **Work restriction** refers specifically to limits on production output set by work group norms. It is such a well-known phenomenon that many people think this is the only direction in which group influences on individual performance operate. The truth is somewhat more complicated.

The Hawthorne bank wiring room studies stimulated considerable research into the nature of group norms and their impact on the performance of individual group members. Taken as a whole, these studies reveal that some highly cohesive work groups have negative work norms (from management's perspective) and some have positive ones. In consequence, highly cohesive groups tend to be among *either* the most *or* the least productive groups in an organization, depending on whether their norms support or undermine organizational expectations for performance. Consistent with the discussion of uniformity in cohesive groups, performance norms serve to reduce the variance of individual performance.

Variance

See pages 40–42

Many experiments and case studies regarding the influence of groups on work performance focus on volume of productivity, but groups also influence other member behaviors related to performance. There are norms about the way things are done as well as about how much is done. A common example is the problem some companies have with work norms that encourage dangerous work practices and can jeopardize individual safety. Other work method norms include the following:

- Norms about the use of resources: "Don't worry about waste—the company can afford it."

- Norms about task priorities: "We always do Clark's work first."

- Norms about customer treatment: "The young ones never buy anything—ignore them."

Learning norms, such as those listed, is part of the process by which a newcomer to a work group becomes an accepted insider (socialization), as the conversation in Exhibit 13–4 illustrates.

Influences on Satisfaction

The classic study of the influence a work group can have on the job satisfaction of its members is described by Roy (1959–60). In a famous report he calls "Banana Time," Roy discusses his experiences and observations as part of an actual four-man work group. The task of these employees consisted of stamping plastic into various shapes with a machine designed for this purpose. The job was repetitive and incorporated very little opportunity for task variety into its 12-hour day.

Banana time was a patterned social interaction in which one member of the group regularly seized and ate the banana another member brought for his own lunch. Each day this "time" went the same way; one group member craftily extracted the banana from the other's lunch and devoured it against the protestations of its owner and the chiding of the third member for "all the fuss." By contrast, "peach time," while equally structured in terms of the social interaction, led to the entire group sharing the peaches brought by one member.

Exhibit 13–4
Learning the
Ropes: Group
Norms and
Performance

For eighteen years Ginny had been doing about the same thing—packing expandrium fittings for shipment. So well practiced was she that she could do the job perfectly without paying the slightest attention. This, of course, left her free to "socialize" and observe the life of The Company as it took place about her.

Today, however, she was breaking in a new packer. It was instructive.

"No, not that way. Look, honey, if you hold it that way, well, then you have to twist your arm when you pack this corner, see. This way it's easier."

"But that's the way Mr. Wolf (methods engineer) said we had to do it."

"Sure he did, honey. But he's never had to do it eight hours a day like me. You just pay attention to what I say."

"But what if he comes around and says I should pack the other way?"

"Oh, that's easy, When he's here you do it his way. Anyway, after a couple of weeks you won't see him again."

"Slow down, you'll wear yourself out. No one's going to expect you to do eighty pieces for a week anyway."

"But Mr. Wolf said ninety."

"Sure he did. Let *him* do it. Look, here's how to pace yourself. It's the way I was taught, and it works. You know the Battle Hymn of the Republic (Ginny hummed a few bars). Well you just work to that, hum it to yourself, use the way I showed you, and you'll be doing eighty next week."

"But what if they make me do ninety?"

"They can't. Y'know you start making mistakes when you go that fast. No, eighty is right. I always say, a fair day's work for a fair day's pay."

From R. Richard Ritti and G. Ray Funkhouser, *The Ropes to Skip and the Ropes to Know.* Copyright 1977 Grid Publishing, Inc. Reprinted by permission of John Wiley & Sons, Inc.

In addition to banana time and peach time, the group had "fish time," "Coke time," "window time," and "pickup time." There were also a number of conversational themes, both comic and serious, that followed an almost unvarying pattern. Among other themes, Roy describes "getting Dannelly a better job" and "George's daughter's marriage."

Roy discusses the meaning of times, themes, and various work games (shutting off his machine every time a member left the work area, for example) in terms of their effects on job satisfaction. In this group, social interaction was being used to inject some satisfaction into a particularly sterile job situation. Roy discovered for himself that this interaction, which initially seemed to him to be meaningless, silly, and irritating, provided psychological support to make the long days relatively easy to endure. In his words: "The 'beast of boredom' was gentled to the harmlessness of a kitten "(p. 168).

Influences on Job Adjustment

It has frequently been suggested that the social aspects of work described so vividly by Roy may help to offset absenteeism, turnover, and job stress. Mossholder, Bedeian, and

Hypothesis
See page 25

Armenakis (1982) investigated this hypothesis by looking at relationships between (a) group member interaction, (b) individual differences in self-esteem, and (c) job performance, reported job tension, and tendency to leave the job. Questionnaires were used to measure subjects' self-esteem, peer group interaction (PGI), experienced job tension, and likelihood of leaving the job. Supervisory ratings were used to measure job performance. Subjects were nurses at a large hospital.

A summary of the major findings of the investigation by Mossholder and his colleagues is presented graphically in Figure 13–2. As had been predicted, both job tension and propensity to leave the job were lower for subjects who reported that social interaction among members of their work groups was high (graphs a and b). The relationship was stronger for low-self-esteem subjects (as indicated by the steeper lines in the graphs), and the performance of these subjects was also related to peer group interaction (graph c). By contrast, the performance of high-self-esteem individuals was high regardless of what happened in work groups.

The results of Mossholder, Bedeian, and Armenakis's study as summarized in the figure highlight the important influence group membership may have on the job adjustment of certain employees. In particular, it may be that low-self-esteem employees function better in work situations requiring interpersonal interaction and teamwork. By contrast, jobs requiring independent performance may be performed better by people with high self-esteem.

Group Influences in Perspective

Group membership is an extremely important aspect of any individual's social environment, at work as well as away from it. It should not be thought, however, that all people conform all the time to the norms of the groups of which they are members.

The psychological force causing one to conform is a complex of individual motives and group expectations. Certain individual characteristics, combined with certain

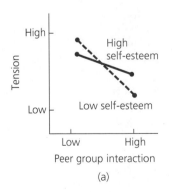
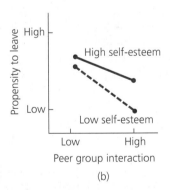
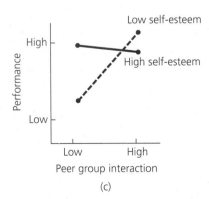

Figure 13–2
Self-Esteem, Peer Group Interaction, and Employee Behaviors and Attitudes

From K. W. Mossholder, A. G. Bedeian, and A. A. Armenakis, "Group Process–Work Outcome Relationships: A Note on the Moderating Impact of Self-Esteem." *Academy of Management Journal*, 1982, *25*, 575–585. Copyright 1982 Academy of Management. Reprinted by permission.

situational factors, produce independence or even occasional anticonformity responses to group influence attempts. (Jewell & Reitz, 1981, p. 67)

Among the individual characteristics that are associated with greater resistance to
group influence are high self-esteem, strong values that run counter to group norms, and
strong confidence in one's own knowledge and abilities. The reaction of a group when
such a member fails to conform to group norms has been studied extensively.

The classic study of individual deviance from group norms by Schachter (1951), and
the work of those who followed this line of research, reveal a pattern. For a time the deviant will be the center of attention as the group members attempt to bring him or her
into conformity. Eventually, the members will give up trying, and the deviant will be ignored or expelled from the group.

The pattern first described by Schachter was modified and refined by later research
in the area. Dentler and Erikson (1959) suggest that some deviance usually will be tolerated in a group merely to help keep group norms clear and defined. Hollander (1964)
provides a detailed analysis of the relationship between member status in the group and
the extent to which deviance is tolerated.

Hollander's idea is that individual group members accumulate what he calls idiosyncratic credits, a sort of credit account against which individual acts of conformity may be
balanced. The higher the individual's status, the greater the credit. The greatest status
usually is accorded a group's leader, and so this individual can often get away with considerable deviance from group norms. Idiosyncratic credits are used up by acts of nonconformity, however, and even a leader is subject to sanctions, being ignored, or being expelled from the group once this credit account is bankrupt.

Group Decision Making

To this point the discussion has concentrated on describing groups and examining the
nature of their influence on individual members. But this is not the only way to look at
groups; many psychologists are interested more in what groups do as groups—that is, in
group behavior. These researchers have studied the processes of group development, the
relationships between groups, and the ability of groups to perform tasks and accomplish
goals.

Group decision making, an aspect of group behavior that has significance both for itself and for its possible motivational implications, is considered in this chapter. A decision-making group is defined as a collection of individuals interacting in some way (usually, but not always, face to face) to make a group decision—that is, one decision that
represents the consensus of the group. The decision may be in the form of a *choice* (such
as which of two sites to choose for a new plant), a *solution* to a problem (such as what to
do about falling market share), or one or more *recommendations* (such as steps that might
be taken for more effective documentation of employment practices).

The increasing use of groups to make decisions is one of the more striking characteristics of modern organizations. Planning, forecasting, setting policy, and solving particular problems are all activities that were long delegated to individuals. Now they are
turning up as the jobs confronting research teams, commissions, task forces, advisory
groups, and committees of various structures, sizes, and purposes. Even letter writing has
become a team effort in many firms.

It is almost certain that a group will take longer to make a decision than would an individual. If time is money, then group decisions will almost certainly cost more than the corresponding individual decisions. The question may well be asked: Why the increasing trend toward group decision making in organizations? The answer lies in expectations about the quality and acceptance of group decisions.

The Quality Assumption

"Two heads are better than one" is an old saying reflecting the general belief that two (or more) people should be able to make better—more accurate, more effective, more creative—decisions than individuals. The use of groups in organizations to make decisions is based on the same principle. When there are more people to work on it, there should be more information and experience available to apply to the decision. Even if one person knows much more about the particular subject, the limited, but unique, knowledge of others could serve to fill in critical gaps. In addition, the different viewpoints that members bring to the situation should stimulate thinking and bring out more ideas on the issues.

The idea that groups should make better decisions than individuals for all of the reasons stated has been investigated quite thoroughly over the years. The conclusions of this older research are stable in themselves, and they also hold up well to more sophisticated, modern experimental methods and analyses (e.g., Cooke & Kernaghan, 1987).

The most basic of the conclusions about individual versus group decision making is that group decisions are *different* from the decisions made by the same persons acting as individuals (e.g., Michaelsen, Watson, & Black, 1989; Sniezek & Henry, 1990). Whether a group makes a *better* decision than its individual members might have made alone, however, depends on a number of factors. These factors, whose relationships are summarized in Figure 13–3, are the nature of the task, group composition (individual member characteristics plus characteristics of the group itself), group goals, and group processes.

The Nature of the Task

An assessment of any group performance situation begins with examining the nature of the task (McGrath, 1984). More than fifty years of research have led to certain well-supported conclusions about the kinds of decisions groups make better than individuals and the kinds they do not. Problems for which groups tend to produce better decisions than even the best individual in the group could do alone have two characteristics: (1) they have multiple parts and (2) these parts are susceptible to division of labor.

An example of a multiple-part problem that meets the criterion of feasible division of labor is selecting a new route for a school bus. This decision, if it is to be effective, requires using knowledge about population distribution, traffic flow patterns, safety hazards, street layouts, local politics, state regulations, cost of operation, and many other facts. Acquiring and making sense of all of this information is a daunting task for an individual, but it is not necessary. A group can generate a satisfactory solution to this problem by pooling information and combining partial solutions.

What kinds of tasks should organizations not ask groups to do? The answer is multiple-stage (as opposed to multiple-part) problems, which "require thinking through a se-

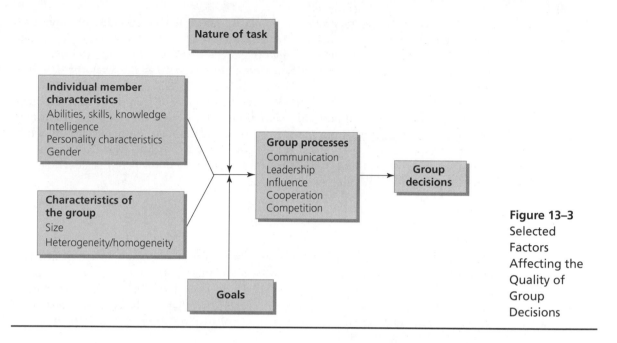

Figure 13–3
Selected Factors Affecting the Quality of Group Decisions

ries of interrelated steps or stages, analyzing a number of rules at each point, and always keeping in mind conclusions reached at earlier points" (Kelley & Thibaut, 1969, pp. 69–70). Multiple-stage problems are not amenable to division of labor, and the large number of possible lines of reasoning any one individual might follow makes it difficult to demonstrate the superiority of any given solution. In most organizations, long-range planning and major policy decisions fall into this category. In this situation, members of decision-making groups often interfere with one another more than they assist one another.

Composition of the Group

A group with very competent, task-oriented members may be expected to produce better decisions than a group without such members, but competence and task orientation do not tell the whole story. The composition of the group on other characteristics, such as sex, race, and decision-making style, is also relevant. A heterogeneous group is composed of individuals who have different levels or amounts of some trait or characteristic. Homogeneous groups have members similar on some trait or characteristic.

Most groups in organizations will be heterogeneous with respect to some traits and homogeneous with respect to others. A group of female employees chosen at random from the ranks of personnel in a large bank will be homogeneous with respect to sex, but heterogeneous with respect to intellectual ability, work experience, and personality characteristics. Psychologists have long been interested in the effects of group heterogeneity or homogeneity on group functioning. The effects of cultural diversity on groups and their members is of particular interest these days.

Consistent with the importance of similarity for greater group cohesion, investigations of culturally diverse groups reveal a general trend toward less cohesion (e.g., Tsui, Egan, & O'Reilly, 1992) and more conflict (e.g., Davis, Strube, & Cheng, 1995) in more diverse groups. When it comes to the quality of group decisions, however, the data support heterogeneity (e.g., Watson, Kumar, & Michaelsen, 1993).

The effect of group member composition on the quality of group decisions has been investigated in many situations with many traits. The implications of these studies are clear; more heterogeneous groups tend to outperform more homogeneous groups, whatever the trait examined or the nature of the decision-making situation. This conclusion is entirely consistent with the basic premise that the source of the potential advantages in group decision making is individual differences.

Group Goals

The individual differences that are a group's strongest potential advantage in decision making are irrelevant unless group processes allow them to be utilized. A first condition necessary for varied viewpoints to be heard and considered in the decision-making process is that the group be cooperatively organized. In other words, a common goal must be more important for the moment than individual goals. (See O'Leary-Kelly, Martocchio, and Frink, 1994, for a review of group goals and performance.)

Members of a decision-making group who use it to pursue individual agendas or to showcase individual talents may dominate the discussion, push their own ideas without listening to others, or refuse to endorse a good idea that comes from someone else (e.g. Mitchell & Silver, 1990). Members who are more concerned with appearing intelligent and competent in the eyes of other group members than with making useful contributions to the problem may withhold valuable insights for fear of being laughed at or ignored.

Even if a group is united in a common goal, there can still be problems. In some groups, this goal is either subtly or explicitly redefined from that of reaching the right or best decision to that of finding a decision with which everyone can agree. "Chris doesn't like applicant A, and Pat feels that B doesn't have enough experience, and Lee doesn't think C will fit in. No one seems to have any strong feelings about D one way or the other, so let's offer D the job." Of interest in this regard is the work of Janis (1972) with the phenomenon known as groupthink. (See also Neck and Moorhead, 1995.)

Groupthink is characterized by "a deterioration of mental efficiency, reality testing, and moral judgement that results from in-group pressures" (Janis, 1972, p. 9). In a group suffering from groupthink, concern with presenting a united front overrides concern with arriving at a good solution to a problem or with making a good decision. As a result, it is particularly vulnerable to the behavior of a strong leader. Janis illustrates the concept of groupthink with a number of interesting examples from political and military history. A brief discussion of one of these examples by social psychologists Tedeschi and Lindskold (1976) is presented in Exhibit 13–5.

Janis believes the disastrous Bay of Pigs decision was a classic example of groupthink. President John F. Kennedy, a strong leader, exploited the group needs for consensus as a means to discourage the discussion of dissenting opinions and to push for his personal preferred solution. Alternatively, Kennedy could have *countered* the groupthink syndrome from his position of strength.

President Kennedy's highly intellectual set of advisors were basking in the euphoria of invulnerability; everything had gone right since the opening of the Kennedy drive in 1956 to capture the 1960 Presidential election. It seemed that nothing could stop them from succeeding in implementing their plans, so they tended to ignore glaring defects in their thinking. The group had an assumed air of consensus. Several of the President's senior advisors had strong doubts about the Bay of Pigs planning, but the group atmosphere inhibited them from voicing criticism. Thinking became simplified into black-and-white, either-or terms. . . .

The way the meetings were conducted served to suppress dissent. When a point of criticism was raised, the President encouraged the CIA planners of the invasion to respond immediately to it. In a specific instance recounted by Janis [1972], Senator Fulbright raised strong objections to the plan and correctly predicted some of the adverse effects the invasion would have on American foreign relations. Rather than discuss Fulbright's criticism, the President returned to taking a straw vote of his advisors on the plan. The group maintained its consensus to support the plan, and Arthur Schlesinger, Jr., one advisor who was known to be in agreement with Fulbright, was not even called upon for his vote because time had run out.

Exhibit 13–5
Groupthink, Leadership, and the Bay of Pigs

Excerpted from J. T. Tedeschi and S. Lindskold, *Social Psychology: Interdependence, Interaction, and Influence.* Copyright © 1976 by John Wiley & Sons, Inc. Reprinted by permission of John Wiley & Sons, Inc.

Group Processes: Leadership and Communication

Be they formal (appointed or elected) or informal (emerging out of the group interaction), leaders play a critical role in any decision-making group. This role is discussed at some length in a classic article by Maier (1967). As he points out, leaders' contributions do not receive the same treatment as those of other group members; whether they like it or not, their position is different. Numerous studies have demonstrated that unless a group leader takes steps to separate his or her discussion-leading function from the functions of contributing and evaluating ideas, the group decision is more likely to reflect the leader's preferred solution than the considered opinion of the group as a whole. The critical steps to be taken include actively encouraging the free expression of ideas, insisting that minority viewpoints be heard, and discouraging the premature evaluation of ideas.

A group leader's ability to have a positive influence on communication in a group is not totally a matter of being willing to take the steps mentioned. The situation also plays a role. As the size of a group increases, for example, communication becomes increasingly difficult to manage. Opportunities for each member to participate decrease and chances that the discussion will be dominated by a few individuals increase. The likelihood that subfactions with different goals will form also increases as the size of the group increases, especially if there is an even number of group members.

As a rule of thumb, decision-making groups of three, five, or seven members reduce such problems, but there are situations when group size cannot be controlled in this way. For example, a decision might require input from all of the department heads in a large firm. The skill and information requirements of many tasks are best met by groups with more than seven members, even though it might be possible to form a smaller group.

Technology, in the form of various modes of electronic communication, offers a possible solution to some of the communication problems in larger groups. Electronic communication channels (such as e-mail, teleconferencing, and computer conferences) make it unnecessary for the members of a decision-making group to meet face to face. This feature has practical advantages—getting people together physically can be difficult to arrange as well as expensive. Electronic communication also makes the task of controlling and guiding group communication processes much easier for a group leader. It is difficult to shout down a computer message in midstream, for example.

The fuller participation by all group members that is made possible by electronic communication means that computer-mediated decision groups almost always complete less of a task in a given time period than do face-to-face groups (e.g., Siegal, Dubrovsky, Kiesler, & McGuire, 1986; Weisband, 1992). Obviously, it takes longer to listen to everyone's views. Is this time worth it in terms of better realization of group potential? In other words, do such groups make better decisions than face-to-face groups?

To date, researchers have not collected much information on the question of how electronic communication affects the *quality* of group decisions. The study summarized in Spotlight on Research is a step toward filling this gap. Half of the subjects in this laboratory experiment took part in traditional face-to-face groups, sitting around a table in a private room in the usual fashion. The other half of the subjects communicated via a computer-conferencing system. Messages were composed and edited on one section of a computer screen. Then they were sent to a common message "board" that was displayed on all group members' screens. Under these conditions, Straus and McGrath (1994) concluded that electronic communication groups are less productive than face-to-face groups, but more research is needed before this conclusion may be generalized.

Communication and leadership are two of the group processes that affect the extent to which group resources are utilized toward the goal of effective decision making. As shown previously in Figure 13–3, influence, cooperation, and competition among group members are also relevant. These topics are examined in detail in introductory social psychology textbooks. Here, the discussion turns to a specific application of the quality assumption underlying the use of groups to make decisions.

Laboratory experiment
See pages 27–28

Generalizability
See page 45

Quality Circles and the Quality Assumption

A typical **quality circle** is a group of six to ten employees who meet regularly to identify and solve work problems. Quality circles in this country meet a few hours a month on company time. (In other countries, they may meet on their own time.) Discussions are limited to areas having to do with the quantity or quality of work; hiring, firing, promotions, pay, benefits, and other such personnel issues are out of bounds, as are any issues restricted by a collective bargaining agreement. Usually, the groups have no power to implement ideas directly; they serve primarily as brainstorming, problem-solving groups whose task is to generate solutions and recommendations.

Relative to many other work improvement programs, quality circles are easy to implement and have a relatively low cost. Managers get the benefit of subordinate ideas and input without having to give up traditional managerial functions. On the other side, quality circles can be effective employee development tools, and there is some evidence that participation enhances individual career advancement (Buch & Spangler, 1990). Along with these very practical advantages, the quality circle concept is a sound use of group decision making.

As usually implemented, quality circles meet the size requirements for better group decision making. Like the quality team described in Psychology at Work, they are ho-

SPOTLIGHT ON RESEARCH

Does the Medium Matter? The Interaction of Task Type and Technology on Group Performance and Member Reactions

Excerpted from S. G. Straus and J. E. McGrath, "Does the Medium Matter? The Interaction of Task Type and Technology on Group Performance and Member Reactions." *Journal of Applied Psychology,* 1994, 79, 87–97.

Research question   How does the productivity of computer-mediated and face-to-face communication groups compare?

Type of study   Laboratory experiment.

Subject   240 undergraduate students working in same-sex groups of three (1/2 groups all male, 1/2 female).

Independent variable   (1)Type of group—Electronic (CM) or face-to-face (FTF) communication (and others not reviewed here).

Dependent variable   Group productivity as measured by the amount of each of 3 decision-making tasks completed in a fixed period of time (and others not reviewed here).

General procedure   Subjects were assigned randomly to experimental conditions. Following briefing and introductions to fellow group members (not real names), subjects read written task instructions. CM subjects were given a brief training session in use of computer conferencing. All groups performed all three tasks, which were designed to vary in complexity of required communication.

Analysis   Analysis of variance.

Results   CM groups completed less of each given task in a fixed time period and made considerably more errors in recording groups' answers or solutions than did members of FTF groups.

Conclusion   ". . . face-to-face modes [of communication] are superior to computer-mediated discussions when productivity is a priority or when the time available to perform tasks is at a premium, especially for highly interdependent tasks" (p. 91).

ANOVA
See page 42

mogeneous with regard to the general area of members' work focus ("medicine"), but desirably heterogeneous with regard to sex, age, work background and experience, and specific job duties. It may also be assumed that most are somewhat heterogeneous with respect to intelligence and approach to problems.

The quality circle concept also conforms to the requirements for good group decision making in the nature of its goals. Organizational practices differ, but quality circle membership is usually voluntary, and action authority, if any, is limited. Members are there to generate ideas and make recommendations to solve problems or improve productivity; there is little or no need for individual grandstanding, bargaining, or compromise solutions that can supersede original goals in other kinds of decision-making groups.

Finally, the quality circle concept qualifies as a situation in which groups are likely to make good decisions given the usual nature of the task. Quality circles examine work-specific problems with production quantity and quality, problems that generally lend themselves to solution by pooling individual experience, ideas, information, and viewpoints. For example, a quality team at Florida Power & Light's Stuart Service Center near Palm Beach got together with a quality coach for weekly brainstorming sessions and eventually came up with a workable method for servicing underground cables without constantly having to shut off consumer power.

In summary, quality circles have a lot going for them as decision-making groups, and viewed from this perspective, there is nothing surprising about the many success stories (e.g., Krigsman & O'Brien, 1987). Nevertheless, not all quality circles are productive. Among the factors that seem to make a difference are the amount and the quality of the training that circle members receive in group problem-solving procedures; the skills of group leaders in facilitating group communication in the ways mentioned earlier; whether participation in the quality circle is voluntary (e.g., Geehr, Burke, & Sulzer, 1995); and the commitment of an organization's upper management to the quality circle idea (e.g., Landon & Moulton, 1986; Tang, Tollison, & Whiteside, 1989).

Greenbaum, Kaplan, and Metlay (1988) also suggest that more rigorous evaluation of quality circle programs than is usually undertaken would increase their effectiveness. Finally, it may be that the life span of such groups should be limited. Evidence is coming to light that quality circles begin to lose effectiveness over time; in one study, three years appeared to be the upper limit for sustaining the benefits of this innovation (Griffin, 1988).

The Acceptability Assumption

The best decision in the world is useless if it is not accepted by those who must implement it. Economists know that increased saving and reduced spending alleviate inflationary pressures in the long run. The implementation of this solution, however, depends on millions of individuals who lose (in the short run) when inflation rates exceed the interest rates on their savings plans. They spend rather than save, and the "known solution" to the problem of inflation is worthless.

The importance of support for decisions provides yet another reason for the increased use of organizational decision-making groups. Insofar as group decision making permits individual participation and influence, it should follow that more individual members are likely to accept decisions made by a group than decisions made by individuals acting alone. Even if some or all of those who must implement the solution are not part of the group, there should be increased confidence in the validity of a decision that is made by several people rather than one. In turn, this greater confidence should lead to greater acceptance.

The acceptability argument for using groups to make decisions is basically an attitude argument. Attitudes are defined as having three consistent components—affective (feeling), cognitive (thinking), and behavioral (acting). If a group, rather than an individual, makes a decision, the acceptability argument states that the affective component of individual members' attitudes toward that decision will be positive. Members will have *feelings* of satisfaction with having been part of the decision-making process.

The cognitive component of attitudes toward a decision should also be favorable in group decision making because people will have increased *understanding* of, and confidence in, the decision. Finally, because the three components of an attitude are, by definition, consistent, the favorable affective and cognitive components of attitudes toward the decision should be followed by *behaviors* that facilitate implementation of the solution.

The results of some 50 years of research support the hypothesis that people who participate in group decision making are more satisfied with the decision than with one made and handed down by one individual (e.g., Carey, 1972; Coch & French, 1948; White & Ruh, 1973). Whether this satisfaction leads to behaviors that are helpful in implementing the decisions is another matter. A pair of studies on reducing absenteeism illustrate the point.

Powell and Schlacter (1971) studied the relationship between (a) degree of participation in decision making about the problem of absenteeism and (b) change in level of absenteeism. They found that employees who participated in groups that developed solutions

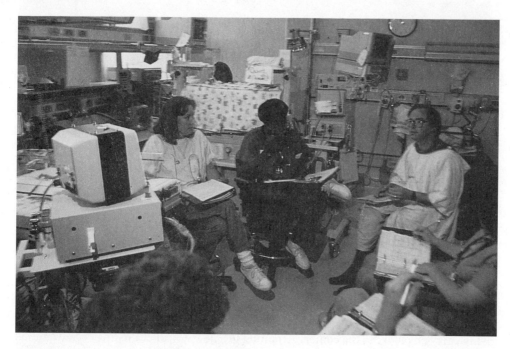

*Quality circles are
decision-making
groups whose pri-
mary function is to
identify and gener-
ate ideas for solving
work problems.*

to the problem expressed greater satisfaction with the solution than did employees who
simply received the solution passed down by management. The subsequent rate of absenteeism for the two groups was the same, however. By contrast, Bragg and Andrews (1973)
found that participation in decision making was associated with a decrease in absenteeism
and an increase in productivity, as well as with an increase in reported job satisfaction.

The inconsistency in the two studies described, as well as in much of the other research in this area, may reflect many factors. Among these are methodological issues,
variation in the kinds of decision-making processes used, and variation in individuals'
private opinions as to the quality of the final decision. More fundamentally, this inconsistency may illustrate a fact often overlooked: an individual's attitude toward a decision
is only *one* of the factors influencing his or her subsequent behavior.

As an example of the minor role that attitudes may play in behavior, consider one
member of a decision-making group who believes the group's decision was not very good.
As a result, he or she is not satisfied with the decision or the group interaction that produced it. Nevertheless, this individual is very active in implementing the decision because
of a strong belief that this behavior is important for career reasons. Another member is
highly satisfied with the group interaction process and confident about the quality of the
ultimate decision, but fails to do anything at all about implementation. For this person at
this time, the matter simply has low priority.

With respect to the acceptability argument for using groups rather than individuals to
make decisions, individual differences and situational factors make it impossible to make
definitive statements about the more effective implementation of group-generated decisions. If satisfaction is an issue, the argument that group decisions are preferred seems to
have validity. In short, the evidence available supports Cooke and Kernaghan's (1987)
statement that quality and acceptance of group decisions are arrived at by different group
processes and the two outcomes are not necessarily related. An interesting theoretical and
empirical review of the group decision-making literature is offered by Davis (1992).

Participative Decision Making

In group decision making, a relatively small number of people interact for the purpose of making one or more decisions. It is not so many steps from here to a wider involvement of employees in more general organizational decision making—that is, to participative decision making or participative management. This participation comes in many forms, including the employee suggestion programs and quality circles already discussed, and many definitions are offered by I/O psychologists who study it. In the current context, **participative decision making** is defined as "higher level individuals' effort to provide those at a lower level with . . . a greater voice in organizational performance" (Glew, O'Leary-Kelly, Griffin, & Van Fleet, 1995, p. 395).

The definition makes it clear that in the I/O psychology literature, participative decision making (PDM) represents a deliberate change from traditional management in which a minority of upper-level management employees make all of the decisions regarding organizational policies and functioning. This change is a philosophical issue to some people, but participative management is essentially a very practical matter. Boxing all employees into one narrow work role places artificial constraints on organizational performance, as the following example illustrates.

Stewart (1995) describes an organization change program at Variety, a Buffalo, New York–based farm equipment manufacturer. Among other aspects, the program involved giving every employee in the company training in a new way of evaluating organizational performance. Following the training, a man who managed the inventory stockroom approached his boss with the following idea.

> "My suggestion . . . is that you put a lock on the warehouse door and throw the key away. We're filling up this warehouse with inventory just because it's there. If you gave us a football field, we would fill up a football field. If you gave us a broom closet, we'd fill a broom closet. So give us a broom closet. Make inventory the responsibility of dispatchers on the line." When his boss asked him why he didn't say this before, he said, "Nobody asked." (p. 118)

Participative decision making might be summed up as an effort to avoid the "nobody asked" syndrome. Jack Stack, CEO of Springfield ReManufacturing Corporation in Missouri, asked everybody. The company was failing and morale was sinking when Stack decided to solicit employee ideas for turning the situation around. He opened every aspect of the company's operation, including its finances, to scrutiny by every worker. In exchange for ideas that improved the business, employees got bonuses and stock in the company. Today the former International Harvester division is profitably on its own.

Along with the expectation that asking will improve the *quality* of organizational decision making is an expectation that people who participate in decisions that affect them will understand the issues better and *accept* the decisions more readily. This understanding and acceptance, together with satisfaction at being part of the process, should be followed by more effective implementation of the decisions. Early reviews of the empirical evidence for these hypotheses usually ended with the conclusion that PDM had few effects on the quality of performance and its effects on satisfaction were too varied for prediction (e.g., Locke & Schweiger, 1979).

Cotton and his colleagues (1988) undertook to re-review the participative decision making literature in light of the possibility that there are different forms of participation and that these may be associated with different, but predictable, outcomes. If true, overall reviews of the evidence would find exactly what Locke and Schweiger found—very little—because effects would be canceling one another out as a result of the different forms of participation examined in different studies.

Beginning with more than 400 articles on the subject, these investigators eventually identified five basic dimensions on which participative decision making varies: (1) formal/informal, (2) direct/indirect, (3) level of influence, (4) content, and (5) short-term/long-term. Working with these dimensions, the investigators found six combinations that were adequate to describe the forms of PDM they found in the literature. When they reanalyzed the studies on the basis of this classification scheme, they concluded that different forms of PDM have different outcomes.

According to the analysis, the most consistent positive performance and satisfaction outcomes were associated with informal participative decision making. This rather homey, undramatic form of PDM is defined in terms of day-to-day interpersonal relationships between supervisors and subordinates. The number of empirical investigations in this category was not large, but results are sufficiently consistent to tempt speculation. One explanation may simply be that employees are more influenced by what supervisors and managers do and say on a day-in, day-out basis than by obvious formalized attempts to involve them in work-related decisions. Alternatively, it may be that employees who are better performers and have better attitudes toward their jobs invite more participation in decision making on a regular basis.

Whatever the explanation for any particular finding, the article by Cotton and his colleagues set off a chain of re-analysis, debate, and rebuttal (e.g., Cotton, 1995; Cotton, Vollrath, Lengnick-Hall, & Froggatt, 1990; Leana, Locke, & Schweiger, 1990; Ledford & Lawler, 1994, Sagie, 1994, 1995; Wagner, 1994). Central to this on-going dialog are two questions. First, does the form of decision-making participation make a difference to its effects on participant performance and satisfaction? Second, are obtained effects large enough to be important? Among other problems, serious measurement issues seem to be blocking efforts to date to obtain consensus regarding these questions (Coye & Belohlav, 1995).

Measurement error
See pages 53–54

In the field, participative decision making continues to gain ground despite disagreements among I/O psychologists as to its effectiveness (e.g., Larson, 1989). Many managers express a belief that PDM will improve the quality of decision making in the organization (e.g., Collins, Ross, & Ross, 1989; Long, 1988). On the other side of the fence, employee attitudes toward participative decision making are affected by a number of factors, including the current quality and quantity of communication between superiors and subordinates (Harrison, 1985); prior experiences, if any, with participation (Marchington, Wilkinson, Ackers, & Goodman, 1994), and the perceived commitment to participation by management (Parker & Price, 1994).

As regards specific individual interest in participation, a survey of more than 700 manufacturing employees by Miller and Prichard (1992) found that younger employees who are more interested in advancement, more active in their unions, and more optimistic about the benefits of PDM report more interest in participation. Among the potential problems identified by Baloff and Doherty (1989) that may accompany individual participation are peer group pressure (against "cooperating with management") and management coercion (to participate) or retribution (for participating).

I/O psychologists' interest in the idea of involving employees in work-related decisions goes back at least as far as the Hawthorne experiments, but significant organizational interest in PDM is much more recent. As organizations move into the 21st century, they face economic, legal, and social challenges to their very survival. To prosper, they must make better use of resources, especially those in human form. Participative decision making is one strategy for doing so. Shifting from a hierarchical, bureaucratic form of organization to a more flexible one based on teams and teamwork is another.

Groups as Work Teams

Beginning sometime in the late 1980s, the words *team, teamwork,* and *teaming* began to appear with ever more frequency in the I/O psychology and other literature concerning organizations. Many experts believe that teams rather than individuals will be the building blocks of successful organizations in the future (e.g., Hackman, 1986, 1987; Peters, 1988). One reason for this belief is the fact that, potentially at least, this form of organization makes better use of human resources. Teams can be designed to be flexible—each member can perform many or all assigned tasks—and to manage themselves, thereby reducing the need for managers and first-line supervisors.

The use of teams in organizations is not new. Teams are the basis of job design in numerous settings, including airline crews, bands and orchestras, construction gangs, and operating rooms in hospitals. Team job design is also used to make certain kinds of work more interesting—the team auto assembly described in Chapter 8 is an example. All of these teams are formal task groups. All have norms and some degree of cohesiveness, and all influence individual members' attitudes and behavior to some extent. So what, if anything, makes teams different from groups?

In one sense, the answer is nothing. All teams are groups. Not all groups are teams, however. Members of a **team** are interdependent; each must perform his or her task correctly if the team is to succeed (think of an orchestra performing a piece of music). Furthermore, the members have "a common goal and a common fate" (Hollenbeck et al., 1995, p. 293). The team's success (or lack of it) as evaluated by one or more outside agents directly affects individual rewards. If a professor assigns term projects to groups of students, and if each member of a group will receive the grade given to the project, the group is a team.

If there is anything new about the use of teams in organizations, it lies most obviously in the extent to which this concept is currently being embraced. In some instances the change may be more apparent than real as company after company substitutes phrases such as "team members," "cast members," and "crew members" for the terms "employees" or "workers." In other cases, commitment to the team concept is obvious and extensive. All of the 700-plus employees of Johnsonville Foods Company, a medium-sized sausage maker in Wisconsin, work in self-managed teams.

As discussed in Chapter 8, a self-managing team is responsible for a whole unit of work. Rather than being directed by a manager, members decide among themselves how the work tasks are to be allocated and no one member need perform the same task all the time unless by choice. The focus is on the completed work, not on its components.

In practice, there can be considerable variation in the actual decision-making freedom allowed self-managing work teams (Manz, 1992). Nor is this job design appropriate in all work settings or for all employees (Glenn, 1995). When conditions are right, however, the self-managed team can be very effective. In a study reported by Cohen and Ledford (1994), more than 1,300 employees of a telecommunications company made up of self-managing teams performed customer service, administrative, managerial, and technical jobs more effectively than comparable traditionally managed groups.

Cross-Functional Teams

Between merely changing what employees are called and reorganizing an entire company around self-managed teams lies what probably is the most common as well as the most quietly revolutionary use of teams in modern organizations—the cross-functional product (or project) team. An example of this form of team structure, in this case called an integrated product team (IPT), is shown in Figure 13–4. Unlike members of auto assembly

teams or sales teams or ambulance crews, each member of this team comes from a different functional unit in the organization, and team duties are in addition to regular duties.

The team depicted in Figure 13–4 was formed at the request of top management to
stimulate business development for the corporation. A leader was appointed to recruit the
other members; whatever their status in their "home rooms" (primary unit of employment),
on the team these individuals are coequal. Their mission is a long-term, open-ended one
that requires extensive interaction with various segments of the organization's environment.

Other work teams are organized in much the same way as depicted in the diagram,
but their goals are more specific and more time constrained and the members usually
work full-time for the duration of a project. In designing its Neon automobile, for example, Chrysler Corporation used a team made up of people from design, manufacturing,
finance, procurement, and marketing groups. The Neon went from design to completion
of the first car in 33 months rather than the usual four to six years.

Among the many other organizations that use cross-functional self-managing teams
for product development, manufacturing, and delivery are Hewlett-Packard, General
Foods, Honeywell, Inc., and Dell Computer Company. The success of this team job approach is to a substantial degree the result of the integrating multiway communication
channel that it creates. Chrysler's Glenn Gardner explains.

> In the past . . . one group—whether of designers, marketers, manufacturing engi-
> neers, procurement experts or finance people—would finish its work and then
> "throw it over the wall" to the next group. If, late in the process, outside suppliers

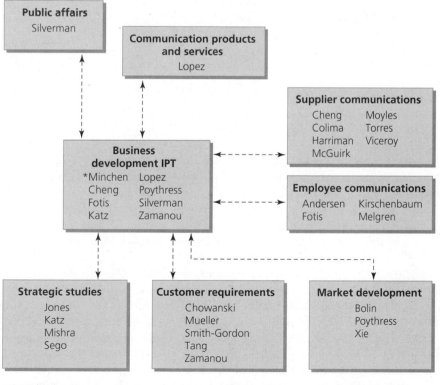

Figure 13–4
A Diagram of a
Cross-
Functional
Marketing
Team

said they couldn't build a motor that engineers had specified, the whole project would go back to the designers for reworking. (Bulkeley, 1994, p. A4)

Accomplishing the purpose for which it is formed is one of the two basic tasks facing any work team. The other may be described as team building—learning to get along and work together. Some teams, like the auto assembly team described in Chapter 8, can accomplish both ends with little or no contact outside of the organization; in this regard they are externally *independent*. Teams like the ones described in this section must usually deal directly with that environment on a regular basis. To a greater or lesser extent, such teams are externally *dependent*.

The way in which a team deals with the relevant parts of its organization's external environment is not a given; most self-managing teams must determine their own strategies for doing so. In a pioneering study of new cross-functional teams in a state education department, Ancona (1990) found that the type of strategy adopted was related to mission success. Specifically, she concluded that externally dependent teams are more effective when they adopt a strategy of high-level environmental probing (seeking information, establishing relationships, identifying needs, and so on) from the beginning, even if these external activities interfere with initial team building. In the teams Ancona studied, a strategy that gave too much attention to internal processes at the beginning was associated with higher individual satisfaction and group cohesion (relative to other teams) but poorer team performance.

As reviewed in the current chapter, many years of small group performance research lead to the conclusion that both getting organized and getting along are necessary to effective task accomplishment. Group interdependency with the external environment (in addition to usual member interdependency with one another) seems to change the picture. Members must develop externally focused roles as well as within-group roles. In Ancona's investigation, team building appeared to be more a result than a cause of effective team performance. At the end of three months, a member of the team with the highest performance rating reported that the group was finally "beginning to be more like a team" (p. 354).

The results of Ancona's study will not generalize to all work teams, but they are valuable in highlighting the need to question direct applications of conclusions from traditional group research to teams. For example, much of the current literature on using work teams in organizations emphasizes providing team members with team building or team development training at the outset (e.g., Laiken, 1994; May & Schwoerer, 1994; Neck & Manz, 1994; Ray, 1995). Such training is consistent with traditional group dynamics research, and it is no doubt very important in many team applications. For teams with a high degree of external interaction, however, it may be counterproductive (or just a waste of time). The same may be true for teams whose various members have differing amounts of prior experience with teams and therefore different ideas about how teams should operate (e.g., Rentsch, Heffner, & Duffy, 1994).

The conditions under which specific training in team development is useful and/or necessary is but one of many questions to be answered about work teams, particularly cross-functional teams. Another is, under what conditions are the strong cohesion and powerful norms that characterize a well-developed group desirable? In a study of a small manufacturing company, Barker and Tompkins (1994) found that workers identified more strongly with their teams than with the employing organization, especially in terms of loyalty.

Barker and Tompkins believe that substituting team-based control for bureaucratic control is not, as some people believe, a way of freeing up or empowering the employees of an organization (see also Barker, 1993). To the contrary, they say, it increases "the iron cage of control." This outcome can occur only if there is a higher level of group cohesiveness than many groups ever achieve. Nevertheless, the point that teams—be they self-managing, cross-functional, closed system, externally dependent, or other—are not appropriate in every situation is important

By way of summarizing this section, a framework for analyzing work teams is presented in Figure 13–5. The basic underlying premise of this framework is that teams are understood in "relation to external surroundings and internal processes" (Sundstrom, De Meuse, & Futrell, 1990, p. 121). In the case of externally independent teams, the organization (context) constitutes the relevant external surroundings. When dealing with externally dependent teams, the lens must be opened to include interaction with relevant aspects of the organization's environment (external process).

The framework lists the major classes of variables discussed in this and other chapters that are known or believed at this time to be relevant to work teams. Output variables are the familiar ones of performance and satisfaction plus a variable here called group development, which refers to the extent to which group members have adapted to one another, matured, and may reasonably be expected to function effectively as a team in the future.

Variables

See pages 25–26

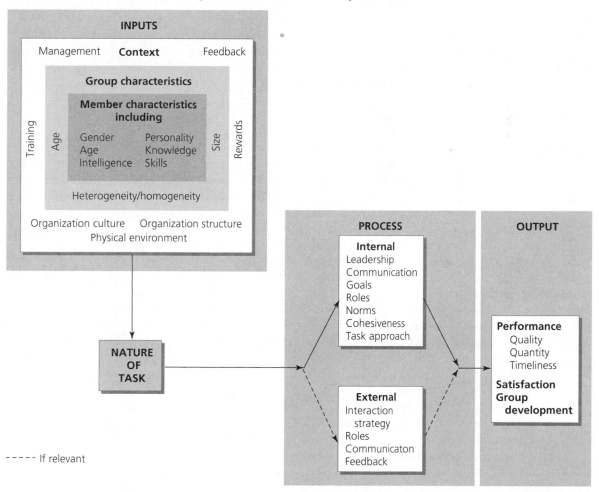

Figure 13–5
A Framework for
Examining Work Teams

Have Unions Outlived Their Usefulness?

More than 65 years ago, Congress passed the Railway Labor Act, the first significant pro-labor legislation in the United States. By 1935, the Labor Relations Act (Wagner Act) had established collective bargaining as a fact of American life. By the 1950s, almost one-third of the American work force was unionized. In 1961, President John F. Kennedy issued Executive Order No. 10988, which extended the right to organize to employees of the federal government.

By the late 1980s, figures from the Bureau of Labor Statistics showed that fewer than 20% of American workers belonged to unions, and the number has continued to fall since that time. Some labor experts predict that private-sector unionization will be down to the 7% of 100 years ago by the arrival of the 100th anniversary of the Labor Day holiday in 2001. The reasons suggested for this decline by people who study organized labor movements vary. One theory is a life-cycle one.

Historically, every labor movement in the world has gone through a predictable pattern of development that is somewhat independent of particular economic, political, and industrial circumstances. A start-up period of resistance from management and apathy from workers is followed by a growth period, a plateau period, and a decline period. Great Britain is generally acknowledged to be in the latter stages of decline, and some experts believe that America entered the early stages in the mid-1980s.

Another theory to account for the declining popularity of organized labor in this country is that unions have been so successful in accomplishing the goals of fair wages and better working conditions that they have worked themselves out of a job. Certainly, anyone who has studied the labor movement in this country knows that unions have indeed been instrumental in making things better, not just for union members but for all American workers. Improvements won for workers by union-supported legislation (and improvements given to nonunion employees by organizations eager to avoid labor organization) have established many of the employment standards we take for granted today. With all of the undeniable improvements, however, the job is not done.

Many people who work still make too little money to achieve anything approximating the standard of living most of us feel is reasonable. Others are at the receiving end of unfair management practices by "rogue" managements. In addition, far too many people are injured or killed on the job or become ill as a result of the use of hazardous substances in the workplace or overstressful working conditions. The question is: Do we need unions to correct these problems?

This question arises for two reasons. First, government regulation of employment practices and working conditions, now very strong, was virtually unknown in the early days of the organized labor movement. Second, new management practices adopted in response to a number of factors have been taking many organizations in the direction of explicit concern for the needs of their employees. They are "adopting management practices that consciously blur the line between workers and managers and create an organizational culture characterized by employers caring more, knowing more and doing more" (Lawler & Mohrman, 1987, p. 294).

The line between management and workers is more blurred today than when Lawler and Mohrman wrote those words, and the question of whether there is a necessary role for unions remains valid. With government and management both looking out for employees, why do we need unions? I/O psychologists Lawler and Mohrman say the answer lies in the checks and balances that unions can provide. They believe that union involvement is needed to insure the permanency of current trends toward more concern with working conditions and increased employee involvement in work-related decisions. To put it another way, unions, with their history of adversarial relationships with management, may be uniquely qualified to keep management honest. Can they halt their downward slide in time to fill this role, or will widespread opinions that they have outlived their usefulness create a self-fulfilling prophecy?

Summary

Organizations are made up of groups, both formal and informal. Some of these groups have important influence over the attitudes and behavior of members that may be greater than the influence of the employing organization. Unions constitute a special case of group membership with important norms that originate outside the organization but affect behavior within it.

I/O and other psychologists study group behavior, such as group decision making, as well as group influence on members. The assumptions that groups will make better decisions than individuals and that people will be more satisfied with and more cooperative in implementing decisions made by groups are subject to a number of conditions. The same is true for the broader assumption that participative management will have similar results.

Teams of all kinds, including cross-functional product or process teams, are taking on a central role in work design in many organizations. Teams are groups and as such are subject to the same internal processes as other groups. But many also must deal with an organization's external environment. This requirement adds a new dimension to the study of groups and throws some doubt upon direct extensions of small-group research to this area.

Questions for Review and Discussion

1. Give one example of a group to which you belong that falls into *each* of these categories: formal group, informal group, reference group, identity group, team. Your answers should show that you understand the differences among them.

2. What is the nature of the relationship between group cohesiveness, norms, and sanctions in the process of influencing the behavior of an individual member? Give an example from a group of which you are (or have been in the past) a member. You may use the "group" of a class if you wish.

3. Describe a decision situation (task) in which a group should be able to make a better decision than an individual. Assemble (on paper) a group from among your classmates or other acquaintances to make this decision and explain your choices (names may be made up).

4. Discuss Barker's (1993, p. 408) statement that self-managing teams in organizations "draw the iron cage [of control] tighter and . . . constrain the organization's [individual] members more powerfully" than bureaucratic management, in the light of what you have learned about groups.

Key Terms

acceptability and group decisions

cross-functional project team

group cohesiveness

group composition

group goals

norms

participative decision making

quality circle

quality and group decisions

reference group

union as group

work team

References

Alderfer, C. P., & Smith, K. K. (1982). Studying intergroup relations embedded in organizations. *Administrative Science Quarterly, 27,* 35–65.

Ancona, D. G. (1990). Outward bound: Strategies for team survival in an organization. *Academy of Management Journal, 33,* 334–365.

Baloff, N., & Doherty, E. M. (1989). Potential pitfalls in employee participation. *Organizational Dynamics, 17,* 51–62.

Baratta, J. E., & McManus, M. A. (1992). The effect of contextual factors on individuals' job performance. *Journal of Applied Social Psychology, 22,* 1702–1710.

Barker, J. R. (1993). Tightening the iron cage: Concertive control in self-managing teams. *Administrative Science Quarterly, 38,*408–437.

Barker, J. R., & Tompkins, P. K. (1994). Identification in the self-managing organization: Characteristics of target and tenure. *Human Communication Research, 21,* 223–240.

Barling, J., Wade, B., & Fullagar, C. (1990). Predicting employee commitment to company and union: Divergent models. *Journal of Occupational Psychology, 63,* 49–61.

Blau, G. (1995). Influence of group lateness on individual lateness: A cross-level examination. *Academy of Management Journal, 38,* 1483–1496.

Bonoma, T. V., & Zaltman, G. (1981). *Psychology for management.* Boston: Kent.

Bragg, J., & Andrews, I. (1973). Participative decision making: An experimental study in hospital. *Journal of Applied Behavioral Science, 9,* 727–735.

Buch, K., & Spangler, R. (1990). The effects of quality circles on performance and promotions. *Human Relations, 43,* 573–582.

Bulkeley, W. M. (1994, Dec. 23). The latest big thing at many companies is speed, speed, speed. *Wall Street Journal,* pp. A-1, 4.

Carey, R. G. (1972). Correlates of satisfaction in the priesthood. *Administrative Science Quarterly, 17,* 185–195.

Coch, L., & French, J. (1948). Overcoming resistance to change. *Human Relations, 1,* 512–532.

Cohen, S. G., & Ledford, G. E. (1994). The effectiveness of self-managing teams: A quasi-experiment. *Human Relations, 47,* 13–43.

Collins, D. (1995). Death of a gainsharing plan: Power politics and participatory management. *Organizational Dynamics, 24,* 23–38.

Collins, D., Ross, R. A., & Ross, T. L. (1989). Who wants participative management? The managerial perspective. *Group and Organization Studies, 14,* 422–445.

Cooke, R. A., & Kernaghan, J. A. (1987). Estimating the difference between group versus individual performance on problem-solving tasks. *Group and Organization Studies, 12,* 319–342.

Cotton, J. L. (1995). Participation's effect on performance and satisfaction: A reconsideration of Wagner. *Academy of Management Review, 20,* 276–278.

Cotton, J. L., Vollrath, D. A., Froggatt, K. L., Lengnick-Hall, M. L., & Jennings, K. R. (1988). Employee participation: Diverse forms and different outcomes. *Academy of Management Review, 13*, 8–22.

Cotton, J. L., Vollrath, D. A., Lengnick-Hall, M. L., & Froggatt, K. L. (1990). Fact: The form of participation does matter—A rebuttal to Leana, Locke, and Schweiger. *Academy of Management Review, 15*, 147–153.

Coye, R. W., & Belohlav, J. A. (1995). An exploratory analysis of employee participation. *Group and Organization Management, 20*, 4–17.

Davis, J. H. (1992). Some compelling intuitions about group consensus decisions, theoretical and empirical research, and interpersonal aggregation phenomena: Selected examples, 1950–1990. *Organizational Behavior and Human Decision Processes, 52*, 3–38.

Davis, L. E., Strube, M. J., & Cheng, L. (1995). Too many Blacks, too many Whites: Is there a racial balance? *Basic and Applied Social Psychology, 17*, 119–135.

Dentler, R. A., & Erikson, K. T. (1959). The functions of deviance in groups. *Social Problems, 7*, 98–107.

Feldman, D. C. (1984). The development and enforcement of group norms. *Academy of Management Review, 9*, 47–53.

Forsyth, D. R. (1990). *Group dynamics* (2nd ed.). Pacific Grove, CA: Brooks/Cole.

Fryxell, G. E., & Gordon, M. E. (1989). Workplace justice and job satisfaction as predictors of satisfaction with union and management. *Academy of Management Journal, 32*, 851–866.

Fullagar, C. J. A., Gordon, M. E., Gallagher, D. G., & Clark, P. F. (1995). Impact of early socialization on union commitment and participation: A longitudinal study. *Journal of Applied Psychology, 80*, 147–157.

Geehr, J. L., Burke, M. J., & Sulzer, J. L. (1995). Quality circles: The effects of varying degrees of voluntary participation on employee attitudes and program efficacy. *Educational and Psychological Measurement, 55*, 124–134.

Glenn, R. R. (1995). A training model for implementing self-directed work teams. *Organization Development Journal, 13*, 51–62.

Glew, D. J., O'Leary-Kelly, A. M., Griffin, R. W., & Van Fleet, D. D. (1995). Participation in organizations: A preview of the issues and proposed framework for future analysis. *Journal of Management, 21*, 395–421.

Greenbaum, H. H., Kaplan, I. T., & Metlay, W. (1988). Evaluation of problem-solving groups: The case of quality circle programs. *Group and Organization Studies, 13*, 133–147.

Griffin, R. W. (1988). Consequences of quality circles in an industrial setting: A longitudinal assessment. *Academy of Management Journal, 31*, 338–358.

Hackman, J. R. (1986). The psychology of self-management in organizations. In M. S. Pallak & R. Perloff (Eds.), *Psychology and work*. Washington, DC: American Psychological Association.

Hackman, J. R. (1987). The design of work teams. In J. Lorsch (Ed.), *Handbook of organizational behavior*. New York: Prentice-Hall.

Hammer, T. H. (1978). Relationships between local union characteristics and worker behavior and attitudes. *Academy of Management Journal, 21*, 560–577.

Harrison, T. (1985). Communication and participative decision making: An exploratory study. *Personnel Psychology, 38*, 93–116.

Hollander, E. P. (1964). *Leaders, groups, and influence*. New York: Oxford University Press.

Hollenbeck, J. R., Ilgen, D. R., Sego, D. J., Hedlund, J., Major, D. A., & Phillips, J. (1995). Multilevel theory of team decision making: Decision performance in teams incorporating distributed expertise. *Journal of Applied Psychology, 80*, 292–316.

Huszczo, G. E., & Hoyer, D. T. (1994). Factors involved in constructive union-management relationships. *Human Relations, 47*, 847–866.

Jackson, J. (1966). A conceptual and measurement model for norms and roles. *Pacific Sociological Review, 9*, 35–47.

Janis, I. L. (1972). *Victims of groupthink*. Atlanta: Houghton Mifflin.

Jewell, L. N., & Reitz, H. J. (1981). *Group effectiveness in organizations*. Glenview, IL: Scott, Foresman.

Johnson, W. R., & Johnson, G. J. (1992). Union performance and union loyalty: The role of perceived steward support. *Journal of Applied Social Psychology, 22,* 677–690.

Kameda, T., & Davis, J. H. (1990). The function of the reference point in individual and group decision making. *Organizational Behavior and Human Decision Processes, 46,* 55–76.

Kelley, H. H., & Thibaut, J. W. (1969). Group problem solving. In G. Lindzey & E. Aronson (Eds.), *The handbook of social psychology* (Vol. 4). Reading, MA: Addison-Wesley.

Kelloway, E. K., & Barling, J. (1993). Members' participation in local union activities: Measurement, prediction, and replication. *Journal of Applied Psychology, 78,* 262–279.

Kelly, C., & Kelly, J. (1994). Who gets involved in collective action? Social psychological determinants of individual participation in trade unions. *Human Relations, 47,* 63–88.

Krigsman, N., & O'Brien, R. M. (1987). Quality circles, feedback and reinforcement: An experimental comparison and behavioral analysis. *Journal of Organizational Behavior Management, 9,* 67–82.

Laiken, M. E. (1994). The myth of the self-managing team. *Organization Development Journal, 12,* 29–34.

Landon, D. N., & Moulton, S. (1986). Quality circles: What's in them for employees? *Personnel Journal, 65,* 23–26.

Larson, J. S. (1989). Employee participation in federal management. *Public Personnel Management, 18,* 404–414.

Lawler, E. E., III., & Mohrman, S. A. (1987). Unions and the new management. *The Academy of Management Executive, 1,* 293–300.

Leana, C. R., Locke, E. A., & Schweiger, D. M. (1990). Fact and fiction in analyzing research on participative decision making: A critique of Cotton, Vollrath, Froggatt, Lengnick-Hall, and Jennings. *Academy of Management Review, 15,* 137–146.

Ledford, G. E., & Lawler, E. (1994). Research on employee participation: Beating a dead horse? *Academy of Management Review, 19,* 633–636.

Locke, E. A., & Schweiger, D. M. (1979). Participation in decision making: One more look. *Research in Organizational Behavior, 1,* 265–339.

Long, R. J. (1988). Factors affecting managerial desires for various types of employee participation in decision making. *Applied Psychology: An International Review, 37,* 15–34.

Mael, F. A., & Tetrick, L. E. (1992). Identifying organizational identification. *Educational and Psychological Measurement, 52,* 813–824.

Maier, N. R. F. (1967). Assets and liabilities in group problem solving: The need for an integrative function. *Psychological Review, 74,* 239–249.

Manz, C. C. (1992). Self-leading work teams: Moving beyond self-management myths. *Human Relations, 45,* 1119–1140.

Marchington, M., Wilkinson, A., Ackers, P., & Goodman, J. (1994). Understanding the meaning of participation: Views from the workplace. *Human Relations, 47,* 867–894.

Mathieu, J. E., & Kohler, S. S. (1990). A cross-level examination of group absence influences on individual absence. *Journal of Applied Psychology, 75,* 217–220.

May, D. R., & Schwoerer, C. E. (1994). Developing effective work teams: Guidelines for fostering work team efficacy. *Organization Development Journal, 12,* 29–39.

McGrath, J. E. (1984). *Groups: Interaction and performance*. Englewood Cliffs, NJ: Prentice-Hall.

Mellor, S., Mathieu, J. E., & Swim, J. K. (1994). Cross-level analysis of the influence of local union structure on women's and men's union commitment. *Journal of Applied Psychology, 79,* 203–210.

Michaelsen, L. K., Watson, W. E., & Black, R. H. (1989). A realistic test of individual versus group consensus decision making. *Journal of Applied Psychology, 74,* 834–839.

Miller, R. W., & Prichard, F. N. (1992). Factors associated with workers' inclination to participate in an employee involvement program. *Group and Organization Management, 17,* 414–430.

Mitchell, T. R., & Silver, W. S. (1990). Individual and group goals when workers are interdependent: Effects on task strategies and performance. *Journal of Applied Psychology, 75,* 185–193.

Mossholder, K. W., Bedeian, A. G., & Armenakis, A. A. (1982). Group process–work outcome relationships: A note on the moderating impact of self-esteem. *Academy of Management Journal, 25,* 575–585.

Mullen, B., & Copper, C. (1994). The relation between group cohesiveness and performance: An integration. *Psychological Bulletin, 115,* 210–227.

Neck, C. P., & Manz, C. C. (1994). From groupthink to teamthink: Toward the creation of constructive thought patterns in self-managing work teams. *Human Relations, 47,* 929–952.

Neck, C. P., & Moorhead, G. (1995). Groupthink remodeled: The importance of leadership, time pressure, and methodical decision-making procedures. *Human Relations, 48,* 537–557.

O'Leary-Kelly, A. M., Martocchio, J. J., & Frink, D. D. (1994). A review of the influence of group goals on group performance. *Academy of Management Journal, 37,* 1285–1301.

Parker, L. E., & Price, R. H. (1994). Empowered managers and empowered workers: The effects of managerial support and managerial perceived control on workers' sense of control over decision making. *Human Relations, 47,* 911–928.

Peters, T. J. (1988). *Thriving on chaos.* New York: Knopf.

Powell, R. M., & Schlacter, J. L. (1971). Participative management: A panacea? *Academy of Management Journal, 14,* 165–173.

Ray, R. G. (1995). A training model for implementing self-directed work teams. *Organization Development Journal, 13,* 51–62.

Rentsch, J. R., Heffner, T. S., & Duffy, L. T. (1994). What you know is what you get from experience: Team experience related to teamwork schemas. *Group and Organization Management, 19,* 450–474.

Rettew, D. C., Billman, D., & Davis, R. A. (1993). Inaccurate perceptions of the amount others stereotype: Estimates about stereotypes of one's own group and other groups. *Basic and Applied Social Psychology, 14,* 121–142.

Ritti, R. R., & Funkhouser, G. R. (1977). *The ropes to skip and the ropes to know.* Columbus, OH: GRID.

Roethlisberger, F. J., & Dickson, W. J. (1939). *Management and the worker.* Cambridge, MA: Harvard University Press.

Ross, R. S. (1989). *Small groups in organizational settings.* Englewood Cliffs, NJ: Prentice-Hall.

Roy, D. F. (1959–60). "Banana Time"—Job satisfaction and informal interaction. *Human Organization, 18,* 158–168.

Sagie, A. (1994). Participative decision making and performance: A moderator analysis. *Journal of Applied Behavioral Science, 30,* 227–246.

Sagie, A. (1995). Employee participation and work outcomes: An end to the dispute? *Academy of Management Review, 20,* 278–280.

Schachter, S. (1951). Deviation, rejection, and communication. *Journal of Abnormal and Social Psychology, 46,* 190–207.

Schmit, J. (1995, May 5). Air Force streamlines its fliers' physicals. *USA Today,* p. 6B.

Shepperd, J. A. (1993). Productivity loss in performance groups: A motivation analysis. *Psychological Bulletin, 113,* 67–81.

Siegal, J., Dubrovsky, V., Kiesler, S., & McGuire, T. W. (1986). Group processes in computer-mediated communication. *Organizational Behavior and Human Decision Processes, 37,* 157–187.

Sniezek, J. A., & Henry, R. A. (1990). Revision, weighting, and commitment in consensus group judgment. *Organizational Behavior and Human Decision Processes, 45,* 66–84.

Stewart, G. B., III. (1995, May). EVA works—But not if you make these common mistakes. *Fortune*, p. 117.

Straus, S. G., & McGrath, J. E. (1994). Does the medium matter? The interaction of task type and technology on group performance and member reactions. *Journal of Applied Psychology, 79,* 87–97.

Sundstrom, E., De Meuse, K. P., & Futrell, D. (1990). Work teams: Applications and effectiveness. *American Psychologist, 45,* 120–133.

Tang, T. L., Tollison, P. S., & Whiteside, H. D. (1989). Quality circle productivity as related to upper-management attendance, circle initiation, and collar color. *Journal of Management, 15,* 101–113.

Tedeschi, J. T., & Lindskold, S. (1976). *Social psychology: Interdependence, interaction, and influence.* New York: Wiley.

Tsui, A. S., Egan, T. D., & O'Reilly, C. A. (1992). Being different: Relational demography and organizational attachment. *Administrative Science Quarterly, 37,* 549–579.

Wagner, J. A. (1994). Participation's effects on performance and satisfaction: A reconsideration of research evidence. *Academy of Management Review, 19,* 312–330.

Watson, W. E., Kumar, K., & Michaelsen, L. K. (1993). Cultural diversity's impact on interaction process and performance: Comparing homogeneous and diverse task groups. *Academy of Management Journal, 36,* 590–602.

Weisband, S. P. (1992). Group discussion and first advocacy effects in computer-mediated and face-to-face decision making groups. *Organizational Behavior and Human Decision Processes, 43,* 352–380.

White, J. K., & Ruh, R. A. (1973). Effects of personal values on the relationship between participation and job attitudes. *Administrative Science Quarterly, 18,* 506–514.

14

Leadership in Organizations

The Post-Heroic Leader

Corporate leadership used to be so simple. You had it, or you didn't. It was in the cut of your jib. And if you had it, you certainly didn't share it. The surest way to tell if you had it was to look behind you to see if anyone was following. If no one was, you fell back to flogging the chain of command. Because the buck stopped with you. . . . Your job was to kick ass and take names. . . .

Then, of course, the world turned upside down. Global competition wrecked stable markets and whole industries. Information technology created ad hoc networks of power within corporations. . . . Middle managers disappeared, along with corporate loyalty. . . . You accepted the new dizzying truth: that the only constant in today's world is exponentially increasing change. . . .

Call it whatever you like: post-heroic leadership, servant leadership, [or] distributed leadership. . . . But don't dismiss it as just another touchy-feely flavor of the month. It's real, it's radical, and it's challenging the very definition of corporate leadership for the 21st century. . . . Leaders are going to resemble not so much captains of ships as candidates running for office. They will face two fundamental tasks: first, to develop and articulate exactly what the company is trying to accomplish, and second, to create an environment in which employees can figure out what needs to be done and then do it well.

If you don't believe it, come to the little Appalachian town of Murphy, North Carolina . . . the old red brick Levi sewing plant. Here you'll meet Tommye Jo Daves, a 58-year-old mountain-bred grandmother—and a living incarnation of [the new] management. . . . Says Daves, "Sometimes it's real hard for me not to push back and say, 'You do this, you do that, and you do this.' Now I have to say, 'How do you want to do this?' I have to realize that their ideas may not be the way to go, but I have to let them learn that for themselves." [The result from Levi's leadership training and team management at this plant is that] flawed jeans have been reduced by a third, time between an order and shipment has fallen by ten days, and the time a pair of jeans spends in process at a plant has shrunk to one day from five. . . .

[Post-heroic leadership] still requires many of the attributes that have always distinguished the best leaders—intelligence, commitment, energy, courage of conviction, integrity. But here's the big difference: It expects those qualities of just about everyone in the organization. . . .

Excerpted from J. Huey, "The New Post-Heroic Leadership." *Fortune*, February 21, 1994, pp. 42–50. Copyright © 1994 Time Inc. All rights reserved. Reprinted with permission.

THE PSYCHOLOGY at Work excerpt illustrates several important aspects of leadership. First, there are the personal *traits* of the leader, such as intelligence and integrity. Second, there are the *behaviors* of the leaders. Third, there are *contingencies* to be considered. As the world and expectations change, so do the kinds of demands placed on a leader. Finally, there is the contemporary focus on leaders providing a *vision* that followers autonomously pursue.

The nature, history, and future of research and theory about leadership in organizations are explored in this chapter. Much of this discussion falls into the categories of trait, behavior, and contingency approaches to the study of leadership. A few of the more contemporary approaches go further, looking at the effects subordinates have on their leaders, the perception of leadership, and team leadership. The discussion opens with a look at some factors that facilitate or inhibit opportunities for leadership behavior in organizations.

What Is Leadership?

Leadership means different things to different people. To some, leadership means that people follow. To others, leadership means that people *willingly* follow. To still others, the essence of leadership is that a leader's influence is effective in getting goals accomplished. But what goals? A leader within an organization might be a person who can influence others, but is this influence in the best interests of the organization? A member of a work group might be very successful in influencing co-workers to hold back and limit group production to the absolute minimum standard set by the supervisor, for instance.

Over the decades, leadership has been defined by I/O psychologists and others who study it in a number of ways—as a focus of group processes, a person's personality and its effects, the art of inducing compliance, the exercise of influence, a behavior, a form of persuasion, a power relationship (Bass, 1990a). For present purposes, the definition of **leadership** provided by social psychologists Katz and Kahn (1978) is most useful.

> We consider the essence of organizational leadership to be the influential increment over and above mechanical compliance with the routine directives of the organization. (p. 528)

The definition conveys all of the ideas about leadership mentioned. Leaders get people to do more than they would do without a leader, and these efforts are in line with accomplishing organizational goals. Leadership gets people to go beyond simple compliance with the system, and helps groups achieve their goals.

According to Katz and Kahn, there are five reasons why organizations need leadership. The greater the need in any of these areas, the greater the opportunity for an individual to exercise leadership.

1. *The incompleteness of organizational design.* No set of rules, plans, procedures, or organization charts can describe perfectly what must happen within an organization if it is to survive and be successful. Leaders help interpret the rules and plans and fill the gaps.

2. *Leadership as a boundary function.* In Chapter 12, organizations are defined as systems of interrelated subsystems. Leaders are the links between these subsystems.

3. *Changing environmental conditions.* The concept of an organization as an open system interacting with its environment is also discussed in Chapter 12. Leaders get resources from the environment and make the environment more receptive to the organization.

4. *The internal dynamics of an organization.* Organizations change and grow. Leaders prevent these changes from hurting the organization and its members and they encourage positive change.

5. *The nature of human membership in organizations.* People come, go, and change. Leadership provides continuity and helps people adapt to change.

Substitutes for Leadership

Katz and Kahn's five factors create opportunities for leadership, but there are also conditions that inhibit these opportunities. Kerr and Jermier (1978) propose that characteristics of the subordinates, the task, and the organization can work to prevent opportunities for leadership. Leadership behavior can be neutralized when characteristics of the situation prevent the leader from leading, and certain built-in substitutes for leadership can make the leader's behavior relatively unimportant.

The characteristics hypothesized to neutralize or substitute for leadership are presented in Table 14–1. To summarize this information briefly, independent, well-trained, and professional subordinates (including the large group of knowledge workers employed in today's organizations) need less leadership of any type. Constant, routine tasks

Table 14-1   Substitutes for Leadership

	Will Tend to Neutralize	
Characteristics	**Relationship-Oriented, Supportive, People-Centered, Leadership: Consideration, Support, and Interaction Facilitation**	**Task-Oriented, Instrumental, Job-Centered Leadership: Initiating Structure, Goal Emphasis, and Work Facilitation**
Of the subordinate		
1. Ability, experience, training, knowledge		X
2. Need for independence	X	X
3. "Professional" orientation	X	X
4. Indifference toward organizational rewards	X	X
Of the task		
5. Unambiguous and routine		X
6. Methodologically invariant		X
7. Provides its own feedback concerning accomplishment		X
8. Intrinsically satisfying	X	
Of the organization		
9. Formalization (explicit plans, goals, and areas of responsibility)		X
10. Inflexibility (rigid, unbending rules and procedures)		X
11. Highly specified and active advisory and staff functions		X
12. Closely knit, cohesive work groups	X	X
13. Organizational rewards not within the leader's control	X	X
14. Spatial distance between superior and subordinates	X	X

From S. Kerr and J. M. Jermier, "Substitutes for Leadership: Their Meaning and Measurement." *Organizational Behavior and Human Performance,* 1978, *26,* 375–403. Copyright 1978 Academic Press. Reprinted by permission.

may not require supervisors to exercise leadership. And inflexible organizations that do not give leaders much control over rewards inhibit opportunities for leadership behavior.

Understanding the conditions that create or inhibit opportunities for leadership in organizations is important to people who study leaders and their behavior. Without this understanding, the possibility of erroneous inference is substantial. If the fact that Company Z does not allow its managers any input into raise and promotion decisions is not considered, for example, subordinates' negative evaluations of Company Z's managerial leadership are out of context. Accordingly, it might be concluded that many of the managers in this company need extensive leadership training or should be replaced. In fact, their perceived ineffectiveness stems in large part from something that has nothing to do with their behavior.

Investigations of substitutes for leadership support the basic premise that under some conditions leadership in the usual sense is unnecessary or even counterproductive. In one study of 612 employees in three different firms, leader behaviors were found to have only a modest impact on employees' performance, whereas the substitutes for leadership accounted for a large amount of employee satisfaction and commitment (Podsakoff, Niehoff, MacKenzie, & Williams, 1993). In a second study, Podsakoff, MacKenzie, and Bommer (1996) examined the relative impacts of leadership and substitutes on 1,539 employees in a variety of job levels, industries, and organizations. Again, substitutes accounted for considerably more of the variance in employee attitudes and performance (20.2%) than did leadership (7.2%).

Inference
See pages 35–43

Variance
See pages 40–42

Leadership and Management

Some I/O psychologists and management scholars believe that a distinction between leadership and management is important. Hersey and Blanchard (1988) see the difference between the two as a focus on influence (leadership) versus a focus on the accomplishment of organizational goals (management). Others believe the distinction lies in routine (management) versus innovation (leadership), or "doing the right thing versus doing things right" (e.g., Bennis & Nanus, 1985).

The belief that there is a difference between management and leadership is accepted by the many organizations that spend considerable time, money, and effort trying to make their managers better leaders, but it is not accepted by everyone (e.g., Krantz & Gilmore, 1990). In this chapter, the discussion is about people in organizations who are given formal responsibility for the work of others. Most of these people are supervisors, managers, or executives and as such they wear many hats (Mintzberg, 1980). They need to be competent both in management activities, such as planning and organizing work, and in leadership activities, such as influencing and communicating a vision (Kim & Yukl, 1995). It is the behaviors that express the leader role that are examined in the current chapter.

Trait Approaches to the Study of Leadership

One of the first attempts to specify the nature of leadership in organizations focused on top management. Chester Barnard's (1938/1968) *The Functions of the Executive* remains a classic in this area. Organizations are systems, and Barnard believed that executives are primarily to be charged with the design and maintenance of these systems through the functions of (1) coordinating the activities and systems necessary to maintain the organization, (2) bringing the necessary people into the organization and securing their cooperation, and (3) establishing the objectives and goals of the organization.

When people talk of what leaders *should* do, as Barnard does, they are implying that there are correct (effective) and incorrect (ineffective) ways of leading, an assumption that underlies most of the early leadership research. In this context, the notion that some individuals have a knack for leadership and others don't seemed a reasonable one; shortly after the turn of the century the hunt was on for a list of personal traits that would distinguish between these two types of people.

The "Great Man" Theory

This early trait theory approach to the study of leadership is often called the "great man" theory because of its focus on obviously successful leaders. (Note the assumption about the sex of a good leader.) Researchers hoped that they could improve organizational functioning by the relatively simple strategy of identifying the characteristics of good leaders, finding people with these characteristics, and putting them in leadership positions.

The general methodology of the early trait theory research was to search for significant differences between the personal traits of successful leaders and those of unsuccessful leaders. In this literature, the definition of success varies from the performance of the leader's group to the personal success of the leader (such as promotion to a top position). In his review of hundreds of trait studies conducted over almost 70 years, Stogdill (1974) summarizes the results of this line of research.

> "The leader is characterized by a strong drive for responsibility and task completion, vigor and persistence in pursuit of goals, venturesomeness and originality in problem solving, drive to exercise initiative in social situations, self-confidence and sense of personal identity, willingness to accept consequences of decision and action, readiness to absorb interpersonal stress, willingness to tolerate frustration and delay, ability to influence other persons' behavior, and capacity to structure social interaction systems to the purpose at hand. (p. 81)

As Stogdill's word picture suggests, the search for the traits that good leaders have and poor leaders do not have was successful insofar as agreement about these traits is concerned. Unfortunately, the list is not very useful for identifying good leaders in advance because it consists mostly of traits that can be assessed only by observing someone's behavior over time. As far as effective leadership is concerned, the personal traits that can be observed or measured easily at the outset (such as sex and personal appearance) refuse to fall into a neat division.

Reliability

See pages 54–58

Despite the fact that many years of research failed to yield a neat division of readily observable personal traits that reliably differentiate successful from unsuccessful leaders, there was (and remains) considerable agreement as to what that division should be. Show people a picture of a tall, silver-haired man in his 60s wearing a tailored business suit, a "power tie," and a serious expression and a second picture of an attractive, dark-haired woman in her 40s wearing a casual, sleeveless dress, dangling earrings, and a big smile, and ask them to choose the leader. The majority will select the man and set the woman aside unless they recognize Donna Karan, chief designer and founder of one of this country's most successful and influential clothing firms.

I/O psychologists know that personal traits are important influences on peoples' perceptions of leadership ability and performance.

The process described also works in reverse. When shown photographs of people identified as leaders or nonleaders, subjects rated the leaders as more attractive and mature than the nonleaders, and as possessing leaderlike status and personality traits (Cherulnik, Turns, & Wilderman, 1990). Yet, the labels "leader" and "nonleader" were assigned randomly to photographs prejudged to be of about equal attractiveness. The qualities the subjects saw in the leader pictures were qualities they *believed* are associated more with leaders than nonleaders.

Leadership in the Eye of the Beholder

In the discussion of psychological approaches to job design in Chapter 8, the role of social information processing in determining individual employee reactions to work is reviewed briefly. The basic premise of this view is that a person's perceptions of his or her job are based, in part, on information from the social environment. There is a similar line of information processing research in the leadership area that emphasizes the role of people's ideas about (1) what real leaders are like and (2) cause and effect connections. Both of these "theories" are affected considerably by the factors in the social environment.

People deal in many ways with the constant barrage of information from the environment in which they must operate. One is by grouping people and their behavior into mental pigeonholes, "already existing, contextually meaningful categories" (Binning, Zaba, & Whattam, 1986, p. 522). The mental classification system serves as a substitute for having to attend to, and make sense of, everything someone does; an action can be evaluated and responded to on the basis of the assigned category.

As regards leadership research, the social information processing model suggests that widely shared ideas (social information) about leader traits and behaviors have significant effects on individual perceptions of leadership (e.g., Lord, DeVader, & Alliger, 1986). These implicit leadership theories are already existing categories for pigeonholing someone as leader or nonleader, and a person in a leadership position is responded to accordingly.

If people have their own ideas about what makes for an effective leader, there should be differences in the ratings of any given individual's leadership according to who is doing the rating. Research generally confirms this expectation. Atwater and Yammarino (1993) found that subordinates respond positively to intelligence and athletic experience, but the leader's superiors are more impressed by his or her general degree of conformity to organizational norms and values.

Norms
See pages 474–475

Other research in the area of implicit theories of leadership find that some people view the ideal leader as superintelligent, while others are certain that a "real leader" is the individual possessed of that elusive quality called charisma. Still another take on the subject is found in a recent study by Kenney, Blascovich, and Shaver (1994). These investigators report that the leader most likely to achieve the greatest acceptance by a new group is one who learns the group's goals, takes charge, is a nice person, and—seems a bit nervous!

The social information processing view of leadership also suggests that perceptions of leadership are affected by outcomes of leader behavior (cause and effect connections) as well as by implicit theories of leadership (what real leaders are like). Many studies have found that evaluations of leadership activity are influenced by information about the performance of subordinates or the group of which the individual was leader, with leaders of successful groups being seen as more effective (e.g., Binning, Zaba, & Whattam, 1986; Phillips & Lord, 1982).

The idea that the success of a group, department, or organization plays a vital role in evaluations of leadership is often overlooked in discussions of leaders and leadership. There are many factors that can affect the success of an organization or of groups within it, only one of which is its leader. To the extent that people evaluate and respond to that leader on the basis of his or her unit's success, this evaluation may rise or fall on factors

In every aspect of life, people have their own "theories" about the characteristics of an effective leader.

beyond the control of any one individual. Nevertheless, much of the writing about leadership continues to focus on traits. In particular, the "trait" of being male or female has come in for considerable attention.

The Gender of Leadership

Throughout the history of formal interest in leadership, no trait has been more firmly linked to most people's concept of a real leader than masculinity (e.g., Lord, DeVader, & Alliger, 1986; Schein, 1973). Analysis of responses to questionnaires about perceptions of men, women, and successful managers usually wind up delivering the same message: men in general are described as more similar to successful managers than are women in general.

The findings described are, perhaps, not that difficult to understand in the sense that managers have been men for most of our country's history. Things have changed enormously in the past few decades, however. Naturally enough, when Heilman and her co-investigators replicated some of the research into the "gender of leadership" in the late 1980s, they expected to find fewer differences in the perceived association between gender and managerial effectiveness (Heilman, Block, Martell, & Simon, 1989). These investigators reasoned that social and legal changes would have helped women progress toward equality as well as equal opportunity in the work environment.

They reasoned wrong. Successful managers were rated more similar to men in general than to women in general in their leadership ability, self-confidence, desire for responsibility, and about 50 other issues. Successful managers were rated more similar to women in general than to men in general in terms of being curious, helpful, intuitive, creative, understanding, neat, aware of others' feelings, and less vulgar. The subjects in the study were all men, but the picture does not necessarily change much when women are included.

Some investigators find that women no longer stereotype managers (e.g., Norris & Wylie, 1995), but in many studies the old pattern persists. Fagenson (1990) reports that both men and women in upper-level corporate jobs rated themselves in more masculine terms than did individuals in lower-level jobs. This "think manager—think male" phenomenon is not only stable but also widespread, having been identified among men and women in Germany, Great Britain, Japan, and China as well as in the United States (Schein, Mueller, Lituchy, & Liu, 1996).

The research findings on how leaders *behave* (rather than what they are "like") at first look mixed. In some cases, men clearly behave in ways that help them emerge as leaders more often than women, but at other times there is no difference. The explanation for these inconsistent findings may lie in the settings of the different studies. In the typical laboratory setting, men dominate (become leaders of) small groups that are meeting to accomplish a specific task in a short amount of time more often than women. In real organizations, however, successful men and women managers seem to be more alike than unlike (Eagly & Johnson, 1990; Powell, 1988).

Laboratory research
See pages 27–28

Despite a high degree of similarity in the behavior of successful managers, research also identifies differences in the way men and women in leadership positions behave. Many leadership scholars believe these differences are very important to effective organizational functioning. Rosener (1990, 1995) states that women are more inclined to use interactive leadership, encourage participation, share power and information, enhance others' self-worth, and get others excited about their work. This different style of leadership, she maintains, is more likely to be effective in contemporary organizations where working together and developing subordinates is increasingly emphasized over traditional my-way-or-the-highway styles.

Some support for Roesner's argument is offered by an interesting examination of leadership style at the top. Adler (1996) found that women heads of state around the world tend to minimize hierarchy, use inclusive processes to build consensus, and focus on creating unity. But even in routine, day-to-day activities at less rarified levels, women managers often adopt a different pace and are more tolerant of interruptions and non-business activities than men. When taking the leadership role, they are more likely to use an interactive process than one-way communication of a vision (Helgesen, 1990).

There may be more women than men who have a talent and a preference for a leadership style that fits some situations better than traditional alternatives, but it is often difficult to prove its effectiveness. As noted, many, perhaps most, people have always expected their leaders to behave in a manner that is stereotypically masculine. Unfortunately, these same people are likely to devalue women who try to lead with the preferred masculine style (e.g., Eagly, Makhijani, & Klonsky, 1992).

Both men and women often react negatively when women attempt to communicate in a forceful way or to behave in a high-status manner. Yet, that's just how people are expected to behave in order to be persuasive and influential (Adler, 1993). Ragins (1989, 1991) believes that the issue is really power, not gender. Women and men managers of equal power are rated by their subordinates as being equally effective; men, however, have much greater access to power in most organizations with "the path to power for women [resembling] an obstacle course" (Ragins & Sundstrom, 1989, p. 51).

To sum up, the research findings that *successful* women and men managers behave in very similar ways are really no surprise. Our society values certain kinds of behaviors more than others in our leaders, and these behaviors are almost unanimously associated with masculinity. In order to reach the top in most organizations, a person (man *or* woman) must behave in accordance with these values, thus perpetuating the preference for this style.

The Ideal Leader

The social information processing view of leadership suggests that personal traits are quite as important to being a successful leader as many people have long insisted, if in a different way from that originally thought. Many I/O psychologists and management scholars have brought their experience and personal philosophies to bear on this subject. Three of these statements describing the ideal leader and his or her leadership style are reviewed here.

The Take-Charge Leader

Bennis and Nanus (1985) sought to identify the characteristics of good leaders through extensive, unstructured interviews with 60 successful chief executive officers (CEOs). Based on these interviews, the authors identified the four successful leader strategies for taking charge described in Exhibit 14–1. These ideas captured the imagination of corporate America for a time, and they continue to stimulate thought and discussion about

Attention through vision

Successful leaders have a vision of what they want to accomplish and they create a focus for achieving their agenda.

Meaning through communication

Successful leaders are able to communicate their visions to others and develop a shared meaning of the desired outcomes.

Trust through positioning

Successful leaders develop trust by being persistent, demonstrating stability, and behaving in ways that back up their vision.

Deployment of self through positive regard

Successful leaders maintain a positive self-image, do not even consider the possibility of failure, and are able to learn from bad experiences.

Exhibit 14–1
Leader Strategies for Taking Charge

leadership vision. The process of communicating that vision has also received attention. Conger (1991) discusses the importance of the leader's use of symbols and rhetoric in "managing by inspiration."

According to Conger, a leader must help followers interpret reality by creating values that inspire, provide meaning, and instill purpose. The leader must communicate through metaphors, analogies, stories, and language that creates vivid images and elicits potent emotions from followers or subordinates. For example, following Conger's idea, a road crew is maintaining the arteries of America and her commerce, not filling potholes.

The Transformational Leader

James MacGregor Burns (1978) discusses the difference between two types of political leaders. The transactional leader views the leader-follower relationship as a *transaction*. The subordinate who does good work is rewarded by the leader. The transformational leader, by contrast, gains more than simple compliance from followers; he or she is able to gain superior achievement and outcomes by *transforming* the followers' basic beliefs, values, and needs. Bass (1985, 1990b) has carried this idea over to organizational leadership, as have Tichy and Devanna (1986).

According to Tichy and Devanna, a transformational leader recognizes the need for organizational change, creates a vision, mobilizes commitment to the vision, shapes the organization's culture to support the change, and looks for new signals of change. The tools of transformational leadership are rhetorical (communication) skills that create an image of strength and self-confidence, trust, and personalized leadership. Even though the leader may not have a personal relationship with each follower, the followers *feel* as if such a relationship exists.

Because followers perceive a personal connection with a transformational leader, they embrace his or her vision, focus on issues greater than themselves, and feel powerful in their pursuit of the vision (Hughes, Ginnett, & Curphy, 1996). Kuhnert and Lewis (1987) maintain that it is personality trait differences that distinguish this leader from the transactional leader. Wofford and Goodwin (1994), on the other hand, believe that the adoption of one style or the other is a cognitive choice people make depending in part on the ways they view the world and their subordinates. It should also be noted that transformational leadership can build on the basic organizational skills inherent in transactional leadership without replacing it.

> Transformational leaders can be directive or participative, authoritarian or democratic. Nelson Mandela is directive when he declares: "Forget the past." He can be participative when he actively supports and involves himself in open, multiracial consultations and mutual agreements. (Bass, 1995, p. 747)

The Charismatic Leader

Charismatic leaders, "by the force of their personal abilities, are capable of having profound and extraordinary effects on followers" (House & Baetz, 1979, p. 399). People identify with this leader and follow willingly. Examples of charismatic leaders from the past might include John F. Kennedy, Jr., Eleanor Roosevelt, and Lee Iacocca, former head of Chrysler Corporation.

The formal measurement and examination of charisma as a defined set of leader traits or behaviors (rather than as some mysterious quality with which some people are born and most are not) is still developing (e.g., House, Spangler & Woycke, 1991; Tepper & Percy, 1994). Among the aspects of behavior that seem to make up charisma are vision and the ability to articulate it, willingness to take personal risk, and sensitivity to individual needs (Conger & Kanungo, 1994).

A comparison of transformational and charismatic leadership is presented in Exhibit 14–2. Clearly, charisma would add enormously to a transformational leader's effectiveness. The combination can have unfortunate consequences as well as desirable ones, however (e.g., Conger, 1990; O'Connor, Mumford, Clifton, Gessner, & Connelly, 1995). The leader may be successful in getting people to work toward a vision that is inaccurate or unrealistic. As history well demonstrates, charisma can also be used to move people toward dark ends (think of Hitler or the leader of the Heaven's Gate cult).

Exhibit 14–2 A Comparison of Transformational and Charismatic Leadership	**Transformational leadership originates with a vision.** The transformational leader creates a vision of change, motivates followers to pursue it, and incorporates the change into the fabric of the organization. Martin Luther King, Jr., is believed by many to have been a leader of this type.
	Charismatic leadership originates with a person. The charismatic leader elicits trust and acceptance of his or her values and goals by force of presence and personality. Relationships with this leader and identification with his or her mission enhance followers' self-esteem. John F. Kennedy, Jr., is believed by many to have been a leader of this type.

Trait Theories of Leadership in Perspective

The old trait theory shopping-list approach to leadership is not very helpful in finding more effective leaders, but the assumption that effective leaders differ in some identifiable and fundamental ways from other people is still very much a part of mainstream I/O psychology (e.g., Kirkpatrick & Locke, 1991). Are successful leaders more intelligent? Do they have higher needs for power? Are they more masculine than feminine? Do they have personalities that are similar to one another, but different from unsuccessful leaders? These and related questions still intrigue investigators the world over.

The renewed interest in personality as a variable of study in I/O psychology has led a number of researchers into the leader characteristics area. Among other findings in this line of research, investigators report that effective leaders have higher scores on measures of the traits of conscientiousness, extroversion, dominance, energy, agreeableness, intelligence, openness to experience, and emotional stability than the average person (Kets de Vries, 1994). In addition, people with high scores on some of these same dimensions of personality are often perceived as leaders in groups that have no formal leader (e.g., Hogan, Curphy, & Hogan, 1994). On the flip side, a number of personal characteristics, such as being mechanical, individualistic, and egocentric, seem to be associated with the ultimate failure of people who occupy leadership positions (Grant, 1996).

To recapitulate, the search for leadership traits has brought I/O psychologists and other researchers a certain distance toward understanding leadership. The possibility of a clear distinction between the individual characteristics of effective and ineffective leaders continues to intrigue investigators, but traits as traditionally envisioned do not allow for an adequate distinction by themselves. The behavior of people in leadership positions must also be examined.

Behavioral Approaches to the Study of Leadership

Early approaches to the study of leader behavior remained linked to trait theories in that they emphasized what were believed to be basic opposing differences in patterns of leader behavior that originated in personalities and personal philosophies. The best-known of these typologies is the authoritarian, democratic, and laissez-faire leadership style distinction of Kurt Lewin and his colleagues.

Authoritarian, Democratic, and Laissez-Faire Leadership

The basic differences among the three leadership styles described by Lewin, Lippitt, and White (1939) revolve around who makes decisions about what the group (of followers) does. The authoritarian leader makes all of the decisions and passes them down. By contrast, the democratic leader encourages and assists group members with participation in all such decisions. The laissez-faire leader is a nonparticipative leader who steps aside and takes no part in decisions unless asked specifically.

The leader behavior differences summarized served as operational definitions in many of the early studies of the way that leadership style influences behavior. The study

Operational definitions
See page 26

SPOTLIGHT ON
RESEARCH

Patterns of Aggressive Behavior in Experimentally Created "Social Climates"

Summarized from
K. Lewin, R. Lippitt,
and R. K. White,
"Patterns of
Aggressive
Behavior in
Experimentally
Created 'Social
Climates.'" *Journal
of Social
Psychology*, 1939,
10, 271–299.

Research question   What are the effects of different climates created by different leadership styles on various aspects of the behavior of group members?

Type of study   Field simulation experiment.

Subjects   Ten-year-old male volunteers.

Independent variable   Leadership style. Operational definition: (a) authoritarian, (b) democratic, (c) laissez-faire.

Dependent variable   Aggressive behavior of subjects. Operational definition: Several based on a variety of social analysis techniques.

General procedure   Four new clubs of 10-year-old boys were organized on a volunteer basis. The clubs engaged in a variety of social activities. Every six weeks each club had a new leader with a different style of leadership. A large amount of observational data were collected according to predetermined methods.

Results

- Under authoritarian leadership, most boys showed extremely nonaggressive, apathetic behavior and notable outbursts of aggression on the days of transition to a new leader.
- Nineteen out of 20 boys liked their democratic leader better than their authoritarian leader, and 7 out of 10 liked their laissez-faire leader better.
- There were two "wars" between clubs and two striking instances of aggression against inanimate objects.

Conclusion   "A general interpretation of the . . . data on aggression can be made in terms of four underlying factors: tension, restricted space of free movement, rigidity of group structure, and style of living (culture)" (p. 299).

Experiment
See pages 29–31

Independent/ dependent variable
See page 29

Research subjects
See page 27

Criterion
See page 63

summarized in Spotlight on Research is a well-known investigation in this area, although this experiment was not a study of leadership in organizations at all. Lewin, Lippitt, and White (1939) were investigating the relationships between (a) the social climates associated with their manipulations of leader behavior (independent variable) and (b) the social interaction patterns of their subjects (dependent variable). But the obvious parallel to organizational leadership excited many I/O psychologists, and the study is considered a classic in this line of research.

Subsequent investigations of authoritarian, democratic, and laissez-faire leadership styles examined the influence of these behavior patterns on the traditional leadership effectiveness criteria of task accomplishment and subordinate satisfaction. Some of these studies confirmed Lewin, Lippitt, and White's finding that people *like* democratic leadership better, an idea that has returned to popularity in recent years in such forms as self-managing work teams, flatter organizational hierarchies, and the concept of employee empowerment. One result is that elaboration and clarification of the democratic style of leadership is again of interest to researchers (Gastil, 1994).

Other studies of Lewin and his colleagues' typology concluded that the best leadership style depends on circumstances, especially as regards task accomplishment (e.g., Vroom & Mann, 1960). In particular, authoritarian leadership appears to be associated with greater productivity when the situation is highly stressful to employees in some way (e.g., Rosenbaum & Rosenbaum, 1971). To the extent that satisfaction is related to successful goal accomplishment, people in this situation tend to be more satisfied with authoritarian leadership. Still, for others, authoritarian styles have been linked with higher productivity but lower job satisfaction (e.g., Smither, 1993).

Two Dimensions of Leader Behavior

The authoritarian/democratic/laissez-faire distinction is based on only one facet of a leader's behavior—how a leader makes decisions. A broader line of research into leader behavior was undertaken by the Survey Research Center at the University of Michigan (Katz, Maccoby & Morse, 1950). Two basic types of leader behavior were identified in this research. Employee-centered behaviors are directed toward interpersonal relationships and the needs of subordinates. Job-centered behaviors are directed primarily toward getting the work done.

Concurrent with the Michigan studies, similar work was being carried out at Ohio State University (Stogdill & Coons, 1957). This group of researchers also identified two general categories of leader behaviors. One category was labeled "consideration" and was defined in terms of behaviors directed toward concern with employee feelings, mutual trust, open communication, and respect. The second category was labeled "initiating structure" and was defined in terms of behaviors directed toward achieving goals, defining, and directing subordinate performance. Sound familiar? The two major categories of leader behavior identified in the University of Michigan research were virtually identical to those identified independently in the Ohio State studies.

The basic results from the Ohio State/University of Michigan research may be summarized fairly simply. Job *performance* outcomes are related more to job-centered (initiating structure) behaviors, whereas employee *satisfaction* outcomes are related more to employee-centered (consideration) behaviors. Over the years, research has continued to support this pattern. In one survey of 256 employees from a number of different companies, for example, Seltzer and Numerof (1988) found that subordinate burnout (defined as feeling fed up, discouraged, and angry about one's work) was negatively correlated with the supervisor's use of consideration behaviors and positively correlated with the supervisor's use of initiating structure behaviors.

Correlation
See pages 37–39

The early behavioral approaches to the study of leadership (as exemplified by the Michigan and Ohio State studies) took a broader view of leadership than older trait approaches, but they shared the assumption that there is one best way to lead. If some concern for people and some attention to the task are both good, then it would seem that the very best leaders would be those who are high on both dimensions of behavior. Some I/O psychologists put this belief into practice, developing training programs to help people in organizational leadership positions change their behaviors to fit the profile believed to be ideal (e.g., Blake & Mouton, 1985).

The idea that the key to effective leadership lies in learning to be a high-high leader (high on both employee and task concerns) was appealing to people looking for a quick fix for effective leadership. As the body of research in this area accumulated, however, investigators began to report inconsistent results. Sometimes a strong emphasis on only one type of behavior (such as employee-centered) proved more successful than a strong emphasis on both types of behavior. At other times, use of the formerly successful behavior did not work out as well as a focus on the other behavior (task-centered). The evidence that high-high leadership was oversimplified mounted, and researchers began to look for characteristics of the situation that might determine when each type of behavior would be appropriate.

Contingency Approaches to the Study of Leadership

A contingency theory in any area of study substitutes "it depends" thinking for "there is one best way" thinking. In leadership, a contingency theory begins with the proposition that there is no one best way for a person in a position of leadership to behave at all times. The appropriate leader behavior depends on (is contingent upon) certain characteristics of the leader, the subordinates, and the situation. During periods of organizational stability, for example, leaders may emphasize their symbolic behaviors. Upheavals such as reorganization, mergers, economic downturns, and the like may call for emphasis on substantive behaviors (Eggleston & Bhagat, 1993). (Contingency theories of leadership are also called situational theories by some writers.)

Fiedler's Contingency Theory

The first well-known contingency theory of leadership was proposed by Fiedler (1967), who attempted to develop a framework that would match leaders to the situations in which they would be successful. The resulting contingency model states that the effectiveness of a leader depends on three variables. First is the leader's need structure, specifically whether the leader is primarily motivated to seek task accomplishment or to seek satisfaction of interpersonal needs. The leader's preference for a task or people orientation is measured with an instrument called the Least Preferred Coworker (LPC) scale.

Variable
See pages 25–26

The second variable is the leader's situational control, his or her confidence that the task will be accomplished. Situational control is hypothesized to depend on (1) the leader-member relations (the degree to which the leader is supported by the subordinates), (2) the task structure (the clarity and specificity of the work), and (3) the leader's position power (the extent to which the leader can reward or punish). Good relations combined with a well-structured task and a strong power base form the most *favorable* (highest situational control) situation for the leader. Poor relations, low task structure, and a weak power position create the least favorable situation.

Finally, there is the interaction between the leader's need structure and situational controls.

> Task-motivated . . . leaders tend to perform best in situations in which they have high control as well as in those in which their control is low. Relationship-motivated . . . leaders perform best in moderate-control situations. (Fiedler & Garcia, 1987, pp. 81–82)

In other words, the interaction of the leader and the situation predict the success of the leader. This interaction is summarized in Figure 14–1.

A review of 24 validation studies found that the proposed contingency relationships in the figure were supported in about half of the laboratory investigations to that time, while field studies yielded only limited support (Peters, Hartke, & Pohlmann, 1985). The authors of the review concluded that additional variables must be added if the model is to increase its predictive power. More recently, Schriesheim, Tepper, and Tetrault (1994) conducted a meta-analysis of research on Fiedler's contingency theory using data from more than 1,200 groups. On the basis of this analysis, these investigators concluded that this approach has promise, but they, too, offered ideas for modifying the theory.

Meta-analysis
See page 43

One of the biggest criticisms of Fiedler's contingency theory is that it takes an overly simplistic view of the work situation. It is also criticized because it does not explain *why*

These situational characteristics ...	Leader-member relations	Good	Good	Good	Good	Poor	Poor	Poor	Poor
	Task structure	High	High	Low	Low	High	High	Low	Low
	Position power	Strong	Weak	Strong	Weak	Strong	Weak	Strong	Weak
Create this type of leadership environment ...	Situational favorableness	Very high			←————————————→				Very low
In which this type of leader is more likely to succeed	LPC score	Low	Low	Low	High	High	High	High	Low

Figure 14–1

The Conditions for Leader Effectiveness According to Fiedler's Contingency Theory

things work (and so it is not actually a theory). But perhaps the greatest criticism comes from challenges to the Least Preferred Coworker instrument, which is supposed to indicate a person's basic people or task orientation. According to one leading researcher in the leadership area, despite more than 25 years of research no one really knows what the LPC instrument measures (Yukl, 1994).

Some years after his original statement, Fiedler and his colleagues (Fiedler & Garcia, 1987; Fiedler & House, 1994) developed the cognitive resource theory (CRT) of leadership effectiveness, which focuses on the relationship between a leader's intelligence and leadership success. As illustrated in Figure 14–2, this relationship is moderated by directiveness (smart + directive = success) and stress (intelligence has more impact on success under conditions of low stress).

Moderator variable
See page 39

Cognitive resource theory, like Fiedler's early contingency theory of leadership, considers the leader's trait and behavior (intelligence and directiveness, instead of LPC) and the situation (stress and group support) in predicting leadership effectiveness. Contingency theory predicts when an effective leader should be directive, however, while CRT focuses more on when a leader's intelligence is most effective.

Research on CRT is still thin, and the evidence available offers only mixed support. In one study of 48 four-person groups, only one of seven hypotheses was supported: leader intelligence was more strongly associated with group performance for highly directive leaders, compared with nondirective leaders (Vecchio, 1990). At present, cognitive resource theory seems to be more controversial than accepted. A recent issue of an international journal that carried a report by Fiedler in support of CRT also held over a half dozen replies critical of the theory (see Fiedler, 1995, and associated articles). Nevertheless, the influence of Fiedler and his colleagues on the field of leadership studies has been, and remains, substantial.

Hypothesis
See page 25

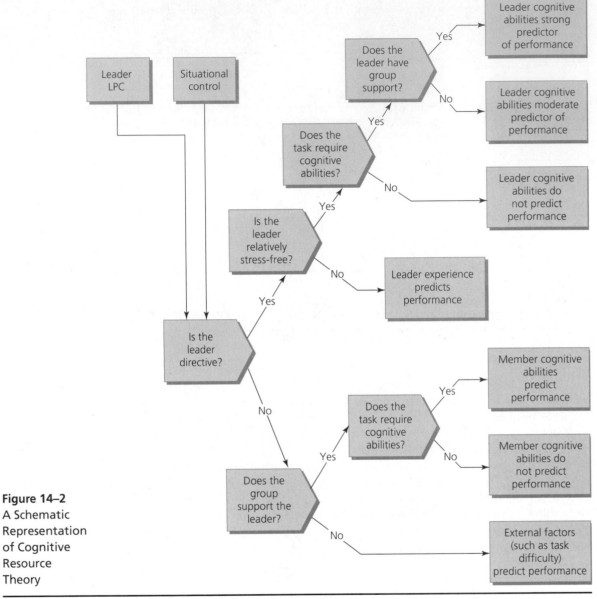

Figure 14–2
A Schematic
Representation
of Cognitive
Resource
Theory

From F. E. Fiedler and J. E. Garcia, *New Approaches to Effective Leadership: Cognitive Resources and Organizational Performance.* Copyright 1987 John Wiley & Sons. Reprinted by permission.

Vroom, Yetton, and Jago's Normative Model

Vroom and Yetton (1973) developed a model of leadership decision making—later refined by Vroom and Jago (1988)—that prescribes certain leadership behaviors in certain situations. Thus, this model is a contingency approach in its rejection of one best way for all situations, but it is also a normative model in its specifications of what leaders *should* do under certain conditions. Underlying the model are three criteria of effectiveness: rationality (it should objectively be a good decision), acceptance (if subordinates are needed to implement the decision, the leader should try to get them to accept it), and time (unless developing teamwork is more important than time).

Based on various combinations of the three criteria, there are five possible basic leadership styles in the normative model. At one extreme is an autocratic style in which the leader makes decisions wholly on his or her own. At the opposite extreme is a group decision-making strategy in which the leader serves merely to facilitate subordinate decision making. Between these extremes lie various consultative leadership styles: the leader makes the decision, but only after soliciting ideas and suggestions from individual subordinates.

In the normative model, different leadership styles are appropriate in different situations. The model includes a procedure for analyzing a situation and identifying which of the styles (called the feasible set) are likely to be both objectively correct and effectively carried out. The final choice from the feasible set depends upon whether the leader would rather save time or create a participative climate.

In an early study of the normative model, Vroom (1976) asked managers to give examples of successful and unsuccessful decisions they had recently made. When these examples were compared with the model, 65% of the managers whose methods fell within the feasible set had successful decision outcomes. Only 29% of those who failed to follow the model were successful. Reversing the process, Field (1982) told subjects in advance which method to use. Of the occasions that fit the feasible set, 49% were successful, and 36% of the decisions outside of the feasible set were effective.

What such research suggests is that following the normative model does not guarantee success, but it does seem to increase the odds. Further research continues to demonstrate the effectiveness of this approach for managers (e.g., Field & House, 1990; Paul & Ebadi, 1989), but its successful use in practice requires knowing quite a lot about one's subordinates and the task at hand. In addition, its applicability, like that of the much earlier Lewin, Lippitt, and White (1939) formulation, is limited to decision making. This is usually a vital part of any leader's role, but it is not the only part.

House's Path-Goal Theory

A third influential contingency approach to the study of leadership is House's (1971) path-goal theory. In this theory,

> the motivational functions of the leader consist of increasing the number and kinds of personal payoffs to subordinates for work-goal attainment and making paths to these payoffs easier to travel by clarifying the paths, reducing road blocks and pitfalls and increasing the opportunities for personal satisfaction en route. (House & Mitchell, 1974, p. 85)

The concept of goal in path-goal theory includes both the leader's performance goals and the subordinate's reward goals. The paths are the behaviors by which the follower can simultaneously achieve both goals. The leader's job is to understand what each subordinate finds rewarding (such as a raise, a promotion, or being left alone), know the performance capabilities of the subordinate (so that the proper performance goals can be set), link achievement of the performance goal to receipt of the desired reward, and help the subordinate achieve the performance goal (and associated reward).

The path-goal leadership theory proposes that a leader's behavior is acceptable and satisfying to a subordinate to the extent that the subordinate believes the leader's actions will lead him or her to personal rewards. Thus this approach, unlike that of Fiedler or Vroom and Yetton, focuses specifically on the relationship between a leader and individual followers. In House's theory, personal characteristics of a follower (such as belief in own abilities and relative need for achievement) and the nature of the work environment (such as the structure of the task and the authority of the leader) affect a leader's ability to lead. The appropriate leader behaviors are contingent on the subordinate's personal goals and characteristics and on the nature of the work environment. There are four general types of leader behavior to fit different combinations of the relevant variables (House & Mitchell, 1974).

1. *Directive leadership* is characterized by letting subordinates know what is expected of them and providing specific guidance as to what should be done and how it should be done. Directive leadership can increase a subordinate's understanding of the job to be done (particularly when task structure is low) and his or her perceptions of contingent rewards.

2. *Supportive leadership* is characterized by friendliness and approachableness and overt concern for the status, well-being, and needs of subordinates. This form of leadership can help reduce boredom and lead to an increased interest in work. It can also build self-confidence by increasing followers' expectations of success and rewards.

3. *Participative leadership* is characterized by soliciting subordinate input and seriously considering the suggestions. Participative leadership helps subordinates feel involved; it also helps to clarify unclear tasks.

4. *Achievement-oriented leadership* involves setting challenging goals, expecting subordinates to perform at their highest level, and showing confidence that the subordinates will achieve the goals. Achievement-oriented leadership makes up for a lack of challenge and leads to harder, but still achievable, goals.

From a path-goal perspective, a leader's job is to diagnose the situation and choose the appropriate behavior style. Unlike Fiedler's predictive model, the path-goal theory is explanatory, drawing on the general expectancy theory of motivation discussed in Chapter 6 to explain why employees should put forth more effort under the appropriate leadership style. Investigators often find support for the basic premises, but Indvik's (1986) extensive review (48 studies and more than 11,000 subjects) suggests that some of the theory's propositions might require fine tuning. Directive leadership does not seem to enhance performance when task structure is low as is predicted, for example.

More recently, two different meta-analyses of the literature have sought to verify the predicted impacts of situational and subordinate characteristics on a leader's ability to bring about positive outcomes (Podsakoff, MacKenzie, Ahearne, & Bommer, 1995; Wofford & Liska, 1993). Both sets of investigators conclude that there is modest support for path-goal theory, although they note that much of the research they examined is methodologically flawed.

Despite problems with some of the research subjected to the meta-analysis reviews, there are individual studies that offer useful possibilities for the fine tuning suggested by Indvik (1986). For example, followers' needs for both achievement (Mathieu, 1990) and clarity (Keller, 1989) have been found to have an effect on which leadership style will be most successful. Followers with a high need for achievement seem to prefer achievement-oriented leadership, whereas those with a low need for achievement prefer supportive leaders. Followers with high needs for clarity are more satisfied with directive leaders than are followers whose needs for clarity are low.

Contingency Theories in Perspective

The basic premise of contingency theories of leadership—that a leader's behavior should vary according to the nature of the specific situation—has been widely accepted. There are disagreements about the subordinate and environmental characteristics that are most important in determining the appropriate style of leadership in a given situation, but all of the theories and models reviewed share the assumption that the people-versus-task distinction is basic to this style. A brief summary of this commonality is shown in Table 14–2.

Despite its common acceptance, the contingency approach to leadership is not accepted by everyone. The deliberate and rational analysis of "the situation" and selection of "a style" of leadership to fit is not, according to some, a practical approach to making people better leaders. Quinn and his colleagues (Denison, Hooijberg, & Quinn, 1995; Hart & Quinn, 1993; Quinn, 1988) go somewhat to the opposite extreme, taking the position that successful leadership depends more on the ability to deal effectively with complexity.

As these authors point out, people in leadership positions in the organizations of today are faced with some difficult conflicting pressures: they are supposed to be flexible (adaptive and innovative) but also stable (able to effectively coordinate and direct ongoing activities). They must maintain an internal focus (help people within the group/organization) as well as keeping a weather eye on the world outside (keep the group/organization aligned with its environment). Therefore, "the test of a first-rate leader may be the ability to exhibit contrary or opposing behaviors (as appropriate or necessary) while still retaining some measure of integrity, credibility, and direction" (Denison, Hooijberg, & Quinn, 1995, p. 526).

In addition to appearing oversimplified to some, contingency approaches to leadership have also been criticized for a view of leadership that is not unlike an independent variable in an experiment—something that is done to or applied to subordinates (e.g.,

Table 14–2	The Task-Oriented Versus People-Oriented Dimensions in Leadership Research	
Source	Task	People
Substitutes for leadership (Kerr & Jermier, 1978)	Instrumental	Supportive
Leadership style (Lewin, Lippitt, & White, 1939)	Authoritarian	Democratic
University of Michigan (Katz, Maccoby, & Morse, 1950)	Job-centered	Employee-centered
Ohio State (Stogdill & Coons, 1957)	Initiating structure	Consideration
Contingency theory (Fiedler, 1967)	Task-oriented	People-oriented
Normative model (Vroom & Yetton, 1973)	Efficiency	Participative
Path-goal theory (House, 1971)	Directive	Supportive

Pfeffer, 1977). There are alternative views of leadership that emphasize psychological and social processes rather than individual and situational characteristics, and it is to these that attention now turns.

Leadership as a Two-Way Street

If leaders have the major influence on subordinate behavior from day to day that leadership theories assume they have, it seems likely that subordinates also influence the way leaders behave. Further, it seems likely that this influence varies from subordinate to subordinate—that is, that leaders interact with subordinates more as individuals than in the aggregate (group) way implicit in most traditional leadership theories.

The possibilities suggested may be taken into account by viewing leadership as a social exchange in which the parties trade benefits. The leader helps subordinates, as individuals, achieve valued rewards by directing them toward goals desired by the organization. Subordinates help the leader achieve status and the privileges that go with authority, influence, and prestige by performing well and making him or her look good.

From a social exchange viewpoint, a leader's behavior or style is influenced to some degree by the behavior of subordinates; that is, there will be some degree of reciprocal causation. Hollander (1958) demonstrated this premise some time ago in a study in which he found that the better subordinates performed, the more the leader demonstrated consideration and the less he or she initiated structure. In other words, the behavior of subordinates influences the way the leader behaves toward them and vice versa; from this perspective, it is the *interaction* of leader and subordinates that is important.

The Vertical Dyad Linkage and Leader-Member Exchange Models

A leadership framework that specifically addresses interactions between leaders and followers is the vertical dyad linkage model (Dansereau, Graen, & Haga, 1975; Graen & Cashman, 1975). One proposition of this model is that leaders tend to separate their subordinates into two groups consisting of a cadre, or in-group, and the hired hands, or out-group. Each group is treated differently, with the cadre being allowed more latitude in behavior and a closer relationship with the leader.

In exchange for the benefits, such as influence, autonomy, and rewards, subordinates in the cadre are expected to be more loyal to the leader, committed to the organization, and more involved with their work. Researchers have found support for the hypothesis in that being a member of a leader's in-group is associated with higher performance ratings, higher actual performance, greater satisfaction with the supervisor, and lower intention to quit. These results were shown to be related directly to the fact that the leader behaved differently towards subjects in the in-group and the out-group (Vecchio & Gobdel, 1984).

Over time, the vertical dyad linkage model has evolved into the leader-member exchange (LMX) model, in which the quality of leader-follower relations (exchanges) can vary on a continuum from high to low (not just in- and out-group). The central idea is that "effective leadership processes occur when leaders and followers are able to develop mature leadership relationships (partnerships) and thus gain access to the many benefits these relationships bring" (Graen & Uhl-Bien, 1995, p. 225).

Illustrating the reciprocal nature of leader-follower interactions, Phillips and Bedeian (1994) found that the more a leader perceived a follower's attitudes to be similar to his or her own, the more positive were the exchanges between the leader and the follower. Similarly, Basu and Green (1995) report the quality of leader-member exchange to be positively related to how similar the leader and the subordinate are in education and attitudes.

There is research support for many aspects of both the vertical dyad linkage model and the leader-member exchange model. The quality of leader-follower relationships does seem to play an important role in a leader's success and a follower's work performance, citizenship behaviors, and satisfaction (e.g., Deluga, 1994; Major, Kozlowski, Chao, & Gardner, 1995; Settoon, Bennett, & Liden, 1996). This is a significant step forward for leadership theory; more research is needed, however, especially in the area of testing specific prescriptions of these models (Yukl, 1994).

The view of leadership as a two-way street might also benefit from a more explicit incorporation of the role played by a leader's relationship with his or her *own* leader. In particular, the leader's upward influence (or perceived influence) has important implications for his or her own behavior toward subordinates. This influence, called the Pelz effect (Jablin, 1980), has been recognized for some time (Pelz, 1951), but it was largely ignored in the leadership literature until recently (see Anderson, Tolson, Fields, & Thacker, 1990). Findings from a related line of research into the nature and effectiveness of specific influence tactics in organizations could also prove useful to researchers in this context (e.g., Kipnis, Schmidt, & Wilkinson, 1980; Yukl & Falbe, 1990).

It Takes Two to Tango: The Power of Followership

The vertical dyad linkage and leader-member exchange models of leadership are reminders that when it comes to leadership it takes two to tango; that is, there can be no leaders without followers. Robert Kelley (1988, 1992) believes the general tendency people have to focus so intently on leaders makes those who are not leaders feel powerless and free from responsibility when neither is true. He points out that if leadership effects account for only 10–20% of an organization's effectiveness, as some research suggests, then followership effects could account for as much as 80–90% of that effectiveness. Support for this possibility is found in results of a recent telephone survey reported in the *Wall Street Journal* ("Ego Deflator," 1996).

In the survey, 41% of the workers who participated said that their supervisor has no effect on their performance, 42% said that their supervisor helps their performance, and 14% reported that the boss made their job harder. To put it another way, fewer than half of those surveyed believed that their superior (leader) was helpful to getting their jobs done. If the secret of effective leadership actually eludes so many people in leadership positions, perhaps Kelley's suggestion that I/O psychologists focus on the other side of the equation as well has merit. To be a follower was at one time an honor (think of King Arthur's knights), and Kelley believes this honor should be restored. "Followers at their best . . . participate with enthusiasm, intelligence, and self-reliance . . . in the pursuit of goals" (Kelley, 1992, p. 26).

The best followers, according to Kelley, are active and demonstrate independent and critical thinking. They are also innovative and creative, and they stand up to superiors when necessary. Thus, they are not in any way the opposite of leaders, but part of the leadership process itself. These views are consistent with the direction in which this field of study and many organizations themselves have begun moving. That direction is toward teamwork and collaboration, and leaders whose role may well come to be described as "first among equals."

New Age Leadership

Chinese philosopher Lao Tzu wrote: "A leader is best when people barely know that [he or she] exists. . . . When . . . [the] work is done, . . . [the] aim fulfilled, they will all say, 'We did this ourselves'" (quoted in Hughes, Ginnett, & Curphy, 1996, p. 61). Several leadership scholars are now defining leadership success in terms of the ability to create followers who don't really need leaders. The idea, as the quotation from Lao Tzu demonstrates, is not new, but its application to leadership in contemporary organizations is a significant departure from the mainstream leadership theory reviewed in this chapter.

The views of leadership described in this section have grown out of the revolutionary changes in the world of work that have been encountered throughout this book. As mentioned in the Psychology at Work feature at the beginning of this chapter, these changes are not just a "touchy-feely flavor of the month." To the contrary, they show every sign of becoming the hallmark of the first years of a new century. For these reasons, the term *new age* seems an appropriate description for these ideas, all of which describe a diminished role for leadership behavior in the traditional sense and an enhancement of the responsibilities of followers.

The Multiple Linkage Model

Yukl's (1994) multiple linkage model states that a group's (or an organization work unit's) effectiveness is dependent on the six elements described in Exhibit 14–3. The leader's job is to discover which of the elements listed are most critical for any particular group and

---

Exhibit 14–3
Yukl's Multiple
Linkage Model

Work unit (group, team, organization) effectiveness depends on:

1. The amount of effort, commitment, and responsibility subordinates bring to the task.

2. The extent to which subordinates understand what they need to do and have the skills to do it.

3. The use of effective performance strategies and appropriate organization of the work.

4. The extent to which work unit members cooperate and work as a team.

5. The resources and support available to the work unit.

6. The degree to which the work unit's efforts are coordinated with other units of the same organization.

whether these are present in sufficient quantity, and then to help the group fill in any gaps. When the work is complex and labor intensive, for example, subordinates' efforts and commitment are particularly critical. The leader's role in this case is to assure that the situation facilitates strong effort and commitment.

If the elements described are weak or missing, the leader should provide them through actions such as creating enriched jobs and rewarding desired behavior. If he or she is effective in this endeavor, the group has all of the conditions for success and leads itself to a productive outcome. So far, research attempting to validate this model is slim, but what has been done has supported the basic premise (Kim & Yukl, 1995; Yukl, 1994).

A similar approach to enhancing the role of subordinates and minimizing the role of leadership in organizations is advanced by Hackman and his colleagues (Hackman & Walton, 1986). From this perspective, a leader's job is to establish and maintain favorable performance conditions for the group. The leader does whatever is required to bring about effort, sufficient skill and knowledge, and task-appropriate performance strategies within the group. For example, by carefully selecting the members of a group and training them in problem-solving skills, the leader can increase the odds that the group will succeed. The perfect group is one where everything runs so well that no leadership in the traditional sense is needed.

As many organizations divest themselves of layers of management, experiment with participatory management, and increase their use of work teams, leadership in these organizations must of necessity move away from the traditional and in the general direction described by Yukl and by Hackman. In the new age, a third dimension of leader behavior may be added to the basic task- and employee-centered behavior dimensions—group-centered behaviors.

Group-centered (or group-facilitator) behaviors include asking questions to help a group identify and solve problems; training the group in job and team skills; advising group members on problem solving; facilitating group interactions by encouraging balanced participation, summarizing differences and agreements, and brainstorming; managing group boundaries; coordinating group activities; and providing formal and informal group recognition (Holpp, 1995). Many of these behaviors are described in Chapter 13 as ways a leader can help a group make more effective decisions. As noted there, traditional research into group dynamics may be slated for a renaissance in the new age.

Superleadership

Manz and Sims (1990, 1991, 1995; Sims & Manz, 1996) have written extensively on the theme that the best leader (the "super leader") is the one who turns the largest number of followers into self-leaders. The basic premise behind superleadership is that a person should first become an effective self-leader; he or she should then teach these same skills to subordinates. Success comes when the subordinates no longer need a leader.

The first step in superleadership is becoming a self-leader. This is accomplished through a combination of behavioral strategies (including self-set goals, self-observation, and self-reward) and cognitive strategies, which use positive and constructive thought patterns (such as positive self-talk, mental imagery, and mental rehearsal) to create opportunities in work and life. The second step is to model this self-leadership for others, letting them see it succeed and rewarding others' self-leadership successes as they occur.

The third and fourth steps in the superleadership plan are for the leader to encourage subordinates to set goals for themselves and to help them create positive thought patterns by expressing confidence in them. The fifth step is to have subordinates build rewards into their own work and to provide constructive reprimands to subordinates when needed. Organizing work around teams is the sixth step. Finally, the superleader facilitates the creation of a positive organizational culture that is conducive to high performance.

Manz and Sims offer anecdotal evidence for their views, but in common with many of the new age conceptions of leadership, there is insufficient research on the superleadership approach to draw any conclusions one way or another. In one study, some of the basic principles were shown to facilitate successful work group performance (Manz & Sims, 1987), but in another, superleadership was not as effective as traditional leadership in stimulating employee organizational citizenship behavior (Schnake, Dumler, & Cochran, 1993).

Citizenship behaviors include altruism, conscientiousness, sportsmanship, courtesy, and civic activity. The Schnake, Dumler, and Cochran finding is damaging to Manz and Sims's concept in the sense that, theoretically, all of these behaviors should flow from effective superleadership. They are also behaviors that can be expected to become increasingly important as many work organizations continue the process of transforming themselves into work communities.

The Study of Leadership in Perspective

Leadership theorizing and research began with the idea that there is something special about effective leaders as people that sets them apart from everyone else. It then moved through the hypothesis that effective leadership is merely a matter of choosing the "right" behaviors and on toward a conception of leadership as a mutual influence process. Currently, ideas about leadership seem to be evolving toward a position that the best leaders are those who work themselves out of a job by training subordinates to lead themselves. The question arises: What has been learned in this hundred-year journey?

A number of inferences can be drawn with confidence from leadership research and theory to date. These conclusions do not come from any one study or line of research, but from an overall consideration of the relevant literature. The context of much of this literature is the traditional work organization, and the related conclusions may seem (or be) inappropriate for different structures. At this time, however, the majority of organizations are still structured partly or entirely on the traditional model.

1. *The behaviors of people in leadership positions may be divided into two general categories—behaviors oriented toward the task and behaviors oriented toward people.* These two sets of behaviors affect different processes, and their outcomes are not necessarily related. In general, task-oriented behaviors affect employee performance more strongly, whereas people-oriented behaviors affect subordinate job satisfaction more strongly. To some extent, then, which emphasis is more important depends on which outcome is more important provided the task is accomplished satisfactorily. There is no evidence that people-oriented behaviors on the parts of leaders can compensate subordinates fully for lack of job success.

2. *Elements of the organizational situation are important in that they offer clues to someone in a leadership role as to what behavioral emphasis is most appropriate.* In general,

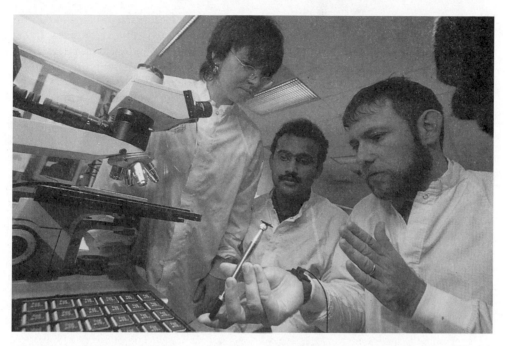

Some directive task-centered behaviors are required of most people in organizational leadership positions.

task-oriented behaviors seem to be more important when the work to be done is not routine, is carried out under emergency or dangerous conditions, and is performed by people who have little experience, job knowledge, or interest in job autonomy.

If work is routine and carried out under comfortable and familiar conditions by people who do not need guidance, people-oriented behaviors are more important; they seem to aid task accomplishment by helping to offset negative aspects of what can be a rather boring job situation. In some cases, as when highly competent and autonomous people are performing work they like and know well, little or no leadership seems to work best; competence and work knowledge act as effective substitutes for leadership.

3. *A leader's personal characteristics are important, not because they correspond in any one-to-one fashion with some natural ability to lead, but because they affect the perceptions of those who are to be led.* These perceptions, in turn, affect willingness to be led and responses to the leader's behavior. The widespread acceptance of stereotypes about the looks and behavior of a "real leader" make the conclusion inescapable that people who match these ideas more closely (or who possess that mysterious quality called charisma) have a head start in becoming effective leaders.

The knowledge that an individual's personal characteristics play an important role in other peoples' evaluation of his or her fitness for the leader role has few directly practical implications for the selection of leaders in organizations. It is not realistic for organizations to choose supervisors, managers, and executives on the basis of whether they look and act the way people *expect* leaders to look and act. Newer research does suggest, however, that certain individual characteristics, as measured by tests (rather than subjectively evaluated by other people), are related to job success. Once such tests are validated, they become useful sources of information for selecting people for leadership positions.

Criterion validity
See pages 63–66

4. *Leadership is not a unilateral phenomenon.* Successful leadership, as Katz and Kahn describe it in the definition at the beginning of the chapter, is an influence process. In organizations this influence is only general to some extent. It depends also on interactions between each person in a leadership position and his or her individual subordinates (and superiors). These interactions are reciprocal; that is, subordinates' responses to a leader affect the way that leader behaves in the future, which in turn affects subordinates' responses, and so on.

5. *Many people now in leadership positions need more and/or different skills than are traditional.* With work more often organized around groups, an increasing number of people in supervisory, management, and executive positions are expected to build these groups into teams and then to train these teams to manage themselves effectively and get the job done with a minimum of outside direction. The skills and behaviors required to accomplish these objectives are not necessarily the same ones that make for leadership success under traditional job design conditions.

Domain

See page 62

Graen and Uhl-Bien (1995) offer a useful framework for summarizing the conclusions discussed and the research that lies behind them. As shown in Table 14–3, the framework is based on three primary domains of the study of leadership—the leader, the

Table 14–3	Three Domain Approaches to Leadership		
	Leader-Based	**Relationship-Based**	**Follower-Based**
What is leadership?	Appropriate behavior of the person in leader role	Trust, respect, and mutual obligation that generates influence between parties	Ability and motivation to manage one's own performance
What behaviors constitute leadership?	Establishing and communicating vision; inspiring, instilling pride	Building strong relationships with followers; mutual learning and accommodation	Empowering, coaching, facilitating, giving up control
Advantages	Leader as rallying point for organization; common understanding of mission and values; can initiate wholesale change	Accommodates differing needs of subordinates; can elicit superior work from different types of people	Makes the most of follower capabilities; frees up leaders for other responsibilities
Disadvantages	Highly dependent on leader, problems if leader changes or is pursuing inappropriate vision	Time-consuming; relies on long-term relationship between specific leaders and members	Highly dependent on follower initiative and ability
When appropriate?	Fundamental change; charismatic leader in place; limited diversity among followers	Continuous improvement teamwork; substantial diversity and stability among followers; network building	Highly capable and task-committed followers
Where most effective?	Structured tasks; strong leader position power; member acceptance of leader	Situation favorability for leader between two extremes	Unstructured tasks; weak position power; member nonacceptance of leader

From G. B. Graen and M. Uhl-Bien, "Relationship-Based Approach to Leadership: Development of Leader-Member Exchange (LMX) Theory of Leadership Over 25 Years: Applying a Multi-Level Multi-Domain Perspective." *Leadership Quarterly,* 1995, *6,* 219–247. Copyright 1995 JAI Press. Reprinted by permission.

follower, and the relationship between the two. Of the approaches to leadership reviewed here, trait theories, early behavioral approaches, and contingency theories fall into the leader-based category in the table. Followership, the vertical-dyad linkage model, and leader-member exchange theory are relationship-based approaches; new age leadership concepts are basically follower-based ideas.

The analysis by Graen and Uhl-Bien makes it clear that all of these approaches have their place. Which is best depends, and *depends* is the watchword of contingency theories. The traditional contingency theories of leadership reviewed in this chapter postulate that the correct way for a leader to behave depends on the situation. Table 14–3 delineates what might be called a meta-contingency theory of leadership; that is, the most appropriate theoretical approach (leader, relationship, or follower-based) depends on the situation.

From this vantage point, the critical question in the study of leadership changes from What makes a good leader? to What makes for good leadership? Such a shift could move leadership theory and research to a new level. Rather than debating the fine points within a particular approach, I/O psychologists and other researchers could move on

> to examine combined and interactive effects of the variables generated by each domain to obtain a more complete picture of the leadership process. . . . Once the proper mix for each of these domains considered in combination is identified, a subsequent question could address the issue of how these domains may be influenced to enhance the effectiveness of leadership. (Graen & Uhl-Bien, 1995, p. 223)

A leader is a person who, when added to followers and a situation, creates leadership—the influential increment that fills gaps and gets people to "go beyond." The time seems to have come for leadership research itself to go beyond traditional boundaries if efforts to enhance the effectiveness of leadership are to progress. A different view of the situation is presented in At Issue.

At Issue

Leadership and the Loch Ness Monster

Calder (1977) maintains that the nature of leadership theories and research is fundamentally different from the nature of the scientific process. Claiming that "what has been attempted is not the development of scientific theory but the systematic and consistent use of everyday thought" (p. 182), Calder has proposed an attributional theory of leadership. The central idea is that if something happens in the world (such as an economic recession) that we believe can be affected by a leader *and* if there is someone around (the president of the United States, for example) who seems to be doing things that we think of as "leadership," then we assume that the leader is the cause of the event. In reality, of course, the leader may have had little or no impact on the

event, but the perception of leadership is colored by our natural tendency to look for causes and effects.

A number of attributional theories about leadership appeared in the 1980s (e.g., McElroy, 1982) and continue through today (e.g., Bresnen, 1995; Meindl, 1995). Meindl and his colleagues (Meindl, Ehrlich, & Dukerich, 1985) examined our "romance with leadership" and found that when the causes of an event are not clear, there is a bias toward viewing leadership as the likely cause. They also note that organizational outcomes (such as profitability) are rated more favorably by observers when the outcomes are attributed to leadership than when they are attributed to other causes (Meindl & Ehrlich, 1987).

Some years ago, Pfeffer (1977) made the following statement:

> Leadership is associated with a set of myths reinforcing a social construction of meaning which legitimates leadership role occupants, provides belief in potential mobility for those not in leadership roles, and attributes social causality to leadership roles, thereby providing a belief in the effectiveness of individual control. (p. 111)

Pfeffer was making the point that people like to believe that individual actions matter and that they too might someday become leaders who can have a significant impact on events. According to this viewpoint, leaders mainly manipulate symbols to maintain the legitimacy of, and member commitment to, the organization. We like to see our leaders' behaviors as being deliberate, results oriented, and consistent (Staw, 1982). More recently, Kets de Vries (1994) discussed the symbolic and psychodynamic qualities of leadership.

> A frequent problem is what Freud described as the phenomenon of a "false connection," meaning that followers may not perceive and respond to their leader according to the reality of the situation, but as if the leader is a significant figure from the past, such as a parent or other authoritative person. (p. 82)

Kets de Vries is saying that followers can project their fantasies onto their leaders, interpret the leader's actions in light of this self-created image, and influence their leaders toward the belief that they are these illusory creatures (Kets de Vries, 1993). For example, an employee may idealize her supervisor, as she did her mother, and play out that old relationship within this new one. Clearly, this process is inappropriate and can become dangerous if the supervisor responds as though he or she were the other party in this transferred relationship and plays out his or her own needs.

Viewpoints such as those described have made some I/O psychologists and organizational scholars wonder about the basic usefulness of the leadership concept. Are we just seeking something that we created with our own lazy perceptual processes, needs, and wishes? Perhaps "leadership" is akin to the Loch Ness Monster phenomenon: We believe that there is something big, mysterious, and powerful out there, we have a rough idea of where to look, and we have launched some elaborate and expensive expeditions. But hard evidence remains sparse, and the pictures we have managed to obtain are fuzzy.

Summary

Leadership is a concept reflecting the ability of one person to affect the behavior of other people in a particular direction. Early approaches to the study of this process focused on the personal traits of leaders. This research was followed by a close examination of how leaders behaved, rather than of what kind of people they were. Contingency theories of leadership try to prescribe the best leadership methods by defining the situation in which each kind of behavior works most effectively.

More recent views of leadership take an interactive perspective, looking at the influence of subordinates on leaders as well as at the influence of leaders on subordinates. The relationship between leaders and individual followers is also receiving attention, as are leader behaviors appropriate in newer group forms of job design that emphasize teamwork and collaboration.

Questions for Review and Discussion

1. Name three people you would call "real leaders" and describe the characteristics they have in common on two lists, one of personal traits and one of behaviors. In terms from the chapter, what can you conclude on the basis of this analysis about your personal theory of leadership?

2. Compare the major contingency theory approaches to leadership discussed in the chapter on the criteria of (a) central concept, (b) empirical evidence for, and (c) usefulness for improving organizational leadership in the field. You may find a table form helpful for this comparison.

3. Of the various contingency theories of leadership, the path-goal model is the most closely tied to a major theory of work motivation (general expectancy theory). Using terms from the general expectancy theory of work motivation discussed in Chapter 6, illustrate this relationship.

4. In what way(s) do social exchange and new age views of leadership represent major departures from traditional leadership theories?

5. Discuss the following: "Some I/O psychologists and organizational scholars wonder about the basic usefulness of the leadership concept. Are we just seeking something that we have created with our own lazy perceptual processes, needs, and wishes?" Your answer should demonstrate knowledge of the material in this chapter.

Key Terms

contingency approach to leadership

gender of leadership

inspirational leadership

leader

leadership

new age leadership

normative approach to leadership

opportunities for leadership

social exchange view of leadership

social information processing and leadership

substitutes for leadership

trait theories of leadership

two dimensions of leader behavior

References

Adler, N. J. (1996). Global women political leaders: An invisible history, an increasingly important future. *Leadership Quarterly, 7,* 133–161.

Adler, T. (1993, April). Competence determined by status characteristics. *APA Monitor, 24,* p. 18.

Anderson, L. R., Tolson, J., Fields, M. W., & Thacker, J. W. (1990). Extension of the Pelz Effect: The impact of leader's upward influence on group members' control within the organization. *Basic and Applied Social Psychology, 11,* 19–32.

Atwater, L. E., & Yammarino, F. J. (1993). Personal attributes as predictors of superiors' and subordinates' perceptions of military academy leadership. *Human Relations, 46,* 645–668.

Barnard, C. I. (1938/1968). *The functions of the executive.* Cambridge, MA: Harvard University Press.

Bass, B. M. (1985). *Leadership and performance beyond expectations.* New York: Free Press.

Bass, B. M. (1990a). *Bass and Stogdill's handbook of leadership: Theory, research, and managerial applications.* New York: Free Press.

Bass, B. M. (1990b). From transactional to transformational leadership: Learning to share the vision. *Organizational Dynamics, 18,* 19–31.

Bass, B. M. (1995). Theory of transformational leadership redux. *Leadership Quarterly, 6,* 463–478.

Basu, R., & Green, S. G. (1995). Subordinate performance, leader-subordinate compatibility, and exchange quality in leader-member dyads: A field study. *Journal of Applied Social Psychology, 25,* 77–92.

Bennis, W., & Nanus, B. (1985). *Leaders: The strategies for taking charge.* New York: Harper & Row.

Binning, J. F., Zaba, A. J., & Whattam, J. C. (1986). Explaining the biasing effects of performance cues in terms of cognitive categorization. *Academy of Management Journal, 29,* 521–535.

Blake, R. R., & Mouton, J. S. (1985). *The managerial grid III.* Houston, TX: Gulf.

Bresnen, M. J. (1995). All things to all people? Perceptions, attributions, and constructions of leadership. *Leadership Quarterly, 6,* 495–513.

Burns, J. M. (1978). *Leadership.* New York: Harper & Row.

Calder, B. J. (1977). An attribution theory of leadership. In B. M. Staw and G. R. Salancik (Eds.), *New directions in organizational behavior.* Chicago: St. Clair.

Cherulnik, P. D., Turns, L. C., & Wilderman, S. K. (1990). Physical appearance and leadership: Exploring the role of appearance-based attribution in leader emergence. *Journal of Applied Social Psychology, 20,* 1530–1539.

Conger, J. A. (1990). The dark side of leadership. *Organizational Dynamics, 19,* 44–55.

Conger, J. A. (1991). Inspiring others: The language of leadership. *Academy of Management Executive, 5,* 31–45.

Conger, J. A., & Kanungo, R. N. (1994). Charismatic leadership in organizations: Perceived behavioral attributes and their measurement. *Journal of Organizational Behavior, 15,* 439–452.

Dansereau, F., Jr., Graen, G. B., & Haga, W. J. (1975). A vertical dyad linkage approach to leadership within formal organizations: A longitudinal investigation of the role-making process. *Organizational Behavior and Human Performance, 13,* 46–78.

Deluga, R. J. (1994). Supervisor trust building, leader-member exchange and organizational citizenship behaviour. *Journal of Occupational and Organization Psychology, 67,* 315–326.

Denison, D. R., Hooijberg, R., & Quinn, R. E. (1995). Paradox and performance: Toward a theory of behavioral complexity in managerial leadership. *Organization Science, 6,* 524–540.

Eagly, A. H., & Johnson, B. T. (1990). Gender and leadership style: A meta-analysis. *Psychological Bulletin, 108,* 233–256.

Eagly, A. H., Makhijani, M. G., & Klonsky, B. G. (1992). Gender and the evaluation of leaders: A meta-analysis. *Psychological Bulletin, 111,* 3–22.

Eggleston, K. K., & Bhagat, R. S. (1993). Organizational contexts and contingent leadership roles: A theoretical exploration. *Human Relations, 46,* 1177–1192.

Ego deflator. (1996, May 21). *Wall Street Journal,* p. A1.

Fagenson, E. A. (1990). Perceived masculine and feminine attributes examined as a function of individuals' sex and level in the organizational power hierarchy: A test of four theoretical perspectives. *Journal of Applied Psychology, 75,* 204–211.

Fiedler, F. E. (1967). *A theory of leadership effectiveness.* New York: McGraw-Hill.

Fiedler, F. E. (1995). Cognitive resources and leadership performance. *Applied Psychology: An International Review, 44,* 5–28.

Fiedler, F. E., & Garcia, J. E. (1987). *New approaches to effective leadership: Cognitive resources and organizational performance.* New York: Wiley.

Fiedler, F., & House, R. J. (1994). Leadership theory and research: A report of progress. In C. L. Cooper (Ed.), *Key reviews in managerial psychology: Concepts and research for practice.* West Sussex, England: Wiley.

Field, R. H. G. (1982). A test of the Vroom-Yetton normative model of leadership. *Journal of Applied Psychology, 67,* 523–532.

Field, R. H., & House, R. J. (1990). A test of the Vroom-Yetton model using manager and subordinate reports. *Journal of Applied Psychology, 75,* 362–366.

Gastil, J. (1994). A definition and illustration of democratic leadership. *Human Relations, 47,* 953–975.

Graen, G., & Cashman, J. F. (1975). A role making model of leadership in formal organizations: A developmental approach. In J. G. Hunt and L. L. Larson (Eds.), *Leadership frontiers.* Kent, OH: Kent State University Press.

Graen, G. B., & Uhl-Bien, M. (1995). Relationship-based approach to leadership: Development of leader-member exchange (LMX) theory of leadership over 25 years: Applying a multi-level multi-domain perspective. *Leadership Quarterly, 6,* 219–247.

Grant, L. (1996, June 24). Rambos in pinstripes: Why so many CEOs are lousy leaders. *Fortune,* pp. 133, 147.

Hackman, J. R., & Walton, R. E. (1986). Leading groups in organizations. In P. S. Goodman (Ed.), *Designing effective work groups.* San Francisco: Jossey-Bass.

Hart, S. L., & Quinn, R. E. (1993). Roles executives play: CEOs, behavioral complexity, and firm performance. *Human Relations, 46,* 543–574.

Heilman, M. E., Block, C. J., Martell, R. F., & Simon, M. C. (1989). Has anything changed? Current characterizations of men, women, and managers. *Journal of Applied Psychology, 74,* 935–942.

Helgesen, S. (1990). *The female advantage: Women's ways of leadership.* New York: Doubleday.

Hersey, P., & Blanchard, K. H. (1988). *Management of organizational behavior: Utilizing human resources* (5th ed.). Englewood Cliffs, NJ: Prentice-Hall.

Hogan, R., Curphy, G. J., & Hogan, J. (1994). What we know about leadership: Effectiveness and personality. *American Psychologist, 49,* 493–504.

Hollander, E. P. (1958). Conformity, status, and idiosyncrasy credit. *Psychological Review, 65,* 117–127.

Holpp, L. (1995, March). New roles for leaders: An HRD reporter's inquiry. *Training and Development, 49,* 46–50.

House, R. J. (1971). A path-goal theory of leader effectiveness. *Administrative Science Quarterly, 16,* 321–338.

House, R. J., & Baetz, M. L. (1979). Leadership: Some empirical generalizations and new research directions. In B. M. Staw (Ed.), *Research in organizational behavior* (Vol. 1). Greenwich, CT: JAI.

House, R. J., & Mitchell, T. R. (1974). Path-goal theory of leadership. *Journal of Contemporary Business, 3,* 81–97.

House, R. J., Spangler, W. D., & Woycke, J. (1991). Personality and charisma in the U.S. Presidency: A psychological theory of leadership effectiveness. *Administrative Science Quarterly, 36,* 364–396.

Huey, J. (1994, Feb. 21). The new post-heroic leadership. *Fortune,* pp. 42–50.

Hughes, R. L., Ginnett, R. C., & Curphy, G. J. (1996). *Leadership: Enhancing the lessons of experience.* Chicago: Irwin.

Indvik, J. (1986). Path-goal theory of leadership: A meta-analysis. Presented at the meetings of the Academy of Management, Chicago.

Jablin, F. M. (1980). Superior's upward influence, satisfaction, and openness in superior-subordinate communication: A re-examination of the "Pelz Effect." *Human Communication Research, 6,* 210–220.

Katz, D., & Kahn, R. L. (1978). *The social psychology of organizations* (2nd ed.). New York: Wiley.

Katz, D., Maccoby, N., & Morse, N. C. (1950). *Productivity, supervision, and morale in an office situation.* Ann Arbor, MI: University of Michigan Institute for Social Research.

Keller, R. T. (1989). A test of the path-goal theory of leadership with need for clarity as a moderator in research and development organizations. *Journal of Applied Psychology, 74,* 208–212.

Kelley, R. E. (1988). In praise of followers. *Harvard Business Review, 66,* 142–148.

Kelley, R. (1992). *The power of followership.* New York: Doubleday.

Kenney, R. A., Blascovich, J., & Shaver, P. R. (1994). Implicit leadership theories: Prototypes for new leaders. *Basic and Applied Social Psychology, 15,* 409–437.

Kerr, S., & Jermier, J. M. (1978). Substitutes for leadership: Their meaning and measurement. *Organizational Behavior and Human Performance, 26,* 375–403.

Kets de Vries, M. F. R. (1993). *Leaders, fools, and impostors: Essays on the psychology of leadership.* San Francisco: Jossey-Bass.

Kets de Vries, M. F. R. (1994). The leadership mystique. *Academy of Management Executive, 8,* 73–89.

Kim, H., & Yukl, G. (1995). Relationships of managerial effectiveness and advancement to self-reported and subordinate-reported leadership behaviors from the multiple-linkage model. *Leadership Quarterly, 6,* 361–377.

Kipnis, D., Schmidt, S. M., & Wilkinson, I. (1980). Intraorganizational influence tactics: Explorations in getting one's way. *Journal of Applied Psychology, 65,* 440–452.

Kirkpatrick, S. A., & Locke, E. A. (1991). Leadership: Do traits matter? *Academy of Management Executive, 5,* 48–60.

Krantz, J., & Gilmore, T. N. (1990). The splitting of leadership and management as a social defense. *Human Relations, 43,* 183–204.

Kuhnert, K. W., & Lewis, P. (1987). Transactional and transformational leadership: A constructive/developmental analysis. *Academy of Management Review, 12,* 648–657.

Lewin, K., Lippitt, R., & White, R. K. (1939). Patterns of aggressive behavior in experimentally created "social climates." *Journal of Social Psychology, 10,* 271–299.

Lord, R. G., DeVader, C. L., & Alliger, G. M. (1986). A meta-analysis of the relation between personality traits and leadership perceptions: An application of validity generalization procedures. *Journal of Applied Psychology, 71,* 402–410.

Major, D. A., Kozlowski, S. W. J., Chao, G. T., & Gardner, P. D. (1995). A longitudinal investigation of newcomer expectations, early socialization outcomes, and the moderating effects of role development factors. *Journal of Applied Psychology, 80,* 418–431.

Manz, C. C., & Sims, H. P., Jr. (1987). Leading workers to lead themselves: The external leadership of self-managing work teams. *Administrative Science Quarterly, 32,* 106–128.

Manz, C. C., & Sims, H. P., Jr. (1990). *SuperLeadership: Leading others to lead themselves.* New York: Berkley.

Manz, C. C., & Sims, H. P., Jr. (1991). SuperLeadership: Beyond the myth of heroic leadership. *Organizational Dynamics, 19,* 18–35.

Manz, C. C., & Sims, H. P., Jr. (1995). *Businesses without bosses: How self-managing teams are building high-performance companies.* New York: Wiley.

Mathieu, J. E. (1990). A test of subordinates' achievement and affiliation needs as moderators of leader path-goal relationships. *Basic and Applied Social Psychology, 11,* 179–189.

McElroy, J. C. (1982). A typology of attribution leadership research. *Academy of Management Review, 7,* 413–417.

Meindl, J. R. (1995). The romance of leadership as a follower-centric theory: A social constructionist approach. *Leadership Quarterly, 6,* 329–341.

Meindl, J. R., & Ehrlich, S. B. (1987). The romance of leadership and the evaluation of organizational performance. *Academy of Management Journal, 30,* 91–109.

Meindl, J. R., Ehrlich, S. B., & Dukerich, J. M. (1985). The romance of leadership. *Administrative Science Quarterly, 30,* 78–102.

Mintzberg, H. (1980). *The nature of managerial work.* Englewood Cliffs, NJ: Prentice-Hall.

Norris, J. M., & Wylie, A. M. (1995). Gender stereotyping of the managerial role among students in Canada and the United States. *Group and Organization Management, 20,* 167–182.

O'Connor, J., Mumford, M. D., Clifton, T. C., Gessner, T. L., & Connelly, M. S. (1995). Charismatic leaders and destructiveness: A historiometric study. *Leadership Quarterly, 6,* 529–555.

Paul, R. J., & Ebadi, Y. M. (1989). Leadership decision making in a service organization: A field test of the Vroom-Yetton model. *Journal of Occupational Psychology, 62,* 201–211.

Pelz, D. C. (1951). Leadership within a hierarchical organization. *Journal of Social Issues, 7,* 49–55.

Peters, L. H., Hartke, D. D., & Pohlmann, J. T. (1985). Fiedler's contingency theory of leadership: An application of the meta-analysis procedures of Schmidt and Hunter. *Psychological Bulletin, 97,* 274–285.

Pfeffer, J. (1977). The ambiguity of leadership. *Academy of Management Review, 2,* 104–112.

Phillips, A. S., & Bedeian, A. G. (1994). Leader-follower exchange quality: The role of personal and interpersonal attributes. *Academy of Management Journal, 37,* 990–1001.

Phillips, J. S., & Lord, R. G. (1982). Schematic information processing and perceptions of leadership in problem-solving groups. *Journal of Applied Psychology, 67,* 486–492.

Podsakoff, P. M., MacKenzie, S. B., Ahearne, M., & Bommer, W. H. (1995). Searching for a needle in a haystack: Trying to identify the illusive moderators of leadership behaviors. *Journal of Management, 21,* 422–470.

Podsakoff, P. M., MacKenzie, S. B., & Bommer, W. H. (1996). Transformational leader behaviors and substitutes for leadership as determinants of employee satisfaction, commitment, trust, and organizational citizenship behaviors. *Journal of Management, 22,* 259–298.

Podsakoff, P. M., Niehoff, B. P., MacKenzie, S. B., & Williams, M. L. (1993). Do substitutes for leadership really substitute for leadership? An empirical examination of Kerr and Jermier's situational leadership model. *Organizational Behavior and Human Decision Processes, 54,* 1–44.

Powell, G. N. (1988). *Women and men in management.* Newbury Park, CA: Sage.

Quinn, R. E. (1988). *Beyond rational management: Mastering the paradoxes and competing demands of high performance.* San Francisco: Jossey-Bass.

Ragins, B. R. (1989). Power and gender congruency effects in evaluations of male and female managers. *Journal of Management, 15,* 65–76.

Ragins, B. R. (1991). Gender effects in subordinate evaluations of leaders: Real or artifact? *Journal of Organizational Behavior, 12,* 259–268.

Ragins, B. R., & Sundstrom, E. (1989). Gender and power in organizations: A longitudinal perspective. *Psychological Bulletin, 105,* 51–88.

Rosenbaum, L. L., & Rosenbaum, W. B. (1971). Morale and productivity consequences of group leadership style, stress, and type of task. *Journal of Applied Psychology, 55,* 343–348.

Rosener, J. B. (1990). Ways women lead. *Harvard Business Review,* 119–125.

Rosener, J. B. (1995). *America's competitive secret: Utilizing women as a management strategy.* New York: Oxford University Press.

Schein, V. E. (1973). The relationship between sex role stereotypes and requisite management characteristics. *Journal of Applied Psychology, 57,* 95–100.

Schein, V. E., Mueller, R., Lituchy, T., & Liu, J. (1996). Think manager—think male: A global phenomenon? *Journal of Organizational Behavior, 17,* 33–41.

Schnake, M., Dumler, M. P., & Cochran, D. S. (1993). The relationship between "traditional" leadership, "super" leadership, and organizational citizenship behavior. *Group and Organization Management, 18,* 352–365.

Schriesheim, C. A., Tepper, B. J., & Tetrault, L. A. (1994). Least preferred co-worker score, situational control, and leadership effectiveness: A meta-analysis of contingency model performance predictions. *Journal of Applied Psychology, 79,* 561–573.

Seltzer, J., & Numerof, R. E. (1988). Supervisory leadership and subordinate burnout. *Academy of Management Journal, 31,* 439–446.

Settoon, R. P., Bennett, N., & Liden, R. C. (1996). Social exchange in organizations: Perceived organizational support, leader-member exchange, and employee reciprocity. *Journal of Applied Psychology, 81,* 219–227.

Sims, H. P., Jr., & Manz, C. C. (1996). *Company of heroes: Unleashing the power of self-leadership.* New York: Wiley.

Smither, R. D. (1993). Authoritarianism, dominance, and social behavior: A perspective from evolutionary personality psychology. *Human Relations, 46,* 23–43.

Staw, B. M. (1982). Counterforces to change. In P. S. Goodman (Ed.), *Change in organizations: New perspectives on theory, research and practice.* San Francisco: Jossey-Bass.

Stogdill, R. M. (1974). *Handbook of leadership: A survey of theory and research.* New York: Free Press.

Stogdill, R. M., & Coons, A. E. (Eds.). (1957). *Leader behavior: Its description and measurement.* Columbus, OH: Bureau of Business Research, Ohio State University.

Tepper, B. J., & Percy, P. M. (1994). Structural validity of the Multifactor Leadership Questionnaire. *Educational and Psychological Measurement, 54,* 734–744.

Tichy, N. M., & Devanna, M. A. (1986). *The transformational leader.* New York: Wiley.

Vecchio, R. P. (1990). Theoretical and empirical examination of cognitive resource theory. *Journal of Applied Psychology, 75,* 141–147.

Vecchio, R. P., & Gobdel, B. C. (1984). The vertical dyad linkage model of leadership: Problems and prospects. *Organizational Behavior and Human Performance, 34,* 5–20.

Vroom, V. H. (1976). Can leaders learn to lead? *Organizational Dynamics, 4,* 17–28.

Vroom, V. H., & Jago, A. G. (1988). *The new leadership: Managing participation in organizations.* Englewood Cliffs, NJ: Prentice-Hall.

Vroom, V. H., & Mann, F. C. (1960). Leader authoritarianism and employee attitudes. *Personnel Psychology, 13,* 125–140.

Vroom, V. H., & Yetton, P. W. (1973). *Leadership and decision making.* Pittsburgh: University of Pittsburgh Press.

Wofford, J. C., & Goodwin, V. L. (1994). A cognitive interpretation of transactional and transformational leadership theories. *Leadership Quarterly, 5,* 161–186.

Wofford, J. C., & Liska, L. Z. (1993). Path-goal theories of leadership: A meta-analysis. *Journal of Management, 19,* 857–876.

Yukl, G. A. (1994). *Leadership in organizations* (3rd ed.). Englewood Cliffs, NJ: Prentice-Hall.

Yukl, G., & Falbe, C. M. (1990). Influence tactics and objectives in upward, downward, and lateral influence attempts. *Journal of Applied Psychology, 75,* 132–140.

15

Organization Change and Development

About 200 postal workers picketed U.S. Postal Service headquarters in Orange County. . . . protesting an automated letter-sorting system they say makes their jobs harder.

"It's making it impossible to deliver the mail," said John Wellen, a spokesman for the National Association of Letter Carriers' Local Branch 1100, which organized the demonstration . . . as part of a one-day "informational picket" at post offices nationwide. . . .

The letter carriers said they are upset about the postal service's increasing use of machines . . . designed to automatically sort mail by destination. . . . the workers contend the new system is slowing [mail delivery] up by causing errors that the carriers are not allowed to correct in a timely manner. Making matters worse, they said, the postal service has begun scheduling carriers' shifts to begin later in the day. . . .

"We want to deliver the mail and we want to deliver it before dark," said George Heim, a letter carrier in Placentia. . . .

"Change is hard for everyone . . . " [said a spokesman for the postal service]. "Changing the way people do their jobs upsets them, but we believe this is the best direction for the post office."

"We're not trying to stand in the way of the machines" [said Heim]. "We're just trying to have some input so we can make them work properly."

THE REPORT in Psychology [*not*] at Work demonstrates two important points about change in organizations. First, the Post Office made major changes in job design (part of the technical system) that are not meshing smoothly with the traditional hands-on service culture (part of the social system) of this organization. Second, the people most involved were not given an opportunity to have input into the proposed changes and perhaps to head off some of the mail delivery problems and resulting employee and customer dissatisfaction that have been encountered.

The report of the Postal Service's difficulties is titled Psychology [*not*] at Work to emphasize that few, if any, I/O psychologists would endorse going forward with such a major change in job design without soliciting input and feedback from those who would be most affected by it. The change has saved money, but it is probable that savings would be even greater if postal employees understood, accepted, and were able to utilize the new system to advantage.

The process of bringing about change in the social system that is an organization is examined in this chapter. Change goes on all the time in organizations, of course, but the concern here is not with drifts, growth changes, stop-gap crisis measures, or other such processes. The focus is on planned changes in the organizational social system that go by the label **organization development**. (The phrase *organizational* development is also used frequently in the literature.)

What Is Organization Development?

As an active and identifiable specialty interest within the field of industrial/organizational psychology, organization development (OD) is a relatively new field, having begun sometime in the late 1950s or early 1960s (Bowers, 1976). One of the first and most quoted formal definitions of this area is that of French:

Organizational development refers to a long-range effort to improve an organization's problem solving capabilities and its ability to cope with changes in its external environment with the help of external or internal behavioral scientists, or change agents. . . . (1969, p. 23)

The world of work has changed enormously since French presented his definition, and both organizations and organization development have changed with it. Today organization development encompasses a broad range of proactive changes that go beyond adaptability to the external environment and improved decision making. Today, the goals of organization development:

> involve improving both organizational performance and the quality of work life experienced by organization members. These aims are attained by applying knowledge about people in organizations, derived from the social and behavioral sciences. (Sashkin & Burke, 1987, p. 393)

Sashkin and Burke's definition of OD (see also Burke, 1982, 1987) takes in more territory than French's, but the two share the same premise: organization development is a deliberate, planned undertaking to bring about specific change. Knowledge from behavioral and other sciences is the foundation upon which this undertaking rests.

The Change Agent

It is usual to refer to the person who plans and carries out formal organization development (OD) efforts as a **change agent.** Some organizations have employees charged with these duties, but it is more common to employ outsiders in this capacity. The people who provide these services usually call themselves management or organizational consultants, and many of them (but not all) are I/O psychologists.

Wherever they come from and whoever they are, effective change agents tend to have certain characteristics in common. The role played by personality as such is a matter for debate (e.g., Hamilton, 1988; Hilton, 1989), but most good consultants do share the ability to relate well to many kinds of people, along with diagnostic and problem-solving skills and goal-setting expertise. Many experts in the field believe that future OD practitioners will also need much greater familiarity with a client's business than has been required in the past (e.g., Beer & Walton, 1990; Sanzgiri & Gottlieb, 1992). An overview of management consulting is provided by Cosier and Dalton (1993).

The OD Contract

The discussion in this chapter is focused primarily on outside consultant change agents whose basic discipline is I/O psychology. Such specialists usually become involved with an organization through a decision made at the upper management level. As shown in Exhibit 15–1, the basis for this decision varies along a continuum from reaction to some current crisis to proaction vis-à-vis upcoming events.

Lying between crisis-stimulated need for change and event-stimulated opportunity for change are the symptoms of deviation from normal or desired states that probably prompt most organizations to seek the services of an organization development specialist. The

Exhibit 15–1
Sample
Conditions for
Initiating
Organization
Development

Reactive		Proactive
Crisis	**Symptoms**	**Opportunities**
For example:	For example:	For example:
• hostile takeover attempt	• high absenteeism/turnover	• change in technology
• dramatic loss of profit	• low quality/quantity production	• moving to a new location
• major new competitor	• increased interpersonal conflict	• key person retiring
• loss of key personnel	• deteriorating labor relations	• upcoming acquisition/merger

symptoms may represent barriers to organizational effectiveness or reduced quality of work life for employees, or they may be early signals of upcoming crises.

The use of an external change agent to help with the kinds of issues in the exhibit or others requires a contract between the parties. This contract includes the terms for the duration of the undertaking and the financial arrangements, of course, but it goes beyond these. A basic issue is the nature of the relationship between the change agent and the employing organization. In some instances, an outside change agent is engaged as an expert who is expected to diagnose any problems, find the solutions, and implement them. Management's role is to provide the information, support, and authority needed to carry out these functions. In a collaborative role, the change agent and members of the organization are partners in the process described. Finally, some organizations know what they want done, and the agent's role is to do it; this might be called a technician role for the change agent.

Given a choice, many I/O psychologists prefer the collaborative role. This arrangement provides the change agent with valuable information and assistance from members of the organization, who are the real experts on the situation of a particular company. In return, members of the organization acquire knowledge and skills to maintain desirable changes and perhaps to undertake new ones on their own in the future. The collaborative role also tends to encourage and facilitate (although not to guarantee) more widespread participation by organizational personnel in the change effort.

The belief that participation on the parts of those to be affected by a change will facilitate acceptance and implementation of the change has a long and honorable history going back at least as far as psychologists Coch and French's (1948) classic work on overcoming resistance to change in the workplace. This belief takes strength from the many reports of negative reactions by employees (like those of the Postal Service described in Psychology at Work) to nonparticipative changes as well as from research. The field study summarized in Spotlight on Research illustrates this line of investigation.

The authors of the Spotlight study (Macy, Peterson, & Norton, 1989) examined attitudinal differences between groups of employee subjects who participated to varying degrees in a long-term joint union-management job redesign program at a power company. As hypothesized, they found that direct participation was associated with more positive reactions to changes than were either indirect participation or no participation.

Field study
See pages 27–34

Research subjects
See page 27

Hypothesis
See page 25

Research question   Will direct and active participation in a change effort be associated more strongly with positive changes than indirect participation or no participation?

Type of study   Longitudinal field study.

Subjects   225 pairs of employees of the engineering division of a major power-generating company and 227 matched pairs in a similar division of the same company in another city (comparison group).

Independent variable   Participation in change effort: direct/indirect/none.

Dependent variables   Job involvement, job satisfaction, organizational trust, and group cohesiveness as measured by surveys, structured and semistructured interviews taken at four points in time.

General procedure   Direct participation group served on Quality of Work Committee to recommend changes and make policy decisions in a change program lasting approximately six years. Indirect participants were surveyed as to their views. A comparison group had no role. Some of the changes recommended and implemented in company were flextime, a modified performance appraisal method, and coordinated work process documentation.

Results   Direct participants generally reported positive changes in the quality of work life, the work environment, and interpersonal participation as compared with the indirect participation and comparison subjects.

Conclusion   "These . . . results make it quite clear that some changes in attitudes associated solely with the participation in the joint union-management re-design effort occurred in the experimental site at the power company" (p. 1127).

SPOTLIGHT ON RESEARCH

A Test of Participation Theory in a Work Re-design Field Setting: Degree of Participation and Comparison Site Contrasts

Summarized from B. A. Macy, M. R. Peterson, and L. W. Norton, "A Test of Participation Theory in a Work Re-design Field Setting: Degree of Participation and Comparison Site Contrasts." *Human Relations*, 1989, *42*, 1095–1165.

Organization Development and Values

"Science" is often portrayed as objective and value-neutral, but this is seldom, if ever, the case. Scientists are people and these people have values. As Carl Rogers (Rogers & Skinner, 1956) points out, even the decision to experiment is a value choice. So is the decision to make a change in some aspect of an organization's functioning—a choice that reflects valuing change as a way of making things better.

Like any psychologist, an I/O psychologist acting as a change agent for an organization is acting within the context of personal and professional values. To return to an issue discussed earlier, a particular OD specialist may place a high personal value on participation in change efforts by those to be affected (whether or not this participation is perceived to be necessary to bring the change about). As a result, this individual will limit his or her involvement with organizations to relationships and activities that allow for a participative approach.

It is not possible to speak for all I/O psychologists, but many of those who do applied work in organizations subscribe to a common set of values. In their well-known paper on this subject, Tannenbaum and Davis (1969) discuss 13 value dimensions that are relevant. The basic positions they believe describe organization development practitioners are listed in Exhibit 15–2. It is possible that the list might be expanded today, but there is little evidence that it should be shortened; the values listed by Tannenbaum and Davis continue to be reflected strongly in contemporary OD literature.

Independent/dependent variables
See page 29

Exhibit 15–2
Some Value
Orientations of
Organization
Development

- A view of people as basically good
- Appreciation of employees as human beings and "whole people"
- A view of people as being always in the process of development
- Accepting and making positive use of individual differences
- Making the appropriate expression and use of feelings possible
- Emphasizing authentic (real) behavior
- Using status only for organizationally relevant purposes
- Trusting people
- Willingness to confront people
- Willingness to risk
- Seeing process work as essential to effective task accomplishment
- Emphasizing collaboration, not competition

Based on the discussion by R. Tannenbaum and S. A. Davis, "Values, Man, and Organizations." *Industrial Management Review,* 1969, *10,* 67–86.

The values underlying OD as a professional activity help individual practitioners make decisions about what they will do and how they will do it, and they are vital if any ethical conflicts arise. Shared values also help give the field respect and credibility and its practitioners a shared identity. Finally, the study of these values can have practical implications, especially if cross-cultural change efforts are to be effective (e.g., Jaeger, 1986; Perlaki, 1994). Techniques and approaches that stem from particular values are unlikely to work (and may offend) in a culture with different values.

An OD practitioner's values also play a role in the success of same-culture organization development efforts in that success is far more likely if they are compatible with the basic values of the organization (Zeira & Avedisian, 1989). Values underlie selection of both the goals and the methods of organization development; if there is a lack of fit in organization-consultant values, there is a strong possibility that the consultant will be unable to perform to client expectations or satisfaction.

Models of Change

Scientific method
See pages 23–24

The scientific study of any phenomenon requires going beneath labels and descriptions and data to the more fundamental issue of explanation. When it comes to organization development, a basic question is: How does change itself (regardless of specifics) come about? The first, and still most generally accepted, model of this process is that proposed by psychologist Kurt Lewin more than 45 years ago.

Lewin's Model of the Change Process

Lewin (1951) viewed the behavior of people in a work situation as resulting from a balance of dynamic forces working in opposite directions. Some of these forces are driving forces and some are restraining forces. As illustrated in Figure 15–1, an observed behav-

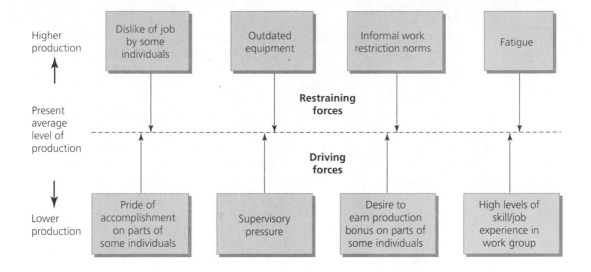

Note. In Lewin's force-field analysis technique, the length of the lines would vary according to the strengths of the different operating forces.

Figure 15–1
A Quasi-Stationary Equilibrium of Work Production

---

ior pattern may be conceptualized as the balance between these forces. The behavior used as an example is that of the production level of a particular work department in which employees are paid a bonus for exceeding set standards.

Typically, production in the hypothetical department fluctuates, but the range of fluctuation is not great. In Lewin's conceptualization, this is because the sum of the forces driving greater production (such as the desire of individuals to earn more money) is about equal to the sum of the forces restraining greater production (such as group work restriction norms). The net result of all of this pulling and pushing is what Lewin called a "quasi-stationary equilibrium"—the typical pattern of work output in that department.

Change will occur in a quasi-stationary equilibrium when something happens to cause an imbalance between the driving forces and the restraining forces. This may occur if one or more of the driving or restraining forces becomes stronger (the bonus for greater production is raised by management, for instance), if one or more of the forces is removed (perhaps a group member who had been extremely influential in setting work restriction norms leaves to take another job), or if one or more new driving or restraining forces is added (the employees join a union).

In Lewin's terms, any of the changes described (or any of many other possibilities) results in an unfreezing of the existing equilibrium. After a period of adjustment (the change), there will be a refreezing of the situation and a new equilibrium. This simple unfreezing-change-refreezing conceptual model of change is a useful tool, both for understanding organization change in the abstract and for bringing about desired change in practice. Each of these stages is considered separately, although they do not necessarily occur in a separate and stepwise fashion.

Unfreezing

The first step in any organization development effort is diagnosis of the current situation and identification of desirable changes. Assuming for the moment that this step has been carried out, Lewin's model dictates that a way must be found to bring about an unfreezing of the current equilibrium before the changes can be implemented. In any deliberate attempt to unfreeze the status quo, it is helpful to understand the general nature of the driving and restraining forces in the situation. These forces will be different in different situations, of course, but as shown in Table 15–1, their origins are the same.

Driving and restraining forces that may be affecting a pattern of behavior can originate with individual employees (resistance, for example), work groups (work norms, for instance), the particular subsystem of an organization that is the focus of change (such as leadership), the entire system that is the organization (structure, for example), and even the organization's external environment (current economic conditions, for instance) or some combination of these. The relevant driving and restraining forces in a situation are the more important factors working for and against bringing about a desired change in an organization.

Theoretically, unfreezing is a matter of increasing any of the driving forces and/or reducing any of the restraining forces so as to upset the existing equilibrium, but a focus on employee attitudes toward change is common. From this viewpoint, unfreezing requires overcoming individual resistance to change itself (reducing an individual restraining force) and stimulating a desire for change (increasing a driving force). The psychological dynamics of bringing these goals about are discussed in a classic article by Schein (1961). At the applied level, involving employees who will be affected by a change in planning the change is a common strategy aimed at accomplishing these ends.

Unfreezing is upsetting the status quo, and, as noted, it is possible to go about this by attempting to change attitudes toward change itself. Alternatively, a direct attack may be made on the behavior that is the focus of change. For example, the goal of change in a marketing organization might be more sharing of ideas and less competition among the people working there so that more good ideas will be generated and developed. As a general rule, however, people are unlikely to change their accustomed ways of dealing with one another unless these old patterns of interaction are unfrozen in some way.

One possibility for unfreezing old interaction patterns is the once-popular laboratory training ("T group" or sensitivity training) technique in which members of a group confront one another in new ways with the help of an experienced trainer. Specifically, they focus on their feelings about one another and their reactions to one another's behavior,

Table 15–1	Sources and Examples of Driving and Restraining Forces in a Work Setting				
Source	**Individual Employee**	**Work Group**	**Subsystem or Unit**	**Organizational System**	**External Environment**
Examples:	• Skills	• Norms	• Technology	• Unions	• Economic conditions
	• Experience	• Goals	• Power in organization	• Structure	• Government regulations
	• Values	• Leadership	• Space	• Culture	• Pressure groups
	• Attitudes	• Cohesiveness	• Resources	• Market position	• Availability of materials
	• Motivation	• Values	• Leadership	• Economic position	• Market characteristics

rather than on objective issues (see Dupre, 1976). With the usual interpersonal interaction and communication patterns disrupted, the way is open for new ones to be learned and adopted.

Sensitivity training is not much used these days, but the basic principle of putting people in new roles and relationships as a way of unfreezing the status quo can be applied in other ways. For example, quality circles, cross-functional project teams, and *ad hoc* (for this special purpose only) problem-solving groups all put people into new roles and new relationships without major disruption to old ones. As unfreezing occurs, formal changes may be introduced more effectively.

The unfreezing strategy described is based on eliciting new behaviors directly rather than attempting to educate people about them (that is, change attitudes). It is consistent with a long line of social psychology research that has found that "behavior forced by new roles or circumstances causes people to endorse attitudes consonant with that behavior, even when their original attitudes conflicted with the behavior" (Beer & Walton, 1990, p. 160).

To put it another way, there is generally more evidence for the hypothesis that attitudes follow behavior than for the reverse hypothesis, and attitudes about change are no exception (Bem, 1968; Festinger, 1957). With few exceptions, it is easier to start unfreezing with behavior rather than attitudes.

Change

Once a situation is unfrozen, the way is open for change. The change under consideration is planned change to meet a particular goal or goals, and the organization development term used to describe the process of bringing this about is **intervention**. One of the meanings given by the dictionary for the term *intervene* is "to come in or between in order to stop, settle, or modify," and this is not a bad description of what an OD change agent does. He or she comes into an organizational social system in order to modify (change) something (which may include stopping or settling something). In the process, he or she may also get between subsystems of the organizational system, and one result can be that the change effort has unintended consequences or fails altogether.

In Chapter 12, organizations were examined as social systems made up of interrelated subsystems that must work together in harmony if the system as a whole is to survive and prosper. One of the many important implications of this view of organizations is that it is virtually impossible to intervene in one part of an organizational system without affecting other parts. To put it another way, a change will create **systems effects** in other parts of the organization. This concept is demonstrated in the current context by Figure 15–2.

The figure illustrates the large number of variables and the proposed relationships among them (Burke & Litwin, 1992) that may be affected by change. For example, among other variables, a simple change in vacation policy might affect

- management practices (supervisor can no longer give preference to certain employees, for example);
- leadership (is now perceived as fairer);
- work unit climate (is more positive); and
- individual-organization "fit" (employees who value justice feel more comfortable with situation).

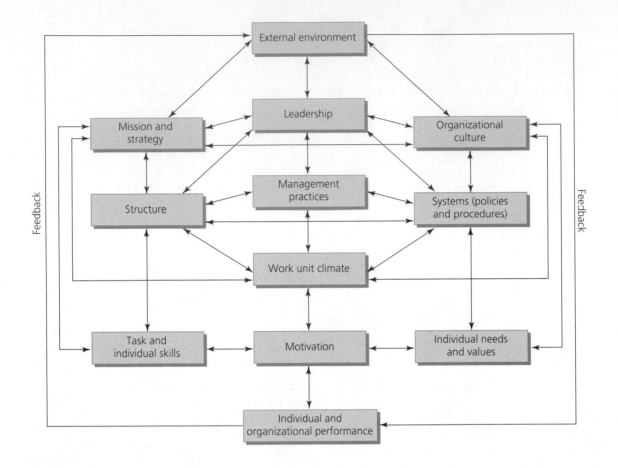

Figure 15–2
A Model of Organizational Performance and Change

From W. W. Burke and G. H. Litwin, "A Causal Model of Organizational Performance and Change." *Journal of Management*, 1992, *18*, 523–545. Copyright 1992 JAI Press. Reprinted by permission.

The positive systems effects of changing the vacation policy are welcome because the purpose of an intervention is to make a change that will benefit the organization and its personnel as a whole. Sometimes, however, the effects are the wrong ones and they act against, rather than for, organization development. The sad story of the Hovey and Beard Company (Strauss & Bevelas, 1955) illustrates the point.

The Hovey and Beard Company made wooden toys. It was quite successful in this enterprise, and the demand for its products had increased substantially from the initial level. To help increase production to meet this demand and continue to grow as a company, management instituted a change in work methods (involving increased mechanization) for one work group (employees who painted the finished toys). The employees worked under a group incentive plan, and a special learning bonus was also added to support the work-methods change. Nevertheless, results were disappointing. Production fell, team spirit decreased, and turnover increased. The change appeared to be a failure, and Hovey and Beard called in a management consultant for help.

In the next chapter of the story, the employees involved in the change were given the opportunity to participate in discussing the problems and what might be done to solve them. Following these discussions, two more changes in the work environment were implemented. Large fans were installed to increase personal comfort, and the workers were given the means to control (within limits) the speed of the chain of overhead hooks that now moved the toys through this department. Did these changes work to bring about the desired goals? Indeed they did, but unfortunately the story does not have a happy ending.

After the new changes went into effect, the employees who were painting toys increased their production far beyond expectations. In the process, they began earning more money than many skilled workers in other parts of the company. These employees complained bitterly, and a general atmosphere of contention began to grow between employees, work engineers, first-line supervisors, and management. In the end, the learning bonus was withdrawn, control of the hook speed was taken away from the painters and reset at the engineered standard, production dropped back, and within a few months, all but two of the employees in the toy painting group had quit.

One way to look at what happened at Hovey and Beard is from the viewpoint of unanticipated systems effects of change. The changes made in one part of the system (painting department) were thought out carefully, supported by a change in the relevant reward system, and modified according to worker input when problems developed. Unfortunately, however, no one seems to have anticipated the negative effects this intervention would have on other parts of the Hovey and Beard organizational system. Effective OD change agents do the best they can to anticipate major undesirable systems effects and to take or to suggest measures to avoid or minimize them.

Refreezing

Refreezing is the last stage in Lewin's model of change. It occurs with or without help because it is merely the new status quo (quasi-stationary equilibrium) in a situation after a change has occurred. When the change has been deliberate and the results are successful, help may be necessary to refreeze the situation at this point. Otherwise, the situation may revert to previous and familiar ways, or things may deteriorate to a state even less desirable than the original one as they did at Hovey and Beard.

Refreezing a desired change in an affected subsystem and integrating it into the larger organizational system is known as **institutionalization** of the change. (The same process at the individual level is called internalization.) When a change has been institutionalized, it has been formally recognized and accepted by organizational personnel as a permanent part of the organization's functioning.

Some changes are relatively easy to institutionalize in the sense that they can be mandated by management; a new policy about performance appraisal is an example. Despite the relative ease of making this change, however, there will be many different individual reactions to the new policy (Buller & McEvoy, 1989). There may also be considerable confusion and resistance before everyone accepts and adjusts to it. Among the strategies that may help to institutionalize a change successfully in the acceptance as well as the formal recognition sense are

- distributing information about the reasons for adopting the change on a permanent basis;

- training current or future employees in ways to help them adjust to the change;

- providing reinforcement for doing things the new ways, and

- setting up a mechanism for individuals and groups to provide management with feedback about how the change is working and what adjustments might be necessary.

Positive reinforcement
See pages 204–206

Other factors that seem to increase the success of an organizational change effort and its institutionalization are a culture that is supportive of the change, general management support (e.g., Doherty, Nord, & McAdams, 1989), and the presence of one or more "evangelists." In this context, an evangelist is a top manager who feels personally responsible for the achievement of change goals and has the power and resources to back up his or her convictions (e.g., Zeira & Avedisian, 1989).

Feedback
See pages 138–140

In the final analysis, refreezing is a relative matter whatever steps are taken. Organizations are dynamic, open systems in which people and conditions are always changing, and organization development is probably seen more accurately as a process than an event.

Models of Organization Development

Kurpius, Fuqua, and Rozecki (1993) describe six stages of an organizational consulting relationship. They are (1) pre-entry; (2) entry, problem exploration, and setting a contract; (3) information gathering, problem description, and goal setting; (4) solution exploration and change intervention; (5) evaluation of the intervention; and (6) termination of the consulting relationship. A particular model for these stages that emphasizes the link between *action* to deal with a situation and *research* to add to scientific knowledge is called the action research model.

Action research is a cyclical process of diagnosis, planning, action, and evaluation. This model, like the general model of change discussed, was proposed originally by Lewin, but a number of other researchers have been involved in expanding upon it (e.g., Frohman, Sashkin, & Kavanagh, 1976). The basic form is shown in Figure 15–3.

The action research model of organization development emphasizes diagnosis, full client participation in the organization development process, evaluation of all interventions, and follow-up action based on this evaluation. This careful, step-by-step, comprehensive approach is useful for generating new behavioral science knowledge that may be used to improve the effectiveness of any organization. In addition, the basic ideas of the model are flexible enough to allow it to be applied in new ways and to new problems (Elden & Chisholm, 1993).

Action research has many potential advantages for organization development practice and research, and many OD practitioners endorse it (e.g., Church, Burke, & Van Eynde, 1994). In common with many models in I/O psychology, however, this one describes an ideal. Many organizations lack the resources to enter into such a comprehensive program, and not all problems require it. It should also be mentioned that action research tends to extend the change process, and it can create client dependency on the change agent.

Client dependency is avoided by an alternative model of organization change, called simply planned change, which places greater emphasis on the use of specific strategies to solve specific problems (Lippitt, Watson, & Westley, 1958). Both it and action research are models of organization development, however, not rigid prescriptions. A particular change agent may prefer one conceptualization over the other, but even so, he or she will likely deviate from the "steps" in many situations. Models of organization change are conceptual tools, and as such, they are not right or wrong, but more or less useful.

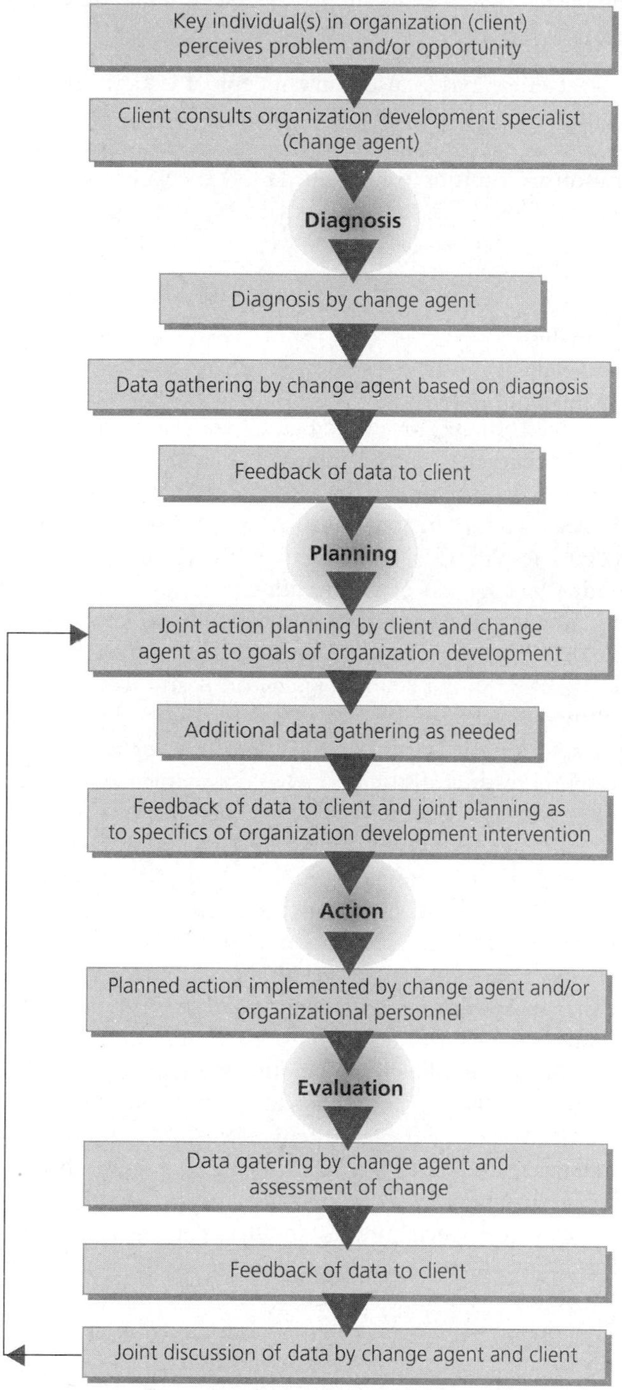

Figure 15–3
Action
Research in
Organization
Development

Key individual(s) in organization (client)
perceives problem and/or opportunity

Client consults organization development specialist
(change agent)

Diagnosis

Diagnosis by change agent

Data gathering by change agent based on diagnosis

Feedback of data to client

Planning

Joint action planning by client and change
agent as to goals of organization development

Additional data gathering as needed

Feedback of data to client and joint planning as
to specifics of organization development intervention

Action

Planned action implemented by change agent and/or
organizational personnel

Evaluation

Data gatering by change agent and
assessment of change

Feedback of data to client

Joint discussion of data by change agent and client

Implementing Organization Change

To this point, the discussion has focused on conceptual issues. What does organization development mean? How does change come about? It is now time to consider some of the practical questions raised by that discussion. What are the goals of a change effort and who are its targets? What kinds of techniques do OD specialists use to bring about organization development? How are results evaluated?

The Goals of Change

In everyday terms, the goal of organization development is to make things in an organization better by means of intervention into some aspect of the organizational system. What does "better" mean? In the Hovey and Beard case, better meant a bigger, more profitable organization for everyone, and one step toward this goal was greater work output from one group of employees. In many instances, however, it is difficult to specify the goals of change in such a clear-cut and quantifiable way. And in some cases, the specific goals of the change that will improve the organization are unknown; the change agent's first task is to conduct a diagnosis of the situation.

Following a study of many organization development interventions in the United States and New Zealand, O'Driscoll and Eubanks (1993) emphasize that the first step in diagnosis is close attention to the client's expectations and requirements. (The number of people working with the change agent at this step, as well as the job positions they hold, can vary enormously; the term *client* is used to cover the range of possibilities.) How are things now? If there is a problem, what do people in the organization think is the cause?

If the stimulus for organization development is not a problem but an opportunity, what is its nature? How should things be after a change? The initial answers to these questions are often referred to collectively as the expressed needs of the client. The diagnosis process may stop right here; it is understood that the client's expressed need will be the basis for action (although not all consultants will work this way).

It must also be acknowledged that the reverse situation is sometimes the case. Some management consultants walk through the door of every organization convinced that they already know what the problem is, and many are successful in selling this view (and their solution of choice) to the client. Because the view of the problem and the preferred solution tend to be the same regardless of the organization (for example, the problem is poor communication and the solution is role-playing seminars), this approach has been called a marketing approach to organization development (Kahn, 1974).

I/O psychologists with a special interest in OD most often recommend a strategy lying between the extremes described. The expressed needs of the client are a starting point, but it is desirable for a change agent to make his or her own diagnosis of the situation as well. This diagnosis may be relatively quick or it may be complex and time-consuming, involving interviews, surveys, observation, and the study of records. The purpose is to come up with an answer to the question: How should things be in the future?

The answer to the question, and so the objectives of any OD program, will vary according to the particulars of the situation, but Sherwood (1971) identifies a number of problems that are common to many organizations. As a result, many traditional OD efforts share certain objectives.

*A basic choice that
an I/O psychologist
seeking to bring
about change in an
organization must
make is whether to
start with trying to
change people or
making a change
in the work
environment.*

- To build trust among individuals and groups.

- To create an open, problem-solving climate throughout the organization.

- To locate problem-solving and decision-making responsibilities as close to the relevant resources and information as possible (rather than in a particular role or level of the organization).

- To increase employees' sense of "ownership" of organizational goals.

- To increase collaboration between individuals and work groups.

- To help individuals and groups become more aware of interpersonal dynamics (such as communication patterns, power struggles, and conflict) and how these affect work task performance.

The objectives listed are relevant to interpersonal processes and relationships, and at one time they were usually themselves the end goals of change efforts. This is still true in some cases, but today they are also likely to be undertaken to help create a favorable climate for changes in organizational structure or technology (Majchrzak & Klein, 1987).

The Target of Change

In the broadest sense, "the organization" is the target of all OD change. In most cases, however, the actual intervention is limited; the assumption is that improvement in one area will improve overall effectiveness or health (or both). In the specific sense, the target of an OD change effort is that aspect (or those aspects) of the organizational system into which a specified intervention will be made.

The problem of excessive employee absenteeism is a convenient one for examining the question of selecting a target for change. In this situation, as in all cases, there are two basic choices. One is the *people* involved; for example, a company might replace the employees who are being absent too frequently. The other is the work *environment* of the people involved; the organization might make a change in its formal policy concerning time off from work. In some cases, it may be possible to work with both targets, but how does the change agent make a choice if a choice must be made?

One basis for making a choice between people or work environments as the primary target of OD is a change agent's personal preference, values, and opinions. As mentioned, some consultants have preset ideas about the appropriate target of (and technique for) change. Others have strong beliefs that influence their choice even if they do not take a marketing approach. A consultant who believes that the only way to bring about *real* change in a situation is to change underlying attitudes, for example, would probably be unsympathetic to changes targeting some aspect of the job environment.

The hypothetical consultant mentioned may do very fine work; nevertheless, he or she is biased. When a problem (such as absenteeism) is the stimulus for OD, a critical part of the diagnosis process is trying to identify the more important causal factors producing the symptoms. If analysis suggests that boring work and an unreliable public transportation system are implicated in the absenteeism, then the environment would seem to be the target of choice (at least initially). If, on the other hand, it turns out that a few employees account for the greater part of the absenteeism and most of these individuals had poor attendance records on previous jobs, then people would be the first logical target for change.

Notice that the current discussion refers to "causal factors," not "the cause of a problem." This is an important distinction. There is seldom, if ever, a single cause of a problem. Beginning a diagnosis with the assumption that there is such a cause, therefore, can lead to overlooking or discounting relevant information. Even if one factor is relatively more important than others (as is often the case), it is necessary to have a broader understanding for practical reasons. Some causes just cannot be "fixed." Examples include a poor decision made in the past that cannot be undone or an entrenched authority figure who will not change his or her ways and cannot be transferred or terminated. In such cases, the question becomes: What *else* might be done?

In the end, the process of determining the most appropriate target for change is a process of collecting information to help understand the situation, weighing it carefully to select what appear to be the more important causal factors, and evaluating these factors in terms of their *practical* potential (whether a change here could likely be accomplished) as well as their *conceptual* potential (whether a change here would solve the problem).

Among the practical issues to be considered in the evaluation described are the time required; the number of people who will be affected and how personal the effects are likely to be; the probable cost in dollars; the degree of disruption to the work of the organization; short-term versus long-term gains; and the possibility of any negative systems effects. In making the final decision, a general guideline is: When there is a choice, the "shallowest" intervention that will accomplish the goals is the preferred intervention (Harrison, 1970).

In organization development terminology, a *shallow* intervention is one that takes less time, affects fewer people, has effects that are less personal, and costs less than alternatives. Any intervention, no matter how well planned and carried out, is a shock to the organizational system to some extent. Creating more shock than necessary to achieve the objectives at hand is counterproductive to the broader objective of making an organization a better place.

*The behavior of
people at work is
the result of a com-
plex interaction of
individual and situ-
ational factors, and
a basic understand-
ing of these factors
is one of the organi-
zation change
agent's most valu-
able tools.*

The basic process of selecting a target for change is the same whether there is an existing problem such as absenteeism or whether the organization development effort is a
more proactive one. In the latter case, however, the diagnosis phase may take longer because the field of vision is wider. The focus is no longer on a particular identified problem, but on the possible existence of general barriers to (or opportunities for) increased
organizational effectiveness.

In closing this section, it must be noted that the people-versus-environment target of
intervention issue, although hotly debated in some quarters, is really a question of means
rather than ends. All organization development interventions are for the purpose of affecting people and their behavior in some way, be it their actual job behavior, the way they
interact with one another, their attitudes toward work, or other behaviors and attitudes.
Selecting a target is selecting a place to make the initial intervention that is likely to bring
about desired changes while minimizing shock to the system.

The Methods of Change

In the organization development literature, the distinction between environments and
people as targets of change is usually presented as the difference between *structure* (or
technostructure) change and *process* change. An example of structure change is a new
policy about vacation time; a change is made in some aspect of an organization's design
or functioning (in this case, a policy). The particular individuals holding positions in the
organization at the time of the change are targets of the change only as representatives of
all employees who will ever be affected by the new policy.

In process change, by contrast, the particular individuals currently holding job positions in the organization are the focus of change as individuals, as work groups, or as a

work force. Instead of setting a new policy about vacation times, for instance, management might arrange for an I/O psychologist to conduct a series of meetings with various organizational units. The purpose of these meetings would be for the particular individuals involved to work out mutually acceptable departmental vacation scheduling policies that would not leave anyone short of staff at a critical time.

The people/environment or process/structure distinction is not always easy to make in an applied situation, because structural or environmental changes almost always affect people. The distinction has importance, however, for a review of representative OD methods. Examination of most formal discussions of OD reveals a strong emphasis on people/process methods. This emphasis is consistent with the set of common OD objectives discussed by Sherwood, as well as with the historical roots of organization development (French & Bell, 1984). At the same time, many I/O psychologists today are involved in organization development efforts that take some aspect of an organization's structure or environment, rather than particular individuals, as the primary target.

In previous chapters, a variety of interventions in organizations have been discussed that fall into the category of environmental/structural changes. A few examples are positive reinforcement programs for desired employee behavior, changing from assembly-line to self-managing group job design in the auto and other industries, hiring for the organization and not for the job, creating cross-functional product design teams, and turning performance appraisal into performance management that takes place on a year-round basis. In every case, there will be effects on current individuals employed by the organization, but the changes, if maintained, will also affect future employees significantly.

By contrast with structural changes, process methods seek to change particular people and/or their interrelationships in some way. A summary list of some well-known people/process methods is provided in Table 15–2. Two of these have been selected as examples of this more traditional organization change approach. The first is survey feedback,

Table 15–2		A Sample of People-Oriented OD Intervention Methods	
Name of Technique	**Target**	**Purpose**	**Means**
• Process consultation	• Work group	• Help members understand the process of interacting with one another	• Group meetings
• Laboratory training (sensitivity training)	• Individual	• Promote self-awareness and sensitivity to others	• Group sessions (lasting up to two days)
• Managerial Grid™	• Individual	• Change management style to one called "team management"	• Seminars and a mix of other techniques
• Management by Objectives	• Individual	• Improve performance and satisfaction through integration of individual and organizational goals	• Joint supervisor-employee goal-setting and progress-evaluation process
• Confrontation meeting	• Management team	• Identify and solve problems	• Group meetings for airing attitudes, problems, and priorities and bringing about commitment to action

one of the first (and still widely used) OD techniques, and the other is team building, one of the most popular techniques in use today.

Survey Feedback

The organization development method known as **survey feedback** is a systematic process of data collection and feedback. Typically, members of one or more work groups in an organization are asked to give their opinions about specific issues (such as leadership or job satisfaction) and/or about problems they see in their work groups or the organization. The change agent collects this written survey information, analyzes it, and summarizes it in a form that is clear and easy to understand. On the basis of these data, he or she then conducts (or trains group leaders to conduct) open feedback and discussion sessions with the employees involved.

What happens after the survey feedback meeting? That depends on the change agent and the client, but experts all agree that *something* should happen. It is seldom practical to address every problem identified by employees, but some must be given attention and solved if at all possible. Putting employees through an involved information gathering and analysis process without taking follow-up steps may do more harm than good. In Lewin's terms, the situation is likely to refreeze in a less desirable place than before; the problems are still there and management has lost some credibility.

The diagram in Figure 15–4 illustrates the nine steps of a full survey feedback program (Nadler, 1977). Up to one full day is usually required for each step; the elapsed time between steps varies according to the situation.

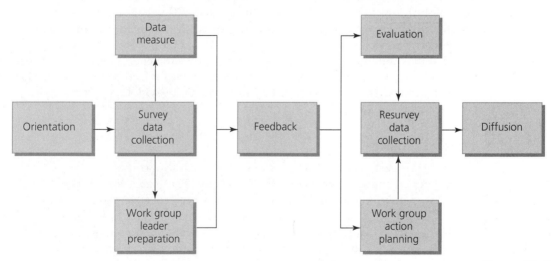

Figure 15–4
A Survey Feedback Program Model

From D. A. Nadler, *Feedback and Organizational Development: Using Data-Based Methods,* (figure 2.1 page 26). © 1977 Addison-Wesley Publishing Company Inc. Reprinted by permission of Addison-Wesley Longman Inc.

Criterion
See page 63

1. *Orientation.* Familiarize the people involved with the program and address questions and concerns.

2. *Survey data collection.* Collect opinion/attitude survey data.

3. *Data measure.* Prepare data for feedback and determine criteria for success of process.

4. *Work group leader preparation.* Train leaders to deal with data, feedback methods, and action planning.

5. *Feedback.* Present data to individuals who participated in the survey.

6. *Evaluation.* Evaluate success of feedback process as per criteria determined in step 3.

7. *Work group action planning.* Plan actions to be taken on the basis of the data collected.

8. *Resurvey data collection.* Repeat survey to determine changes and guide future action planning.

9. *Diffusion.* Continue and expand process as needed.

Survey feedback is first of all a diagnostic tool for a change agent. Results of the survey help him or her assess the current situation in an organization. For example, an opinion survey in an acute-care hospital facility revealed that more than one-third of the employees believed there were problems of some kind in the areas of communication, compensation, performance evaluation, identifying staffing needs, the operation of the cafeteria, and career development (Gray, 1995).

Survey feedback may also be viewed as an unfreezing mechanism. The heart of the technique is one or more feedback meetings conducted to help employees as a group accept the data they have generated as accurate (that is, to overcome defensiveness), to take appropriate responsibility for their roles in any identified problems, and to commit to taking part in finding and implementing solutions to the problems (Neff, 1966). This process has been found to be an effective unfreezing technique for facilitating change, especially in organizations that have multiple problems interfering with their effectiveness.

Team Building

In an OD context, **team building** is an intervention into a work group for the purpose of strengthening the group's effectiveness as a group. The change agent's primary role is to help the members find and eliminate such barriers to effective performance as strained interpersonal relationships, inefficient decision-making processes, or conflicts over group leadership. At the same time, he or she is working to increase the group's cohesiveness and its ability to handle future problems on its own (Beer, 1976).

Group cohesiveness
See pages 472–474

The goals of team building are approached via meetings in which group members explore issues and problems. The change agent takes the role of facilitator, making sure that all members participate, working through any interpersonal conflicts that arise, and clarifying ideas as necessary. There are many variations of this process, however. Some are ongoing; some are short-term. Some are general; some are problem-specific. A team-building program created by Buller and Bell (1986) consisted of six meetings with a general focus; subjects worked on finding and solving problems getting in the way of working effectively, efficiently, and safely as a team.

Team building in the Buller and Bell study was conducted within the context of a field experiment in which the authors investigated the effects on productivity of two different kinds of interventions into work groups of underground miners. As far as the effectiveness of team building itself was concerned, results were positive. There were also some improvements on the performance criteria. More of these improvements occurred in a goal-setting treatment, however, than in the team-building treatment. In addition, the researchers do not believe they can say with confidence that any of the observed improvements were *caused* by their organization development interventions.

In evaluating the results of their experiment, Buller and Bell discuss a number of uncontrolled variables in this field setting that may have confounded their results. This difficulty is more of a problem in some cases than others, but it plagues most research into the effectiveness of OD interventions to some extent. It is to this topic, evaluating organization development activities, that attention now turns. A complete discussion of team building can be found in Dyer (1987).

**Experimental
treatment**
See page 29

Evaluating Organization Development Activities

As discussed in Chapter 2, the practice of I/O psychology rests upon scientific research. The primary goals of this research in an organization development context are to increase the field's knowledge of change and to evaluate the effectiveness of various strategies for bringing it about. Many OD interventions are effective in meeting both these specific goals and the more general goal of making an organization a better place, and research is being carried out that is both sound and applicable. Nevertheless, a number of problems interfere with acquiring more systematic knowledge about planned change in organizations.

Research in Organization Development

A major problem in the field of organization development in general is that very often no attempt is made to evaluate the effectiveness of an intervention at all beyond informal assessments of how people felt about it. The knowledge that most participants like a particular technique is useful (and gratifying) to the OD practitioner, but such opinions have limited potential for advancing knowledge of organization development. As Kahn (1974) and many others have noted, the practice of OD has always tended to exceed research in OD.

A second problem with OD research lies in the nature of the situation. By definition, organization development takes place in an organizational setting. Useful information about the dynamics of a particular technique may be acquired in a laboratory setting, but the generalizability of this information is limited. To a very substantial degree, information about the effectiveness of organization development must be acquired in field settings with all of the associated control problems.

Generalizability
See page 45

The number of possible confounding variables in a field setting is large. These affect research efforts, the inferences to be drawn from them, and even the OD intervention itself. Petty, Singleton, and Connell (1992) describe a pilot organizational incentive plan experiment that was not continued despite its success because of conflict between management

**Confounding
variable**
See page 28

Inference
See pages 35–43

and the company's union. In another company, the withdrawal of support from an absence control intervention quickly undermined the strong and constructive changes that the program had brought about (Miners, Moore, Champous, & Martocchio, 1994).

Reduced control in a field setting is a basic research problem, and considerable creativity may be required to get around it and to design a study that has sufficient methodological rigor to qualify as scientific. In one of the more provocative examinations of organization development research, Terpstra (1981) undertook to investigate the relationship between such methodological rigor and the reported outcome of a study. On the basis of his analysis of 52 OD research reports, he concluded that the more rigorous the methodology of a study, the less likely it was that the reported intervention was deemed successful.

What might such findings mean? Terpstra suggested there might be an unconscious bias on the parts of OD practitioners to interpret ambiguous results in favor of OD—a phenomenon commonly referred to as the "positive-findings bias." Certainly less rigorous research tends to produce ambiguous results in any field, and vested interests in a successful OD outcome (Staw, 1981) might affect the evaluation of an ambiguous result. On the other hand, as Bass (1983) points out, there is also the possibility of a bias *against* OD on the parts of researchers who carry out more rigorous research.

In the years since Terpstra's paper was published, many investigators have sought to lay the question of a positive-findings bias in organization development research to rest one way or another. In some cases, analyses have yielded results consistent with such a bias (e.g., Golembiewski & Sun, 1990; Guzzo, Jette, & Katzell, 1985). In other cases, they have not (e.g., Barrick & Alexander, 1987; Neuman, Edwards, & Raju, 1989). On the basis of their own three-phase analysis of 52 organization development studies conducted in organizations between 1967 and 1987, Roberts and Robertson (1992) reached the following conclusion that probably is a fair summation of consensus on this issue at this time.

> . . . we are not optimistic about a final empirical resolution of the positive-findings bias issue. However, it is an important issue and one that evaluators should be aware of. In the end, evaluators who are knowledgeable and conscientious are the most important safeguards against bias. (p. 923)

Whether the matter is ever resolved or not, the positive-findings bias issue cautions against the uncritical acceptance of claims for the effectiveness of any particular organization development intervention. It also highlights what many believe to be a basic problem with OD research; the majority of the studies examined by Terpstra and other investigators received low scores for methodological rigor. Given the difficulties of conducting rigorous research in field settings, this is not so surprising. At the same time, it must be acknowledged that some of the problems appearing in OD research are more a function of the research design than of the setting.

The Measurement of Change

A common problem in organization development research design is the use of success criteria that are not appropriate to the intervention undertaken (Nicholas & Katz, 1985). For example, the literature on the relationship between job satisfaction and work production is clear about the fact that there is no direct causal relationship between these two variables. This being the case, the likelihood that an OD program designed to increase job satisfaction will increase work production as well is not very good. Therefore, a measure of work output is not an appropriate measure of the program's effectiveness.

The use of a criterion measure that is inappropriate for the nature of the intervention is a particular instance of a broader issue. How is change to be measured when evaluating the effectiveness of an OD intervention? Change in work production is an example of what has been called *alpha* change (Golembiewski, Billingsley, & Yeager, 1976), which is movement along a basic measurement scale that is relatively stable from one measurement to the next. By contrast, *beta* change occurs when an OD intervention leads to a recalibration of the measuring scale—that is, to a shift in the standards by which people are evaluating the criterion. Managers might rate their ability to relate effectively to other people *lower* after a sensitivity training weekend than they did before, for instance, but not because their abilities have deteriorated as a result of the sensitivity training.

The managers are exhibiting a form of the response shift bias mentioned in Chapter 5. Because they now know more *about* interpersonal dynamics, they are making more realistic assessments of their abilities in this area. Most I/O psychologists would consider this increased knowledge and realism to be a positive outcome of the OD intervention. If the effectiveness of the program is evaluated in alpha change terms (pretraining and posttraining scores on a particular questionnaire), however, the program would appear to be a failure.

The third type of change that may be brought about by an OD intervention is *gamma* change, a complex form of change reflecting a postintervention *redefinition* of the basic issue around which the change effort was structured. Perhaps team-building sessions do not lead to a more cohesive and effective work group, but to a consensus by participants that the type of work they do makes effective teamwork impossible. In this instance, the issue becomes redefined from process (teamwork) to structure (job design), and pre-OD evaluations of teamwork are meaningless for evaluating the outcome of the intervention.

Most formal efforts to evaluate organization development-related change use alpha change measures despite the fact that many interventions are for the purpose of bringing about changes in process, and such changes are far more likely to involve beta or gamma change. The measurement of alpha change is relatively less difficult, but it is an inappropriate measure in many situations and can lead to erroneous inferences. In their study of newcomer organizational commitment over a six-month period, Vandenberg and Self (1993) found that the presence of gamma change made it impossible to interpret what had at first appeared to be significant alpha change over the course of the investigation.

Vandenberg and Self note that their finding was only uncovered because they deliberately tested for beta and gamma change as well as alpha change. This procedure is seldom employed, despite mounting evidence that researchers cannot assume subjects will interpret self-report measures the same way at different points in time (see also Millsap & Hartog, 1988; Tennis, 1989). Eventual acceptance of this basic criterion issue may yet prove to be the key to moving the study of the change process forward (Armenakis, Bedeian, & Pond, 1983).

Related to the question of what type of change is to be measured is the question of the time frame. Bass (1983) points out that short-term evaluations of what may be long-term effects distort the view of organization development effectiveness. He also suggests the possibility that various effects of an OD intervention may cancel one another out in some cases, leading to the erroneous inference that no change took place.

To summarize, organization development research is neither abundant nor outstanding for its rigor. The situation is improving (e.g., Sashkin & Burke, 1987), but it is fair to say that the field has some catching up to do. The issue is one of making OD successes more predictable and using research to link these successes to increased scientific knowledge of change and organizational effectiveness. In this regard, Bowers's (1976) comment would still seem to be appropriate: "any assemblage of techniques capable, under certain circumstances, of significantly improving productivity while substantially raising levels of human satisfaction deserves and very likely will receive more systematic attention and support" (p. 62).

The Management of Change

Few dispute the need for more good research into organization change and more coordination between research and practice in the field of organization development. At the same time, few dispute the fact that organization development is a growth industry. Pressures on organizations to change are increasing, not decreasing. Changes in the economic, technological, social, and political aspects of the external environment are accelerating and triggering corresponding needs for changes within organizational systems if they are to survive and prosper.

The needs organizations have for change cannot be set aside while I/O psychology research catches up. To reflect this practical reality, this chapter closes with a set of 10 recommendations for managing change in organizations. The list, drawn from the relevant literature by Umstot (1988), is relatively independent of technology, the type of organization involved, and the specifics of an organization intervention.

1. *Take a systems perspective of change;* remember that changes in one part of an organization affect other parts and these effects must be recognized in planning for change.

2. *Analyze resistance to change.* Try to anticipate and formulate plans for removing major obstacles to change.

3. *Identify the major driving and restraining forces* for change to help with the unfreezing process.

4. *Take actions to unfreeze the situation* before attempting to implement a change.

5. *Establish clear goals for change and communicate them* to those who are involved in the change.

6. *Build expectations for success.* Strong top management support and commitment are critical.

7. *Involve those to be affected by the change* in the planning and implementation to the extent possible.

8. *Refreeze successful changes.* Do not overlook this important step; establish rewards and structural support for the change. Remove any that support the old way of doing things.

9. *Take the "organization's pulse" after change.* Consider how well goals have been met, how things are going now, and what further action is needed. Action research is a useful model for this step.

10. *Be aware of relevant values, norms, and cultural factors* throughout any change process.

At Issue

Who Benefits?

I/O psychologists and others who work as organization development specialists help organizations plan and make transitions from one state to a different one. In theory, the changed organization will be "a better place to work" with "people working together better," and all employees will benefit. But some people believe that organization change agents too often are merely pawns in high-level power games played by and for those members of organizations with lots of power at the expense of those with little power (see Palazzoli et al., 1986; Schein, 1987).

A trend toward "flatter," more democratic organizational structures may be observed as the century turns, but most organizations are still pyramids in which a larger number of people at lower levels work for a smaller number of people at upper levels. The people at the upper levels almost always have more to gain if organization development makes an organization more effective and profitable. They are also the individuals who usually have the power to instigate and implement changes and to control both the nature and the extent of the change effort.

The situation described holds considerable potential for abuse of the professional change agent's skills. A management consultant may be brought into an organization more as a sign to others that management is "serious" about change than as a resource for bringing about changes that will benefit the organization as a whole. In such a case, the result may be a surface change that alters the appearance of things for a time but leaves them essentially unchanged. Alternatively, the result of organization development may be a real change that benefits only a few or that serves to strengthen the existing power structure.

Most I/O psychologists and others who work as change agents for organizations are committed to trying to bring about changes that benefit organizations as systems, not just particular individuals in them. If they are to achieve this goal and avoid being used for purposes they find unacceptable, they must retain a strong sense of personal ethics and reject client–consultant relationships that violate their standards. Argyris (1982) discusses the role that the action research model, with its emphasis on fact finding and joint client–change agent diagnosis, can play in this process.

The action research model is one tool to help a change agent make his or her own evaluations, not only of what is to be changed in organizations and how, but of whether to implement change at all. Organizations are complex systems. Just as a surgeon may have to cut through skin, muscle, and bone to reach a targeted area for surgery, so may a change agent have to disrupt many aspects of an organization in order to achieve desired changes in one part of it. In neither case should the enterprise be undertaken lightly; like the surgeon, the I/O psychologist must evaluate the potential costs and benefits of any procedure on the basis of his or her own knowledge and values and handle sharp objects with care.

Summary

Organization development today encompasses a wide variety of activities and research relating to deliberate interventions into organizational systems for the purpose of making them more effective and better places for people to work. Several models of this process have been proposed.

Diagnosis of the need for, and goals of, change is usually the first step in organization development. This is followed by planning the nature of the change and the means for bringing it about; there is some evidence that participation in this step by those organization members to be involved in the change is desirable.

The implementation of organization change is called intervention. Traditionally, OD interventions have focused on people and interpersonal processes. Today, many organization development activities take the environment rather than people as the main target. In either case, there should be some formal evaluation of the effort—that is, some measurement of the change that has occurred (or not).

Questions for Review and Discussion

1. Use Lewin's quasi-stationary equilibrium concept to analyze the general forces you can think of that will work for and against change in a work situation with which you are familiar. Use Figure 15–1 as a model in this analysis. (Figure 15–1 analyzes the forces for and against a *particular* change. You are asked to consider change in *general* in your organization.)

2. Consider a college or university changing from a quarter system (three 10-week terms in a nine-month academic year) to a semester system (two 15-week terms in a nine-month academic year). Identify as many positive and negative systems effects of this change as you can.

3. Compare and contrast survey feedback and team building as techniques for OD intervention. In this discussion, you should consider the goals of change, the target of change, the type of change that is likely to occur, the relative depth of the intervention, and any other relevant chapter concepts.

4. Using this chapter's Spotlight on Research as a model, outline an investigation of an OD change effort in an organization with which you are familiar; indicate (in general terms) how you would try to get around the research problems discussed in the chapter.

5. "What we face today are serious questions of values and ethics. In the face of (a) companies being bought and sold more rapidly than ever before, and (b) activities such as downsizing, undoubtedly a significant change is underway in the nature of the psychological contract between employer and employee. . . . What is fair treatment of employees today? Do we [OD] practitioners support the organization from whence our salary comes or the individual being considered for outplacement?" (Sashkin & Burke, 1987, p. 410). Make a case for one side of this issue or the other.

Key Terms

action research	organization development
change agent	positive-findings bias
change measurement	survey feedback
change target	systems effects
intervention	team building
Lewin's change model	

References

Argyris, C. (1982). *Reasoning, learning, and action.* San Francisco: Jossey-Bass.

Armenakis, A. A., Bedeian, A. G., & Pond, S. B. (1983). Research issues in OD evaluation: Past, present, and future. *Academy of Management Review, 8,* 320–328.

Barrick, M. R., & Alexander, R. A. (1987). A review of quality circle efficacy and the existence of positive-findings bias. *Personnel Psychology, 40,* 579–592.

Bass, B. M. (1983). Issues involved in relations between methodological rigor and reported outcomes in evaluations of organizational development. *Journal of Applied Psychology, 68,* 197–199.

Beer, M. (1976). The technology of organizational development. In M. D. Dunnette (Ed.), *Handbook of industrial and organizational psychology.* Skokie, IL: Rand McNally.

Beer, M., & Walton, E. (1990). Developing the competitive organization: Interventions and strategies. *American Psychologist, 45,* 154–161.

Bem, D. J. (1968). Attitudes as self-descriptions: Another look at the attitude behavior link. In A. G. Greenwald, T. C. Brock, & T. M. Ostrom (Eds.), *Psychological foundations of attitudes.* New York: Academic Press.

Bowers, D. G. (1976). Organizational development: Promises, performances, possibilities. *Organizational Dynamics, 5,* 50–62.

Buller, P. F., & Bell, C. H., Jr. (1986). Effects of team building and goal setting on productivity: A field experiment. *Academy of Management Journal, 29,* 305–328.

Buller, P. F., & McEvoy, G. M. (1989). Determinants of the institutionalization of planned organizational change. *Group and Organization Studies, 14,* 33–50.

Burke, W. W. (1982). *Organization development: Principles and practices.* Boston, MA: Little, Brown.

Burke, W. W. (1987). *Organization development: A normative view.* Reading, MA: Addison-Wesley.

Burke, W. W., & Litwin, G. H. (1992). A causal model of organizational performance and change. *Journal of Management, 18,* 523–545.

Church, A. H., Burke, W. W., & Van Eynde, D. F. (1994). Values, motives, and interventions of organization development practitioners. *Group and Organization Management, 19,* 5–50.

Coch, L., & French, J. R. P., Jr. (1948). Overcoming resistance to change. *Human Relations, 1,* 513–533.

Cosier, R. A., & Dalton, D. R. (1993). Management consulting: Planning, entry, performance. *Journal of Counseling and Development, 72,* 191–198.

Doherty, E. M., Nord, W. R., & McAdams, J. L. (1989). Gainsharing and organization development: A productive synergy. *Journal of Applied Behavioral Science, 25,* 209–229.

Dupre, V. A. (1976). Human relations laboratory training. In R. L. Craig (Ed.), *Training and development handbook* (2nd ed.). New York: McGraw-Hill.

Dyer, W. G. (1987). *Team building: Issues and alternatives* (2nd ed.). Reading, MA: Addison-Wesley.

Elden, M., & Chisholm, R. F. (1993). Emerging varieties of action research: Introduction to the special issue. *Human Relations, 46,* 121–142.

Festinger, L. (1957). *A theory of cognitive dissonance.* Stanford, CA: Stanford University Press.

French, W. L. (1969). Organization development: Objectives, assumptions, and strategies. *California Management Review, 12,* 23–34.

French, W. L., & Bell, C. H. (1984). *Organization development: Behavioral science interventions for organization improvement* (3rd ed.). Englewood Cliffs, NJ: Prentice-Hall.

Frohman, M., Sashkin, M., & Kavanagh, M. (1976). Action research as applied to organization development. *Organization and Administrative Sciences, 7,* 129–142.

Golembiewski, R. T., Billingsley, K. R., & Yeager, S. (1976). Measuring change and persistence in human affairs: Types of change generated by OD designs. *Journal of Applied Behavioral Science, 12,* 133–157.

Golembiewski, R. T., & Sun, B. C. (1990). Positive-findings bias in QWL studies: Rigor and outcomes in a large sample. *Journal of Management, 16,* 665–674.

Gray, T. R. (1995). A hospital takes action on employee survey. *Personnel Journal, 74,* 74–77.

Guzzo, R. A., Jette, R. D., & Katzell, R. A. (1985). The effects of psychologically based intervention programs on worker productivity: A meta-analysis. *Personnel Psychology, 38,* 275–291.

Haldane, D. (1996, June 20). Workers protest mail-sorting system. *Los Angeles Times,* p. B–3.

Hamilton, E. E. (1988). The facilitation of organizational change: An empirical study of factors predicting change agents' effectiveness. *Journal of Applied Behavioral Science, 24,* 37–59.

Harrison, R. (1970). Choosing the depth of organizational intervention. *Journal of Applied Behavioral Science, 6,* 181–202.

Hilton, T. F. (1989). A critique of "The facilitation of organizational change: An empirical study of factors predicting change agents' effectiveness." *Journal of Applied Behavioral Science, 25,* 201–203.

Jaeger, A. M. (1986). Organization development and national culture: Where's the fit? *Academy of Management Review, 11,* 178–190.

Kahn, R. L. (1974). Organizational development: Some problems and proposals. *Journal of Applied Behavioral Science, 10,* 485–502.

Kurpius, D. J., Fuqua, D. R., & Rozecki, T. (1993). The consulting process: A multidimensional approach. *Journal of Counseling and Development, 71,* 601–606.

Lewin, K. (1951). *Field theory in social science.* New York: Harper & Row.

Lippitt, R., Watson, J., & Westley, B. (1958). *The dynamics of planned change.* New York: Harcourt Brace Jovanovich.

Macy, B. A., Peterson, M. R., & Norton, L. W. (1989). A test of participation theory in a work re-design field setting: Degree of participation and comparison site contrasts. *Human Relations, 42,* 1095–1165.

Majchrzak, A., & Klein, K. J. (1987). Things are always more complicated than you think: An open systems approach to the organizational effects of computer-automated technology. *Journal of Business and Psychology, 21,* 27–49.

Millsap, R. E., & Hartog, S. B. (1988). Alpha, beta, and gamma change in evaluation research: A structural equation approach. *Journal of Applied Psychology, 73,* 574–584.

Miners, I. A., Moore, M. L., Champous, J. E., & Martocchio, J. J. (1994). Organization development impacts interrupted: A multiyear time-serial study of absence and other time uses. *Group and Organization Management, 19,* 363–394.

Nadler, D. A. (1977). *Feedback and organizational development: Using data-based methods.* Reading, MA: Addison-Wesley.

Neff, F. W. (1966). Survey research: A tool for problem diagnosis and improvement in organizations. In A. W. Gouldner & S. M. Miller (Eds.), *Applied sociology.* New York: Free Press.

Neuman, G. A., Edwards, J. E., & Raju, N. S. (1989). Organizational development interventions: A meta-analysis of their effects on satisfaction and other attitudes. *Personnel Psychology, 42,* 461–489.

Nicholas, J. M., & Katz, M. (1985). Research methods and reporting practices in organization development: A review and some guidelines. *Academy of Management Review, 10,* 737–749.

O'Driscoll, M. P., & Eubanks, J. L. (1993). Behavioral competencies, goal setting, and OD practitioner effectiveness. *Group and Organization Management, 18,* 308–327.

Palazzoli, M. S., Anolli, L., DiBlasio, P., Fiossi, L., Pisano, I., Ricci, C., Sacchi, M., & Ugazio, V. (1986). *The hidden games of organizations.* New York: Pantheon.

Perlaki, I. (1994). Organizational development in Eastern Europe: Learning to build culture-specific OD theories. *Journal of Applied Behavioral Science, 30,* 297–312.

Petty, M. M., Singleton, B., & Connell, D. W. (1992). An experimental evaluation of an organizational incentive plan in the electric utility industry. *Journal of Applied Psychology, 77,* 427–436.

Roberts, D. R., & Robertson, P. J. (1992). Positive-findings bias, and measuring methodological rigor, in evaluations of organization development. *Journal of Applied Psychology, 77,* 918–925.

Rogers, C. R., & Skinner, B. F. (1956). Some issues concerning control of human behavior: A symposium. *Science, 124,* 1057–1066.

Sanzgiri, J., & Gottlieb, J. Z. (1992). Philosophic and pragmatic influences on the practice of organization development, 1950–2000. *Organizational Dynamics, 21,* 57–69.

Sashkin, M., & Burke, W. W. (1987). Organization development in the 1980s. *Journal of Management, 13,* 393–417.

Schein, E. H. (1961). Management development as a process of influence. *Industrial Management Review, 2,* 59–77.

Schein, E. H. (1987). *The clinical perspective in field work.* Newbury Park, CA: Sage.

Sherwood, J. J. (1971). An introduction to organization development. *The Experimental Publication System,* Issue no. 11.

Staw, B. M. (1981). The escalation of commitment to a course of action. *Academy of Management Review, 6,* 577–587.

Strauss, G., & Bevelas, A. (1955). Group dynamics and intergroup relations. In W. F. Whyte (Ed.), *Money and motivation.* New York: Harper & Row.

Tannenbaum, R., & Davis, S. A. (1969). Values, man, and organizations. *Industrial Management Review, 10,* 67–86.

Tennis, C. N. (1989). Responses to the alpha, beta, gamma change typology: Cultural resistance to change. *Group and Organization Studies, 14,* 134–149.

Terpstra, D. E. (1981). Relationship between methodological rigor and reported outcomes in organizational development evaluation research. *Journal of Applied Psychology, 66,* 541–543.

Umstot, D. D. (1988). *Understanding organizational behavior* (2nd ed.). St. Paul: West.

Vandenberg, R. J., & Self, R. M. (1993). Assessing newcomers' changing commitments to the organization during the first six months of work. *Journal of Applied Psychology, 78,* 557–568.

Zeira, Y., & Avedisian, J. (1989). Organizational planned change: Assessing the chances for success. *Organizational Dynamics, 17,* 31–45.

Useful Addresses

American Psychological Association
750 First Street NE
Washington, DC 20002

American Psychological Society
1010 Vermont Avenue, Suite 1100
Washington, DC 20005

Society for Industrial and Organizational Psychology, Inc.
745 Haskins Road, Suite A
Bowling Green, OH 43402-0087

American Board of Professional Psychology
2025 Eye Street NW, Suite 405
Washington, DC 20006

American Association of State Psychology Boards
100 Corporate Square
555 S. Perry Street, P.O. Box 4389
Montgomery, AL 36101

APA Committee on Professional Practice
4545 42nd Street NW, #304
Washington, DC 20016

APA Divisions of Particular Interest to I/O Psychologists*

Division 5
Evaluation, Measurement, and Statistics

Division 13
Consulting Psychology

Division 14
The Society for Industrial and Organizational Psychology, Inc.

Division 19
Military Psychology

Division 21
Applied Experimental and Engineering Psychology

Division 23
Society for Consumer Psychology

Division 42
Psychologists in Independent Practice

---

*Addresses for any of the divisions may be obtained from the American Psychological Association. See Appendix A.

Professional Journals of Particular Interest to I/O Psychologists

Academy of Management Executive

Academy of Management Journal

Academy of Management Review

Administrative Science Quarterly

American Psychologist

Ergonomics

Group and Organization Studies

Human Factors

Human Performance

Human Relations

Industrial Engineering

Journal of Applied Behavioral Science

Journal of Applied Psychology

Journal of Business and Psychology

Journal of Experimental Psychology: Human Perception and Performance

Journal of Industrial Psychology

Journal of Military Psychology

Journal of Occupational and Organizational Behavior

Organizational Behavior and Human Decision Processes

Organizational Dynamics

Personnel Psychology

Psychological Bulletin

Public Personnel Management

A Summary of State Laws Regulating I/O Psychologists

State	Law	Title	Degree Required
Alabama	L*	Psychologist	Doctorate
Alaska	L	Psychologist Psychological Associate	Doctorate Master's
Arizona	L	Psychologist	Doctorate
Arkansas	L	Psychologist Psychological Examiner	Doctorate Master's
California	L	Psychologist Psychological Assistant	Doctorate Master's
Colorado	L	Psychologist	Doctorate
Connecticut	L	Psychologist	Doctorate
Delaware	L	Psychologist	Doctorate
D.C.	L	Psychologist	Doctorate
Florida	L	Psychologist	Doctorate
Georgia	L	Psychologist	Doctorate
Hawaii	L	Psychologist	Doctorate
Idaho	L	Psychologist	Doctorate
Illinois	L	Clinical Psychologist	Doctorate
Indiana	L	Psychologist	Doctorate
Iowa	L	Psychologist	Doctorate Master's

*L = Licensure (regulates use of title and defines activities that constitute the practice of psychology)

**C = Certification (regulates use of a title only)

Data from the American Psychological Association

Kansas	L	Psychologist	Doctorate
Kentucky	L	Psychologist	Doctorate
	C**	Psychological Associate	Master's
Louisiana	L	Psychologist	Doctorate
Maine	L	Psychologist	Doctorate
		Psychologist Examiner	Master's
Maryland	L	Psychologist	Doctorate
Massachusetts	L	Psychologist	Doctorate
Michigan	L	Psychologist (Limited License)	Doctorate Master's
Minnesota	L	Psychologist Psychological Practitioner	Doctorate Master's
Mississippi	L	Psychologist	Doctorate
Missouri	L	Psychologist	Doctorate
	L	Psychologist	Master's
Montana	L	Psychologist	Doctorate
Nebraska	L	Psychologist	Doctorate
Nevada	L	Psychologist	Doctorate
New Hampshire	C	Psychologist	Doctorate
New Jersey	L	Psychologist	Doctorate
New Mexico	L	Psychologist	Doctorate
	L	Psychological Associate	Master's
New York	L	Psychologist	Doctorate
North Carolina	L	Psychologist	Doctorate
North Dakota	L	Psychologist	Doctorate
Ohio	L	Psychologist	Doctorate
	L	School Psychologist	Master's
Oklahoma	L	Psychologist	Doctorate
Oregon	L	Psychologist	Doctorate
	L	Psychological Associate	Master's
Pennsylvania	L	Psychologist	Doctorate Master's
Rhode Island	C	Psychologist	Doctorate
South Carolina	L	Psychologist	Doctorate
South Dakota	L	Psychologist	Doctorate
Tennessee	L	Psychologist	Doctorate
	L	Psychological Examiner	Master's
Texas	L	Licensed Psychologist	Doctorate
	C	Certified Psychologist	Doctorate
	C	Psychological Associate	Master's

Utah	L	Psychologist	Doctorate
Vermont	L	Psychologist	Doctorate
		Psychologist	Master's
Virginia	L	Psychologist	Doctorate
	L	School Psychologist	Master's
Washington	L	Psychologist	Doctorate
West Virginia	L	Psychologist	Doctorate
	L	Psychologist	Master's
Wisconsin	L	Psychologist	Doctorate
Wyoming	C	Psychologist	Doctorate

Glossary

ability test: test to assess an individual's potential for learning something or performing some activity

action research: cyclical organization development process of diagnosis, planning, action, and evaluation

adverse impact: situation that occurs when a selection procedure results in a selection rate for any protected group that is less than 80% of the rate for the highest group

affirmative action plan: formal, written plan for reducing female and minority group underrepresentation in an organization

analysis of variance (ANOVA): set of quantitative techniques for comparing amount of variance (in dependent variable) explained by experimentally manipulated variables with amount explained by error

assessment center: approach to employment screening and employee development based on a group multiple-technique testing procedure typically lasting from one day to one week

behavior checklist: performance appraisal method requiring rater to record, but not evaluate, a list of specific job behaviors

behaviorally anchored rating scale: graphic performance rating scale with specific behavior examples, rather than adjectives or other descriptive phrases, as anchors

burnout: response to chronic emotional stress characterized by lowered job productivity, physical and/or emotional exhaustion, and a tendency to think in impersonal terms, even of oneself

change agent: individual who plans and carries out formal organization development efforts

citizenship behavior: helpful, constructive behavior that is not part of a job description

clinical prediction: evaluating the likelihood of an applicant's job success on the basis of human judgment

cognitive psychology: study of mental processes by which people selectively take in, store, remember, and use the stimuli from their environments

communication: exchange of information, ideas, or feelings between two or more individuals or groups

communication network: overall patterning of the formal upward, downward, and horizontal communication flow in an organization

comparable worth: equal pay for jobs whose satisfactory performance contributes equal value to the organization

compressed work week: redistribution of the standard 40 hours of work; in its most common form, people work four 10-hour days

confounding variable: extraneous variable that can affect conclusions from research because it has an important effect on a variable that is being investigated

content-related evidence of validity (of test): evidence that test items are relevant and representative of the test domain

construct-related evidence of validity (of test): evidence that a test measures what it is intended to measure

contingency approach: approach to organizational functioning characterized by rejection of the idea that there is one best way to do something; the best way varies with the particulars of the situation

correlates: variables found to be associated with one another in a predictable fashion

correlation: relationship between variables such that they change in a predictable manner with respect to one another

correlation coefficient: a measure of the nature and strength of the relationship between variables that change in a predictable manner with respect to one another

criterion: external measurement of some attribute or behavior against which to make some evaluation (plural: *criteria*)

criterion-related evidence of validity (of test): evidence that scores on the test are related systematically and significantly to some other measure (criterion)

cutoff score: test score (or ranking of some sort) that cuts off those below it from further consideration for a job, training class, school entrance, or other opportunity

dependent variable: subject behavior of interest in a research experiment

determinants: factors accounting for the measurement variance on some variable

differential validity: situation in which the criterion-related validity is significantly different for two population subgroups, such as males and females

domain: content or space including all items or units with defined characteristics

electronic performance monitoring: computer-based methods for collecting, storing, and analyzing information about employee work attendance, speed, and accuracy

Equal Employment Opportunity Commission: agency that enforces federal equal employment opportunity legislation

equity theory of motivation: theory that people exert the effort required to maintain equity between their own work inputs and rewards versus the inputs and rewards of relevant others

evaluative set: characteristic tendency on the part of a rater to use only a narrow range of a performance appraisal scale

experiment: observations of subject behavior made under different states of the environment created by experimenter

experimental conditions (also called treatments): particular states created by the manipulations in an experiment

feedback: return information from some process or behavior

field study: study in which the researcher relies on existing circumstances to provide clues to the relationships between important variables

flexible working hours (flextime): a range of variations in the distribution of work time characterized by some number of core hours during which employees must be at work, together with some flexibility in starting and stopping times on either side of the core

flexiplace: expansion of acceptable work-site options beyond the physical location of the employer

forced-choice scale: performance appraisal method requiring rater to pick statement most characteristic of ratee from sets of equally favorable or unfavorable statements

forced-distribution ranking: performance appraisal method requiring raters to assign a certain percentage of ratees to each of a set number of categories

general expectancy theory of motivation: theory that people exert effort in activities that they expect will lead to valued outcomes (rewards)

generalizability: extent to which an inference from a study can be applied beyond the particular circumstances of the study

graphic rating scale: performance appraisal method calling for rater to assess degree to which each ratee exhibits the behaviors and/or traits shown on the scale

group cohesiveness: degree to which members of a group are attracted to one another and to being in the group

group participative instructional methods: training methods in which trainees interact with and learn from each other as well as from materials and trainers

halo error: tendency to evaluate all of the behaviors or traits of a ratee in a manner consistent with some global impression or evaluation of the ratee

Hawthorne effect: changes in behavior brought about through special attention to the behavior

historical study: study in which research observations are made from records

human factors approach to job design: designing jobs, equipment, and work environments to be compatible with human physical and mental capabilities and limitations

human factors psychologists: psychologists with a major professional interest in the physical aspects of job design

hypothesis: statement of a predicted answer to a research question

independent variable: manipulated variable in an experiment

individual participative instructional methods: training methods that allow for active participation and individual learning pace

industrial/organizational psychological services: development and application of psychological theory and methodology to problems of organizations and problems of individuals and groups in organizational settings

inference: process of deriving conclusions from observations

institutionalization (of change): integrating a specific change into the structure and ongoing functioning of an organization

integrity test: test to identify people likely to be dishonest or create problems on the job

intervention: process of making a deliberate change in an organizational system (organization development)

job: all of the identical or similar positions in an organization

job analysis: data collection and analysis procedure through which systematic information about job tasks and requirements is obtained

job description: factual statement of tasks, responsibilities, and working conditions of a particular job

job enlargement: psychological job design strategy to make jobs "bigger," or larger, by adding to the number of work tasks each person performs

job enrichment: psychological job design strategy to make jobs "richer" by giving employees more responsibility and decision-making authority with respect to planning, scheduling, and controlling their own work

job evaluation: formal process for determining the financial worth of a job to an organization

job family: group of jobs that are similar in terms of the demands they make on employees

job satisfaction: attitude toward a job based on an affective (feeling) evaluative response to the job situation

job specification: statement of the employee characteristics needed to perform a particular job

leadership: influential increment over and above mechanical compliance by subordinates with the routine directives of an organization

matching model: the idea of achieving a fit between individual abilities and skills/job requirements and individual needs, values, and expectations/job rewards and opportunities

mean: average obtained measurement on a particular scale; the center point of a normal curve

measurement: assignment of values to observations according to a defined system

mentor: organization insider who provides information, support, and assistance and takes a personal interest in a newcomer and his or her success

meta-analysis: set of quantitative methods for summarizing findings across independent research studies

moderator variable: variable that has a predictable influence on the nature of the relationship between two other variables

motivation: sum of the forces that produce, direct, and maintain effort expended in any particular behavior

need theories of motivation: theories that people exert effort in behaviors that allow them to fill what they believe to be deficiencies in their lives

nonparticipative instructional methods: training methods that limit a trainee's role to that of a passive recipient of information

normal curve: bell-shaped curve describing a large number of measurements of a normally distributed variable

norms: unwritten standards for behavior, values, and attitudes that grow out of social interaction

Occupational Safety and Health Administration: created in 1970, the primary external regulatory agency for the safety and health of American workers

open system: whole that is made up of parts that function together in an interdependent fashion and that also interacts with its environment

operational definition: definition of a variable in terms of the process by which it is measured

operator-machine system: system in which human and machine work together, performing different functions, to accomplish a job

organizational behavior: application of psychology, sociology, anthropology, and related fields to the study of organizations and the people in them

organizational climate: consensus of employee perceptions about how a particular organization and/or its subsystems deals with its members and its external environment

organizational commitment: the degree of connection an individual feels with the organization in which he or she is employed

organizational culture: collective experience of the people in a particular organization about the meaning of their social environment

organization development: systematic effort applying behavioral science knowledge to the planned creation and reinforcement of organizational strategies, structures, and processes for improving an organization's effectiveness

paired-comparison ranking: performance appraisal method requiring a rater to compare each ratee with every other ratee

participative decision making: deliberate management policy of giving employees a voice in organizational decisions

performance appraisal: process of evaluating the extent to which people are doing their assigned work satisfactorily

personality test: test intended to compare an individual with the "average" individual (the "norm") on one or more traits, such as conscientiousness or extraversion

population: all of the people (organizations, departments, or other units) that have characteristics relevant to a research question of interest

position: basic building block of an organization, defined by the sum total of the tasks performed by one employee

positive reinforcement: strengthening of behavior that occurs when the behavior has been rewarded by its consequences

predictor variable: variable that explains a significant portion of the variance observed in measuring another variable

procedural justice: ideal of arriving fairly at a decision or course of action

psychological approach to job design: designing jobs to be compatible with human psychological needs

psychology: the study of human behavior

quality circle: group of six to ten employees that meets regularly to identify and solve work problems

quality of work life: impact of the total work situation on the personal life and health of employees

quantitative prediction: evaluating the likelihood of an applicant's job success on the basis of a predetermined numerical decision rule

quasi-experiment: research design that is similar to, but does not meet all standards for, an experiment

ratee-based rater bias: performance appraisal bias based on a rater's response to specific individuals being evaluated

realistic job preview: presenting job applicants with all pertinent information about a job in a straightforward, nonselling manner

recruiting: process of finding and attracting people to fill positions in an organization

reference group: group that an individual uses as a source of personal values, beliefs, or attitudes, and/or as a standard for evaluating his or her own behavior

reinforcement model: set of principles relating behavior to its outcomes

reliability: consistency or stability of measurement

research design: a plan for making research observations consistent with the rules of the scientific method

restriction of range: problem encountered in research where test scores or other measurements do not cover the full measurement scale

sample: defined portion of a specified population

sampling error: bias that reduces the extent to which a sample is representative of the relevant population

scientific method: investigation of phenomena by an orderly process of observation, inference, and verification

screening: process of identifying individuals likely to be successful in a job from among a pool of applicants

selection ratio: number of applicants from among whom to choose one employee for a position (expressed as a ratio or percentage)

self-efficacy: a person's judgment about his or her capability to carry out action necessary to accomplish a goal

shift work: work hour scheduling strategy in which different groups of full-time employees perform the same job duties in different blocks of time during a 24-hour period

simulation experiment: experiment in which the experimenter reproduces certain aspects of the real world while controlling selected confounding variables

simulation training: training method in which certain aspects of a job are reproduced in a controlled setting

social environment: conditions created by other people, an individual's relationships with them, and the relationships among them

social facilitation: principle that simple and/or well-learned behaviors are enhanced by the presence of an audience

socialization: process by which newcomers to a group acquire the attitudes, values, and norms necessary to become accepted members of the group

sociotechnical view of organizations: systems perspective of job design emphasizing the necessity for a balanced relationship between the human/social and the technological components of an organization

specialization approach to job design: strategy limiting the number of job tasks performed by one person to one or a few

standard deviation: standard mathematical unit describing the variability of a distribution around the mean of the distribution

standard error of measurement: standard deviation of a normal curve

statistic: number that is the result of a defined set of mathematical computation procedures

statistical significance: a measure of the likelihood that the results obtained from a defined procedure are not due to chance

straight ranking: performance appraisal method in which ratees are ordered from best to poorest on some dimension, such as overall quality of work

stress: energized physical/emotional response to events and conditions in the environment that are perceived as threatening in some way

structured interview: interview in which questions to be asked by interviewer and order of asking are specified in advance; replies may be recorded on a standardized form

structured questionnaire: detailed written guide that standardizes questions asked and answers reported; subject may complete on his or her own

subject: one individual (or other unit) in a sample

success rate for hiring: percentage of employees hired who are successful on the job (also called *base rate*)

survey feedback: organization development technique consisting of systematic data collection and feedback

survey research: research in which observations are made by means of written questionnaires

systems effects: changes in one part of a system that come about because of changes in another part of the system

task: assigned piece of work to be finished to some standard within some time period

task analysis: breaking down a general description of job duties into individual task elements required to accomplish them

task-based rater bias: bias characterized by a consistent form of oversimplification of the performance appraisal task

team: group whose members are interdependent; successful goal accomplishment depends on each doing his or her tasks correctly

team building: intervention into a work group for the purpose of strengthening the group's effectiveness as a group

test: defined procedure for making an estimate of an individual's relative or absolute position on some physical, psychological, or behavioral scale of measurement

test battery: combination of selected tests given for a specified purpose

Title VII of the Civil Rights Act of 1964: law that prohibits employment discrimination based on race, color, sex, religion, and country of national origin

training: structured learning experience for transforming abilities into specific skills, knowledge, or attitudes

transfer of training: generalization of what is learned in a training setting to a real-life job setting

treatments: see **experimental conditions**

underrepresentation: marked discrepancy between the number of people in the labor force available for a job or occupation and the number actually employed in it

validity: appropriateness, meaningfulness, and usefulness of a measurement

validity generalization: extending ("transporting") evidence for test validity acquired in one situation to another situation judged to be similar in basic respects

variable: some aspect of the world that can take on at least two different measured values

variance: measured differences around a true or an average measurement

verification: confirming or substantiating results

workforce diversity: mix of sexes, races, ages, cultural backgrounds, personalities, and lifestyles in an organization's work force

work methods: physical movements by which job tasks are performed

workplace flexibility: organizational policies designed specifically to help employees manage conflicts between work and personal lives

work restriction: limits on production output set by work group norms

work sample test: screening test consisting of a standardized sample of one or more behaviors important to performing a job successfully

workspace envelope: space assigned to, and occupied by, an individual employee in the performance of his or her primary job duties

Name Index

583

584

591

Subject Index

Index of Tests and Research Instruments

Photo Credits

Chapter 1: p. 7, UPI/Corbis/Bettmann; p. 10, George Gibbons/FPG.

Chapter 2: p. 34, Robert Brenner/PhotoEdit; p. 44, Spencer Grant/FPG.

Chapter 3: p. 60, Janice Sheldon/Photo 20-20; p. 73, Jay Daniel/Photo 20-20.

Chapter 4: p. 92, John Terence Turner/FPG; p. 95, Cindy Charles/PhotoEdit; p. 97, PhotoEdit/Tom McCarthy; p. 118, Reg Parker/FPG.

Chapter 5: p. 141, Ron Chapple/FPG; p. 151, Dennis MacDonald/PhotoEdit; p. 165, Gary Conner/PhotoEdit; p. 170, Rhoda Sidney/PhotoEdit; p. 178, Amy C. Etra/PhotoEdit.

Chapter 6: p. 195, Michael Nelson/FPG; p. 221, Jeffry W. Myers/FPG.

Chapter 7: p. 260, Mark Richards/PhotoEdit.

Chapter 8: p. 291, Mark Harmel/FPG; p. 312, Jonathan A Meyers/FPG.

Chapter 9: p. 334, John Neubauer/PhotoEdit; p. 338, D. Young-Wolff/PhotoEdit; p. 349, D. Young-Wolff/PhotoEdit.

Chapter 10: p. 368, Mark Richards/PhotoEdit; p. 373, Mark Richards/PhotoEdit; p. 380, Mark Harmel/FPG; p. 391, Stephanie Rausser/FPG.

Chapter 11: p. 428, Ron Chapple/FPG.

Chapter 12: p. 444, Richard Laird/FPG; p. 460, Jeff Kaufman/FPG.

Chapter 13: p. 470, Leverett Bradley/FPG; p. 487, Mark Richards/PhotoEdit.

Chapter 14: p. 507, AP/Wide World; p. 508, AP/Wide World; p. 527, Mark Richards/PhotoEdit.

Chapter 15: p. 552, Jeff Greenberg/PhotoEdit; p. 553, Michael Neuman/PhotoEdit.

TO THE OWNER OF THIS BOOK:

I hope that you have found *Contemporary Industrial/Organizational Psychology,* Third Edition, useful. So that this book can be improved in a future edition, would you take the time to complete this sheet and return it? Thank you.

School and address: _____

Department: _____

Instructor's name: _____

1. What I like most about this book is: _____

_____

_____

2. What I like least about this book is: _____

_____

_____

3. My general reaction to this book is: _____

_____

4. The name of the course in which I used this book is: _____

_____

5. Were all of the chapters of the book assigned for you to read? _____

    If not, which ones weren't? _____

6. In the space below, or on a separate sheet of paper, please write specific suggestions for improving this book and anything else you'd care to share about your experience in using the book.

_____

_____

_____

_____

_____

Optional:

Your name: _____ Date: _____

May Brooks/Cole quote you, either in promotion for *Contemporary Industrial/Organizational Psychology,* Third Edition, or in future publishing ventures?

Yes: _____ No: _____

Sincerely,

L. N. Jewell